1-50

CW0065520

NAPOLEON AND RUSSIA

Napoleon and Russia

Michael Adams

hambledon
continuum

Hambledon Continuum, a Continuum imprint
The Tower Building, 11 York Road, London SE1 7NX, UK
80 Maiden Lane, Suite 704, New York, NY 10038, USA

First Published 2006

ISBN 1 85285 458 8

A description of this book is available from the
British Library and from the Library of Congress.

Typeset by Egan Reid Ltd, Auckland, New Zealand.
Printed in Great Britain by MPG Books Ltd, Cornwall.

Contents

Illustrations

Plates

Between Pages 296 and 297

Maps and Text Illustrations

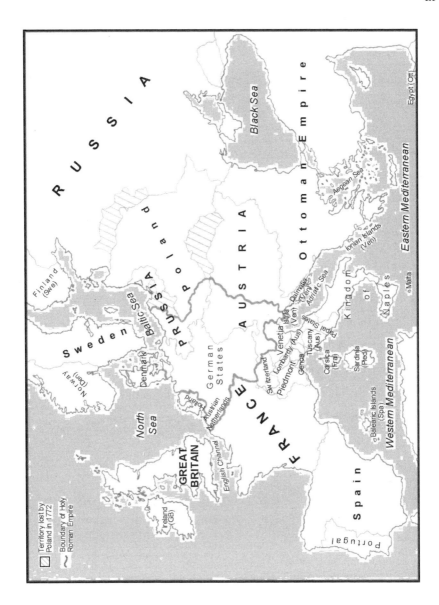

Europe in 1792

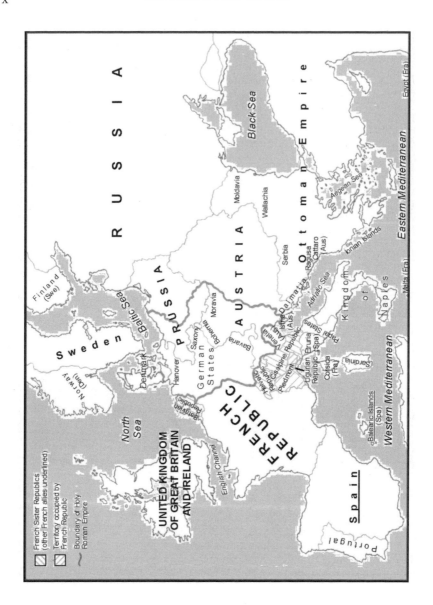

Europe in 1801

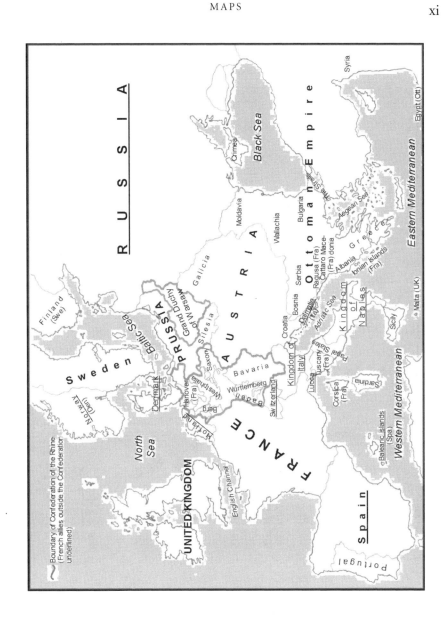

Europe in 1807

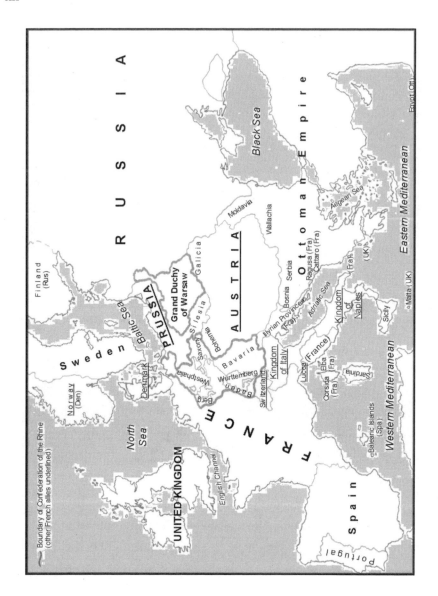

Europe in 1812

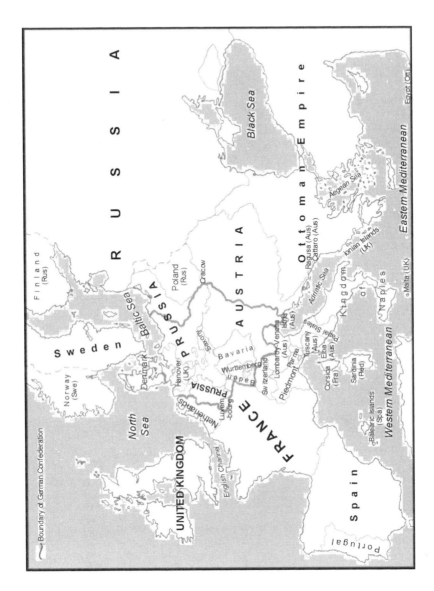

Europe after 1815

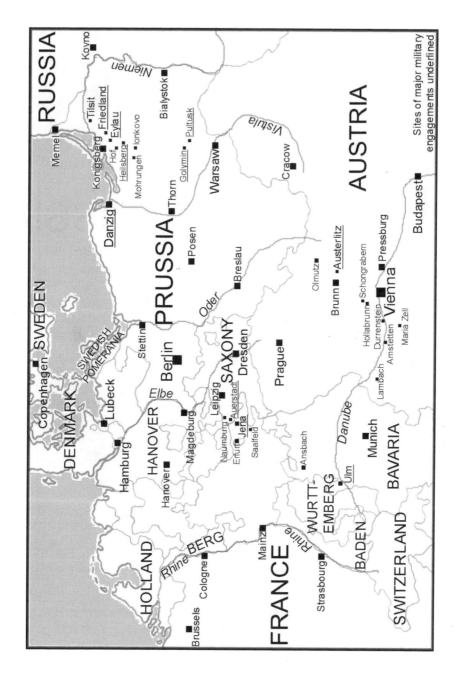

Napoleon's Campaigns in Central Europe, 1805–07

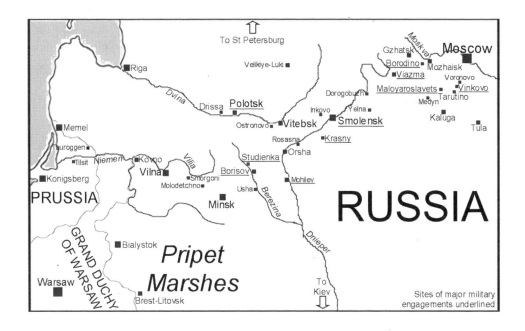

The Russian Campaign, 1812

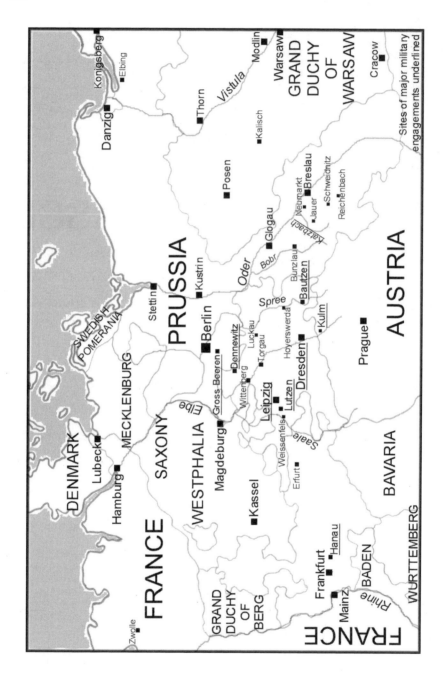

Napoleon's Campaigns in Central Europe, 1813

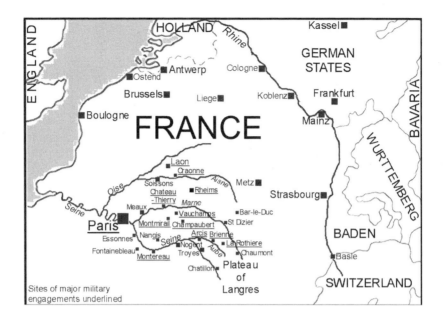

The French Campaign, 1814

1812 and All That

Picture a scene of utter devastation. In a desolate area of open countryside just a few square miles in size lie the corpses of thousands upon thousands of soldiers. Scattered among the human wreckage are the bodies of many hundreds of horses, as well as the material debris of conflict; helmets, muskets, breastplates, smashed artillery and so on. This grisly landscape is given an added horror, moreover, by the fact that it is covered with a thick blanket of snow, the brilliant whiteness of which serves to make the blood and entrails of the fallen stand out with a grotesque vividness. For the past two days this has been a battlefield fought over with incredible endurance and ferocity by two opposing armies. One of those armies has retreated in the night, but the other is in no fit state to pursue its adversary, so great have its losses been.

The corpses lie more thickly in some places than others. One particularly densely packed location, ironically enough, is a cemetery near the small town after which this battle will be named. Another, perhaps the worst, is the section of a shallow valley to the east of the town. Here, a corps of some 9,000 men had stumbled, blinded by a vicious snowstorm, into the muzzles of a terrifying battery of seventy enemy cannon, and had then been charged by hordes of cavalry. In a matter of a few ghastly minutes, a proud, fearsome body of soldiers had been torn to bloody ruin to such an extent that it would soon be disbanded and its survivors allocated to other units.

Not all the dead that litter this battlefield, however, are victims of their wounds. The clash had been fought amidst swirling blizzards in temperatures barely above freezing, but the wintry chill of the day must have seemed positively mild when compared to the biting cold of the night that followed. By the morning, many of the wounded who had not been fortunate enough to be attended to and provided with shelter had simply frozen to death. Their petrified bodies, along with all the other corpses, will remain unburied until the weather has warmed up sufficiently for graves to be hacked out of the frozen ground.

Throughout the icy night just passed and into the following day, surgeons have been working feverishly to save as many men as they can in field hospitals hastily set up in local barns. Their job, difficult at the best of times, is made even harder by the fact that the intense cold numbs their hands. Still, the piles of amputated limbs that are to be seen in the corners of the buildings they have commandeered for their work provide graphic testimony to their perseverance despite the horrendous conditions. Many of the soldiers whom the surgeons treat will die anyway. Others, if sufficiently wounded, will be sent on the lengthy journey home. Incredibly, they will be considered lucky, in spite of their injuries, by many of their comrades, who long to leave this godforsaken part of Europe and return to the more hospitable lands of their birth.

In recent weeks, the soldiers have had more than just the enemy to worry about. The army has struggled to keep them supplied with even the basics, and many have been forced to live off potatoes dug from the rock-hard earth. Horses have been kept alive by being fed the thatch stripped from cottages. This, of course, has bred resentment among the local peasantry, some of whom have availed themselves of the opportunity to take bloody revenge on isolated individuals or small groups whenever they have been presented with such a chance. Completing the men's woes, there is the ever-present threat of disease; a danger to all armies at all times, but especially prevalent in the cold, barren lands in which this latest campaign is being fought.

These soldiers who have endured so much and yearn so keenly for home are, of course, Frenchmen in the service of their emperor, Napoleon. Equally predictable is the fact that their adversaries are Russians. After all, everything one might classically associate with the phrase 'Napoleon and Russia' is here – the snow, the cold, the carnage, the suffering. Indeed, the picture painted above might, in the popular imagination, be said to encapsulate in a few hundred words the very essence of Bonaparte's disastrous invasion of Russia in 1812, a campaign that has been commemorated in works as famous as Tolstoy's *War and Peace* and Tchaikovsky's *1812 Overture*.

Yet the vision depicted above does not describe events of 1812. The setting is not even Russia. The scene outlined above dates from February 1807, the location the environs of a town then known as Eylau, a settlement in East Prussia a little over twenty miles south of the Baltic port of Königsberg.

These facts make a simple but crucial point. The story of Napoleon's relationship with the Russians is about much more than the famous and ill-fated invasion of 1812. There is a longer tale to be told, some of which, like the battle of Eylau, broadly fits in with the popular conceptions of what typified the relationship, but other parts of which contrast with those perceptions markedly.

None of this is to deny the vital importance of the 1812 campaign. Indeed, it was probably the most significant episode in the whole of the Napoleonic era. Nevertheless, it was only part of a greater whole; a whole, moreover, that has never been properly and systematically explored before. Almost all books that deal with Napoleon and Russia focus very heavily – in fact often exclusively – on the invasion of 1812. While this is understandable, it does mean that the bigger picture is missed. One of the main aims of this book, therefore, is to tell the full story.

And what an extraordinary story it is! Right through the Napoleonic era, from the late 1790s when Bonaparte came to power, to the mid-1810s and his fall, the influence of Russia can be discerned. When Napoleon was at both his highest and lowest point on the international scene, the Russians were central to his fortunes. At many of his greatest victories, as at his worst defeats, the Tsar's men, and sometimes the Tsar himself, were there. Frenchmen fought Russians not only in their respective homelands, but in many of the countries in between also. The struggle between the two powers literally ranged across a whole continent.

Yet the story of Napoleon and Russia is not just one of enmity and war. For several years, France and the land of the Tsars were allies. At this time, Europe seemed genuinely to be at a crossroads. Had the alliance held, it seems likely that French hegemony throughout much of the European mainland would have proved longer lasting than it did, something which would have had profound implications for the future. Instead, the alliance disintegrated, paving the way for the re-establishment of a balance of power on the Continent and a divided Europe of separate nation states.

All cultures are wont to view history from a biased perspective, and that is especially true of the Napoleonic period. In the English-speaking world, there is a tendency for the Napoleonic Wars to be seen primarily as a struggle between France and Britain, with other nations reduced most of the time to bit parts in the drama. English-speakers (or Anglo-Saxons as they are often, if inaccurately, referred to in France) are often conditioned to believe, moreover, that it was the British who played the key role in defeating Napoleon, the battles of Trafalgar and Waterloo typically being seen as the critical French defeats of the period. It is similar to the way in which the Second World War is generally viewed in the 'Anglo-Saxon' world, the key role in Hitler's downfall being played by the English-speaking nations, with the Battle of Britain and D-Day replacing Trafalgar and Waterloo. The truth is, however, that in both cases this is a distortion of reality. That is not to argue that Trafalgar, Waterloo, the Battle of Britain or especially D-Day were unimportant, or that the role of the 'Anglo-Saxon' powers was anything less than highly significant in either massive struggle, but the fact is that in both conflicts Napoleonic France and Nazi Germany suffered their worst defeats not in western Europe but in Russia. It was in fighting the Russians that the fate of both nations, indeed of the whole of Europe, was primarily decided.

Russia was the graveyard of Napoleon's ambitions. Before he invaded in 1812, he may have had problems, especially in the Iberian Peninsula, but he basically looked secure as master of the Continent. After the invasion, the tide had turned and he was on a downward trajectory towards ruin. More than any other event or factor, it was the failure to defeat Russia, and the horrendous losses sustained trying to do so, that ultimately brought down one of Europe's greatest conquerors.

But, as emphasized above, there is so much more to the story of Franco-Russian relations in the early nineteenth century than the invasion of 1812, crucial as it clearly was. Before that pivotal year, Russia's relationship with France had already influenced the course of European history in profound ways. For example, Russian adherence to the Second Coalition against the French Republic at the end of the eighteenth century brought about the situation that created the opportunity for Bonaparte to become France's ruler. Then, in the opening years of Napoleonic rule, a dramatic switch in Russian foreign policy to a more pro-French, anti-British stance played a significant role in bringing peace to Europe for the first time in a decade. Shortly thereafter, Russia, under a new tsar, Alexander I, changed policy again. The resultant formation of the Third Coalition compelled Napoleon to abandon his plans to invade Britain and led him and his army instead to the magnificent triumph at Austerlitz, which cleared the way for France to reorganize much of central Europe as her ruler wished. Despite the crushing defeat at the end of 1805, Russia remained hostile to France, and this was an important factor in Prussia's decision to go to war with Napoleon in 1806. The result was the smashing of the Prussian army and state, which extended French power on the Continent even further. It took one more campaign, in 1806–7, and two more of Napoleon's greatest battles, at Eylau and Friedland, finally to bring Russia to the peace table with France.

It was at the peace table in summer 1807 that the Russians once more made a remarkable *volte-face* and aligned themselves with their recent enemies. The treaty of Tilsit not only confirmed the subjugation of Prussia, the rebirth of a semi-independent Polish state, and the Napoleonic mastery of western and central Europe, it also brought into being a Franco-Russian alliance that, had it lasted, could only have spelled disaster for the British and prolonged French dominance on the European mainland. Napoleon was never more powerful than in the aftermath of Tilsit, and the sense of near omnipotence that the Russian alliance gave him perhaps helps to explain some of the more high-handed and aggressive actions he took in subsequent years, starting with the attempt to take control of the Iberian Peninsula.

Of course, history tells us that the dramatic upturn in Franco-Russian relations did not last. Instead, the relationship spiralled downwards so that by 1811 Napoleon had decided to get his blow in first in what seemed to be an imminent and inevitable war with his erstwhile ally. The ensuing invasion of Russia in the following year was an unparalleled catastrophe for Napoleonic France and her ruler, and an even greater one for the hundreds of thousands of troops and civilians who suffered and died as a result of it. It has gone down in history as an example of sheer folly, of megalomania exceeding rational thought, but was it really such a ridiculous enterprise? Can a case not be made for the attack? This author contends that it can and that the general idea of an invasion, if not perhaps the way in which it was conducted, can be presented in coherent terms.

Almost as important as Napoleon's defeat in Russia was the decision of Tsar Alexander to continue the war against France into central Europe in 1813, and not, as many of his key aides, including his chief military commander, advised him, to stop at Russia's borders. This decision played a critical role in determining the policies of Prussia, Austria and other European states in 1813 in their campaign to smash French hegemony in Europe. The culmination of the fighting that year came at the battle of Leipzig (the largest ever fought during the Napoleonic wars), at which the Russians were present in force. Leipzig effectively destroyed the French Empire, and the Russians were in again at the kill, playing a major part in the invasion of France in 1814. Indeed, the lasting image of ultimate French defeat in 1814 is that of Cossacks watering their horses in the Seine and camping on the Champs-Elysées. Even in 1815, that famous reprise of the Napoleonic saga, the Russian influence could be felt. It was primarily the prospect of hundreds of thousands of Russian (and Austrian) soldiers invading France from the east that prompted Napoleon to attack the British and Prussians in Belgium in an effort to deal with them first before the bigger armies arrived.

The tale of Napoleon and Russia, then, is one of huge importance. It is a story of great figures and great events. Throughout there are examples of human heroism and barbarity, endurance and tragedy. It is history writ large, the chronicle of people and proceedings that played a genuinely fundamental role in shaping the future of Europe and the world. English-speakers are likely to know something of Trafalgar and Waterloo, of Nelson and Wellington, but are far less likely to know anything of the battles of Friedland and Borodino, or of Tsar Alexander and Field Marshal Kutuzov. When 'Anglo-Saxons' think of Napoleon and Russia, they are likely to conjure up only images of bitter winters, horrendous suffering and disastrous French defeat, but not blazing summers and spectacular Napoleonic victories. It is hoped that this book will do something to change all this by offering a fresh, less Anglocentric perspective on one of the most fascinating and crucial periods in world history.

Revolution and War

In 1789 the French had a revolution, and Europe was never quite the same again. The Revolution had many causes, but at root it was about replacing an old system of unfair privilege that was based on tradition and custom, and in which one's birth was the prime determinant of one's perceived worth, with a new, more coherent and rational system built on equality before the law and greater political representation, in which every individual's perceived merit depended more on their ability than their social background. In short, it was about the overthrow of the *ancien régime* and its replacement with the beginnings of a modern nation state.

The French Revolution stood for many of the things that we today cherish, yet its reputation in the English-speaking world has been severely tarnished, thanks in no small part to the many years of international strife that followed it. This is unfortunate, as responsibility for the conflicts that have been labelled by historians the French Revolutionary Wars lay by no means exclusively with the French revolutionaries. Nevertheless, the fact remains that the 1790s were a decade of turmoil and struggle in Europe and it would be fair to say – choosing one's words carefully – that much of that upheaval was related to the revolutionary events that took place in France from 1789 onwards.

Historians who seek to place most of the responsibility for the outbreak of the French Revolutionary Wars on the French are keen to point out that initial reactions to the Revolution throughout Europe were far from all bad, that people who defended the revolutionaries could be found throughout the continent. This is basically true, but it obscures the prevailing reality. By and large, those liberal, progressive individuals who welcomed the events in France were few in number and not the people in power. The rulers of Europe – the established monarchies, aided and abetted by similarly well-established aristocratic families – were generally far from enthusiastic about the French Revolution and its doctrine of liberty and equality. In that they reacted with any kind of eagerness towards developments in France, they did so because they believed that internal upheaval would effectively remove the French from the international equation for a time, giving Britain, Prussia, Austria and Russia a freer hand in foreign affairs.

The general attitude of Europe's rulers towards the Revolution was, or swiftly became, hostile. There was widespread disgust among European elites when the revolutionaries in France abolished noble privileges, including feudal rights, without compensation. There was repugnance at the attitude the new French government adopted towards that staunchest of supporters of established authority and the *ancien régime*, the Catholic Church, seizing its lands throughout France and demanding that its clergy swear an oath of allegiance to the French nation. Most of all, there was abject horror at the way the French people treated their 'divinely appointed' monarch, Louis XVI. By failing to support, and often opposing, the changes that were proposed after 1789, Louis increasingly lost the support of the French people, resulting in him being bullied into agreeing to reform, and in the royal family being kept under effective house arrest in Paris. When, in summer 1791, he unsuccessfully attempted to flee the country in order to unite with those beyond France's borders who opposed the Revolution and its changes, it resulted in a massive upsurge in republicanism, the King's temporary suspension, and even tighter confinement for himself and his family in Paris. The ruling elites of Europe were shocked and horrified. War between revolutionary France and the *ancien régime* was now only months away.

Nowhere in Europe was hatred for the French Revolution and its supporters more keenly felt than in Russia. At the dawn of the nineteenth century, European Russia alone was equivalent in size to all other European countries combined. Her vastness made her seem broodingly menacing to other Europeans, but, in truth, it was arguably more of a weakness than a strength at this time. To be sure, the sheer scale of European Russia was to play a vital role in defeating the French in 1812, but the great distances between major settlements severely retarded the development of both the economy and infrastructure of the state. That Russia was administratively and economically more backward than other European nations was largely a result of the immense difficulties involved in trying to master her enormous size.

Dwarf other European states as she might geographically, however, Russia enjoyed a less pronounced advantage in terms of population. At around forty million, she was certainly the most populous country in Europe, but it was only thanks to conquests in the last quarter of the eighteenth century that her population had moved noticeably ahead of the second most populous European nation, France, with around thirty million (by way of comparison, the Austrian Empire at this time had twenty million inhabitants, the British Isles sixteen million and Prussia nine). Theoretically, Russia's large population should have enabled her to field the largest armies in Europe, but the much greater administrative efficiency of France meant that the French could almost always raise bigger armies than the Russians, a pattern only reinforced as more and more of the Continent came under Paris's influence.

With the possible exception of the hotchpotch of nationalities that was the

Austrian Empire, Russia was the most ethnically and culturally diverse of all the major powers. The majority of the population was, appropriately enough, Russian, but even if one, rather questionably, includes Ukrainians and Belorussians in a broad 'Russian' grouping, it still only accounted for three-quarters of the Tsar's forty million subjects. The rest were an eclectic mix of other Slavic peoples, such as Latvians, Lithuanians, Estonians and, most numerous of all, Poles, in the west, some Finns in the north, various Caucasian groups in the south, and, back in the west again, a small number of Germans. This ethnic diversity was largely mirrored and reinforced by religious differences. The bulk of the Tsar's subjects were, like him, Orthodox Christian, but most Poles were staunchly Catholic, the Germans Protestant and many of the Caucasians Muslim. There were also a considerable number of Jews, predominantly in the non-Russian Slavic areas. While France was a more or less ethnically and religiously homogenous state, Russia in the early nineteenth century was a multicultural empire dominated by one nationality.

In terms of her social structure, Russia was again more extreme than other European countries. Although, technically, she did have both a middle class and an urban proletariat, both were so small and politically insignificant as almost to be not worth mentioning. Whereas in France one in five people lived in towns or cities by this time, in Russia it was only one in twenty-five, representing the lowest degree of urbanization among the great powers. The vast majority of Russians lived in the country, almost all of them peasants.

There was nothing especially unusual about the fact that just one per cent of the Russian population, the 400,000 nobles, held almost all the wealth and power, nor was the continued existence of serfdom in Russia at all unique. What did make Russia stand out, however, was the sheer scale of serfdom. In the early nineteenth century, there were some ten million adult male serfs in Russia. In other words, over half of all Russian men were effectively owned by just one per cent of the population. Nor did it end there. In addition to the ten million full adult male serfs, there were around five million more so-called state serfs, men whose status lay somewhere between that of a full serf and a free peasant (of which Russia had very few). State serfs mostly worked on the vast estates owned by the Tsar, far and away Russia's biggest landowner. The restrictions placed upon them were generally less confining than those endured by full serfs and their treatment by their government-appointed masters usually better than that meted out by Russian nobles to their chattels, but they were still far from enjoying the free status of the peasantry in countries like Britain and France.

If the gargantuan scale of serfdom in Russia was remarkable – including the women and children of serf and state serf families, something in the area of ninety per cent of Russians were unfree – the typically brutal life of Russian serfs was barely less notorious. To equate serfdom with slavery is not *quite* accurate, but the difference between the two institutions in practice was so narrow as to be almost non-existent. Serfs and their families, like slaves, could be bought or sold and were routinely abused by their masters in all manner of ways.

Only two things enabled serfdom in Russia to survive. First was fear, pure and simple. Most serfs lived in a state of constant dread of what might happen to them or their families should they step out of line in even the most trifling way. Serf revolts were not unknown, but Russia's vast distances made effective coordination of resistance all but impossible and any rebellion that did erupt was always ruthlessly and brutally crushed by the army to dissuade others from joining the rebels.

Serfdom's second prop was the Russian Church. As was typical elsewhere in Europe, poor rural folk in Russia were almost all religious, yet the Orthodox faith of the bulk of them – or, more accurately, its priesthood – betrayed the material needs of the vast majority of its followers. Utterly lacking in even rudimentary education and without any alternative source of information, such as a free press, Russia's serfs were entirely at the intellectual mercy of the Orthodox Church's priests, and the social doctrine they preached was ultra-conservative. Even more than the Catholic Church elsewhere in Europe, the Orthodox Church in Russia went arm-in-arm with society's elite to maintain the established, strict, social hierarchy. Everyone, the serfs were taught, was put in their place by God and to seek to upset His plan was a sin. One had simply to endure whatever God had ordained for one. Serfs should not seek to improve their worldly wellbeing, but instead concentrate on their spiritual welfare, which, of course, involved going to church every week and doing what they were told by their superiors. To disobey was to court eternal damnation. It is not hard to see why European liberals of the age often regarded monolithic, organized religion with contempt.

Needless to say, serfdom was an appallingly inefficient mode of agricultural production, akin in some ways to the disastrous collectivization of Russian agriculture under Stalin. This meant that, indigent as the serfs were, Russia's nobles, at least when compared to rival aristocracies elsewhere in Europe, were also considerably less well-off than they might have been. To be sure, some Russian families, including the ruling Romanovs, were fabulously wealthy, but most nobles lacked the pecuniary assets of their European counterparts. It is no wonder that a man's wealth in Russia was measured not in money but serfs.

Russia's political system in many ways reflected its social structure, in that it was strictly hierarchical, largely inefficient and propped up by religion. At the top of the tree was the Tsar. At this time, established absolute rulers were very much the norm in Europe, but Russia's emperor was the most absolute of the established rulers. The Tsar enjoyed a position of political supremacy that was matched by only one other European ruler in the early nineteenth century; ironically enough, this was the master of the country which underwent the anti-autocratic French Revolution, Napoleon.

If Napoleon and the Russian Tsar were similar in the powers that accrued to them, the political machines over which they presided were radically different. French administration was the most efficient in the world, thanks in no small part to Bonaparte, whereas Russia's was the worst in Europe. The inadequacies and backwardness of Russian governmental administration were nicely expressed by one of the Tsar's ministers: 'Anywhere else a minister thinks, orders, dictates, corrects, confers, discusses, and attends council meetings; but in Russia he also has to be a clerk, and yet we have three hundred employees in the College of Foreign Affairs, not including foreign missions and the Moscow archives.'

Of course, the Tsar could not run the government single-handedly, especially one as inefficiently organized as that of Russia. He needed advisers, ministers and officials, and the most important of these were drawn almost exclusively from the nobility and given a rank according to their eminence, the highest being chancellor. It was entirely within the Tsar's power to appoint and dismiss at will, to listen to and act upon advice he was given or to ignore it, to pursue policies favoured by the aristocracy or to follow a line to which they objected, but he had to be aware that to upset too many nobles could provoke a drastic response.

Justification for Russia's political system was simple. As the Orthodox Church taught, the Tsar was appointed by God to act as a father to his subjects. It was a ruse used to vindicate the existence of almost all monarchies before the modern era, when people at last began to question the validity of such concepts and generally found them wanting. In western Europe, the divinity of monarchy had come under attack from British radicals as long ago as the mid-seventeenth century and opposition to the idea had culminated in the uncompromisingly anti-monarchical stance of the French radicals of the mid 1790s. In truth, however, enmity to monarchical government remained restricted to small radical groups, even in the more advanced European countries like France and Britain, until well into the nineteenth century. Until education became more widespread and the power of conservative, established churches declined, it remained possible to convince people that God did indeed order society according to a plan and that everyone had a place, the monarch's being to rule. In the Russia of the early nineteenth century, of course, it was easy to promote the idea of the divine right of kings, so strong was the Orthodox Church's grip on the intellectual life of the vast majority of people. Indeed, it is probably fair to say that most serfs loved the Tsar, and in fact saw him, rather perversely and inaccurately, as being on their side against the hated nobility.

Just as Russia's social and political systems seem incredibly backward to us now, her economy in the period was similarly undeveloped. The inefficiency of Russian agriculture, far and away the country's biggest economic activity, has already been mentioned, and her industry was certainly in no position to make up for it. Russia had undergone practically no industrialization as we would recognize it today. To be sure, some goods were produced in the towns, but most Russian production was on a very small scale; cottage industry in effect. Urban centres were much more commercial markets than bases of production, and even the great cities, like St Petersburg, had only a handful of what could possibly be called factories. It is telling that the great bulk of Russian exports were raw materials, not finished goods.

Of all Russia's institutions, the one that was held in the highest esteem abroad was the army. Perhaps the greatest strength of the Russian military was the rank and file of the infantry. Predominantly recruited from among the serfs by a quota system (an irregular form of conscription), the average Russian foot soldier was appallingly educated, brutally disciplined, and poorly armed with a musket that often misfired and was prone to explode. Nevertheless, Russian infantry was widely acknowledged, as it would be in the Second World War, as the toughest and most resilient in Europe. The Tsar's footsoldiers bore hardships and losses with a stoicism rarely found elsewhere in the continent.* This could make them difficult to repel when they attacked and even harder to dislodge from a defensive position.

Russia's cavalry was also renowned. Its horses were generally considered the best in Europe and its riders were typically brave, if tactically unimaginative. Most of the regular Russian cavalry was of the heavy type, used as a shock weapon in battle, for Russia's light cavalry was largely made up of the famous Cossacks. Vaguely Asiatic in dress, riding small but incredibly hardy mounts, and armed with lances, sabres and pistols, the Cossacks were highly skilled at scouting, harassing the flanks and rear of an army, and pursuing a defeated enemy. In battle, however, they were frequently less useful as they lacked the organization and discipline necessary to excel in such circumstances. Indeed, their conduct in battle could be described as cautious to the point of cowardice. As one French cavalry general who fought the Cossacks testified:

> if you keep up a bold front and are not intimidated by their deafening cries they will not press home the attack, but stop dead or fall back in order to prepare a new charge. The moment the artillery opens up they make themselves scarce. Threaten them with a pistol or any kind of firearm and they will keep out of your way. They never hold their ground or risk a personal combat unless they have odds in their favour of several to one.

Russian cannon were both plentiful and well made, but their effectiveness was seriously limited by organizational weaknesses. Russian armies were generally

---

* The explanation often proffered for this is the exceptional hardness and brutality of Russian peasant life which allegedly inured the soldiers to extremes of adversity and privation, but it seems that the serfs' religious attitudes also played a significant role by encouraging them to view material hardship as something to be endured uncomplainingly.

not good at moving their artillery around the battlefield to make its impact tell at key points and, even worse, batteries often ran out of ammunition due to poor commissariat arrangements. When the Russians did get their guns in the right place at the right time and provided them with sufficient rounds, though, the result could be devastating.

Given the undeniable qualities of the three main branches of the Russian army, it is fortunate for those who faced the Tsar's men that the institution had major flaws. One such flaw was the deficiency of the auxiliary arms, such as engineers and surgeons (almost non-existent). Russian logistics were also poor, combining frequent supply shortages with habitually slow and cumbersome baggage trains carrying a ludicrous amount of officers' personal belongings.

Another serious weakness of the Russian military was its officer corps. Although in this period Russia produced a few decent generals, most were mediocre at best, and the average Russian junior officer was an uninspiring figure. Part of the problem was that although the officer corps, as in almost all European countries at this time, was effectively restricted to the nobility, Russian aristocrats generally showed little passion for military service. Indeed, Napoleon once commented that a French private took a greater interest in the planning and conduct of a battle than senior Russian officers. While this may be an exaggeration, it nevertheless highlights the frequently lackadaisical attitude of Russian officers to their job.

The final major flaw of the Russian army was a prevailing outmodedness in its way of doing things. The epitome of infantry tactics was still widely held to be the bayonet charge, for example, and the Russians very rarely made use of skirmishers to spearhead or break up attacks or shield blocks of troops. Organizationally, the Tsar's army lacked flexibility, its various regiments tending to act monolithically, and coordination between the three main arms was often weak. Perhaps most reactionary of all, the Russians made no real attempt to establish a proper staff system for the efficient communication of orders and planning of campaigns. Whenever possible, these vital administrative tasks were handed over to the staff officers of allied armies, which, of course, raised language problems. Otherwise, Russian commanders simply improvised.

Overall, then, the Russia of the early nineteenth century can perhaps best be described by the single word 'backward'. In every major respect, socially, economically, politically, religiously, even culturally and militarily, she was what we today would regard as less modern than the other major European powers. It was a feature, moreover, of which contemporaries, both in Russia and elsewhere, were aware and it set the Russians apart from the rest of Europe. They were widely perceived, with semi-racist overtones, as being not quite European, Asiatic even, partly a legacy of the fact that Russia had been overrun by the Mongols in the Middle Ages. When Napoleon described them in January 1807, a time when he was at war with Russia, as 'a swarm of fanatics and barbarians', he was merely expressing what most politically-aware Europeans felt.

Yet contemporaries feared Russia too. They feared her size. They feared her hordes of people. They feared her armies. They feared that her ultimate aim in foreign affairs was to conquer as much of Europe as possible. Disdain or fear the Russians as they might, however, every statesman in Europe knew that they had a crucial part to play in the power politics of the period.

Russia had only really emerged onto the European political scene during the reign of Peter the Great, at the start of the eighteenth century, when she had ousted Sweden as the major power in the Baltic region. Since then, she had engaged in a number of European conflicts, her most consistent enemies being Poland, the Ottoman Empire* and Sweden. Traditionally, France enjoyed good relations with all three of these, and this, plus the fact that the French showed a desire throughout the eighteenth century to keep Russia out of European affairs, made for generally poor Franco-Russian relations, even before 1789. After the Revolution, the relationship between Paris and St Petersburg reached a new low.

In the early 1790s, Russia was once again being ruled by a monarch who would be granted the epithet 'the Great'. She had been born in 1729 at Stettin on the Baltic, the daughter of a minor German royal, the Prince of Anhalt-Zerbst. Christened Sophia Frederica Augusta, she is better known to posterity as Catherine.

Married off as a teenager to Grand Duke Peter of Russia, Catherine came to power in the most sordid of circumstances in July 1762, when her husband, Tsar for just six months, was ousted and subsequently murdered by one of the Tsarina's many lovers, the nobleman Gregory Orlov. Swiftly proving herself a master of the dark arts of politics and court intrigue, Catherine, despite being both German and a woman, became undisputed autocrat of the Russian Empire, a position she would hold for more than three decades and during which time her armies would almost double her subject population. Hers was a truly exceptional reign.

Catherine admired what she saw as the masculine attributes of strength, vigour and ruthlessness. She enjoyed a string of young lovers (the famous story of the horse is, however, a fabrication made up by her enemies) and she ruled with a heart of stone, showing not the least remorse, for example, when she ousted from the Polish throne a man she had once loved.

Alongside virile young men and ruthless territorial expansion, Catherine's most fervent passion was the preservation of traditional political and social

---

* The Ottoman Empire was centred upon modern Turkey and had its capital at Constantinople (modern Istanbul) but also covered the bulk of south-east Europe, parts of the Caucasus and much of what we now refer to as the Middle East.

structures. Inevitably, this made her a bitter enemy of the French Revolution and all its machinations. She referred to the revolutionaries as 'scum' and said, 'We must wipe out even the name of France'. As early as October 1789, she broke off diplomatic relations with Paris. Her police were ordered to look out for any French-inspired propaganda or meetings in Russia and to crush them. She even forbade Russians from travelling to France and demanded that all French people in Russia swear an oath of hatred for the Revolution or leave her realm forthwith. Catherine would have had little to learn from the McCarthyites of post-war America when it came to repressing a loathed ideology.

Despite holding an interest in the progressive, eighteenth-century, western European movement known as the Enlightenment, the Tsarina believed passionately, as did almost all her fellow monarchs, that rebellion and revolution anywhere ultimately threatened the established order everywhere, and that the menace could only be effectively dealt with by armed force and repression. To this end, she pleaded repeatedly with the rulers of Austria and Prussia to attack France and overthrow the Revolution, yet she herself was destined never to go to war against the French revolutionaries she detested so fervently.

The reason for Catherine's failure to take on France militarily was simple. Her forces were too busy elsewhere in the early 1790s. Although undoubtedly a great power, Catherine's Russia should in no way be confused with the superpower that was the Soviet Union in the four decades after the Second World War. She was in no position to send troops off hither and yon to fight any number of enemies. Odd as it may seem to us now, it was perfectly possible in the late eighteenth century for the likes of Sweden, the Ottoman Empire and Poland (at least in combination) to keep Russia's armed forces fully occupied.

When the Revolution erupted, Russia was engaged in bloody wars over territory against both the Ottoman Empire and the Swedes. Peace was restored in 1792, although continued poor relations with Stockholm and Constantinople necessitated the retention of large numbers of troops on the borders. In the event, the fragile peace held, but Catherine's attention was soon taken by developments elsewhere. In Poland, a third of whose extensive territory had been grabbed by Russia, Prussia and Austria in 1772, national pride began to stir once more and efforts were made to strengthen the state. This was anathema to the Tsarina, who was only prepared to tolerate Poland's existence so long as it remained firmly under her own thumb. The reaction of Catherine and her fellow rulers in Berlin and Vienna was consequently ruthless, but, to France's great benefit, the destruction of Polish independence and the partition of Poland would keep the Russian army occupied until 1795.

When Catherine's armies invaded Poland in May 1792, the series of conflicts that have become known as the French Revolutionary Wars had just broken out. The tension between the revolutionaries and the champions of the *ancien régime* had been building since 1789, and in spring 1792 the dam finally burst.

There are a number of reasons why war did not break out until 1792. Russia's restraint, at least militarily, towards France has already been dealt with, but the other three great European powers all had reasons for holding back in the first years after 1789 as well. In Britain, much as the traditionalist Tory administration detested the Revolution, it was not prepared to undergo the great expense of a war – at least not while France remained quiescent on the international stage, the more radical revolutionaries in Paris were kept out of power, and the conservative Louis XVI was still king. The rulers in Berlin, meanwhile, although eager to fight the French revolutionaries, realized that, weakened by its internal problems as France supposedly was, she would still probably prove too strong for Prussia's military unless it received the aid of another major power. The obvious such power was Austria, but Vienna, like St Petersburg, was busy fighting a war against the Turks until early 1792.

It is instructive to note that as soon as Austria's war with Turkey started to wind down, the Habsburgs began to take a more aggressive line towards the French revolutionaries. In August 1791, Austria's ruler, Leopold II, joined the King of Prussia in issuing the Declaration of Pillnitz. This was ostensibly a response to the treatment of the French royal family since 1789, and especially since its failed flight that June. The Pillnitz Declaration not only invited all European rulers to join with Austria and Prussia in promoting monarchical government in France in whatever way possible, it was also issued in the name of the royal and aristocratic *émigrés* who had fled France since 1789 and had openly committed themselves to the complete overthrow of the Revolution. It is hard to imagine a more provocative piece of diplomacy, and the French, quite understandably, erupted in fury when they heard of it.

War did not come yet, however, although a major step had been taken towards it. The catalyst proved to be the *émigrés* in whose name the Declaration of Pillnitz had been issued. Led by Louis XVI's youngest brother, the ultra-reactionary Comte d'Artois, the *émigrés* had begun to gather just across the border in the Rhineland in the immediate aftermath of the Revolution. Funded by the rulers of Russia, Austria and Prussia, as well as many of the umpteen princelings who controlled Germany at this time, they raised armed forces and prepared for war to restore the *ancien régime* in France.

The activity of the *émigrés* posed a threat that the French government could not and did not ignore. In autumn 1791, the French Assembly voted to confiscate the lands of *émigrés* who refused to return to France and to deny them citizenship, only to have its law vetoed by Louis XVI. Severely riled by this, the revolutionaries were rendered nothing short of apoplectic at the end of the year when the Austrian government explicitly warned them that any move against the *émigrés* in the Rhineland would not be tolerated by Vienna. The French, by now more determined than ever to crush the menace across their border, responded in early 1792 by demanding that Austria make a public declaration of peaceful intentions towards France or face war. The sudden and unexpected death of Leopold II and his replacement by his brother Francis in March 1792 changed nothing. Austria maintained her menacing attitude, so France declared war in April. The following month, Prussia entered the conflict.

The era of war between France and the other European powers that would not end until 1815 thus broke out primarily over the ideological issue of whether the Revolution and all it had unleashed should stand or be destroyed. That initial core cause would soon become just one of a number of reasons for the fighting to continue, but the period of conflict that marked the turn of the nineteenth century was always about more than just the acquisition of territory. It was ultimately about two radically different visions of the future.

The war started badly for the French; in fact, very badly. Their armies had been severely weakened by the loss of many of its predominantly aristocratic officers, and the raw enthusiasm of their inexperienced volunteer troops proved insufficient on its own to overcome the professional forces of the Prussians and Austrians. Before long, France had been invaded from both Belgium (then a Habsburg possession known as the Austrian Netherlands) and Germany. It seemed only a matter of time before Paris fell; and with it the whole Revolution.

This was exactly, of course, what the Austrians, Prussians, émigrés and French royal family had hoped for, yet the joy would prove short-lived, especially for Louis and his family. The revolutionaries blamed the alarming trend of the war not on the army's problems, but on treachery, and the prime suspects were the King and his court. The accusations were far from groundless. Louis and his supporters certainly wished for the defeat of their own country, and many of them took the extra step and actively contrived towards it. Marie-Antoinette, wife of the King and sister of the Austrian ruler, was particularly prominent in this regard, sending France's enemies valuable information.

In June, the people of Paris, more convinced than ever of the royal family's ill-will towards the Revolution by Louis's recent vetoing of measures designed to improve the country's ability to wage war effectively, acted. They stormed the Tuileries palace in the heart of the capital. For once, Louis produced a sure-handed performance to survive the crisis, donning a red bonnet of liberty and toasting the health of the nation. The mob dispersed.

It is perhaps just conceivable that the by now thoroughly discredited monarchy might have survived had no further crises emerged before the French armies managed to turn the tide of war, but in late July, the commander of the enemy forces marching on Paris sealed its fate. The Duke of Brunswick issued a stark warning to the revolutionaries that if the French royal family was in any way harmed, he would order his armies to raze Paris to the ground. The response to the Brunswick Manifesto was swift, dramatic and predictable. In early August, the people of Paris stormed the Tuileries once again, massacred the Swiss Guards who endeavoured to protect the King, and arrested Louis and his family. This time, his removal from the throne would prove permanent. The gauntlet that Brunswick had so rashly thrown down had been sensationally picked up.

Within just a few months, the struggle had assumed a remarkable bitterness. The threat to destroy Paris had resulted in the deposition of the King, an extremely powerful message that was lost on none of Europe's other crowned heads. The desire of the *ancien régime* to crush the Revolution was greater than ever, the need for the revolutionaries to defend it equally inflated, as now they could expect no mercy whatsoever should they lose.

In spite of the King's deposition, Paris remained under threat from the approaching enemy armies, but on 20 September 1792, near the town of Valmy to the east of the capital, one of history's truly critical events took place. The French revolutionary armies won their first major victory; a triumph, moreover, that sent the enemy reeling back towards the border and saved both Paris and the Revolution. In a wave of euphoria, the French Republic was formally announced the next day.

Valmy, of course, only removed the danger temporarily, but in its wake the revolutionaries enjoyed further stunning successes and upped what was at stake in the struggle still further. The great victory of 20 September was all well and good as far as it went, but it was not going to guarantee the security of France or the Revolution in the long term. The restoration of good relations with the other major powers of Europe might have done that, but that simply was not an option in the autumn of 1792. France, by making herself a republic, had become a pariah, every bit as loathed and detested by European ruling elites as the Soviet Union was to be in the twentieth century. Therefore the French, as the Soviets would do after them, looked to solve their long-term security problems in a hostile world in a more confrontational manner. If Europe as currently configured would not accept Republican France, then Republican France would have to change the configuration of Europe.

In early November 1792, the French won a second major victory, at Jemappes in the Austrian Netherlands, which cleared the way for them to take over the whole region. The Rhineland too, a nest of the venomous *émigrés*, was invaded and overrun, while to the south east Savoy, an area inhabited predominantly by French-speakers but whose rulers had foolishly declared war on France the day after Valmy, was also occupied. It would not be until January 1793 that it was formally announced as French policy, but what the revolutionaries were doing was fighting for the completion of what they termed France's 'natural frontiers'

– the ocean, the Pyrenees, the Alps and the Rhine. The motivation was primarily defensive, but to others, just like the Soviet occupation of Eastern Europe after the Second World War, it looked aggressive.

The quest for the 'natural frontiers' was one of three developments in late 1792 and early 1793 that served to expand the conflict dramatically. The first of the other two was the Edict of Fraternity of November 1792, by which the French Republic declared that it would 'accord fraternity and help to all peoples who wish to recover their liberty'. It proved to be little more than hot air in practice, and was withdrawn four months later, but that did not stop it seriously alarming the established authorities of Europe against whom it was directed; much as the Bolsheviks' calls for world revolution scared other governments after 1917.

The third development that escalated the war was the execution of Louis XVI on 21 January 1793 for treason. If his deposition had been greeted with horror by the other crowned heads of Europe, his death was met with wails of shocked abhorrence. Within a few short weeks, France was at war with the Dutch, the Spanish and the British, for whom the execution, which had particular poignancy for a monarch whose ancestor had also been beheaded by his subjects, was the final straw. As far as London was concerned, the French had gone beyond the pale by killing their 'divinely appointed' ruler, threatening to export their Revolution, and, most alarming, occupying part of the Low Countries, an area which Britain believed was as vital to her security as did the French.

It was as well for the French that there was one European power that they did not end up at war with in spring 1793. That, of course, was Russia. Much as Catherine and the vast majority of the Russian elite approved of and encouraged efforts to crush the Revolution, the Tsarina's troops did not go to fight the French because they were needed elsewhere. The Russian campaign against the Poles in summer 1792 had proved easy, resulting in early 1793 in the second partition of the country, by which Russia annexed further large tracts and the Prussians were given lands on the Baltic. Although Poland had been defeated and further reduced in size, however, the threat of a major Polish rising was very real and necessitated the retention of large numbers of soldiers in the area. Troops were also still required to guard against a possible renewal of war with either Sweden or the Ottoman Empire. Besides, France was already facing three of the other four great powers of Europe, as well as sundry other states. Surely Russian troops would not be needed to annihilate the 'cancer' of revolution? Leaving the Prussians and the Austrians to conduct the bulk of the campaign against France, moreover, could only weaken their position *vis-à-vis* Russia in the east, a factor that was certainly not lost on the calculating Tsarina.

If Catherine still refused to send soldiers to fight the French, she was prepared to take almost all measures short of that. She was allegedly so stunned by news of Louis XVI's execution that she had to retire to her sick bed – conveniently forgetting that she was effectively a regicide herself, having connived in her own husband's murder. She gave vent to her disgust by declaring economic war on France. From spring 1793, all Russian ports were closed to French trade and Russian ships in the Baltic were instructed to harass French vessels. There really was only one step she could take beyond this.

Had Catherine bitten the bullet and despatched soldiers west in considerable numbers in spring 1793, the fate of the French Republic might well have been sealed. As it was, the extension of the war soon put France firmly on the back foot once more. The introduction of conscription to meet the increased commitments of the struggle sparked a massive revolt in the royalist and staunchly Catholic Vendée region of western France. This was quickly followed by the heavy defeat of a major French army at Neerwinden in the Low Countries, which resulted in loss of control of what is now Belgium and the base defection to the enemy of General Dumouriez, the victor of Valmy and Jemappes.

Desperate times called for desperate measures. At the start of summer, men who were prepared to take those measures, the Jacobins, came to power following a coup by the people of Paris. This only served to ignite further revolts in the provinces, with regional centres such as Lyon rising up against the new government, which was felt to be too centralist and in the pocket of the Paris mob. The most alarming example of such rebellion came in August, when the Mediterranean city of Toulon, with its great naval base, went over to the British.

Toulon's defection proved to be the nadir. After that, the French Republic embarked upon a string of successes that would be practically uninterrupted for the next five years. Crucial to the turning of the tide was the introduction in late summer 1793 of the famous *levée en masse*, by which the whole French nation was called upon to serve in defence of *la Patrie* in whatever way they could, whether by fighting, making weapons, providing food or even just stirring up hatred of the Republic's enemies. It was a remarkable effort and it gave France armies that outnumbered those of her many enemies.

Alongside the *levée en masse* went a brutal repression of the Republic's internal enemies known as the Terror. This is not the place for a detailed discussion of this controversial campaign. Suffice it to say that it was savage and bloody, and that it undeniably claimed the lives of many innocent people, but the great bulk of its victims were enemies of the state and it did help the Republic overcome its adversaries and save the Revolution.

The final major factor in the turning of the tide of war from autumn 1793 was the emergence of a crop of skilled French commanders who adopted new tactics and strategies and made them work. The most famous of these men is, of course, one of the main subjects of this book, but there were many others, all of whom benefited from the opening up of careers to talent rather than aristocratic birth in the wake of the French Revolution.

In October 1793, one such commander, General Jean-Baptiste Jourdan, who had served in the American War of Independence as a mere private, led a French army to victory at Wattignies, thereby saving Paris. Two months later, another rising star, destined to shine brighter than all the others, won Toulon back from the British and their rebel allies. In summer 1794, General Jourdan won another great victory, this time at Fleurus, opening the way for the reconquest of what is now Belgium and the left bank of the Rhine. With the crisis passed and the Terror getting out of hand, the radical Jacobins were ousted the month after Fleurus, but the Republic continued to enjoy success. In January 1795, French troops overran their enemies in Holland and set up the Batavian Republic, a sister republic closely allied to and dominated by France …

If Catherine the Great had refused to send troops when she thought the French would be defeated anyway, why did she not revise her decision when it became clear that she had been mistaken and that the hated Republic would survive? The answer is simple. In spring 1794, a massive revolt erupted in Poland. It required armies from Russia, Prussia and Austria to crush the rising, and even then it took many months. Warsaw did not fall until November, its capture being preceded by scenes of carnage and horror that almost make the Terror in France look like child's play.

Even then, the Polish saga was not over. All three eastern powers were determined to wipe Poland from the map in a third partition, but the question was how the spoils were to be divided. Initially it looked like agreement would not be reached and that war would break out between the Russians, Prussians and Austrians. Eventually, though, peace was preserved and a distribution of territory agreed upon, but not before Prussia had determined to make peace with France so as to prepare for a showdown to secure what she saw as her rightful share of the spoils in Poland.

In truth, it was likely that the Prussians would have made peace with the French in 1795 anyway. They were the least of the five great European powers and three years of war had left them exhausted. Austria had always been their traditional enemy and they feared that to continue the struggle against a French Republic that showed no signs of being defeated any time soon would leave them dangerously weakened *vis-à-vis* Vienna and St Petersburg. Prussia desperately needed peace and a chance to rebuild and absorb its Polish gains of recent years. Despite the continued ideological opposition of the Prussian elite to the Revolution, they would keep Prussia out of war for more than a decade.

Practicality overcame ideology for other nations in 1795 also. Spain made peace with France in July 1795, just three months after Prussia. Over the previous century, her main enemy had been the British rather than the French, and Madrid had become increasingly worried in recent years about Britain's growing naval preponderance; as great a potential threat to Spain's colonial possessions as it was an actual one to those of France. Within a year, to the delight of Paris, the Spanish joined in the war against the British on the Republic's side.

Russia might, of course, have taken the place of Prussia and Spain in fighting the French, and indeed was strongly pressed by both the Austrians and the British to do so. Vienna and London were disappointed, however. Catherine's armies were far too busy over the next year absorbing their latest Polish conquests and keeping a watchful eye on the Swedes and the Turks to make fighting a war with France possible. So, hate it as she did, the Tsarina, like the rest of the European crowned heads, had little choice in summer 1795 but to accept – for the moment at least – a *fait accompli*. The French Republic had taken on practically the whole of monarchical Europe and not only survived, but expanded its territory and influence into the bargain. And it had not finished yet.

The history of France, indeed of Europe, was dominated for the two decades after 1795 by one man, Napoleon Bonaparte. Few individuals have had such an impact upon the world or provoked such controversy. To some a glorious saint, to others an unmitigated sinner, Napoleon was in reality neither. One's view of the man is always coloured by one's general attitudes and beliefs. While traditionalist right-wingers and radical left-wingers both tend to despise him, for example, progressives on the right and moderates on the left have both found much to admire about him. One's nationality is often critical in determining one's view as well. To most French he is a hero, while to many British he is a bogeyman, and the main reason in both cases is the same: Napoleon almost made France rather than Britain the most powerful nation in the world in the nineteenth century. Historians often like to think that they are more objective in their analysis of the past than the common man, but the nationalistic sensibilities of authors writing about Bonaparte and his era are frequently palpable even today.

Napoleon's personality was complex. At turns charming and brusque, generous and mean-spirited, frank and dishonest, pragmatic and romantic, it is little wonder that he has been seen in so many different ways. One fallacy about him should, however, be dismissed out of hand. He was not a proto-Hitler or Stalin. There may be similarities in their careers and in some of their attitudes – Bonaparte was undeniably authoritarian – but the differences between the Emperor of the French and the twin monsters of the twentieth century are far more important than the resemblances.* It simply was not in Napoleon's

---

* His defenders include, among others, Winston Churchill, who kept a bust of the great man on his desk at Chartwell. The very fact that Churchill, a man who is famed above all for his staunch opposition to the regimes of Hitler and then Stalin, retained his esteem, fondness even, for Napoleon throughout his life is as good a reason as any to question the validity of lumping Bonaparte in with that diabolical pair. Chartwell was Churchill's beloved home in Kent.

character to annihilate an entire race or to butcher tens of thousands of potential or imagined domestic opponents. He was no fanatical, racist bigot, nor was he a cold, paranoid brute whose ruthlessness knew no bounds. His defenders have always been able to point out a wide variety of reasons to admire and even like him.

Napoleon displayed many of the personality traits common to most strikingly successful individuals. He was egotistical, highly self-confident, fiercely ambitious, strong willed, hard-working, extremely charismatic, and prepared to be duplicitous if necessary. He abounded with energy and imagination, and there is no doubt that he was a genuine genius with quite brilliant mental powers. He was able, for example, to dictate several letters at once, hopping around amongst them and returning to each one seamlessly. His memory for facts and figures was stunning, his mathematical understanding exemplary, and his ability to discuss complex issues with specialists impressed a range of acknowledged experts in a variety of fields, from philosophy to science. His understanding of his fellow man, furthermore, was extraordinary and played a key role in his success. There can rarely, if ever, have been a better leader of men.

Napoleon's views are often difficult to fathom, as all manner of things he said (or is alleged to have said) at different moments in differing circumstances have been recorded for posterity. While no misanthrope, he struggled to make close connections with people; but that is not unusual for a person of such abilities who was for most of his life isolated by holding high office. Contrary to the image promoted by his enemies, he was not callous or especially careless with the lives of his soldiers and countrymen, whose plight often touched him deeply, but he does seem to have had an ability to distance himself from suffering and sacrifice (including his own) when conditions made such an attitude propitious. Again, the same could be said of many great leaders in wartime.

Although Napoleon's will stated, 'I die in the Roman Catholic Church into which I was born', his personal religious outlook for the majority of his life was deistic: he believed in some form of divine force but wasn't sure what it was and didn't believe that it had much to do with the everyday world. He felt that his life, and the lives of others, were guided not by God, but by a combination of personal ability and hard work, luck and, oddly for a generally rational man, destiny.

Politically it is common to see Napoleon as a man of the right, but this needs qualification. As a young man, he was radical in some ways and strongly supported not only the Revolution in general but also the left-wing Jacobin regime of 1793–4. As he grew older and came to power, he certainly became more conservative, but his was never the conservatism of the *ancien régime*, whose advocates always saw him as a figure on the opposite side of the political divide from themselves. This contributed in no small part to the conflicts which raged between Napoleonic France and the established monarchies. Certainly,

Napoleon's early radicalism never entirely left him. While, for example, he restored Catholicism to something of its former position in France, he also ensured that Protestants, Jews and people of no faith were free to worship (or not) as they chose. Similarly, although his imposition of autocratic rule* and, later, his assumption of the title of emperor can only be seen as shifts to the right, he always retained a liberal's respect for the rule of law and never became an entirely arbitrary ruler. The odd, but appropriate, phrase 'liberal authoritarian' has been coined to describe both his regime and his personal political outlook.

The question of what drove Napoleon is a knotty one for which many answers have been posited. Some can fairly safely be discarded. That his career was an attempt to overcome or mask some deep-seated inadequacy – whether to compensate for lack of height (he wasn't actually that short for his time), a sense of social inferiority, a lack of, for want of a better phrase, 'manly stature' (none of his various lovers ever mentioned that he was underendowed), or anything else – just doesn't add up. Rather than a sense of inadequacy, Napoleon felt a clear sense of his own superiority, at least in the areas that really mattered to him. Nor is there any real sense of Bonaparte ever being strongly driven by either hatred or a desire for vengeance, despite his coming from an island notorious for its culture of the vendetta. He was not a man to bear grudges (one could even argue that he was too lenient towards those who crossed him) and he never allowed himself to become consumed with hate, even for his most inveterate opponents.

The desire for financial gain did play some role in driving him, but not a major one. True, it was important to him to ensure that he and his close relatives never had to worry about money as they had in the first decades of his life, when his father's premature death (amongst other things) threatened the family with serious hardship. It is also fair to comment that he took some pleasure in wealth, though mostly the pleasure of being able to provide those close to him with luxuries (his own tastes always remained rather frugal, most extravagance that he indulged in being to maintain the splendour of his position as head of state). There is no real feeling, though, that he ever sought money for money's sake, at least beyond the level at which he and his family achieved a good degree of comfort and security, a point reached pretty early in his career.

No, what really drove Napoleon was altogether more abstract than simple cupidity. At the heart of it lay the – arguably very French – desire for *la gloire* (glory). Immersing himself in ancient history as a youth, there seems no doubt

---

* I prefer the words 'autocratic' and 'autocrat' to 'dictatorial' or 'dictator' in referring to Napoleon as the latter words have become so loaded following their application to men of vastly lesser worth and calibre than Bonaparte. There is no doubt that Napoleon rightly would not have seen himself as a 'dictator' in the wholly pejorative light in which it has come to be understood today.

that Bonaparte became impassioned to emulate men who became his heroes. Nearly all these figures, such as Julius Caesar, Alexander the Great or Hannibal, were great military commanders and conquerors, and this furthers our understanding of the nature of the glory that Napoleon craved. Success in war and conquest were always part of his envisioned path to glory, and while it is easy to criticize him for this, we must judge him in the context of his day, not ours. War and conquest were inextricably linked to glory in his era, and not just in France but throughout Europe. Catherine of Russia was given the honorific 'the Great' not because she was a woman operating successfully in a man's world (possibly her greatest achievement) but because she oversaw a massive expansion of Russian territory and influence. Wellington became a hero to the British public not because he pushed through Catholic emancipation in the United Kingdom (his great political success) but because his military victories brought martial glory to Britain and helped her remain the dominant colonial power. Indeed, war and glory were so intertwined in this period (as in most before the twentieth century) that it was almost inconceivable to obtain the latter without resort to the former. Now, we may from our own perspective damn Napoleon for wanting such glory, but then we must damn too practically every other major figure of the era, for in truth they almost all sought such glory.*

In any case, war and conquest were never the only aspects of glory that Napoleon desired. It was never enough for him *just* to be a brilliant general. He was always even more a political animal than a military one, and his political achievements were every bit as important to his own sense of glory as his martial ones. Of course, to achieve anything politically he needed power, and his desire for this is often held up as a prime driving force for him. This is a broadly accurate analysis, but only up to a point. The image of the power-crazed megalomaniac is wide of the mark. Rather like money, Napoleon never wanted power just for power's sake, but for what he could do with it. There are aspects in his desire to wield power in the political realm of nationalist feeling – of the longing to secure both prosperity and a position of pre-eminence for the French – as well as of the wish to see the triumph of (certain) Revolutionary ideals, such as 'careers open to talent'. It is perhaps better, though, to state simply that Napoleon hoped to use his power to draw glory to his name in the political sphere by making the world a better place. Of course, this is a vague and highly subjective concept, and it is easy to point to aspects of his career in which he demonstrably failed to do this,

---

* Including those who condemned Napoleon for his lust for *la gloire*, such as Wellington. True, Wellington never revelled in glory *per se* in the way that Napoleon did, but he was exceptionally prickly whenever anyone called into question the high esteem in which his military skills and achievements were held. His pride in those achievements (which was perfectly justified) is surely just a more reserved (more English?) form of basking in glory.

but that does not mean that that is not what he yearned to do. Like most political figures, Bonaparte always had an eye on what history might say of him and he was deeply concerned that what it said would be positive, which meant being seen to have improved the world in some way. We in the English-speaking world may find it natural to question the idea that acquiring autocratic power for himself or attempting to secure French predominance in Europe would make the world a better place, but that should not necessarily lead us to dismiss the notion that that is how Napoleon saw things. From his point of view – and the viewpoint of a good many others, both at the time and since – he was the man and France was the nation best suited to improving the world during his era, so it logically followed that the more power each had, the better.

If trying to fathom what Napoleon's views were and what drove him are often the most fascinating (and controversial) aspects of studies of the man, where he is placed by those assessing him on the moral compass is perhaps the most otiose. To talk of him as a 'good' man or a 'bad' man tells us little more than the particular prejudices of each of his judges. The truth is that Napoleon was neither a Gandhi nor a Hitler.[*] Like the vast majority of people, particularly those who live out their careers on the political stage, his personality and life defy (or at least should defy) the assertive application of such simplistic and highly subjective adjectives as 'good' or 'bad'. Much as we might baulk at describing Bonaparte simply as 'good' or 'bad', though, one word we can unquestionably apply to him is 'great'. He was clearly a great man; indeed one of the greatest ever to have lived.[†] In the opinion of Charles Maurice de Talleyrand, a French statesman of the period (and a figure who ultimately became an opponent of Napoleon), 'He was clearly the most extraordinary man I ever saw, and I believe the most extraordinary that has lived in our age, or for many ages', while another contemporary (and detractor), the eminent writer René de Chateaubriand, came to sum Napoleon up simply as 'the mightiest breath of life which ever animated human clay.'

Born on 15 August 1769 on the Mediterranean island of Corsica to parents of middling social rank, Napoleon exploited luck, the tide of events and, above all, his own outstanding talents to rise from this relatively humble, obscure beginning

---

[*] Neither of whom was quite the epitome of 'good' or 'evil' that they are often made out to be. Gandhi's legacy to India was far from entirely beneficial, while even Hitler is widely acknowledged to have been kind to animals and children (this is not intended as a flippant point – it shows that, for all the horrendous things that he was responsible for during his career, Hitler was recognizably human and, much as we may find that fact uncomfortable, we should endeavour to understand him and what he did in that context, not portray him crudely and inanely as some otherworldly demon).

[†] The use of the phrase 'great man' is not intended to indicate any moral judgement. Josef Stalin was as much a 'great man' as Nelson Mandela, for example; indeed, more so.

to become master of France and Europe, before losing it all in a few short years. There is, quite simply, no more remarkable story in the whole of history.

Napoleon enjoyed a fairly comfortable, contented first decade on his home island, before being packed off to France and military school. He had shown an interest in all things martial from an early age, and this, plus the fact that the army offered a stable income, decided the course of action of his parents, Carlo and Letizia.

As his parents' names suggest, Napoleon's first language was not French but Italian (his own name originally was Napoleone Buonaparte). Corsica had been owned for centuries by the Genoese and had only been taken over by France in 1768. The young cadet struggled with his new language, for which he was teased by his schoolmates, who also mocked his humble lineage (most of them were from established French noble families) and lack of aristocratic airs and graces. Unsurprisingly, Napoleon did not enjoy his school days, becoming surly and solitary, making few friends, and devoting most of his spare time to extra study. The study paid off. He excelled at mathematics, history and geography, and, aged fifteen, won a place at the prestigious Ecole Militaire in Paris. He completed two years' study in one, electing upon graduation in 1785 to join the artillery, the least hidebound and most professional of the military's arms.

The rest of his life should have been unspectacular. As an officer of undistinguished origins in the French Royal Army, a glass ceiling barred his progress to the senior ranks, which were reserved solely for the 'great' noble families of France. The Revolution changed all that. With careers opened to talent rather than birth, and with the Republic desperate for men of military skill to save it, Napoleon's future suddenly became one of tremendous opportunities.

For the first years after 1789, he spent much time in Corsica, hoping to carve out a path to riches, glory and power by dabbling in the convoluted politics of his native land. He enjoyed a few minor successes, such as his election to the lieutenant-colonelcy of a volunteer regiment, but he was ultimately forced to flee the island in 1793 when he fell out with its leading figure, Pasquale Paoli.

From now on, Napoleon's future lay very much in his adopted home, France, and an opportunity that would propel him into the limelight was just weeks away. Given command of the artillery of a Republican army besieging Toulon, he soon came up with the plan that enabled the French to recapture the city and evict the British fleet from its harbour. Promoted to the dizzying heights of brigadier-general, Bonaparte was the Republic's latest hero.

Heroism was no guarantee of lasting favour in the turbulent France of the mid-1790s, however. Just eight months after his dazzling success at Toulon, Napoleon was imprisoned and in danger of facing the guillotine. He had strong connections to the Jacobins, and when they were ousted from power in July 1794, the young Corsican general suffered from the political repercussions.

Napoleon's luck held. He was released without charge. For more than a year, however, his career seemed to be going nowhere. He realized that now France's hour of greatest need had passed, he needed more than just talent to secure another plum appointment. Over the summer of 1795, therefore, he worked on building up contacts among Paris's new social and political elite. It bore fruit. When a royalist uprising broke out in the capital in October, it was Napoleon who was called upon to put it down. He did so with ruthless efficiency. His reward was a promotion to full general and, at the age of just twenty-six, appointment to the command of the French Army of Italy. The latter came, it was said, as a wedding present from the powerful politician Paul Barras, for shortly before he took up his new post in March 1796, Napoleon married Joséphine de Beauharnais.

Previously married to an aristocrat who had been executed during the Terror, six years older than her new husband, and with two young children, Joséphine was not the kind of woman a man whose star was very much in the ascendant would have been expected to choose for a wife. Nevertheless, Napoleon was genuinely besotted in the early years of their marriage and would retain profound feelings for her (and her children) even after their divorce in 1809.

Much would happen between their wedding and their separation, and it all started in Italy. At this time, the Italian peninsula was a motley collection of states, not the unified country it is today. The Austrians dominated northern Italy, and they and their allies from the kingdom of Piedmont had been waging war along France's south-eastern frontier for almost four years by the time Napoleon took command in the theatre. The struggle had been typified by stalemate, with no great French victories to match those in the north. That would all soon change.

Taking command of a rag-tag army of ill-fed, ill-paid soldiers low in spirit, General Bonaparte turned it into the Republic's most successful force in a matter of weeks. He addressed his troops' woes, lifted their morale, and led them with a strategic and tactical flair that can only be described as brilliant. By the end of May 1796, he had routed the Austrians and their Piedmontese allies in north-west Italy, and forced the King of Piedmont to sue for peace. He went on to conquer Lombardy and then defeated every attempt by Austria between mid-1796 and early 1797 to come to the relief of the vital fortress town of Mantua, south of Lake Garda. When Mantua finally fell to the French, the route to Vienna via north-east Italy was open, and Napoleon and his all-conquering army lost no time in marching along it. Shattered both physically and psychologically, and fearing that their capital would fall to the dashing young Corsican, the Habsburgs sued for peace in spring 1797. Napoleon and his men had defeated the mighty Austrians and, in so doing, brought peace to the Continent for the first time in half a decade. It was a quite stunning achievement.

Napoleon's spectacular success in Italy alarmed the crowned heads of Europe, none more so than Catherine the Great. Indeed, it was sufficient for her at last to compromise Russian security against the Poles, Turks and Swedes by ordering an army 60,000 strong to be readied to go to the aid of the reeling Austrians. With the force nearing readiness for despatch, however, Catherine died in November 1796.

The man who succeeded the Tsarina as ruler of Russia was her son, Paul. His fame, such as it is, rests primarily upon his madness, but this is unfortunate, as the general consensus among modern historians is that he was not clinically insane. That said, he was certainly emotionally unstable, veering from raging tantrums to bouts of deep despondency and covering most moods in between. His rule would prove equally turbulent, both domestically and in international affairs.

Born in 1754, Paul grew to idolise his murdered father and detest his ruthless mother. His hatred for Catherine is hardly surprising. For most of his life, she kept him in seclusion, and she even tried to remove him from the succession in favour of his own son, Alexander. Much of what he became and did was a conscious rejection of his mother. Whereas Catherine was a German who worshipped all things Russian, Paul was a Russian who adored all things German.

There were certain ways, however, in which mother and son were strikingly similar. Both fervently believed in the preservation of established hierarchies, in rigid order and discipline, and both, therefore, loathed the French Revolution and all it stood for with a passion. Like Catherine, Paul saw the revolutionaries and their ideas as a cancer eating away at the 'divinely ordained' system of *ancien régime* Europe.

With that in mind, one would naturally expect the 60,000 Russians Catherine had been about to despatch to Italy to have been sent by her successor, but instead he ordered them to stay put. The exact reasons for this decision, as for so many of the volatile Paul's decisions, are open to speculation, but it seems likely that it was partly simply to counter one of his hated mother's schemes.

There were certainly more rational factors that might have influenced the decision, though. It took time for Paul to gain control of the Russian diplomatic machine, for example, as his erratic manner encouraged resistance. The old difficulties regarding the Poles, Swedes and Turks remained very much alive, moreover, and neutral Prussia now needed to have an eye kept on her as well. Added to that, Russia was in debt following her frequent war-making under Catherine and, perhaps most alarming, there was a spate of serf revolts throughout the country in the mid-1790s that gave rise to genuine fears of a revolution that the army would be needed to crush. On his accession, therefore, although Paul sent out a note to foreign courts promising all possible opposition to what he called the 'frenzied French Republic', he nevertheless stated that Russia could not participate directly in the ongoing war as yet.

If the new Tsar was not yet ready to take up the sword, neither was he prepared to sit on the sidelines doing nothing. Thus in the early spring of 1797 came Paul's first major foray into European affairs with an attempt to mediate a general peace. His aim was simple: if France and the Revolution could not be contained by war, as it seemed they could not, then perhaps they could be contained by peace. The Tsar was not so callow as to suggest that the French, in their currently predominant position, give up all the territorial gains they had made since 1792, but he did suggest that French influence be removed from Germany and the left bank of the Rhine. Almost as soon as the initiative was launched, however, it was rendered superfluous by Austria's agreement to the preliminary peace of Leoben in April 1797, which acknowledged France's position in the Rhineland. Typically, Paul took umbrage at this, and, as if to demonstrate to the rest of Europe that Russia and not Austria was now the focus of opposition to the French Republic on the Continent, he gave shelter both to the Comte de Provence, Louis XVI's brother and heir to the old French throne, and to *émigrés* who had fought against France.

The terms of the peace of Leoben between France and Austria were effectively rubber-stamped after a few months of diplomatic wrangling by the Treaty of Campo Formio in October 1797. Vienna formally acknowledged the French annexation of Belgium, recognized France's predominant position in northern Italy, including the two recently formed sister republics, the Cisalpine, centred on Milan, and the Ligurian, centred on Genoa, and accepted the transfer of the strategically important Ionian Islands at the entrance to the Aegean Sea from Venetian to French possession. The Habsburgs even, albeit only in a secret clause, acceded to French control of the left bank of the Rhine. In return, Austria was given most of north-east Italy, Istria at the head of the Adriatic Sea and Dalmatia along its eastern shore, all of which had until its recent conquest by Napoleon's army been the territory of a nominally independent Venetian state. The War of the First Coalition, as the five-year struggle became known, had ended in a magnificent French triumph.

News of Campo Formio sent the French into raptures of delight and made its architect, General Bonaparte, the darling of the nation. True, peace had not been made with the British, but they had been left without a major ally in their conflict with France and were in no position to do the French much harm on the Continent with their own small army. Besides, with financial problems growing in Britain and the Royal Navy in mutinous mood over conditions of service, it seemed perfectly possible that London would soon be forced to yield to common sense and give up the struggle.

Thus, by the end of 1797, the French Republic – and the Revolution – had not only been saved, but had greatly increased its power, influence and security through the achievement of the 'natural frontiers' and the establishment of friendly, buffer republics in Holland and northern Italy which would help keep the antagonistic Prussians and Austrians at arm's length in future. Thanks to the great exertions of her people and the brilliance of her commanders, France had gone from the brink of utter defeat to the summit of triumph. Within just two more years, however, in a spectacular reversal of fate, the French Republic would once more be on the verge of collapse; and the Russians would have played a key role in putting it there.

2

Unintended Consequences

One could debate endlessly whether there was a genuine opportunity after 1797 for Europe to settle down peacefully. Maybe, having failed to crush the French Republic and mindful of its obvious power, the established rulers of the Continent would have accepted its right to exist and acquiesced in its recent conquest of the Low Countries, the left bank of the Rhine and most of northern Italy. But then again, maybe not. After all, the Tory administration in London, in spite of its serious domestic troubles, refused to make peace with Paris while the French retained control of the Low Countries, while Austria undoubtedly resented the loss to France of her dominant position in Belgium, the left bank of the Rhine and northern Italy. And still, of course, there was the ideological divide. The continued existence of the French Republic, and, even more, its prosperity, seemed to pose a potentially mortal threat to the *ancien régime* everywhere. With its attractive doctrine of liberty, equality and fraternity, and clear proof that a revolutionary republic could more than compete with a powerful combination of monarchical states on the international stage, there was a real danger that the unprivileged majority throughout the Continent would soon demand to go the way of the French.

Whatever the chances of the French securing lasting peace after 1797 actually were, their government's actions in 1798 undeniably helped to make a reignition of widespread hostilities more likely. Having in the end won the War of the First Coalition so convincingly, the regime in Paris became brashly overconfident. It decided that, with Austria defeated, Prussia neutral, and Russia still showing no signs of being about to go to war, now was the time to further increase the Republic's security, power and influence in an antagonistic world.

In the early months of 1798, France exploited revolutionary insurrections in both the Papal States of central Italy and the cantons of Switzerland to send in troops and create two new sister republics, the Roman and the Helvetic. These acts were followed over the summer by increasing pressure upon the defeated kingdom of Piedmont in north-west Italy to conform with French wishes and policies, culminating, when they were resisted by the King, in his overthrow and the occupation of the whole country at the end of the year.

The key French move of 1798, however, was the expedition to Egypt. The brainchild of the Republic's Foreign Minister, Charles Maurice de Talleyrand, a man who had no equal in regard to his unctuousness, venality and instinct for self-preservation, the Egyptian project swiftly won the support of France's greatest general, Napoleon Bonaparte.

The scheme was intended as a means of attacking the British indirectly, a major invasion of Britain not being judged feasible in the near future, but it was never wholly realistic in its aims. Insofar as French occupation of Egypt might damage British trade with the eastern Mediterranean region, the plan had some merit, but the bolder idea of using the country as a base from which to launch an overland attack upon the heart of Britain's imperial power in India always had more than a dash of fantasy about it. Nevertheless, the project was approved, largely due to Napoleon's strong support for it. One suspects that the Corsican's emotions overrode his intellect on this occasion and that his prime motivation in undertaking the scheme was to emulate the feat of one of his idols, Alexander the Great, in founding an Egyptian colony and then, opportunity permitting, campaigning through the Middle East. As far as the government in Paris was concerned, it was happy simply to remove the obviously ambitious and hugely popular General Bonaparte from the capital, where he was perceived by many of those in power as a potential rival.

Setting sail from Toulon in May 1798, Napoleon's 40,000-strong expeditionary force landed first on the central Mediterranean island of Malta in June. Its strategic location made possession of Malta vital were Egypt to be turned into a lasting French colony, but although the island was easily captured from its rulers, the medieval chivalric order of the Knights of St John, the conquest would have damaging repercussions for France.

Egypt itself was reached in July and its ruling elite, the Mamelukes, swiftly overthrown following a crushing Napoleonic victory at the battle of the Pyramids. Although a campaign to mop up the remnants of the Mameluke forces had to be fought over the next several months, French control was successfully established in Cairo within weeks of the initial landing. Then, at the start of August, a British force under the command of Admiral Horatio Nelson arrived off the Egyptian coast and, in an engagement in Aboukir Bay known to the British as the battle of the Nile, annihilated the fleet that had carried Napoleon's men across the Mediterranean. Suddenly, Bonaparte's army was stranded hundreds of miles from home, and all thought of doing anything more in the foreseeable future than trying to hold onto Egypt disappeared. The French Republic had suffered its most serious reverse in years, a fact that did not go unnoticed in the capitals of Europe's monarchs.

Nelson's great victory in Aboukir Bay was crucial in bringing about a Turkish declaration of war on France the following month. Although the Mamelukes had ruled Egypt before the French came, the country had officially been part of the

Ottoman Empire and so a *casus belli* had existed between Constantinople and Paris since July. It was only in the wake of the destruction of the French fleet in the eastern Mediterranean, however, that the Turks felt bold enough to declare war. While the fleet had remained in being, the French would only have had a relatively short voyage north by sea from Egypt to Constantinople. That journey would be much harder by land.

Vital as it was for the Ottoman Empire, the great British naval triumph was much less significant in bringing into play the most important member of what soon became known as the Second Coalition; Russia. From his palace in St Petersburg, Tsar Paul had watched the detested French Republic grow in power and influence after its defeat of Austria with increasing alarm, and it seems certain that he would have decided to go to war with France whether Nelson had crippled French sea power in the Mediterranean or not. To be sure, the British victory opened up one or two minor strategic options for the Russian navy, but it was not a major factor in the Tsar's decision finally to send troops west to fight the French Republic.

Concerned as Paul had been about French expansion in Italy, Germany and Switzerland, it was the Egyptian expedition that at last made up his mind for war. Russia had mercantile interests in the eastern Mediterranean in the 1790s that had already been threatened by French control of the Ionian Islands and which the Republic's possession of Egypt further endangered. The greatest Russian fear, though, was that French control of territory in southern Europe and the eastern Mediterranean would give them a springboard for further, more extensive expansion at the expense of the Ottoman Empire. As far as St Petersburg was concerned, the lands of the declining Turkish power should fall to no one but Russia. Catherine the Great had done much in her reign to advance this cause by conquering huge tracts of Turkish territory around the Black Sea, but that was only the start. The ultimate aim of Russian ambition in regard to the Ottoman Empire was indicated by the fact that Catherine insisted upon her second grandson being christened Constantine, her vision being that her eldest grandson would rule Russia while Constantine would one day reign in the Turkish capital of Constantinople.

Perhaps the most important factor in Paul's *personal* decision for war in 1798, however, was the French occupation of Malta. In January 1797, just two months after he had come to the throne, the Tsar had signed a treaty with the island's rulers, the Knights of St John, whereby he agreed to provide them with funds and effectively became their protector. Partly this had been an attempt to increase Russian influence in the Mediterranean, but mostly Paul took the Knights of St John under his wing simply because his hated mother had refused to do so.

It may seem odd to us today that a man's pique at the sweeping aside of a medieval relic he had elected to sponsor just to spite his dead mother could be a major factor in the outbreak of war between two great powers, yet in the late eighteenth century the sensitivities and whims of autocratic rulers were often of considerable significance in determining policy of all kinds. Paul took the French conquest of Malta personally as a direct snub to his dignity and prestige. He resolved as a consequence to organize a crusade of Europe's ruling elites against the Republic and the Revolution.

If the Tsar took such umbrage at the occupation of Malta in June 1798, it may reasonably be asked why he did not declare war on France at once. The simple fact is that almost nothing happened quickly under the *ancien régime* (which is one of the reasons why the French did so well against it). It took time to call up troops, ready ships, arrange alliances, discuss war aims, and in a society in which nothing moved faster than a horse, that could be a lengthy process. So the Russians bided their time.

It was the following year before the Tsar's land forces were ready to engage the French, but his navy went into action as early as autumn 1798. Exploiting the opportunity given them by Nelson's victory in Aboukir Bay and the Ottoman Empire's entry into the war, the Russians sent a fleet under Admiral Ushakov into the eastern Mediterranean where it joined with Turkish forces to attack the French-held Ionian Islands. It was something the French had never expected to see; those old enemies, the Russians and the Turks, not only on the same side, but actually fighting shoulder to shoulder. By the following spring, the unlikely allies had cleared the last of the strategically significant islands of Frenchmen, before, eventually, handing them over to the nominal control of local aristocrats.

In the grand scheme of things, France's loss of the Ionian Islands was of no great importance. The Republic was certainly not going to fall, or even have its prestige seriously eroded, because of its failure to hang on to a few rocky islands at the entrance to the Adriatic Sea. The fate of France would be decided, as it always had and always would be, on the European mainland. In that light, the signature of a formal alliance between Russia and Britain at the end of 1798 was of far greater concern to Paris, for it signified the intention of St Petersburg not to restrict itself to peripheral actions, but to take the Republic on seriously.

The fact that Russia was now in the unaccustomed position of being on the same side as the Turks meant that she was better able than at any point in the past decade to send troops west to fight the French. Thanks to continued uncertainty over both Sweden and Poland, however, it was likely that those soldiers would be numbered in the tens rather than the hundreds of thousands. Moreover, as things stood at the start of 1799, the only way those Russians could reach the west was by sea, which would require a number of ships not readily available, even to the navally preponderant British. The attitude of Austria thus became of vital importance, and Russia would play the key role in coaxing her into the Second Coalition.

Somewhat peculiarly, the British government was not particularly eager in early 1799 to get the Austrians to join the war against France. It considered the treaty of Campo Formio a gross violation of the terms and spirit of alliance of the First Coalition, and so deemed Austria to be an unworthy, unreliable ally. Showing greater sense, the Russians realized that, as Prussia evinced no signs of abandoning its recuperative neutrality soon, the help of the Austrians was vital if the Second Coalition were to have any realistic chance of seriously weakening, let alone overthrowing, the French Republic. It was therefore left up to the Tsar's diplomats to get Vienna to adopt the desired course of action.

In some ways, they had an easy task. Hatred of the Republic and the Revolution among Austria's ruling elite had not dimmed over time. Indeed, desire to restore the losses the Austrians had suffered fighting the French gave them even greater reason to wish for France's defeat than before. Balancing this, however, was the simple fact that Austria's previous attempt to crush the Republic had resulted in an expansion of the French revolutionaries' power and influence, mostly at Vienna's expense. During the final diplomatic wranglings that had preceded the treaty of Campo Formio, Napoleon had dramatically threatened to destroy the Habsburg monarchy should the Austrians not sign. It had been a bold threat, but who was to say that if a second war against France turned out as badly as the first, that it might not happen?

Another serious concern for Vienna was the Prussians. Traditionally, Berlin had been an enemy of Austria, and in recent years some of the former hostility had re-emerged into the relationship. The Habsburgs were thus anxious that Prussia might exploit a renewed Franco-Austrian conflict to extend her influence in central or eastern Europe at Vienna's expense.

Skilful Russian diplomacy overcame Austrian fears. St Petersburg would stand by the Habsburgs as a firm ally and together they would smash the French Republic. To this end, Russia would send tens of thousands of soldiers and, just as important, their best commander to help Vienna and London take on France along a wide arc running from the Low Countries, through Germany and Switzerland, and into northern Italy. To keep Berlin in check, moreover, a large Russian army would be left menacingly on the Russo-Prussian border. The Habsburgs were sufficiently reassured and, in March 1799, declared war on the French Republic.

In the event, Austria provided, by some way, the largest contingent that fought on the allied side in the War of the Second Coalition. But for the Russian promise of assistance, however, it is debatable whether Vienna would have taken up the sword again. Russia thus proved the key in the formation of a second coalition strong enough to do the French Republic serious damage. Russia would also, as we shall see, prove to be the key factor in ensuring that serious damage was actually done. And that in turn would prove to have momentous consequences for the future of a young Corsican general, the French nation and, indeed, the whole of Europe.

In contrast to the War of the First Coalition, the War of the Second Coalition did not start badly for the French. One of the minor adherents to the anti-revolutionary alliance, the kingdom of Naples, jumped the gun, invading the neighbouring, pro-French Roman Republic in November 1798. Although the sudden attack succeeded in capturing Rome, none of the great powers were yet ready to come to Naples' assistance, and the French swiftly drove the impudent Neapolitans from their sister republic, invaded the southern Italian kingdom, and forced the royal family to flee ignominiously to Sicily under the protection of Nelson's Mediterranean fleet. In January 1799, the French defiantly proclaimed the creation of a new sister republic, the Parthenopean, to accompany their others in Italy. This was certainly not how the war was supposed to go.

A simple perusal of a few basic facts, however, indicated that France's success in southern Italy was unlikely to be followed, in the near future at least, with many more such triumphs. By the spring of 1799, the Second Coalition could muster around 400,000 soldiers to fight in Europe, the bulk of them Austrians. To confront them at that time, the French Republic could call on fewer than 200,000 effectives. The huge numbers that had been put under arms in the wake of the one-off *levée en masse* in 1793 had mostly been allowed to return to their former occupations once the crisis had passed. It was in order to address this dramatic decline in troop numbers that, with the renewal of war in Europe imminent, a controversial law had been passed in the autumn of 1798 introducing a permanent system of conscription. It would be late June 1799, however, before the law came into force, and then it would encounter widespread resentment and resistance, all of which would result in the Republic gaining precious little benefit from the new measure in its hour of need.

Lack of numbers was not the only problem the French faced. Just as worrying was the fact that many of their best commanders were stranded in Egypt. The most notable of these was Bonaparte, but sharing his current exile were several other highly talented generals. Their absence left France about to take the field for the big match with their star player and half of the first eleven sidelined.

In spite of the Republic's obvious problems, the Austrians, mindful of the beatings an inferior number of Frenchmen had given them before, were determined to remain on the defensive until their Russian allies arrived. The French should have exploited this pusillanimity on the part of their Habsburg foes to increase their preparedness to meet the Russo-Austrian onslaught when finally it came. Instead, emboldened by previous successes, including the recent victory in Naples, Paris ordered its armies in southern Germany and northern Italy to attack. Outnumbered and lacking in leadership, the French were checked on both fronts in early spring 1799. Still the Austrians remained unwilling to launch an offensive of their own until the Russians arrived.

The first wave of the Tsar's troops reached northern Italy in mid-April, and with them came Russia's greatest commander, Field-Marshal Count Alexander Vasilievich Suvorov. Despite his sixty-nine years, Suvorov remained as bold, dashing and dynamic as he had been in his youth. He was eccentric, mercurial, flamboyant, uncouth and supremely confident, a combination which meant that he attracted both animosity and loyalty. Mostly, the animosity came from fellow nobles who considered him graceless and from politicians who found him too bullish. His soldiers adored him, and it was his ability to get the most out of them, as well as his audacity and doggedness, that made him a formidable general. He has been criticised, with some justification, for a lack of great strategic or tactical flair – Napoleon once famously commented that Suvorov was 'a man with the soul, but not the brain, of a great commander' – but the fact remains that he got results.

Suvorov had made his name as one of Europe's best commanders fighting the Poles and Turks in the reign of Catherine the Great. Given the failure of any other *ancien régime* general to shine against the military talent the French Republic had unearthed in recent years, he was widely looked to throughout Europe as the man to give the impudent revolutionaries the thrashing the ruling elites so desperately wished to see handed out. Indeed, in such high esteem were his military abilities held that the Habsburgs agreed, indeed practically insisted, that the Russian be made supreme commander of the predominantly Austrian forces in Italy. For his part, Suvorov looked forward to the opportunity to fulfil the European ruling elites' most fervent desires. A devout Orthodox Christian who believed as passionately as any king in monarchical authority, he despised the Revolution and its supporters because of their disdain for both monolithic, organized religion and the supposed divinity and legitimacy of established monarchies.

The impact of the arrival in northern Italy of Suvorov and his Russians was both immediate and dramatic. Without delay, the Allied forces abandoned their defensive stance and advanced against the French. At the battle of Cassano on 27 April, he won the Second Coalition's first major victory of the campaign. For the loss of fewer than 2,000 men, the Allies killed, wounded or captured 7,500 Frenchmen and twenty-seven guns. The following day, having pushed the enemy back over a hundred miles in just a week and a half, Suvorov entered the capital of the Cisalpine Republic, Milan. A month later he was in Turin, having reconquered most of Piedmont from the French. Short on numbers and desperate to halt Suvorov's advance before he invaded France herself, the French withdrew their troops from southern and central Italy, opening the way for bloody, bitter and vicious anti-revolutionary uprisings that overthrew the Roman and Parthenopean republics. The wily old field-marshal moved to meet the emerging threat from the south and handed out another heavy defeat at the battle of Trebbia in mid-June. For the next two months, and against the aggressive Suvorov's natural instinct, he was ordered by his temporary political masters in Vienna not to invade southern France, but to reduce the series of garrisons that remained in French hands throughout northern Italy.

Thus, within the space of just four months, French dominance throughout almost the whole of Italy had been overthrown. In Germany and Switzerland, too, the forces of the Second Coalition had advanced, the Swiss city of Zurich falling in early June, for example, but these successes, significant as they were in adding to the growing sense of crisis in France, were less spectacular than Suvorov's in Italy. They owed a great deal, furthermore, to the opportunities the Russian field marshal's victories had created by focusing French attention on his actions.

The Austrians may have provided the bulk of the soldiers for the Second Coalition, but everyone knew to whom the greatest laurels should go. Suvorov had so far more than lived up to the hopes placed in him by infusing the men under his command with the spirit, energy and belief necessary for success, while his tens of thousands of Russian troops had tilted the numerical balance definitively in the Allies' favour. It had taken many years for the Russians to commit themselves militarily to the struggle against the French Republic, but now they had, their intervention was beginning to look like being decisive.

The current French regime had been in place since the fall of the Jacobins, and, as such, was the longest surviving of any of the post-1789 regimes so far. Partly, this was because, up to late 1798, it had not done badly in running the country. The War of the First Coalition had been won, many of the anti-Catholic excesses of earlier, more radical revolutionary governments had been curbed, and even France's precarious economic predicament, which went back to before the Revolution, had shown some signs of improvement. To be sure, the regime had always had opponents to both left and right who sought its overthrow in order to bring about either greater political representation for the less well-off and more radical reform, or a return to some form of pro-Catholic, monarchical government. To date, however, it had defeated all challenges to its continued existence with some ease, if not necessarily always within the strict bounds of the law and constitution.

How much longer the regime might have remained in place had events gone differently is impossible to say. What can be said, though, is that the crisis of 1799 finished it off. Its image may have been tarnished by its notorious venality and occasional illegal purging of the legislative chambers, but it was smashed by the string of serious reverses on the international front. The humiliation of losing so much of the territory that had been gained in recent years so quickly was bad enough, but when this was added to the domestic difficulties caused by the dramatic escalation in the war, it made a lethal combination. Economically, the country was near to collapse by the late summer of 1799. Inflation was running rampant and the price of even basic commodities, such as butter and cheese, was going through the roof; assuming they could be got at all. With the treasury empty, taxes shot up; never a popular move even in less volatile times. Law and order, meanwhile, was threatened by widespread resistance to the newly introduced conscription. Parts of France, such as the Vendée, erupted into rebellion while elsewhere many young men preferred to take to the hills and woods to live as brigands rather than join the army. And behind everything, of course, there was the re-emergence of a major threat to the very existence of the Republic and all the changes wrought by the Revolution.

The question in France in the late summer of 1799, therefore, was not so much whether the current regime would be replaced, but what would replace it. To left and right, the Jacobins and the Royalists were both ready and waiting for either a popular rising or a senior military figure with the support of a substantial part of the army to champion their cause. The prospect of a lurch in either political direction alarmed those in the centre, but maintaining support for an increasingly discredited government that had hitherto stood in the way of such a development was becoming ever less feasible, so there was just as much talk of plots and coups from this quarter too.

News of the parlous state into which the Republic had fallen reached Napoleon in Egypt in mid-August. Here at last was the chance the ambitious young Corsican had been waiting for since his successes in Italy had given him his first taste of real power. In the past year, he had strengthened France's tenuous hold on Egypt by organizing a colonial administration, putting down a revolt, and smashing two Turkish armies sent to oust the French, one at Mount Tabor in Syria in April 1799, another at Aboukir, near the scene of Nelson's earlier victory, in July. Now, though, he had bigger fish to fry.

One month on from his latest battlefield triumph, with the French government looking certain to fall, there was only one place for the general to be, and that was Paris. Political power was up for grabs and Napoleon had no intention of missing out. On 23 August 1799, he handed command of the Army of Egypt over to General Kléber and, risking capture by the British Navy, set sail for France.

By the time Bonaparte headed for home, France's fortunes had slumped even further. Having already lost almost all of Italy and having been pushed back in Switzerland and Germany, the over-stretched French now had to contend with a fourth European front after an Anglo-Russian force of more than 30,000 landed in Holland, seized the Dutch fleet, and advanced towards Amsterdam. As if this were not bad enough, on 15 August – the day, incidentally, that Napoleon turned thirty – Suvorov had won his greatest victory yet in northern Italy. A reinforced French army, led by one of the Republic's rising stars, General Barthelémy Joubert, had been routed after a series of desperate attacks by the Russian field marshal's men near the town of Novi. The French had lost 4,500 dead or wounded, including the unfortunate Joubert, who was shot in the head while leading an attack, and 6,500 prisoners. Worse, in the headlong retreat that followed the defeat, thousands more had deserted, so that the overall effect of Suvorov's triumph had been to reduce France's effective force in Italy by fully a third.

In the wake of his victory at Novi, Suvorov's reputation in the countries fighting the French Republic reached new heights. Already elevated to the title of Prince Italijsky (Prince of Italy) by Tsar Paul in July, his portrait now appeared all over monarchical Europe like some latter day saint. The British even went so far as to mint medals with him on them. But then, from the jaws of total victory, the Allies began to pluck eventual defeat.

Despite being made commander-in-chief of all Allied forces in Italy at Vienna's insistence, Suvorov did not enjoy a good relationship with Austria's leading statesmen and bureaucrats. They thought him uncouth, arrogant and alarmingly independent-minded, while he viewed them as grasping, ineffectual and ignorant of military and strategic affairs. Both sides were broadly correct in their opinions of each other. Even when things went well for the Second Coalition over the summer of 1799, there had been problems brewing. Suvorov had been appalled at the Austrians' failure to provide his Russian troops with a level of supplies and equipment that he considered necessary, and had made no bones about stirring up a diplomatic storm over the issue. Having thus blotted his copybook with the Austrian government as soon as he had arrived in Italy, the field marshal had proceeded to worsen relations by refusing, except under extreme duress, to obey orders sent to him by the civilians in Vienna, or even to consult with them on his proposed course of action.

What really soured the relationship, though, was Austrian acquisitiveness. Suvorov, like Tsar Paul, saw his mission as being the weakening – ideally the overthrow – of the French Republic and the restoration of established rulers whom the revolutionaries had dispossessed. Vienna agreed with these objectives, but also wanted to augment its own territory and influence at the same time. One target the Habsburgs had in mind was Piedmont, from which they hoped to shave some land to add to the traditionally Austrian-dominated province of Lombardy. When, therefore, Suvorov had unilaterally announced the uncon-ditional restoration of the King of Piedmont, after his capture of Turin in late spring, the Austrians had been livid.

Relations between Suvorov and Vienna had worsened over the summer, his continued victories notwithstanding, so that it was decided that the field marshal and his Russian troops should be removed from northern Italy, leaving the Austrians a free hand there, and sent to join another Russian army in Switzerland.

The idea was that Suvorov's all Russian force would then take the lead in invading the French Republic itself, while Austrian armies in Italy and Germany advanced on either flank and the Anglo-Russian force in Holland applied pressure from that direction too.

As strategies went, it was not bad *per se*, although, when he received his marching orders at the end of August, Suvorov was understandably vexed that he was being prevented from completing the destruction of French forces in Italy around Genoa and then invading France from the south. Where the new Allied strategy went awry was in its application. The idea was that an Austrian army currently stationed in Switzerland in support of a Russian force under General Korsakov would move north into Germany when Suvorov's Russians arrived from Italy to replace them. Unfortunately for the Allies, Austro-Russian relations had become so thorny that the Austrian commander in Switzerland, the Archduke Charles, younger brother of the Habsburg emperor, Francis, ordered his soldiers to march north before Suvorov was anywhere near Korsakov's army around Zurich. The French had been presented with a glorious opportunity to deal their adversaries a major blow in the centre.

Suvorov immediately recognized the danger into which Korsakov's army had been thrust by the premature Austrian move and ordered his loyal Russians to march to their compatriots' aid as fast as they could. Given that this necessitated them crossing the Alps, the journey was never going to be easy in the best of circumstances. One can readily imagine Suvorov's ire, therefore, when the Austrians failed to provide him with the mules he had requested for the crossing, holding the Russians' progress up by several crucial days as they scoured the countryside for beasts.

Consequently, it was not until 23 September that Suvorov's men made it through the lofty St Gotthard pass. As they started their descent, they began to encounter opposition, most especially at two bottlenecks called, appropriately enough, the Devil's Hole and the Devil's Bridge. The first of these was a 200 feet long tunnel, the latter a 400 yard long span across a deep gorge, and both were dominated by French guns. Typically, the aggressive Suvorov ordered both stormed, and it was only his troops' fanatical belief in and respect for their commander that enabled them to endure the brutal pounding they took to secure both objectives, albeit at a heavy cost in lives lost.

No sooner had Suvorov's tough Russians broken through, however, than the news they had been marching so desperately to avert arrived. The French commander in Switzerland, General André Masséna, a former smuggler from Nice and one of the finest military leaders the Republic had unearthed in recent years, had grasped the opportunity his enemies had unexpectedly presented him with. Recognising as swiftly as Suvorov that Korsakov's army of under 30,000 had been left in an extremely vulnerable position around Zurich by the premature

Austrian withdrawal north, he fell upon the unfortunate Russians with his numerically superior forces. In the subsequent battle, fought on 25 September, the French had routed their opponents, inflicting losses of 8,000 men, 100 guns and large numbers of prisoners. Korsakov's army had been smashed and the whole Allied strategy thrown into confusion as a result.

The crushing French victory at Zurich also left Suvorov and his men in a predicament. With the remnants of the army they had been marching to support now in headlong retreat, the field marshal's hardy veterans faced the prospect of being surrounded and annihilated by Masséna's triumphant soldiers. Suvorov's response to the crisis was characteristically dogged. The thought of surrendering or seeking an armistice never even crossed the old campaigner's mind. Instead, he led his men east, through yet more treacherous terrain, fighting yet more bloody skirmishes, until, finally, they shook the French off. Their losses in recent weeks had been very considerable, but they had remained a force in being, battered but not bowed. It is no wonder that when, in the dark days of the Second World War, the Soviet leadership wanted to institute an award to be given to Russian soldiers who displayed exceptional heroism and bravery in fighting the enemy, it chose to call it the Order of Suvorov.

Switzerland was not the only area in which the Second Coalition's plan to crush the French Republic began to go awry in autumn 1799. In Holland, the Anglo-Russian army that had landed in August was checked by a Franco-Dutch force under the sometime writer and ardent republican general Guillaume Brune at Bergen on 19 September. Two and a half weeks later, Brune and his men gave the Allies a sound beating at the battle of Castricum, and this, together with a worsening in the weather and the spread of disease among the invading force, led to the British and Russians evacuating Holland by the end of October.

The serious Allied reverses in Switzerland and Holland were partially made up for by a rare Austrian victory over the French near Genoa in early November, but there was no similar Habsburg success in Germany. As winter approached, the overall strategic situation had undoubtedly improved markedly for the French, yet if the threat of imminent defeat had been lifted, the Republic was far from being entirely safe in the longer term. Large Austrian armies remained poised on its south-eastern and north-eastern frontiers, and, despite their recent ordeal, there was no reason why the Russian armies of Suvorov and Korsakov could not be reformed, reinforced, and returned to the fray next year, the bold field marshal at their head.

France thus remained in danger and so needed strong, effective leadership. In spite of the recent successes of generals Masséna and Brune, few believed that the current regime in Paris was the one to provide that able guidance. The memory of the summer crisis was too vivid, the humiliation of the loss of Italy in just a few months too severe. Any credibility the government had built up over its years of rule had been scattered to the four winds. The desire for political change accordingly remained, and on 9–10 November it came.

Napoleon had arrived back in France on 9 October, having been fortunate to evade the attentions of the many British ships that now patrolled the Mediterranean Sea. His timing had been impeccable, for just ahead of his arrival had come news of his most recent battlefield triumph, that over the Turks at Aboukir in July. He was consequently fêted as the hero come to save his country in her hour of need wherever he had gone on his weeklong procession north to Paris.

The returning general had found France poised at a political crossroads. Almost anything – except the long-term survival of the present regime – seemed possible. Power might be seized by the Jacobins, as it had been in 1793, or maybe there would be risings or a coup to restore the monarchy. Either of these courses would have been extremely divisive, however, so the most likely development was always that a new regime would emerge in the centre to keep both the left and the right out. Plotting to bring about such a change was, indeed, already well underway. All the conspirators needed, in case things turned violent, was a sword; the backing of a popular general who could call upon the support of a powerful element of the army. Bonaparte, after quickly deciding that a return of the Jacobins he had supported earlier in the decade would have the backing of too little of the nation at this time, was only too willing to oblige.

Despite being practically bloodless, the two-day *coup de Brumaire,* as it is known, ultimately only succeeded because troops loyal to Napoleon were on hand to purge the legislature of members hostile to the plot, leaving a rump prepared to vote for the changes the conspirators wanted. The government was dissolved, two commissions charged with drafting a new constitution were to be set up under the control of the plotters, and a body of three consuls was to take over the running of the country in the meantime. Needless to say, one of those consuls was General Bonaparte.

In the weeks that followed the coup, Napoleon comprehensively outmanoeuvred his main conspiratorial allies in the negotiations for a new constitution, not only securing for himself the position of prime political importance as First Consul, but also ensuring that, as such, he would have almost total power in governing the nation. France remained, for the moment at least, a republic, but she was adopting a quasi-monarchical form of government.

Why did Frenchmen, who had, after all, revolted against autocratic rule (among other things) just ten years earlier, accept this, even voting for it in a plebiscite held in the new year? Partly, of course, they were just glad to see the back of the previous regime, but that can only be considered a minor factor in explaining why they voted *for* the new regime. Also of less significance than one might initially imagine was active desire *at this point* for the country to be led by Bonaparte, for although he was the nation's great hero, many were unsure about him becoming its ruler too (once he did become ruler, though, and proved adept in the role, the number of those actively supporting his regime swelled). More important in 1799–1800 than specific pro-Bonaparte feeling was the fact that he and his government provided a bulwark against the return of either the Jacobins or the *ancien régime*: Napoleon and his political allies were initially more attractive for what they were not than for what they were. However, the main reason most Frenchmen acquiesced, or even supported, a return to more autocratic rule was simply that it offered, and seemed to have the potential to deliver, what the great majority of French people wanted above all else by this stage – stability.

No regime since 1789 had managed to achieve lasting stability. In many ways, the government that Bonaparte and his fellow conspirators kicked out had come closest, but that had all been set at nought when the Second Coalition had been formed and plunged France into her worst crisis since 1793. Russia, of course, had played the key role both in building that coalition and in it enjoying the level of military success necessary to throw the Republic into turmoil, and this is why the Russians merit a significant part in the drama of Napoleon's accession to power; a part rarely accorded them.

Accept the Corsican and his autocratic rule as they were initially prepared to do, however, the bulk of the French people undoubtedly viewed the young general who had grabbed the reins of government at the end of 1799 as being very much on probation. If he could not make good his pledge to restore stability to France, his regime was likely to prove short-lived. In the mid to long term, he would largely be judged on his domestic policies, but in the short term, it was in the international arena that it was most pressing that he be successful. At the dawn of the new century, the Republic was still at war and still in danger. Napoleon needed a great victory to cement his rule. And that meant that what the Russians did would continue to play a major part in shaping this extraordinary man's destiny.

3

The World Turned Upside Down

Napoleon came to power towards the end of 1799 knowing that if he failed to deliver the stability the bulk of the French people craved, he was unlikely to retain his pre-eminent position for long. The First Consul was consequently extremely active in his first months in charge. The revolts that had plagued the final months of the previous regime were swiftly put down and bands of brigands suppressed. French finances were put on a sounder footing by the establishment of the Bank of France and the raising of large new loans. A whole new governmental structure that centralised power in Napoleon's hands, but made it much easier for decisive action to be taken by the state, was also set up. This was all done within a matter of weeks over the winter of 1799–1800, and both the French Republic and the Napoleonic regime were rendered considerably more stable as a result.

No matter what Bonaparte did domestically, however, he knew that events on the international stage might set all his internal achievements at nought. He therefore wrote to the rulers of Britain and Austria on Christmas Day 1799 appealing for peace. His approach was summarily rejected by both London and Vienna. Indeed, the militantly anti-republican British Prime Minister, William Pitt, who drafted his monarch's response to Napoleon's letter, used the opportunity to unleash a virulent diatribe against the French Republic and Revolution which concluded by baldly stating that Britain would only make peace if the Bourbon monarchy were restored in France. Given that General Bonaparte had certainly not come to power just to hand it tamely over to the bloated younger brother of the dead king, the prospects for peace did not look good.

The most interesting thing about the First Consul's peace initiative of Christmas 1799, though, is not that it was spurned by the British and Austrians, but that the Russians were not included in it. To be sure, if France made peace with Austria and Britain, the Russians would then have little sensible choice but to follow suit, as their troops would be unable to get to grips with the French. Nevertheless, the decision not to write to the Tsar can only be seen as a flagrant snub, and one that the French were lucky the ultra-sensitive Paul did not take to heart. It seemed that the new regime's attitude towards St Petersburg would be in accord with the long-established French policy of trying to exclude Russia from European affairs.

The failure of Bonaparte's Christmas peace moves meant that active hostilities would be resumed once the weather improved in the spring, so much of the First Consul's energy in the first months of 1800 was devoted to getting the army into a better state to fight. To this end, the recently introduced conscription laws were tightened and the process made more efficient, moves which were broadly accepted by the French people in light of the stark refusal of the Republic's enemies to consider peace. Napoleon ensured that the distribution of pay and supplies to the army was improved, and inefficient or greedy civilian contractors were replaced wherever possible by permanent, professional services under direct military control. Perhaps the most significant military reform of this brief period, though, was the formal introduction, at the start of March 1800, of the corps system. This greatly enhanced the strategic flexibility of the French army by essentially making it a collection of many mini-armies (or corps), each of which included infantry, cavalry and artillery, as well as other elements such as a staff and engineers. The corps system would give the French a great advantage over their enemies until they also adopted it.

As spring, and the new campaigning season, approached, Napoleon's confidence in the future was growing. Perhaps the best indication of this was his decision in February 1800 once more to offer peace to the Austrians, this time explicitly on the basis of the treaty of Campo Formio. At first sight, this may seem more like a confession of weakness, but its boldness is made plain when one recollects that the French had lost almost all of Italy in 1799. Bonaparte was thus effectively asking Vienna to give up its gains of the previous year without so much as a fight. It was a remarkably brazen gambit, impertinent even, and the Austrians unsurprisingly rejected it.

If Napoleon's audacity in offering the Austrians peace on the basis of Campo Formio owed much to the improving domestic and military situation within France, it was also based on the dramatically changing international situation. It had been clear in autumn 1799 that the Allied disappointments in Switzerland and Holland had damaged the Second Coalition, but just how severely did not become apparent until the new year. Most of the success the Allies had enjoyed in 1799 had been down to Suvorov and the Russians. By the time hostilities recommenced in 1800, it was clear to everyone, the First Consul included, that Russia would not be taking part.

To say that Tsar Paul took the defeat of his armies in Switzerland badly is an understatement, for it fails to convey the extraordinary level of rancour he came to feel towards his Austrian allies. Like Suvorov, Paul had been less than happy to see Vienna's expansionist ambitions undermining Allied strategy, such as when the old campaigner had been ordered to consolidate the Allied position in northern Italy in summer 1799 rather than invade southern France. The Austro-Russian alliance had survived that episode, but the Swiss debacle had dealt it an altogether more serious blow. The fact that the whole affair had had its genesis in Vienna's desire to get the troublesome Suvorov out of northern Italy, so that the Austrians could do as they pleased there, was always going to cost the Habsburgs dear in the Tsar's eyes. Things had been made even worse, though, by the manner in which events had unfurled. Archduke Charles's premature withdrawal from Switzerland, compounded by the Austrian failure to provide Suvorov with the mules he needed to cross the Alps, made it easy for Paul to blame the subsequent rout of Korsakov's army at Zurich, and the close-run escape of Suvorov's force from sharing the same fate, solely on the Austrians. On 22 October 1799, in a private letter to the Habsburg emperor, Paul had written, with an all too obvious acrimony:

> Seeing my troops abandoned and thus delivered to the enemy by the ally on whom I counted most, his policy contrary to my views and the safety of Europe sacrificed to the plans of your monarchy for its own aggrandisement ... I declare to you ... that from this moment I abandon your interests, to occupy myself solely with my own.

It is perhaps just possible that the Tsar might have been coaxed into cooperating with the Austrians again, but any chance that may have existed had been blown out of the water by crashing Austrian insensitivity over events at the Italian port of Ancona. The town had been captured in autumn 1799 by Habsburg troops aided by a Russo-Turkish fleet, but, incredibly, the Austrian general on the spot had only allowed Austria's flag to be raised. Worse than that, he had actually ordered the Russian flag to be torn down when a group of tsarist sailors had taken it upon themselves to hoist their standard over the docks. Paul had been apoplectic upon hearing the news, and the light punishments that had subsequently been handed out to the offending Austrians by Vienna had only made the Tsar even more furious.

After Ancona, there had been no turning back. Paul had sent secret instructions to Suvorov in early November to prepare the remnants of his and Korsakov's armies to return to Russia. On 8 January 1800, the formal order finally came and the Russians began the long march home. It turned out to be a less than glorious end to the career of one of Russia's greatest generals, for just a few months later, in May, Suvorov died.

The emotional Paul's fury at the Austrians was such, however, that the mere withdrawal of his troops from central Europe was not enough. Early in 1800, St Petersburg approached Berlin in the hope of securing a strongly anti-Austrian alliance with Prussia. The Prussians were stunned by the move, which seemed to them to be aimed at the ultimate destruction of the Habsburg state. To be sure, Berlin did not object in principle to the idea of Vienna being taken down a peg or two, especially in Germany, where the Prussians hoped to replace the Austrians as the dominant power, but the intensity of the Tsar's current stance alarmed the

King and his advisers. They feared a future in which France and Russia would be all-powerful on the Continent and in which Prussia would consequently rue the loss of Austria as a potential major power ally. Berlin therefore politely rejected the Russian approach, settling merely for a renewal of an old defensive alliance between the two countries.

Although he retained his new-found distaste for the Austrians until his dying day, the volatile Paul's enmity began to be increasingly turned from early 1800 onwards towards one of his other allies in the Second Coalition; Britain. The sources of this nascent dislike of the British were several. Just as he saw the damage done to Russian military prestige in Switzerland as the fault of the Austrians, the Tsar viewed the Dutch reverse as the responsibility of the British. He perhaps exaggerated British blame, but there was undoubtedly some justification for the general charge. London had never been quite sure what it wanted from the campaign in Holland, an attitude typified by the fact that there had been calls for the troops to be withdrawn as soon as the Dutch fleet had surrendered. In the event, the Anglo-Russian force had stayed, but its British commander, the Duke of York (he of the children's rhyme), had hardly exerted himself to move his men swiftly south towards France, and thus had allowed the French and Dutch to contain and ultimately defeat his army. Moreover, when the tally of losses had been evaluated at the end of the short-lived campaign, the Russians had not been pleased to discover that their men made up three-quarters of the casualties despite constituting a minority of troops deployed.

The Dutch fiasco was only the start of the rot in Anglo-Russian relations. Just as damaging was the poor treatment the Russian soldiers, evacuated from Holland by the Royal Navy, received at the hands of their British allies. London had crassly refused to allow the Tsar's men to disembark on the English mainland, but had sent them instead to the Channel Islands as if they somehow needed to be quarantined. Once there, their treatment was little better, as they were forced to subsist with poor facilities and on an inadequate level of supplies. The British then threw further fuel onto the fire of Paul's growing anger by publicly denigrating the abilities of the Russian army and refusing to exchange Russian prisoners of war for Frenchmen. London even had the nerve to begin to quibble over the subsidy they had agreed to pay for the use of Russian troops in the Dutch campaign.

With Anglo-Russian relations teetering on the brink of collapse in early 1800, the British government belatedly tried to turn things around by offering St Petersburg the Spanish island of Majorca should Russia remain an active member of the Second Coalition. It is unlikely that Paul would have found the offer attractive at the best of times, as Russia's interest lay in the eastern, not the western, Mediterranean, but the Tsar was in no mood to do a deal with London anyway. The final nail came when Britain chose to ally more closely with the hated

Austrians in the build up to the renewal of hostilities in spring 1800. Paul took it as a personal snub and consequently expelled the British ambassador from St Petersburg as he had earlier thrown out the Habsburg representative.

Although they were not party to much of what went on among the Allies over the winter of 1799–1800, the French could not help but pick up on the fact that all was not well within the Second Coalition. They did not need a copy of the Tsar's order to Suvorov's men to march home, for example, to discover that Russian troops were being withdrawn from central Europe in the early months of 1800. The expulsion of the Austrian and British ambassadors from St Petersburg in the spring merely confirmed what Paris had suspected for some time: Russia was withdrawing from the Second Coalition.

If the Russians looked unlikely to engage in hostilities with the French in 1800, they nevertheless still technically remained at war with France. We have seen how Napoleon initially did not seek peace with St Petersburg, but in the light of the Tsar's changing attitude towards his erstwhile allies, the French sensed an opportunity. Paris therefore approached neutral Berlin to act as an intermediary with Russia in the hope of improving Russo-French relations and perhaps securing a formal peace deal. The Prussians agreed to adopt the proposed role, but then carried it out without enthusiasm or energy.

In truth, it is improbable that, even if the Prussians had behaved with more vigour, there would have been much movement in relations between Paris and St Petersburg in spring 1800. Russian policy was still evolving, and if the Tsar was sure he did not like the Austrians or the British, he was far from convinced yet that the French were any better. So far, though, France's new ruler had impressed him. Paul was pleased by both the First Consul's autocratic style and his conciliatory attitude towards the French nobility and the Church. Napoleon's talk of drawing a line under the Revolution and restoring stability to a country that had known little but upheaval for a decade also appealed to the ultra-conservative Tsar. Of course, Bonaparte remained an upstart and France a republic, and Paul would undoubtedly have preferred to see a Bourbon restoration, but at least this latest French regime seemed less 'revolutionary' than its predecessors. His overall attitude towards the First Consul was thus hesitant and sceptical, but not unhopeful.

As spring 1800 neared its end, therefore, there seemed to be a chance to improve Franco-Russian relations, but before Napoleon could turn his full attention to that issue, there was a more pressing matter to deal with. Active hostilities had once more erupted in Europe and it was time for France's greatest general to take to the field.

The absence of direct Russian involvement in Napoleon's Second Italian Campaign of 1800 was arguably the single most important factor in its outcome.

Indeed, had the Russians deployed an army in northern Italy in 1800, as they had the year before, along maybe with another in Germany, the entire strategic situation would have been transformed. Perhaps Napoleon would still have adopted a bold, offensive plan of operations. Perhaps also the French would still eventually have emerged victorious. The chances of either, however, would have been seriously diminished. On hearing news, as the campaigning season approached, of the withdrawal of Russian troops from central Europe, therefore, the young Corsican must have thought that his thirty-first birthday had come early. Now, he would have a real opportunity to restore France's fortunes fully.

The details of Bonaparte's Second Italian Campaign need not delay us too long, for vital as it was, there was no direct Russian participation. Ordering the talented but conceited General Jean Moreau to launch a limited offensive in southern Germany with the French Army of the Rhine, Napoleon led the Army of Reserve, *à la* Hannibal, on a bold drive through Switzerland and over the Alps into northern Italy in an attempt to catch the large Austrian force there, under General Melas, between himself and General Masséna's Army of Italy. French plans were thrown out somewhat by an unexpectedly vigorous Austrian attack in northern Italy, but the First Consul nevertheless managed to cross the Alps successfully in mid-May, outdoing Suvorov's Alpine feat of the previous year by taking a larger force over a higher pass at a less propitious time of year. Still the campaign was far from won, however, for within days of the Army of Reserve arriving in northern Italy, capturing Milan and placing itself astride the Austrians' line of communications to Vienna, Masséna, driven back into Genoa by the earlier Austrian attack, asked for and received terms from General Melas by which he yielded the city in return for safe passage to France. All hope of catching the Austrians between two French armies was gone.

News of Genoa's fall led Napoleon to seek a battle with Melas as soon as possible in an effort to destroy his army before the Austrian general decided to withdraw into the coastal city, from which, supplied by sea by the Royal Navy, it would have been extremely difficult to remove him. Racing to close with the enemy, Bonaparte unexpectedly found a sizeable Austrian force near the town of Alessandria, some thirty miles north of Genoa. Usually so good at second guessing his opponent's intentions, this time the First Consul got it wrong. Expecting Melas to withdraw south towards the coast, Napoleon dangerously divided his army in the face of the enemy, sending part of it to outflank the Austrians and block their anticipated retreat towards Genoa. The following morning, however, 14 June, Melas attacked Bonaparte's force near the village of Marengo.

Outnumbered and outgunned, the First Consul was forced to fight a defensive battle, seeking to hold his line as long as possible in the hope that the troops he had precipitously despatched the previous day could rejoin him in time to save the situation. By late afternoon, it seemed that the day was lost. The French had fought magnificently against the odds, but without reinforcement their line could not take much more pressure before breaking. With the battle (and possibly the Napoleonic regime) on a knife edge, General Louis Desaix and the soldiers Napoleon had despatched the day before reached the field in the nick of time. Organizing and leading a brilliant counter-attack, Desaix threw the Austrians back and routed their centre, only to fall tragically to an Austrian bullet at the moment of triumph.

The death of Desaix, a man with whom Bonaparte had built up a close friendship over recent years, grieved the First Consul sorely, but things could, of course, have been far worse. Although losses in dead and wounded at Marengo had been comparable, at about 6,000 each, the French had captured no fewer than 8,000 Austrian prisoners and forty guns, making the battle a resounding French victory. Even more important than the figures was how the Austrians reacted to their defeat. It temporarily shattered their confidence and Melas sued for an armistice on terms that Bonaparte was only too willing to accept. All Austrian forces were to withdraw from the whole of Liguria, Piedmont and Lombardy. At a stroke, the Italian front was pushed 200 miles east and Napoleon was put in a position to re-establish French dominance throughout most of northern Italy. Shortly afterwards, Vienna agreed to a general truce and entered into peace negotiations, ultimately unsuccessful, which lasted five months. Although Marengo failed to end the war with Austria, it nevertheless showed that the danger to the French Republic had been lifted, that the lost empire in Italy could, and would, be regained, and that French arms were once more the envy of Europe. The First Consul got all the credit for this and so, more than any other single event, it was Marengo that stabilized his nascent regime.

After Marengo, Napoleon never looked back. As secure in his position as he could ever realistically have expected to be so soon after coming to power, the young Corsican could look forward in midsummer 1800 to a rosy future. And now the Austrian threat had been temporarily dealt with, he could turn his attention once more to relations with Russia.

Throughout the eighteenth century the usual state of Franco-Russian relations had been uncooperative and distant, if not downright frosty. In the late 1790s, however, a radical new conception of Russo-French relations had begun to circulate in France's foreign ministry. This called for nothing less than a full Franco-Russian alliance aimed initially at carving up the declining Ottoman Empire's possessions in south-east Europe and north Africa. The two nations would then continue to work closely together to make themselves the dominant powers in western/southern and eastern/northern Europe respectively. The scheme had a maritime aspect, too, for it was envisaged that, if France and Russia dominated the Continent, Britain's naval supremacy in European waters could be seriously weakened.

In theory, the design offered enormous benefits for France in the ongoing struggle for pre-eminence in which every major power in this period was engaged. The trouble was that to most French diplomats it just seemed like so much pie in the sky. For a start, there was considerable scepticism that the Russians would be prepared to share the spoils of the declining Ottoman Empire with anyone, at least without a fight. And then, of course, there was the matter of the Tsar's well-known loathing for the French Republic and Revolution. The plan was consequently seen as little more than an intriguing curiosity. Until, that is, Russia fell out so spectacularly with her Second Coalition partners.

As foreign minister, Napoleon had appointed the experienced, if odious, Charles Maurice de Talleyrand. A former bishop who had nevertheless helped to sell off church lands in France in the 1790s, Talleyrand was self-serving and cynical. He led a notoriously debauched personal life, his propensity for accepting bribes knew no limits, and his general outlook was neatly summed up, in his own words, by the phrase, 'The only good principle is to have none'. Unpleasant and untrustworthy an individual as he undoubtedly was, however – Napoleon would one day succinctly describe him, to his face, as 'nothing but shit in silk stockings' – Talleyrand was also undeniably good at his job. And by summer 1800, he sensed that there might be opportunities for France in St Petersburg after all.

Talleyrand took it upon himself to press upon the First Consul the advantages which might accrue to the Republic should relations with Russia improve. Napoleon, back from the Marengo campaign, listened with interest and responded with enthusiasm. Some token of goodwill was needed to break the ice, however, and fortunately the French had one to hand. In mid-July 1800, France was still holding some 6,000 Russian prisoners of war from the 1799 campaigns in Holland and Switzerland. Now, Napoleon wrote to Tsar Paul offering to return the men, fully equipped, with no *quid pro quo*, and commenting, not entirely inaccurately, that any success the Second Coalition had had against France had been due to the Russians. The approach was further sweetened by an offer to return Malta to the Knights of St John and, a particularly nice touch, a gift of the sword of La Vallette, the most renowned of the Knights' grand masters.

Paul received this barrage of Napoleonic generosity with some interest but no little scepticism. He was suspicious of French motives and saw the offer to evacuate Malta as the cheap gesture it was – the French garrison on the island would clearly soon have to surrender to a British force which had been landed on the island anyway. Nevertheless, Bonaparte's flattery certainly struck a chord with the Tsar, who, upon hearing news of Marengo, had exclaimed with excited vindictiveness, 'See what a drubbing they give the Austrians in Italy now that the Russians are no longer there!' The Tsar therefore accepted the offer to return the prisoners, but, for the moment, maintained an outwardly aloof attitude towards the French Republic. Privately, however, Paul began to muse on the possibility of Russia and France 'uniting and maintaining harmonious relations' in order to 'hinder the other powers from adversely affecting their interests'.

Paul's nascent interest in improving relations with France owed a great deal to his deteriorating relations with his former allies, Britain and Austria. As summer progressed, those relations, especially with the British, got even worse. The first key source of increasing Anglo-Russian tension in the second half of 1800 was the issue of the rights at sea of neutral states. Essentially, the greater their naval superiority had grown, the more overbearing the British had become in their treatment of neutral merchant ships. It was generally acknowledged that a combatant nation had the right to prevent contraband from reaching its enemies in times of war even if it was carried in neutral hulls, but that was about all that there was agreement on between London and the neutral states. The definition of contraband was hotly disputed, the neutrals favouring a narrow interpretation covering only materials of a direct military nature, such as gunpowder and weapons, the British wishing to include just about any good they could associate with the means to wage war, even food. Then there was disagreement over whether neutral ships should be allowed to carry non-contraband trade between a belligerent and its colonies in time of war when they were not allowed to do so in times of peace. Finally, and perhaps most divisive, was the issue of the Royal Navy's insensitive handling of neutral ships at sea. Because they had the naval superiority to do so, many British captains inspected the cargo of almost every neutral ship they came across, often dragging the vessels off to a British port to do so.

Britain's high-handed attitude towards the issue of neutral rights at sea undoubtedly hindered and damaged the trade of neutral states. What really stuck in the neutrals' craw, though, was not so much the harm done to their trade as the sheer arrogance, hypocrisy and selfishness of the British position. As Britain had the most powerful navy, it was she who effectively decided what international maritime law was in practice, and this was considered less than fair by the neutrals. Worse, the British were not averse to violating their own blockade and trading with their enemies when it suited them, yet strenuously denied any such rights to other nations. The thing that irked neutrals more than anything else, though, was the impression that Britain was exploiting the blockade of her enemies to boost her own trade and undermine that of her commercial rivals. It was not an inaccurate view. As one British chancellor of the exchequer of the period candidly admitted, the aim was 'to subordinate the trade of the whole world to the development of the navy and the shipping of Great Britain'. London was no less self-serving in waging war in the eighteenth and nineteenth centuries than any other major power. It was just generally better at getting away with it than anyone else.

By the early 1800s, however, there was a clear and powerful body of opinion forming throughout continental Europe and in the United States that Britain's wings needed to be clipped. She was seen as having grown rich and powerful by using her naval superiority to gobble up overseas colonies while other Europeans were distracted in fighting each other on the Continent. The France of the Republic and Napoleon had been and would be condemned for its desire to dominate areas beyond its borders on the European mainland, but Britain was just as guilty of having a lust for hegemony; in her case for global trade, overseas colonies and naval mastery.

In July 1800, the Baltic neutrals of Denmark and Sweden (who also controlled Norway and Finland respectively) decided that they had finally had enough of Britain's oppressive and unjust restriction of their trade. Aware that there was little they could do against a major power on their own, they looked to recruit a powerful sponsor for their cause, and that turned them towards St Petersburg.

The Tsar was only too willing to oblige. A man who seems to have had an almost congenital need to fight a crusade against something or other, Paul, now that he had stepped back from leading the effort to weaken the French Republic, seized upon the opportunity of challenging Britain's dominance at sea. With the enthusiastic encouragement of the French, he proposed the resurrection of the League of Armed Neutrality of Baltic States (also known as the Northern League). This had been formed, ironically enough, under the leadership of Paul's hated mother, Catherine, in 1780, during the War of American Independence, when it closed off Baltic trade to Britain and seriously threatened the island's economy. The issues back then had been the same as they were now: neutral rights at sea and a desire to clip British wings. It would be mid-December before the arrangements were finalised and the Northern League, including Prussia as well as Russia, Denmark and Sweden, was officially brought back to life, and a few months after that before all its members hardened their attitude towards Britain. Nonetheless, the trend of Russian policy was clear from late summer 1800, and it was unmistakably anti-British.

If news of Tsar Paul's moves to resurrect the League of Armed Neutrality had got them breaking open the crates of champagne in Paris, what happened in the autumn will have sent the corks flying from the bottles. Back in December 1798, London had pledged to recapture Malta from the French and then return it to the Knights of St John. When the island finally fell to the British in September 1800, however, the commanding officer on the spot, Admiral Nelson, declared that Britain would hold on to Malta until its future could be decided at a peace conference.

Tsar Paul, who had been elected Grand Master of the Order of the Knights of St John in summer 1799, was livid, and his response was swift and resolute. In early October, all British ships in Russian ports were impounded and their crews sent to detention camps. Trade between Russia and Britain was severed and British goods seized. Finally, lest London doubt the Tsar's resolve, he ordered all Russian Baltic ports to be prepared against naval attack and a fleet of forty warships to be readied in the northern sea. Russia and Britain stood on the brink of war.

Shortly before Paul had imposed his embargo on commercial relations with the British, one of his senior advisers, Count Nikita Panin, had tried desperately to arrest the recent trend of Russian policy. A committed Anglophile, quite possibly in receipt of bribes from London, Panin remained unswervingly opposed to the French Republic, once commenting that he would 'never sign a treaty with France except after the re-establishment of the monarchy'. It was anti-French, pro-monarchical sympathies that Panin attempted to reawaken in the Tsar in September 1800, urging upon him a resumption of active hostilities against the Republic and the Revolution. Paul, however, was not listening. Indeed, before the year was out, Panin would be sacked.

The man who had the ear of the Tsar in autumn 1800 was Count Fyodor Vasilievich Rostopchin. Rostopchin in turn seems at this time to have been strongly influenced by pro-French figures in St Petersburg, and this is certainly reflected in a memorandum he wrote for Paul in early October. As we shall see, this paper bore a remarkable similarity to ideas which had been circulating in the French foreign ministry in recent years, and, although it cannot be proved, it seems more than possible that the content of Rostopchin's memorandum was inspired by Paris via a convoluted chain of shady individuals including a favourite of the Tsar and a high-class French prostitute.

The Rostopchin memorandum was firmly anti-British, heavily censuring Britain for 'her greed and insolent behaviour on the seas, the dominion of which she wants exclusively for herself', and supported the resurrection of the Northern League. More significant than that, though, was another recommendation for future Russian policy. Rostopchin proposed that St Petersburg join with Paris and Vienna in partitioning the Ottoman Empire. Russia would gain Moldavia and Wallachia (provinces which make up two-thirds of modern Romania) as well as Bulgaria and territory south of there as far as the Straits, Austria would get Bosnia and Serbia, while France would keep Egypt and gain Greece and the Greek islands. Prussian support for the scheme would be obtained by allowing Berlin to annex Hanover, the British King's ancestral possession in north Germany, and a few other small bits of German territory. Once all this was achieved, the powers of continental Europe would be in a strong position to overturn Britain's dominance of the seas, at least in European waters.

Unfortunately, we simply do not know for certain what Paul's reaction to the Rostopchin memorandum was, and whether he approved of it or not. What is certain, though, is that by this time the Tsar was clearly interested in exploring the possibilities of closer relations with France. To this end, he despatched to Paris an emissary, General Georg Sprengporten, a Finn in Russian service, in late autumn. The French treated him like royalty, wining and dining him lavishly, the First Consul himself playing a key role in the wooing – and this despite the resumption of hostilities with Austria in late November.

In the wake of Marengo, Napoleon had once more offered Austria peace on the basis of Campo Formio, arguably a generous position considering his recent victory. The Austrians, however, remained keen to gain something for their recent efforts, and so, abetted by substantial English bribes not to sign a treaty, they had pursued a policy of continual stonewalling in the peace negotiations that had gone on over the summer and autumn of 1800.

The talks finally broke down in November and war resumed before the month had ended. Just as in late spring and early summer, it proved short-lived. The decisive battle this time came in southern Germany. On 3 December, in hilly, wooded country near the village of Hohenlinden, thirty miles east of Munich, the poorly-led army of Archduke John, the eighteen-year-old nephew of the Habsburg emperor, was hammered by General Moreau's Army of the Rhine. The Austrians lost 20,000 men, 60 per cent of them as prisoners, as well as 90 guns. French losses were just 5,000.

Austrian morale held a little longer this time, before seeking an armistice, than after Marengo. Fighting in Germany stopped on Christmas Day, with Moreau heading purposefully towards Vienna. In northern Italy, where General Brune enjoyed a series of minor victories before the year was out, a truce came into effect in mid-January 1801. The following month, the Habsburgs finally signed a peace deal, the treaty of Lunéville. This essentially reaffirmed Campo Formio, but Austria now recognized French possession of the left bank of the Rhine more explicitly, as well as acknowledging France's dominant position in Holland and Switzerland. The Second Coalition, mortally wounded since Russia's withdrawal, was at long last dead.

One of the reasons Napoleon himself had not taken the field when hostilities had resumed with Austria at the end of autumn 1800 was his desire to be in Paris to meet and greet the Tsar's emissary, General Sprengporten. The First Consul had been growing increasingly enthusiastic about the possibilities of forging strong Russo-French links since the summer, and his conversations with Sprengporten served only to fuel this enthusiasm further.

On 21 December, Napoleon wrote a fulsome letter to Paul in which he frankly stated that 'both for political considerations as well as for considerations of esteem for you, I want to see the two strongest nations in the world promptly and irrevocably united'. It was an extraordinarily bold comment, given the fact that

France and Russia were still technically at war. Yet Bonaparte's boldness was not entirely misplaced, for the First Consul's missive of 21 December crossed in the post with a message to him from Paul. The Tsar's letter was certainly less effusive, but there was much in it to encourage the French. For a start, he seemed to be willing to bury the hatchet regarding 'the principles of different governments that each country has adopted', something which hitherto had been a major obstacle to closer relations between the post-revolutionary Republic and the staunchly *ancien régime* tsardom. Moreover, in writing, 'I am ready to listen and to treat with you ... in re-establishing the general peace', Paul clearly showed that he was prepared to work with France in at least some capacities.

Crucially, the Tsar matched words with actions. Shortly after sending his letter, he restored full trade relations with the Republic for the first time in almost a decade. He followed this by peremptorily evicting the dead Louis XVI's brother, the Comte de Provence, from his sheltered exile in Russia, and rounded it all off by announcing that he would shortly be sending Stepan Kolychev, one of his senior advisers, to Paris.

The most spectacular example of Russia's increasingly favourable attitude towards the French, however, came when Paul took the extraordinary step of piling pressure on the Habsburgs to make peace with the French. He even went so far as to move large Russian forces to the border with Austria to reinforce his point. It is possible, of course, that even without this action, Vienna would have signed the treaty of Lunéville, though it is worth noting that, in spite of their recent defeats in Germany and Italy, the Austrians still had large armies in the field, and that some senior figures, including the Chancellor,* wished to continue the fight. Russian pressure gave the doves in Vienna the ammunition they needed to silence the hawks.

It was not just the Austrians that the Tsar was prepared to tighten the screw on either. Having resurrected the League of Armed Neutrality against the British in December, Paul was determined to make sure that it had bite as well as bark. Anglo-Russian trade had already been severed in October 1800, but, in the early weeks of 1801, St Petersburg strongly urged its partners in the Northern League to follow its lead and, even more dramatically, to enforce an embargo on all British trade with the Baltic region by occupying states and cities outside the League. As a result, by the end of March, Denmark had marched into the north German ports of Hamburg and Lübeck, Prussia had occupied Hanover, and Britain's trade with the whole of northern Europe had been severed.

The British were confronted with their worst crisis for a generation. Their inability to sell goods to Baltic nations was certainly problematical in financial terms, but it would take time to do really serious damage to the economy. Far

---

* The Habsburg emperor's chief minister.

graver was the abrupt severing of Baltic imports, especially naval supplies (such as timber, hemp, pitch and tar) and grain. Britain relied heavily upon her trade with Northern League states for both these crucial types of commodity, and she could not hope to make up the shortfall from other sources, such as the New World, before the loss of Baltic supplies began to have dire consequences. It was no coincidence that wheat prices reached their highest ever level in Britain in March 1801; and the situation only promised to get even worse.

Just as worrying for the British as the sudden severing of Baltic imports was the potential naval power of the League. Prussia had no navy to speak of, but Russia had eighty-three major warships, forty-eight of them currently in the Baltic, Denmark twenty-three, and Sweden eighteen. True, nearly all the Russian ships were icebound in early 1801, and the Swedes currently only had eleven vessels ready for sea, the Danes seven or eight, but the potential was frightening, especially considering that the Royal Navy already had to contend with the French and Spanish fleets.

Russia did not only present a threat to Britain at sea at this time. In a truly extraordinary move, Paul despatched an army of 22,000 Cossacks in early 1801 to central Asia, from where they were to march on British India. This shows the depth to which Anglo-Russian relations had by this stage sunk. The two nations were at war in all but name – and it did not look like it would be long before the real fighting started.

On 14 March 1801, the fervently anti-republican administration of William Pitt fell in London. Ostensibly, the critical issue had been the King's refusal to agree to Catholic Emancipation, but there can be little doubt that the state of the international situation had played a major part too. There was a growing feeling in Britain that it was time to seek at least a temporary peace with France, even if the terms she could expect to be offered were likely to be less than favourable. The resignation of Pitt, and his replacement as Prime Minister by Henry Addington, cleared the way at last for serious efforts at securing an Anglo-French settlement. It would be overstating the case to argue that London began to seek peace in 1801 *only* because of St Petersburg's increasingly hostile attitude, but the danger of sliding into war with Russia undoubtedly weighed heavily upon British minds at this time.

When he came to power in late 1799, Napoleon could not have dreamed that the international situation would have changed so drastically in France's favour in little more than a year, much of it down to the sensational realignment of Russian policy. By dropping out of the Second Coalition, Russia had greatly facilitated France's successful military campaigns against Austria. Through her increasingly anti-Austrian and anti-British stance, she had helped make Vienna sign a peace treaty and London enter into negotiations – and all while still technically at war with France. It had been an extraordinary turn of events, and, as the winter of 1800–1 approached its end, the First Consul was keen to take the next, dramatic step.

That Napoleon was interested in extending French influence into the eastern Mediterranean is beyond doubt. His annexation of the Ionian Islands in 1797 had been largely prompted by the idea of using them as a forward base from which to ensure that France got a share of the spoils if the declining Ottoman Empire collapsed. Even more explicitly, of course, he had invaded and conquered Egypt. Now, in March 1801, Bonaparte approached his recent adversaries, the Austrians, about the possibility of a tripartite division of Turkey's European possessions.

The French had hoped to discuss the Turkish project directly with the Tsar's envoy when he arrived in Paris, but Kolychev, a haughty aristocratic Francophobe, gave them a rude shock. Rather than showing any willingness to talk about carving up the Ottoman Empire, the Russian stunned his hosts by demanding that they return Egypt to the Turks as a precondition of any Russo-French peace settlement. The Tsar was prepared to acknowledge France's annexation of the left bank of the Rhine, Kolychev added, but in Italy the kings of Piedmont and Naples must be restored to their thrones.

The last demand did not trouble the French much. They had already pledged to restore the King of Naples under the terms of the treaty of Lunéville and Talleyrand informed Kolychev that the King of Piedmont would be put back on his throne if that was what Paul really wanted. Over Egypt, however, Napoleon would not budge. *L'Egypte française* had been won by French blood and the First Consul was not prepared to give it up without a fight.

Relations between Kolychev and his hosts rapidly became strained, and the French, who were still entertaining the much friendlier General Sprengporten, became convinced that the Russian was simply misrepresenting the Tsar's views. Perhaps Kolychev's general tone and manner were more bullish than Paul would have liked, but insofar as the demands to quit Egypt and restore the Piedmontese and Neapolitan monarchs were concerned, the Tsar's envoy was undoubtedly following his master's orders. Paul had expressly instructed Kolychev to bring up these points in his negotiations in Paris. Whether the Tsar saw the demands as genuine *sine qua nons* or merely as possibilities that he hoped to see fulfilled, we cannot be sure. Either way, the fact that he asked the French to abandon Egypt, an area of the Ottoman Empire that, under the terms of the Rostopchin memorandum, was to go to France, strongly suggests that Paul had reservations about the prospect of carving up Turkish territory with the French.

Perhaps the Tsar was just not ready *yet* to divide up the Ottoman Empire with two powers, France and Austria, with which he had had a less than stable recent relationship. On the other hand, maybe he simply hoped to secure all of the Turks' possessions for Russia alone. Or perhaps he was not interested in partitioning the Turkish Empire at all. Unfortunately, the evidence to prove any of the above hypotheses does not exist. What is clear is that, whatever Paul's views on the Rostopchin memorandum and its scheme to carve up the Ottoman Empire, Russia was, in early spring 1801, on far better terms with the French than she had been before Napoleon had come to power. Equally certain is the fact that St Petersburg's relations with France's one remaining major power enemy, Britain, were but a whisker away from outright war. The French Republic was in the strongest position internationally it had ever been in.

4

Alexander and Amiens

The night of 23–24 March 1801 was, predictably enough, an icy one in St Petersburg. The chill of the Russian winter, however, was more than matched by the coldness of the plot that unfurled in the early hours of the morning. Tsar Paul had suspected something was afoot earlier in the month, but had been uncertain against whom he should act or how. His indecisiveness cost him dear. He retired to his chambers in the Mikhailovsky Palace on the evening of 23 March anxious about the unexpected change of guards protecting the residence that night. The new soldiers had been drafted in especially by the plotters, but, although he suspected their disloyalty, Paul unwisely did nothing to secure a different set of guards. It was almost as if he wanted whatever was brewing to be over and done with, preferring to deal with the consequences of a revealed conspiracy than the fear of a hidden one.

Shortly before one o'clock in the morning, the intrigue was played out. A cabal of conspirators almost twenty strong and led by General Count Levin Bennigsen walked past the palace guards they had themselves selected for the night and headed for the Tsar's rooms. Most of the band had been drinking heavily, but their inebriation did not prevent them from knowing precisely what they were doing. Paul's only protection was his two valets posted outside his bedroom door, no match for the drunken mob that descended upon them. They were swiftly overwhelmed and the Tsar's chamber door broken down. The conspirators found Paul cowering behind a screen in a corner of the dimly-lit room. Bennigsen announced that he was being deposed, and when the Tsar futilely cried for help, a handful of the mob set about him with whatever objects came to hand. Within moments, Paul was dead, battered and strangled until he no longer drew breath. He was just forty-six years old.

Later that day, it was announced in St Petersburg that the Tsar had died naturally in the night of an unfortunate bout of apoplexy, a fiction that was officially maintained by the Russian state for over a hundred years. Few people believed the authorized story, however, even in the early nineteenth century.

It is generally maintained by historians that Paul's murder was predominantly a reaction to his domestic policies rather than to his volatile conduct of Russia's foreign affairs. Certainly, the Tsar had trodden on more than a few toes in his brief reign. He had been determined to strengthen central authority at the expense of local vested interests, an approach that alienated the bulk of the powerful Russian nobility. He had also made efforts to curb the aristocracy's and gentry's more flagrant abuses of the downtrodden peasantry, and had further upset established interests by trying to rationalise Russia's political, military and economic systems. Then there had been his general style of rule, undeniably so autocratic and capricious that not even his closest advisers at any given time had been able to feel entirely secure in their position. Indeed, many were the former favourites who had been exiled to their estates on a whim of the Tsar (Suvorov had died while enduring just such an exile). Together, his domestic policies and his erratic personality led to Paul being viewed as a tyrant by the elite in Russian society. The murdered tsar was viewed more favourably by many peasants and common soldiers, both groups whose lot he had endeavoured to better, but it was the small minority of wealthier Russians that counted politically, and they mostly celebrated Paul's passing when news of it reached them.

The opposition of many of Russia's privileged minority to Paul's domestic programme and a distrust of his capricious character only takes us so far in accounting for his assassination, however. After all, these were ongoing gripes and so pose the question why he was not removed earlier. It seems highly probable, therefore, that the Tsar's erratic foreign policy had a lot more to do with his deposition than is generally allowed. Of course, there might have been a coup in March 1801 regardless of what Paul did on the international stage, but the fact is that he was overthrown just at the point when his new anti-British foreign policy was really beginning to bite. In this context, it is intriguing to note that almost all the plotters were pronounced Anglophiles and that the man who fathered the conspiracy was the most ardent Anglophile of them all, Paul's former adviser, Count Nikita Panin. Some historians have inevitably gone the final step and asserted that the Tsar was murdered as a direct result of English bribes. The accusation would have been supported by Napoleon, who, according to an aide, upon being informed of Paul's demise 'uttered a cry of despair and gave himself up at once to the idea that his death was not natural and that England was a party to the coup'. This charge cannot be proved, although the British government at this time was certainly not averse to paying people to try to kill important individuals they did not find to their taste (Bonaparte himself survived several English-backed assassination attempts).

Quite possibly, English gold was the factor that finally turned discontent with the Tsar into a plot to kill him. Or maybe the conspirators were simply convinced that Paul's anti-British policy was both dangerous and harmful, and were unwilling for Russia to become embroiled in war with the hegemon of the seas. Either way, it is likely that the timing of the palace coup of March 1801 was predominantly due to the Tsar's foreign policy. His domestic agenda and erratic personality were undoubtedly crucial in building up hostility to Paul – indeed, it is hard to imagine there having been anything so drastic as a coup without them – but it was his direction of foreign affairs that finally led to discontent turning into action.

Intriguing as the issues of responsibility for the coup and the chief motivation of the plotters are, however, they were not the key ones for the rulers of Europe in early spring 1801. What most concerned them was what Paul's demise meant for the future of Russian foreign policy. And everyone knew that the answer to that question lay above all with the murdered tsar's young successor.

Alexander Pavlovich Romanov was just twenty-three years old when he came to the throne of Russia as Alexander I. He had been born on 24 December 1777 and named after St Alexander Nevsky, a thirteenth-century warrior-king and one of Russia's greatest heroes. Like Napoleon, a man with whose fate he would become closely entwined, he came from a large family, having three brothers and five sisters.

His grandmother, Catherine, played at least as big a role in the young Alexander's upbringing as his parents, and she ensured that he was given a fashionable education and learned to speak both French and English fluently. It was Catherine too that chose his wife, a German princess from Baden who adopted the name Elizabeth. The pair married in October 1793 while still in their mid-teens. It seems that Elizabeth genuinely came to love her husband, a feeling that he never fully reciprocated. In May 1799, the pair had a daughter, but she tragically died just fourteen months later. A second child, another girl, was born to them in 1806, only to last four months longer than the couple's first baby. As if this were not heartbreaking enough for Alexander, his three other children, all daughters and all born to his favourite mistress, died young as well, two in infancy and one aged eighteen.

As an adult, Alexander was widely considered handsome, although portraits show him to have had a prematurely receding hairline and a chubby face. Tall and well-built, he walked with a slightly awkward gait, the result of an injury to his hip sustained after falling from a horse. He was also deaf in one ear (the left) and grew increasingly short-sighted from his late teens onwards. His strawberry blond hair was curly, his eyes blue, and he wore contemporarily stylish mutton-chop sideburns.

Alexander's personality was complex. Indeed, he is often referred to by historians as the enigmatic tsar. Napoleon, ever an astute judge of character, came to sum him up by saying, 'I find there is something missing in him; and I have never managed to discover what it is'. Certain things can be said about Alexander with confidence, however. He undeniably had presence, largely a result of his imposing physique. He could also be charming and was religious, his faith intensifying as he grew older, so that by the time of his death he was practically living the life of a monk. He was typically cautious and had a tendency to be fickle, both with projects and people, one moment seeming to be solidly committed, the next abandoning them, usually when the going got tough. Although he projected an image of modesty, this belied an inner arrogance. As tsar, he expected his advisers and ministers to agree with him and rarely listened to counsel with which he dissented. His sense of his own importance led him to develop an urge to have a finger in every pie, to play a personal role in all manner of state activities, great and small. This attitude extended to foreign affairs, where Alexander always wanted and expected to have his views listened to and respected by other statesmen and rulers. He came to believe that he was a man with a mission, chosen by God to lead his people, although he did not always know quite where he should lead them.

Alexander's fickleness and hollow modesty help to explain another feature of his character which contemporaries often picked out; his apparent insincerity and ability to dissimulate. This deceptive streak appears to have extended to himself as well as to others. Alexander was a chronic fantasist, able to spout all manner of platitudes with seeming conviction while conspicuously failing to put his ideals into practice and, indeed, allowing their antithesis to flourish.

The classic example of this self-delusory aspect of Alexander's personality is his supposed liberalism. In his youth, he learned of the enlightened ideas of eighteenth-century thinkers such as Voltaire and Rousseau and outwardly took them to heart. Indeed, an old friend alleged that, at one point, the young ruler-to-be stated that 'hereditary monarchy was an unjust and absurd institution, and that the supreme authority should be granted not through the accident of birth but by the votes of the nation'. Fine words, echoed in less radical fashion by Alexander's frequent claims to be determined to give Russia a constitution, to give limited political power to some of the people. Practice, however, proved rather different. In reality, although as tsar he oversaw an investigation into the possibility of introducing a form of constitutional monarchy to Russia, he did nothing to implement such a plan. Instead, he ruled in as autocratic a way as any of his predecessors.

Alexander also claimed to be passionately committed to improving the lot of the poor Russian masses, but again reality tells a different story. As tsar, while he instigated exploration of how the conditions of the masses might be ameliorated, as soon as it became clear that this could not be done without undermining the position of the social elite, he effectively abandoned the idea. One senses that, at heart, Alexander always believed vehemently in political and social hierarchy.

In foreign affairs too, Alexander liked to project the image of a liberal statesman. He talked repeatedly of his desire for peace, but then so did all rulers of this period. In practice, though not an unbridled warmonger, he was at the same time far from averse from using war as an instrument of state policy. He would also often claim to be working not in Russia's interests but in those of the whole of Europe, but again this can be brought into question when one looks at what happened in reality. Russia emerged from the Napoleonic Wars with her territory and influence hugely expanded, something which was not achieved by accident.

In the final analysis, it is hard not to agree with Lenin's judgement that Alexander was merely 'playing at liberalism', that he spoke the language of the Enlightenment without ever really understanding it or genuinely taking it to heart. He was more interested in appearing liberal, enlightened and progressive than actually being it. This was, after all, a man who could condemn the slave trade while maintaining serfdom at home, apparently unaware of the blatant hypocrisy of such a position.

In reality, Alexander was no liberal, although the myth that he was persists to some extent even today, especially among those eager, for whatever reason, to argue that France's monarchical enemies during this period were not, ultimately, just reactionaries whose prime aim was always to maintain their own unjustly privileged positions. To be fair, the new Tsar was by no means the most reactionary of his contemporaries, but he was a prisoner of his background, incapable, both emotionally and intellectually, of doing anything that might seriously undermine the position of Russia's established elite. He thus lived shrouded by fantasy, a conservative who ever tried to fool himself that he was a liberal.

Self-delusion, or at least gross naivety, was also a strong feature of Alexander's role in his father's downfall. Realising that they would need the tacit backing of Paul's heir for their coup to proceed as smoothly as possible – as well as for the plotters to avoid retribution – one of the conspirators, Count von Pahlen, had secretly met Alexander at the end of February 1801. Paul's young heir was initially reluctant, but von Pahlen appealed to his vanity, always a sure route to winning Alexander round. Paul was behaving like a despot and Russia needed Alexander to come to her rescue. It was just the sort of thing likely to entice a man with a fantastical notion of himself as a modern, enlightened monarch-in-waiting. It is interesting to note that there were also rumours flying around St Petersburg in early 1801 that Paul might be about to replace his eldest son as his heir with the Tsarina's nephew, though how far, if at all, this affected Alexander's thinking is unclear. What we do know, however, is that he agreed to the idea of the establishment of a regency in Russia, with Paul being held under house arrest while Alexander took over the reins of state.

In the event, no regency was needed because Paul was murdered. Although it is generally accepted that Alexander, as a condition of his agreeing to the coup, had insisted that no physical harm come to his father, it is clear that he was naive in so doing. Paul was simply not the kind of man to take an attempt to remove him from power lying down. His murder was an inevitable result of the coup, something of which the conspirators were fully aware. When asked by a fellow plotter what would happen were Paul to resist the attempt to overthrow him, von Pahlen answered obliquely, but nonetheless clearly, 'you cannot make an omelette without breaking eggs'.

The fact that news of his father's death came as a genuine and terrible shock to Alexander showed that his appeal for Paul not to be harmed had been sincerely meant. Indeed, so grief-stricken was he that he initially proclaimed himself unable to rule, though that swiftly passed. What remained, however, was a deep sense of guilt over his father's murder. He had, after all, known of the conspiracy, even of its timing, yet had said nothing, and the new tsar was not so credulous as to believe for one moment the declaration that his father had died from an apoplectic fit. If nothing else, the bruises and strangle marks must have disabused him of that notion.

Alexander's first public pronouncement upon becoming tsar was that he would rule Russia as his grandmother had. It was intended to reassure the politically all-important Russian nobility, elements of which had, of course, just killed his father. Catherine the Great had done her best throughout her reign to avoid antagonising the social elite, heeding its opinions and respecting its privileges, which included the right to abuse, oppress and exploit the bulk of the population. Encouraging as this undoubtedly was to Russia's aristocracy, the most pressing issue in early spring 1801 was not the manner in which Alexander wished to conduct domestic policy but the course he intended to set in foreign affairs. Paul had left Russia on the brink of war with Britain, so it was with bated breath that London and Paris as much as St Petersburg awaited the new tsar's first moves on the international stage.

It is part of the Nelson myth that the great admiral almost single-handedly saved his country in early April 1801 when he destroyed the dangerous League of Armed Neutrality by smashing the Danish fleet as it lay at anchor in Copenhagen harbour. However, like the greatest of Nelson's triumphs, Trafalgar, the significance of the action at Copenhagen has been exaggerated.

For a start, Copenhagen was not the crushing British victory it is sometimes painted as. Fought on 2 April 1801, it was a brutal affair lasting several hours in which both sides took a pounding. Indeed, Nelson himself later freely admitted that it had been the most terrible battle he had endured. To be sure, the British emerged from the battering with a narrow advantage, but it was by no means decisive. Nelson won the day not because he smashed the Danish fleet but simply because he and his men proved to have just a little more stomach for the carnage than the Danes and held out long enough to get them to agree to talks leading to a truce.

That truce, moreover, was not the end to the League of Armed Neutrality it is often held to have been. All it provided for was a fourteen-week armistice during which Denmark would temporarily withdraw from the League in return for the Royal Navy not recommencing hostilities. Given that the British had demanded before the battle that the Danes not only withdraw from the League permanently but also accept a defensive alliance with Britain, a more accurate reflection of the scale of Nelson's victory is revealed.

The failure of the battle of Copenhagen to destroy the Northern League was further highlighted by the fact that the British fleet proceeded from there through the Baltic towards the Russian bases of Reval and Kronstadt. Nelson was straining at the leash to attack the real heart of the League, aware that it was only by taking on the Russians directly that British military action could dissolve the coalition that was so threatening to Britain. Far from quaking in his boots, however, the new tsar of Russia sternly warned of the dire consequences that would follow an attack on his territory.

In the event, Nelson never got his chance to bait the Russian bear, for it was clear to London by mid April that such drastic action was entirely unnecessary. Alexander simply had no interest in fighting the British. After all, he had come to power as a result of a coup largely brought about by opposition to his father's staunchly anti-British policies, so he was unlikely to seek to continue them. On the very first day of his reign (more than a week before the action at Copenhagen), Alexander recalled the 20,000 Cossacks Paul had despatched towards India at the start of the year. The following day, he put out feelers for a rapprochement with Britain. Then, as his first foreign minister, Alexander appointed the arch-Anglophile, Count Nikita Panin. In that the new tsar was affected at all by what happened at Copenhagen in early April, it served to irritate him and struck him as utterly unnecessary, for the League of Armed Neutrality was already dying, at the hands of the Russians, not the British.

Sensibly, London opted not to allow Nelson to attack the Russians (a potentially hazardous action anyway), but instead to let diplomacy, which was now moving in its favour, take its course. In May, the embargo on British goods and ships in Russia was lifted, and the following month an Anglo-Russian convention was signed regarding the thorny issue of neutral rights at sea that lay behind the crisis. Significantly, it was a compromise which resulted in London agreeing to a number of concessions it had hitherto strenuously resisted. With Russia having resolved its differences with Britain, the Danes and Swedes had little choice but to agree to the Anglo-Russian convention as well, leaving Prussia to negotiate its own accord with the British and withdraw from Hanover in October 1801.

Predictably, Count Panin had strongly supported Alexander's efforts to reach a rapprochement with Britain, just as he approved of the step the young Tsar took towards mending fences with the Habsburgs in late May when he restored full diplomatic relations by sending a new ambassador to Vienna. The key question now was what approach would Alexander take towards France?

Given his view that Paul's death was a result of British intrigue at St Petersburg, Napoleon never expected the new tsar to follow anything but a less antagonistic policy towards Britain than his predecessor. His main concern in the spring of 1801 was simply that Russia should not become too friendly with London nor too hostile towards France. In writing to Alexander to express his condolences over his father's death, the First Consul stressed both his desire for peace with Russia and the importance of neutral rights at sea. Bonaparte also sent a trusted friend, General Geraud Duroc, to St Petersburg to meet the young Russian ruler.

Although Alexander informed Duroc that he had 'always desired to see France and Russia as friends', other noises emanating from St Petersburg in the spring of 1801 were more alarming for the French. Shortly before Paul's death, the French had overrun the enemy kingdom of Naples and signed a peace treaty with the Neapolitans which allowed them to occupy ports in southern Italy and close them to British trade. Not only did the Russians object to this specifically, but Alexander called upon France to retreat from her position of hegemony in Italy in general. At this stage, however, to the chagrin of his foreign minister, the new tsar was not prepared to take meaningful action to back his demands up. Panin was strongly in favour of Russia renewing active hostilities with the French Republic, which he hoped to see overthrown and replaced with a Bourbon restoration, but Alexander was, as yet, disinclined to take such a line. His main aim in foreign affairs at this time was simply to settle differences with the other major powers and then concentrate on domestic issues, such as much needed administrative reform. Alexander's initial unwillingness to regard Napoleonic France as an enemy may also have reflected that the country and its ruler were widely seen as the most progressive in Europe; setting himself up in opposition to them could only tarnish the new Tsar's cherished claims to be enlightened.

As his confidence grew after a few months of ruling, Alexander felt secure enough to offend his foreign minister and other influential Anglophiles in St Petersburg by sending a new ambassador to Paris, thereby restoring full diplomatic relations with France, and initiating negotiations for a formal Franco-Russian peace treaty. The talks, which commenced in September 1801, distressed the British and were fiercely criticised by Panin. They continued nonetheless and resulted the following month in the signing of an accord that, at last, officially brought the state of war between France and Russia to an end. By the terms of the treaty, Russia effectively accepted French hegemony in Italy and agreed to help Paris make peace with the Ottoman Empire. In return, France agreed to Alexander having a voice in the much needed reorganization of the jumble of German states, shortly to be effected, and promised to compensate those German rulers, including the Tsar's father-in-law, who had lost territory on the left bank of the Rhine to the French. France and Russia also both recognized the independence of the Ionian Islands and agreed that they should be demilitarized.

Finally, although technically a follow-on from the main treaty, both countries pledged to suppress within their borders the activity of *émigrés* hostile to the other power; French aristocrats in Russia, Polish nobles in France.

Disgusted by the thought of reaching an agreement with the French, Panin offered to resign as foreign minister in mid-October, a move Alexander was quick to accept. The relationship between the two men had never been easy, even before the initiation of talks with France, and the way was now clear for the Tsar to appoint a close friend to the foreign ministry. Victor Pavlovich Kochubei never wanted to be foreign minister, preferring instead to focus on domestic issues, but at the time of his appointment, in the autumn of 1801, his reticence was not a major problem. Alexander also wanted to concentrate on domestic matters in the near future and so was more than happy to go along with Kochubei's proposed isolationist foreign policy, now that relations with all the other great European powers had been put on an even keel.

Thus, a little over six months into the new tsar's reign, statesmen on either side of the Channel had reason to be both pleased and disappointed with the recent trend of Russian foreign policy. The British had seen the League of Armed Neutrality dissolved but had been frustrated in their hopes that Russia might re-enter the fray against France, while the French had finally formally made peace with the Russians but seen their hopes of an anti-British alliance with St Petersburg evaporate. Now, the great eastern power was seemingly withdrawing from European affairs and turning inward.

Just as the prospect of war with Russia in early 1801 had played a major role in spurring the British to enter into peace talks with France, the initiation of Franco-Russian treaty negotiations in the autumn helped London finally decide to sign the preliminaries of an Anglo-French settlement. A renewal of active hostilities towards France on the part of the Russians had been the British government's last hope for a major improvement in its bargaining position in the near future, and now it was disappearing it seemed better to make peace sooner rather than later. Despite the dissolution of the League of Armed Neutrality, the British economy remained badly battered and in desperate need of a respite from the expense of war.

Although the treaty of Amiens was not formally ratified until 25 March 1802, peace effectively returned to Europe with the signature of its preliminaries on 1 October 1801. The terms agreed demonstrated clearly which of the two great powers had emerged the more triumphant from the past eight and a half years of conflict. Among the specific clauses, the British agreed to withdraw from Malta along with all their other colonial conquests made since the outbreak of war, except Trinidad in the West Indies and Ceylon (modern Sri Lanka). The French only promised to evacuate Egypt, which, in any case, they were presently being removed from by a large British expeditionary force. Given protestations made later by London, it is important to note that no pledges were made regarding either the protection of British trading rights on the Continent or the formal independence of France's satellite republics. Indeed, by ratifying the treaty in March 1802, the British government was effectively acknowledging all territorial and governmental changes wrought by the French up to that point, as well as Napoleon's mastery over the bulk of western Europe. Of course, no British statesman was likely to admit that openly, especially as so many of them saw the treaty as a mere armistice rather than as a settlement genuinely designed to last.

In France, although many of the more politically-aware doubted the willingness of the Tory administration in London to accept permanently the results of the past decade of warfare in Europe, the Republic's citizens were nonetheless overjoyed that they were at peace with all the other major European powers for the first time in ten years. Napoleon's popularity with the French people was possibly never higher than in the spring of 1802. Having already restored political and economic stability, he had now, at least temporarily, achieved international stability. When religious stability followed in April with the unveiling of the Concordat, which not only repaired the breach between the Republic and the Catholic Church, but also guaranteed the sale of church lands in the 1790s, acclaim for Bonaparte reached greater heights still.

Rarely one to miss an opportunity, Napoleon exploited his enormous popularity at this time to arrange a plebiscite on whether he should be appointed First Consul for life. The vote in May was an overwhelming 'yes'. His rule may have been highly autocratic, certain liberties, such as the freedom of the press, may have been restricted by his regime, he may not even have been a 'proper' Frenchman, but it was clear nevertheless that the thirty-two-year-old Corsican had the bulk of the people of France firmly behind him.

The European peace that played a part in Napoleon being so handsomely voted ruler for life was not to last long. Fourteen months after the treaty of Amiens was ratified in March 1802, France and Britain would be at war again. Less than two and a half years on from then, a third anti-French coalition would be formed, followed by a fourth shortly after that, and then, in subsequent years, a fifth, sixth and seventh.

Viewed as a whole, the conflicts that raged from late spring 1803 to midsummer 1815 have come to be known as the Napoleonic Wars. In the sense that they were essentially a struggle by various combinations of other European states to defeat Napoleonic France, the name is a good one, but the nomenclature has also been used by many historians as evidence that the sole cause of the wars was one man, Bonaparte himself. Like most extreme opinions, it is erroneous. Wars are never started by just one side, let alone one person. Even in the most seemingly exceptional cases, war is not the sole responsibility of one country or man. To call even the Second World War in Europe Hitler's war is a gross oversimplification which ignores many vital factors, not least of which was the fact that Hitler never wanted to fight the British and only did so because London declared war on Germany. Of course, all things considered, there are few who would not place the lion's share of responsibility for the Second World War in Europe on the Führer, but that is still a markedly different and more sophisticated position than simply blaming him alone. It acknowledges that there are other processes at work, that other players have options to exercise, and that, in exercising those options, they are taking at least part of the responsibility for events upon themselves.

Nor can we quite leave Hitler and the Second World War there, for the experience of 1939–45 has had a major impact upon how the earlier Napoleonic Wars have been viewed, especially in 'Anglo-Saxon' culture. Too often, Bonaparte has been seen in the English-speaking world as a prototype Führer, a warmongering megalomaniac bent on conquering the rest of Europe and beyond. In Hitler's case, the view has much justification – after all, he wrote openly in *Mein Kampf* of his desire to dominate the European Continent, to carve an empire out of central and eastern Europe, and to achieve it all through the medium of warfare. As far as Napoleon is concerned, there is no *Mein Kampf*, no blueprint for war and conquest. Indeed, in the case of most of the conflicts that make up the Napoleonic Wars – that against Britain from 1803, the Third Coalition in 1805, the Fourth Coalition in 1806–7, the Fifth in 1809, and the Seventh in 1815 – it was France's adversaries, not France herself, that initiated hostilities. On each occasion, moreover, the decision for war against the French was a genuine choice, not a clear-cut matter of national security that necessitated military action. Only by invading the Iberian Peninsula in 1807–8 and Russia in 1812 did Napoleon initiate war, and in both cases, there was an element of pre-emption.

None of the above is to contend that Bonaparte was not a man eager to extend French power and influence in Europe, to make France the dominant nation on the Continent, or to build and maintain an empire. Nor would it be fair to argue that everything Napoleon did was ultimately justified and defensive, while all his adversaries did was unjustifiable and aggressive. The point is that it is hardly fair to do the opposite either. Napoleonic France was far from the only state in Europe at this time vying to expand its power and influence. Every one of the major European powers, *without exception* (as well, it might be said, as most of the smaller nations), followed a policy of extending the bounds of their own authority and control in this period. If France was different, it was simply because she was generally better at it than her rivals. Or, perhaps one should say, than her continental rivals, for of course the British, great espousers as they were of the cause of 'freeing' Europe from French hegemony, were already well on the way to building an empire that would one day encompass fully a quarter of the globe; vastly more if one includes the Royal Navy's domination of the seas.

If one is to criticise Napoleon and the French for their expansionist tendencies, then, one ought also to condemn all powers that held similar ambitions. To maintain, as many English-speaking commentators effectively have, that the principle of French dominance in continental Europe was unacceptable whereas the idea of British empire-building elsewhere in the world and London's hegemonic control of the seas and global trade were perfectly acceptable is nothing short of nationalistic hypocrisy.

In practice, of course, not all empires and imperial projects are equally bad or good. Only a madman, for example, would argue that the USA's current global dominance is not hugely preferable to the nightmare of a world controlled by a Nazi Germany that had emerged victorious from the Second World War. Going back two centuries, one can also argue that certain of the European powers were 'better' imperialists than others. The British Empire has always had its defenders, and with some justification. The role of the Royal Navy in suppressing the slave trade in the nineteenth century, for instance, perhaps goes at least some way towards making up for the prominent role Britons played in setting up the slave trade in the first place. The Russian Empire, on the other hand, with its typically brutal repression, backward institutions and oppressive social structure, has generally been viewed as a more or less unmitigated curse for the vast majority of those it encompassed.

Of the two, the Napoleonic Empire was very much more akin to the British than the Russian empire in its overall impact. True, hundreds of thousands of non-French Europeans were taxed by France, tens of thousands were conscripted into armies directed by her ruler, and thousands of others were the victims of acts of suppression aimed at maintaining French control. It is hard to argue that these were not ills visited upon the people who endured them, but then such things happen in all empires. Crucially, moreover, it must be remembered that France was operating in a world in which the other major European powers frequently displayed hostility towards her. It is this environment that provides the context for the Napoleonic Empire's taxes, conscription and repression; a context that Napoleon's detractors are apt to ignore. It would have been fascinating to see how the French Empire would have developed in the long term had Bonaparte succeeded in establishing a lasting and stable peace.

It has also become fashionable in recent years to talk of the Napoleonic Empire as being little more than a grand spoils system administered by Bonaparte, in the guise of a prototype Mafia don, handing out parcels of land in Germany, Italy and elsewhere to his key henchmen. This wholly negative image overlooks certain highly significant points. For a start, Napoleon's redistribution of land to his supporters becomes rather less repellent when one considers that the great bulk of such territory was taken not from 'ordinary' people but either from engorged Churches or long-established noble families who had opposed the French. Unlike those who were dispossessed by the French, furthermore the majority of the marshals, generals and government officials that Bonaparte rewarded had at least done something to merit the material fortune with which they were bestowed. Also worth considering is the fact that, benefit greatly as many of Napoleon's main supporters undeniably did from the French Empire, the extension of his power and influence indubitably brought advantages, as well as drawbacks, to non-Frenchmen as well – the abolition of feudalism, a more equitable redistribution of land, superior administration, and a more enlightened, rational legal system, to mention but a few. Moreover, the extension of benefits to all those within the French Empire was a definite aim of Napoleon and his supporters, who hoped to win over the educated throughout the Continent to their vision of a Europe built upon meritocracy, efficient administration, good order and Enlightened views. To be sure, the spread of French-inspired benefits was limited in parts of the Empire, especially those which came under the Emperor's sway after 1805, but that was primarily because a fuller introduction of French methods and laws would have provoked a potentially dangerous backlash from local established elites in these areas, which France's enemies would have been sure to exploit. The more relevant fact is surely not that the French failed to introduce all their beneficial changes everywhere, but rather that they made the effort to introduce as many of their reforms in as many regions as they felt they safely could.

Although Napoleon was certainly an imperialist, and despite the fact that he expected himself, his supporters and France to benefit most from the extension of French power, he did anticipate that others would gain in substantial ways as well.* Most interesting in this regard is his vision, which developed as he became ever more successful on the international stage, of what French hegemony in Europe would ultimately mean for all Europeans. As he explained to his secretary in 1805, 'there is not enough sameness among the nations of Europe. European society needs a regeneration. There must be a superior power which dominates all the other powers, with enough authority to force them to live in harmony with one another – and France is best placed for that purpose.' It was unquestionably an arrogant vision, but by no means an ignoble or entirely selfish one, encompassing, as it did, notions of spreading to other Europeans the post-Revolutionary benefits that France enjoyed and establishing in Europe the kind of stable, durable peace that it had not enjoyed since the days of the

---

* There is perhaps a comparison to be made here with the forward policy adopted by the American government since 11 September 2001 – although acting primarily in the US's interests, Washington's more active approach in foreign affairs arguably stands to bring notable benefits to many non-Americans as well.

Roman Empire. Admittedly, the price of such a *Pax Napoleonica* would have been French pre-eminence in Europe and the repression of national independence, but it could be argued that it might nevertheless ultimately have been in the best interests of the majority of Europeans. It is too big and complex an issue to develop at any length here, but it is hard, for example, to see how a Europe dominated by France could have given birth to the two enormously bloody and fratricidal conflicts known as the world wars.

Of all the conflicts that made up the Napoleonic Wars, the one whose causes are most consistently distorted in the English-speaking world is that between France and Britain. While the French and their leader are typically accused of an insatiable and outrageous appetite for aggressive aggrandisement, the British are portrayed as reluctant warriors, taking up the sword against an over-mighty France purely in self-defence. To say that this is a partisan view is an understatement. While the British undoubtedly did have concerns for their security arising from French dominance on the Continent, the French also had fears for their security which at least partly explain their expansion. If this expansion cannot accurately be seen as purely defensive, moreover neither can the British desire to reverse it; for statesmen in London were far from unaware that a limited France and a divided Continent left them able to dominate the waves, overseas colonies and global trade.

Ultimate culpability for the breakdown of the ephemeral peace of Amiens, then, can maybe only fairly be shared equally between France and Britain. The determination of each to be the greatest power in the world effectively made conflict inevitable until one or the other emerged definitively triumphant. Responsibility for the actual rupture of the peace when it came, though, lies mostly at London's door.

The fact that as its new ambassador to France the British government chose Lord Whitworth, a renowned opponent of the treaty of Amiens, hardly suggests that many in a position to influence policy in London saw peace with the French as anything more than a breathing space in the struggle to reduce France's power on the Continent. Even more damning is London's abject failure by the end of 1802 to withdraw its forces from Malta or Egypt, as it had pledged to do under the terms of the peace settlement. For his part, Bonaparte had swiftly removed his troops from southern Italy as he had promised.

In late February 1803, Napoleon summoned Whitworth to protest at his country's refusal to honour its pledges. The ambassador replied that no action had been taken because of French policy in Piedmont and Switzerland. In autumn 1802, Piedmont had been formally annexed to France after its exiled king refused to return when Napoleon invited him back to rule, albeit as little more than a puppet. Around the same time, Switzerland had been given a new constitution by Paris and Napoleon made its Mediator (the man who was to be turned to if the Swiss could not resolve problems among themselves).

The British counter-protest concerning their failure to implement the terms of Amiens was unconvincing for a number of reasons. For a start, the affairs of Piedmont and Switzerland, unlike Malta and Egypt, were nothing to do with the treaty of Amiens. Napoleon's activities in the two areas, moreover, were hardly the egregiously provocative measures the British made them out to be. Both had already been firmly under French influence and the changes wrought were effectively little more than tinkering, certainly not a substantial alteration in the European balance of power as London attempted to claim. In any case, the British were hardly in a position to attack Napoleon for changing the official status of other areas of Europe, for in 1801 Ireland had been formally incorporated within the United Kingdom.

London arguably had more legitimate cause for complaint regarding trade, where Napoleon had introduced high tariffs on all British goods entering French-controlled Europe. Much as this harmed British exports, though, it was chiefly a justifiable attempt by France's ruler to protect French producers and merchants from fierce competition from their more successful counterparts across the Channel, and hardly a reason for war in any case. Moreover, the British government can hardly be absolved of creating tension itself, refusing to do anything about the virulent and hugely insulting personal attacks upon Napoleon in the English press, which undeniably stirred up anti-French sentiment. (London's claim that it could do nothing about the attacks as England famously had a free press is nonsense. Pro-French sentiment in the press had been ruthlessly suppressed by the government in the 1790s.)

Confronted with British intransigence over Malta and Egypt, Napoleon unfortunately tried to break the deadlock through intimidation. An article was published in *Le Moniteur*, the official newspaper, warning that, if the British did not fulfil their pledges in the Mediterranean as he had, France might be forced to reconquer Egypt. It was a crass and, given the Royal Navy's domination of the inland sea, empty threat, but London skilfully leapt upon it as alleged evidence of Bonaparte's expansionist desires and committed enmity to Britain. The momentum for war in Britain grew, fuelled largely by the belief that renewed efforts to reduce the old enemy's power had to be made before France became too powerful for her recent expansion in Europe to be reversed. In early March 1803, King George III made a speech declaring that Britain had been put on a war footing. This infuriated Napoleon, who roundly berated Whitworth and his government in public. Once he had calmed down, though, the First Consul tried frantically to prevent the now looming renewal of hostilities. First, he suggested that he would acquiesce in the British acquiring a base on Crete or Corfu, if they evacuated Malta, only to have London suddenly raise the stakes by demanding not only that Britain retain control of the island for ten years, but also that the French withdraw immediately from Holland and Switzerland. Bonaparte refused, which prompted Whitworth to ask for his passport, the standard sign that war would shortly follow. Napoleon now offered to accept a three-year British tenure of Malta, after which the island would be handed over to the Russians. Again, London rejected the compromise offered them, insisting upon their previous ultimatum. Finally, Bonaparte suggested that Britain retain control of Malta for ten years as she was demanding, provided London accept France reoccupying Taranto, a southern Italian port she had evacuated the previous year in accordance with the terms of the treaty of Amiens. The British government simply was not listening. In mid-May, even though it was they who had failed to fulfil their side of the peace settlement, the British declared war on France.

The renewal of conflict between Britain and France provided the backdrop for so much that happened in the international sphere over the following twelve years. It was the classic showdown of land power versus sea power, the elephant against the whale, the new Rome versus the new Carthage. France's best hope for defeating Britain was to overturn, at least temporarily, her mastery of the seas, thereby clearing the way for an invasion. For the British, the hope was that the continental powers would join them in the struggle against French dominance and use their armies to overthrow Napoleon on land. For both Paris and London, therefore, the attitude of the other three major European powers was crucial. With their help, Britain might prevail. Without it, with the French free to concentrate solely on the war against the British, it seemed likely that France would eventually be able to build enough ships to wrest control of the Channel from the Royal Navy long enough for Bonaparte to ferry a large army across.

Hitherto, the French Republic's most consistent continental adversary had been Austria, but from 1803 that would change. Indeed, the position the Habsburgs had enjoyed for several centuries as France's main rival on the European mainland would be challenged by a more recent member of the great powers club and its new, young and ambitious ruler. It would not be Habsburg Austria that joined the western European powers as one of the three key arbiters of the continent's fate, but the Russia of Tsar Alexander.

5

Russia's Road to War

At the beginning of his reign, Tsar Alexander had withdrawn from international affairs and turned inwards to address domestic issues. Within a matter of just months, however, the young ruler was losing interest in the problems of internal reform and looking for ways to play a role on the European stage. Having failed miserably in his initial plan to modernize his empire, he began increasingly from mid-1802 to view his role in international terms. Essentially, he came to see himself as Europe's arbiter. It was not the first (and would certainly not be the last) time a political leader came to power promising sweeping domestic change, only to shy away from tackling the tough issues that that involved and to compensate for their failure by moving instead into the supposedly easier realm of international statesmanship.

The first significant indication of Alexander's burgeoning interest in European affairs came as early as June 1802, when he arranged to meet the Prussian King and Queen at Memel in east Prussia. The purpose of the meeting was ostensibly to discuss the future of Germany, but really it was more an exercise in establishing contacts that might one day prove useful. In this regard, it was not without result in that the young Tsar got on very well with his fellow monarchs, flirting openly with Queen Louise and falling completely for the over-the-top flattery and deference shown him by the ineffectual Frederick William III.

In the aftermath of the Memel meeting, Alexander raised the issue of German reorganization with the man in the prime position to effect a settlement in Germany; Napoleon. The Tsar asked the First Consul to favour princes who had dynastic links to Russia, a request the latter was happy enough to accede to, but Alexander then put his nose out of joint by reminding him that Russia also retained an interest in the affairs of Piedmont and Switzerland, areas the Corsican considered very much part of France's sphere of influence.

By the autumn of 1802, it was clear to the Tsar's foreign minister that the isolationist foreign policy he favoured was no longer supported by Alexander. In the past six months, Kochubei had become more and more superfluous and disregarded, and in September the Tsar finally consented to his transfer to another department of state. He was replaced by Count Alexander Vorontsov, a senior member of a prestigious family and a man who had served prominently during much of Catherine the Great's reign. Worryingly for the French, Vorontsov's younger brother was the staunchly pro-English ambassador in London.

No sooner had Vorontsov replaced Kochubei than a mini-crisis erupted in Franco-Russian relations following Bonaparte's annexation of Piedmont. Although northern Italy had previously been an area of Habsburg influence, the Austrians acquiesced in this move, doubtless realising that it altered very little strategically, but the Russians pointedly refused to acknowledge the change unless the French compensated the King of Piedmont by finding him a suitable kingdom elsewhere. Napoleon was exasperated. Piedmont, like Switzerland or, for that matter, western Germany, was of no significant strategic or economic interest to Russia, yet here was the Tsar complaining, even though he himself had refused to compensate the King of Georgia for the loss of his realm in the Caucasus to the Russians at the end of Paul's reign (indeed the new tsar continued to follow an expansionist policy in the Caucasus in subsequent years). Unsurprisingly, Bonaparte ignored the protest from St Petersburg, assuming that the young Tsar would do nothing concrete to back it up and hoping that he would soon get over his irritating propensity to interfere in what the First Consul considered matters of no concern to Russia.

Bonaparte's decision to ignore Alexander's complaints seemed to prove justified in early 1803. First, although the introduction of the Act of Mediation in Switzerland, an area Alexander had expressed an interest in, brought a few murmurs from St Petersburg, the Russians basically accepted it. Then, in the same month, February 1803, Napoleon oversaw the long overdue reorganization of Germany. Some 112 independent small estates and forty-one free cities were incorporated into the larger German states, including Bavaria, Saxony and, of course, Prussia and Austria. Berlin had worked closely with Paris in effecting the settlement, Vienna had ultimately decided that it was better to accept it and gain something than oppose it and receive nothing, while states such as Bavaria and Saxony were delighted with it, and the majority of Germans seem to have approved of it. Ostensibly, Russia accepted the reorganization too. Indeed, Alexander had been consulted by Napoleon as agreed in the Franco-Russian peace treaty of 1801 and had given his consent.

In reality, however, the Tsar was unhappy with the whole affair. He had hoped that, by encouraging Bonaparte to treat states such as Bavaria, Baden and Württemberg favourably, a pro-Russian buffer against the further extension of French influence would be created in south and west Germany. Instead, these states all now inclined towards France, grateful for the generosity of the First Consul and eager to play the French off against the traditional power in their region, Austria. What really irked the Tsar, though, was the dramatic realization of his inferior position in Europe relative to Bonaparte. He continued to complain of not being consulted over the rearrangement of Swiss affairs and the annexation of Piedmont (though quite why he should have been consulted is unclear) and he moaned about the fact that France had very much been the key actor in the settlement of Germany, his own role being little more than that of a rubber stamp. The dangerous seeds of a potent jealousy towards the French ruler were taking root in Alexander's mind.

Following the renewal of hostilities between Britain and France in late spring 1803 (an event which, notably, almost all Europe's leaders, including the increasingly anti-Napoleonic tsar, held to be mainly London's fault), French troops swiftly occupied Hanover, George III's German electorate, and reoccupied the Neapolitan ports they had withdrawn from in accordance with the treaty of Amiens, closing them once more to British trade. As these were the only ways for France to strike at her enemy across the Channel in the immediate future, neither move came as a great shock. What was surprising was the fact that it was the distant Russians who once again seemed to be most irritated by the French actions, Alexander taking by now familiar umbrage at not being consulted by Napoleon before he acted.

The First Consul was perhaps beginning to become concerned about Russia's increasingly hostile attitude by June 1803, for in that month he invited Alexander to mediate in France's conflict with Britain. The move could not have been better calculated to flatter and please the vain, young Tsar, and he accepted the offer with delight. A month later, he forwarded his proposals to Paris and London.

When he read Alexander's plan for peace, Napoleon was horrified. Britain was to hand Malta over to Russia but receive the central Mediterranean island of Lampedusa instead. France, meanwhile, although being assured natural frontiers and a dominant position in north-western Italy, was to cede her current pre-eminent influence in the rest of Italy, Switzerland, south and west Germany and Holland. A Russian-sponsored peace was thus to be founded almost entirely on French sacrifices, a proposition Bonaparte can hardly have been expected to accept, at least without some kind of reciprocal retreat by the British, such as a withdrawal from Ireland and India. Inevitably, Napoleon rejected the Tsar's proposals, concluded from them that Russia was veering very much towards the British, and began to speak of the Russians from summer 1803 onwards as potential enemies.

Interestingly, London too rejected Alexander's proposals, which, given their heavy bias in Britain's favour, indicates just how far the British government's determination to restrict French power went. It was perhaps fortunate for the First Consul that the Tory administration was equally unamenable to the Russian scheme, for the Tsar took its rejection very much to heart. Having believed he had finally been accepted as Europe's arbiter in June, it was clear by the end of August that respect for his views was not as great as he had hoped. Upset with both western European powers, it was nevertheless Bonaparte, the man who had invited his mediation in the first place, for whom Alexander reserved a special resentment.

Two developments in the final third of 1803 pushed Alexander further down the road towards war with France. The first came in late September, when Napoleon openly accused the Russian ambassador in Paris, Count Arkady Morkov, of colluding with the First Consul's enemies both in France and abroad, and demanded his replacement. The charge was not without justification, but the Tsar was furious at the public manner in which Bonaparte had aired his grievance. Alexander did recall Morkov but showed his displeasure at the First Consul by awarding the ambassador Russia's highest honour when he returned to St Petersburg.

The second development in autumn 1803 that made war between Russia and France more likely was altogether more important, and beyond Napoleon's control. Vorontsov's deputy at the Russian foreign ministry since September 1802 had been an old friend of Alexander's called Prince Adam Czartoryski. With the foreign minister now becoming increasingly ill (he was to die in 1805), his deputy effectively took over, and he was to have a profound impact upon Russian foreign policy.

Czartoryski was a handsome, intelligent man in his mid-thirties with a reputation as something of a charmer (indeed, he may even have cuckolded Alexander himself, although if he did, the Tsar was either unaware or did not care). The key facts about him, though, were that he was a member of a prominent Polish family and a passionate nationalist.

Czartoryski's prime aim was his desire to see some form of Polish state recreated. His friendship with Alexander, and what little realism he allowed into his otherwise mostly naive or inconsistent thoughts, led him specifically to target the resurrection of a kingdom of Poland under the suzerainty of the Tsar. For his part, Alexander encouraged his friend to believe that he would one day put Poland back on the map, but when he finally did so, at the end of the Napoleonic Wars, the reconstituted kingdom swiftly proved to be a great disappointment to the Poles themselves. There was only one power in this period that would grant the Poles anything approaching an independent state and that, ironically enough, was the one power Czartoryski did more than anyone else to push Alexander into war with; France.

To be fair, Czartoryski could not have succeeded in getting the Tsar to pursue a policy that was likely to embroil Russia with France unless Alexander was, at some level, already amenable to the idea. Nevertheless, by skilfully manipulating his friend's character, the Pole encouraged the Tsar to set himself ever more firmly against the French.

Aware that his prime goal, the restitution of a Polish state, was not one that, on its own, would much appeal to Alexander, and even less to the Russian nobility, Czartoryski formulated an overall foreign policy programme that he hoped would lead to his cherished aim being fulfilled. He outlined his scheme in a crucial memorandum of 1803.

Appealing to Alexander's vanity, the deputy foreign minister called for Russia to become Europe's saviour from the 'menace' of the French Republic and its leader. Czartoryski made much of the idea of what would become known in the twentieth century as national self-determination, strongly advocating that nations such as the Dutch or Swiss should be free to rule themselves. The intention was clear. If Alexander accepted the right of these nationalities to govern themselves, then surely he could not oppose self-determination of at least a limited kind for the Poles.

Czartoryski weakened his case for the rights of small nationalities to rule themselves, however, in much of the rest of his memorandum. Aware of Russia's expansionist aims regarding the Ottoman Empire, he advocated direct annexation of Moldavia and Wallachia and the founding of a Russian 'protectorate' over the whole of the Balkans, arguing that 'no other European power must establish posts there'. The idea behind this blatant appeal to Russian acquisitiveness was that, if he were seen to play a part in the achievement of the long-cherished Russian goal of taking over the lands of the declining Ottoman Empire, Czartoryski's reward might be a Polish state.

Elsewhere in Europe, the Pole advocated the establishment of both an independent north Italian state and a German federation which excluded Prussia and Austria, the aim being to deny those two powers (as well as France) influence in those regions and thus reduce their relative strength *vis-à-vis* Russia. This was especially important given that Austria and particularly Prussia currently possessed large tracts of Polish territory that the deputy foreign minister hoped Alexander would be able to 'liberate' from them.

Czartoryski had the sense at least to realize that his highly ambitious programme could not be achieved by Russia alone, so he promoted the idea of an alliance with what he saw as the least directly threatening to the Russians of all the other European powers; Britain. The British would acquiesce, he hoped, in Russian expansion in the Balkans in return for the breaking of French dominance on the Continent. They too, he felt, would support the establishment of neutral states along France's borders as a limit on the influence of the three 'central' powers.*

What Czartoryski was effectively proposing, therefore, was the reduction of French, Prussian and Austrian power to the benefit of some of the smaller nationalities of Europe (most notably the Poles) and of the British and Russians. Of course, it would not do to be too obvious about elements of the scheme,

---

* Prussia, Austria and France.

especially the expansionist ones, so the whole plan was to be wrapped in a veneer of altruism. Russia and her tsar would be acting purely in the interests of Europe, their aim being simply to bring stability, peace and justice to a continent ravaged by war and turmoil.

Over the following year, Alexander came to accept most of Czartoryski's programme, although, significantly, he would never commit himself fully to the restoration of a Polish state. He adored the prospect his friend laid before him of becoming Europe's 'saviour' and was attracted to the Pole's scheme for expanding Russian influence and territory at the expense of the Ottoman Empire. Like most politically significant figures in Russia at this time, the Tsar tended to view the Balkans and the Near East as Russian spheres of influence. Their hope was that Russia would be able to persist in gradually taking over Turkish lands as the Ottoman Empire continued to decline. Their fear was that other powers might also cast covetous eyes on the Turk's territory and that, were the Ottoman Empire suddenly to collapse in the near future, Russia might not be strong enough to secure the whole of it for herself.* This is why the French occupation of Egypt had troubled St Petersburg, why the Russians had shown such concern over the fate of the Ionian islands and Malta, both potential staging posts for expansion in the eastern Mediterranean, and why the French presence in Italy, next door to the Balkans, worried them too.

Napoleon's empty threat of early 1803 to reoccupy Egypt also had a profound effect in Russia. Indeed, it was perhaps one of the most important events on the road to a renewal of Franco-Russian hostilities. In fact, although Bonaparte did send agents to Egypt and the Levant, and does seem to have been toying with the idea of mounting an expedition to reclaim the land of the Pharoahs for France, the likelihood of him actually doing so was never great. The Royal Navy had amply demonstrated the dangers of such a project when it had been attempted the first time, and it is highly improbable that Napoleon would again have risked the destruction of an invasion force at sea or its cutting off from France once it landed.

None of this seems to have registered with the Russians. The spectre of the French 'stealing' Ottoman territory from them loomed large from early 1803 on, and indeed grew. Soon, the Russians were wildly imagining French armies

---

* In this light, the outbreak of a major Serb revolt against Turkish rule at the start of 1804 provoked something of a panic in St Petersburg. Some argued that Russia should exploit the opportunity by championing the Serb cause and then replacing Turkish domination of Serbia with Russian. Instead, more cautious counsel prevailed. It was feared that a successful Serb revolt would trigger the collapse of the Ottoman Empire and precipitate a free-for-all among the great powers that would see Russia lose territory to others that she craved for herself. The Russians judged that they simply were not yet strong enough to guarantee the lion's share of the spoils, and so the Serbs were left to their fate.

crossing the Adriatic from Italy and marching through the Balkans; even advancing on the southern lands bordering the Black Sea won from the Turks in the reign of Catherine the Great. Crucially, Czartoryski played on these fears with Alexander, exaggerating the French threat, and thereby helping to promote his pro-British, anti-French foreign policy programme.

It is no coincidence that just a few weeks after Czartoryski effectively became Russian foreign minister, St Petersburg made its first attempt in several years to secure an anti-French alliance. It was not at the most obvious target, London, that this effort was directed, however, but at Vienna. After all, if the Russians were going to intimidate or fight the French, they would stand a far better chance of success if they had the support of the Habsburgs and their large army.

The Russian proposal of December 1803 and its aim were simple. In order to stop any further French expansion, Austria would mobilize her entire army while Russia would send 80,000 additional troops. Although the alliance was theoretically to be purely defensive, it is hard to see how Vienna could have kept all its forces mobilized without sooner or later going to war. The Habsburgs, appreciating where the Russian alliance was likely to lead and unwilling as yet to risk fighting a French army and leader who had already soundly beaten them twice, politely rejected the proposal. Nevertheless, the course of Russian foreign policy was now clear. It was heading unmistakably towards war with France.

The next step on Russia's road to war, in late March 1804, was the most extraordinary yet. For the past several years, the ultra-reactionary Comte d'Artois, backed and funded by the British government, had led a royalist cabal in London which aimed to assassinate Napoleon and put Artois's fat and useless elder brother, the Comte de Provence, on the throne of France. They had nearly succeeded in killing Bonaparte at Christmas 1800, when the First Consul's carriage had narrowly avoided being blown to pieces by a cart loaded with gunpowder. The plots continued over the following few years, and by early 1804 the latest plan was to intercept Napoleon's carriage, murder him and foment rebellion throughout France.

The conspiracy was foiled by the First Consul's efficient police and spy network before it could be put into effect, but interrogation of the initial captives brought to light a web of intrigue that extended to General Moreau, the victor of Hohenlinden and a man bitterly resentful of how much further Bonaparte had risen than him, and an unnamed Bourbon prince. Towards the treacherous Moreau, Napoleon was merciful, merely sending him into exile, but France's ruler determined to make an example of the Bourbon prince in the hope of discouraging any future plots.

The trouble, of course, was identifying the prince. Even today, it is not clear to whom the interrogated conspirators were referring when they talked of an anonymous Bourbon prince returning to France to lead a royalist rebellion. The obvious candidate was Artois, although he was safely ensconced in London. The suspicions of Napoleon's police therefore fell on the Duc d'Enghien, a member of a lesser branch of the Bourbon family, who lived just across the border from France in the German state of Baden. Certainly, Enghien was an ardent royalist in English pay who had talked of leading troops against his homeland, though whether he was directly implicated in this latest plot is by no means clear. Nevertheless, on the night of 20 March 1804, a small unit of French troops crossed the frontier into Baden, abducted Enghien from his estate, and took him back to Vincennes, where he was rapidly tried by court martial, convicted of conspiring against France and shot in the early hours of the following morning.

There is no doubt that the French action was ruthless, rash and of dubious legality, but the killing of Enghien does not appear to have damaged the First Consul's standing among the French people and it did effectively end the threat of Bourbon-sponsored conspiracies for the remainder of his rule. The affair was not without its costs to Napoleon, though, for it brought on him the opprobrium of the established ruling elites of Europe, who sanctimoniously accused him of murder most heinous while conveniently ignoring that it was a direct result of efforts to kill him.

The deepest umbrage at Enghien's execution was taken in the socially most conservative of Europe's states, Russia. To be fair, the Tsar had more cause for complaint than most in that it had been his father-in-law's territory of Baden from which Enghien had been abducted, but what really offended both him and the Russian nobility – indeed established rulers and aristocrats throughout Europe – was the affront to the 'sanctity' of royal blood. By killing a prince as if he were a common criminal, the Napoleonic regime had gone beyond the pale in the eyes of Europe's elite. It reminded them that, unlike them, France's leaders were no respecters of privilege based solely upon a person's birth and reignited the ideological, class-driven antagonisms of the 1790s. Rarely was Alexander more his grandmother's grandson than when, in the wake of Enghien's death, he echoed Catherine the Great's melodramatic reaction to news of King Louis XVI's execution by breaking off all diplomatic relations with France, ordering the Russian court into official mourning, sending a strong note of protest to Paris, and abruptly demanding that French troops be withdrawn from Hanover and the Neapolitan ports.

Understandably, Napoleon regarded the Tsar's protest note as unwarranted interference in the domestic affairs and internal security of France, and he responded to it incisively in the official newspaper of his regime, *Le Moniteur*: 'If, when England prepared the assassination of Paul I, the Russian government had discovered that the organizers of the plot were no more than a league from the frontier, would it not have seized them at once?' Few things could have been more calculated to throw Alexander into a furious frenzy, reminding him, as it did, of his failure to prevent his father's murder and stirring up the deep-seated guilt that never entirely left him. Nor was the Tsar's anger assuaged by Bonaparte's brusque rejection of his absurdly belated demand to withdraw from Hanover and Naples or his counter-protest at Russia's use of French *émigrés* in diplomatic positions at Dresden and Rome, from where they spied and conspired against the Republic.

Unsurprisingly, St Petersburg sought to exploit the animosity felt by the established ruling elites of Europe towards Napoleon in the wake of the Enghien affair. In April 1804, the Russians went back to the Austrians in search of an alliance on the same terms they had put forward the previous December, except with their own contingent increased to 100,000 men. Once more, however, the Habsburgs, still fearful of the possible consequences of a new war with the French, politely turned them down.

The Russians had more success the following month in Prussia, where the Tsar was still looked upon favourably by the king and queen after the Memel meeting two years earlier. From Berlin, Russia managed to extract a secret pledge to defend north Germany against any French encroachments so long as the Russians provided 40–50,000 men themselves and got other states, like Denmark and Saxony, to help too. It was better than nothing, but it still left the Prussians, who were even more anxious about French might than the Austrians, a number of get-out clauses. Nevertheless, it was a start to the fulfilment of the Tsar's by now unmistakable desire to build a third anti-French coalition.

If the execution of Enghien had opened a wound for Alexander and the Russian aristocracy, Napoleon's transition in May 1804 from First Consul for life to Emperor of the French rubbed salt in it. The change was brought about chiefly to provide lasting stability in France. The recent large-scale plot to assassinate Bonaparte, though foiled, had brought home to the French people, as well as to Napoleon himself, just how fragile all he had achieved potentially was. One bullet, one bomb or one dose of poison could remove at a stroke the man who was the central prop for all that had been achieved since late 1799 in the way of political, economic and religious stability. France would be thrown back into a political maelstrom in which reactionary royalists and radical Jacobins could again be expected to vie for power.

It was mainly in order to establish a fixed succession, and thereby, he hoped, secure his legacy, that First Consul Bonaparte opted to become Emperor Napoleon, a move strongly endorsed by the French people in a plebiscite held that November. The adoption of the imperial title rankled with the established European ruling elite, however, placing Napoleon on a titular par with the rulers of Austria and Russia and ahead of the kings of Prussia and Britain, an 'affront' made all the more 'impertinent' by the fact that Bonaparte was widely seen by the snobbish nobility of Europe as a 'Corsican upstart'. Unhappy as they were with the change, the Prussians and Austrians at least recognized a *fait accompli* when they saw one and so acknowledged Napoleon's new status. The British government, on the other hand, adopted an altogether more petulant attitude to the situation, refusing to refer to Napoleon as Emperor or even to use his first name, by which he was to become universally known.

As over the Enghien affair, though, it was the Russians who proved most affronted. Alexander refused to recognize the new title, which he felt demeaned all similar titles, including his own. Indeed, so outraged was he that he went so far as to block recognition of the imperial title in Constantinople by threatening the Turks. It was a wild reaction, and one that perhaps denotes the young Tsar's deep-rooted feelings of inferiority and jealousy toward Napoleon. Having already demonstrated how much more important he was than Alexander on the international stage, as well as how much more successful as a domestic reformer, Bonaparte was now undermining the one area in which the Tsar felt superior his rank.

Alexander's distress at Napoleon's adoption of a monarchical status that he felt should be bestowed by God alone through birth served to strengthen further his commitment to the path of confrontation with the French. Such a policy, however, required the adherence of Austria and, if possible, Prussia in order to have the greatest chance of success, and so far both had proven somewhat reticent about the prospect of fighting France and her new emperor. Nevertheless, the Russians kept pressing and in early November 1804 their efforts in Vienna finally bore some fruit. After almost a year of spasmodic urging by St Petersburg, the Habsburgs at last agreed to an alliance; though not the kind the Russians had ideally wanted. This was a purely defensive arrangement by which Austria agreed to provide 235,000 soldiers and Russia 115,000 in the event of France directly provoking a conflict with either power. As such it was a containing move against possible further French expansion rather than a pact that would seek to roll French influence back, but, like the agreement made with Prussia back in May, it was at least a move in the right direction as far as the Russians were concerned.

Predictably, St Petersburg and Vienna now endeavoured to persuade Berlin to join their alliance, but the Prussians remained unwilling to commit themselves to anything that might involve them in hostilities with France over an issue not of direct concern to them. Russian disappointment was only marginally eased by the decision of Sweden, which had entered into an alliance with Britain in December 1804, to ally itself with Russia also early in the new year.

Alongside these efforts at securing the cooperation of the Continental powers, St Petersburg had finally opened talks with the British in autumn 1804 aimed at forging an alliance. Alexander took the initiative by despatching Nikolai

Novosiltsev, another of his old friends, to London with a set of proposals for the settlement of Europe. In many regards, these were similar to Czartoryski's memorandum of the previous year, although, notably, the issue of Poland was omitted. They certainly reflected the tendency to dress up hard-nosed power politics in high-minded, vague and empty rhetoric about bringing lasting peace, stability and independence to the peoples of Europe. The more concrete propositions certainly told a less selfless story than the airy waffle. First, the French were to be ordered to give up all their conquests of recent years and to return to (non-Napoleonic) monarchical rule, with Britain and Russia choosing who should wear the French crown. Then, Italy and Germany (excluding Prussia and Austria but including Holland and Switzerland) were to be organized into ostensibly neutral federations under Anglo-Russian 'protection', a euphemism Napoleon himself would soon use to veil his own dominant influence in a region. The Russians were also keen to reach some kind of arrangement regarding the Ottoman Empire, suggesting that, were the Turks to ally with the French in the event of war, Britain and Russia should partition their territory between them. That St Petersburg hoped to reserve Turkish gains for itself, however, was made clear by its proposal that, in the projected conflict with France, it should hold back the bulk of its army for possible use against the Ottoman Empire.

So, Napoleonic ascendancy in Europe was to be replaced with Anglo-Russian pre-eminence instead and, the greatest impertinence of all, other countries, particularly Austria, were clearly to do most of the fighting against the French required to bring it about. Novosiltsev's proposals took the British government by surprise. William Pitt, who had returned to the office of Prime Minister in May, thought all the high-minded talk just so much hot air and was unwilling to engage in discussions about the future of the Ottoman Empire, fearing that it would distract from Britain's cardinal objective, the defeat of France. He also could not see how the Russian plan for Europe would appeal to Prussia or Austria. Instead, Pitt favoured strengthening each as a buffer against the French by giving Berlin territory in northern Germany, Vienna land in Italy, and both shared supremacy over a German confederation. Nevertheless, the British government remained keen to make some kind of alliance with Russia and so kept negotiations going.

Those talks dragged on for months, first in London, later in St Petersburg, with no agreement being reached on several key issues, such as Germany or the Ottoman Empire. Finally, on 11 April 1805, to prevent the negotiations collapsing entirely, representatives of the two sides signed a draft treaty of alliance that encompassed what they could both agree on. This envisaged an ultimatum being presented to France to withdraw from her conquests, which, if rejected, would result in war. It was hoped that the coalition would be able to call upon upwards of 400,000 troops, all heavily subsidized by the wealthy British. However, although Russia agreed to provide 115,000 of those soldiers, the rest would have to come from elsewhere, it being anticipated that Austria might provide a quarter of a million men. Following France's projected defeat, it was agreed that a series of 'neutral' states would be set up along the French borders, but other crucial issues of the post-war settlement, such as the nature and alignment of a German federation, were not resolved.

It soon became apparent that both London and St Petersburg were reluctant to ratify the agreement their representatives had reached. The Tsar remained eager before formalising the alliance to resolve all manner of issues related to the post-war settlement, including the future of Malta, which Alexander wanted returned to the Knights of St John, and neutral rights at sea. This infuriated the British, who just wanted Russia to agree to fight the French and leave the talking until after Napoleon was defeated.

With the prospect of an Anglo-Russian alliance seemingly stalled, Napoleon clumsily and inadvertently gave the project a fillip. First, in late May 1805, he had himself crowned King of Italy in Milan. Although this new kingdom only incorporated the former Cisalpine Republic, not the whole peninsula, and would be governed on a day-to-day basis by his stepson, Eugène de Beauharnais, the ruling elite of Europe was once again galled at the impudence of the 'Corsican upstart'. Then, early the following month, Napoleon made things even worse for himself by annexing to France the north-west Italian Ligurian Republic, centred on Genoa.

The opposition of both Britain and Russia to these acts was sufficiently strong for an alliance between the two to be ratified at the end of July. Its terms, essentially those of the pact signed in April, undoubtedly pleased the British more, leaving, as it did, key issues of the post-war European settlement unresolved and making no provision for Russian expansion at the expense of the Ottoman Empire. The Russian idea of presenting the French with an ultimatum to cede all their conquests since the early 1790s was also dropped, it being decided that military operations aimed at achieving that would simply be initiated instead. Alexander thus chose to settle, for the moment at least, for a leading role in ridding Europe of the twin 'scourges' of Napoleon and French pre-eminence, hoping that he could become chief architect of the peace and take land from the Turks afterwards.

Of course, the Anglo-Russian alliance would seriously lack teeth unless Austria could be persuaded to join the nascent coalition, but Napoleon's recent actions in the Italian peninsula made that more likely. The Habsburgs were just as affronted as other established crowned heads by Napoleon's annexation of Liguria and adoption of the title King of Italy, and still deeply resented having lost their dominant position in northern Italy and southern Germany to the French. Indeed, they very much hoped one day to be able to win it back, but what had restrained them since 1801 was fear of the consequences of a third defeat at the hands of Napoleon. Austria thus wavered in the early summer of 1805, with some in Vienna, led by the emperor's brother, Archduke Charles, arguing that the country was not ready for war either economically or militarily, while others, championed by General Mack, took a more optimistic and hawkish approach.

With the Austrian decision for war or peace finely balanced, the Russians decisively entered the equation. Alexander tried to overcome Habsburg fears by blindly promising that he would build an allied army of 600,000 men by providing more Russian troops and getting others, particularly his friends the King and Queen of Prussia, to join the coalition. Seeing the Austrians not convinced by this, the Tsar played his trump card. Unless Vienna joined the coalition, he would withdraw Russia from European affairs altogether and leave Austria at the potential mercy of the mighty French Empire. It was almost certainly a bluff, but would the Habsburgs call it?

They did not. Alexander's threat finally tilted the argument in Vienna in favour of war. If the Tsar followed his promise to withdraw from European affairs, the Habsburgs felt they would never have a realistic chance of reversing the trend of recent years and restoring their previous position of pre-eminence in northern Italy and southern Germany. In early August Austria therefore acceded to the Third Coalition and joined the Russians in mobilizing for war. Aware of the danger, Napoleon demanded that Vienna stop its mobilization and declare its neutrality. It refused, with consequences clear to all.

There are two things not commonly appreciated about the outbreak of the War of the Third Coalition. The first is that the key role in the coalition's formation was played not, as is usually held, by Britain but by Russia. Tsar Alexander had pushed for alliances with all manner of countries in 1804–5 and it was he who had ultimately tipped the balance in favour of Austria entering the fray, just as his father had persuaded the Habsburgs to join the Second Coalition in 1799. Of course, the British had been seeking to build a coalition too, but their efforts were irrelevant to Russia's decision for war and secondary to Austria's. (Prussia remained uncommitted for the moment, but here too it would be the Russians rather than the British who proved decisive.)

The second thing not commonly appreciated about the slide into war in 1805 is that in no meaningful way can Napoleon be said to have *forced* the Tsar into building the coalition against him. Indeed, there was a significant body of opinion in St Petersburg, including the ministers of commerce, finance and the interior, who saw no reason for opposing France and wished to avoid war. While it is true that many of the French ruler's actions in the previous few years had angered or irritated Alexander, none of them posed a direct threat to any significant Russian economic or strategic interest. Nor, moreover, did any of Bonaparte's unilateral actions make any serious difference to the overall strategic situation in Europe. French dominance in Piedmont and Liguria was well established even before their annexation. Similarly, the reorganization of the Swiss constitution and the transformation of the Cisalpine Republic into the Kingdom of Italy made little appreciable difference to the extent of French ascendancy in those areas. Admittedly, the occupation of Hanover and the reoccupation of the Neapolitan ports did denote an extension of France's influence, but they were also justified as a legitimate response to the renewal of hostilities with Britain. From Napoleon's perspective, all he was doing in 1802–5 was either modifying the administration of regions over which he believed he had been ceded authority by the peace treaties he had made with other powers or seeking justifiable ways of striking at a country with whom he was at war. It was a slanted view to be sure, but a far from indefensible one.

None of this is to suggest that Napoleon was entirely blameless for the outbreak of war in 1805. He certainly acted insensitively at times, and if other rulers feared he had plans to expand his mastery beyond what he already held during the brief period of peace in 1802–3, then he must take much of the responsibility for making them think that way. That does not mean that Napoleon forced the Tsar, or for that matter any other member of the Third Coalition, to take up arms against him in 1805. They *chose* to do so and, in the event, did it with the intention not to uphold treaties they had previously made with the French, but to overthrow them and strip France of all her gains since the early 1790s. It was not Bonaparte but his enemies who sought a radical alteration in the European situation that had been agreed to in 1801–2. Of course, one can quite legitimately argue that it was perfectly reasonable for the other European powers to seek to reduce French power and influence, but given that they did so purely in order to increase their own, it is unfair to malign Napoleon for wishing to consolidate France's hard-won position of pre-eminence.

In the final analysis though, the formation of the Third Coalition was never *just* about considerations of power politics, crucial as they undoubtedly were. It also owed much to personal factors. Just as the established ruling elites of Europe had decided in the 1790s that they hated the French Revolution and all it stood for, they had decided by 1805 that that didn't like its heir either, the royal-killing *parvenu* from Corsica who had the 'effrontery' to call himself Emperor of the French and King of Italy. The dislike was especially keenly felt by the coalition's main architect, Alexander of Russia. In him, a fierce jealousy of the 'Corsican upstart' mixed with a burning desire to usurp his place as Europe's leading figure. In order to fulfil the Tsar's hopes, however, France's *arriviste* ruler and his armies would have to be defeated on the field of battle – and that was to prove no easy task.

6

Austerlitz

Napoleon had always hoped to fight a campaign in 1805, but not the one he ended up fighting. After two years of preparation, the Emperor finally felt ready that summer to attempt to get some 200,000 Frenchmen across the Channel and march on London. In his way was the Royal Navy. He knew that Britain's ships would have to be swept aside, at least temporarily, for the invasion to be launched, but the chances of it happening in 1805 were, in reality, never good. The simple fact was that the Royal Navy had such a pronounced superiority in both overall leadership and the skill of its crews by this time that it would have taken either a truly inspired French admiral, a remarkably inept British error or an overwhelming Franco-Spanish numerical advantage for mastery of the Channel to have changed hands. In 1805, none of these existed.

It is in this light that one must view Nelson's much-lauded triumph off Cape Trafalgar in late October of that year. Widely heralded ever since as the battle that saved Britain from invasion, and thus possibly the most important engagement of the Napoleonic Wars, it was in fact nothing of the sort. By the time Nelson got to grips with the Franco-Spanish fleet of Admiral Villeneuve, the invasion of England had been indefinitely postponed and the army that was to have conducted it had moved from the Channel coast to central Europe. To be sure, by sinking or capturing almost twenty enemy ships at Trafalgar (a tremendous achievement in a battle which famously cost Nelson his life), the British strongly reinforced the sense of the Royal Navy's superiority and seriously dented Napoleon's efforts to assemble an overwhelming numerical advantage at sea. The battle did not, however, shatter French or Spanish naval might entirely, nor did it prevent the Emperor from continuing to try to build an irresistibly large fleet to overthrow the Royal Navy. Indeed, given time, as even a British First Lord of the Admiralty of the period acknowledged, Napoleon would have 'sent forth such powerful fleets that our navy must eventually have been destroyed, since we could never have kept pace with him in building ships nor equipped numbers sufficient to cope with the tremendous power he could have brought against us'. What ultimately saved Britain from invasion was not Nelson's victory at Trafalgar, crushing as it was, but the fact that Napoleonic France would be vanquished on land before she could defeat the British at sea.

Which leads us back to affairs on the Continent at the end of summer 1805.

By late August, some 300,000 troops, a third of them Russian, most of the rest Austrian, were massing in central and eastern Europe to fight the French, with more to follow. In such circumstances, Napoleon had little choice but to turn his attention from invading Britain (the impracticability of which in the near future was becoming clear to him anyway) towards the mounting threat on land. On 27 August, the Army of France, now redesignated *La Grande Armée*, broke camp along the Channel coast and began the march east to meet France's new foes. The future of Europe would be decided not at sea, but on land.

Napoleon considered the *Grande Armée* of 1805 'the finest army that has ever existed'. The reasons for this judgement were many. One of the most obvious is that during the two years from 1803–5 that it was posted along the Channel coast, it underwent a process of rigorous training that left the men fitter, more familiar with the tactical manoeuvres required of them, and with higher morale than any contemporary force.

A particular strength of the *Grande Armée* was its officer corps. While the officers of all other European armies in this period were drawn almost exclusively, especially at the higher levels, from the aristocracy, France officered her army on the basis of merit rather than birth. The useless were weeded out, regardless of wealth or background, while the deserving were promoted. In an age when it was a great rarity for a soldier to rise from the ranks, fully half the officers of the French army of 1805 were ex-rankers, promoted on merit. Admittedly, the vast majority of those were low ranking officers, but the more restricted presence of people from humbler backgrounds higher up in the army was a reflection of the greater educational opportunities of the better-off in society rather than a policy of exclusion. Indeed, many of the army's most prominent leaders, such as Joachim Murat (the son of an innkeeper), André Masséna (a former cabin boy) and Jean Lannes (an ex-dyer's apprentice), were of very modest origins, and even the Emperor himself, although from a less lowly background, was very much able to converse with the rankers on their level (often by swearing like a trooper). French officers, moreover, were as a whole demonstrably braver than those of any other nation. Because they led from the front, their losses in the Napoleonic Wars were far greater proportionally than those of the officers of all other powers, a trend which continued all the way up to the very top levels of the army.

If the quality of its officers was perhaps the greatest strength the *Grande Armée* enjoyed, close behind it was the calibre of its ordinary soldiers. Fifty per cent of the French army in 1805 were veterans of at least one previous campaign; often indeed of more than one. This not only made those particular troops better, but it ensured that their experience and expertise was passed on to the conscripts who made up the rest of the army. The ordinary French soldier was also generally better motivated than the rankers of other armies. Whereas the lash remained the preferred means of maintaining order outside France, corporal punishment was banned in the French army. Napoleon's men were driven less by fear of their officers than by respect for them, as well as by love of their homeland or Emperor, passion for honour and glory, and, perhaps most important, the promise of receiving a genuine reward for their efforts, such as promotion from the ranks.

Turning to the individual branches of the French army of 1805, the elite corps of an already exceptional whole was the Imperial Guard. Some 7,000-strong at this time, it was made up, like all corps in the *Grande Armée*, of all arms, its men selected on the basis of especial ability. Although only occasionally committed to battle by Napoleon, who preferred to hold it back as a reserve, when its soldiers did move forward and attack, resplendent in full dress uniform, it would almost always be decisive. The higher pay and preferential treatment accorded to the Imperial Guard certainly caused some resentment in the rest of the army, but the psychological and military value of having such a powerful body at his disposal more than outweighed this for the Emperor. Besides, the possibility of joining the Guard was a further motivation for many soldiers to perform to their utmost.

With the exception of the immaculately turned-out infantry of the Imperial Guard, the *Grande Armée*'s foot soldiers generally looked a rather dishevelled, scruffy bunch. On campaign, however, the French infantry, armed with the 1777 Charleville musket, a good basic weapon, more often than not got the better of their more elegantly presented, tidier opponents. The more unkempt appearance of France's foot soldiers often reflected an independent, practical spirit that contrasted favourably with the more rigid, almost robotic behaviour typical of many elements of rival armies. It is interesting to note in this context that the French usually produced much better skirmishers than their Continental adversaries.

If scruffiness was a trademark of the French infantry, impeccable tailoring was just as much a feature of France's cavalry. They may not have had the best horses in Europe, nor, for that matter, all that many of them, but the French horsemen always looked magnificent. More importantly, they knew how to fight as well. The heavy cavalry rode fairly slow-moving steeds, but they handled them with a tactical skill and cohesion few in Europe could match. The light cavalry, meanwhile, could throw themselves into battle as boldly and bravely as anyone, but truly excelled at more strategic tasks, such as scouting ahead of the army or pursuing a defeated enemy. Finally, the dragoons, the medium cavalry, displayed a tremendous flexibility, being able to fight either on horseback with sabres or dismounted with their carbines, a shortened version of the Charleville musket.

Seeing as Napoleon was an artilleryman by training: one would not expect that branch of the *Grande Armée* to have been anything other than excellent. True, France did not produce the most or even the best cannon, but the French artillery remained superior thanks to the skill with which the guns were deployed.

The various batteries were organized in such a way that cannon could be massed or dispersed with relative ease, and French artillerymen and commanders were encouraged to make full use of this flexibility. The result was that even in engagements in which the enemy deployed a greater number of guns than the *Grande Armée*, the French artillery often had a greater impact upon the outcome because of the skill with which it was moved around the battlefield.

Of course, the *Grande Armée* of 1805 was not perfect. The relative shortage of both horses and cannon has already been mentioned, but it was the auxiliary branches of the army in which the greatest deficiencies were to be found. Although French military engineers were generally of a high calibre and plentiful enough, the medical services were not great. There were certainly prominent individual surgeons, most notably Dr Dominique Larrey, who invented the field ambulance, but he and his associates were never given an organization worthy of their prodigious efforts in caring for the wounded and sick (that said, French medical services were at least as good as anyone else's and better than most). The *Grande Armée*'s logistics also left something to be desired, especially if compared to the tremendous system Wellington was to establish in the Iberian Peninsula, but then French doctrine was based on foraging for supplies. This enabled the army to move faster but brought with it other problems, particularly the resentment that it bred among local populations and the hardships it imposed upon French troops when there was little to forage.

Despite these shortcomings, the *Grande Armée* remained a truly formidable weapon of war. What turned it into arguably the best army of all time, however, was the man at its head. Running a highly centralized but efficient command system that it took a genius to master, Napoleon combined brilliant strategic nous and phenomenal administrative proficiency with unparalleled leadership skills. He could motivate men, charm them and win their admiration, respect, and even love better than perhaps any other leader in history. Together, Napoleon and his *Grande Armée* were to achieve truly great things.

The ultimate aims of the Third Coalition, which was soon joined by the kingdoms of Sweden and Naples, were nothing if not bold. Essentially, they were to roll back French power and influence in Europe to what they had been before the French Revolutionary Wars and, if possible, to install in France a government more to the Allies' liking (in all probability, a Bourbon restoration). For their part, the Austrians doubted if such aims were feasible and so focused on the more immediate goal of restoring their lost pre-eminence in southern Germany and northern Italy. For the Russians and especially the British, the ultimate aims were firmly fixed in their minds.

The strategy adopted by the Allies highlights the extent of their ambitions. In the north, a Russo-Swedish army was to move west from Swedish Pomerania, an enclave on the southern shore of the Baltic, into Hanover and then Holland. It was hoped that it would be joined by a Russo-Prussian army to make this thrust more dangerous, but that obviously depended on the attitude of Berlin. In the south, meanwhile, an Anglo-Russian expeditionary force was to land in southern Italy, link up with the forces of the King of Naples and move northwards up the peninsula. Finally, in the centre, there were to be the two most powerful thrusts, one north and one south of the Alps. The Austrians expected northern Italy to be the key theatre once more in their struggle with Bonaparte and so posted their largest army, 95,000-strong, there under the Habsburg Emperor's brother, Archduke Charles. His main task was to capture Lombardy, but, if the war went well, he would also be in a good position to invade France from the south east. Further north, the second largest Austrian army was to invade Bavaria and then await the arrival of two Russian armies before pushing west into France via Strasbourg.

Napoleon would not have been the military genius he was if he had not quickly appreciated his enemy's strategy, recognized its threats and weaknesses, and then devised a strategy of his own to counter it. With numbers in the Allies' favour, the Emperor realized that he had to prioritize and move swiftly to redress the imbalance. He immediately focused upon southern Germany as the key theatre. From there would eventually come the greatest threat; there lay potential French allies, and through there ran the most direct route to the capital of the least enthusiastic major member of the Coalition, Austria.

For the 1805 campaign, Napoleon divided France's forces into four main bodies, one of which was very much larger than the others. In Italy, he gave one of his most able commanders, Marshal Masséna, 50,000 men to keep Archduke Charles's army at bay, while a further 20,000 or so under General Laurent Gouvion St Cyr, a former artist, were to counter the threat from Naples. In the north, meanwhile, the Emperor left some 30,000 troops at Boulogne under Marshal Brune to oppose either an Allied advance into Holland or a British descent on the French coast. The bulk of the army that had originally been intended to invade England, nigh on 200,000 soldiers, Napoleon took command of personally. Divided into seven regular corps, a cavalry corps and the Imperial Guard, this massive force was, at the end of August, spread out all the way from Hanover in the north, through Holland and Belgium, and along France's northern coast to Brittany in the far west. It seemed far too large an army to move in a coordinated fashion, but the flexibility of the corps system and the brilliant, meticulous planning of the Emperor and his invaluable chief of staff, Marshal Louis-Alexandre Berthier, nicknamed 'the Emperor's wife' so closely did he work with his master, were to astound the world.

Having ordered his *Grande Armée* to gather initially along the Rhine after it broke camp in late August, Napoleon turned his attention to diplomacy. The attitude of Prussia during the coming months might well prove crucial, for should she join France's enemies once more, the balance of forces against the French might prove insurmountable. The Emperor therefore sought to counter Allied efforts to win the Prussians over by despatching to Berlin his trusted aide, General Duroc, with the offer of Hanover as a reward for siding with France, or even just remaining neutral. Fear of French might and the tempting offer were enough to prevent Berlin from joining the Third Coalition in the immediate future.

If Prussia was the key target of both Napoleonic and Allied diplomatic efforts, the allegiance of other, smaller states was also sought by both sides, and in this area the French did much better than their adversaries. The Allies had hoped to persuade all manner of minor powers to join their coalition, from Denmark in the north, to Saxony in the east, and the southern German states of Bavaria, Baden and Württemberg in the centre. They were to be bitterly disappointed. While the first two chose to remain neutral, the latter three all formally allied themselves with France between late August and early October after Napoleon skilfully offered their rulers territory currently belonging to Austria and a promotion in their ruling status. The early diplomatic rounds thus went to the Emperor, but it was the initial military confrontation that was really to stun Europe.

With the bulk of the *Grande Armée* less than a week into its march towards France's eastern frontier along the Rhine, an Austrian army of some 70,000 men under the command of General Karl Mack invaded Bavaria on 2 September. The move's initial aim was to 'persuade' the Bavarians to join the Third Coalition, a goal which was not achieved, but more important was its intent to reassert Austrian authority in southern Germany and pave the way for an invasion of France. Arriving at Ulm on the Danube, some hundred miles west of Munich and a similar distance short of the Upper Rhine to the east, Mack called a halt to the first phase of his campaign. Here, the Austrian commander felt entirely secure. To his south lay the Alps, to the west was the Black Forest, while to the north was the Prussian territory of Ansbach, whose neutrality Mack was convinced the French would never dare to violate in the current diplomatic climate. Moreover, by his own calculations, with which almost every expert in Europe agreed, there was no way Napoleon could move a superior force, let alone anything like 200,000 soldiers, from the Channel coast to southern Germany before the two Russian armies heading west to join the Austrians at Ulm more than doubled his strength.

Bonaparte learnt of the Austrian invasion of Bavaria on 13 September, and a week later that Mack's army was gathering around Ulm. His own army's move to the Rhine was proceeding quickly thanks to the ability of each corps to advance by different roads, the absence of large, cumbersome baggage trains to slow the army down, and the fitness, discipline and morale of the highly trained troops. By the 27th, some 200,000 Frenchmen were aligned in a great arc stretching north along the upper Rhine and east into Hanover. Napoleon now unleashed them in one of the most brilliant manoeuvres in military history. Ordering part of his force, under Marshals Murat and Lannes, to advance through the Black Forest and keep Mack's attention fixed to the west, the Emperor launched the bulk of the *Grande Armée* on a sweep around Ulm from the north east aimed at cutting the enemy off from both Austria and their slowly advancing Russian allies.

The manoeuvre came off magnificently. Advancing at a pace that their opponents did not dream was possible for such a large army, Bonaparte's troops had Mack's men practically encircled by the second week in October. Belatedly, the Austrians endeavoured to break out of the trap that was closing around them, but with little success. By the 16th, the French had closed the noose around Ulm tight enough to commence a bombardment of the town. Utterly demoralized by recent events, the Austrian troops pressed their commander to capitulate. Faced with the possibility of a mutiny, Mack had little choice but to agree, and on 20 October, with the nearest Russians still well over a hundred miles away, the Austrian army at Ulm surrendered.

Something like 27,000 Austrian soldiers laid down their arms at Ulm itself, but the disaster was far greater than that. Of the 70,000 men Mack had commanded in Bavaria, just 10,000 managed to escape back east. French losses around Ulm, at only 2,000, were almost ridiculously low by comparison. It was an astounding victory, won primarily by the *Grande Armée*'s ability to put into practice the minutely detailed marching orders of its commander. As French soldiers soon began to quip, 'the Emperor makes war not with our arms but with our legs'.

Outstanding a triumph as the destruction of Mack's army was, Napoleon knew that it would not end the war. The Austrians might have received a shattering blow in southern Germany, but they retained large forces in the field, especially in northern Italy, from where Archduke Charles's 100,000 men, upon hearing of the disaster at Ulm, began to march north east in the hope of defending Vienna. The Habsburgs' Russian allies, moreover, had not yet been blooded and remained eager for the fight. True, the first of the two Russian armies which had been marching to reinforce Mack had now turned around and was heading back east, but only to join up with the second of the Tsar's forces moving west.

By late October 1805, the Third Coalition had been given a severe pounding, but it remained powerful nonetheless, and if the French gave it time to recover, would soon pose a serious threat once more. Napoleon thus needed to land a second telling blow on his enemy, a real knock-out punch, and the obvious target for such a strike was the Russian army nearest him. The 1805 campaign was far from over yet.

In the wake of the Austrian capitulation at Ulm, Napoleon swiftly rearranged his forces. Detaching three corps, around a third of the *Grande Armée*, to prevent Archduke Charles from reaching Vienna or linking up with the Russians, the Emperor led the rest of his men eastwards down the Danube.

His new target was the nearest Russian army, commanded by General Mikhail Ilarionovich Kutuzov. Sixty years old in 1805, Kutuzov had made a name for himself serving as the great Suvorov's right-hand man in Russia's wars against the Turks. Easily recognized by his corpulent frame, loss of one eye, and propensity for wearing a sailor-style hat, he came across as indolent, blunt and coarse. This masked a devious nature, however, and he was capable of showing considerable resilience and tenacity. Although not without merit as a general, many commentators, especially Tolstoy in *War and Peace*, have exaggerated Kutuzov's abilities. In truth, he was generally not a particularly gifted commander.

Having begun his march west at the head of over 45,000 soldiers, Kutuzov arrived on the Bavarian border in late October with just 27,000 men still under his control, thanks to a combination of straggling, desertion and exhaustion on the long trek from Russia. Fortunately, he was joined there by around 16,000 Austrians, but he remained heavily outnumbered by the main French body now advancing towards him. Sensibly, Kutuzov decided to do what he always did best – retreat.

The chase was now on. If Napoleon could catch Kutuzov before he could join up with the second Russian force still some way off to the north-east, the chances were that the Emperor would utterly destroy a second Allied army. His own forces were, however, beginning to feel the strain of their prodigious physical efforts since late August. By the start of November, some 8,000 French soldiers were on the sick list and large numbers of horses had died as a result of the pace of the advance from the Channel.

With tiredness already slowing the French rate of march, their speed was further reduced by poor weather, the predominance of pine forest along the Danube valley, and the adoption by the retreating Russians of a scorched earth policy, which made foraging much more difficult. Nevertheless, Napoleon's advance guard, under his exceptional commander of cavalry, Marshal Murat, caught up with the rear of the Russo-Austrian column at the beginning of November at Lambach, some 125 miles west of Vienna. The Allies successfully extricated themselves from the ensuing skirmish, but at the cost of 500 prisoners.

The Allied force divided after Lambach, most of the Austrians heading off south east in the hope of joining Archduke Charles. Instead, they were chased down and destroyed at Maria Zell in the foothills of the Alps by the most gifted of the Emperor's military subordinates, the bald-headed nobleman Marshal Louis-Nicolas Davout. Meanwhile, on 5 November, the spearhead of Napoleon's main army clashed at Amstetten with Kutuzov's rearguard. The combat cost the Russians a further 2,000 men, but it also bought them a brief breathing space. Thus, a fortnight into the second phase of the 1805 campaign, although the French had dealt the Austrians another hefty blow, 'We have only hurt the Russians a little', Napoleon admitted in a letter to his Archchancellor back in Paris: 'as rapidly as we march, they retreat more rapidly'.

If the Russians were proving harder to trap than their allies, though the hope of catching them remained very much alive. But then the headstrong Marshal Murat blundered. So far, Kutuzov had retreated along the south side of the Danube, thereby covering Vienna, but on 8–9 November, while still some forty miles west of the city, he crossed to the north bank. Confusing the essential (the destruction of Kutuzov's army) with the peripheral (the capture of Vienna), Murat charged headlong for the weakly defended Austrian capital. By the time the Emperor realized what had happened, it was too late. The Russians had as good as got away.

Then Kutuzov too made a mistake. Murat's dash for Vienna had left the advance guard of the one small French corps that had been advancing down the north bank of the Danube suddenly vulnerable to counter-attack and the Russians could not resist the temptation. On 11 November, some 15,000 of Kutuzov's men fell upon a division of 6,000 Frenchmen from three sides at Dürrenstein. A savage battle ensued in which the heavily outnumbered French, with their backs to the Danube, outfought their enemy. Nevertheless, it took the arrival of elements of a second division to save them from being overwhelmed. The following day, the French retreated across the river by boat, allowing the Russians to claim the victory, even though they had lost 4,000 men to their opponents' 3,000. More worrying than the number of casualties, though, was the fact that the time spent fighting at Dürrenstein had once again created an opportunity for Napoleon to trap Kutuzov's army.

Entering the practically undefended Austrian capital on 12 November, Murat had soon made up for his error in going there in the first place by securing the city's vital bridge to the north side of the Danube. This allowed Napoleon to conjure up a new plan for ensnaring the retreating Russians. He ordered Marshal Jean-Baptiste Bernadotte, a vain, arrogant, jealous man and unfortunately one of the less able of his commanders, to cross the Danube near where Kutuzov had and continue the pursuit along the path taken by the Russians. Meanwhile, the rest of Napoleon's army, spearheaded by Murat, was to march north from Vienna towards the town of Hollabrunn in the hope of putting themselves between Kutuzov and the second Russian army still heading west.

A combination of Bernadotte's slowness in crossing the Danube and a renewed sense of urgency on the part of Kutuzov foiled Murat's efforts at placing himself across the Russian line of retreat. Nevertheless, the French advance guard did manage to catch up with the Russian rear guard at Schöngrabern near Hollabrunn on 15 November. Had Murat attacked at once, which would have been his usual approach in such a situation, the chances are that he would have swept the Russians aside and been in a position to catch up with Kutuzov's main body shortly afterwards. Unfortunately for Napoleon, however, the typically bold marshal chose this moment to develop a bout of anxiety. Mistakenly judging the Russian rear guard to be stronger than it was, and with the tardy Bernadotte nowhere to be seen, Murat negotiated a brief armistice with the enemy to give more French troops time to arrive. The Russians could not believe their luck and used the opportunity to put a greater distance between their main body and the French.

It was late on the following day, 16 November, that, following a severe reprimand from the Emperor for making an unauthorized armistice, Murat finally attacked at Schöngrabern. The encounter took place almost entirely after dark, which made it easier for the Russians to stage a fighting withdrawal, but it was fiercely contested even so. By the time the battle ended around eleven, the Russians had lost almost 2,500 men, but they had bloodied French noses enough to escape.

On 18 November, the rear guard that had fought so bravely at Schöngrabern rejoined Kutuzov's main body. The following day, they finally linked up with the second Russian army and an Austrian force near the town of Olmütz (modern-day Olomouc) in Moravia (the eastern part of today's Czech Republic), around a hundred miles north-northeast of Vienna. Here, the long retreat stopped.

The French advance halted a couple of days later near the Moravian capital of Brünn (modern-day Brno) a little way south-west of Olmütz. The men and horses who had advanced all the way from the Channel coast in under three months were shattered and in desperate need of a rest. Besides, the numerical advantage the French had enjoyed at the start of the chase of Kutuzov had now been overturned. Because of the need to detach corps to protect his extended supply lines and guard against the possibility of Archduke Charles marching to join with the Russians, Napoleon's effective combat strength in Moravia had fallen to around 70,000. The Allies, meanwhile, now had almost 90,000 soldiers around Olmütz, all but 15,000 of them Russians.

Nor did the Emperor's worries end there. If he could take some comfort from the fact that there was as yet little danger to his empire from Allied forces in either northern Germany or southern Italy, Archduke Charles's large army greatly troubled him. Despite the detachments he had made to prevent the Austrian from taking the shortest route to Moravia, Bonaparte did not have the men to stop him from going the longer way round via Hungary. It was with more than a hint of anxiety, therefore, that he wrote on 22 November to Marshal Masséna, who had already been shadowing Charles's retreat from northern Italy for several weeks, ordering him to 'pursue the enemy with your sword in his ribs so that he may not be able to attack us, as we are now in the presence of the whole Russian army'.

Even Archduke Charles was not Napoleon's greatest concern in late November 1805 though. After all, should the Austrian manage to unite with the Russians in Moravia, the Emperor would at least be able to withdraw to southern Germany and draw all his forces to him. By so doing, he would undoubtedly forfeit the advantage he and his army had worked so hard to gain, but he would nevertheless remain very much alive in the war. The real nightmare confronting Napoleon was that the Prussians would join the Third Coalition.

Late November 1805 would have been about the worst time for Prussia to have entered the war against the French. Not only would her intervention have dramatically shifted the numerical balance against them after they had fought so hard in recent weeks to even it out, it would also have threatened the Emperor's main force in Moravia with being cut off from its easiest route home back along the Danube. For some time now, ominous noises had been coming from Berlin, so one can imagine Napoleon's apprehension when, on 28 November, Count Haugwitz, a prominent member of the Prussian government, arrived to meet him.

Before revealing what passed between Bonaparte and Haugwitz at their crucial meeting, it is worth tracing what had happened with regard to Prussia since the end of the summer. It will be remembered that Napoleon had despatched his trusted aide, General Duroc, to Berlin in late August. He had arrived on 1 September in a city fraught with tension. For several weeks, the Russians had been pressing the Prussians in the most vigorous manner to join the Third Coalition and threatening that, even if they did not, elements of the Tsar's army would cross Prussian territory on their way to fight the French. The figure behind this extraordinarily bullish policy was Russia's deputy foreign minister, Prince Czartoryski. His hope, astoundingly, was that he would manoeuvre Prussia into war *against* Russia. Czartoryski detested the Prussians and planned to incite his fellow Poles in the large chunk of Poland earlier annexed by Berlin to stage an uprising. Alexander would then declare himself their champion, enter Warsaw, and establish a semi-independent Polish state under Russian 'protection'.

Perhaps the only thing more incredible than the fact that Czartoryski could be developing such a scheme at a time when Russia had just gone to war with the greatest power on the Continent was the fact that Alexander was actually thinking of supporting it. Throughout September and into October, the Tsar mulled over authorizing Czartoryski to incite a Polish rebellion. Meanwhile, Duroc was making some progress towards a formal Franco-Prussian alliance, by the terms of which France would guarantee the integrity of Holland and Switzerland, pledge to make no new annexations for herself in Germany as a result of the current war, and hand over the French-occupied British territory of Hanover to Prussia.

Regrettably for the French, Berlin did not take the bait offered it quickly enough. In early October, elements of the *Grande Armée* marched through the

Prussian territory of Ansbach in southern Germany in order to get behind the Austrian army of General Mack at Ulm. Although extremely helpful militarily, this violation of Prussia's neutrality was highly damaging diplomatically. As soon as he heard of the move, an indignant King Frederick William gave the Russian army permission to cross Prussian territory and requested a meeting with the Tsar. Alexander arrived in Berlin on 25 October.

Czartoryski was appalled that his master had chosen to negotiate with the Prussians instead of make war on them, but it was clearly the sensible thing to do. By 3 November, the Tsar had secured the treaty of Potsdam. Under the terms of this agreement, the Prussians were to deliver an ultimatum to the French demanding that they withdraw from the bulk of their conquests over the past dozen years or Berlin would join the Allies. In a secret clause, Alexander promised to do all he could to try to secure Hanover for Prussia as a reward.

Berlin's course was even yet not quite set, however. Given that in early November Napoleon had just smashed one Allied army and had another on the run down the Danube, the Prussians, despite beginning to mobilize their army, thought it wise to delay approaching Napoleon for several weeks to see how events in central Europe worked out. By the end of the month, with most of Kutuzov's army having evaded French clutches, the timorous King Frederick William felt confident enough to despatch Count Haugwitz to present the ultimatum to the French emperor.

And so we return to the fateful meeting on 28 November. Given the fact that in recent weeks the Prussian king had entertained the Tsar of Russia for over a week in Berlin and had started to mobilize his army when Alexander had left, Napoleon must have guessed why this prominent Prussian minister wanted to see him. Luckily for the Emperor, however, Frederick William had selected the wrong man for the task in hand. Haugwitz was, if anything, even more cautious than his master and he wanted proof of French vulnerability before delivering an ultimatum that would effectively commit Prussia to war against Europe's greatest power. By late November, that proof had yet to be delivered, for Napoleon's forces had done nothing so far this campaign but advance and win victories. So the meeting that should have paved the way for Prussia to join the Third Coalition instead turned into little more than a friendly chat.

Of course, Haugwitz's failure notwithstanding, the treaty of Potsdam still stood, and so the threat of Prussian intervention had been delayed rather than lifted. In this extraordinary campaign that had led opposing armies from as far apart as the Channel coast and Russia to within a few dozen miles of each other in Moravia, it was clear that whatever happened next was likely to prove decisive.

The almost 90,000 strong Allied army, some five-sixths of it Russian, which gathered around Olmütz in mid-November 1805 had the dubious honour of being joined by the rulers of both Austria and Russia. As always, the strapping Alexander cut an impressive figure, but his Habsburg counterpart, Francis, had the unfortunate look of a man who was already thoroughly defeated. Seeming much older that his thirty-seven years, the Austrian emperor's demeanour was typified, as so often, by melancholy and pessimism. Needless to say, Alexander, like almost all the Russians who met Francis, was far from impressed.

Nevertheless, the Habsburgs and the Romanovs remained allies, and that meant that they had to decide what to do next in the war against Napoleon. One option was swiftly ruled out. The army around Olmütz could not stay where it was much longer, as it was proving impossible to keep it properly supplied there. It was thus a straightforward choice between advancing towards the French around Brünn and offering battle, or retreating further east towards Russia or Hungary, awaiting the arrival of Archduke Charles and Prussian entry into the war, and switching to the offensive then.

The second option was clearly the safer, if the more timid. Inevitably, therefore, it was the one Emperor Francis inclined towards, as did most of the senior Austrians with him. One leading Austrian, however, General Weyrother, who had been appointed to serve as chief of staff to the Allied army's commander-in-chief, Kutuzov, ardently supported attacking the enemy in the near future.

The senior Russians, whose opinion clearly mattered more given the preponderance of the Tsar's forces in the Allied army in Moravia, were more evenly divided. Their top military commander, Kutuzov, strongly favoured a further withdrawal east, but one of his two key subordinates, General Buxhöwden, an Estonian German lacking in ability but who had been promoted primarily because of his marriage to one of Catherine the Great's illegitimate daughters, advocated attacking. Buxhöwden was supported by almost all the young aides around the Tsar, most especially Prince Peter Dolgoruky, the scion of one of Russia's most prominent noble families, who sought to egg his master on by repeatedly referring to the need to crush 'the usurper Bonaparte and his horde' as soon as possible.

With opinions divided, the view of the Tsar was crucial. Given that his most senior general, several of his other commanders, most of the Austrians and his fellow monarch all advocated withdrawing, one might have expected Alexander to side with them. He was, however, disinclined to agree with the timorous Francis, nor did he care overly for Kutuzov, whom he disliked, distrusted, and had only appointed commander-in-chief because of his seniority and standing in the Russian army. More importantly perhaps, the Tsar, having been trained for military command as a youth, considered himself a competent military judge and so did not feel in any way reliant upon Kutuzov, or indeed anyone else, for advice. He was extremely keen, moreover, to exercise real military leadership, an urge that was only reinforced by the arrival of a courier from St Petersburg who sycophantically declared, 'All Russia is quivering with joy, Sire, at the thought of their beloved leader taking into his own hands the fate of the army'. This was just the kind of flagrant flattery to which Alexander so often responded. As an aide observed, he was soon dreaming of 'a victory that would place him at one stroke above the man who as yet had no equal, let alone a rival, on the battlefield'.

Just as Alexander's jealousy of Napoleon had played a significant role in the formation of the Third Coalition in the first place, so now it was exerting a powerful influence upon him at a crucial time for the fate of that alliance. What the Tsar wanted more than anything else was to replace Napoleon as Europe's leading statesman, and what an opportunity he seemed to have now. Napoleon was hundreds of miles from home at the head of an outnumbered and exhausted army within just a few days march of the Allied force at Olmütz. The last time Russians had fought the French, in 1799, they had won almost every encounter, and only lost when the numerical odds were heavily stacked against them. Bonaparte might defeat the Austrians easily enough, but they, like their ruler, obviously lacked the spirit of Russia's sons. So why retreat? To wait for Archduke Charles to join up with them or for the tardy Prussians finally to intervene would mean sharing the glory of defeating the 'Corsican upstart'. To take him on and crush him now would make that sweet victory belong predominantly to Russia and her Tsar. Alexander therefore sided with Weyrother, Buxhöwden and Dolgoruky, and arrangements began to be made for the forces around Olmütz to move out. On 27 November, the Allies, many of them reluctantly, began the slow advance towards Brünn.

It is claimed in most accounts of the 1805 campaign that Napoleon lured the Allies into advancing towards him in late November by cleverly feigning that he was in a much weaker position in Moravia than he really was. This is not entirely accurate. For a start, it ignores the desire of key figures within the Allied army to fight, most particularly Alexander, and it also disregards the fact that the Allied decision to advance was taken before most of the Emperor's much lauded chicanery was played out. Nonetheless, it is true that Napoleon deliberately tried to make himself appear weaker than he was in order to bring about a decisive encounter with the enemy near Brünn. This deception did, furthermore help to convince the Allied advocates of a battle that they had made the right decision in advancing and so prevented a possible change of policy at the last moment.

As soon as he arrived at Brünn, the Emperor decided that the best way to extricate himself from the vulnerable position he was now in was to tempt the Allies at Olmütz to attack him on a battlefield of his choosing, inflict a decisive defeat upon them, and thereby hopefully end the campaign. To this end, he skilfully arranged the forces still under his own immediate control. Of the 75,000 or so men available to him for a battle, he kept just 53,000 with him near Brünn, despatching Bernadotte's corps north west towards Bohemia to keep an eye on a small Austrian army gathering there and Davout's corps south to Vienna to watch for Archduke Charles. Both detached corps he intended to order to march to rejoin him as soon as he felt a battle was imminent, for now, their absence made the French army near Brünn seem considerably more vulnerable than it was. This undoubtedly encouraged those in the Allied camp inclined to fight to have the courage of their convictions and was probably the most important ruse Napoleon utilised.

The Emperor's second piece of deception came on the day the Allied army started to advance towards his own. Despite agreeing to send his small force forward with the much larger Russian contingent, the Austrian emperor remained reluctant to take on the French before Archduke Charles and his army could join him. He therefore went behind Alexander's back and sent envoys to Napoleon suggesting an armistice in the hope of buying time for reinforcements to arrive. Napoleon, of course, saw straight through the Austrian ploy but nevertheless received the envoys politely and displayed an exaggerated interest in making peace. This effectively doomed any hope of a truce, for when the hawks in the Allied command heard of Napoleon's supposed eagerness for ending hostilities, it only made them more convinced that he was ripe to be crushed.

Soon after, Prince Dolgoruky arrived at the French camp brusquely demanding an audience with the Emperor. At their meeting, the arrogant young Russian aristocrat disdainfully offered the French peace if they agreed to abandon their conquests and generally spoke to Europe's most powerful statesman as if he were his inferior. Napoleon was livid at being so blatantly insulted but managed to control his temper and so sent Dolgoruky back to Alexander convinced that the French army must indeed be in dire straits.

The final piece of Napoleonic deception came as the Allied army neared the French force at the end of November. The Emperor ordered his units nearest the enemy to withdraw, feigning panic as they did so. With the two armies now close, there could be no turning back for the Allies. Napoleon and Alexander would soon get the battle they both wanted to determine who was the true master of Europe.

As soon as he was certain a battle was imminent, the Emperor recalled the corps of Marshals Bernadotte and Davout. For once, Bernadotte bestirred himself, arriving at the head of his corps on the evening of 1 December with almost half a day to spare before the fighting started. He had covered an impressive sixty miles in thirty-six hours (by way of comparison, it took the Allied army more than twice the time to travel half the distance to the battlefield). Davout, who had further to travel than Bernadotte, set a similar pace, in person reaching Napoleon in the early hours of 2 December to promise him that the leading elements of his corps would join the line of battle no later than eight that morning. That was enough for the Emperor.

Bonaparte had picked out the area on which the decisive battle with the Allies would be fought as early as 21 November and had made sure since then that both he and his subordinates were thoroughly familiar with it. The presence to the north of the battlefield of the Moravian mountains effectively dictated that the Allied army would approach the French position from the east, passing by the town after which the battle would be named Austerlitz (modern day Slavkov).

The main feature of the battlefield, around 15 miles east of Brünn, was the large area of mostly open higher ground in the centre known as the Pratzen Heights. Aligned roughly south–west to north–east and around four miles in length, the slopes on the eastern (Allied) face were notably steeper than those on the western (French) side. Had he merely been planning a defensive battle, Napoleon would have occupied the heights, but he had something altogether more dramatic in mind and so abandoned them to his enemies.

A little way west of the Pratzen Heights, and running roughly parallel to them, were the Goldbach and Bosenitz streams, behind which the bulk of the French force was drawn up. North of the heights, the Bosenitz ran past a low hill, named by Napoleon's men the Santon, the ground to the east of which was fairly open. In the south, meanwhile, the Goldbach flowed through broken terrain studded with villages, woods and marshes, to the east of which, just south of the Pratzen Heights, were two sizeable but shallow lakes, the Satschen and Menitz Ponds.

The Emperor's plan took full advantage of the terrain he had chosen to fight over. Just as he had helped lure his enemy to challenge him in the first place by feigning weakness, Napoleon deliberately left the right, or southern, section of his line looking vulnerable in order to entice the Allies to concentrate their attack in that area. The broken terrain in that sector along the Goldbach was ideal for defence, and any assault upon it would end up getting funnelled between the southern end of the Pratzen Heights and the lakes. That flank would also receive steady reinforcements as various elements of Davout's corps arrived throughout the morning.

While the anticipated Allied attack on the French right developed, hopefully drawing in ever more troops from the centre, Napoleon's men would hold the enemy in the north around the Santon and then, when the moment was right, unleash a sudden assault upon the Allied position on the Pratzen Heights. Following this dagger thrust at the heart of the enemy line, the French left would ideally push forward as well and begin to encircle the entire Allied force; but even if that were not feasible (it was a very bold scheme), occupation of the Pratzen Heights might still enable the Emperor's soldiers to destroy in detail the southern half of the enemy host.

Of course, for Bonaparte's plan to succeed, the Allies would have to fight the kind of battle he wanted and expected them to fight, and it is testimony to his genius that that is exactly what they were intending to do. The Austro-Russian battle plan was drawn up by General Weyrother, with the wholehearted approval of Tsar Alexander. In the north and centre, the Allies were simply to hold the French initially, while to the south, tens of thousands of troops were to assault the French right along the Goldbach between the villages of Telnitz and Sokolnitz. Once they had swept the enemy aside here, thereby cutting Napoleon off from his line of retreat back to Vienna, they would drive north, rolling up the entire French line and putting the 'upstart' Emperor and his 'Great Army' to rout.

As Weyrother explained his plan to the assembled Allied generals in the early hours of 2 December, the general mood was one of apathy. Most of the commanders had opposed fighting the French, and even those Russians who had supported the idea of offering battle showed little interest in the details of the Austrian general's scheme. Kutuzov, with a lack of concern disgraceful in an army's commander-in-chief, spent most of the meeting sleeping in the corner.

Napoleon, by contrast, was extremely active on the night before the battle. Having cheerfully chatted with his staff as he dined on a favourite meal of potatoes fried with onions earlier that evening, Napoleon then toured his units to buoy the men up and make last minute checks that administrative arrangements, such as field hospitals and ammunition supplies, were in hand for the morrow. The troops' morale was further lifted by a Napoleonic order of the day, read out to them that evening by their officers. By entreating them to make one last effort to end the campaign, defeat the enemy and save the nation's honour, it appealed to the men's sense of patriotism, their hunger for glory, the rightness of their cause, and their desire to finish the war and go home.

It was a bitterly cold night, temperatures falling as low as minus six. As he reconnoitred the southern end of the French position, Napoleon's entourage narrowly avoided a Cossack patrol. Still, the danger of capture had been worth it, for the mass of enemy campfires to be seen opposite the French right confirmed that the Allies were intending to concentrate their efforts tomorrow exactly where he wanted them to.

Returning to his headquarters in the early hours of the morning, Napoleon received an altogether warmer welcome than that which the Cossacks would have given him. A group of soldiers suddenly realized that, it now being 2 December, it was the anniversary of the Emperor's coronation. Building makeshift torches from straw, they lit up the night sky in their commander's honour and soon the whole area was echoing with hearty cries of 'Vive l'Empereur!' Napoleon was deeply touched by this spontaneous and widespread show of affection, and went to bed for a couple of hours of much deserved sleep declaring, 'It has been the finest evening of my life'. He was just hours away from one of the greatest military victories of all time; and he knew it.

Monday, 2 December 1805, dawned with a heavy mist covering the lower-lying ground over which a great battle was about to be fought. Having observed over the past fortnight the regularity with which such fog formed in the morning in this area of Moravia, the Emperor was pleased to see that the weather had not let him down. Not only would the mist slow the Allies' attack on his southern flank, as their troops stumbled to find their way, it would also help the French obscure their preparations for the decisive attack on the Pratzen Heights, the higher parts of which could be seen above the fog.

With the arrival of Bernadotte's corps the previous evening, the French army had risen to 66,000 men and 139 guns stretched out over a six mile front running from the Santon in the north, down the Bosenitz and Goldbach streams, to around the village of Telnitz in the south. Throughout the morning, some 7000 additional soldiers of Davout's corps, along with a small number of cannon, would reinforce the army's southern flank, but that would still leave the Allies 89,000 men and 278 guns, around half of which was earmarked for the massive assault on the French right, with a distinct numerical advantage. Important as mere numbers are in war, however, it is how one uses the forces at one's disposal that is the key to victory, and at Austerlitz Napoleon would give a master class.

The day started for the Allies on the southern flank much as it would end; in chaos and confusion. By first light, many commanders were still to receive their orders, and as the attempt was made to set in motion the assault on the French right between Telnitz and Sokolnitz, columns soon began marching across each other in the fog. Eventually, the mess was sorted out and individual units were given the directions they needed, but the Allies had lost valuable time in which the leading elements of Davout's corps had drawn ever nearer the battlefield.

It was around 7 a.m. before the Allied attack in the south finally got underway. Even once the problem of columns getting in each others' way had been sorted out, the advance had still been slow, hindered as it was by the nature of the terrain in this area. Woods, marshes, vineyards, orchards, lakes, slopes and, everywhere, cloying mud reduced the Austrians and Russians to a snail's pace. And then, of course, they ran into the French.

Napoleon initially deployed just 11,000 men from Marshal Nicolas Soult's large corps, the third best in the *Grande Armée* after that of Davout and the Imperial Guard, to defend his right flank. They would be strengthened from 8 a.m. by the arrival of successive elements of Davout's expertly trained corps, but by the time those first reinforcements arrived, the Allies would have committed over 40,000 men under the command of General Buxhöwden to the assault in the south, with more scheduled to join them.

Given the disparity in numbers, it was almost inevitable that the Allies would make some headway against the French right, but the Emperor had gauged the situation deftly. Using large numbers of skirmishers to take advantage of the

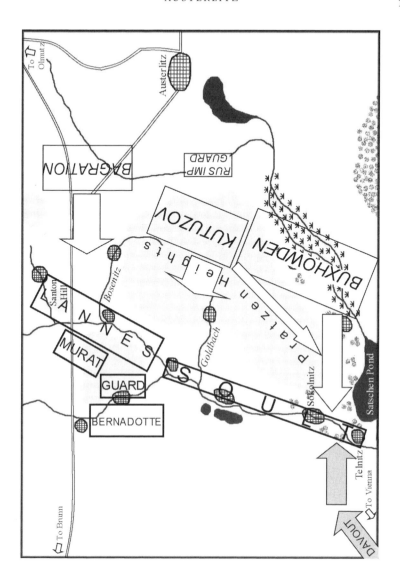

Battle of Austerlitz: Phase One

broken terrain, Soult's men slowed the enemy advance even further. The sheer weight of the Allied attack nevertheless pushed the French back into the villages of Telnitz and Sokolnitz, which both eventually fell after tough fighting in the streets.

But then, as promised, Davout's soldiers began to arrive. The bald-headed victor of Maria Zell took responsibility for the French right and, reinforced by men from his own corps, launched an immediate counter-attack that recaptured the key villages. The settlements would change hands several times over the following few hours, but the Allied hordes never broke the southern wing of the French army. The Russian and Austrian troops in this area fought bravely enough, but they were poorly led by General Buxhöwden, who gave little direction to his soldiers and indeed seems to have been drunk. Davout, by contrast, had a magnificent battle, constantly riding up and down the French right to steady the men and direct the defence of the whole sector.

Nor was Davout the only French hero in the south. The commander of one of his divisions, General Friant, had no fewer than four horses shot under him during the battle, and in the village of Sokolnitz, two French sergeant-majors were seen using regimental eagle standards as cudgels. In fact, almost every Frenchmen who fought on the right wing of the army at Austerlitz was a hero, and their resistance surprised even the Emperor, who, although confident that his fine troops would not break, had anticipated that they might have to fall back further than they did.

The remarkable skill and tenacity of the French soldiers in the south stunned the Tsar too. He had expected that the enemy's right wing would collapse under the weight of the massive Allied assault, but there it was, holding firm. Alexander became increasingly irritated as time passed and ordered ever more men to be committed to the attack from his position atop the Pratzen Heights.

Away to the west, from his vantage point on high ground behind the French left-centre, Napoleon had been watching the Allies thin their ranks on the heights and send more and more men down into the foggy Goldbach valley below. At around a quarter to nine, he turned to Marshal Soult, one of his best battlefield generals and the man who had been ordered to lead the planned assault on the Allied centre. 'How long will it take you to storm the heights?' the Emperor asked. 'Twenty minutes, sire,' replied Soult. Bonaparte nodded. His right flank was holding magnificently, his relatively strong left had so far only been involved in skirmishes with the Allied right, and there had been no fighting at all in the centre. 'Very well,' he said. 'We will wait another quarter of an hour.' The French thunder-stroke would be unleashed with impeccable timing.

By 9 a.m., the Allied position on the Pratzen Heights had been sufficiently weakened to enable Soult to overrun it, while their left was still not strong enough to break the French right in the near future. It was the scenario Napoleon had envisioned in planning the battle, and his genius as a military commander allowed him to recognize exactly when it had come to pass on the morning of 2 December. Hidden by the fog in the valley to the west of the heights, the divisions of Generals Vandamme and St Hilaire, their troops fortified by a triple ration of brandy, crossed the Goldbach stream and began their long ascent.

As if Providence were bestowing its blessing upon the French attack, the sun burst through the clouds at the very moment the men of Soult's corps emerged from the mist part way up the north-west slope of the Pratzen Heights. The Allies were stunned, but they had weakened their centre too much to prevent the French gaining possession of the plateau which dominated the battlefield. During the attack, Tsar Alexander, Emperor Francis and General Kutuzov all came under fire from the soldiers of Vandamme and St Hilaire. The Allied high command was scattered, destroying any hope of the Austrians and Russians being able to fight a properly coordinated battle. Kutuzov, indeed, was hit in the cheek by a musket ball, but refused the attention of the Tsar's personal physician, allegedly pointing to the advancing French and stating that that was where the real wound was.

To the credit of some of the Russian commanders, including Kutuzov, they quickly managed to arrange a counter-attack on the southernmost of Soult's attacking divisions, that of St Hilaire, by recalling units that had recently been ordered off the heights to join the assault on the French right. St Hilaire's men came under intense pressure from the Russians, who slowly started to push the French back across the open plateau. It was arguably the most decisive moment of the day, for if St Hilaire had given way, Napoleon's whole plan of battle might have begun to unravel.

The flexibility and skill of the *Grande Armée*'s artillery now proved invaluable. French guns were brought forward to within close range of the enemy, from where they were able to wreak havoc. Soon, the Russian counter-attack was halted and then thrown back. By 11 a.m., the French had secured the Pratzen plateau and the Emperor then moved his command post there. A spectacular victory was within his grasp.

In contrast to the tough time St Hilaire's division had in storming the Pratzen Heights, Vandamme's division advanced almost as if it were taking a stroll in the park, but that was largely due to the efforts of the French left wing to the north. As Soult's divisions had swept aside the initial weak opposition on the plateau, Napoleon had ordered the units at the northern end of the French line to press forward against the forces on the Allied right flank, thereby preventing them from moving to reinforce their comrades on the Pratzen Heights.

The French left wing was strong, including, as it did, the three divisions of Marshal Lannes's corps and several thousand horsemen of the cavalry corps

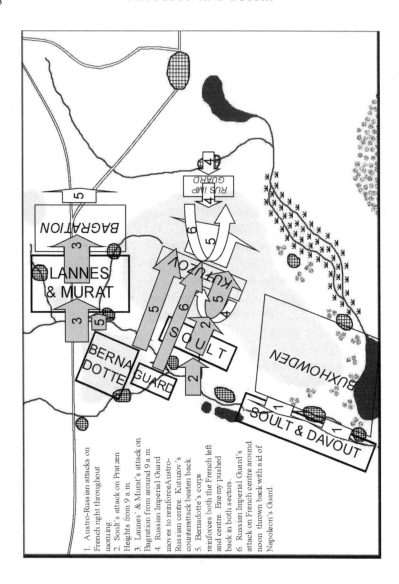

1. Austro-Russian attacks on French right throughout morning.

2. Soult's attack on Pratzen Heights from 9 a.m.

3. Lannes' & Murat's attack on Bagration from around 9 a.m.

4. Russian Imperial Guard moves to reinforce Austro-Russian centre. Kutuzov's counterattack beaten back.

5. Bernadotte's corps reinforces both the French left and centre. Enemy pushed back in both sectors.

6. Russian Imperial Guard's attack on French centre around noon thrown back with aid of Napoleon's Guard.

Battle of Austerlitz: Phase Two

under Murat. The Austro-Russian forces opposite them were similar in number and were commanded by arguably the best Allied general on the field, Peter Bagration. A nobleman of Georgian descent, and bearing the swarthy features that betrayed it, Bagration was another of Suvorov's disciples, having served with him in Italy and Switzerland in 1799. Taciturn, tenacious and prone to losing his temper, he was not a gifted strategist or tactician, but he did have the ability to inspire his men.

As the struggle for the Pratzen Heights got underway, the hitherto sporadic skirmishing that had typified the fighting in the northern sector of the battlefield intensified. The French pushed forward and were soon reinforced by elements of Bernadotte's corps. Napoleon's great hope was that the Allied right might give way, enabling his left flank forces to sweep round the back of the Pratzen Heights and encircle the whole of the enemy army. That would have led to an even greater disaster for the Allies than was to befall them, and it is thanks to Bagration and his men that it did not happen.

The combat raged back and forth across the open ground east of the Santon, attacks being repulsed and then followed by counter-attacks, which in turn were beaten back. Lannes's infantry, many of them conscripts on their first campaign, battled bravely but could not make a breakthrough against the tough Russian foot soldiers. The French cavalry proved equally unable to smash the Allied horsemen, despite becoming embroiled in a long-running series of clashes that eventually drew in some ten thousand horses and their riders.

The addition of Bernadotte's men to the struggle in the north gave the French the advantage and helped push the Allies slowly back, but Bagration's line held. On a day that the Russians and Austrians would otherwise have liked to forget, the performance of the men under the Georgian general's command was one of which the *Grande Armée* itself would have been proud.

As Bagration's forces gradually began to give ground in the north, the Allies made a last throw of the dice in the centre. Around noon, the Russian Imperial Guard, which had been posted near the town of Austerlitz as a reserve force whose services were not expected to be required, began to advance against the northernmost of Soult's two divisions on the Pratzen plateau. Just as St Hilaire had had to face the first counter-attack aimed at regaining the key central ground, Vandamme now had to confront the second.

The infantry of the Russian Imperial Guard stormed in first. Resplendent in their green uniforms, these elite foot soldiers charged Vandamme's men from fully three hundred yards up a relatively steep slope, yet still broke through his first line. The overly long dash to close with the enemy had exhausted the Russians, however, and the French, reinforced by elements of Bernadotte's corps, held them and began to inflict heavy casualties.

Now it was the turn of the Russian Guard cavalry, who launched their assault less recklessly. Falling in among units already shaken by the infantry attack, the horsemen sent large numbers of Frenchmen streaming back past their Emperor and threatened to recapture the northern end of the Pratzen plateau for the Tsar.

Napoleon had also kept his Imperial Guard as a reserve, however, and now it proved its worth. To counter Alexander's elite cavalry, the Emperor unleashed his own superlative squadrons. Catching the Russians disorganized and tired by their initial charge, the French horsemen smashed into their foes and put them to rout before turning on the Tsar's infantry and scattering them too. With the cream of the Russian Army pouring back down the slopes of the Pratzen Heights, the Allied centre was on the verge of disintegration.

Following the rout of the Russian Imperial Guard, Napoleon turned his attention to making his victory as decisive as possible. Ordering Lannes and Murat to continue pressing Bagration's forces back in the north, and commanding Bernadotte to move his corps into the centre and complete the rout of the enemy there, he instructed Soult's two divisions on the plateau, along with the Imperial Guard, to move against the enemy left.

This final phase of the battle commenced around half past one. Over two hours earlier, foreseeing what might happen if the French could not be dislodged from the commanding Pratzen Heights, Kutuzov had written an order instructing Buxhöwden to pull his forces back from their assault on Napoleon's right. It was 3 p.m. before the messenger finally found the Estonian, by which time it was utterly superfluous. The French were now driving in the Allied left from west, north and east.

Many of the soldiers trapped in the southern pocket fought on bravely, but many more, suddenly finding the enemy attacking them from the flank or behind, panicked and attempted to flee. The half of the Allied army that had been supposed to win the day for the Third Coalition effectively collapsed as a fighting force. As snow started to fall in mid-afternoon, thousands upon thousands of mostly Russian troops took flight in the one direction in which they were not confronted by Frenchmen. That led them into the area of the large Satschen and Menitz Ponds, but the cold of this time of year had frozen the surface of these shallow lakes, providing a slippery escape route. As ever – more soldiers rushed onto the ice, however, the sheer weight of numbers, exacerbated by a bombardment from French artillery at the southern end of the Pratzen Heights, opened up huge holes through which large numbers of Allied troops and guns fell. It is unclear how many men drowned or froze to death in the icy waters – certainly nowhere near the 20,000 claimed by the French at the time, but possibly as many as 2,000. Whatever the true number, pandemonium resulted as the Allied left disintegrated.

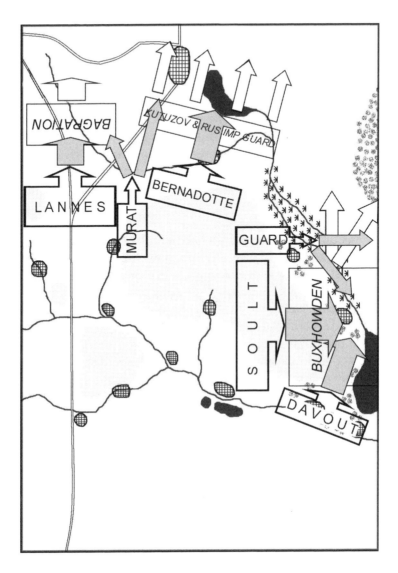

Battle of Austerlitz: Phase Three

As the cold winter's night fell around half past four, the fighting died out all over the battlefield. In the north, Bagration had conducted a largely successful fighting retreat, his sterling efforts keeping at least part of the Allied army more or less intact. In the centre, Bernadotte had pushed east from the Pratzen Heights against weak Austro-Russian resistance, reaching the town of Austerlitz by dark. In the south, that portion of the Allied left wing that had not been killed, wounded or captured had been scattered to the four winds, some never to return to their regiments, others only after some time. An army of nigh on 90,000 men that had come to this place expecting to annihilate the *parvenu* French Emperor and his self-proclaimed *Grande Armée* had been all but destroyed as a fighting force.

The butcher's bill for the battle of Austerlitz told a stark tale. For the small loss, given the intensity of much of the fighting, of 2,000 Frenchmen killed, 7,000 wounded and 500 captured, Napoleon's *Grande Armée* had killed or wounded 15,000 Allied soldiers and captured 12,000 prisoners, 180 guns and some 50 regimental standards. As if that were not bad enough for the Allies, many thousands more of their troops died as a result of a typhus epidemic in the following weeks. The one thing they had to be grateful for was the fact that the French had so exhausted themselves through their prodigious efforts on 2 December that they were in no position to launch a vigorous pursuit of their enemy and tear what was left of the Allied army to shreds. But then they didn't need to. So thoroughly battered and demoralized were the Allies by their defeat that the Tsar's men were set on returning to the safety of Russia, while the Austrians were desperate simply to end the war.

And what of the trio of rulers who had been present at Austerlitz (and give it its alternative name of the battle of the Three Emperors)? In one of the great understatements of history, Francis of Austria wrote to his wife as he fled with what was left of his small force, 'A battle was fought today which did not turn out very well'. Psychologically shattered, he was already bracing himself for a punitive peace treaty and a further diminution of Habsburg power and prestige.

Tsar Alexander cut an even more pathetic figure that night. Missing for some time following the disastrous defeat, he was eventually found sitting underneath a tree many miles from the battlefield sobbing profusely into a handkerchief. Rather than crying for the thousands of soldiers, most of them from his own army, who had died that day, his tears were those of humiliation and self-pity. He had wanted the battle, indeed the whole war, in order to crush the 'upstart' Corsican, show the world that he was the better man, and replace the French emperor as the greatest ruler in Europe. Now, his dreams lay in tatters as the Continent's true master had asserted his superiority in the most unmistakable and mortifying fashion.

In contrast to his rivals, Napoleon was preoccupied that evening not with the fate of his dynasty or his own prestige, but with the wellbeing of the remarkable soldiers of his *Grande Armée* to whom he owed so much. Touring the battlefield after dark, Napoleon personally searched for wounded Frenchmen, giving every one he found a stiff drink of brandy to dull their pain and ensuring that they received whatever treatment could be given them. Perhaps he was also already mulling over the pledge he would subsequently give to provide the widow of every one of his soldiers killed at Austerlitz with a handsome pension. Certainly, he gave thought to a proclamation he intended to write and have read out to his victorious army that night, but sheer exhaustion took over as he returned to his new headquarters in Austerlitz.

The proclamation was completed and read out the next day. Eschewing the florid phrases he might have used, but which most of his plain-spoken men would not really have appreciated, the Emperor began his short and, above all, grateful message to his troops with an understated sentence that summed up his sentiments perfectly. It read simply, 'Soldiers, I am pleased with you!'

7

Prussia's Gambit

In the wake of Austerlitz, with what was left of the Russian army that had fought there streaming headlong back towards home, Archduke Charles's army still some way away, and Vienna firmly in French hands, the Austrian emperor felt he had little choice but to agree to an armistice and peace talks. Meeting Napoleon face to face on 4 December, Francis quickly agreed to a truce that brought an end to fighting between Frenchmen and Austrians and called for all Russian troops to leave Habsburg territory. The following day, Tsar Alexander assented to Francis's plea for him to withdraw his men, who were in any case already set on returning to Russia after their mauling.

It is a measure of how far Austrian morale had been sapped by recent events that, whereas it had taken six months for them to agree to a peace treaty with France in 1797 and two months following Hohenlinden in 1800-01, the Habsburgs agreed to this latest covenant almost as soon as it was presented to them. Furthermore, the treaty of Pressburg, signed on Boxing Day 1805, was the most punitive settlement Napoleon had yet formulated. Having warned Austria earlier in the year not to got to war with France again on pain of dire consequences should she lose – an attempt to dissuade Vienna from joining the Third Coalition which failed – Bonaparte had effectively tied his own hands when it came to making peace. The threat having been made, he had to carry it through: not that he was at all unwilling to do so.

By the terms of the treaty of Pressburg, Emperor Francis lost lands which contained 2,500,000 of his subjects (around 10% of the total) and which generated a sixth of his revenues. Much of the lost territory had only been in Austrian hands since the earlier treaty of Campo Formio when Napoleon had given it to them. These were the former lands of the Venetian Republic – a large chunk of north-eastern Italy, Istria at the head of the Adriatic Sea and Dalmatia on its eastern shore – which the Emperor now put under the jurisdiction of the Kingdom of Italy. Francis also ceded Habsburg territory of longer standing, though, in southern Germany and the Tyrol, almost all of which went to Napoleon's three key German allies; Baden, Württemberg and especially Bavaria (whose territory expanded by a third). Austria further had to acknowledge the promotion of the rulers of these three south German states, in the first case to grand duke in the latter two to king. Finally, Vienna agreed to pay an indemnity of 40,000,000 francs to the French, accepting that until the sum was paid in full, elements of the *Grande Armée* would remain on Austrian soil.

The treaty of Pressburg is sometimes cited as the point where Napoleon sowed the seeds of his future defeat by making an intractable enemy of Austria to add to his other across the Channel. It is a view coloured perhaps by the experience of Germany's hostile reaction to the treaty of Versailles at the end of the First World War. To the extent that both treaties engendered a potent sense of animosity in the countries upon which they were imposed, the argument is valid, but it neglects a further, equally important point. Vienna undoubtedly *wanted* to overturn Pressburg, just as Berlin desired to overthrow Versailles in the 1920s and 1930s, but that does not mean it *could*, or even that it would necessarily try. Austria had been hesitant in taking up the sword in 1805 through fear of defeat. That fear only increased in the aftermath of Pressburg, especially as a fourth humiliation at the hands of Napoleon might imperil the very existence of the Habsburgs' multinational empire. Austria's future foreign policy would thus be dictated more by how confident she was that France could be beaten and the terms of Pressburg overthrown than by her simple sense of grievance at those terms. It was similar with German foreign policy in the 1930s. It was ultimately shaped more by the fact that Britain and France *allowed* Hitler to overturn the terms of Versailles, which they had the power, if not the will, to uphold, than by his mere desire to do so.

Just as Napoleon determined to treat his defeated Austrian enemy harshly at the end of 1805, he was disinclined to be generous towards the power that had almost joined Vienna in fighting him; Prussia. In plain power political terms, it was imperative for Napoleon that the Prussians did not simply replace the Austrians in an anti-French coalition, but the fact that news of Austerlitz caused Berlin to cease the preparations for war it had been making since early November indicated that that was not likely in the immediate future. Further evidence of Prussia's new-found passion for the neutrality she had so nearly abandoned was provided when Count Haugwitz, the man who was to have delivered the bellicose ultimatum to Napoleon in late November, instead in early December extended his king's compliments to the Emperor on his fine victory.

Bonaparte was less than impressed by this shameless fawning, knowing, as he did, what the Prussians had originally planned to do. Prussian intervention had been his greatest concern in the weeks before Austerlitz, and the fact that Berlin had so nearly made the nightmare a reality had a profound impact upon the Emperor. This was only exacerbated by his feeling of betrayal in that his offer to the Prussians of friendship and, more particularly, Hanover had been spurned. Ungrateful, unreliable Prussia might have abandoned all thought of joining the ranks of France's enemies for now, but Napoleon determined that she should also be dissuaded from doing so in the future. While he held the whip hand once more, therefore, he resolved to put his relations with Berlin on a sounder footing.

Meeting with Haugwitz again on 15 December, the Emperor presented him with a draft Franco-Prussian treaty of alliance. Berlin was still to be offered Hanover, but the *quid pro quos* had greatly grown. Prussia was now to hand over territory of her own in return: the small enclave of Neuchâtel in Switzerland (which was to go to Marshal Berthier, Napoleon's loyal and able chief of staff, as reward for his services); Ansbach in southern Germany (which France's loyal ally, Bavaria, was to get); and Cleves in western Germany. This last territory was to be combined with the small, Bavarian-owned Grand Duchy of Berg and given to Marshal Murat, husband of Napoleon's sister Caroline, but Berlin was expected to pay Bavaria compensation for the transfer. Finally, Prussia was to guarantee all Bonaparte's territorial adjustments throughout Europe. These terms were certainly less generous than those offered to Berlin just a few weeks earlier (essentially Hanover in return for continued Prussian neutrality) but, recognizing the radically changed circumstances that Austerlitz and the imminent making of peace between France and Austria had wrought, Haugwitz signed.

The treaty still needed to be ratified by the Prussian king, however, and in early 1806 he showed that he was disinclined to do so; at least without modifications. Frederick William suggested that Prussia's cession of territory should be postponed until a general European peace, to be mediated by Berlin, was reached, that Prussia should receive further lands in northern Germany, such as Hamburg and Bremen, and that she not be expected to guarantee the status of Italy.

Napoleon reacted to the King's proposals with anger. As far as he was concerned, Frederick William was lucky the *Grande Armée* was not currently marching on Berlin in retaliation for Prussia so nearly joining the Third Coalition and the King should be thankful he was still being offered Hanover. The Emperor therefore responded by making yet further demands of Prussia. She should close her ports to British ships, break off relations with Britain, and pledge to support France in any future war she might fight. Prussia was, in essence, to become a subordinate partner of the Napoleonic Empire. Nevertheless, on 15 February 1806, Frederick William, fearing the probable consequences of refusing to do so, ratified the treaty of alliance with France. Within weeks, Prussia and Britain were at war, albeit one that neither waged very actively.

Bonaparte's treatment of Prussia in winter 1805–6 was certainly rough and undoubtedly contributed to Berlin's decision to go to war with France later in the year, but it must be put in context. The Prussians had to a large degree brought their fate upon themselves. Had they not prepared to fight France in autumn 1805 but instead maintained their neutrality sincerely, they would have got Hanover with far fewer strings attached. It is admittedly likely that Napoleon would still have pressed them to become a formal ally, like Bavaria, but at least then they could have expected rewards for their support and loyalty, as, indeed, the south German states had been rewarded for theirs. The fact is that, by effectively abandoning their position of neutrality in autumn 1805, the Prussians made a return to such a status all but impossible. They could never expect Napoleon to trust them again; hence his efforts to bind them to France by alliance. Perhaps a more generous attitude on his behalf would have made them more likely to abide by that alliance, but maybe not, and one must surely understand the Emperor's reluctance to show too much generosity to a power that had so nearly stabbed him in the back.

Austria's decision to make peace and Prussia's new-found quiescence in the wake of Austerlitz placed France's two remaining great power enemies, Britain and Russia, in an awkward position. The Tsar's first reaction was to send his aide, Prince Dolgoruky, to Berlin on 6 December to plead with the Prussian king to fulfil the obligation he had made in early November to enter the war against Napoleon, but his entreaties fell on deaf ears. Despite Dolgoruky's promises of assistance, the Prussians knew the Russians would be in no position for some time, following their recent crushing defeat, to offer the level of help Prussia would need to take on the French.

With both central European powers thus unwilling to fight, the armies the Russians and British had despatched in autumn 1805 to northern Germany and southern Italy, and which had achieved next to nothing, were suddenly rendered extremely vulnerable. Humiliatingly but sensibly, both London and St Petersburg now withdrew those forces. In northern Germany, Russian troops which had landed on the Baltic coast east of Denmark in early October began to trudge back home via Prussia in early 1806, while a British expeditionary force was re-embarked and sailed back across the North Sea with similar promptness. In southern Italy, meanwhile, where Anglo-Russian soldiers had arrived as recently as mid-November to reinforce the Neapolitan Army, a similar skedaddle occurred, although in this case the British only went to Sicily and the Russians to Corfu in the Ionian islands.

Their departure was none too premature either, for Napoleon determined that the rulers of Naples, like those of Austria and Prussia, needed to be taught a lesson in the basics of international power politics. Just as the French had endeavoured in autumn 1805 to get the Prussians to guarantee they would not join the Third Coalition, they had entered negotiations with the Kingdom of Naples, and indeed had succeeded in late September in getting the Neapolitans to sign a neutrality pact. To back this up, Napoleon had warned the reactionary Queen of Naples, just as he had cautioned the Austrian emperor, that she and her family would be punished should her kingdom go to war with France. Having broken the neutrality pact just weeks after signing it and ignored Bonaparte's warning to boot, the rulers of Naples did not have long to wait after Austerlitz to discover their fate. On 27 December, the day after the signing of the treaty of Pressburg, Napoleon declared the Neapolitan royal family deposed, and within a fortnight Marshal Masséna, freed from his task of shadowing Archduke Charles, was leading an army down the Italian peninsula to give force to the Emperor's words. Realising that resistance was futile, the King and Queen of Naples fled with the British to Sicily, where the ships of the Royal Navy could protect them. Their capital was occupied in mid-February 1806 without a fight and at the end of March Joseph Bonaparte, Napoleon's elder brother, was officially appointed the new King of Naples, a change which most, though not all, Neapolitans greeted with indifference. (Another Bonaparte brother, Louis, was made King of Holland by Napoleon in May 1806. As French influence was already dominant in Holland, the change here was largely cosmetic. Still, it was not well-received by the established rulers of Europe, who felt it further debased the notion of 'legitimate' monarchy.)*

Despite leading Russia into a war that had gone disastrously wrong, Alexander returned to St Petersburg in December 1805 to a warm welcome from the city's population. As so often happens when people are unwilling to see the faults of a 'divinely appointed' monarch, it was against the Tsar's young friends and advisers that most influential groups and figures in Russia, including Alexander's own family, turned when looking for someone to blame for the recent catastrophe. The Polish deputy foreign minister, Czartoryski, came under particularly heavy fire for his role in forming the Third Coalition, and, to his discredit, Alexander also soon decided to make his old friend the scapegoat for the ill-starred 1805 campaign. Inevitably, relations between the two men broke down, but, bizarrely, the Tsar still would not accept Czartoryski's offer to resign for several months.

Alexander in the opening weeks of 1806 seems to have been mentally and emotionally paralysed by his crushing defeat at Austerlitz and was entirely unsure what to do. Czartoryski, on the other hand, had very firm ideas and continually pressed for them over that winter and into the spring. He advocated a policy of continued resistance to the French, favoured maintaining close relations with Britain and Austria (Prussia, the Pole's *bête noire*, was noticeably omitted), and proposed an active extension of Russian influence on the Continent. He was especially alarmed, as were most politically significant Russians, by the expansion

---

* From a more modern perspective, there remains something distasteful about Napoleon's placing of his siblings on thrones, for although it can be argued that he had earned his monarchical position, his brothers owed theirs solely to his influence. That said, of course, there was nothing particularly unusual about a European monarch seeking to place members of his own family in positions of power. Under the *ancien régime*, for example, the Bourbons had managed to provide the rulers of several states.

of Napoleonic power in southern Italy and, most particularly, the eastern coast of the Adriatic. This was seen as a major threat to Russia's own ambitions in the Balkans and eastern Mediterranean, but Czartoryski had an answer to the envisaged menace. Russia should cooperate with the British to check France in the Mediterranean at Malta and Corfu, while pre-empting any possible French ambitions in south-east Europe by working to construct two new Balkan states, one Slavic and one Greek, which would nominally be under Ottoman suzerainty but in reality be dominated by St Petersburg. Furthermore, the Pole strongly suggested that, should the Turks, as seemed possible, draw closer to Paris, Russia should threaten to occupy Moldavia and Wallachia.

Hard as Czartoryski promoted his ideas, however, Alexander, having made his friend the scapegoat for the disasters of 1805, was unwilling or unable to adopt them fully, at least at this stage. The Tsar did act in early 1806, though, to counter the expansion of French influence in southern Italy and Dalmatia by ordering the army which had been evacuated from Naples to retire no further than Corfu. Even more contentiously, he instructed Cattaro (modern Kotor), a key strongpoint on the eastern Adriatic coast that Austria had ceded to France under the terms of Pressburg, to be seized in early March. The Russians then pressured the tiny but strategically significant independent republic of Ragusa (modern Dubrovnik) to side with them, a move which only resulted in French forces sent to Dalmatia, occupying the city in late May 1806. There followed a localized Franco-Russian war in this part of Europe which went on until summer 1807 and in which the Russians generally had the better of the fighting, thanks to their naval supremacy in the Adriatic (which they only enjoyed because of the Royal Navy's domination of the Mediterranean). Despite their best efforts, however, the Russians could not shift the French from Ragusa or seriously threaten their control of the majority of Dalmatia.

If Czartoryski was in accord with the Tsar's position in regard to the Mediterranean and Adriatic, though, the differences between them were high-lighted by Alexander's attitude towards Prussia. Although the Tsar did not let relations with Britain and Austria lapse entirely in 1806, he showed himself far more interested in securing an accord with the King and Queen of Prussia, his good friends since 1802. Politely rebuffed by them in December 1805, by the following spring, Alexander found Frederick William and his domineering wife, Louise, more ready to entertain a demarche from a Russia which was beginning to recover from the shock of Austerlitz. The Tsar proposed an anti-French military alliance and suggested that, in order to buy time for both countries to prepare fully for hostilities, the arrangement should remain secret and be given cover by Russia entering into peace talks with the French. Frederick William responded eagerly, informing Alexander that he now considered his recent alliance with France effectively annulled and claiming that he was determined to join the

Russians in fighting the French as soon as it was feasible. On 1 July, the treaty of alliance was duly signed. Another major war on the Continent was now all but inevitable.

By the time the Russo-Prussian pact was signed, one of Czartoryski's frequent offers of resignation had at last been accepted by Alexander. As he left office, the Pole fiercely criticized the Tsar's close links with Prussia and, perhaps fearing that war in alliance with the Prussians would only make things worse for Russia, suggested that Alexander should try for a peace settlement with Napoleon, even though he doubted it would meet with success. The Tsar, as we have seen, was already thinking of launching a peace initiative as cover for his successful wooing of Prussia, so, in June, Pierre d'Oubril, the former Russian *chargé d'affaires* at the Paris embassy, was despatched as a special envoy to Paris, where he arrived early the next month.

How seriously St Petersburg took the negotiations that followed is, to say the least, open to question. Indeed, d'Oubril was instructed to sign a deal with the Emperor only 'should such an arrangement present infinitely marked advantages for Russia'. More specifically, the Russian envoy was directed to secure Dalmatia, Ragusa and Albania as a new kingdom for the deposed rulers of Naples, the idea being that this state would then act as an anti-French buffer protecting Russian designs in the Balkans. Given the deep animosity between Napoleon and the former Neapolitan king and queen, this aim was never likely to be fulfilled and, indeed, was duly rejected by the French.

Nevertheless, Oubril did sign a peace settlement on 20 July. Under its terms, the Russians were to evacuate Cattaro, reduce their forces based in Corfu, and recognize Joseph Bonaparte as King of Naples and Napoleon as Emperor of the French and King of Italy. In return, the French undertook to withdraw from Ragusa, pull their troops out of Germany within three months of the treaty's ratification, and even endeavour to have the hated former Neapolitan rulers given the Balearic Islands as compensation for their recent loss. Finally, both sides would guarantee the integrity of the Ottoman Empire.

Although Napoleon was aware that many Francophobic courtiers had the ear of Alexander in St Petersburg, he nonetheless expected the Tsar to ratify what he saw as a perfectly reasonable peace treaty. The news which reached Paris in early September that Alexander had rejected the accord therefore greatly frustrated the Emperor. Russia's new foreign minister, Andrei Gotthard Budberg, a Latvian general of Germanic descent, former tutor of the Tsar in military affairs, and a man of very limited diplomatic ability or knowledge, had vehemently opposed the treaty when he saw it, but it had been all but inevitable that Alexander would refuse to ratify it anyway. As we have seen, the Tsar was only willing to agree to a settlement that gave Russia significant gains, most especially the removal of the

French presence from south-east Europe. Nor, clearly, did he expect, or probably even want, to get such a deal, for Russia spent much of the summer of 1806 gearing up for a renewal of large-scale active hostilities against the French and urging the King of Prussia to do likewise. Alexander expected that by the end of October Russia would have an army of 60,000 ready to march west, with a second, similarly-sized force standing by to follow within a fortnight. Both armies, Frederick William was promised, would come to Prussia's aid the moment she went to war with France.

The Tsar thus never really took the peace talks of summer 1806 seriously. Napoleon, on the other hand, did, but he did not help his cause by courting the Ottoman Empire at the same time. The Emperor's reasons for trying to improve relations with Constantinople were twofold. First, he hoped, rather crassly perhaps, that by wooing Russia's traditional enemy it would increase the pressure on St Petersburg to agree a settlement with France, and second, he felt that, should the peace talks with the Russians fail, he might be able to make an alliance with the Turks to help him in the continuing war. The Sultan, Selim III, responded warmly to the courtship, seeing in good relations with France a chance to regain some of the influence and territory the Ottoman Empire had lost to Russia in the past half century. The Russians were understandably both alarmed and irate to see closer relations developing between the French and the Turks, but rather than making them more eager for peace, as Bonaparte had hoped, it made them more inclined towards war; and not just against the Emperor, but the Sultan too.

So the peace that Napoleon had hoped to make with Russia in 1806 never materialized. In addition to the original reasons the Tsar had in going to war in 1805, he now also wanted the French presence removed from south-east Europe, but the Emperor was not prepared to give up control of Dalmatia while Russian and French forces continued to fight there, as to do so would look like a defeat.* The state of war between France and Russia would thus continue, but geography dictated that, in order for the Tsar's armies to take on Napoleon's forces in any serious way, they needed one of the central European powers to go to war with the French too. It was thus with some pleasure that, in late summer 1806, the hawks in St Petersburg watched the Prussians mobilize to fight the nation they had become a supposed ally of just a few months earlier.

We have already seen how the Prussian government had put itself on a collision course with France by the start of July 1806, and events in the following weeks

---

* One is reminded of the attitude of successive British governments to the status of Northern Ireland – no concessions to the Republicans while the IRA continued an active paramilitary campaign.

only made Berlin move faster towards the looming clash. The first major episode was the announcement by Napoleon in the middle of July of the creation of the Confederation of the Rhine (also referred to as the Rhenish Confederation or the *Rheinbund*). This was a federal grouping of the states of south and west Germany with the French Emperor as its Protector and responsible for its foreign and military affairs. It was formed primarily as a defensive buffer between France and the central and eastern European powers, thus reflecting Napoleon's conviction that the security of his realm in a potentially or actually hostile Europe would be best served by the consolidation of French power and influence, but it also helped disseminate some of the benefits of post-Revolutionary France, such as improved administration and more rational laws, throughout Germany.

Inevitably, though, the *Rheinbund*'s creation provoked something of a stir among France's great power rivals. Neither Britain nor Russia, both still at war with Bonaparte, were happy to see the French consolidate their dominant influence in south and west Germany, but it was the Germanic powers, Austria and Prussia, that were most affected by the Confederation's formation. The Habsburgs theoretically had most cause to be affronted, for the creation of the *Rheinbund* effectively killed off the Holy Roman Empire, a loose affiliation of Germanic states established many centuries ago and headed for hundreds of years by the ruler of Austria.* In the event, though, Vienna took the demise of the ancient institution fairly sanguinely, Francis abdicating as the final Holy Roman Emperor in early August without much fuss. The fact is that the Austrians had seen that the writing was on the wall for the moribund pan-German organization for some time. That is why Francis had adopted the new title Emperor of Austria in summer 1804, so that he could retain an imperial nomenclature once the Holy Roman Empire finally died. Of course, Vienna was not pleased at the consolidation of French predominance in south and west Germany that the formation of the *Rheinbund* signalled, and still ideally wished to see it overthrown and Austrian pre-eminence restored, but it recognized that its loss of primacy in the region to France had already happened before the new body was formed.

The other major German power, Prussia, reacted with less *sang froid* to the creation of the Confederation of the Rhine. Berlin had dreamed for many decades of replacing Vienna as the dominant capital in Germany. In recent years, it had witnessed Habsburg influence in central Europe decline dramatically, but only to see it replaced by that of France. For the Prussians, therefore, the message of the formation of the *Rheinbund* – that French authority in south and west Germany was here to stay – was a particularly depressing one.

Napoleon clearly sensed the strongly negative manner in which Berlin might

---

* Ironically enough, the Holy Roman Empire had been founded by Charlemagne, one of Napoleon's heroes.

react to the Rhenish Confederation, for he shrewdly suggested to the Prussians at this time that they might form a north German confederation under their own influence to complement his own creation. It was an astute diplomatic move that might have diffused much of the anti-French feeling building in Prussia, but the Emperor soon undermined it by advising several independent coastal trading centres, such as Hamburg, and Prussia's southern neighbour, Saxony, not to join Berlin's proposed grouping. Napoleon had good reason for this, as he was still, rightly, unsure of how trustworthy his Prussian 'allies' were and so, having already given them Hanover, was reluctant to see them extend their authority too far, but his obstructiveness unsurprisingly frustrated Berlin by restricting the gains it hoped to make. An offer which the Emperor saw as generous and hoped would ameliorate relations with Prussia was thus seen by the Prussians as unfairly curbed and even irritating.

If Napoleon's proposal for a limited north German confederation failed to improve Franco-Prussian relations in the wake of the creation of the *Rheinbund*, though, information which reached Berlin on 7 August brought the relationship to its nadir. It was then that the Prussians discovered that, in ultimately futile efforts to reach a peace deal with Britain, Bonaparte had proposed arranging to return Hanover, the one great gain Prussia had made from the French alliance so far, to the British king. Understandably, Frederick William, Louise and all their ministers were enraged. Indeed, so furious were they that preparations for war against France were immediately initiated, Prussian ports were reopened to the ships of Napoleon's British adversaries, and a peace treaty to end the desultory Anglo-Prussian war that had officially been in existence since early spring was requested from London by the Prussian king. Not missing a trick, Tsar Alexander reiterated that Russia would stand by Prussia should she take up arms against France and urged Berlin on to war.

It is easy to blame Napoleon entirely, as many historians indeed have done, for the outbreak of war between Prussia and France in 1806 that would soon become the War of the Fourth Coalition – easy, but simplistic. Of course, Napoleon's offer to return Hanover to Britain was diplomatic dynamite in Berlin and was never likely to provoke anything other than justifiable fury from the Prussians. However, the Hanoverian issue was only part of the origins of the Franco-Prussian conflict of 1806. The Prussians were already on the road to hostilities with France many weeks before they learnt of the Emperor's offer in his talks with the British, as signified by the signing of the treaty of alliance with Russia, a country still at war with the French. Taking the cause of war back further still, Berlin's closer relations with St Petersburg were admittedly partly a reaction to the rather peremptory manner in which Napoleon had made Prussia an 'ally', but it must not be forgotten that that treatment was a result of Prussia's decision to join the Third Coalition. True, in the event, the Prussians failed to declare war in 1805, but the fact that they had been about to before the French won so handsomely at Austerlitz was surely an even greater and more justifiable *casus belli* for France than the offer to return Hanover was eight months later for Prussia. Just as Napoleon might reasonably have chosen to make war on the Prussians in December 1805 but didn't, the Prussians might reasonably have decided not to go to war with him in August 1806 but did. Looked at from this perspective, responsibility for the outbreak of war between France and Prussia takes on a different hue. The Prussians made a choice for war in summer 1806; they were not forced into it.

Of course, the Prussian choice was by no means unreasonable. The idea that Napoleon might have taken Hanover from them was an affront to their dignity and a potentially serious blow to their power and influence. Certain other factors should be considered, though. First, his motives in offering Hanover back to the British were, for want of a better word, good. He hoped, albeit naively, that it would secure a peace treaty with his most inveterate opponents. Secondly, if the British had accepted his offer, it is unlikely that the Emperor would simply have stripped Hanover from his Prussian allies. More likely is that he would have found Berlin some form of compensation, perhaps Saxony, in the hope of preventing Prussia from becoming an enemy (that would have been tough on the Saxons or whoever, but that is not the issue here). Thirdly, whereas the Prussians were already displaying signs of an eagerness to fight the French even before the Hanoverian crisis broke, Napoleon showed no interest in going to war with Prussia in 1806. True, the bulk of the *Grande Armée* had remained stationed in Germany since Austerlitz, but its deployment there was entirely defensive and was intended primarily to guard against a possible renewal of hostilities with Austria. Besides, Napoleon had begun to make preparations for his troops' withdrawal from Germany by the end of summer 1806, only to feel compelled to cancel them in early September when Prussia's warlike intentions became increasingly apparent and the Tsar refused to ratify the peace treaty with France. Moreover, as relations with Prussia became acutely strained in late summer, the Emperor repeatedly stressed to his ministers that he did not want to fight the Prussians and ordered his marshals stationed in Germany to avoid offending Prussian officials. He even pleaded with Frederick William directly not to initiate hostilities, an unusual move from a man more used to adopting a much tougher stance in such circumstances.

Napoleon's efforts to maintain peace were to no avail. Initially unable to believe that Prussia, the weakest of the major powers, was really about to attack the mighty French Empire despite having no meaningful source of support immediately to hand (Russians troops, slow as ever to mobilize, would not be ready to assist the Prussians until late autumn), Bonaparte made no significant military preparations of his own until mid-September. By then, two things finally convinced him that war was imminent. One was news that Prussia had bullied its neighbour to the south, Saxony, into joining her as an ally and allowing Prussian troops into Saxon territory, from where they could march directly south or west into the Confederation of the Rhine. The other was word that the Tsar had refused to ratify the peace treaty d'Oubril had signed in late July. Immediately, Napoleon correctly guessed that Russia had decided to fight alongside the Prussians and surmised, not inaccurately, that this promise of Russian support had played a significant role in bringing the typically pusillanimous Frederick William to risk war. It was almost 1805 all over again; two major continental powers marching to fight the French in Germany. The key question now was whether the result would be the same.

Extraordinarily, the Prussians, just like the Austrians the previous year, chose not to wait for their Russian allies to reinforce them before advancing towards the French, and by early October they had around 140,000 men deployed in Saxony within striking distance of Napoleon's ally, Bavaria. By this time, the Emperor had assembled no fewer than 180,000 men of his *Grande Armée* in southern Germany to meet this threat. As in the previous year, Marshal Brune on the Channel coast had been ordered to guard against a possible British descent, while Louis Bonaparte was instructed to defend his new Dutch kingdom should either the Prussians or British attack it. The direct route to France from central Germany over the Rhine was protected by a corps stationed at Mainz, while Austria was encouraged to remain quiescent by the presence near her borders of a large army in the Kingdom of Italy and, north of the Alps, a Bavarian force. The Emperor had covered almost all eventualities.

Despite being outnumbered in Germany, the Prussians generally remained imprudently positive. Convinced that they had the best, if not necessarily the largest, army in Europe, they in fact had one of the worst. The glory days of Frederick the Great in the middle of the eighteenth century had long since gone and the Prussian Army had not moved on one iota. It used the same muskets now it had used then, its artillery was too heavy to be moved around a battlefield easily, its tactics and organization were stuck in the rigid patterns of fifty years earlier, and more than half its generals were over sixty (the most senior ones being in their seventies or even eighties). With an army such as this, the sensible thing to do would have been to withdraw behind the mighty River Elbe, to try to stop the French crossing it should they advance, and to await the Russian armies gathering in the east before undertaking an offensive. Even then, the chances are that the Prussians would have been soundly bested before the Tsar's soldiers arrived, but that at least would have been preferable to what happened instead. By advancing the bulk of their army prematurely into Saxony, the Prussian commanders, who were for some strange reason convinced that the French would stay on the defensive in Germany, put themselves in a terrible position against a man and an army better able than anyone else to exploit their enemies' mistakes.

For the sake of form, the Prussian government belatedly issued an ultimatum to Napoleon for him to withdraw west of the Rhine, but the Emperor only received it on 7 October, the day before it was due to expire. Berlin had never expected or desired its demands to be accepted anyway, but was set on resolving its differences with the French by a war it was naively confident it would win. It would not take long for the Prussians to be disabused of their illusions.

On 8 October, the day the Prussian ultimatum expired and war officially started, Napoleon led his army in southern Germany north into the Thuringian Forest towards Saxony. He had divided the bulk of his force up into three columns of two corps each that advanced on parallel roads around a day's march apart (he christened this formation the *bataillon carré* or battalion square as, like a square on the battlefield, it was perfectly arranged to meet threats from any direction). The Emperor's strategic aim was simple; to position his army between the Prussians and the Russians and destroy the former – essentially a repetition of the manoeuvre on Ulm in 1805.

Within forty-eight hours, all three columns of the *Grande Armée* had made contact with elements of the Prussian army and briskly swept them aside. The biggest encounter took place on 10 October at Saalfeld, on the French left, where the corps of the dashing Marshal Lannes ran into a Prusso-Saxon force around half its size. For the loss of fewer than 200 men, Lannes inflicted casualties on his opponent that were around twenty times as great.

The humiliation of Saalfeld belatedly removed the Prussians' rose-tinted spectacles and the decision was swiftly reached to retreat back towards Berlin. Eager to prevent them escaping, Napoleon despatched his best subordinate, Marshal Davout, with his superb corps forty miles north to Naumburg astride the anticipated Prussian line of retreat. Davout got there, with his usual speed, by the evening of 12 October. The rest of the *Grande Armée*, meanwhile, was probing to find the main body of the Prussian army and force it into battle.

It found it, or so the Emperor thought, about half way between Saalfeld and Naumburg on 13 October, west of the town of Jena. The broken and wooded terrain in the area prevented Napoleon from seeing more than a few tens of thousands of Prussian troops when he reconnoitred, but he felt sure that the bulk of the rest of the enemy army was nearby. He therefore ordered the majority of his own force to converge on Jena from the east as swiftly as possible, while the corps of Davout and Bernadotte were to advance south-west from their present position further north to envelop the Prussian left flank.

The next day, 14 October, dawned with a thick fog blanketing this whole area of central Germany. With 55,000 men already assembled near Jena, 40,000 more due to join him by noon, and even more expected to come up after that, Napoleon saw no need for hesitation and ordered an attack. The assault developed slowly in difficult conditions and was not the best coordinated the Emperor ever oversaw, but, nevertheless, the French soon began to push the Prussians steadily back. By early afternoon, the pressure on the Prussian line had become too much and it broke. As the French started to pursue, they ran into a large body of enemy reinforcements, but these men could do no more than stem the tide temporarily and they soon joined the flight. The Prussian army at Jena had been smashed. For the loss of only 5,000 men killed and wounded, the French had inflicted 11,000 casualties upon their adversaries and captured a further 15,000, as well as 200 cannon and 30 flags.

It had been a surprisingly easy victory. By the time all meaningful fighting had stopped, Napoleon had around 96,000 men on the field, but almost half of them had not seen action. The 50–60,000 French troops who did engage the enemy should certainly not have been able to rout so swiftly or readily the 100,000 or more Prussians the Emperor had guessed were near Jena. The fact was, however, that the Prussian army put to flight by Napoleon on 14 October had not been as strong as he had thought. By the end of the battle, just 53,000 Prussian soldiers had fought at Jena, no more than half the number the Emperor had expected to face and comparable to the size of the French force that actually engaged them. So where were all the other Prussians Napoleon had imagined were confronting him?

The answer arrived at the Emperor's headquarters that evening in the form of a courier sent by Marshal Davout. The aide reported, incredibly, that Davout's corps had earlier that day faced, and defeated, the main force of the enemy army near Auerstädt, some fifteen or so miles to the north-east. Napoleon at first refused to believe what he was hearing, informing the courier that his famously short-sighted marshal 'must be seeing double!' It soon dawned on him, however, that Davout's poor eyesight had not, in fact, deceived him.

Advancing south-west from Naumburg on the morning of 14 October as per his instructions from the Emperor, Davout and his corps had unexpectedly run into major Prussian opposition east of the town of Auerstädt. Using the advantages afforded him by the fog and the broken terrain in the area, the bald marshal had drawn up his 27,000 crack soldiers and 40 guns in a superb defensive position. As the attacks on his corps intensified as the morning wore on, Davout began to realize that he was standing in the path of the retreat towards Berlin of the largest Prussian force in the area. In fact, the army confronting him comprised no fewer than 63,000 troops and 230 guns, and was led by the Prussian king, his chief military adviser, and Prussia's senior field commander. Nevertheless, Davout and his men bravely stood their ground against overwhelming odds, the marshal appearing wherever he was most needed on the battlefield, expertly siting his limited number of cannon and throwing even his sappers into the front line to hold the enemy back.

Merely to have fought the Prussians to a standstill in such circumstances would have been truly remarkable, but Davout and his corps went one better than that. By early afternoon, with Prussia's senior field commander, the Duke of Brunswick, having been killed, the king's chief military adviser, Marshal von Möllendorf, having been captured, and news beginning to filter through of the disaster unfolding to the south at Jena, Frederick William lost his nerve and ordered a retreat. Seizing the moment with quite brilliant judgement and nerve, Davout boldly ordered his heavily outnumbered men to advance and the Prussian army broke and fled. The day's fighting had cost Napoleon's greatest subordinate almost 8,000 men killed or wounded, over a quarter of his total force, but his corps had, incredibly, inflicted 12,000 casualties on its opponents and captured 3,000 prisoners and 115 guns. It was possibly the single most outstanding battlefield achievement of the entire Napoleonic Wars.

Davout's victory, for which he was subsequently made Duke of Auerstädt, should, however, have been a lot less arduous than it was. Bernadotte, stationed near his fellow marshal at Naumburg at dawn on 14 October, had refused to march south-west under Davout's nominal command and instead headed south. Even worse than this petty fit of pique, though, Bernadotte had ignored Davout's repeated and urgent requests for him to bring his corps to his aid at Auerstädt, despite only being a handful of miles away.

When Napoleon heard of Bernadotte's appalling behaviour he was outraged and drew up a court martial order. Unfortunately, in light of future events, he tore it up before issuing it. He knew that it could only result in the marshal's execution for gross dereliction of duty and he was unwilling to upset so grievously Bernadotte's wife, a woman to whom Bonaparte had once himself been engaged. Instead, he gave the wayward marshal another chance. If he excelled himself in the pursuit of the defeated Prussian army that the Emperor now ordered in the wake of Jena and Auerstädt, he would be forgiven.

The fearsome harrying of the battered forces of Frederick William in the three weeks following 14 October 1806 is rightly regarded as one of the most spectacular pursuits in history. It went from Saxony all the way north to the Baltic coast and resulted in the almost complete annihilation of the Prussian army. Wherever the chasing French troops caught up with their adversaries, the Prussians surrendered in droves. Even well-provisioned fortress cities, like Magdeburg and Stettin, fell without much of a fight. The morale of Frederick William's shattered army simply disintegrated in the face of the ruthless and brilliant French pursuit. The honour of entering Berlin first rightly went to Davout's magnificent corps, which marched in unhindered on 25 October. Napoleon himself followed two days later, having visited the tomb of the present Prussian king's far more illustrious predecessor, Frederick the Great, on the way. By the end of the chase in early November, the French had rounded up no fewer than 140,000 prisoners and 2,000 cannon, a quite staggering total. In summer 1940, Hitler's *Wehrmacht* would overwhelm the French armed forces in just six weeks; an astounding feat. In autumn 1806, however, without the benefits of mechanization or air power to assist them, Napoleon's *Grande Armée* crushed the Prussian Army within a month; an even more amazing accomplishment. Never had one supposed major power been so clearly, comprehensively and speedily vanquished by another.

It is tempting to see Jena-Auerstädt and their aftermath as an even more crushing reprise of the Emperor's great victory at Austerlitz, but, in some ways, they were more akin to his triumph at Ulm. To be sure, Prussian power in October 1806 was smashed to a far greater extent than Austrian power had been in the same month a year earlier, but, just as Ulm failed to end the War of the Third Coalition, Jena-Auerstädt and the pursuit which followed them did not terminate what posterity has come to call the War of the Fourth Coalition. In both cases, moreover, the key reason the conflict continued was the same; the Russian armies had yet to enter the fray. As 1806 entered its penultimate month, tens of thousands of the Tsar's men were on their way west to take on the French and their emperor once again.

8

The Bloodbath in the Snow

The scale of Napoleon's victory over Prussia in autumn 1806 was so great that it seemed almost inconceivable that a peace treaty would not swiftly follow. Indeed, Frederick William had requested an armistice in the immediate aftermath of Jena-Auerstädt, but the Emperor had rejected the idea, realizing that it was an attempt to buy time for the Prussian Army to regroup and reorganize after its recent humiliations. Just a few days later, with his armed forces disintegrating before his eyes, the Prussian king bowed to the seemingly inevitable and asked for full peace negotiations, fully aware that the settlement offered was likely to be harsh.

Peace talks began on 21 October, while the *Grande Armée* was still mopping up the scattered Prussian forces, and the terms presented to Frederick William's delegates were even more stringent than they had expected. Prussia was to lose all territory west of the Elbe river, acknowledge French dominance in Germany, pay a huge indemnity, guarantee the integrity of the Ottoman Empire, and become a French ally once more, which would mean terminating trade with the British again. Bonaparte also insisted, perfectly reasonably, that Russian troops must not be allowed to march onto Prussian soil and, indeed, should be prevented from doing so by all means possible, including the use of force; although, if it came to that, the French pledged to assist the Prussians.

Unsurprisingly, the Prussian government was divided by the terms put forward. Frederick William himself favoured accepting them before the situation, and possibly the terms, got even worse. He was opposed by his chief minister, the hawkish Count Hardenberg, and his fiercely anti-French wife, Queen Louise, a woman once pithily described by Napoleon as 'the only real man in Prussia'. They were both eager to fight on with whatever forces could be mustered and placed enormous faith in the ability of the Russians to reverse Prussia's plight. While Prussia's rulers dithered and her delegates at the peace talks tried in vain to win better terms, the *Grande Armée* continued to occupy ever more territory and capture ever more troops.

In the end, the decision for war or peace was effectively taken out of Prussian hands. The Russians were fully committed to waging war on the *Grande Armée* at this point and had been pressing their Prussian allies since mid-October not to agree to an armistice or separate peace with the Emperor. Alexander personally pledged to fight on until the French were pushed back across the Rhine and warned Frederick William darkly that should Prussia stop fighting, it would not affect the movement of Russian troops. It was thus clear that reaching an accord with the French would result in the Prussians having to fight to remove Russian armies from Prussian soil. Peace simply was not an option for Prussia in late 1806; it was just a question of which power she would fight. Caught in a cleft stick, the Prussians understandably chose to continue fighting the French in the hope that their Russian allies might yet be able to save the day and obviate the need to sign a punitive peace settlement with Napoleon. In mid-November, Frederick William broke off talks with the French. To the Prussian king's dismay, the war he had initiated would go on, and his shattered country would continue to be Europe's latest battleground.

It was not only Frederick William who was disappointed to see war go on in late autumn 1806. The majority of the soldiers of the *Grande Armée* had expected peace and a return to less taxing duties to follow their stunningly successful whirlwind campaign in Prussia. The mood of the French people too was much less euphoric than after Austerlitz and the Senate sent a deputation to Napoleon at Berlin urging him to make peace. He replied simply that he would do so once he had dealt with the Russians, whose determination to fight him in northern Europe at this time was such that he realistically had little choice but to take up their bellicose challenge.

The Emperor learnt in early November that an army of around 60,000 Russians, with tens of thousands more following it, had crossed the Prussian border and was heading west towards the French. There was also a 15,000 strong force in eastern Prussia that was the remnant of the Prussian field army and many thousands of troops currently garrisoning key towns along the eastern Baltic coast and in Silesia (immediately to the north of the modern Czech Republic and Slovakia). Together, these Russian and Prussian forces posed a serious threat to the *Grande Armée* that Napoleon chose to deal with in his usual way – boldly.

Napoleon was undoubtedly aware of the difficulties involved in campaigning in eastern Prussia in late autumn and early winter, although he probably underestimated them. The poor weather, inhospitable terrain, appalling roads and limited options for living off the land all militated against continuing active operations at this time, as did the fact that his army was now at the end of a long line of supply which stretched all the way back to France. The arguments in favour of moving further east in the final months of 1806 seemed, however, more compelling. Napoleon realized that if the *Grande Armée* could just reach the banks of the mighty Vistula river before halting field operations for the winter, the prospects for campaigning the following spring (assuming that were necessary) would be greatly improved. For a start, it would prevent the enemy from fortifying the line of that formidable water obstacle. It would also, by cutting off the garrisons in Silesia and along much of the eastern Baltic coast and covering the sieges of those towns, preclude any attempt by the Prussians to gather all their remaining forces together. The occupation of yet further Prussian territory would additionally deprive Frederick William of potential recruiting grounds, while the advance of French soldiers into the former Polish lands which constituted much of eastern Prussia would present the Emperor with opportunities to enlist the military services of many thousands of Poles. Napoleon's overall reasoning was sound, but it meant that his men were in for a tough few months. Just how tough, few, if any, could have predicted.

The threat of enemy forces in eastern Prussia was not the only thing weighing on the Emperor's mind in late 1806. Another problem he gave much thought to that autumn was the question of how to bring Britain to the peace table. Invasion remained an option, although it was clear that it was a long-term one, and Napoleon was never a patient man. He therefore took what was to prove one of his most fateful steps. On 21 November 1806, he issued the Berlin Decree prohibiting French-controlled Europe and its allies from engaging in 'all commerce and all correspondence with the British Isles'. Thus was instituted the Continental Blockade, which soon evolved into the Continental System. The aim of the Blockade was to destroy Britain's export trade, thereby, at best, bringing on economic collapse or, at worst, seriously undermining Britain's ability to fund its own and other states' war effort against France. As Napoleon himself put it, the goal was to 'conquer the sea by mastery of the land'. In many ways, it was the logical culmination of earlier measures attacking British commercial interests of 1793 and 1803, which had banned British goods from France and then extended the ban to cover French subject states as well, but its scope was greater than these for it envisaged shutting off the whole of continental Europe to British trade.

The Continental System, which soon developed out of the Blockade, highlighted the extent of the Emperor's economic ambitions even further. The System incorporated the Blockade but added to it an attempt to enable France to replace Britain as the leading trading and manufacturing power in Europe. The idea was that French merchants and manufacturers would fill the gaps in the European market created by the exclusion of British goods. To this end, they were given advantages over their rivals throughout the rest of French-controlled Europe, a move which inevitably and understandably fostered considerable discontent outside France.

In concept, the Continental Blockade was arguably brilliant, but, in practice, it never quite worked. Although it did cause strain and distress in Britain, at times severe, the rapidly industrializing British economy proved more resilient than expected and, to general amazement, was able to maintain not only the immense costs of funding Britain's own war effort but also much of that of her allies as well. An important factor in this was the development of a widespread system of smuggling into French-controlled Europe of British goods, which were often either cheaper or better than Continental alternatives, or which manufacturers and traders on the Continent, where industrialization was yet really to get going, were simply not capable of providing. Indeed, so far short of Napoleon's expectations did Continental (especially French) traders and manufacturers fall in replacing British sources of supply that the French government itself was ultimately forced to undermine its own system and condone a limited amount of importation of goods from Britain.

Significant as these factors were, there were two even more crucial reasons why the Continental Blockade failed to debilitate the British as drastically as had been hoped. First, and perhaps most vital, London had learnt the lesson that the resurrection of the League of Armed Neutrality in 1800–1 had offered them. Ever since then, when the abrupt cessation of trade with the Baltic countries had caused such economic turmoil, the British had assiduously sought out new markets, especially in the Americas, and after 1806 these proved crucial to the maintenance at a tolerable level of both Britain's imports and exports. Secondly, in the event, the Continental Blockade could never be applied as vigorously for as long as was needed to bring truly decisive results. The continuation of wars on the European mainland after 1806 opened up gaps in the attempt to cut British trade off from the Continent and these were fully exploited to help keep Britain's economy functioning.

Napoleon realized, of course, that in order for his Continental Blockade to produce the desired effect in crippling the British, as many gaps as possible would have to be plugged, but his attempt to plug those gaps had seriously damaging consequences for France. The more rigorous the denial of British goods from entering Europe was, for example, the greater the discontent it caused because of the resulting shortages or enforced reliance on second-rate replacements. Efforts to enforce the Blockade as vigorously as possible also played a role, as we shall see, in the outbreak of further conflicts after 1806.

Given the problems it created for the French, the Continental System can only really be seen as a blunder. In Napoleon's defence, however, it must be stressed that almost everyone, including the British themselves, were surprised at just how resilient Britain's economy proved to be. Had the Blockade worked quickly, within a year or two, as Napoleon expected it to, things might look rather different in hindsight. That said, the advantages given to French manufacturers and merchants under the system were an entirely predictable mistake. The resentment they caused was both profound and justified, and inevitably made the alternative of British economic dominance in Europe seem less oppressive, and even preferable, by comparison. The Emperor's determination to stick with the Continental System, moreover, even when it became clear that it would not achieve the decisive results he had hoped for as quickly as he had expected, can certainly also be questioned, especially as the problems the System was causing were all too patent. From the perspective of late 1806, however, those problems lay in the future and the introduction of the Continental Blockade seemed much more likely to spell ruin for Britain than it did to create major difficulties for France.

If his relations with Russia, Prussia and Britain were the most important of his concerns in late 1806, Napoleon nevertheless had a number of other significant issues to address. One such was the matter of making peace with two recent enemies; Saxony and Sweden. In the first case, a deal proved remarkably easy to reach. The Emperor was fully aware that the Saxons had been unwilling allies of Prussia in the latest campaign and so was prepared to be generous to them in victory. Their ruler, Frederick Augustus, was promoted to the rank of king in return for which Saxony joined the Confederation of the Rhine in January 1807. At a stroke, an enemy became an ally.

The Swedes turned out to be less amenable. In November 1806, the French approached Stockholm, which, having joined the now defunct Third Coalition, remained technically though not actively at war with France, on the basis that, if Sweden did not make peace, Napoleon would feel compelled to order his troops to occupy Swedish Pomerania on the southern coast of the Baltic. Most members of the Swedish government appreciated the logic of this position, felt that the Emperor had been reasonable in giving them a choice, and advocated accepting the offer of peace. The King, however, vetoed the idea. Gustavus IV of Sweden detested the 'upstart Corsican' with what can only be described as a passion verging on mania. He genuinely seems to have considered Bonaparte to be the Antichrist and ordered copious pictures and busts of the French ruler just so he could deface or smash them. Given this kind of attitude, peace with France was never likely. Indeed, in early 1807, Gustavus arranged with the British and Russians for Sweden to join actively in the war against Napoleon again, although the contribution Swedish forces were to make in the event was negligible.

A power which was to play a more significant role in the struggle between the French and their enemies was the Ottoman Empire. Exploiting Russia's preoccupation with fighting the Emperor and emboldened by his improving relations with France, at the end of summer 1806 the Turkish Sultan took a step that created great consternation in St Petersburg. Selim III had wanted to rid himself of the *hospodars* (effectively viceroys) of the provinces of Moldavia and Wallachia for some time, believing that they were involved in plots to challenge his authority as ruler of the Ottoman Empire, maybe even to overthrow him. They were also, he considered, much too pro-Russian. At the end of August, therefore, the Sultan peremptorily replaced them.

This action had ramifications beyond internal Ottoman politics. Under the terms of treaties signed during the reign of Catherine the Great, the Turks had pledged to get the consent of St Petersburg before removing or appointing the *hospodars* of the Principalities (as Moldavia and Wallachia were often referred to). Selim's unilateral action was thus clearly a snub to the Russians. More serious than that, though, was the impression the Sultan's action created in Russia that her influence in south-east Europe was declining at the expense of France. The new *hospodars* were viewed, with some justification, as pro-French and it was suspected, wrongly but strongly nonetheless, that Selim had been pushed into acting by Paris.

Russia's response to Selim's action was prompt and vigorous. An ultimatum was delivered to Constantinople demanding the Sultan reinstate the recently deposed *hospodars* or face Russian occupation of the Principalities. Initially, Selim seems to have been inclined to resist, even closing the Straits (between the Black Sea and the Aegean) to Russian warships in early autumn, another act which contravened treaties dating from Catherine's reign. Soon, though, with the Russians moving large numbers of troops towards the Moldavian border, the Sultan lost his nerve and, to French dismay, restored the deposed *hospodars* and reopened the Straits in mid-October.

That should have been an end to the crisis, but St Petersburg now decided to press matters further. A string of additional demands was delivered to Constantinople, the acceptance of which would have humiliated the Sultan. Nonetheless, Selim tried to accommodate the Russians as far as he felt able, but it was not enough. On 23 November 1806, some 60,000 Russian soldiers invaded the Principalities. The troops made swift progress and overran both Moldavia and Wallachia in just six weeks.

The Russian invasion alarmed not just the Turks, but also the British and especially the Austrians, who saw it as the first step in a Russian effort to conquer the whole of south-east Europe. Napoleon too, whose aim at this point was to strengthen the Ottoman Empire, was not pleased by the ease with which the Russians had advanced in the Principalities, but in so far as it diverted tens of thousands of Russian soldiers that might otherwise be facing his *Grande Armée* in eastern Prussia, the situation was not without its benefits.

With hindsight, the Russian invasion was, if not inevitable, certainly very likely. We have seen how Czartoryski had consistently pushed for a Russian advance in south-east Europe during his tenure of the Russian foreign ministry. Although the Pole had now gone, his successor, Budberg, essentially continued his policy. In May 1806, indeed, St Petersburg had suggested to London that Russia should annex the Principalities and Britain Egypt, a move the British had rejected for fear that it would only trigger a scramble to take over the whole of the Ottoman Empire, in which the French might do rather well. By the autumn of 1806, with

Turkey clearly moving towards a close friendship with France, Russian minds were even more keenly exercised by the desire to occupy Moldavia and Wallachia. The Turks were so in awe of French might and the triumphs of Ulm, Austerlitz and Jena–Auerstädt that a strong show of Russian force was necessary, it was argued, in order to restore Russia's influence at Constantinople and undermine that of France. Occupation of the two provinces would also put Russia in a much better position to check any possible French advance in south-east Europe from Dalmatia. Finally, Russian dominance in the Principalities would facilitate the expansion of St Petersburg's influence elsewhere in the Balkans, most notably in the Slav lands that bordered Wallachia. Indeed, the arguments in favour of occupying the Principalities seemed so powerful to the Tsar that he decided in early autumn to go ahead with the operation regardless of how the Sultan responded to Russian demands that he restore the *hospodars*. Selim's sudden about-turn in mid-October thus came as an unwelcome surprise to Alexander and necessitated the subsequent additional demands to provide a pretext for the invasion.

If the Russians thought that the Turks would be impressed and cowed by their display of military force, they were soon proved wrong. When he heard of the attack in early December, Napoleon, doubtless mindful of Selim's retreat in the face of Russian pressure in mid-October, immediately wrote to the Sultan urging him that, if he wanted to restore the Ottoman Empire's former power and prestige, now, while the French were fighting them too, was the moment to take on the Russians. In truth, the Emperor's encouragement was not really needed. News of the Russian invasion of the Principalities was greeted in Constantinople with indignation and fury from all quarters, effectively forcing the Sultan's hand. On 22 December 1806, he declared war on Russia. Suddenly, St Petersburg's hawkish attitude to south-east European affairs began to look a little reckless.

We left the *Grande Armée* as it was about to embark upon what Napoleon expected to be a brief winter campaign in eastern Prussia. Detaching units to isolate Prussian garrisons on the Baltic coast, such as Danzig, and sending a whole corps into Silesia to reduce the fortresses there, the Emperor ordered the bulk of his forces for this new campaign to advance into eastern Prussia to occupy the west bank of the mighty Vistula river. Napoleon was aware of the demands that these operations would place upon his armies and took steps to address them. Although 80,000 new recruits of the class of 1806 joined the *Grande Armée* in the last month of that year, he realized that the need to garrison occupied Prussia and protect his long lines of supply meant that he might require even more troops by the following spring and summer when he expected the real fighting against the Russians to take place. He therefore ordered the class of 1807 to be called up in January instead of autumn so that an extra 80,000 soldiers would be able to take the field by around the middle of that year. His allies too were urged to increase their recruiting efforts.

Alongside these measures to bring more men into his armies, the Emperor set about tackling the much thornier problem of supplying his soldiers in the inhospitable lands of eastern Prussia. Parts of Germany were ruthlessly milked for supplies and money, a step hardly likely to endear the Germans in those areas to the French. Prussia especially was plundered for masses of equipment and tens of millions of francs, a move which ignited a powerful Francophobia in that defeated country. To get the provisions and their pay to the soldiers, Napoleon established practically from scratch a supply system that would not have been unfamiliar to the armies of the eighteenth century. The reliance upon baggage trains would, of course, slow the *Grande Armée* down, but it was the only hope it had in this region at this time of year of being properly fed, equipped and paid. It was something of an administrative *tour de force* that Bonaparte managed to set up a supply system so quickly, but, in the event, it proved only partially successful in keeping the soldiers provisioned. Conditions were simply too difficult to be overcome entirely and it did not help that the French had grown unaccustomed to large scale baggage trains, for a great many draft animals were simply worked too hard and broken down by their inexperienced handlers.

Far and away the greatest and the most intractable of the difficulties confronting Napoleon and his men in late 1806, however, were the climate and conditions of the lands in which they now campaigned. Good roads were almost literally non-existent in eastern Prussia, a fact which helped slow movement to a crawl. Even worse than that was the appalling weather, which oscillated between torrential rain and freezing frosts from mid-November through to the end of the year. This meant that, at times, the fastest the various corps of the *Grande Armée* could move was a meagre one and a quarter miles an hour. After particularly heavy downpours, the soldiers could find themselves trudging through sodden earth almost up to their knees. The scale of the problem was best described by Napoleon himself. After just a few days in eastern Prussia his verdict on the land was typically succinct – 'God has created a fifth element – mud.'

The terrible weather and the impossibility of supplying the troops effectively in such wretched conditions soon bred further problems. It was at this time that the Emperor coined the (mostly affectionate) nickname for his soldiers of *les grognards* (the grumblers) in response to their willingness to express to him their thoughts on their current predicament. To try to stem the growing discontent and drop in morale, Napoleon increased his men's pay and ordered extra provisions to be distributed, but still the grumbling continued. More seriously, disease increased markedly, a chief surgeon in the *Grande Armée* later recording that only a quarter of the men admitted to hospitals in the army's rear areas over the winter of 1806–7 had been wounded in action. Alongside the upsurge in sickness among the soldiers came a similar rise in indiscipline, with looting, straggling and desertion all showing a marked increase in these hard conditions. The situation was worse in some corps than others, but even strict disciplinarians like Davout could not entirely prevent these ills from affecting their ranks. Predictably, in areas where indiscipline became especially serious, the local peasantry who suffered as a result took any opportunity presented to them to seek revenge against isolated individuals or small groups of soldiers. This limited form of guerrilla warfare never became a major issue during this campaign, but it did provide a pointer to the altogether more serious difficulties French soldiers would face from civilian populations in the future elsewhere.

If the French were often not welcomed in the countryside through which they marched in late 1806, however, they could take some comfort from the reception they were given in the eastern Prussian towns of former Poland. In Posen (modern Poznan), Davout's men were, according to Napoleon, welcomed 'with an enthusiasm difficult to portray' by all sections of Polish society, and when Murat's advance guard reached Warsaw, the capital of former Poland, at the end of November, it was greeted with similar fervour. By the time the Emperor himself reached the city in mid-December, the Poles had erected a triumphal arch upon which was inscribed 'Long live Napoleon, the Saviour of Poland. He was sent to us straight from Heaven'.

Needless to say, the adulation given the French by the Poles caused considerable alarm in Russia. St Petersburg had, after all, been the prime beneficiary of the destruction of Poland in the late eighteenth century. Were the Emperor to respond to the clamour from the Poles to establish a new Polish state from the former Polish lands annexed by Prussia, it might stir up unrest in Russia's Polish provinces. To meet this threat, Czartoryski, who was returning to favour with the Tsar, pressed him to proclaim a Polish kingdom under Russian suzerainty before Napoleon could create one under French. Alexander mulled the idea over but then rejected it on the grounds that it would upset the other two powers who had shared in the partition of Poland; Prussia, an ally, and Austria, who the Tsar hoped might yet rejoin the fight against Napoleon.

In turning down Czartoryski's scheme, Alexander had acted rationally, but if the instructions he gave to the Orthodox Church at this point are anything to go by, one is tempted to conclude that his fear and jealousy of Napoleon were beginning to border on the hysterical. The Tsar decided, essentially, to turn the war against the French into a crusade. The Orthodox clergy were consequently ordered to denounce the Emperor as 'the accursed foe of Christendom' and to declare him 'The principal enemy of Mankind, one who worships idols and whores'. In every city, town and village in Russia, priests announced to their flock that Napoleon's aim was to destroy the Church and proclaim himself Messiah.

It is doubtful that the defamation of his character in Russian churches greatly bothered the Emperor, who had more pressing concerns in December 1806. By the middle of the month, his men had successfully gained possession of the west bank of the Vistula and operations in Silesia were progressing satisfactorily (the fall of the key fortress of Breslau in the new year would effectively end resistance there). There had been very little contact with the enemy's forces so far, as they had retreated in the face of the strong French advance, yielding even Warsaw without a fight. Now, however, cavalry probes north from the Polish capital across the Vistula discovered that the Russians had halted their withdrawal around thirty miles away in the vicinity of the town of Pultusk. The 60,000 Russian soldiers who had advanced into eastern Prussia only to fall back at the approach of the *Grande Armée* were now reinforced by 35,000 of their comrades and put under the command of the seventy-six-year-old Field Marshal Kamenski, a man of rapidly declining mental and physical capacity. Napoleon should perhaps have stuck to his original plan to halt operations for the winter as soon as his army had secured the line of the Vistula, but the presence of his Russian adversaries within striking distance proved too great a temptation. Rather than ordering his exhausted men into winter quarters, therefore, the Emperor instructed his five corps in the area to manoeuvre so as to fall on the Russians from south, west and north. If all went well, there might be no need for a spring campaign next year after all.

All did not go well. As the French corps began their manoeuvres shortly before Christmas, they were confronted with the same intractable problems of rain, frost, mud and lack of supplies that they had endured on the long march east from central Prussia. In such conditions, coordination rapidly deteriorated and Napoleon's plan, sound in theory, began to unravel. Davout added yet another feather to his cap by successfully mounting a crossing of the Narew river at night, a notoriously difficult undertaking, but the losses, at around 1,400 per side, suggested ominously that the Russians would prove no walkover.

It was doubtless fortunate, given the difficulties the French were enduring, that there was no Russian commander with sufficient strategic nous to exploit the situation. Indeed, the Russian high command was typified by confusion at this time. Kamenski baffled his subordinates with a perplexing series of orders instructing them to march first one way and then another. In the end, the field marshal himself retreated north east, away from the advancing French, with around two-fifths of the forces under his command, but that left the remaining three-fifths within range of Napoleon's closing corps.

It was now the Russians turn to be fortunate, for the French were in no position, thanks to the climatic and geographical conditions, to organize and conduct their assault on the remaining enemy forces with much coordination or alacrity. There were, nevertheless, two battles fought on Boxing Day 1806, one near the town of Golymin, the other at nearby Pultusk.

At Pultusk, the corps of the redoubtable Marshal Lannes took on a much larger force under General Levin Bennigsen. Bennigsen was a Hanoverian in his early sixties who had served the Russian crown for over three decades. Described by a contemporary as 'a pale, withered personage of high stature and cold appearance, with a scar across his face', he was a competent, if unexceptional, general whose greatest contribution to European affairs up to this point had been the prominent role he had played in the murder of Tsar Paul. On 26 December, he drew up his 37,000 men in a defensive position centred upon the town of Pultusk itself. Lannes reconnoitred the ground as effectively as he could, but the lay of the land obscured a large portion of the enemy from sight. Having been informed by Napoleon, who was himself relying on faulty intelligence, that Pultusk was only lightly held as the bulk of the Russian army was in retreat, the marshal decided to attack with his 20,000 men.

Despite the discrepancy in numbers, and the fact that the Russians were fighting the kind of defensive battle to which they were best suited, Lannes's corps did remarkably well, smashing their way into the town of Pultusk in the afternoon. Bennigsen counter-attacked, however, and his numerical advantage soon began to tell. The French were forced out of the town and were slowly driven back to their original positions by the time the fighting ended in the darkness of the evening. In the wet, windy and muddy conditions it had been fought in, the battle had degenerated into a slugging match in which Lannes's soldiers, gratefully reinforced by the timely arrival of a division from Davout's corps, had done well to avoid a heavy defeat. Losses in engagements throughout the whole of the campaign of 1806–7 in eastern Prussia are among the most disputable of the Napoleonic period, but, given the intensity and duration of the fighting, it seems likely that each side lost somewhere between 5,000 and 7,000 men.

The battle at Golymin, a dozen miles to the north-west of Pultusk, was a less draining affair for both sides. Here, almost 40,000 Frenchmen – elements of the corps of Marshals Murat, Davout and Augereau, the last a coarse Parisian who had once served in the armies of Catherine the Great – faced fewer than 20,000 Russians under General Gallitzin. Three factors saved the Russians from what should otherwise have been a crushing defeat. First, the dreadful prevailing conditions of mud, rain and wind. Secondly, Gallitzin had chosen his ground excellently. He deployed his men in a superb defensive position with woods and marshes hindering the advance of enemy forces. Thirdly, as it was half past three in the afternoon on a midwinter's day before the serious fighting got underway, the imminent fall of night prevented any proper plan of attack from being carried out and the engagement was more a series of isolated skirmishes. Casualties again are debatable, but 1,000 Russian losses to 600 French seems about right.

In the wake of the battles of Pultusk and Golymin both Bennigsen and Gallitzin withdrew under cover of darkness on the first leg of a march to rejoin the forces under the inept Field Marshal Kamenski some way to the north-east. Normally, the French would have pursued, but recent events had made it clear to the Emperor that conditions in this region at this time would in all probability make such a pursuit futile. Besides, the men had had enough. In late December, therefore, he finally ordered his soldiers into winter quarters. His bold decision to seek a decisive battle in the final weeks of 1806 had proved a misguided one. Of the five corps manoeuvring against the Russians, only one, that of Marshal Lannes, had managed to engage the enemy on Boxing Day in a significant manner. True, the French had been denied a crushing triumph much more by the weather than by the Russians, but that did not alter the outcome of their failure to come to grips properly with the Tsar's forces. As they retired to winter quarters, the troops of the *Grande Armée* knew that their services would be called upon yet again over the coming months.

Napoleon returned to Warsaw on New Year's Day, 1807, where he was once again fêted as the Poles' saviour. So far, however, he had done little in regard to the tricky Polish question. Talleyrand urged him to resurrect Poland as a bulwark against Russia and the Emperor himself was fully aware of the potential advantages such a move would bring in terms of gaining France an ally in eastern Europe and more troops for his *Grande Armée*. He was also alert, though, to the potential problems of re-establishing Poland. As he confessed to his secretary at one point, 'I should like to make Poland independent, but that is a very difficult matter. Austria, Russia and Prussia have all had a slice of the cake; when the match is once kindled, who knows where the conflagration will stop?' Unilaterally to declare Poland restored would not only make it even harder to make peace with the Russians, but might also goad the Austrians into joining the coalition against him. The Emperor therefore adopted something of a fudge as his Polish policy. To appease the Poles and retain at least some of their early enthusiasm for him, he set up a provisional Polish administration in mid-January to oversee the territory of former Poland captured in recent weeks from Prussia. He would not, however, call upon the Poles, either in eastern Prussia or elsewhere, to revolt and refused to promise them independence. The furthest he would go was to let it be known that he would resurrect some form of Polish state provided they could put 40,000 men in the field. The Poles were frustrated by this, but Napoleon justified his position by arguing that there was no point in him recreating a Polish state that would not be able to defend itself.

The Emperor's policy did enough to retain him the support of the majority of Poles. After all, where else were they going to turn in their hope of regaining at least some of their lost independence? The intensity of their affection for the French ruler, though, undoubtedly dimmed a little from its initial ardour. Nevertheless, the Polish charm offensive continued unabated. General Savary, one of Napoleon's aides, recalled January 1807 in Warsaw as an almost ceaseless succession of concerts, balls, parties, fêtes and other spectacles. More subtly, the leading Polish statesmen put intense pressure on a young noblewoman to whom the Emperor had taken a fancy to become his mistress and thereby, it was hoped, gain influence over him in the campaign for a Polish state. The young woman was initially very reluctant, but the intensity of the pressure and her innate patriotism eventually persuaded her at least to meet with Napoleon. The relationship was somewhat frosty on her part at first, but soon the Emperor's charm began to work its magic and her reticence receded. Before long, she fell deeply in love with him.

The young Polish woman's name was Countess Marie Walewska. Just twenty years of age at this time, she was already married to a septuagenarian aristocrat who, it seems, did not overly object to his wife being used as a pawn in attempts to wrangle a Polish state from the French. Blonde and beautiful, Marie exuded the same powerful femininity that had attracted Napoleon to Josephine. Smitten at first by her physical attractiveness, Bonaparte came to grow very fond, perhaps even genuinely to love, the young Polish woman, but her feelings for him were certainly stronger. She would bear him a son in May 1810 and remain loyal to him to the very end. How far his affection for her influenced his attitude towards the Poles in general is impossible to say, but as Napoleon undoubtedly had a strong romantic streak, it is possible that it coloured his judgement. What it did not do, however, was what the Polish aristocrats who had pressed the match on Marie had hoped it would – induce the Emperor to resurrect Poland immediately.

If the events of the final weeks of 1806 had been frustrating for Napoleon and the French, they had been an even greater disappointment to the Emperor's adversaries. Not only had Russian and Prussian forces been compelled to withdraw in the face of the *Grande Armée*'s advance, thereby yielding yet further territory, the Turkish declaration of war on Russia had been an unexpected development that complicated the military situation considerably. Some 20,000 soldiers who had been intended to join the campaign in eastern Prussia had to be diverted south, and the intense diplomatic pressure the Russians persuaded the British to put on the Sultan to get him to back down in his dispute with St Petersburg only resulted, in late January 1807, in a Turkish declaration of war on London.

Selim was fortified in his increasingly belligerent mood by promises of French support. Having requested a formal alliance and military aid from Napoleon in the wake of his declaration of war on Russia, the Sultan received a positive response the following month. The Emperor offered him a perpetual anti-Russian alliance should Turkey's eastern neighbour, Persia, join too, he also suggested that the Turks should aim at reconquering not just the Principalities but the northern shore of the Black Sea, and offered Selim the assistance of 25,000 French soldiers to fight in western Wallachia and six warships.

Because of the unpropitious time of year, there was very little fighting in south-east Europe in the weeks following the outbreak of war. The Russians, having occupied the Principalities, halted for the moment and simply fortified the line of the Danube. The only major action in the region in the first two months of 1807 was an attempt by the Royal Navy in February to force its way past the Straits and close on Constantinople in the hope of forcing the Turks to make peace. Just as in the better-known effort conducted in 1915, the British attack failed miserably, in this case due to a combination of adverse winds and unexpectedly stout resistance, partly organized by French military advisers. Following the failure of this expedition, St Petersburg decided to offer the Sultan a peace deal, but destroyed any hope it had of success by drawing up terms that were only likely to be accepted by a foe that had already been heavily defeated. The can of worms the Russians had opened by invading Moldavia and Wallachia was clearly not going to be easily closed.

Napoleon dispersed his army in eastern Prussia at the turn of the year along an arc running from Warsaw in the south-east to the Baltic coast in the north-west. Thus spread out, the men had the best chance of living off what little the land had to offer, supplemented, as far as conditions allowed, by supply trains from further west. The problem with such dispositions, however, as the Emperor well knew, was that it left the flanks of his stretched line vulnerable to possible enemy attack. As January went by with little sign of Russian or Prussian activity, though it began to seem as if the *Grande Armée*'s adversaries were as keen to spend the remainder of the winter resting and recuperating as it was itself.

Then, towards the end of the month, the campaign was suddenly resumed with a vengeance. Shortly after New Year, Kamenski, pleading ill health, had resigned his command of Russian forces in eastern Prussia before he was pushed. To replace him, the Tsar had appointed General Bennigsen, a man whose stock had risen unjustifiably high after he had managed to beat off the attack by Lannes's corps at Pultusk.

Upon taking command, Bennigsen had put into operation an imaginative plan. Leaving three divisions to watch the French near Warsaw, he had led his seven other divisions on a long winter march north-east and then west in order to link up with the small Prussian field army under General Lestocq near the temporary Prussian capital of Königsberg (modern Kaliningrad) on the Baltic coast. By taking such a circuitous route, he hoped to be able to hide his manoeuvre from the French and then fall upon their left wing by surprise, destroying it in detail and perhaps even severing the *Grande Armée*'s important line of supply from Berlin.

To an extent, the bold Russian move did catch the French by surprise. The left-wing corps of Marshals Bernadotte and Ney, a fiercely courageous, flame-haired warrior from Alsace, were forced to fall back in the face of the abrupt appearance to their front of a large enemy army. Indeed, had the Russians been better able than they were to manoeuvre rapidly and flexibly, they would probably have dealt the French left a powerful blow. As it was, Bernadotte's corps had to fight a stiff action against elements of Bennigsen's army at Möhrungen (modern Morag) on 25 January in order to buy a breathing space for his force to withdraw. Both sides sustained a couple of thousand casualties in the engagement.

Bizarrely, the slowing of the Russian advance at Möhrungen, valuable as it was to Bernadotte's men, was not in the best interests of the *Grande Armée* as a whole. Ordering his whole army out of winter quarters on 27 January and leaving some forces to cover Warsaw, Napoleon instructed the bulk of his men to concentrate on tackling Bennigsen. His plan to deal with the threat to his northernmost corps was typically daring and dynamic. He commanded Bernadotte and Ney to continue their retreat in order to lure Bennigsen further west and enable the Emperor to thrust north and cut the Russians off from both their homeland and the major Baltic port and fortress of Königsberg.

As the bulk of Napoleon's men manoeuvred to isolate Bennigsen's force and then crush it, the Russian commander continued with his westwards advance determined to smash the retreating French left and blithely unaware of the trap into which he was falling. Mindful of the inability of the *Grande Armée* to move swiftly and coordinatedly in the wet and mud of late December, Bennigsen never imagined the French would be able to close on him from the south as speedily as they now did. By late January, the torrential rain and cloying earth of the end of 1806 had given way to snow and frozen ground, hardly ideal conditions for a march but certainly much better than those of a month before. The Hanoverian's bold scheme to surprise and devastate the French was being expertly turned to the Emperor's advantage.

Then an unexpected event changed everything. Just as the French used their light cavalry to scout and gather intelligence, the Russians employed the famous Cossacks for the same purpose. At the very end of January, a small group of these hardy horsemen came across a French messenger carrying orders from Napoleon to Bernadotte. The courier had only recently arrived from military academy in France and had got lost in the unfamiliar lands of north-east Prussia in which he now found himself. Realizing he could not escape, the young French officer tried to destroy his despatches but the Cossacks got to him in time to prevent him from doing so. A quick perusal of the captured orders revealed their vital importance and they were raced at once to Bennigsen. Napoleon's plan was laid bare and the Hanoverian suddenly realized the mortal danger into which he was leading his army. He immediately ordered his forces to concentrate at the town of Ionkovo and hoped that he would be able from there to march his men north to Königsberg and safety.

It did not take Napoleon long, once he became aware of the abrupt Russian retreat, to appreciate that the enemy had discovered his plans. Adapting his strategy with his usual aplomb, he now ordered his various corps to fall upon the fleeing Russians as rapidly as possible. On 3 February, he found his foe near Ionkovo. He had to hand just five divisions, part of the Imperial Guard and Murat's reserve cavalry, although the rest of the Guard and Augereau's corps were nearby and closing fast. The Emperor therefore determined to pin the Russians with a frontal attack while two divisions and some of the cavalry under Soult conducted an outflanking manoeuvre to prevent the enemy from withdrawing. It was late in the day before the French assaults on the disorganized Russians got going, and the imminent fall of night thwarted both the pinning and outflanking moves. In that regard, it was Golymin all over again, for Bennigsen, realizing that further French forces were closing on him, ordered his army to retreat north under cover of darkness.

Napoleon was predictably frustrated by the failure to ensnare the Russians at Ionkovo, but was determined not to let them get away easily. The following morning he ordered the enemy to be pursued and brought to battle. The chase took place through a landscape of intermittent plain and forest, all of it blanketed in thick snow. Bennigsen's men, fleeing to escape the trap into which their commander had almost led them, marched hard and were undoubtedly more used to the wintry conditions than their pursuers. Nevertheless, the French had the scent of victory in their nostrils and chased their quarry unrelentingly. On 6 February, Napoleon's advance guard caught up with the Russian rearguard at Hof, some thirty miles south of Königsberg and safety. A sharp action resulted but the French were unable to prevent the enemy from continuing their flight.

The *Grande Armée* was now snapping at the very heels of the fleeing Russians, and on 7 February Bennigsen decided to call a halt to the retreat and prepare for battle the next day. He determined to make his stand along the line of a low ridge some 1,200 yards to the north-east of a hitherto utterly insignificant town around twenty miles south of Königsberg. It was called Eylau.

The leading elements of the French army, Murat's cavalry and Soult's corps, arrived south of Eylau that afternoon, and before long fierce fighting erupted over possession of the settlement. The Russian rearguard under Bagration* defended the town against the determined assaults of French soldiers desperate to secure

---

* When the Soviets annexed this area during the Second World War they renamed Eylau Bagrationovsk in the Georgian's honour.

shelter for themselves for the coming night. This scrappy combat, over which neither army's commander-in-chief was able to exercise real control, lasted from mid-afternoon until well after dark, ebbing and flowing in Eylau's streets and across the town's cemetery. Eventually, the Russians yielded the hotly contested ground to their enemies and withdrew to rejoin the bulk of their comrades on the ridge to the north-east, but not before each side had suffered around 4,000 casualties. Given the limited number of men committed to the battle for the town, such losses were severe, but they would soon pale into insignificance in the light of the carnage that was to be unleashed the following day.

The night of 7–8 February 1807 was bitterly cold. Those Frenchmen who had fought so hard to capture Eylau from its Russian defenders were fortunate enough to have some shelter against the biting wind and snow, although many of the buildings had been stripped of their thatched roofs by cavalrymen who had been able to find nothing else upon which to feed their horses. The majority of the French, though, and almost all the Russians, slept that night outdoors, huddled around fires for warmth. Compounding their misery, the troops on both sides lacked food. The standard meal that evening was the uninspiring one of potatoes and water.

The area in which the two opposing armies spent this unhappy night was an undulating, featureless landscape. In warmer times, there would have been streams and a few ponds, but these were all frozen over and covered in thick snow. The only things that protruded through the deep, white blanket were a few areas of woodland and some equally dispersed settlements. The town of Eylau itself sat a little way from the foot of a spine of higher ground parallel to which, around a mile to the north-east, was the low ridge along which Bennigsen had drawn up his forces. Napoleon had deployed his army more or less to mirror the Russians, with Eylau and its cemetery forming a strongpoint in the left-centre of his line.

By dawn on the 8th, the Emperor had just 45,000 men and around 200 guns with which to face the 67,000 Russians and 460 cannon of Bennigsen. The odds did not, therefore, look good, but Napoleon took heart from two factors. First, he did not rate his opponents highly. As he had commented after Austerlitz, 'The Russian troops are brave, their generals inexperienced, their soldiers ignorant and sluggish which in truth makes their armies little to be feared'. There was certainly some truth in this view, but it ignored the fact that the Russians tended to fight best when on the strategic defensive and especially when they felt cornered. Secondly, Napoleon expected to receive substantial reinforcements during the day. Davout's 15,000 men were already nearing the battlefield and the Emperor was also counting on the 14,500-strong corps of Ney, as well as that of Bernadotte, to arrive at some point. Altogether, that would give the French a healthy numerical advantage over the Russians, even if the latter were joined by General Lestocq's

9,000 or so Prussians who were known to be in the area. (Bennigsen had, in fact, called for Lestocq to march to his aid the previous day.)

The Russian battle plan was, first and foremost, to hold a strong defensive line along the ridge upon which the army was drawn up, but should the day go particularly well, Bennigsen intended to pummel the French centre with the large artillery batteries he had deployed in the middle of his position and then storm the town of Eylau, breaking the enemy line in two. Napoleon's plan was more complicated. The forces he had with him at dawn would initially aim to pin the Russians down while Davout to the south-east and Ney to the north-west manoeuvred to envelop the enemy on both flanks. Once the envelopment had begun in earnest, the Emperor, whose main line would hopefully have been reinforced by Bernadotte, would then send forward Augereau's corps to punch a hole in the Russian left-centre which Murat's cavalry would then exploit. It was a brilliant scheme that promised an annihilation of Bennigsen's army far greater even than that suffered by Kutuzov's men at Austerlitz.

Rarely in war do things go exactly to plan, however, and the battle of Eylau is a classic example of that. The day, which dawned grey, windy and freezing cold, started well enough for the French. The Russians commenced the hostilities at around 8 a.m. with a big artillery bombardment, mostly concentrated on the centre of the enemy line. Napoleon's gunners, of course, responded in kind, and the consequent duel was kept up for much of the day. Surprisingly, given the disparity in number of cannon, the French suffered least from the exchange, for their line was more thinly spread than that of the Russians and many of their troops benefited from the cover which the town of Eylau provided.

At around 8.30, the Emperor ordered Soult on the left to advance against the Russian right and pin it down. It was from this point that things started to go wrong. Soult encountered considerably stiffer resistance than Napoleon had anticipated, and before long the men on his left, through no want of courage or skill on their part, were being pushed back by sheer weight of numbers, and taking a serious mauling in the process. To add to the worsening situation, news soon reached the Emperor that the Russians were also having the better of a cavalry engagement on his extreme right.

It was clear by around half past nine that the French were losing the initiative in the battle and Napoleon determined to wrest it back. There was as yet no sign of either Ney or Bernadotte, and it would be a few more hours before Davout's corps reached the field in force and was in a position to attack. The Emperor therefore had to fall back upon the units under his direct command. Adapting his grand battle plan, he ordered both Augereau's 9,000-strong corps in the French right-centre and the division of General St Hilaire to its right to advance against the Russian line opposite them and thereby take some of the pressure off the French flanks.

Marshal Pierre Augereau was not a well man on the morning of 8 February, suffering, as he was, from a severe bout of rheumatism. Indeed, he had asked Napoleon's permission to hand over command of his corps only to be asked to remain in charge one more day. Even if the marshal had been well, though, it is unlikely it would have seriously altered the tragedy that unfurled over the next hour or so. As Augereau's and St Hilaire's soldiers began their march forward, a ferocious snowstorm suddenly blew in from the east. The foul weather slowed the advance to a crawl and reduced visibility for the French to as little as fifteen yards (because the snow was blowing in from behind the Russians rather than into their faces like the French, Bennigsen's men could see rather further). In the inevitable confusion, Augereau's corps began to drift inexorably and unknowingly to the left.

The first the wandering troops knew of their error was when the seventy cannon of a massed battery in the centre of the Russian line opened fire on them at lethally close range shortly after ten o'clock. The shot and canister tore into the French ranks in a whirlwind of death and destruction. As the unfortunate men reeled from the shock of the violent blast to their front, cannonballs began thudding into them from behind. Blinded by the blizzard to the deviation of Augereau's soldiers, the artillery in the centre of the French line had maintained its steady bombardment of the Russians opposite, only now their missiles were killing their compatriots as well as their enemies.

No body of men could take the punishment being meted out to Augereau's ill-fated troops for long, and they inevitably began to retreat back towards their own line. That they did not break and run at once is testament to the courage and discipline under fire of the *Grande Armée* in its prime. The Russians were not going to let an opportunity like this slip, however, and infantry and cavalry units charged the battered Frenchmen as they withdrew. Some troops ran, many more held firm and conducted a successful, if debilitating, fighting retreat, while some were unlucky enough to find themselves surrounded by the advancing Russians. Even in these circumstances, few surrendered willingly but rather fought on to the bitter end in defence of the eagles the Emperor had given each regiment. The tale of Augereau's men's bravery is perhaps told most eloquently by the fact that the Russians succeeded in capturing just one of those prized standards.

For all their valour and heroism, however, Augereau's soldiers could not alter the fact that their corps had been smashed. An eyewitness estimated that by the time the marshal, who had himself been wounded by a musketball, was able to rally his shattered force, he found himself in command of no more than 3000 men. St Hilaire's division, which had broadly managed to hold its line of advance to the right of Augereau's corps, had fared considerably better in the ill-starred attack, but, without support to its left, it too had been driven back towards the French line by numerically superior forces.

In the Russian counter-attack that swept Augereau's soldiers right back across the battlefield, a body of some 6,000 infantry penetrated the town of Eylau itself. Their arrival, which had been obscured by the raging snowstorm still blowing in from the east, took the French completely by surprise and almost changed the course of history. Napoleon was using the bell tower of a church in this forward part of the town as an observation post and the only troops he had immediately to hand were his personal escort. It was a moment of tremendous peril for the Emperor, but displaying the calmness in dangerous situations so typical of his soldiers, he maintained a remarkable *sang froid*. A single squadron of his personal escort charged fearlessly at the oncoming Russians, heroically buying just enough time for the infantry of the Imperial Guard to arrive on the scene. This elite of the *Grande Armée* threw themselves at the disorganized Russians with a fury, driving them from the town and tearing their ranks to bloody ruin. Napoleon had been saved, but the centre of his line remained in a fragile state. A strong push from the Russians now and it might give way, Guard or no Guard. The Emperor and his indomitable army were on the verge of defeat.

What happened next epitomized Napoleon's aggressiveness as a commander and underlined his military genius. Most generals in his situation on the late morning of 8 February 1807 would have gone on the defensive, pulling back their forces and hoping that reinforcements could arrive in time to save them before the numerically superior Russians overwhelmed them. Instead, Napoleon took the remarkably audacious step of ordering Marshal Murat to gather up almost the whole of the French cavalry contingent and, unsupported by infantry or artillery, charge the enemy centre.

By 11.30, with the ferocious blizzard having died down, some 10,700 French horsemen were ready to launch one of the most spectacular cavalry actions in history. At their head, bedecked in an assortment of striking and stylish furs and sporting an equally distinctive beard, Joachim Murat, Napoleon's brother-in-law and Grand Duke of Berg and Cleves, prepared to lead the charge in person. As the first wave of horsemen thundered towards the enemy centre they crashed into the infantry and cavalry that had chased off the unfortunate soldiers of Augereau and St Hilaire. Catching the Russians in a disordered state, Murat and his men ploughed through them, routing many and relieving the immediate threat to the French position near Eylau.

With subsequent waves following behind, Murat and his lead units rode on. Chasing fleeing Russians before them, they came up to the cannon that had so brutally hammered Augereau's corps before the gunners could unleash the same devastation upon them. They overran the guns and sabred as many artillerymen as they could in vengeance for their comrades' terrible ordeal.

Still the French cavalry charged on, their horses panting heavily and the riders

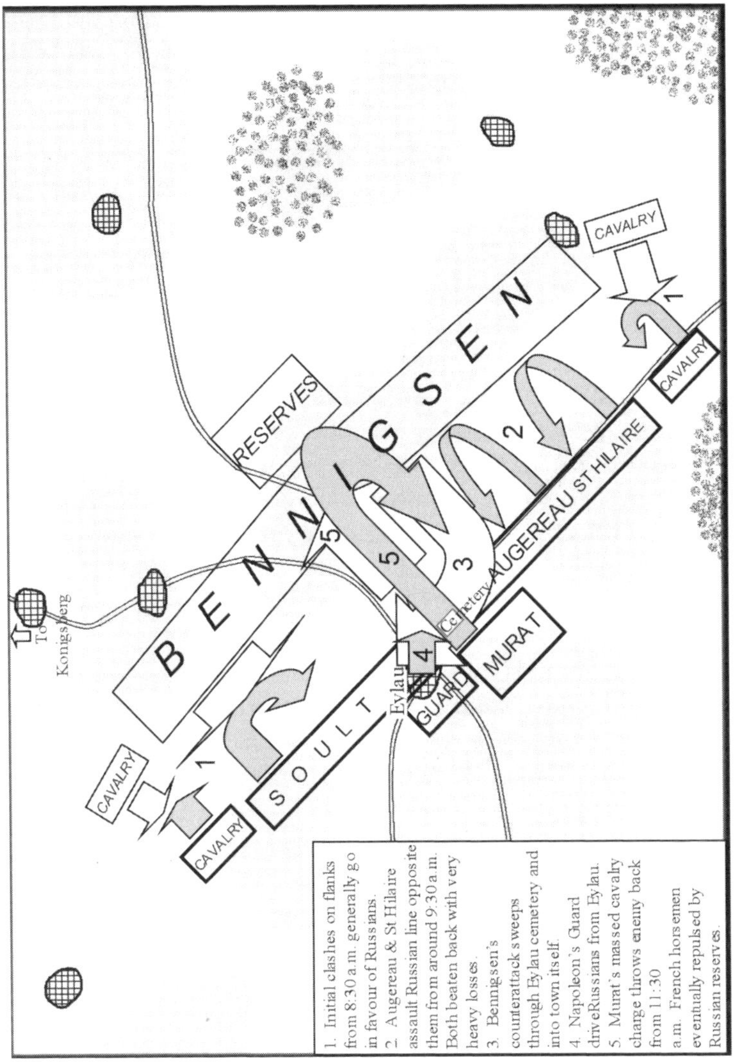
BENNIGSEN
RESERVES
CAVALRY
CAVALRY
CAVALRY
CAVALRY
SOULT
AUGEREAU
ST HILAIRE
MURAT
GUARD
Eylau
Cemetery
To Konigsberg
1. Initial clashes on flanks from 8:30 a.m. generally go in favour of Russians.
2. Augereau & St Hilaire assault Russian line opposite them from around 9:30 a.m. Both beaten back with very heavy losses.
3. Bennigsen's counterattack sweeps through Eylau cemetery and into town itself.
4. Napoleon's Guard driveRussians from Eylau.
5. Murat's massed cavalry charge throws enemy back from 11:30 a.m. French horsemen eventually repulsed by Russian reserves.

Battle of Eylau: Morning

bellowing their war cries. As the Horse Grenadiers of the Imperial Guard came under fire from the enemy, their colonel, Lepic, was outraged to see some of his men ducking and roared at them, 'Heads up, by God! Those are bullets – not turds!'

The fearsome charge only stopped after some 2,500 yards, having cut a swathe through the Russian centre and erupted into Bennigsen's rear. The Russian reserves, powerfully supplied with cannon as they were, were simply too formidable a final obstacle for the *Grande Armée*'s valiant horsemen to take on with their steeds as exhausted as they by now were. So the cavalry turned and charged back towards the French centre, fighting their way past anyone who dared try to stop them.

It is estimated that the magnificent action by Murat and his fellow horsemen cost them around 1,500 casualties, a heavy but not overly grievous loss. It almost certainly saved the day for the French. Not only did it lift the immediate threat to Napoleon's weakened centre, it also dissuaded Bennigsen from going over to the offensive to exploit his enemy's difficulties. Instead, both sides now stabilized their positions and awaited the next move on what was fast becoming one of the bloodiest days of the Napoleonic Wars.

By around 1 p.m., the corps of Marshal Davout was finally ready to launch a concerted assault on the Russian left flank. Having marched hard that morning, Davout's veterans showed little sign of weariness as they crashed against the end of the enemy's line. Alarmed by the fierce assault, Bennigsen moved troops to reinforce his left, but they could not prevent that wing from gradually bending back as the afternoon wore on, until the Russian position came to resemble a giant fishing hook. When Napoleon reinforced the marshal's attack with the rallied division of St Hilaire, it began to look like Bennigsen's flank would give way and that the French would win a victory after all.

But then, around half past three, the momentum of this extraordinary battle swung yet again. In the nick of time, 7,000 Prussians under the command of General Lestocq arrived on the field and were directed at once by Bennigsen to reinforce his wavering left. Smashing into Davout's right flank, the Prussians drove the French back until, sometime after dark and with the fighting in this sector still raging, the Russian line was more or less restored to its original position.

Still the remarkable ebb and flow of the day was not quite over, for at 7 p.m. Ney's corps finally arrived on the Russian right. Although he immediately sent his men into action, he was too late to have much impact upon the course of the battle. In confused fighting in the dark, Ney's soldiers drove the enemy back but were unable to threaten Bennigsen anywhere near as seriously as they would have had they arrived several hours earlier. By ten o'clock, peace at last reigned once more over this barren area of north-eastern Prussia.

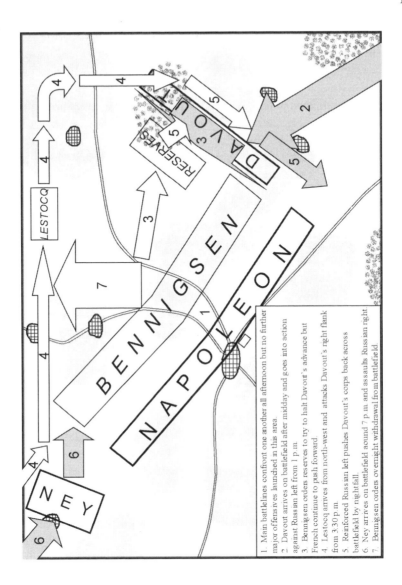

Battle of Eylau: Afternoon and Evening

1. Main battlelines confront one another all afternoon but no further major offensives launched in this area.

2. Davout arrives on battlefield after midday and goes into action against Russian left from 1 p.m.

3. Bennigsen orders reserves to try to halt Davout's advance but French continue to push forward.

4. Lestocq arrives from north-west and attacks Davout's right flank from 3.30 p.m.

5. Reinforced Russian left pushes Davout's corps back across battlefield by nightfall.

6. Ney arrives on battlefield around 7 p.m. and assaults Russian right

7. Bennigsen orders overnight withdrawal from battlefield

Why had Ney arrived so late? And what had happened to Bernadotte? These are questions that have exercised historians ever since the battle. The answer to the latter question is shrouded in mystery. Napoleon subsequently blamed his failure to crush the Russians at Eylau on the non-appearance of his often wayward marshal, and suspicions of incompetence or even treachery have been directed at Bernadotte ever since. In his defence, Bernadotte claimed that he never received the Emperor's order to march to the battlefield, an assertion that could not be successfully challenged as the messenger sent with the instructions had been killed in the battle. The truth of the matter will never be known.

The matter of Ney's tardy arrival is easier to explain, and blame for it is generally put at Napoleon's door. The fact is that the Emperor did not despatch the order for Ney to march to Eylau until first light on the morning of the battle, when he might have summoned him the previous evening. There was, however, good reason for the delay. Time after time since Ionkovo, Bennigsen had used the cover of darkness to withdraw his forces and Napoleon could not be sure on the evening of 7 February that he would not do so again. Until he was certain the enemy was going to fight at Eylau, it seemed wise to leave Ney where he was, for his was the only French corps in a position to intercept the Russians should they withdraw towards Königsberg.

Nor does mitigation of Napoleon's decision to delay recalling Ney end there. Almost twelve hours passed on 8 February between the Emperor despatching his order to Ney and Ney reaching the battlefield, far longer than the former could ever have expected. Partly, Ney was slowed by enemy action, for Lestocq, who also began the day to the north-west of Eylau, skilfully detached 2,000 of his 9,000 Prussians to hinder the French contingent's advance, a task they carried out with some success. That by no means accounts for all, or even most, of the unexpected delay in Ney's arrival, though. The key reason for the marshal's tardy arrival was the fact that he did not receive his orders to march to Eylau until 2 p.m. Given that he was then able to move almost 15,000 soldiers to the battlefield in five hours despite being slowed by Lestocq's Prussians indicates just how late the lone, mounted messenger had been in reaching him. Again, the weather had undone Napoleon's plans, for in the snowy, windy conditions which prevailed on the morning of 8 February, especially after the fierce blizzard blew in from the east, the Emperor's messenger had simply got lost. Compounding the misfortune, the wind and snow had also prevented Ney from hearing the noise of the battle to his south and thereby pre-empting Napoleon's command by marching to the sound of the guns. Seeing as Ney's arrival on the Russian right around mid-afternoon, when Napoleon must have been expecting him, would almost certainly have been decisive, it is not stretching the point to suggest that it was the weather more than the Russians who denied the French victory at Eylau.

The Emperor claimed a victory anyway, for Ney's late arrival persuaded Bennigsen to withdraw from the battlefield overnight and resume the retreat to Königsberg. It certainly didn't feel like a victory to the French survivors, however. Eylau had been a bloodbath. Casualty figures are the most contentious of any of his battles and Napoleon deliberately falsified them in his official bulletin to mask the scale of his own army's suffering, admitting to just 1,000 killed and 4,000 wounded. The truth is that losses in Augereau's corps alone amounted to 5,200 dead and wounded, including every single general and colonel, with a further few hundred men taken prisoner. Indeed, the corps's losses were so terrible that Napoleon felt compelled after the battle to break it up and redistribute its remaining soldiers to other units throughout the *Grande Armée*. Soult's much larger corps, which included St Hilaire's division, suffered grievously as well on 8 February 1807, the marshal officially recording no fewer than 8,250 casualties. Davout's losses, at around 5,000, were very heavy too, and it seems likely that Ney's corps, the Guard and Murat's cavalry sustained at least 5,000 casualties between them. Overall, then, our best guess for French losses is around 25,000, fully a third of those engaged.

Calculating Allied losses is even harder. Bennigsen subsequently admitted to 12,000 killed and almost 8,000 wounded at Eylau, but it would have been extraordinary for the number of fatalities to have been higher than the number of injured, so a French eyewitness estimate of 25,000 Russian losses may be more accurate. To this must be added perhaps a couple of thousand Prussian casualties. In other words, like the French, at least one in every three soldiers who fought on the Allied side at Eylau was killed, wounded or captured.

Much as Napoleon endeavoured to disguise the scale of his losses to the world at large, he was more honest with those close to him. In the early hours of the morning of 9 February, he wrote to Josephine informing her, 'There was a great battle yesterday which I won ... but I have lost a great many men'. To his fellow soldier, Soult, the Emperor despondently acknowledged later that day, 'Marshal, the Russians have done us great harm', to which Soult defiantly responded, 'And we them. Our bullets were not made of cotton.' Napoleon, hardly a man unused to the aftermath of battles, seems nevertheless to have been genuinely shocked by the sheer scale of the carnage at Eylau, admitting that his 'soul was oppressed to see so many victims'.

The true horror of the scene on the morning of 9 February is perhaps only hinted at in this stark testimony from a French surgeon: 'Never was so small a space covered with so many corpses. Everywhere the snow was stained with blood ... The bodies were heaped up wherever there were small groups of firs behind which the Russians had fought. Thousands of guns, helmets and breastplates were scattered on the road or in the fields.' It must truly have been an icy vision of Hell.

For the Russian survivors of the maelstrom, there was some consolation in the fact that their enemy was too exhausted after Eylau to impede their retreat to Königsberg, but the French were confronted with the painful fact that all their efforts and losses had practically been for nought. Marshal Ney summed up their feelings when, upon touring the battlefield in the cold light of day, he remarked to an aide, 'What a massacre! And it has achieved nothing.' As ever, the Emperor's loyal troops were not averse to sharing their opinion with their commander. Visiting his units on 9 February, Napoleon was greeted with more cries of '*Vive la paix!*' than of '*Vive l'Empereur!*'

Bonaparte knew after Eylau that he had no choice but to order his battered forces back to winter quarters and to begin preparations for a summer campaign in eastern Prussia. He delayed giving the command all his men were eagerly awaiting, however, for a good couple of weeks. Aware that the bloody stalemate on 8 February might dent his reputation for invincibility throughout Europe, he was understandably loath to give an indication of the extent to which his army had been damaged by suspending operations too promptly. His soldiers were naturally disappointed by the delay but loyally obeyed the Emperor's orders to shadow Bennigsen's retreat at a distance.

The final fortnight of the renewed winter campaign passed relatively uneventfully. The only significant action took place on 15 February at Ostrolenka away to the south-east, where Lannes's corps, commanded while the marshal was ill by General Savary, drove off the three divisions Bennigsen had left to mask Warsaw in early January. In the north, the *Grande Armée* barely made contact with the retreating Russians after Eylau, a state of affairs that suited both sides. There was only one brief encounter of any note when Davout's corps pushed back a small force of two and a half thousand Russian cavalry. Normally, such a minor skirmish would barely merit attention, but its location was portentous. The town near which Davout's men scored their small success was to feature much more prominently in the story of Napoleon's relationship with Russia in less than four months' time. Its name was Friedland.

9

Friedland

The bloodbath in the snow at Eylau shook the normally imperturbable Emperor. He had not wanted this war against the Russians in the first place, and he desired it even less now that it had done such damage to his *Grande Armée*. His thoughts in the weeks after the great slaughter of 8 February therefore turned towards peace. The problem, of course, was how to get it.

His first move came just six days after Eylau when he wrote to the Prussian king offering to restore all his lands east of the Elbe in return for a restitution of the Prusso-French alliance of 1806. Were Frederick William to accept the offer, all hope of a resurrected Polish state would disappear, a bitter blow to the many Poles who hoped Napoleon would give them back at least part of their country. In the final analysis, however, all nations put their own interests first in the conduct of foreign policy and French interests seemed to be best served in mid-February 1807 by an effort to restore the Prussian alliance and thereby either end the war against the Russians or at least gain an ally in it. Keen as Frederick William personally was to make peace with the Emperor, he was unwilling to sign a deal with the French if that would embroil him with the Russians. When the Tsar informed the King that Russia remained fully committed to waging war against France after Eylau, the Prussian monarch felt he had no choice but to reject Napoleon's approach.

Frustrated by the failure of Frederick William to accept a separate peace, the Emperor shifted strategy at the end of February, raising the idea of a European congress aimed at reaching a general settlement for the whole continent. All the current major combatants (France, Russia, Prussia, Britain and the Ottoman Empire) were to be invited but an armistice would have to be arranged before the congress convened.

The Prussian king leapt on this proposal with some eagerness, pressing the idea upon his Russian allies. For his part, Alexander took this latest French peace move as evidence that Napoleon and his army were in trouble and should not be allowed to escape easily. He did not wish to risk driving Frederick William into the arms of the Emperor, however, and so, rather than rejecting the idea of a congress out of hand, said that Russia would attend such a conference, but only if she were made aware of (and therefore approved) the basis upon which the French would negotiate in advance.

Even more negative about the proposed congress than the Tsar was the Tory administration in London, which came to power in March 1807. The new foreign secretary, George Canning, was cut from much the same cloth as the former Prime Minister, William Pitt, and was every bit as committed to a policy of uncompromising resistance to Napoleonic France as the deceased premier had been. Canning made it clear that 'the only conditions to which England could listen to any proposal of peace or mediation were such that Napoleon would be certain to reject'. Essentially, the British government wanted a restoration of the balance of power on the Continent, a situation which enabled London to play the other European powers off against each other while concentrating on maintaining Britain's dominance at sea and using it to increase British power and wealth. The Emperor was clearly never going to agree to that, but then he too expected his great rival across the Channel to swallow an unrealistically bitter pill. What he wanted from London was the handing back of all the French, Spanish and Dutch colonies that the British had been assiduously collecting since the resumption of hostilities in 1803 and a guarantee of free navigation in all waters. In return for this, Napoleon was not willing to do much more than withdraw from Prussia east of the Elbe. Between Britain and France, the stage was set for a fight to the finish.

Despite the almost non-existent prospect of a general peace, the Prussian king persevered in trying to put the wheels of a congress in motion. By the middle of May, he had succeeded in getting the Emperor's approval of neutral Copenhagen as a site for the conference and of the presence of both Sweden and Austria at the peace talks in return for France's allies attending too. He had also got Napoleon to explain that his basis for negotiating was 'equality and reciprocity between the two belligerent groups'. Whether the Russians or British would have gone ahead with the congress on this basis we shall never know for events in late May and early June dramatically altered the whole international situation, as we shall see. It is highly unlikely that they would have, however, for both London and St Petersburg wanted the French to do far more than engage in bartering territory on a reciprocal basis. They wanted a major rolling back of French power and control in Europe at as little cost to themselves as possible. As far as Britain and Russia were concerned, exchanges such as French evacuation of Prussia east of the Elbe in return for cession of the captured French, Spanish and Dutch colonies were not an acceptable basis for peace. Conversely, Napoleon could see no reason why he should be expected to give up substantially more than his adversaries. Any European congress would thus almost certainly have quickly ended in an impasse. Minds needed to be changed if peace was to be achieved and that put the emphasis firmly back on efforts to gain the upper hand in the War of the Fourth Coalition.

Napoleon's efforts at making peace in the wake of Eylau did not denote as great a level of anxiety as Alexander imagined they did. To be sure, the Emperor's confidence was temporarily knocked by the immense difficulties and heavy losses of the winter campaign, but never to the extent that he felt he would be defeated or that he would have been willing to accept a peace settlement in which France came off worse. He sought peace simply as a means of avoiding further suffering for his army and of terminating a costly conflict he had never wanted. In early spring 1807, he desired nothing more of the Russians than that they stop fighting him. The Russians, however, or at least those that mattered most politically, were not yet prepared to end hostilities without French power in Europe being reduced. Napoleon sensed this and so, alongside his efforts at making peace in the aftermath of Eylau, increased his preparations for further war.

Two military matters occupied the Emperor above all others in the weeks after the slaughter of Eylau: numbers and supplies. Despite already having several hundred thousand troops in his armies throughout Europe, Napoleon decided in late winter 1807 that he needed more in order to replace his recent heavy losses and make anyone who might be thinking of joining his enemies, particularly Austria, think twice before doing so. He therefore called up part of the class of 1808 some eighteen months ahead of schedule and chivvied his allies into providing more soldiers. This latter move was particularly successful and significant: by early summer, more Germans, Italians, Spaniards, Dutch and Poles than ever before were serving under Napoleon's banners. The *Grande Armée* was becoming a truly European army.

The difficulties of the supply situation in eastern Prussia posed an altogether trickier problem. When Marshal Ney, never one to hide his feelings, complained to the Emperor in winter 1807 of the hardships his men were having to endure, Napoleon replied, 'I am pained to hear of all you are suffering. You must still have patience. Provisions are ready here for your corps; it is transporting them that is the difficulty.' The fact was that, thanks largely to Napoleon's earlier efforts at securing supplies, sufficient food, clothing and other equipment was indeed available for the army, but getting it forward to the men along eastern Europe's appalling roads at this time of year was proving extremely difficult. The Emperor was determined, though, to do all he could, instructing his subordinates in late February, 'Procure what you can for me. Spare no money for the engaging of transports.' Slowly but surely the situation improved over the following weeks. The key factor was the better weather as winter turned to spring, but the monumental efforts of Napoleon (and, of course, many others) should not be discounted.

At the start of April, the Emperor ensconced himself in Castle Finckenstein, some eighty miles south-west of the main enemy base of Königsberg, making it the temporary centre of Imperial government and also the location for his blossoming love affair with Marie Walewska. Already the supply situation had eased greatly, and it would improve further over the coming weeks. By early summer, as Napoleon well knew, he would finally be in a position to deal the Russians a truly telling blow.

In the wake of Eylau, Napoleon's enemies had much the same military priorities as the Emperor, but they proved considerably less adept at dealing with them. Despite having the advantage of control of the Baltic Sea and generally much shorter supply lines, the Russians failed to provide their soldiers with adequate provisions. Indeed, the Tsar's troops suffered more, as a rule, from deprivation than did the Emperor's. As one observer noted, 'the Russian army is so distressed that the men actually pass whole days without a morsel of bread'. The result was predictable and unfortunate. Russian soldiers frequently looted and pillaged the territory of their Prussian allies for whatever they could find.

The supply situation in north-eastern Prussia troubled the Russian government rather less, however, than the issue of troop numbers. The unusual move of establishing a peasant militia, in mid-1806, had already proved very disappointing by spring the following year, freeing up far fewer regular soldiers from internal duties than had been hoped. Moreover, following the invasion of Moldavia and Wallachia, St Petersburg had to find troops for the southern front against the Turks as well as the northern one against the French. The Russian army was becoming disturbingly stretched and needed help. But from where?

The Prussians provided some assistance, of course, but Frederick William's kingdom was very much a broken reed, incapable of playing more than a subsidiary role in the ongoing struggle against Napoleon. The Russians therefore looked to their other allies, the British and the Swedes, to take some of the pressure off Bennigsen's army in north-eastern Prussia. Both London and Stockholm said the right kind of things, agreeing to mount a diversionary attack on the north German coast at some point, but neither were able (or willing) to move Heaven and Earth to make the assault happen as promptly as the Russians desired. St Petersburg was therefore compelled to fall back on the hope that the clearly reluctant Austrians could be persuaded to cast their worries aside and join the Fourth Coalition. Great diplomatic efforts were put into coaxing and cajoling Vienna in the late winter and spring of 1807, but all to no avail. The Austrians remained unconvinced that Napoleon could be beaten, terrified of the consequences of failure should they go to war with France a fourth time, and deeply suspicious of Allied, and especially Russian, motives in the conflict. All Vienna was prepared to do in spring 1807 was offer to mediate between the warring parties, a mediation that neither side wanted nor felt was necessary.

Given their inability to supply their armies properly or win over the Austrians, the most sensible course for the Russians in spring 1807 would probably have been to try to make peace with Napoleon. Some influential figures, such as his old friends Czartoryski and Novosiltsev, advised the Tsar to do just this, but Alexander remained committed to the armed struggle. Indeed, in April, he joined the Prussian King and Queen in the northernmost city of their kingdom, Memel, and pressed them to sign a statement of war aims. The result, at the end of the month, was the Convention of Bartenstein. By its terms, the Russian and Prussian rulers pledged to continue the fight until the French had been driven back across the Rhine and never to make a separate peace with Napoleon. Then a new European system would be arranged. Germany would be federated under (nominal) Austrian and (effective) Prussian leadership. Prussia would be fully restored and given a more defensible military frontier in the west. In a blatant effort to win support for the scheme from London and Vienna, Hanover was to be returned to the British, although it would be tied to Prussia militarily, and north-eastern Italy was to be given to the Austrians. Territory would also be found for the deposed ruling families of Holland and Piedmont. The Ottoman Empire was to be preserved, but under dominant Russian influence.

In some ways, the Convention of Bartenstein marked a greater realism on the part of Napoleon's enemies in regard to their war aims. There was no specific commitment to overthrow the Emperor and restore the Bourbons, and it even seemed to envisage France retaining the Low Countries, north-western Italy and a dominant position in Switzerland. It retained severe weaknesses, however, as a rational programme. For a start, the Allies had so far shown little sign of pushing the French back across the Vistula, let alone the Rhine. Just as serious, Bartenstein was quite clearly intended to benefit its formulators, the Russians and Prussians, considerably more than anyone else, thereby restricting its appeal. The British and Swedish governments both thought little of the scheme, though in the case of the former that was partly because it did not propose reducing French power as much as London would have liked. Bartenstein held no appeal for the Austrians either. Indeed, they were so unenthusiastic about it when the Russians asked them to sign up to it in May that St Petersburg tried to bully Vienna into joining the convention (and the war) by threatening, should it refuse, to make a separate peace with Napoleon that would be unfavourable to Austria. It is a measure of just how cowed the Austrians were by French might that even such a threat as this (similar to one made in 1805 to get Austria to join the Third Coalition) failed to move Vienna towards war. The Tsar would have to rely primarily on his own soldiers to dig him out of the hole he and his government had got Russia into by late spring 1807.

After the bloodbath at Eylau, both sides were happy to allow the bulk of their forces in eastern Prussia a break from active campaigning until early summer. That is not to say, however, that there were no military operations at all in the spring of 1807. Napoleon sent a corps under Marshal Adolphe Mortier, a burly, half-English soldier affectionately known as the Big Mortar, to occupy Swedish Pomerania on the Baltic coast east of Denmark, but the Swedish soldiers were rather less interested in fighting the French than their Bonaparte-hating monarch, Gustavus IV. Following what can only be described as desultory manoeuvring aimed primarily at avoiding any serious combat, Mortier, with the Emperor's approval, concluded a ceasefire with the Swedes at the end of April.

The second area of active operations in northern Europe that spring was some miles to the east of Swedish Pomerania and was altogether more determinedly contested and significant. The great Baltic port city of Danzig (modern Gdansk) lay three miles from the mouth of the mighty Vistula. In 1807, not only was it full of provisions the French would benefit from capturing and denying to their enemies, but its garrison also posed a potential threat to the *Grande Armée*'s stretched lines of supply that ran back into Germany. In early March, therefore, Napoleon made Danzig's capture his immediate operational priority.

The siege, led by Marshal François Lefebvre, a slow-moving but broadly competent commander, got underway on 11 March, but it was 24 April before the French got into position to begin bombarding the defences. Several sallies from the mostly Prussian garrison were defeated, but the real threat to the successful conclusion of the siege of Danzig came on 11 May, when an 8,000-strong Russian army under General Kamenskoi landed at the mouth of the Vistula. Napoleon, though, had anticipated such a move and had despatched the ever-reliable Marshal Lannes to the city with his corps to meet the new challenge. After spending four days bottled up in the forts at the mouth of the Vistula awaiting Prussian reinforcements that were meant to be coming overland, Kamenskoi finally attacked elements of Lannes's force in the wooded, broken terrain north-east of Danzig at dawn on 15 May. After several hours of tough fighting in which the redoubtable French marshal had his horse shot from under him but continued to command on foot, the Russians were finally driven back into the forts from which they had come, both sides sustaining around 1,500 casualties.

The next day, the Prussian reinforcements Kamenskoi had been waiting for finally arrived, only to be easily beaten off by the French. Five days later, Marshal Mortier's corps, following orders issued at the start of May by the Emperor, arrived on the scene from Swedish Pomerania. The French and their allies now had an overwhelming numerical advantage, and this, combined with Lefebvre's sappers advancing the siege trenches close enough for the city itself to come under bombardment, persuaded the garrison to sue for terms. Agreement for the capitulation of Danzig was reached on 25 May, Lefebvre gallantly allowing the Allied soldiers to march out of the city as free men and with their arms provided they took an oath not to engage in active hostilities against Napoleon's armies for a year. The same day, Kamenskoi sensibly decided to evacuate the forts at the mouth of the Vistula, re-embark his remaining troops and head back east.

The fall of Danzig was undoubtedly the greatest French victory in the east Prussian campaign so far. Huge stocks of food, drink, cloth, weaponry and ammunition were captured, the threat the garrison had posed to the *Grande Armée*'s supply lines had been lifted, and, most important, many thousands of troops were freed for operations further east. The victory came, moreover, at a propitious time, for less than a fortnight after Danzig fell, the main Russian army under Bennigsen resumed active operations south of Königsberg.

The Russian decision to launch an offensive south of Königsberg, in the first week of June 1807, has been widely criticized ever since. We have already seen how the Tsar's armies generally performed much better on the defensive rather than when attacking, but more important even than that is that Allied forces in eastern Prussia were heavily outnumbered by early summer by the *Grande Armée*. Although Bennigsen could call upon the services of around 116,000 Russians (100,000 under his direct control south of Königsberg, 16,000 some miles north-east of Warsaw) and some 20,000 or so Prussians on his right near the Baltic coast, Napoleon now had around 220,000 soldiers available to him in eastern Prussia, 30,000 under Masséna north-east of Warsaw and the remainder under the Emperor's personal command confronting Bennigsen. True, many of those Napoleonic troops were earmarked for non-frontline duties, such as garrisoning and protecting supply lines, but that still left him with a sizeable numerical advantage for the coming campaign. In these circumstances, Bennigsen would probably have been best advised to pull back a little and await the arrival of 30,000 reinforcements currently making their way to join him from Russia. Instead, he launched an attack on the forwardmost elements of the *Grande Armée* opposite him.

It seems that the prime reason for Bennigsen's offensive was more political than military. Following the fall of Danzig, the Prussians had complained bitterly to Alexander that the Russian commander had not done anywhere near enough to help save the city. They had expected him to launch a major diversionary attack on Napoleon's main army south of Königsberg to coincide with Kamenskoi's relief attempt in mid-May. Instead, Bennigsen had merely ordered a few very limited attacks which were easily repulsed. Even had greater efforts been made, though, it is very doubtful whether the fate of Danzig would have been changed. The Emperor also expected a bigger push from Bennigsen and had prepared his forces to meet it. Nevertheless, the Prussians claimed that the city could have been saved and the Tsar, eager to appease his allies, consequently upbraided his commander-in-chief for showing lack of spirit.

The result of Bennigsen's scolding was his offensive of early June. Yet it was not perhaps quite as rash a move as has usually been portrayed. Bennigsen's hope was to destroy individual elements of the Emperor's army before they could be supported, thereby reducing the Allies' numerical disadvantage. As such, it was, rather, Napoleonic in concept. The Russian soldiers were not, however, as flexible and astute in the attack as the French. Moreover, Napoleon's soldiers were generally just as adept on the defensive as the Tsar's men. Bennigsen's chances of success were thus slim.

Relying on the Prussians, reinforced by some Russians, to keep the northernmost of the French corps, that of Bernadotte, busy near the Baltic coast, Bennigsen attacked the corps of Marshal Ney with the bulk of his army on 5 June. Ney's force was stationed to the right of Bernadotte and, pushed forward a little from the main French line, was nearest to the vital Allied base of Königsberg. It was therefore the obvious target for any Russian attack, which was precisely why Napoleon had entrusted that position to Ney, one of his most redoubtable fighting commanders. The fiery Alsatian marshal did not disappoint his Emperor. Ney fell back steadily and in an orderly fashion in the face of the powerful Russian attack, losing 2,000 casualties in the process but inflicting the same number on his opponents. This stout defensive action bought Napoleon the time he needed to begin to effect a concentration of his army and plan a counterstroke. By the evening of 7 June, Bennigsen realized his offensive had already miscarried and ordered his men to commence a withdrawal under cover of darkness that night to a prepared defensive position some twenty miles north-east along the River Alle at Heilsberg.

The following morning, the Emperor set in motion a scheme to divide the enemy armies confronting him in north-eastern Prussia and destroy them in detail. The round-faced and jolly General Victor, commanding Bernadotte's corps as the marshal had received a head wound a couple of days earlier, was ordered to pin down the mostly Prussian force under General Lestocq near the Baltic coast and prevent it from uniting with or reinforcing Bennigsen's main body. Marshals Davout and Mortier, meanwhile, were to march north so as to place themselves between Bennigsen and his main stores and arms dumps at Königsberg. Finally, the corps of Murat, Soult and Lannes were instructed to pursue the retreating Russians directly along the Alle, with Ney and the Guard under Napoleon following and acting as a reserve. Napoleon was determined that, this time, the elusive Russians would not be allowed to escape his clutches.

With over half a day's head-start and marching with an alacrity that Russian armies of this period seem to have reserved for such withdrawals, Bennigsen's men reached the entrenched camp at Heilsberg before the French units pursuing them could catch up. The Russians had prepared their position there well. To the south of the small town, which stood on the west bank of the Alle, ran a crescent of high ground that had been heavily fortified with redoubts and other defensive earthworks. Forward of this main line were other more isolated posts that could be used to slow an enemy assault. The country round about was broken up by woods and tributaries of the Alle. All in all, it was a formidable prospect for any would-be attacker.

There is little doubt that instead of trying to force Bennigsen out of this strong position by direct assault, the French should have attempted to manoeuvre the Russians out by outflanking them and threatening their rear and line of retreat to either Königsberg or Russia. Instead, when the advance guard of the *Grande Armée* under the hot-headed Marshal Murat approached on 10 June, it began to attack the enemy forward positions and thereby initiated an entirely unnecessary combat.

To be fair, the initial French assaults went well, driving the Russians from their advanced positions and compelling them to fall back toward the main defensive line on the high ground south of Heilsberg. But then things started to go awry for the French. With the bit firmly between his teeth and his blood up, Murat used the unofficial authority being the Emperor's brother-in-law gave him to order his fellow marshal Soult to instruct his newly-arrived corps to attack the main Russian line at 2 p.m. Soult obeyed, only to be duly beaten back from a defensive position brimming with cannon and protected by earthworks. By now, Napoleon himself was present, but he had one of his worst days as a commander. Indeed, he didn't really exercise command properly at all; at least not in any meaningful or constructive manner. Rather than call Soult's attacks off, he allowed the marshal to make repeated attempts to breach the strong enemy position throughout the afternoon and early evening, with the result that by the time the last such assault had been driven back at 8 p.m. the corps had sustained around 6,000 casualties. Then, to compound his error, the Emperor failed to stop Lannes from joining in the day's madness when he finally arrived on the scene with his corps as night was falling. The normally shrewd Lannes ordered his men to launch a night attack on the beleaguered Russian line in a desperate effort to win the day. Predictably, this final French assault ended much like all the others, in a bloody repulse that cost the corps over 2,000 casualties.

The battle of Heilsberg was a completely unnecessary tragedy that resulted in death or injury to more than 10,000 men of the *Grande Armée* and around 8,000 Russians. Murat has rightly been censured for recklessly setting the combat in motion. General Savary, for example, commented of the impulsive marshal after the battle that 'it would be better for us if he were less gallant and had a bit more common sense'. Soult and Lannes too had both fallen well short of their normally high standards. The most severe criticism, however, must go to Napoleon himself for failing to take a firm hand when he arrived and call an end to the repeated attacks. One can only assume that he (as well as Soult and Lannes) got into their minds on 10 June that just one more push would break the Russian line. With assault after assault being beaten back, however, albeit at heavy cost to the defenders as well as the attackers, Napoleon would have been wise to desist before dark eventually put an end to the fighting. The Emperor's doggedness was more often than not a great boon, but at Heilsberg it was badly misguided and thousands paid the price.

The two armies were both too exhausted by the fighting on the 10th to seek a renewal of the combat the following day. Then, on the evening of the 11th, Bennigsen received intelligence of the manoeuvre of Davout and Mortier that threatened to outflank him and cut him off from Königsberg. He responded by promptly ordering the withdrawal under cover of darkness that he would have issued even without the slaughter of the previous day. Detaching 9,000 men under Kamenskoi to reinforce Lestocq, who was falling back directly on Königsberg to defend that vital Allied base, Bennigsen pulled the rest of his army across to the right bank of the Alle. The Russians then resumed their retreat northwards, hoping to put enough ground between themselves and the French to allow them to make an abrupt turn west in a few days time and march to reunite with the forces defending Königsberg.

Napoleon soon learned of the Russian moves, but faulty intelligence from a cavalry patrol estimated Kamenskoi's detachment to be considerably larger than it was. The Emperor therefore ordered no fewer than 60,000 men, the corps of Murat, Davout and Soult, to march directly towards Königsberg to take over General Victor's task of pinning down Lestocq's force and preventing it from joining with Bennigsen. Victor himself was to march east to join the corps of Ney, Lannes, Mortier and the Imperial Guard under Napoleon himself. This force would shadow Bennigsen's retreat along the left side of the Alle, thereby remaining between the two enemy armies and holding a central position from which the corps could easily move to concentrate against either Lestocq or Bennigsen.

The key to Napoleon's dispositions in the wake of Heilsberg, was, as usual, flexibility, and before long that flexibility was proving its value. On the evening of 13 June, cavalry units from the French corps nearest the Alle, that of the forthright Marshal Lannes, ran into a strong scouting party of Russian horsemen that Bennigsen had sent across the river at the small town of Friedland (modern Pravdinsk), some thirty miles south-east of Königsberg. The French were driven back to the village of Posthenen, two miles to the west of Friedland, before the action was terminated and the victorious Russians withdrew to the town. Realizing that there were few places at which the deep and steeply-banked Alle could be crossed, and aware that Bennigsen's whole force was currently massing in his vicinity on the river's opposite bank, Lannes assumed that the enemy general was planning to return to the western side of the Alle here at Friedland. He therefore immediately sent a despatch to the Emperor informing him of the Russian presence and requesting instructions.

In actual fact, Bennigsen had not originally intended to cross the Alle at Friedland but to continue further north before turning west towards Königsberg. As soon as he learnt of the presence of Lannes's corps on the west bank of the river, however, he formulated an opportunistic plan. Assuming that Napoleon and the great majority of the French army were currently heading directly towards Königsberg, and that Lannes's force was an isolated detachment ordered to watch his own movements, Bennigsen made an impromptu decision to march his army over the Alle and attempt to destroy the marshal's corps before the Emperor could come to his assistance. It was a bold plan but it had one glaring flaw. Napoleon was not closing on Königsberg on the night of 13–14 June, but was instead at Eylau, around half the distance from Friedland that Bennigsen imagined.

As soon as he received Lannes's report of the cavalry skirmish at Friedland, and the presence of Bennigsen's whole army on the right bank of the Alle there, the Emperor jumped to the conclusion that the Russians were planning to cross the river. He therefore instructed Lannes to do all he could to ensure that the enemy did traverse the Alle at Friedland and then pin them down while he rushed reinforcements to the scene. The cavalry of Generals Grouchy and Nansouty were ordered to lead the move towards Friedland, followed by the corps of Mortier, Ney, Victor (Bernadotte was yet to recover from his wound) and the Imperial Guard. The scene was set for the following day, 14 June 1807, to witness the climax of the war in eastern Prussia.

Having resolved on the evening of 13 June to lead his whole army over the Alle at Friedland, Bennigsen ordered three bridges to be constructed overnight alongside the one permanent crossing between the town and the right bank of the river. By dawn on the 14th, however, the Russians had only got 10,000 men across to the Alle's western side, just a sixth of Bennigsen's total force. With four bridges now operational, though, the 50,000 soldiers currently on the right bank could be expected to cross in rather less time than it had taken the first 10,000.

Facing the Russian army at first light on 14 June were the 9,000 infantry and 3,000 cavalry of Lannes's corps, although they would shortly be reinforced by the 5,000 horsemen of Grouchy and Nansouty. With these 17,000 soldiers, Lannes had to hold whatever Bennigsen could throw at him before more substantial reinforcements arrived from mid-morning onwards.

The first Russian attacks came as early as 4 a.m., but with the great bulk of Bennigsen's army still on the wrong side of the Alle, these posed no serious threat to the French position west of Friedland. After a couple of hours, however, the pressure was mounting and a potentially dangerous Russian thrust, north-west of Friedland towards the village of Heinrichsdorf, was taking shape. Promptly, Lannes ordered Grouchy and Nansouty to ride to the village to prevent the

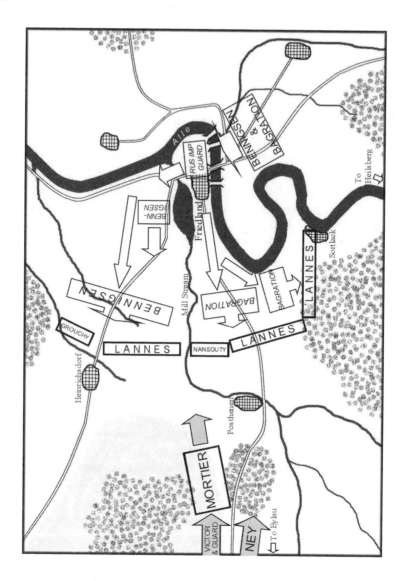

Battle of Friedland: The Russian Assault

French line from being outflanked. The cavalry generals rose to the occasion well and had driven the enemy back from Heinrichsdorf by 7 a.m.

By now, Lannes's force was beginning to become seriously outnumbered but the marshal was having an excellent day in command. He moved his limited units about continuously – Grouchy's horsemen, for example, rode from the south of the battlefield to the north then to the south again and finally to the north once more before the morning was out, charging and reforming umpteen times in the process. This constant reshuffling of his forces not only enabled each Russian thrust to be parried but also fooled the enemy into believing Lannes commanded more men than he did. The marshal also exploited what little cover the terrain provided expertly, holding up attacks on the southern end of his line by luring the Russians into the village and wood of Sortlack and using the height of the wheat in the fields west of Friedland to conceal large numbers of sharpshooting skirmishers.

For all Lannes's skill, however, the Russians might have done better than they did. After all, by 9 a.m. they had no fewer than 45,000 troops on the west bank of the Alle, facing the marshal's 17,000. True, Bennigsen's men were tired from their recent exertions – they had marched thirty-four miles in forty-eight hours prior to the battle, receiving very little food as they did so – but then the French had marched just as hard in the last couple of days. Perhaps more injurious to their attack, was the habitual slowness with which Russian armies organized and carried out major offensive manoeuvres. Despite the fourfold increase in bridges across to Friedland by dawn on 14 June, it still took some five hours for the bulk of Bennigsen's army to cross to the western bank. Even once units had crossed, there ensued a prolonged period of reorganization before they were deemed ready to assault the French line. Had the great Suvorov still been alive and in command at Friedland, events might have followed a rather different course. In the absence of such inspired guidance, the Russians could generally be depended upon, as Napoleon well knew, to take an age to mount a large-scale attack.

By the time Bennigsen was finally in a position to launch a concerted assault against Lannes's position west of Friedland, his substantial numerical advantage had all but evaporated with the arrival between 9.30 and 10 a.m. of some 23,000 French reinforcements. With numbers on the west bank of the Alle now roughly equal, the Russian commander had no chance of winning the crushing victory he had anticipated the previous evening. Nevertheless, he continued to order sporadic attacks, which Lannes was comfortably able to repel, until midday. Then, despite nearly all the 60,000 Russians having finally crossed to the western bank of the Alle, the arrival of yet further heavy French reinforcements evened out the numerical balance and persuaded Bennigsen to go over to the defensive. His dream of annihilating one of the great Napoleon's corps had vanished – and his disappointment would get bitterer still before the day was out.

Along with the French reinforcements who arrived at noon came a man whose presence on a battlefield would famously be said to be worth 40,000 men.* Napoleon was in excellent spirits, reminding all and sundry that today was the anniversary of his great victory seven years earlier at Marengo. Upon surveying the terrain and the enemy's dispositions, his mood was lifted still further. Immediately, he recognized just what an invidious position Bennigsen had got himself into. The battlefield was delimited to both north and south by woods, while to the west, masking the approach of French reinforcements until they actually arrived, ran a spine of higher ground. The area between this high ground and the Alle was almost wholly given over to wheat fields, the crops currently standing tall where they had not already been trampled underfoot. The key features of the battlefield were the River Alle and the town of Friedland itself. North of the town, the Alle ran roughly north–south, but as it passed Friedland it made a sharp turn westwards and then proceeded to trace a large 'S' shape before resuming a broadly north–south course. Just north of Friedland, meanwhile, flowing west to east and dissecting the battlefield, ran a tributary of the Alle known as the Mühlen Floss or Mill Stream, a more formidable obstacle than its name suggests – the Russians had to throw bridges over it on the morning of 14 June to facilitate the passage of troops – especially to the north-west of the town where it spread out into a small lake. Friedland thus stood on the left side of the deep and steeply-banked Alle at the end, effectively, of a peninsula. As Napoleon surveyed the battlefield shortly after midday, the Russian line ran more or less north–south some way to the west of the town, with the peninsula to the rear of its left-centre. The only Russian escape route appeared to be the four bridges over the Alle at Friedland. The Emperor, therefore, resolved to attack the Russian left, drive it back down the Friedland peninsula, capture the town, and thus trap the entire enemy army. First, though, he would wait for the arrival of his remaining reinforcements, the bulk of Victor's corps and the Imperial Guard, so that when he struck he would do so with a significant numerical advantage.

Bennigsen was not so inept as to be entirely unaware of the danger in which he found himself by early afternoon on 14 June, but he was reassured by the failure of the French to launch an attack on his line for several hours after the Emperor arrived. Assuming that Napoleon would not go over to the offensive before further substantial reinforcements arrived, and unaware that those reinforcements would reach the battlefield sooner rather than later, the Russian general was happy to sit on the defensive until nightfall and then use the cover of darkness to undertake the hazardous operation of pulling his army back across the Alle.

---

* The comment is usually attributed to the Duke of Wellington but it may first have been uttered by the Prussian commander Blücher.

The only action for most of that baking hot afternoon, therefore, was regular artillery exchanges between the opposing lines, a duel in which the French, enjoying the advantage of slightly higher ground, came off rather better. The Emperor spent his time riding up and down his lines, encouraging his soldiers, ensuring they had enough ammunition, and generally making sure that everything was in order for the attack he planned for later.

At 4 p.m., the bulk of Victor's corps and the Imperial Guard finally arrived, swelling Napoleon's numbers to around 80,000 and giving the French (and their German, Polish and Dutch allies also present among the corps) an overall advantage of some 20,000 men over the Russians. Bennigsen realized that the unexpected arrival of these reinforcements made an attack on his army in the remaining five of six hours of daylight probable and he began to contemplate ordering his men to commence their withdrawal to the right bank of the Alle before the afternoon was out. This would have been an extremely dangerous move that might well have descended into chaos under the inevitable heavy pressure from the French that would have accompanied it. Before Bennigsen could initiate such a withdrawal, however, Napoleon's cannon thundered to signal the start of his assault on the Russian left. Having crossed the Alle to destroy a single French corps, Bennigsen's army would now have to fight desperately to stave off its own destruction.

By half-past five on the late afternoon of 14 June, everything was in position for the Emperor to crush Bennigsen's army. While the corps of Mortier, including the cavalry of Grouchy and Nansouty, on the left of the French line and Lannes's corps in the left-centre pinned down the Russian forces north of the Mill Stream, Marshal Ney's corps, supported as necessary by elements of General Victor's corps, would deliver the crucial assault in the south. The Imperial Guard, as ever, formed the reserve behind the centre of the French line.

Ney opened his attack in typically ebullient style, his troops storming through the woods and village of Sortlack at the southern end of the battlefield. The Russian defenders here were soon overwhelmed and the marshal directed his forces on the extreme right of the line to wheel northwards, driving the enemy left back towards the neck of the Friedland peninsula. This manoeuvre, however, exposed the corps' right flank to a withering fire from the opposite bank of the Alle where the commander of the Russian left, General Bagration, had deployed much of his artillery. Ney's advance faltered and then stopped under the impact of the enemy guns, but Napoleon had foreseen this eventuality and, before long, a battery of French cannon which the Emperor had ordered forward to support the marshal's attack had hammered Bagration's artillery into ineffectiveness.

The defeat of the Russian guns was by no means the end of Ney's travails. When his corps's drive towards the Friedland peninsula resumed, it was suddenly

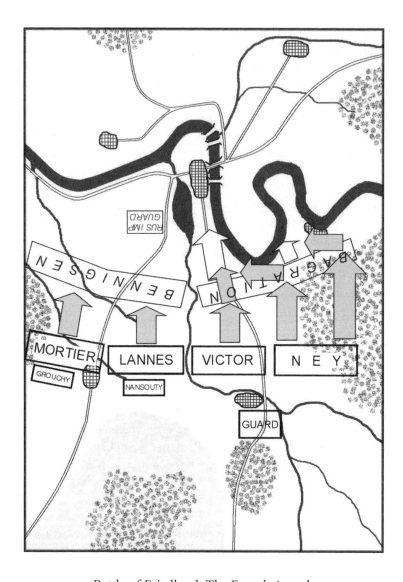

Battle of Friedland: The French Assault

hit by a powerful charge from Bagration's cavalry. Again, Ney's soldiers halted and indeed began to pull back a little under the intense pressure. Once more, though, Napoleon had prepared for such an eventuality. The infantry division of General Dupont, an element of Victor's corps, was sent forward to crash into the Russian horsemen and drive them off.

Bagration's cavalry withdrew to the neck of the Friedland peninsula to reform, but, before they could organize another massed charge, Victor displayed a tactical skill that would win him a marshal's baton in the wake of the battle. Realizing that the Russian left, which had now been bottled up in the narrow tongue of land between the Mill Stream and the bend of the Alle south of Friedland, presented an unmissable target for artillery, the general moved up a strong battery of 36 guns. Opening fire on the Russians at 600 yards, the cannon soon advanced to 300 yards, then 150, and finally just sixty yards. The slaughter inflicted upon Bagration's unfortunate troops was devastating, comparable even to the bloody ruin that the Russian guns at Eylau had visited upon Augereau's corps. Within just half an hour, it was estimated that some 4,000 soldiers on Bennigsen's left were blown away.

The Russian position had now become truly desperate and Bennigsen made his last throw of the dice to try to stabilize his battered left wing, sending in the infantry and cavalry of the Russian Imperial Guard. At Austerlitz, these elite troops had caused consternation among the French when they had been sent in, but at Friedland they were beaten back with relative ease. Dupont's division met the Russian foot soldiers head on and drove them off, while Victor's artillery battery smashed the horsemen of the Guard with a well-timed blast of canister at point-blank range.*

With the Russian Imperial Guard having been repulsed, the corps of Ney and Victor resumed the offensive, pushing determinedly east down the Friedland peninsula. The remnants of Bennigsen's left wing withdrew in the face of the French advance into the town itself, which soon went up in flames. The cause of the conflagration is uncertain – it may have been started by French artillery fire, or the retreating Russians may have deliberately set the town ablaze in the hope of slowing their enemy's advance. Either way, it soon spread to the bridges which spanned the Alle, and all four, which also came under direct fire from French cannon, were destroyed before more than a fraction of the Russian army could escape to the right bank.

The only known escape route gone, panic began to set in among the soldiers of Bennigsen's left. Ney and Victor maintained their intense pressure, the older Russian officers who had the misfortune to face them this day swearing that they

---

* Canister was a type of ammunition used by cannon at close range. It consisted of a tin filled with musket balls that exploded when the gun was fired, turning it into a giant shotgun.

had never endured such concentrated fire. Friedland itself became a nightmare of unbearable heat, choking thick smoke and searing flames that consumed the bodies of the dead and wounded as they piled up in the streets. Unsurprisingly, the entire left wing of the Russian army collapsed, some surrendering, some managing to flee north across the Mill Stream, many unwisely heading for the Alle, where most who tried to swim it drowned. Others simply died where they fought. War can rarely have been more terrible than it was for these wretched Russian soldiers in the Friedland peninsula on 14 June 1807.

By 8 p.m., Ney and Victor had utterly destroyed the Russian left and, so, turned north to attack the flank and rear of the centre of Bennigsen's army. Of course, the Russian troops north of the Mill Stream had not just been sitting idly by for the past two and a half hours while their comrades to the south were annihilated. Some had been despatched by Bennigsen to try to assist the beleaguered left wing, but the great majority had been successfully pinned down by the corps of Mortier and Lannes. As the crisis in the Friedland peninsula had approached its climax, Bennigsen had ordered his right and centre to assault the French forces opposite them in the hope of compelling Napoleon to withdraw units from the attack south of the Mill Stream, but it had been a futile gesture that had been dealt with comfortably. Now, as Victor and Ney seized the bridges over the Mill Stream and moved against the Russian centre, the Emperor finally ordered Lannes and Mortier to advance vigorously against the forces to their front. Assaulted from west and south, the Russians began to recoil towards the Alle, their destruction or surrender a seeming certainty.

Then came a remarkable piece of good news. An uncharted ford had been discovered to the Russians' rear. Bennigsen's men had an escape route once more. Quickly, the general ordered his infantry to form squares in order to cover the retreat of the artillery to the east bank of the Alle from where it could then provide covering fire for the subsequent withdrawal of the Russian foot soldiers and horsemen. Napoleon responded to Bennigsen's move by ordering the French artillery to pummel the tightly packed enemy formations. Again, the Emperor's cannon wrought havoc among the Russian lines, but the stout infantry held firm long enough for a sufficient number of Bennigsen's guns to be massed on the Alle's right bank to cover their own retreat. The French continued to press hard, but they were, unsurprisingly, tiring. Towards the end of the battle, indeed, Grouchy severely marred his record, after his heroics in the morning, by allowing several thousand Russian cavalry to escape north along the left bank of the Alle. One can only assume that he and his men were too exhausted to put up much of an effort to stop them.

By 10 p.m., as darkness fell and the firing at last died down, the Russians had successfully managed to get much of their centre and right across the ford. They had left many thousands of dead and wounded, however, on the western side of

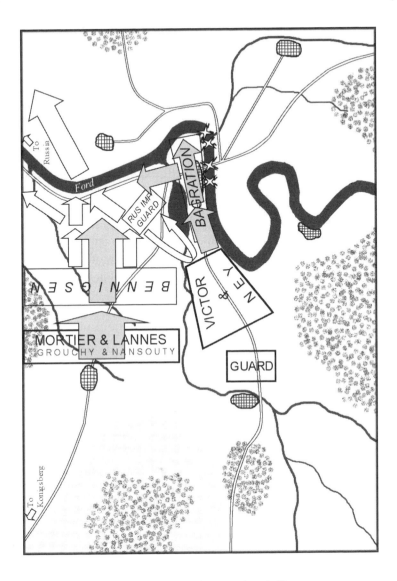

Battle of Friedland: The Russian Collapse

the river. Indeed, the scene on the plain, north of the Mill Stream, the following morning was truly horrendous. Rank upon rank of corpses marked where the soldiers had been mown down by cannon fire, while closer to the river the places where the Russian squares had stopped during their retreat, in an effort to repel the pursuing French, were marked by further piles of dead bodies.

Those Russians fortunate enough to have escaped the battlefield were less an army than a rabble of desperate individuals, glad simply to be alive and determined to put as great a distance as possible between themselves and the French by morning. As usual with the campaign in eastern Prussia, casualty figures are debatable, but given the utter destruction of the Russian left and the severe mauling of the rest of Bennigsen's army, it does not seem unreasonable to suggest that the Russians may have suffered as many as 15,000 dead and a similar, if not greater, number of wounded; in other words, fully half of the force engaged at Friedland. Bennigsen also lost eighty cannon and several thousand prisoners, including a score of senior officers. These were appalling losses, but if the ford had not been found, and if Grouchy had stirred himself to greater efforts in the evening, they would have been even worse.

The French, of course, hardly emerged from the battle unscathed, the corps of Lannes and Ney and the cavalry of Grouchy and Nansouty having had particularly arduous days, and a figure of around 10,000 casualties is generally accepted for Napoleon's army. Given that Bennigsen's entire force had been smashed, however, it seemed a light enough price to the Emperor, who wrote with evident and understandable satisfaction to Josephine that night that his soldiers had 'worthily celebrated the battle of Marengo; the battle of Friedland will be just as famous and just as glorious to my people ... It is a worthy sister of Marengo, Austerlitz, Jena'. What Napoleon and his men needed now to seal their triumph was peace.

10

Tilsit

Upon hearing news of the disaster at Friedland, General Lestocq wisely decided to abandon Königsberg before he was trapped there and began to withdraw his mixed Prusso-Russian army north-east towards Memel. Murat and Davout followed closely behind, while Soult occupied the deserted Baltic port, sequestering masses of provisions in the process.

The forces under Napoleon's direct control, meanwhile, lost contact with the fleeing mob that had been Bennigsen's army on the night of 14–15 June, but then a vigorous pursuit hardly seemed necessary – the Russian commander managed to maintain effective control over just 5,000 soldiers in the immediate wake of his catastrophic defeat. The headlong flight north towards the Niemen, which, for much of its course, marked the boundary between Prussia and Russia, continued throughout the 15th, the Russian troops stopping only to burn bridges in order to slow their French pursuers. The Emperor's advance guard nevertheless did catch up with the enemy rearguard on a few occasions over the coming days, but nothing more than isolated skirmishes developed. Partly, the French were too exhausted after their recent endeavours to press their fleeing foes as hard as they might, but also there was a sense that the job had already been done, that the Russians could surely not fight on after a defeat as crushing as Friedland.

Bennigsen seems to have agreed with the French, for he wrote an urgent letter to the Tsar on 15 June asking that steps be taken to stop hostilities. Hitherto, Alexander had been one of the prime movers in keeping the war going, but Friedland was simply too great a calamity to ignore. With Bennigsen's army shattered and his Prussian allies' territory now almost entirely overrun, there seemed to be little to stand in the way of the *Grande Armée* marching on into Russia herself – and the Tsar's third largest city, Vilna (modern Vilnius), was within striking distance of the Prussian border.

Budberg, Alexander's foreign minister, tried desperately to maintain his master's belligerent spirit by arguing, somewhat dubiously, that Russia could outlast the French Empire in a prolonged war of attrition. Almost all others who had the Tsar's ear, however, were less sanguine. Nearly every Russian general, for example, now advocated making peace with Napoleon, while Czartoryski warned Alexander that, if the French advanced into Russian Poland, the Poles might well rise up in revolt against him. Even more alarmingly, others whispered that an invasion of Russian soil by the former standard bearers of the French Revolution might trigger a massive serf rebellion.

The possible repercussions of Friedland may have been the most pressing of the reasons for Alexander to make peace with the Emperor in June 1807, but they were not the only ones. For a start, Russian forces were in trouble not just in north-eastern Prussia. Further south, to the north-east of Warsaw, Marshal Masséna and his 30,000-strong army had thrown the 16,000 Russian troops left there by Bennigsen into full retreat after soundly beating them in a battle near the Narew river on 12 June. Further south still, in the Balkans, the war against the Turks had started to go badly. The Serbs, in revolt against their Ottoman overlords since 1804, had failed to prove as valuable allies as St Petersburg had hoped, while the Turkish army had recovered from its initial defeats in the Principalities. In April, with the aid of cannon sent by the French forces in Dalmatia, it had thwarted the efforts of the Serb rebels to link up with the Russians in western Wallachia. Then, in late May, the Turks had crossed the Danube and advanced speedily upon the Wallachian capital of Bucharest, besieging the city from early June. Finally, there was pressure upon Russia's flank in the Caucasus, where elements of the Tsar's army had been engaged in fitful hostilities with Persia ever since Georgia had been annexed several years earlier. Unwilling to agree to an arrogant peace offer, put forward by the Russians in early 1807, that would have preserved their gains and allowed for further expansion at Persia's expense in the future, the Persian Shah had turned to France for help. An alliance had subsequently been signed in early May by which the French pledged to send the Shah both advisers and material in order to increase the effectiveness of the Persian armies.

Compounding Russia's military predicament, it was clear that Austria was not going to join the war against Napoleon and that little effective assistance could be expected from either the British or the Swedes. The situation seemed truly hopeless, Grand Duke Constantine, the Tsar's brother and heir, bewailing to Alexander: 'If you do not wish to make peace with France, then give a loaded pistol to each of your soldiers and ask them to blow their brains out! You will obtain the same result as will a new and final battle, which will unfailingly open the gates of your empire to French troops, trained for battle and always victorious.' With such despair gripping almost all his chief advisers and generals, the Tsar had little choice. He despatched the courteous and tactful Prince Dmitri Lobanov-Rostovsky to request a truce.

Alexander's envoy met Marshal Berthier, Napoleon's chief of staff, on 19 June at the town of Tilsit (modern Sovetsk) near the left bank of the River Niemen some forty miles east of Königsberg. Rather than adopting an overweening, combative tone, as might have been expected, the Emperor's representative had been instructed to do all he could to charm the Russian prince. Despite having established a powerful military advantage, Napoleon had no desire to press on into Russia. Instead, he had decided to use his crushing victory at Friedland to try to effect a stunning diplomatic coup and win the Tsar as an ally, an idea that had been in the back of his mind for some time but which only now seemed conceivable. To that end, Lobanov was told to reassure his master that in the peace talks, which the French naturally insisted must follow an armistice, the Emperor would not seek to impose humiliating terms on the Russians. Alexander was pleased to hear of the very positive tone of the conversation his envoy had with Berthier on the 19th and then with General Duroc, another of Napoleon's closest aides, the following day. The Tsar duly authorized the signing of a one-month armistice on 21 June, with negotiations for a Franco-Russian settlement to follow.

The Emperor took his charm offensive one step further on the evening of the 22nd when he dined with Prince Lobanov. Drinking the health of the Tsar and flattering his envoy, Napoleon asserted that 'The reciprocal interest of our two empires calls for an alliance between them'. He then pointed to the Vistula on a map and declared, 'Here is the boundary of our two empires. Your master must dominate one side and I the other.' The message seemed clear. Rather than seeking to reduce or restrict Russian power and influence in Europe, the Emperor appeared to be offering Alexander the chance to share in the domination of the Continent.

Upon hearing of Napoleon's conversation with Lobanov the next day, the Tsar's pessimistic demeanour of recent days transmuted into an excited mood of hope. Suddenly, it seemed that Alexander might be able to restore through peace the prestige he had lost in war. Instead of ending the struggle against France with his tail between his legs, the Tsar had a chance to exploit the Emperor's proffered hand of friendship to increase his and Russia's power and international standing. Of course, making an alliance with Napoleon would involve a reversal of foreign policy even more spectacular than that engineered by his father in 1800–1, but that does not seem to have troubled him. He saw only a profitable way out of an unpleasant situation and he determined to grasp it with both hands. He therefore instructed Lobanov to return to Bonaparte the next day and inform him (the barefaced cheek is almost comical) that 'union between France and Russia has been constantly the object of my desires and that I have the conviction that this alone will ensure the happiness and tranquillity of the world'.

Napoleon was thrilled (and doubtless somewhat amused) to be told on 24 June of the Tsar's burning passion for an alliance. Seizing upon another of Alexander's comments as reported to him by Lobanov, that the two rulers should negotiate without intermediaries, he immediately suggested a meeting between himself and the Tsar the next day. The trouble was to decide where such an encounter should take place. Napoleon, as the victor, was disinclined to go to Alexander, while to summon the Tsar to him might undermine his attempt to woo the

Russian ruler. The Emperor himself came up with the imaginative solution. His engineers would assemble a massive raft in the centre of the Niemen river, which demarcated the limit of the French advance at the time of the armistice of 21 June, and the two men would meet there, on neutral 'territory'.

As promised, the Emperor's engineers had the raft on the Niemen constructed and securely tethered to the piles of a bridge recently destroyed by retreating Russian soldiers by the following morning. Upon it, they had erected two pavilions made of wood and draped with canvas and white linen. The larger of these two pavilions was where the meeting would take place and the French troops had taken the care of painting an 'N' on the side facing the French-held western bank and an 'A' on the Russian side.

Alexander arrived at the right bank of the Niemen as early as 11 a.m. on 25 June and had to hang around for two hours until Napoleon appeared shortly before one o'clock on the opposite shore. The two rulers then clambered aboard boats and were rowed towards the raft, their progress marked by the cheering of troops lined up on both sides of the river and by a salute from the French artillery.

Having the better oarsmen, the Emperor reached the raft first and proceeded to march through the pavilion to greet the Tsar as he finally arrived. Disembarking from his boat, Alexander towered over Napoleon, a result of the Tsar's unusual height of six feet, more than of the Emperor's shortness (at around 5 foot 3 inches he was just a couple of inches below average height for a man in this period). The two men shook hands warmly before disappearing into the seclusion of the pavilion. They emerged almost two hours later, both smiling broadly.

There is no contemporary record of what the two emperors actually said to each other on the raft in the middle of the Niemen, but what is certain is that Alexander was bowled over by Napoleon's charm and intellectual brilliance to such an extent that he underwent an almost religious conversion in his view of his former enemy. The Tsar returned to his side of the river boldly declaring 'If only I had seen him sooner! The veil is torn aside and the time of error is past.' Soon after, he confessed 'I never had more prejudices against anyone than against him, but after three-quarters of an hour of conversation, they all disappeared like a dream.' Alexander was ever vulnerable to flattery and Napoleon, with his superb judgement of character, was just the man to apply it to maximum effect.

The Emperor too was favourably impressed by the young Tsar, writing to Josephine that evening, 'I have just seen the Emperor Alexander and have been very pleased with him'. Much of his pleasure was due to the attitude Russia's ruler had displayed towards Napoleon's most inveterate enemies, the British. Indeed, Alexander's first words upon meeting Bonaparte allegedly were, 'Sire, I hate the British as much as you do', to which the Emperor had supposedly replied, 'In that case, peace is made'. Whether that exchange really did take place is uncertain, but there is no doubt that the Tsar gave Napoleon the impression during their long conversation that he had no love for the British and, indeed, would be prepared to cooperate with the French in trying to force London to agree to a peace settlement with Paris.

The final upshot of the first meeting between the Emperor and the Tsar was that Napoleon agreed to Alexander's request that the King of Prussia be invited to join in the peace talks in the coming days. Frederick William was therefore in attendance on the raft when the Russian and French rulers met again on the 26th, but his presence somewhat soured the atmosphere. Although an armistice between Prussian and French forces was formally signed, the King adopted a cold attitude towards the Emperor. A sense of his mindset can be gauged from a letter he wrote to his wife, Louise, that evening: 'I have seen him, I have spoken to that monster, choked out of hell, formed by Beelzebub to be the scourge of the earth … Never yet have I passed through a more rude trial; all my faculties were in revolt during that terrible interview.' Frederick William's frosty manner towards Napoleon might have eased his frustration at seeing all but a tiny sliver of his kingdom overrun by the 'demonic' French, but it did his country no favours, for it destroyed any hope there might have been that the Emperor would not impose an extremely harsh settlement upon Prussia. Pointedly, Napoleon invited Alexander to dine with him that evening but not Frederick William.

The day after the second meeting on the raft, 27 June, the Tsar took up Napoleon's offer to set up base in Tilsit on the southern side of the Niemen where the Emperor had established his own headquarters. Frederick William was provided with lodgings in the town, too, though nowhere near such fine ones as were found for the Russians. Over the next week and a half, there was a succession of dinners, parties, parades and inspections. Although, somewhat ominously, the level of friendship between the rival army commanders rarely went beyond standard civility, Alexander and Napoleon met every day, talking amiably about world affairs and their visions for the future. They shared long horse rides in the country, exchanged cravats and embroidered handkerchiefs, and asked politely after the wellbeing of each other's families. It was all too much for the Tsar's passionately anti-French foreign minister, General Budberg, who left Tilsit for St Petersburg, the more pliable Prince Lobanov becoming chief Russian negotiator at the peace talks which began at the end of the month.

Those peace talks soon resulted in what is usually erroneously referred to as the Treaty of Tilsit. In actual fact, there were three treaties reached, two between the French and Russians, signed on 7 July and ratified two days later, and one between France and Prussia, signed on 9 July and ratified on the 12th. Between them, they revolutionized European relations and provided a basis for the long-term hegemony of Napoleonic France over most of the Continent. Their terms therefore deserve close attention.

It is easiest to begin with the fate of Prussia, where French occupation of practically the entire kingdom gave Napoleon the whip hand. In short, the Emperor determined that she should no longer be a great power. He remembered how Berlin had come within a whisker of declaring war and putting him in a most unfavourable predicament in the days before Austerlitz. He also recalled that, having given Prussia a second chance (as he saw it) in 1806 by making her an ally of France and giving her Hanover, she had insulted him and compromised French security by making an alliance with Russia, a country with which he was at war. Finally, he bore in mind the foolishly discourteous manner Frederick William had adopted towards him during their recent encounters. Napoleon's attitude was, therefore, ruthless but logical. If the Prussians could not be relied upon not to challenge France, they would be reduced to the status they had occupied before Frederick the Great had made them a major force on the European scene; that of a local power only. To this end, Prussia was stripped of no less than a third of her territory and half her population. A massive indemnity of 160,000,000 francs was imposed upon her and French occupation forces were to remain in the country until it had all been paid. The Prussian government acknowledged all Napoleon's territorial and political changes in Europe, including the Confederation of the Rhine, rejoined the Continental Blockade of Britain, and, once more, formally became a French ally.

Unsurprisingly, the Prussians were horrified and many felt betrayed by their erstwhile Russian allies for failing to compel Napoleon to ameliorate his terms. In truth, there was little the Russians could have done, short of threatening to renew the war, and that was not something the Tsar was any longer at all minded to do. In any case, Alexander did not renege on his friendship with Prussia entirely. He did adamantly, and successfully, resist a French proposal to strip her of Silesia, and he also seems to have persuaded the Emperor not to depose the Hohenzollern dynasty. Indeed, it was openly stated in the text of the treaty of 9 June that Frederick William and Louise were only being allowed to retain their thrones out of 'considerations of the wishes of His Majesty the Emperor of All the Russias'.

By imposing such a draconian settlement upon the Prussians, Napoleon was of course potentially sowing the seeds of future problems borne of resentment and anger. The point has already been made with reference to the peace deal made with Austria after Austerlitz, however – resentment and anger there may have been, but Prussia was in no position to do much about it unless Napoleonic France was weakened by someone else. As we shall see, the Prussian elite did not dare take up arms against the French again until Napoleon had suffered a truly horrendous military reverse.

Besides, the dismemberment of Prussia in 1807 was by no means as intolerable and unacceptable in the long term as is sometimes supposed. It was more the break up of an empire than of a homogeneous state, akin perhaps to the partition of the Soviet Union in the early 1990s. The heartlands of old Prussia were left intact, the vast bulk of what was stripped from her being more recent acquisitions west of the Elbe River or in former Poland. Over time, there is no reason why Prussia could not have come to accept that she was no longer a great power, as many other former major powers have had to do.

So what happened to the lands Prussia lost? Those west of the Elbe either went to French allies, such as Saxony, or (the majority of them) were formed into the new kingdom of Westphalia. This realm, which joined the Confederation of the Rhine and was ruled by Napoleon's younger brother Jerome, was intended by the Emperor to be an example to the rest of Germany of what could be achieved if French ideas and practices were followed. To that end, it was given the first constitution in German history; one, moreover, which embodied many of the ideals of the French Revolution. It was also provided with modern, efficient administration and law. Admittedly, Westphalia never turned out to be quite the flaming beacon Napoleon had hoped, partly because the frivolous Jerome was not perhaps the ideal candidate to carry the torch, but it was nonetheless a clear and progressive step forward in the modernization of Germany.

In eastern Europe, the important Baltic port of Danzig was officially made a free city, but it was to be garrisoned by the French. More significantly, the former Polish lands annexed by Prussia in the 1790s were made into the Grand Duchy of Warsaw. This was effectively a resurrected Polish state, but one with limitations. It was to be ruled, at least officially, by King Frederick Augustus of Saxony rather than by a Pole, although Poles were to dominate the government. It was also, pointedly, not called Poland. Its foreign policy was to be dominated, through its anomalous membership of the Confederation of the Rhine, by Napoleon. Finally, no pledge or suggestion of any kind was made that it would ever extend beyond the boundaries established in 1807 to incorporate the vast Polish lands lost to Austria and especially Russia. Indeed, the small province of Bialystok on the Russian border was handed over to the Tsar to create a more coherent frontier between the new state and Russia.

Interestingly, the creation of the Grand Duchy of Warsaw had not been the Emperor's first thought of how to deal with the Polish question. Initially, during the Tilsit negotiations, he had suggested that, in return for Alexander agreeing to Prussia being stripped of Silesia, Prussia's former Polish lands could be given to the Tsar, provided that he amalgamate them in a resurrected Kingdom of Poland, united to Russia in the person of the Russian ruler. This, Napoleon hoped, would at least partly satisfy Polish national aspirations whilst also estranging Russia and Prussia. Alexander was tempted by the offer but ultimately declined, allegedly out of 'what was left of my regard for unfortunate Prussia'. That his regard for Prussia was negotiable, however, was proved by his suggestion that Russia simply be given all Prussian territory east of the Vistula. Clearly, the Tsar felt that if a permanent wedge were to be driven between St Petersburg and Berlin, he would have to receive as compensation a substantial territorial gain over which his rule could be assured, not one that was to be absorbed within a semi-autonomous greater Poland whose loyalty to Russia might well prove considerably less than absolute. Napoleon, however, his words to Prince Lobanov on 22 June regarding the Vistula marking the dividing line between French and Russian spheres of influence notwithstanding, was not prepared to accede to Alexander's proposal. Perhaps he baulked at the idea of Russia's *direct* control being advanced that far westwards. Or maybe he genuinely felt some kind of debt to the Poles who had helped him in his recent campaign and so did not want to hand large areas of Polish territory over to the Russians without a pledge from the Tsar to recreate a Polish state. Either way, the failure to reach agreement on Napoleon's and Alexander's initial suggestions paved the way for the establishment of the Grand Duchy of Warsaw. This broadly satisfied the Emperor because it went some way towards appeasing Polish national aspirations whilst giving him a dominating influence over Polish military and diplomatic affairs. It was just acceptable too to the Tsar on the grounds that Napoleon had clearly made some effort to take Russian sensitivities into account by not calling the new state Poland, not assigning it a Polish king, and not giving the Poles any reason to hope to expand at Russia's expense.

If the Franco-Prussian treaty signed at Tilsit provided for sweeping territorial and political changes, the accord re-establishing peace between the French and Russians was less dramatic. Both nations pledged to resume normal diplomatic and commercial relations as soon as possible, and each side recognized the titles and possessions claimed by the other – this included Russian acknowledgement of the Confederation of the Rhine, the Grand Duchy of Warsaw and even French control over Dalmatia, as well as acceptance of Napoleon's brothers as rulers of Naples, Holland and the new kingdom of Westphalia. In the Adriatic, where a small scale Franco-Russian conflict had been going on since spring 1806, Russia agreed to evacuate Cattaro and the Ionian islands, both of which were to be occupied by the French. Finally, the Tsar undertook to withdraw his troops from Moldavia and Wallachia on condition that Ottoman forces did not reoccupy them until a settlement had been signed between St Petersburg and Constantinople.

The terms of the Franco-Russian peace treaty signed at Tilsit, then, seemed mild in light of the military reverses recently suffered by Russia in north-eastern Prussia and elsewhere, but it paved the way for the secret treaty of alliance the French and Russians also signed on 7 July. By the provisions of this agreement, the two countries not only pledged to come to each other's aid should another of the European powers go to war with either of them, but also swore not to make a separate peace should they find themselves fighting on the same side in a conflict.

Those promises were monumental enough for the future of European relations, but the new Russo-French alliance did not stop there, for it also addressed the fate of specific areas. One such was Sweden and her vassal state Finland. Over these two nations, the Emperor conceded to Russia a free hand at Tilsit. Alexander was delighted, as in a war against the Swedes to annex Finland he saw a chance for Russian arms to recover some of the prestige they had recently lost.

Another area whose fate was much discussed at Tilsit was the Ottoman Empire. In late June, news had arrived that Sultan Selim had been overthrown in a revolution. Napoleon leapt upon this as an excuse to adopt a rather different line towards the Turks than the one he had been pursuing for the past eighteen months. By the terms of the alliance treaty with Russia, the Emperor pledged to join the Tsar in his war against the Turks unless Constantinople accepted French mediation and made peace with St Petersburg within three months. Even more significant than that, Napoleon raised the issue at Tilsit of a possible future partition of the Ottoman Empire and agreed that, should the Turks not accept his mediation, they would forfeit all their European territory with the exception of Constantinople and its hinterland (effectively what constitutes modern European Turkey). Beyond this, no specific French promises were made, but Alexander left Tilsit with the firm impression that the Emperor would concede to him a free hand in at least the eastern half of south-east Europe. Ideally, of course, the Russians wanted to take over all the Ottoman Empire's European possessions, but, given the establishment of a strong French presence in Dalmatia, the dominant influence France had won for herself at Constantinople over the past year, and Russia's recent military travails, an equal share in a Turkish partition seemed attractive enough in summer 1807.

Just as Napoleon seemed ready to abandon his improved relations with the Turks at Tilsit, so Alexander was prepared to make an equally dramatic *volte-face*. By the terms of the secret treaty of alliance, Russia undertook to offer to mediate a peace between France and Britain based upon recognition of the freedom of the seas and the exchange of Hanover for the British-occupied former French, Spanish and Dutch colonies around the world. Should London refuse such mediation by 1 November 1807, the Tsar pledged to declare war on Britain and to join the Continental Blockade. Then Russia and France would jointly 'invite' Denmark, Sweden and Portugal to close their ports to British trade and go to war against Britain too. If they refused, they were to be treated as enemies. The French and Russians would also put pressure on Austria to join the Continental Blockade and declare war on Britain, although no proviso was included in the Tilsit treaty for treating the Austrians as enemies should they refuse. In essence, therefore, Britain was to be given a choice between making peace on terms favourable to the French or having the whole of the Continent turned against her.

The Emperor's sudden readiness, in summer 1807, to abandon the Turks in favour of a Russian alliance is easy enough to explain. After all, he had courted Constantinople primarily as a means of putting pressure on Russia. Now that such pressure no longer seemed to be necessary, the rationale behind maintaining good Franco-Turkish relations had been undermined. Besides, we have seen how an alliance with Russia had been something that Napoleon had considered would be of great advantage to France ever since 1800. As recently as March 1807 he had reiterated to Talleyrand that, 'I am of the opinion that an alliance with Russia would be very advantageous, if the idea were not fantastic'. By mid-June, in the wake of Friedland and with the Tsar finally willing to make peace, the idea no longer seemed quite so implausible, so it is little surprise that he tried for an alliance, even though such a move was certain to compromise his relations with the Ottoman Empire.

Alexander's leap from arch-enemy of Napoleon to his closest ally, in the space of a month, takes rather more explanation, as it involved the abandonment of relationships upon which Russia had placed considerable importance for some time, and the adoption of a radically new stance in foreign affairs. For the past five years, the Tsar's foreign policy had been characterized by a growing personal animosity towards the Emperor, and by efforts to build and maintain coalitions dedicated to opposing France and her ruler. A major aspect of that had been attempts to work, sometimes closely, with nations such as Austria, Sweden and Britain against which Russia was now turning to varying degrees. Why, then, did Alexander take up Napoleon's offer of alliance so readily instead of settling for merely signing the lenient peace treaty put forward at Tilsit?

To a large extent, we have already answered that question. The Tsar's personal animosity towards Napoleon seemingly evaporated within an hour of meeting the great man. The suggested alliance actually offered Russia something positive (the prospect of territorial aggrandizement in Scandinavia and south-east Europe), whereas the peace treaty, though lenient, gave the Russians nothing other than an end to hostilities. And, of course, the main reason why the peace settlement at Tilsit was less unfavourable to Russia than it might have been was that Napoleon knew that his former enemy was becoming his ally. Had Alexander rebuffed any notion of an alliance with France, the Emperor might well, for example, have broken up Prussia more severely than he did and have created a larger, more threatening Polish state on Russia's borders.

As well as what we might term the 'pull' factors in favour of making a French alliance, however, there were also significant 'push' factors driving Russia apart from her allies of recent years. By early summer 1807, the Russians had become exasperated with the recalcitrant Austrians and their refusal to enter the war, so they went into the negotiations at Tilsit without the slightest feeling of debt to, or consideration for, Vienna. The Swedes, of course, had been at war with the French, but as far as the Russians were concerned, they might as well not have been for all the use they had proved. Their willingness to agree an armistice in Swedish Pomerania at the end of April 1807 had, after all, freed Marshal Mortier's corps to arrive at Danzig in May and campaign with Napoleon in June.

It was towards the British, however, that many Russians had developed an especial bitterness by summer 1807. There was anger at London maintaining an essentially unfriendly attitude towards Prussia for having annexed Hanover even after Berlin had gone to war with Napoleon, a posture that made cooperation within the Fourth Coalition even trickier than it already was. More damaging, there was frustration at the British not making the kind of military contribution to the war against France on land that the Russians felt they should have. St Petersburg was desperate for tens of thousands of British soldiers to be landed in the Baltic to relieve pressure on the Prusso-Russian forces in eastern Prussia, but by the time a small expeditionary force did finally arrive in summer 1807 it was far too little far too late. This created the dangerous (and not entirely unjustified) impression in Russia that Britain was fighting the Emperor to the last European. This insidious belief was exacerbated, moreover, by the fact that the British managed to find plenty of troops to send to attack the Spanish Empire in South America in the winter of 1806 and to invade Egypt in March 1807 (campaigns which both ended in defeat and withdrawal in summer 1807). As far as many Russians were concerned, they were being played for fools by London. While Russia bore the brunt of the effort to reduce French dominance on the Continent, the British exploited the situation to try to expand their power and influence overseas. Such powerful negative feelings might have been obviated if Britain had proved more forthcoming on economic issues in 1807, but even here the Russians felt sorely disappointed. Not only did London renege on a promise to loan Russia £5,000,000, but all the discussions the British and Russians had regarding political and strategic affairs in the first half of 1807 were hindered by demands for greater privileges for British merchants in Russia. Finally, adding insult to injury, the adoption in early 1807, in response to Napoleon's introduction of the Continental Blockade, of a more rigorous obstruction of French trade by the Royal Navy increased the instances of British interference with Russian ships and reinvigorated hostility towards Britain's domination of the seas. By the time Alexander met Napoleon on the Niemen, therefore the Tsar had become so embittered towards his British allies that he felt no compunction in committing Russia to an alliance that might well result in war between the two countries.

Powerful as the 'push' factors were, the factors pulling Alexander towards an alliance with France in summer 1807 were undoubtedly the more important.

For the past five years, the young Tsar had pursued a policy of opposition to the French Emperor that had only resulted in military defeat and the extension of Napoleonic influence to the very borders of Russia. Now, having met and been charmed by the 'Corsican upstart', having indeed been proffered the hand of friendship and a chance to expand Russian power and influence in alliance with France, Alexander decided to try a radically different course in foreign affairs.

On 8 July, the day after the two treaties between France and Russia were signed, a great military parade was held at Tilsit. In the new spirit of amity between the two nations, Napoleon bestowed upon the Tsar, his brother Constantine and all the senior Russian generals present the Grand Cross of the Legion of Honour, France's highest award. Then, in a typically Napoleonic moment of poignancy and drama, the Emperor halted his inspection of the Russian Preobrazhensky Guards, an elite unit, to ask who the bravest soldier in the regiment was. Upon being told, Napoleon stepped forward to the man, removed his own cross of the Legion of Honour and presented it to him. Alexander was not able to match such splendid theatricality, but he did award Napoleon the Cross of St Andrew, Russia's highest order of chivalry.

That evening, the Tsar and the Emperor dined together one last time and then stayed up long into the night talking as if they had been companions since childhood. The following day, the Franco-Russian treaties were ratified at Alexander's lodgings, where the two rulers were again to be seen conversing affably and pledging eternal friendship. Napoleon then escorted the Tsar to the Niemen, embraced him warmly and waved him off as he was rowed back across the river. It had been a monumental past fortnight during which the Emperor, by successfully forming an alliance with Russia, had established a basis upon which French hegemony throughout most of Europe might be maintained in the long term. Never had Napoleon or France been in a stronger position than they were now. With Prussia smashed, Austria cowed, Russia friendly and Britain isolated, it seemed that the struggles of the past fifteen years must soon draw to a close, leaving the French and their Emperor spectacularly victorious.

11

At the Crossroads

In late 1806, the Austrian emperor had sent his most promising young diplomat to Paris as ambassador. Still only in his early thirties, Count Klemens Lothar Wenceslas von Metternich was already building a formidable reputation both as an ardent womaniser and, more pertinently, an astute statesman. Within three years, he would be recalled to Vienna from where he would play a crucial role in European as well as Austrian politics for the next four decades, but his introduction to our story at this point is owed to a comment he made shortly after the conclusion of the Tilsit settlement in summer 1807. With the ink still practically drying on the treaties, he confidently reported to his masters in Vienna that 'the day when the French and Russian emperors will fall out is inevitable, and, according to my innermost feelings, much nearer than many people suppose'. This bold assertion reflected a common belief in Europe at the time, and one, moreover, which has been shared by many historians since: that the Franco-Russian alliance established at Tilsit was, in reality, a charade, that it could not possibly last, and that future enmity between the two countries was unavoidable.

On the face of it, this idea that France and Russia were never real allies and were certain to confront each other again before long has much to support it. It seems clear, for example, that Alexander's popularity in Russia dropped in late 1807 as the extent to which he had tied his country to Napoleonic France became clear. Among Russia's peasant masses, the Tsar's decision to enlist the support of the Orthodox Church in deriding the French emperor as some kind of Antichrist in late 1806 backfired after Tilsit, when Alexander found himself allied to this supposedly demonic figure. Given that the great majority of Russia's lower orders remained as politically ignorant as they were politically insignificant, however, and so knew nothing and cared even less about their ruler's diplomatic tergiversations, there was no mass opposition to Alexander's new policy.

Among the Russian upper and middle classes, the picture that emerges post-Tilsit is one of pretty considerable disquiet and often downright hostility to the new French alliance. There were even rumours of plots against Alexander's life in autumn 1807. The reasons Russia's more privileged citizens had for disliking the Tsar's diplomatic *volte-face* were several. For a start, many of the Russian elite felt a sense of humiliation at their country's recent heavy defeat at the hands of the French. This was only exacerbated by the creation of an, albeit restricted, Polish state and the continued presence after summer 1807 of large numbers of Napoleonic troops throughout Prussia, both of which were widely seen as an affront to Russian prestige and a threat to her security. Then there were what might be termed social considerations. Much of the Russian nobility was unhappy with the new French alliance on the grounds that they still saw Napoleon as the figurehead of the French Revolution's assault on the *ancien régime*. Many Russian aristocrats were also strongly influenced by the large number of noble French *émigrés* who had been allowed to settle in St Petersburg and who assiduously fanned the flames of anti-Bonapartism in the hope that their Russian hosts might do all in their power to help restore the old Bourbon regime in France. Certainly, the refined *émigrés* were much more to the snobbish taste of most Russian aristocrats than the man Napoleon initially sent to the Russian capital as his representative. General Savary, one of the Emperor's most trusted aides, could be vain, tetchy and arrogant, and he did not help his case by making little effort to conceal his disdain for Russia and its backward ways. He was also hamstrung from the start by the fact that he was known to have played a key role in the abduction and execution of that favourite 'martyr' of Europe's nobility, the Duc d'Enghien.

The issue most often cited by historians who have agreed with Metternich's claim that the Franco-Russian alliance was doomed from the start, however, is that of Alexander's agreement to break with the British if they did not make peace on terms favourable to the French. There was certainly a powerful Anglophile party among the Russian nobility who could hardly be anything but perturbed by the Tsar's abrupt anti-British, pro-French move. Many of these aristocrats had significant commercial interests and they, along with many of the rest of Russia's merchants, were alarmed by the threat to trade with Britain that Tilsit posed. In fact, it is often claimed that British trade was so important to the Russian economy that there was no way that Alexander could have maintained the French alliance for long in the face of the economic devastation and political unrest that adherence to Napoleon's Continental Blockade was bound to bring. Commerce, and their geographical position as the flank powers in Europe, made Britain and Russia natural allies, it has been argued, so it was only a matter of time before the Tsar brought Russia back into the anti-French fold. The Franco-Russian alliance, was bound to fail.

Or was it? Certainly, some of the obstacles threatening its survival were serious, but none of them was insurmountable, as sometimes claimed. For example, the unpopular Savary did not stay long in St Petersburg. Before 1807 was out, a new Napoleonic representative had arrived in Russia to supersede him. The thirty-four-year-old General Armand de Caulaincourt was much more to the taste of the St Petersburg nobility. An aristocrat of the *ancien régime* who had wholeheartedly accepted the new Napoleonic order in France, the new French ambassador was sophisticated, tactful and gracious, and soon became popular within Russian high society.

If Caulaincourt's arrival removed a potentially damaging personal factor in St Petersburg, another was soon dealt with in Paris too. Russia's first ambassador to France following Tilsit, Count Petr Alexandrovich Tolstoi, was a strong Francophobe and did little to hide his opposition to the alliance he was theoretically supposed to help uphold. When Alexander was made aware of the extent of his representative's hostility towards the French alliance by complaints from Napoleon, the Tsar recalled him and sent in his stead Prince Alexander Kurakin. Kurakin was a wealthy, vain and ostentatious character in his mid-fifties, but he was also a skilled diplomat and, most important, had something of a stake in the Franco-Russian alliance as he had helped to negotiate the Tilsit treaties.

Perhaps the most significant changes in personnel in the early months of the Russo-French alliance, however, were those at the head of the foreign ministries in both Paris and St Petersburg. In August 1807, the unctuous Charles Maurice de Talleyrand resigned as Napoleon's foreign minister. The split had been some time coming, for the two men never really liked each other and had grown further and further apart in the past couple of years over the direction of French foreign policy. Talleyrand had opposed any alliance with the Russian 'barbarians', so the Emperor's decision to make one in summer 1807 provided an appropriate opportunity for his resignation. Somewhat surprisingly, Napoleon retained Talleyrand in a senior domestic role and called upon his diplomatic skills on an *ad hoc* basis over the next couple of years. The former foreign minister, typically, would repay this continued Imperial favour with treachery. Still, he could do less damage to the Franco-Russian alliance outside the foreign ministry than he could have done had he remained at its head. His replacement was Jean-Baptiste de Champagny, a less able but more loyal statesman.

In Russia, meanwhile, the Francophobic foreign minister General Andrei Budberg found the French alliance so distasteful that he tendered his resignation shortly after Tilsit. It was characteristic of Alexander that he did not accept straightaway – the Tsar always found parting with his ministers difficult, even if he had diverged with them intolerably over policy – though in this case he had good reason. The abrupt departure of Budberg from the foreign ministry might have made the fact that there was disquiet with the new direction of Russian policy too obvious for comfort. For the rest of the summer of 1807, therefore, Budberg continued to say the right things in public, albeit without enthusiasm, while taking a totally different line in private. Indeed he even went so far as to flirt with treason by informally telling the British ambassador in St Petersburg that the settlement reached at Tilsit 'must be considered as a momentary respite and by no means as affording any prospect of permanent tranquillity' between France and Russia. By early September, following repeated pleas from Budberg that he be allowed to resign, the Tsar finally decided to make the break, officially on grounds of ill health. One of the most senior and ardent opponents of the Franco-Russian alliance had been removed.

Budberg's replacement at the foreign ministry could not have been better suited to serving the Tsar's new policy of friendship with France and enmity towards Britain. Count Nikolai Petrovich Rumiantsev was the son of one of Catherine the Great's foremost generals, a man who had made his reputation by repeatedly defeating the Turks. Fabulously wealthy, very affable and generally charming, Rumiantsev was in his early fifties when Alexander offered him the post of foreign minister that he had long craved, allowing him to retain his current position as minister of commerce at the same time. He was a passionate Russian nationalist whose two great hopes were the establishment of a more independent and thriving Russian trade, especially in the Black Sea and Balkans, and the extension of Russia's borders in south-east Europe to incorporate Constantinople, the Straits and as much of Ottoman Europe as possible. If not an uninhibited Francophile, he had at least consistently opposed war between Russia and France, viewing it as futile and a distraction from the pursuit of Russia's real interests. He had argued against breaking relations with France following the Enghien affair in 1804, opposed the Tsar's efforts to form the Third Coalition, and urged that an immediate arrangement be sought with Napoleon in the wake of Austerlitz. Right through to its achievement at Tilsit, Rumiantsev had advocated that peace should be made with the French. As if this were not enough to recommend him as the ideal spokesman for Alexander's new foreign policy, he also, as the British ambassador in St Petersburg sadly confessed to his masters in London, had 'no very favourable sentiments towards Great Britain'. Indeed, he welcomed the opportunity to try to weaken the powerful commercial influence the British had in Russia and fervently hoped one day to see the destruction of what he called 'the despotism which [England] exercises on the seas'.

Crucial as it was for the survival of the nascent Franco-Russian alliance to have a foreign minister in Russia favourable to its maintenance, even more important was the attitude of the Russian autocrat. Given the Tsar's pivotal position in Russian politics, the alliance could not hope to last without his genuine support. The innermost thoughts of the complex character of Alexander Romanov are often difficult to fathom at a distance of two centuries, but it seems clear that he was committed to the Franco-Russian alliance in the wake of Tilsit and not, as is sometimes claimed, that it was just a sham on his part, a measure solely to buy time before lining up again in the ranks of Napoleon's adversaries. While still at Tilsit negotiating the treaties of peace and alliance, he had written to his favourite sister, Catherine, with whom he was generally honest, to tell her of his pleasure with the way things were going. 'God has saved us,' he wrote. 'Instead of sacrifices, we have emerged from the contest with a sort of lustre.' Once back in St Petersburg, the pro-French feelings that had been awakened on the Niemen remained. Unpopular as General Savary was with much of the Russian nobility, the Tsar wined and dined him warmly, frequently informing the Frenchman of his affection for the Emperor and his dedication to the new alliance. One time, for example, he told Savary, 'I shall never forget the tokens of friendship afforded me by the Emperor Napoleon. The more I think of them, the more happy I am to have known him. What an extraordinary man!' On another occasion, Alexander sought to allay Savary's concern about opposition to the French alliance among the Russian aristocracy by telling him frankly, 'General, I have made my choice and nothing will change it'. This reassuring Francophilia continued, and indeed was perhaps even strengthened, by the arrival of Caulaincourt. Alexander and the young Frenchmen were the same age and got on excellently. Soon, Caulaincourt was being accorded preferential treatment among the foreign representatives in St Petersburg, accompanying the royal family on parade ground reviews and sitting with them at the theatre. The fact is that, far from viewing Tilsit and the French alliance as nothing more than a breathing space, Alexander saw it as a triumph and believed that, where war had failed, diplomacy had won him and Russia a free hand in Scandinavia and much of south-east Europe, and made the Tsar joint arbiter with Napoleon of Europe's affairs. Why shouldn't he support an arrangement like that?

Vital as Alexander's position was to Russian policy, though tsars could be, and sometimes were, brutally removed if they followed a course that was sufficiently unpopular with significant elements of Russia's elite. Russia's ruler was acutely aware of this fact, having seen his own father murdered by a cabal of disgruntled aristocrats in 1801. Moreover, there were rumours of plots to oust Alexander in the second half of 1807. The threat to the young Tsar's throne should not, however, be exaggerated. That Alexander felt able to leave his capital in mid-October to tour Belorussia indicates that he, a man more sensitive than anyone to the possibility of a coup, considered that opposition to his foreign policy was not sufficient to provoke an attempt to overthrow him. While not discounting the possibility of a British-funded assassination attempt on the Tsar at some point in the future if he continued to support the French alliance, the chances of Alexander being removed from power by a coup were only likely to become serious if the major issues that worked against the maintenance of the French alliance could not be resolved, ameliorated or ignored. Having examined how most of the key personalities involved were, by early 1808 at least, favourable to the maintenance of the alliance reached at Tilsit, it is time to look in detail at the issues that potentially divided the French and the Russians.

The threat to the Franco-Russian alliance by the negative image in Russia of

Napoleon and the French was unlikely to go away completely, but equally unlikely to prove intense enough to have any real impact on Russian policy. The grievance felt by some against France for losses suffered in war, or against her emperor for his professed connections with either the assault on the *ancien régime* or irreligion, were all things bound to fade over time, especially if the alliance produced the benefits Alexander and its supporters hoped of it. The belief that Bonaparte was the Antichrist was never, one presumes, taken at face value by the bulk of Russia's educated and politically significant citizens, and Napoleon, 'upstart' and moderniser as he was, was never as fierce an antagonist of the *ancien régime* as the revolutionary radicals who had executed Louis XVI and overseen the Terror in the 1790s – he did, after all, repress the 'dangerous' idea of democracy, make peace with the Church, and re-establish a form of monarchy and (in 1808) nobility.

The more substantial issue of France's domination of much of Europe was, it must be acknowledged, potentially a considerably greater threat to the future of Franco-Russian relations. By 1807, however, most politically significant Russians appear to have drawn the lesson from the events of recent years that French hegemony in western and central Europe was unbreakable without a monumental effort. The shattering defeats of first Austerlitz and then Friedland had demonstrated French military superiority beyond contention. The enormous relief with which peace was greeted by the great majority of Russians in 1807 showed also that they no longer saw the sense in expending ever more money and lives in trying to break Napoleonic mastery over areas far from Russia's own borders and in which she had few interests. Rumiantsev, therefore, was far from unique in post-Tilsit Russia in being prepared to concede to France a free hand in western and central Europe, provided Russia was given one in return in areas that were of direct interest to her. It is instructive to note in this context that Russia made no objection to Napoleon's efforts to extend or cement his control in Iberia or Italy in 1807–8.

Of course, there were certain European issues that remained of considerable importance to Russia. Alexander was always sensitive to any slight to his family's honour and, given the presence of some of his relatives among the ruling circles of various minor European states within France's area of dominance, such as the Grand Duchy of Baden and the Duchy of Oldenburg, there was potential for trouble, though only if the French behaved tactlessly in their dealings with these states.

Prussia was ostensibly a thornier issue in Russo-French relations. To the Russians, the truncated country left after the peace signed at Tilsit should, like Austria, be an independent buffer state between the French and Russian empires, not a kingdom occupied and held in thrall to France by large numbers of Napoleon's troops. The Emperor, however, was loath to give up his best guarantee of the duplicitous Prussian government's future good behaviour by withdrawing his men and restoring full Prussian independence. Given the greatly reduced power of Prussia after Tilsit, though as well as the presence elsewhere in Germany of large numbers of Napoleonic soldiers capable of keeping the Prussians cowed, it seemed likely that Russian desires could be met without undue harm being done to French security.

The trickiest European difficulty confronting the maintenance of the Franco-Russian alliance was the future of Poland. It was also, unfortunately, the issue of most concern to most politically significant Russians. Although the existence of the new Grand Duchy of Warsaw had been accepted by Alexander at Tilsit, its creation was a cause of much anxiety in Russia. A small Polish state whose foreign affairs were dominated by a country allied and friendly to Russia was, superficially at least, nothing for the Russians to worry about, but the problem was more complex than that. Poles and Russians were traditional enemies and rivals, and having played a major role in the three eighteenth-century partitions that destroyed the old Kingdom of Poland, it stuck in the craw of many of the Tsar's subjects to be asked to tolerate the recreation of even a much reduced Polish state.

More alarming than the affront to Russian dignity and pride was the potential threat the Grand Duchy of Warsaw posed to the stability of the north-western areas of the Russian Empire (what today broadly constitutes the Baltic States, Belorussia and part of the Ukraine). These areas had been ruled, before the various partitions, by Poland, so many Russians were understandably concerned that this new Polish state might endeavour to reclaim them, either by stirring up discontent among Poles and other non-Russians within the Tsar's realm or by trying to persuade its patron, Napoleon, to commit himself to the recreation of a greater Polish kingdom, which might replace Russia as France's key ally in eastern Europe. In many ways, therefore, the Polish question was, for the Russians, the main gauge of the Franco-Russian alliance. If the Emperor were to support the expansion of Polish power and promote, or even simply allow to flourish, a sense of Polish nationalism, the alliance would face a very uncertain future. If, on the other hand, he were to suppress Polish nationalism and power, perhaps even return the Grand Duchy of Warsaw to Prussia or cede it in some way to Russia, the threat the Polish issue posed to Franco-Russian relations could be stemmed.

Just as Poland was the yardstick of the Russo-French alliance for most Russians, the issue of Russia severing relations with Britain, in accordance with the agreement reached at Tilsit, was the acid test as far as Napoleon was concerned. For the Russians, however, such a move posed serious problems. The thought of going to war with Britain was only mildly disconcerting from a purely military point of view, for there was little that the British armed forces could do to hurt Russia directly. Severing commerce with Britain, though, was an altogether more worrying prospect.

The British were Russia's most important trading partners. Indeed, the impression was that Britain dominated Russian commerce in the early nineteenth century. How, then, could Russia possibly remain faithful to the French alliance by cutting off trade with the British, especially over the long term? It would, of course, prove difficult, but not impossible. Rumiantsev, like many others, positively welcomed the prospect of weakening the grip Britain had on Russian trade in the hope that it would allow indigenous manufacturers and merchants to prosper. There was also an expectation that the severe reduction in Russia's seaborne trade that would inevitably follow a break with London would be remedied by an equally dramatic increase in trade over land.

Still, there is no denying that Russia's implementation of Napoleon's Continental Blockade hurt her economically. It is erroneous to argue, however, that this meant that Russia's eventual abandonment of the French alliance and return to good relations with Britain was inevitable. The damage done to the Russian economy by the severance of trade with the British was not as calamitous as is sometimes claimed. Trade as a whole only made up 10 per cent, via tariffs, of the state's revenues. To be sure, merchants who made a living from trade with the British suffered as a result of Russia's adherence to the Continental Blockade, but these only formed a small, and moderately important, section of politically significant Russian society. A greater number of the rich were affected by the reduction in the availability and increase in price of seaborne luxury colonial items, such as spices and coffee, but this was an inconvenience rather than the kind of serious grievance that might lead to a coup. In short, distressing as in some ways Russia's observance of the Continental Blockade was, it was not so devastating as to necessitate its abandonment.

Just because it was not *essential* that Russia restore commercial relations with Britain, of course, does not mean that it was not *desirable*, but that only made it important that Russians felt there were benefits to be gained from breaking with the British or from the French alliance in general. The hope of allowing Russian manufacturers and merchants to prosper was one such advantage, although it grew less significant over time as the wish was left largely unfulfilled. The other, even greater hope of Russia joining the Continental Blockade was that it would eventually force Britain to make peace and acknowledge some form of freedom of the seas as well as Russia's joint domination of the Continent with France. This aspiration too was to be frustrated, however.

That still left the French alliance in general to bring benefits to offset the economic harm caused by the break with Britain. There was undoubtedly great potential for it to do so. The Tsar believed that he had been granted at Tilsit a predominant position for Russia in much of the Baltic and south-east Europe and looked forward, along with Rumiantsev and other supporters of his new foreign policy, to recovering much of the prestige lost in recent years by expanding Russian influence at the expense of the Swedes and the Turks. Were these aspirations to be fulfilled with French blessing, perhaps even help, as Alexander fully expected them to be, support for the Franco-Russian alliance in his realm could only be tremendously strengthened.

Europe stood at a crossroads in 1807. The Franco-Russian alliance concluded at Tilsit was not a sham, nor was it inevitably doomed. There were, of course, difficulties to be surmounted, some of them considerable, but the potential for the construction of a lasting, mutually beneficial partnership between France and Russia based on the division of continental Europe into French- and Russian-dominated zones was undoubtedly there. It was the greatest opportunity Napoleon would ever have – perhaps could ever have wished for – to secure his own dynasty's future, to cement French dominance over western and central Europe, and to force the British either to make peace on his terms or face ruin. It is the greatest irony of the period, therefore, that the man who would do most to prevent history from following this path was the Emperor himself.

For the Emperor, the Russian alliance offered two great advantages. First, with Russia friendly to France, Austria and Prussia were that much less likely to oppose French domination of western and central Europe in future, much as they might dislike it (plus, of course, if either *were* foolish enough to confront France regardless, they would be much easier for Napoleon to defeat). This alone was enough to make the Russian alliance something to be treasured, but it also brought a second great advantage to the Emperor: namely the prospect that having Russia side with him would compel the recalcitrant British to make peace on Bonaparte's terms or, failing that, enable Britain finally to be brought to her knees.

It was in accordance with the agreement made at Tilsit that, at the start of August 1807, the Russians offered their services in London as mediators in the ongoing Anglo-French struggle. The move was met, unsurprisingly, with the deepest suspicion by the British government and it was the end of the month before it gave an official reply to the Russian offer. Contrary to the expectations of many, including Napoleon, London's attitude towards the idea of peace with France had not been softened by the Franco-Russian peace and rapprochement at Tilsit but hardened. Displaying the same kind of dogged resistance against logic and hope that was to surface again in 1940, the British resolved to fight on against the odds. They believed, quite rightly, that the only kind of peace that could have been made in 1807 was one which would acknowledge French hegemony in most of Europe. That was unacceptable to London on the grounds that any power in control of so much of the Continent's resources would be in a position, at least in time, to pose a major threat to British security and independence.* The British also shared Metternich's belief that the Emperor and the Tsar would inevitably fall out before too long (again there are echoes of 1940 when there was hope that the alliance between Nazi Germany and Soviet Russia would not last) and so felt that if only they could survive for a few years, maybe even just a few months, good opportunities to chip away at the Napoleonic Empire would surface once more. Meanwhile, the Royal Navy's supremacy would allow Britain to snatch yet more overseas colonies from the French, Spanish, Dutch and anyone else allied to Napoleon or within his empire. Indeed, British colonial expansion during this era reached its zenith after mid-1807.

Opposed as they were to pursuing the possibility of peace with France, however, the British were keen not to offend the Russians by too blunt a rejection of their mediation offer. They therefore expressed vague interest but insisted that certain requests be met before they could accept mediation. These were that the full terms of the agreements reached at Tilsit be divulged to them, that they be made aware of the bases upon which peace talks would be conducted in advance, and that the Tsar provide a statement of his general views on foreign policy, details of any engagements he had entered into with any other power, and some form of proof of his continuing friendship towards Britain. The Russians responded to this immediately, informing London in early September that they could not possibly divulge the terms of the secret treaty made with France at Tilsit but duplicitously assuring the British that there was nothing in them hostile to Britain.

Sensibly, the British were not in the slightest reassured by this Russian reply. Information which had reached London via circuitous routes over the summer all suggested that the secret treaty made at Tilsit was a Franco-Russian alliance aimed, at least partly, at Britain. This development, the British government decided, warranted a bold response and it came at the expense of the unfortunate Danes.

It will be remembered that Denmark had been on the receiving end of a major British naval attack in spring 1801 when a fleet led (in practice if not officially) by Admiral Nelson had battered the Danish Navy at anchor in Copenhagen. That attack had at least been justified by Denmark's membership of the anti-British League of Armed Neutrality, but there was no such excuse for what happened in late summer 1807.

The second British assault on the Danes in the early nineteenth century in some ways came out of the last abject failure of the moribund Fourth Coalition.

---

* This was a fair point, but it is worthy of note that those who governed Britain at this time were not interested even in exploring the possibility of peaceful co-existence with a French-dominated Europe.

Far too late to help the Russians in north-east Prussia, the British despatched an expeditionary force to the Baltic in summer 1807. Encouraged by its imminent arrival, Sweden's unbalanced king, Gustavus IV, foolishly repudiated in July the ceasefire his commanders had made with French forces in the spring, only to see Napoleon's troops sweep effortlessly into Swedish Pomerania and drive the Swedes entirely from the southern shore of the Baltic. This left the British expeditionary force without its envisaged base of operations, but London soon came up with another use for the little army it had spent so much money on despatching to the Baltic. Guessing, quite reasonably, that now he had secured peace with Russia, Napoleon would try to build an anti-British naval coalition, to which Denmark's fleet would be an excellent addition, London decided to pre-empt the Emperor. In mid-August, therefore, after the Danes had refused a peremptory demand that they ally themselves with Britain and surrender their navy into British custody, the expeditionary force landed on the Danish island of Zealand, in the east of which lies the capital, Copenhagen. Over the following fortnight, the city was placed under siege by the British army while a large Royal Navy fleet prevented the Danish warships in the harbour from escaping. As in 1801, the Danes put up a stronger fight than expected, but it was always a David versus Goliath struggle. When, in early September, the British began to bombard Copenhagen heavily, the game was soon up and the white flag was raised above the city's ramparts. Fully a third of the Danish capital had been destroyed and some 2,000 civilians killed by the British bombardment, but London had achieved its main goal. The fifteen warships of Denmark's navy were sailed back to Britain.

The British attack on neutral Denmark in 1807 has caused controversy ever since (at least outside Britain). Legally, it was entirely without justification, but in terms of *realpolitik* it was a perfectly rational, if undeniably brutal, thing to do, just as the sinking of the French fleet in North Africa 133 years later would be. It was also, like that later action, intended to send a message of Britain's determination to fight on and ability to hurt those who opposed her. This latter point was, in 1807, especially intended for St Petersburg, in the hope that this dramatic show of force would dissuade the Tsar from pursuing too anti-British a policy and strengthen the hand of those in Russia who still felt that she should ally with Britain against France and not the other way around.

If the message from Copenhagen that the British were not going to make peace was received loud and clear, however, any hope that it would bring Russia round to a less anti-British position was soon dashed. Alexander was furious when he heard news of the British action, and any concern he might have felt about the vulnerability of Russia's Baltic coast to the depredations of the Royal Navy should he break with London was as nothing compared to the fear of what Napoleon's army might conceivably do should the Tsar renege on the agreements he made at Tilsit. With anger at the assault on Copenhagen adding to frustration at Britain's refusal to accept Russian mediation, the break could not be long in coming. The Tsar ramped up the tension as the autumn progressed by stridently denouncing British interference with neutral vessels at sea, turning the issue, indeed, into a *casus belli*. By the start of November, as Alexander had pledged at Tilsit she would be, Russia was officially at war with Britain. If ever proof were needed of the genuineness of the Tsar's commitment to the French alliance in 1807, this was surely it.

For the next five years, Russia and Britain remained enemies, with British ships banned from Russian ports in accordance with the Continental Blockade. Military encounters between the two powers were minimal – a Russian flotilla surrendered to the British at Lisbon in 1808 without a fight, there was an insignificant Anglo-Swedish attack on the Russian coast that same summer, and there were a few inconsequential encounters at sea resulting in the capture of a handful of small Russian ships – but that was more a reflection of the difficulty each side had in getting to grips with the other in any meaningful way rather than indicative of a lack of real enmity; at least on the part of those in charge at St Petersburg.

By late autumn 1807, then, the agreements made at Tilsit had not restored peace throughout Europe but had instead resulted in the outbreak of a new conflict between the intractable British and Napoleon's Russian allies. Where diplomacy had failed in bringing London to the peace table, the Emperor now decided that other, potentially more problematic measures would have to be tried. And Russia's adherence to the Continental Blockade made one such plan genuinely viable.

Although Napoleon never gave up on the possibility of launching a successful invasion of England, he realized by 1807 that it was not a project that was likely to be feasible for a good few years, so dominant had the Royal Navy become. He therefore came to put an increasing emphasis on economic warfare as the means to force Britain to the peace table. To be really effective, however, the Continental Blockade that he had introduced in late 1806 had to be as tight and widespread as possible, and his new alliance with Russia was the key to achieving that.

At a diplomatic reception in Paris on 23 September 1807, Napoleon, fuming at the recent British attack on Denmark and angered by London's refusal to accept Russian mediation, made a momentous pronouncement. He declared: 'I will no longer tolerate a single English envoy in Europe; I will declare war on any power that has one two months from now. I have 300,000 Russians at my back, and with this powerful ally I can do anything. The English declare that they will no longer respect neutrals at sea; I will no longer recognize them on land.' It was a proclamation that held profound consequences for the Continent's remaining neutral states, as would swiftly become apparent.

By Britain's refusal to recognize neutrals at sea, the Emperor was referring to measures introduced earlier in the year by London in retaliation for the introduction of the Continental Blockade. These prohibited neutral vessels from trading with all ports closed to British ships unless they called first at a British port and paid a reshipment duty on all goods going to Napoleonic Europe. The British hoped thereby to make up at least some of the money they would lose from having most of Europe cut off to their trade by forcing neutral traders, in effect, to pay them for the right to sell their goods on the Continent. Any vessel which failed to comply with the British demands stood to have its cargo confiscated. Bonaparte's reply to this intensification of economic warfare by London was to ratchet up the tension further still. In late 1807, he introduced the Milan Decrees, which outlawed throughout all countries within the Continental Blockade all neutral shipping which submitted to the British demands. The prime aim of this measure was to stop British (or British colonial) goods from entering Europe aboard neutral ships, thereby increasing the economic pressure on Britain dramatically. The Emperor was aiming at nothing short of the complete strangulation of British export trade to the Continent.

The intensification of the Continental Blockade in late 1807 undeniably posed a massive threat to Britain. In 1808, for example, British trade with the Continent fell to just half what it had been in 1802, and it would have been even worse but for a few continental outlets remaining open. By 1810–11, Britain was suffering from severe economic difficulties, exacerbated in 1811–12 by serious social unrest. In the event, the British economy survived all the trials and tribulations the Continental Blockade threw at it, but it was a close-run thing.

Just as the intensification of economic warfare hurt the British, however, Continental Europe was also left far from unscathed by it. With practically all official overseas trade cut off by the combination of the Blockade and the Royal Navy, the Continent was forced to rely on smuggling to get hold of products such as coffee, tea, sugar, spices and cheap British manufactured goods. This inevitably sent the cost of such commodities spiralling upwards in order to cover the overheads of running the gauntlet of Napoleon's customs officials or, alternatively, bribing them. Exacerbating the situation, the ban on exporting to Britain hit sales of such continental products as wine, grain, wool, wood and fruit. Alongside the continued wars after 1807, and the consequent demand for men and money to fight them, the economic dislocation caused by the Continental System was the key factor in turning many Europeans, including Frenchmen, against Napoleon.

With hindsight, the Emperor would probably have been better off had he ignored the British after 1807 instead of trying to force them to the peace table. After all, so long as he maintained his alliance with Russia, Britain, with her small army, was unlikely to be able to do much to weaken his hegemony in western and central Europe. Alternatively, he could have played the long game and concentrated on building up his naval power over a period of years until it reached the point where the British faced a real threat of invasion should they refuse to make peace. Napoleon was not a patient man, though, and neither was he one to give up a fight short of a victory that he felt confident could be achieved. Hence the Continental Blockade was intensified rather than abandoned or more loosely maintained. Given the problems it created, this can only be seen as an error, but it must be said that, from the perspective of late 1807, the prospects for bringing Britain to her knees economically looked good. With France in control of much of the Continent, and Russia an ally, Napoleon was in a position to sever British commerce with practically the whole of mainland Europe, a move which, had it been successfully achieved for any length of time, seemed certain to compel London to sue for peace.

The Emperor therefore determined after Tilsit to use the diplomatic leverage his new alliance with Russia gave him to force the remaining neutral states of Europe into joining the Continental Blockade. Potentially the most problematic such state was Austria, but, in the event, she put up little resistance to Napoleon's 'request' of autumn 1807 that Vienna break with Britain unless the British accepted demands to return the Danish fleet and recognize neutral rights at sea. But for the existence of the Franco-Russian alliance, made patent by St Petersburg's declaration of war on London that autumn, the Austrians might well have been inclined to reject the peremptory French 'request', but they realized they were on their own should they choose to resist. Austria duly complied, urging the British at the same time to make peace so that she would not have to break with them. Britain ignored the pleas from Vienna, so, in mid-January 1808, the Austrian ambassador was withdrawn from London and his country joined the Continental Blockade. All four of mainland Europe's major powers were now lined up, with varying degrees of willingness, against the British.

If the Habsburgs proved perhaps surprisingly biddable, the Pope provided unexpected resistance to French demands. By late 1807, the peace between the Papacy and the French government, achieved early in Bonaparte's rule, was rapidly breaking down, principally over the issue of Pope Pius VII's refusal to close the ports of the Papal States, which straddled central Italy, to British trade. As far as Pius was concerned, he was a neutral observer of the conflicts raging throughout Europe at this time, but Napoleon saw this as unacceptable. France was a predominantly Catholic country fighting a Protestant nation in the British, so how could the Pope possibly be neutral? Pius simply would not budge on the issue of closing the ports under his jurisdiction, however, and in early 1808 the Emperor's patience ran out. On 2 February, French troops marched into Rome and two months later Napoleon demanded that the Pope either enter into an alliance with France or lose his temporal power – control over the Papal States.

As Pius did not even reply, the French remained in occupation of papal territory, transferring some parts of it to the Kingdom of Italy in spring 1808 and formally annexing the rest to France in June 1809. The whole sorry story was completed shortly after when the Pope excommunicated the Emperor and was consequently put under arrest, where he remained, in relative comfort it must be said, for half a decade.

An even trickier obstacle to the completion of a Europe-wide Continental Blockade was to be found in the form of Portugal. Although Spain was allied to France in 1807, and had therefore already severed trade with Britain, the Portuguese were neutral and maintained thriving commercial relations with the British. As early as 19 July, therefore, Napoleon instructed the foreign ministry in Paris to inform the Portuguese ambassador that his country would either have to close its ports to British trade or face occupation.

The French demand put the Portuguese government in a most unenviable position. Resist and Portugal would be overrun, comply and the resultant war with Britain would mean the loss of her overseas trade and, probably, colonies. Unsurprisingly, therefore, Lisbon stalled for time. By mid-October, Napoleon had tired of the Portuguese prevarication and, after clearing it with his Spanish allies, instructed an army he had ordered to assemble north of the Pyrenees to cross into Spain and march on Portugal's capital. In November, the French force, commanded by the Burgundian General Andoche Junot, one of Napoleon's oldest acquaintances, invaded Portugal, occupying the capital on the last day of the month. It was another triumph for French arms (not that there had been much fighting required) and a further extension of Napoleonic control, but the victory had its limits. Just days before Junot reached Lisbon, the Portuguese royal family, government and fleet all sailed for the colony of Brazil under the protection of the Royal Navy. As with Denmark, the Emperor had been denied access to a neutral state's ships to help in his aim of challenging Britain's dominance at sea. Junot's army had also arrived in a most ragged condition, his men having endured hunger and thirst on their rapid march through some of the most barren land in Europe where it was extremely difficult to live off the land as was the French wont. Still, Portugal had been occupied and its trade with the British could now be severed. The economic noose around Britain's neck was drawing tighter.

Although it required military force to close Portugal's ports to British trade, the French had no such need for force in getting neutral Denmark, and the Danish colony of Norway, to join the Continental Blockade. The Danes were effectively driven into Napoleon's arms by the British attack on Copenhagen and soon became his allies. The other Scandinavian power, however, Sweden, which also controlled Finland, remained hostile to France and friendly to Britain. Once his troops had driven the Swedes from the southern shore of the Baltic in summer

1807, though, there was little the Emperor could do to bring direct pressure to bear on them, protected as they were by the Royal Navy's domination of the Baltic Sea.

Fortunately for Napoleon, his desire to see Sweden included in the Continental Blockade coincided with the aspiration of his new Russian allies to expand their control in Scandinavia. Though not the prime aim of Russian foreign policy, it had long been thought desirable in St Petersburg to occupy Finland in order to enhance Russian power in the eastern Baltic and provide better security for the capital against the Swedes by pushing the north-western frontier further west. In late 1807, moreover, a war against Sweden would provide the Russian army with a chance to regain some of the prestige it had lost in recent years following its defeats at Napoleon's hands, as well as providing a means of pressuring Stockholm to break its relations with Britain, a development which would make it harder for the Royal Navy to control the Baltic Sea and threaten the Russian coast.

From autumn 1807, therefore, with the Emperor's enthusiastic encouragement, Russia began putting diplomatic pressure on Sweden to sever its links with London. Like the Portuguese in the face of similar French demands, the Swedes prevaricated. Alexander was little more patient with Stockholm than Napoleon had been with Lisbon, and when King Gustavus IV delivered a dramatic snub to St Petersburg in January 1808 by signing a new alliance and subsidy treaty with the British, the Tsar's forbearance came to an end. An ultimatum was promptly delivered to the Swedish government, only to be rejected. In February, to Napoleon's considerable satisfaction, Russia declared war on Sweden.

The chief Russian aim in this new Baltic conflict was to wrest control of Finland from the Swedes. An army of 24,000 men, under the command of the uninspiring General Buxhöwden (the same commander who had so failed to distinguish himself in leading the Allied left wing at Austerlitz), was therefore assembled on the border and crossed over in late February. Confronting this invasion force were 20,000 Swedish soldiers, though these were scattered throughout Finland. Swiftly puncturing the widely spread curtain of defenders, the Russian army drove purposefully towards the Finnish capital of Helsinki, entering the city within three weeks. Now, however, the invaders met their first serious resistance in the form of the fortified island of Sveaborg in Helsinki harbour. This promised to be a very tough nut to crack, but on 3 May the garrison abruptly surrendered, probably with the aid of Russian bribery, thus completing the Russian occupation of the Finnish capital. In a mood to celebrate, Alexander declared the whole of Finland incorporated within the Russian Empire.

The Tsar's celebration soon proved a little premature. Following the capture of Helsinki, the Finns suddenly rose in revolt against their new masters, enabling the Swedes to reorganize and launch a series of successful counter-attacks which pushed the Russians back. It took 12,000 reinforcements for Buxhöwden to stabilize the situation, and the arrival of further troops, bringing his army up to 45,000, before he felt ready to resume the offensive, which had stalled and been rolled back over the summer. When he did go over to the attack again, in early September 1808, however, it was with some success and the Swedes soon requested an armistice. Showing a typical lack of judgement, Buxhöwden agreed and a truce was arranged by the end of the month. St Petersburg repudiated the agreement as soon as it heard of it and angrily ordered its commander in Finland to resume his offensive. Heavily outnumbered, the Swedish troops were forced yet further back until, in mid-November, they signed a convention agreeing to evacuate all Finnish territory.

Even now, however, the war did not cease, for the Swedes still refused to break with Britain, ostensibly the cause of the conflict in the first place. Certainly, as we have seen, St Petersburg had its own reasons for wanting the Swedes to sever their links with the British, but there is undoubtedly also an element of Russia playing the faithful ally to France in continuing the war after her main goal of capturing Finland had been achieved. The biggest beneficiary of a Swedish break with Britain, after all, would be Napoleon rather than Alexander, a fact highlighted by the Emperor's constant encouragement of the Russians throughout 1808 to keep fighting the Swedes until they agreed to ditch London and join the Continental Blockade.

Perhaps one should not read too much goodwill towards France into the Tsar's decision to prolong the Swedish war, however, for by late autumn 1808 cracks had begun to appear in the edifice of the Franco-Russian alliance. And one of the most serious had been put there by disagreement over the future of the Ottoman Empire.

In accord with the agreements made at Tilsit, in summer 1807 Napoleon offered his services as mediator in the Russo-Turkish war, which had been going on since the end of the previous year. By August, an armistice had been made under which the Russians pledged to withdraw from Wallachia and Moldavia within thirty-five days, and both sides agreed to nominate plenipotentiaries for peace talks. With any hope of French assistance in their war now gone, the Turks were more than happy to accept a settlement that merely involved Russian withdrawal from the Principalities and a return to the *status quo ante bellum*, but despite the Tsar's professed willingness at Tilsit to accept Napoleonic mediation to end the Turkish conflict, peace was not on the agenda in St Petersburg. With the Ottoman Empire seemingly in chaos following the deposition of Sultan Selim III at the start of the summer, the Russians felt that the long-anticipated collapse of Turkish rule in south-east Europe might be imminent, and Alexander and his new foreign minister, Rumiantsev, were determined to exploit the situation to extend Russia's frontiers. In early autumn, therefore, the Tsar denounced the armistice the French had mediated, refused to withdraw Russian troops from the Principalities, and denied his ambassador in Paris the authority to negotiate with his Turkish counterpart there for peace.

Somewhat naively, Napoleon seems to have believed that his new Russian allies would willingly accept a settlement of their war with the Turks that gave them no tangible reward. The renunciation of the armistice soon disabused him and the Tsar's expectations were made clearer still at the end of September 1807 when the Russian ambassador in Paris, following instructions from Alexander, proposed to the Emperor that he should mediate a Russo-Turkish peace in which Russia obtained not only Moldavia and Wallachia but also important territories and fortresses in the Caucasus.

Just as Alexander's attitude towards Britain was the acid test of the Franco-Russian alliance for Bonaparte at this time, for the Tsar, the value of the new friendship was to be assessed in these early months in relation to the Ottoman Empire. As we have seen, the Russians gave Napoleon ample proof of the genuineness of the alliance by breaking with the British, but the Emperor was to fall far short of Russian hopes in return. Rather than responding positively to the Russian proposal, as the Tsar had expected him to, Napoleon replied with a counter-proposal. Although he did not rule out trying to mediate a peace that was very favourable to the Russians, he wanted something in return. Specifically, he argued that if Russia was not going to withdraw from the Principalities, which, as he pointed out, he had not formally agreed to cede to the Tsar at Tilsit, then France should also make a new gain in the form of Silesia.

The Russians were dismayed by this for a number of reasons. First, they felt that Prussia had already been dismembered enough. To tear Silesia from her too would destroy any remnant of dignity or pretension to great-power status that Alexander's former ally retained. Secondly, French possession of Silesia would establish a continuous belt of Napoleonic controlled territory stretching all the way from France, through Germany and Poland, to the borders of the Russian Empire. Should Russo-French relations ever deteriorate, this would become an issue of some concern for St Petersburg. Even more worrying, it was feared that Napoleon might give Silesia to the Grand Duchy of Warsaw in order to connect that state with its nominal ruler's Saxon kingdom. Such an expansion of Polish territory and power was anathema to the Russians. Finally, and perhaps most significant, the Emperor's insistence upon receiving Silesia in return for accepting Russian occupation of the Principalities and mediating with the Turks in Russia's favour seemed to Alexander to be a breach of the spirit, if not the word, of the Tilsit alliance. To be sure, Napoleon had given no specific promise of Russian gains at Ottoman expense, but he had certainly given the forceful impression that St Petersburg could expect to see its dominion extend in south-east Europe as a result of the French alliance. The Silesia proposal was thus a slap in the face for the Tsar. Feeling unable to accept it, Alexander simply determined that if Napoleon was not going to help Russia secure the gains she desired then her armies would have to do the job themselves. In late autumn 1807, the Tsar ordered his forces to resume active operations in the Principalities, and by early the following year they had successfully re-established Russian control throughout Moldavia and Wallachia. The Turks, however, confident that Russia's new French allies would not join in the conflict against them, refused to make peace on the basis of ceding the provinces. As a result, the war dragged on for several more years.

The fact that the Russians were less than pleased with his attitude over Ottoman affairs did not escape a man as perspicacious as the Emperor, which of course begs the question why did he adopt the stance he did. The answer is to be found in the secret instructions Napoleon wrote for Caulaincourt on 12 November 1807, shortly before the general was sent to St Petersburg to be France's ambassador. In this document, Bonaparte explicitly stated, 'The true desire of the Emperor *at this moment* (author's italics) is that the Ottoman Empire should remain in its present integrity and should live at peace with Russia and France.' (In this light, it seems probable that Napoleon had expected and hoped all along that the Russians would reject his Silesian proposal.) This poses two further questions: why was Napoleon so eager to preserve the Turkish Empire at this time, and had he ruled out its partition permanently?

Both questions can be answered together. While not averse to partitioning the Ottoman Empire in principle, the Emperor felt that the present time was unpropitious for such a move. Two things particularly concerned him. First, with the Royal Navy dominant in the Mediterranean, Napoleon was worried that to initiate a Turkish carve-up would result in Egypt falling to the British, and for both emotional and strategic reasons, Napoleon remained keen to regain *l'Egypte française* some day. Secondly, and most important, the Emperor knew that the main prize upon which St Petersburg would insist, were the Ottoman Empire to be divided, was Constantinople, yet he was utterly determined that it should not fall to Russia. Indeed, in early 1808, after Russian armies had gained the upper hand following the renewal of fighting with the Turks in the previous couple of months, he even went so far as to talk with Metternich, the Austrian ambassador in Paris, of the possible need for France and Austria to take action to counter any effort by his Russian allies to seize the Ottoman capital.

It is hard to justify the attitude Napoleon took over the fate of Constantinople, for the city was not the strategic prize that Napoleon seemed to think it was – on St Helena, he would refer to it as 'situated for being the centre and seat of universal domination', a viewpoint which presumably came of his extensive reading of ancient and medieval history, periods in which Constantinople had indeed been strategically crucial. In the early nineteenth century, however, although possession of the city would have completed Russia's control over the Black Sea and given her a strong base from which to exert influence over the Aegean and possibly the eastern Mediterranean, none of that was necessarily especially problematic for France, particularly if the Russians remained allies. Napoleon, then, clearly miscalculated when it came to assessing the importance of the Turkish capital, yet there was perhaps more to his resolve to stop the Russians gaining Constantinople than just that. The distinguished French historian of the early twentieth century, Edouard Driault, argued that Bonaparte was driven to emulate the emperors of Ancient Rome and that this made him determined to secure as much of the old Roman Empire, and especially its second greatest city, for himself. This hypothesis cannot be proved or disproved, but either way, it is certain that the Emperor was not prepared to see Constantinople fall to any of the great powers – except perhaps France.

Aware, of course, that his position regarding the Ottoman Empire was not one that would find any favour in St Petersburg, Napoleon informed Caulaincourt in late 1807 that he should prevaricate and stall as politely as possible should the Russians raise the issue of partition when he took up his post as ambassador. At all costs, the idea of a partition was not to be shattered completely. As the Emperor commented, 'This ancient project of Russian ambition is a bond which may hold Russia to France, and from this point of view it is necessary to guard against the danger of destroying her hopes.'

Thus Napoleon's attitude to the Turkish question, at least in late 1807, was that the Ottoman Empire should not be partitioned but, also, that Russian hopes of partitioning Turkish territory in Europe should be maintained. The intrinsic contradiction in the position was obvious, and it was highly improbable that the Emperor would not have to abandon one of those two aims at some point in the near future. Indeed, the Russians soon proved less willing to be fobbed off by Caulaincourt over the Turkish issue than Bonaparte had hoped they would. The French ambassador had been in St Petersburg barely a month when, in early 1808, Rumiantsev, who was particularly desperate to see progress made on the partition of the Ottoman Empire, complained to Caulaincourt: 'You dispose of territories at your will ... but we never get what we ask for ... You must be fair; what we have done for you is apparent to everyone, but what have you done for us?' The growing tension that the less than cooperative French attitude over the Turkish question was generating was also palpable to General Savary, who remained in Russia for the first few weeks after Caulaincourt arrived. Shortly before he returned to France, he felt compelled to warn his master that it would be beneficial 'to show that the French had not had a monopoly of the advantages that resulted from the system of Tilsit', and that 'France herself was interested in seeing that the alliance should become popularised in Russia'.

Napoleon's response to the worrying news from St Petersburg was his famous letter to the Tsar of 2 February 1808. In it, he dramatically wrote, 'An army of 50,000 men, Russian, French, perhaps even a few Austrians, going by Constantinople into Asia, could not arrive at the Euphrates without making England tremble and putting her on her knees before the Continent.' The Emperor then formally proposed that negotiations should take place between Caulaincourt and Rumiantsev over the division of the Ottoman Empire. This was, of course, exactly the kind of thing the Tsar and his foreign minister had been hoping to hear from the French ruler, and when the letter reached St Petersburg, on 25 February, Alexander read it with obvious joy, assenting to the proposed Rumiantsev–Caulaincourt talks at once.

It seemed that the Emperor had decided after all to plump for partition rather than preservation of Turkish territory in the interests of maintaining relations with his Russian allies. The secret instructions he sent Caulaincourt along with the letter, however, cast a different light on the situation. The ambassador was ordered to drag his feet in the proposed discussions and on no account to give way over the issue of control of Constantinople and the Straits, a matter upon which the Russians were bound to insist. It is thus not unreasonable to conclude that Napoleon hoped and envisaged that the proposed talks would fail to reach agreement, thereby at least postponing the issue. His chief preoccupation in early 1808, as we shall see, was with affairs in the Iberian peninsula and it seems that the only way the Caulaincourt–Rumiantsev negotiations might have succeeded was if the Russians proved unfeasibly charitable and offered the Emperor a deal he simply could not refuse.

The talks between the French ambassador and the Russian foreign minister went on throughout spring 1808 and it would be otiose to cover them in any detail. The key point is that the Russian made all the running in trying to find ways past the disagreements that arose. For example, Rumiantsev yielded to a French demand that they go Bosnia and offered France Egypt and Syria, as well as gains in Europe, in return for the French granting Russia the cherished territories of Serbia, Constantinople and the Straits. Despite all the efforts of the Russian foreign minister, however, the talks eventually broke down, although both sides agreed to prepare statements of their final positions to form the basis of envisaged future negotiations between the two emperors.

Once again, the statements showed the Russians prepared to go to lengths the French were not in trying to reach an accord. Indeed, there was agreement on many issues. Both sides concurred that Russia was to get the Principalities and Bulgaria while to France would go Bosnia, Albania, Macedonia, Greece and her islands, Syria, Egypt and even the south-western area of what is modern Turkey, encompassing the Aegean and Mediterranean coastlines. The Russians were thus prepared to cede to the French the bulk of territory in the partition and even offered to send troops to help France conquer the non-European areas and possibly then to march on British India. All St Petersburg wanted in return was French agreement to Russian control of most of Serbia (the French wanted all of Serbia to go to Austria) and, most importantly, Constantinople and the Straits. The French, however, insisted that Constantinople and the Straits must either go to France, in return for which she would yield Dalmatia and Bosnia to Austria, or be made an autonomous principality.

The concessions the Russians made and the way they were prepared to bend over backwards to try to reach agreement with France over the partition of the Ottoman Empire highlights how much stock the Tsar and Rumiantsev put on the French alliance at this stage. They yielded to almost every French demand or suggestion but could not give way over Constantinople and the Straits. The symbolic value of the city was even greater for the Russians than it was for Napoleon, and control of the Straits was considered vital to guaranteeing the security of Russian trade and territory in the Black Sea area as well as in allowing Russia unfettered access to the Aegean and Mediterranean, where it was hoped a thriving commerce could be established. Given the less than crucial significance of Constantinople and the Straits to France, it almost beggars belief that a man as intelligent as Napoleon was not prepared to cede them to Russia in return for the gains he would make and especially in the interests of maintaining good relations with his new Russian allies.

Unsurprisingly, Bonaparte's attitude over the Turkish question did severe damage to the Franco-Russian alliance. Indeed, Edouard Driault identified it as the key cause of the demise of the relationship. French prevarication, stalling and ultimate unwillingness to reach an agreement that offered them even greater gains than it did the Russians not only frustrated and angered the Tsar and his foreign minister, but also denied them the prize both men most looked to in order to justify and popularize the French alliance in Russia. It seems extraordinary that the Emperor could have allowed such damage to be done to an alliance that ever since he had come to power he had viewed as a possible basis of France's enduring hegemony within western and central Europe. In the final analysis, one can only put it down to his dangerous state of mind after Tilsit. Flushed with outstanding success, he seems to have come to believe that he and his army were invincible, that the limitations on his power and influence were less than they in fact were, and that, having finally achieved the Russian alliance, he no longer needed it. Instead of treating Russia as an equal, a genuine partner, Napoleon, by failing to cooperate with his ally over the Ottoman Empire, effectively sent the message that she was just a much larger version of Bavaria or the Grand Duchy of Warsaw or any other French client state. It was, unsurprisingly, not an attitude for which Alexander, Rumiantsev or any other Russian cared.

Yet if the Tsar and his foreign minister were exasperated by the Emperor's unaccommodating stance over the Turkish question during the year after Tilsit, they were certainly not yet prepared seriously to consider abandoning the French alliance altogether. They would stick with it and try to make it work, doing what they could in the meantime to extend Russian power and influence in south-east Europe (as well as Scandinavia) without French help. Partly this attitude was based on an unwillingness to ditch a relationship in which both men had invested so much hope and reputation, partly it was simply founded on acknowledgement of France's preponderant military strength and the desire not to get on the wrong side of it. But then, in the summer of 1808, events in the Iberian peninsula conspired to alter the political situation in Europe, and consequently to make Alexander less willing to tolerate an ally that did not live up to his expectations.

The Spanish ulcer: so Napoleon came to describe the conflict in the Iberian peninsula that erupted in May 1808 and grumbled on for five and a half years, culminating in the total ejection of French forces from the region. It would cost the French Empire over 200,000 men, as well as vast amounts of money. It would tie down up to a third of a million of Bonaparte's soldiers at any one time, and their inability to crush all opposition to them would encourage those who sought to resist French hegemony throughout Europe. It would eventually even do much to undermine support for the Napoleonic regime within France herself. And yet, by itself, it could never have proved fatal to the Emperor's cause, and but for other developments would most likely have eventually been resolved in France's favour.

The basic cause of what became known, in the English-speaking world at least, as the Peninsular War, was the Emperor's attempt to install a Bonaparte dynasty in Madrid. The reasons for this fateful move were several. Although Spain was a French ally, Napoleon decided that she, and he, stood to benefit from a change of government in the country. He hoped that a new administration, inspired by French ideas and methods, would apply the Continental Blockade more effectively than the current inept, backward-looking regime, that it would be able to tap the resources of Spain and her empire much more efficiently in the ongoing struggle with Britain, and that it would improve the lives of the Spanish people. There was also a further factor that is often overlooked. Although the Spanish regime had reluctantly rejoined the war against Britain at the end of 1804, it had soon proved a disaster for Spain, her overseas trade being crippled by the Royal Navy and Nelson's fleet administering a crushing blow to Spanish naval strength at Trafalgar. By 1806, Madrid had decided that it had backed the wrong horse. Naively expecting the Prussians to put the *Grande Armée* in its place that autumn, the Spanish government had recklessly flirted with going to war against France. Following the Prussian thrashing at Jena–Auerstädt, the Spanish had swiftly returned to playing the loyal ally, but Napoleon neither forgave nor forgot. Once the east Prussian campaign was over, the Emperor turned his attention to dealing with his recalcitrant ally. Unable to trust the regime in Madrid any longer, he determined to effect some kind of change, for, as he himself put it, 'my policy demands that I shall not leave in my rear, so close to Paris, a dynasty hostile to mine'.

A vital miscalculation also played a key part in Bonaparte's decision to intervene in Spain's governance. French diplomats in Spain, mixing solely in circles in Spanish society favourable to France, informed their Emperor that his intervention would be welcomed south of the Pyrenees as that of a saviour who would reverse the decline of the past two centuries and restore Spain to her glory days by deposing the old, reactionary royal dynasty and replacing it with a French one. Napoleon placed undue faith in such information and thought that any popular resistance that might flare up could be comfortably dealt with, as it had been in other parts of Europe. He certainly did not for one moment envisage that a French take-over in Spain might unleash a furious and widespread backlash, much less a major war.

Early in 1808, Bonaparte fed large numbers of French troops into Spain on the pretext of supporting the occupation force in Portugal, but in reality to provide the muscle to suppress any opposition to the Emperor's imminent actions. Then, in mid-March, before Napoleon had decided exactly what to do in Spain, a sudden and unexpected coup against the ineffectual King Charles IV in the name of his heir, Prince Ferdinand, forced his hand. As Spain descended into political anarchy, Napoleon ordered his senior commander in the country, Marshal Murat, to occupy Madrid on the pretext of guaranteeing order. He then invited both Ferdinand and Charles to come to him at Bayonne in southern France where he offered to mediate in the dispute between them. Both men responded to the summons willingly, but once they reached Bayonne the Emperor first pressured Ferdinand into abdicating in favour of his recently deposed father, before then pressing Charles to abdicate in favour of a candidate of Napoleon's choice. The Emperor finally settled on his elder brother, Joseph, whose old kingdom of Naples went to Murat, Napoleon's brother-in-law, with the marshal's Grand Duchy of Berg and Cleves being absorbed by Jerome Bonaparte's Kingdom of Westphalia. Ferdinand and Charles were both given large pensions to retire as private citizens on French estates.

An effortless, if rather shady, palace coup thus appeared to have been effected, and Napoleon tried to win the support of Spaniards for it by drawing up a new Spanish constitution and declaring to the people of Spain in late May: 'Your monarchy is old: my mission is to rejuvenate it. I will improve your institutions and will make you happy, if you support me, with the benefits of reform without annoyances, disorders or convulsions.' Nor was this mere rhetoric.

The constitution Bonaparte drew up in 1808 was a predominantly progressive document,* including such reforms as the abolition of the Spanish Inquisition and of feudalism, a rationalization of law and improved prospects for commercial development. Unfortunately for the Emperor (and arguably Spain), however, many Spaniards were unwilling to accept the rule of King Joseph despite – indeed, often because of – its modernizing outlook.

For a long time, Spanish resistance to the French was predominantly explained by historians as a demonstration of passionate nationalism. The Spanish were a proud people who, unlike the bulk of the nationalities within the rest of the Napoleonic Empire, had firmly rooted legends of national greatness and independence, and they took Napoleon's high-handed deposition of their royal family and the subsequent French take-over as a considerable affront. There is *some* truth to this, but modern research has shown its importance to have been greatly exaggerated. Although positive nationalist feeling undoubtedly stirred some Spanish hearts, far more prevalent in fomenting Spanish resistance to the French was the negative side of nationalism; xenophobia.

Another key factor working against acceptance of the new regime was religion, or, more accurately, the Catholic Church. Although Joseph was himself a Catholic and his government was by no means anti-Catholic *per se*, the irreligion of many French soldiers (a legacy of the Revolutionary period), the increasingly bitter dispute between Napoleon and the Pope, and, most important, the fact that Joseph's regime sought to reduce the extremely powerful and stifling influence of the Church on Spanish life won the French the implacable hatred of a huge number of Spanish clerics who did their utmost to stir up hostility to the new government among the devoutly religious Spanish peasantry.

Finally, there was the impact of the war that developed out of initial Spanish resistance. Heavy-handed French reprisals against Spanish insurgents created martyrs and generated further hostility to the foreigners, while the hardships that resulted from the struggle to quell the rebellion (including taxes, requisitioning, plunder and loss of loved ones) were blamed by most Spaniards on the French more than on the rebels, thereby rendering resistance largely self-perpetuating.

The insurrection that would soon develop into a major war began on 2 May 1808 in Madrid – the famous *Dos de Mayo* immortalized by the painter Goya – while the shenanigans at Bayonne were still unfolding. Incited by supporters of Ferdinand, rebels killed some 150–200 French soldiers in the city, only to see

---

* It was, in fact, rather similar to the constitution produced by the Spanish Cortes (parliament) in 1812 which has been much lauded by historians for its progressiveness. Sadly, the liberal Spaniards that drew up that constitution were very much a minority within Spain. When Ferdinand returned in 1814, he overthrew their constitution with the aid of the army, thereby helping ensure that Spain remained a backward country well into the twentieth century.

around 2,000 rioters summarily executed by Murat's troops in reprisal. This brutal action succeeded in restoring order to the Spanish capital, but bloody revolts soon started to erupt throughout Spain. At first, French efforts to suppress these risings were successful, and whenever the Spanish army confronted Joseph's forces in the field it was routinely thrashed, most notably on 14 July at Medina de Rio Seco. But then, just a few days after this great triumph, at a small town in the south of Spain called Bailén, disaster struck. Through incompetence, a French general, Pierre Dupont, allowed his corps of nearly 20,000 conscripts to become surrounded by Spanish forces: he then promptly surrendered. It was the first time a French army had surrendered in the field since the beginning of the Revolutionary Wars and the capitulation gave the revolt an enormous boost as word spread like wildfire throughout Spain of how the supposedly invincible French had been soundly bested. Then, incredibly, King Joseph idiotically compounded the disaster of Bailén by panicking and ordering Madrid to be abandoned in its wake. The psychological impact of the French forces retreating north to take up defensive positions behind the River Ebro was immense, its repercussions felt not just in the Iberian peninsula but throughout Europe.

Nor were French woes over yet. Unsurprisingly, insurrection spread to Portugal as well in that frantic summer of 1808, and, having decided to help the Spanish with provisions, the British went one better with the Portuguese and sent them an army as well. For Britain, Napoleon's intervention in Spain was to prove something of a godsend. Not only did it improve the islanders' strategic position by removing the Spanish fleet from the lists of the Royal Navy's adversaries, it also greatly eased the strain imposed by the Continental Blockade by opening up lucrative markets for British goods both in Spain herself and in the Spanish Empire. The widespread resistance to the French also, of course, provided the British with a tremendous opportunity to attack their great adversaries directly, starting with an attempt to liberate Portugal. An expeditionary force landed there at the start of August and had soon been bolstered to around 17,000 men by the addition of local troops. Rashly, the French commander in Portugal, General Junot, decided to attack the Anglo-Portuguese force at Vimeiro, north of Lisbon, despite being outnumbered, and was duly soundly repelled, another blow to French pride and further encouragement for those in revolt.* With communications to his rear through a largely hostile Spain less than secure, Junot

---

* Interestingly, Junot would not have been outnumbered at Vimeiro had the admiral of the Russian fleet which had taken shelter in Lisbon harbour on its way back home from the Mediterranean agreed to land the troops he was carrying to help his French allies garrison the Portuguese capital. Given that until summer 1807, those soldiers had been fighting the French for control of Dalmatia, however, his refusal is perhaps understandable.

soon agreed to the Convention of Cintra, by which he agreed to evacuate his force from Portugal, provided it was returned to France aboard English ships.[*]

By late summer 1808, therefore, things had begun to go more than a little awry for Napoleon in the Iberian peninsula, with Portugal having been temporarily abandoned, Joseph having foolishly fled his new capital, a whole French corps having marched into captivity, and with Spain in widespread and bloody rebellion. Unwittingly, the Emperor had stirred up a veritable hornets' nest which even he was ultimately to admit had been a mistake, lamenting on St Helena, 'I should never have started this adventure'. Yet he had started it, and by the end of August he had come to realize that the situation in Iberia had become so serious that it required his personal attention.

Before Napoleon could go to Spain to try to reverse French fortunes there, he needed to resolve two interconnected problems: to gather enough veteran troops to make his direct intervention in the Iberian peninsula decisive, and to secure his position in central Europe. The veteran troops could only come in sufficient numbers from Prussia, where tens of thousands of members of the *Grande Armée* remained in occupation of all Frederick William's territory, bar Königsberg and north-eastern Prussia, as security for the payment of the indemnity imposed at Tilsit and as a means of keeping the humbled Prussians down. This occupation had led to numerous complaints from the Russians from late summer 1807 on, protestations to which Napoleon had either turned a deaf ear or had retorted that so long as Russian troops remained in Moldavia and Wallachia in violation of the terms agreed at Tilsit, French troops would stay in Prussia. Technically, the Emperor's point was not an unreasonable one, but it was hardly conducive to fostering a spirit of amity with his Russian allies.

The tide of events in Iberia forced Bonaparte to rethink his Prussian policy. Much as he needed the bulk of the soldiers stationed there for his imminent campaign south of the Pyrenees, he was prepared to withdraw neither entirely nor unconditionally. He therefore pressured the Prussian government into entering negotiations for a revised accord between the two nations. Fearing that they would be forced to sign a second humiliating agreement within the space of little over a year, the Prussians secretly pleaded with St Petersburg to come to their aid or at least put pressure on Paris to adopt a lenient line in the talks. Frustrated as the Russian foreign minister and his master had become with Napoleon's attitude over Prussian and, especially, Turkish issues, however, neither was yet prepared to break with France nor even to risk angering her emperor by interfering in the bilateral Prusso-French discussions.

---

[*] Under the terms of the same agreement, the Russian fleet in Lisbon harbour was taken over by the British but the men onboard were sent home.

By the terms of the Convention of Paris, signed on 8 September 1808, Napoleon agreed to withdraw the bulk of his occupation force from Prussia, including her capital, Berlin, and also to reduce the indemnity Frederick William's defeated nation had to pay from 160 million francs to 140 million. In return, though, Bonaparte ensured he got his pound of flesh. The Prussian army was to be limited to just 42,000 men for the next ten years, the crucial fortress city of Magdeburg on the right bank of the Elbe, Prussia's western frontier since Tilsit, was to be ceded in perpetuity, and three further key fortresses, at Stettin, Glogau and Küstrin, all of which stood on the Oder running through Prussia's heart, were to remain occupied by the French until the indemnity was paid in full.

The Emperor thus procured the veteran troops he needed for his Iberian campaign whilst ensuring that the Prussians would remain no real threat to his empire. As such, it was a successful, if ruthless, piece of diplomacy, but it created two problems for Napoleon. First, the continued presence of French troops on Prussian soil did little to assuage Russian anxieties or frustrations. St Petersburg was only too aware that the withdrawal that did take place was not a token of friendship towards Russia but a result of military necessity, and the fact that two of the Oder fortresses which the French remained in control of were in Silesia only added to fears that Bonaparte intended to annex the region at some point despite Russian objections.

The second unfortunate repercussion for the French of the Convention of Paris was even more serious than the first. The tens of thousands of troops Napoleon had kept in Prussia since the end of the war of the Fourth Coalition not only helped keep the Prussians quiescent, but also the Austrians. Their withdrawal therefore reduced the Emperor's ability to dissuade Vienna from once more adopting a hostile attitude towards France and it came, moreover, at a most unpropitious time. Bonaparte's peremptory overthrow in Spain of the ruling house of one of France's allies not only shocked the Habsburgs but also convinced them that, sooner or later, the French emperor was bound to depose the ruling family of Austria too. As French forces increasingly ran into problems in Iberia, therefore, the idea grew in Vienna that the Habsburgs should confront the French a fourth time, taking advantage of the fact that France would have to fight on two fronts. Having been defeated by Napoleon three times already, few Austrians held out too much hope that the result would be any different next time, but in their funk over the deposition of Spain's ruling family, the Habsburgs felt that the gamble of war might be the only way to preserve their dynasty.* Throughout the late summer and into the autumn of 1808, therefore, Austria called up and mobilized large numbers of troops in preparation for a possible war with France.

---

* In fact, Napoleon had no plans for deposing the Habsburgs.

Austria's bellicose activities might have been expected to lead the Emperor to halt, or at least dramatically reduce, the flow of French soldiers from central Europe to Spain, but Napoleon remained determined to lead a major army south of the Pyrenees to reverse France's setbacks there. The Habsburg threat had still to be dealt with, of course, and Bonaparte tried his usual tactic of darkly warning of dire consequences should Austria force the French to fight and be defeated again. Aware, though, that such cautionary words would have a weaker and weaker impact the more his veterans left central Europe, he looked elsewhere for assistance in coercing Vienna to remain at peace with France. Specifically, he turned to St Petersburg, resurrecting the idea of a second meeting between himself and Tsar Alexander. The Russians had suggested such a conference back in the spring, hoping to use it to thrash out an agreement over the partition of the Ottoman Empire, but Spanish affairs, and the Emperor's reluctance to reach an accord over the Turkish question, had meant that one had not taken place, much to the Tsar's disappointment. Now, however, Napoleon needed his ally's help and so Alexander was invited to the German town of Erfurt, roughly halfway between Paris and St Petersburg, for a summit. The Tsar duly accepted and the Emperor prepared to enchant his fellow monarch as he had the previous summer at Tilsit. Unfortunately for the French ruler, he would find his task much harder this time around.

Napoleon determined not only to charm Alexander at Erfurt but also to awe him. As well as ensuring that the Russian lodgings were resplendent and that the food, wine and entertainment provided were the very best available, the Emperor summoned to the conference all the German heads of state allied to France in order to remind the Tsar just how powerful he was. As Bonaparte himself put it, 'I wish the emperor Alexander to be dazzled by the spectacle of my power'.

The Tsar, however, needed no reminding of the power of his ally and was in no mood to be wooed by him. Although he had swiftly recognized Joseph Bonaparte's new regime in Spain, in spite of being given no warning of the Emperor's actions and in the face of widespread dismay among the Russian aristocracy at the deposition of the 'legitimate' Spanish royal family, frustration and irritation over Napoleon's failure to satisfy Russian desires concerning Prussia and particularly the Ottoman Empire had seriously jaded the French alliance in Alexander's eyes by the autumn of 1808. This is shown by a letter he wrote to his mother in response to her plea that he should not go to Erfurt. In his reply, he talked of building up Russia's forces and hinted that one day they might be turned against France again, concluding ominously, 'The wisest of all policies is to await the right moment to act'. It seems likely that, to some extent, the Tsar was playing up his disillusionment with the French alliance in order to placate the vehemently anti-French Dowager Empress, lest she try to stir up trouble over his decision to meet with Napoleon a second time. Nevertheless, it is highly significant that the thought of abandoning the French alliance and going to war with France once more had entered Alexander's mind after his every word and deed for many months after Tilsit had shown him to be vigorously in favour of the arrangement established then.

While growing disappointment with the French alliance made the Tsar disinclined to give way to Napoleon too much at their forthcoming meeting, it was developments in the Iberian peninsula and elsewhere that provided him with the confidence to follow through on his feelings and adopt a more independent stance. The French entanglement in Spain, the prospect of a fourth Franco-Austrian war and the withdrawal of large numbers of Napoleonic troops from Prussia all placed Alexander in a much stronger position in the autumn of 1808 than he had been in the summer of 1807. He therefore determined that he would yield nothing without receiving something concrete in return. No more would the Tsar settle for the vague notions or unspecified assurances that Napoleon had dispensed at Tilsit, and which had since allowed the Emperor to evade making the kind of commitments to Russia that Alexander wanted without technically breaking the word of their agreements. The Tsar had not quite finished with the French alliance as he prepared to set off for Erfurt, but its long-term survival certainly now depended on Napoleon doing something substantial to justify its continued existence in any meaningful sense.

Bonaparte was given warning that his ally might not prove as amenable to his wishes as he had at Tilsit when, on the way to Erfurt in September 1808, Alexander broke his journey at Königsberg to visit Frederick William and his wife, Louise. The Prussian monarchs used the opportunity to plead with the Tsar in person for him to do something to help reverse the misfortunes they had suffered in the past two years. Alexander listened to their pleas sympathetically but made no commitments. Nevertheless, the fact that he had chosen to call upon two such well-known haters of Napoleon was alarming to the Emperor.

The two rulers of France and Russia were both approaching the small central German town of Erfurt at about the same pace on 27 September when Napoleon, as the conference's organizer and host, decided to spur ahead. He consequently met Alexander and his retinue around four miles east of the town in the early afternoon. All seemed to start well. The two monarchs embraced and exchanged fulsome pleasantries before riding side by side to Erfurt. As they entered the town, bells pealed, drums rolled, cannon fired salutes and troops roared. The townsfolk, unused to such illustrious company, turned out in large numbers to see the rulers arrive. Alexander undoubtedly cut the more impressive figure in his pristine Guard's uniform, sitting tall in the saddle and riding elegantly. Yet it was to Napoleon, slouching in the saddle, riding awkwardly, and dressed in his usual plain uniform, that almost everyone's eyes were drawn. The Tsar can hardly have failed to notice that he was very much second billing and that can only have infuriated a man as sensitive to his own prestige as he was. Still, he retained enough composure to spend the rest of the day talking amicably in the Emperor's company.

For the next week, it was a continuous round of friendly chats, rides, dinners, balls, concerts, theatre performances, parades and inspections. The two monarchs seemed to get on as well as they had at Tilsit, bestowing upon each other lavish gifts and compliments. Napoleon showed Alexander around the nearby battlefield of Jena, explaining to the Tsar how he had won, and was so content with how the first few days had gone that he made one of his more peculiar remarks in a letter to Josephine of 2 October: 'I am well pleased with Alexander and he must be with me,' he wrote. 'If he were a woman, I think I would make him my mistress.'

Sooner or later, however, the allies had to get down to business, and once they did, the atmosphere cooled noticeably. The key aim of the conference as far as Napoleon was concerned was that he should get Russia's agreement to help pressure Austria into remaining quiescent. To this end, the Emperor asked the Tsar to undertake joint Franco-Russian military demonstrations on Austria's borders. In response, Alexander sidestepped Bonaparte's request and instead suggested that a conference of all members of the Continental Blockade should be called at which they could each discuss their grievances and problems. Napoleon was appalled and showed his disgust by throwing his hat on the floor and stamping on it. The Tsar remained placid but was not impressed by the Imperial show of petulance. 'Anger will gain nothing with me,' he calmly told the Emperor. 'Let us talk, let us reason – or else I shall go away.' Bonaparte regained control of his passion and resumed the talks in a cooler mood, but could not get Alexander to agree to joint action on Austria's borders.

Russo-French discussions continued for around a week and covered issues such as Prussia, Spain, the Ottoman Empire, Scandinavia and Britain, as well as Austria. To Napoleon's consternation, the Tsar proved considerably less forthcoming than he had at Tilsit, driving a hard bargain for every concession he granted the Emperor. Alexander would have taken such a line anyway, but he was reinforced in his approach by the treachery of former French foreign minister, Talleyrand. Despite falling out with Napoleon and resigning in summer 1807 from the key diplomatic post he had held for eight years, Talleyrand had remained a senior figure in the French government, holding the offices of Grand Chamberlain and Grand Vice-Elector. Bonaparte invited him to Erfurt in recognition of the limitations of his successor at the foreign ministry, the loyal but uninspiring Jean-Baptiste de Champagny, hoping to benefit from the slippery but highly effective Talleyrand's vast diplomatic experience. Instead, Talleyrand used his presence at Erfurt to meet the Tsar secretly each evening, when he gave away confidential information about the French position and encouraged Alexander not only to resist Napoleon's current requests, especially regarding Austria, but also to cooperate in future with Vienna in opposing the Emperor. Subsequently, the former foreign minister tried to justify his treachery by arguing that he had been acting in France's true interests and had only sought to restrain Bonaparte's dangerous ambitions. This defence would have considerably more credibility had Talleyrand not been in the handsome pay of Austria at the time of the Erfurt conference, and indeed for quite some period beforehand.

Given the Tsar's mood before he even got to Erfurt, it seems improbable that Talleyrand's treachery had much impact upon how things unfolded at the conference. Some form of agreement was eventually reached on most of the issues discussed, but that provided little satisfaction to the Emperor. Over Napoleon's key concern, Alexander made no pledge to pressure Austria into disarming, giving only a verbal promise that he would try to dissuade Vienna from war. Indeed, in a secret Franco-Russian treaty signed on 12 October, all the Tsar would commit himself to on paper was that, in the event of the Austrians attacking the French Empire, Russia would 'make common cause' with France, a rather ambiguous phrase that offered St Petersburg the opportunity to provide its ally with little more than moral support. The Russians did marginally better in the treaty by getting the French to pledge to assist them in their ongoing war with the Turks should another power intervene on Constantinople's behalf. Regarding the Turkish question overall, the idea of partitioning the Ottoman Empire was not pressed by the Russians, so convinced were they that it would prove futile, but they did push instead for formal French acknowledgement of Russian possession of Moldavia and Wallachia. This they duly got, as well as recognition of Russia's annexation of Finland, although the price was an agreement that the rest of the Ottoman Empire was to remain under the Sultan and its territorial integrity was to be respected by both Paris and St Petersburg. It was not what the Tsar and his foreign minister had ideally wanted, but at least it gave them the Emperor's written acceptance of part of the territorial expansion they had hoped to make in south-east Europe. Certainly, it was more satisfactory than Napoleon's continued evasiveness concerning Prussia and refusal to pledge to withdraw his remaining troops from that country. Elsewhere in the new treaty, France and Russia designated Britain 'their common enemy and the enemy of the continent', but the only positive action it committed both parties to was to launch a fresh personal appeal to King George III for peace (the subsequent letters predictably achieved nothing). The two nations did agree, though, not to make a separate peace nor enter into bilateral negotiations with London, and recognition of French domination of Iberia and Russian possession of Finland and the Principalities was made a *sine qua non* of any future settlement with Britain.

Overall, then, the Russians probably had more to be pleased with from the

Erfurt conference than the French. They received at least partial satisfaction on the prime issue to them of the Ottoman Empire, whereas Napoleon had to make do with mere verbal assurances and loosely worded commitments regarding his chief worry, Austria. Russia's continuing hostile attitude towards the British was certainly encouraging, but the pledges made concerning the reaching and terms of a future settlement were as much designed to try to ensure that Paris could not easily forsake Russian interests in making peace with London as to attempt to maintain St Petersburg's adherence to the anti-British struggle.

Despite failing to arrange the partition of the Ottoman Empire or to secure complete French withdrawal from Prussia, then, the Erfurt conference and its secret treaty did just enough to persuade Alexander and Rumiantsev that the French alliance might yet prove a beneficial foundation for Russian foreign policy. That Franco-Russian relations remained far from perfect, however, was highlighted by events in the final days of the congress. For some time, Napoleon had been thinking of divorcing Josephine in the hope that a new marriage would bring him the son and heir he desperately wanted to secure his dynasty. Looking to kill two birds with one stone, he had decided that his projected second matrimonial partnership should also serve French diplomacy and had consequently turned his attention to the elder of Alexander's younger sisters, the twenty-year-old Catherine. After all, what better symbol of the Franco-Russian alliance could there be than a marriage between the Emperor and the Tsar's favourite sister? As pen was being put to paper on the secret treaty signed at Erfurt, therefore, Napoleon prompted Talleyrand and Caulaincourt, who had accompanied Alexander from St Petersburg, to raise the idea of such a marriage with the Tsar. Alexander listened to the French proposal politely but was clearly unenthusiastic. He could give no commitment, he said, because according to his father's will the final decision regarding the marriage of his sisters rested with his mother, the Dowager Empress Maria Feodorovna. Given her well-known anti-French feelings, this response was about as negative as it could have been without the utterance of an undiplomatic outright 'no', and so the matter was tactfully left by the French. Within a month, in a dramatic snub to France's ruler, it was announced in St Petersburg that the Grand Duchess Catherine would marry Prince George of Holstein-Oldenburg, a very minor German royal and political nobody.

Even before the announcement of Catherine's engagement, however, the Emperor knew that all was not well with the Russian alliance. The discussions at Erfurt had provided plenty of evidence of that. The conference had broken up on 14 October and the two rulers had ridden out together that morning on the road back towards Russia accompanied by the same fanfare and ceremonial that had greeted their arrival in late September. After a few miles, the pair had dismounted and talked amiably enough for some time. They had then embraced before

Alexander climbed into the carriage that would bear him all the way back to St Petersburg. Napoleon had remounted his horse, watched the Tsar go and then turned back towards Erfurt. Throughout the ensuing ride he had maintained a sullen silence, doubtless pondering the precarious state of the Franco-Russian alliance.

Some time later, the Emperor put his finger on what had gone wrong at Erfurt. The Tsar, he said, had been 'defiant and unspeakably obstinate. He wanted to treat with me as between equals.' No comment better elucidates the fundamental cause of the ultimate failure of the Tilsit system. In summer 1807, Napoleon believed that he had secured Russian acceptance of a position as junior partner in France's domination of the Continent. He expected Alexander to behave in much the same way as his less powerful allies, men such as the kings of Bavaria and Württemberg: in other words, to do pretty much what the Emperor wanted in the diplomatic sphere in return for a few territorial gains and the removal of the active threat of being overrun by the awesome *Grande Armée*. For the likes of Bavaria and Württemberg, that was enough to satisfy them, at least until the sacrifices required from the French in the form of men, money and adherence to the Continental System began to force a serious rethink in the final years of Napoleon's reign, but Russia was a great power and needed more adept and sensitive handling. Although he would never have admitted it, the Tsar was prepared, in effect, to accept a slightly junior role in the Franco-Russian partnership – the concessions the Russians were ready to make in order to secure a partition of the Ottoman Empire show that – but he was not prepared to tolerate as inferior a position as the Emperor had marked out for him. Alexander believed that the arrangement reached at Tilsit had been for the division of Europe into two spheres, one dominated by France, the other by Russia, with Britain excluded from the Continent until she made peace and accepted the new *status quo*. Russia was to be, if not quite in practice then in theory at least, France's equal. Napoleon's failure in the first year of the Franco-Russian alliance to mollify the Tsar over Prussia or, especially, to accede to Alexander's and Rumiantsev's burning desire to partition the Ottoman Empire demonstrated that he did not view the Russians in quite the same light as the Russians wished, and expected, to be seen by him. This put the alliance in serious jeopardy and the agreements reached at Erfurt provided only a temporary relief. The Tsar and his foreign minister still ideally wanted an agreement to carve up Turkish possessions, they still wanted French soldiers withdrawn from Prussia entirely, and, what was to become an increasingly major problem, they also wanted some kind of satisfactory settlement of the Polish question. None of these was unachievable but they all required a change of outlook on the Emperor's behalf regarding his relationship with Russia. The Russo-French alliance was not quite dead in the wake of Erfurt, but it was in need of some serious attention if it was to survive intact.

12

Death of an Alliance

Barely three weeks after the end of the disappointing Erfurt conference, Napoleon launched what would be his one and only campaign south of the Pyrenees. Following the reverses of the summer, the French forces in the Peninsula had retreated and formed a strong defensive line behind the River Ebro in the north of Spain, where they awaited the arrival of the Emperor with the tens of thousands of veteran troops he was bringing from central Europe. On 7 November, Napoleon and his reinforcements finally crossed the border, and before long the Spanish armies on the southern banks of the Ebro were sent reeling back. Within a month, Madrid was back in French hands.

After a brief period of consolidation and rest, the Emperor was on the move again, though not after the Spanish armies which had retreated into southern Spain, nor towards Lisbon to reassert French control in Portugal. Instead, he went north-west from Madrid in pursuit of a British army which had advanced from Portugal into Spain during the autumn. As soon as the British force's commander, Lieutenant General Sir John Moore, realized the danger in which he now found himself, he ordered a precipitate retreat towards the port of La Coruña (usually rendered Corunna in English histories) in north-western Spain. A chase ensued through mountainous terrain on appalling roads in harsh, wintry conditions in which the smaller British force managed to retain its lead over the pursuing French. By the end of December, the Emperor realized that his army was moving too slowly to encircle Moore's men and so, secure in the knowledge that the British were at least abandoning the Peninsula for the moment, the chase was handed over to Marshal Soult on 2 January 1809. Remarkably, by an almost superhuman effort, the advanced elements of Soult's force did manage to catch up with the British at La Coruña itself in mid-January, but a brief battle, in which Moore held the enemy off but was mortally wounded, failed to prevent the escape of nearly all the army aboard the ships of the Royal Navy.

Despite the failure to destroy Moore's army, by early 1809 it looked like Bonaparte's Iberian campaign had been a triumph. The British had been driven from the Peninsula at the tips of French bayonets, French rule reinstated in much of Spain, and the Spanish given a bloody nose. The successful suppression of resistance throughout the rest of Iberia seemed the most likely course of events in the rest of 1809. And perhaps that is what would have happened had the

Emperor not received news in early January that compelled him to rush back to Paris forthwith.

Clear intelligence reached Napoleon in the first weeks of 1809 that Austria was mobilizing for a spring campaign. At once, the Emperor hurried back to Paris. Although it would be a number of weeks before hostilities commenced, he deemed his presence in his capital necessary in order to oversee a renewed wave of conscription and to organize the defence of both southern Germany and northern Italy against imminent Austrian attack.*

Despite Bonaparte's dramatic advances in Spain, a definite decision for war had been taken in Vienna in December 1808. Indeed, it was perhaps partly spurred by the Emperor's success in Iberia, for it must have seemed to the Austrians that, if they did not strike soon, the Spanish entanglement they hoped to take advantage of might disappear altogether. The only thing likely now to stop the Habsburgs going to war against post-Revolutionary France for a fourth time was Napoleon's ally, Russia. Apprised by Talleyrand, their mole at the heart of the French government, of the Tsar's more independent stance at Erfurt, the Austrians dared to hope that the Franco-Russian alliance was a dead letter. This seemed to be confirmed in January 1809, when Alexander welcomed the King and Queen of Prussia to St Petersburg and fêted them to the skies. Indeed, so strongly did the Austrians interpret this as a sign that Russia might be won over that they secretly approached the Tsar for assistance in their imminent war against France, offering to recognize Russian possession of Moldavia and Wallachia in return.

Alexander, though, was not at all keen on the idea of a fourth Austro-French war. Another Austrian defeat, the probable outcome as far as the Russians were concerned, would most likely mean further French expansion at Habsburg expense, quite possibly in the area now known as Croatia, which was dangerously close to the Serbian lands over which Russia wished to extend her sway. Even more worrying, should Austria go down to a sufficiently catastrophic defeat, she might even be dismembered by Napoleon, making it easier for him to establish a dominant French influence over the constituent parts. That would be a nightmare for Russia as France would then dominate practically the whole of the Continent west of the Tsar's borders and be in a position to swallow up all the Ottoman Empire's European territories if the Emperor so wished. The Russians were no great friends of the Austrians, but they valued the existence of the Austrian Empire as a vital buffer between themselves and French-controlled Europe, as well as as a potential ally should Franco-Russian relations deteriorate

---

* Talk of a possible plot against him had also encouraged Napoleon to return to Paris in early 1809, but the threat turned out to be not serious.

sharply. Fearing the worst, therefore Alexander spurned the Austrian offer of alliance, urged the Habsburgs not to go to war, and gave no assurances that he would not side with the French. Believing that actions speak louder than words, however, the Austrians noticed the Tsar's lack of military preparations along their borders and assumed that if the Russians were not going to fight with them then at least they would not fight against them.

Meanwhile, Napoleon pressed St Petersburg repeatedly throughout early 1809 to make some kind of military demonstration against Austria as the only hope of averting the imminent conflict. Alexander refused, fearing that such a move would do irreparable damage to his relations with the Habsburgs. Russian policy thus fell between two stools: they did not want the war that was about to break out, yet they would not do the one thing that might prevent it. It was now Napoleon's turn to become exasperated with his allies.

Russia's refusal to put military pressure on Austria effectively made war inevitable. Fortunately for Napoleon, so ambitious were the Austrians to use the conflict to extend their influence in all directions that they committed themselves to a plan that involved a potentially dangerous dispersal of effort. Instead of concentrating all offensive efforts on assaulting the Emperor's key allies in southern Germany, sizeable forces were detached and detailed to attack northern Italy, the Grand Duchy of Warsaw and Dalmatia. Nevertheless, when war broke out on 9 April, several weeks earlier than Bonaparte had expected, the French were caught by surprise and the Austrians, whose military had much improved since 1805, consequently did well in all theatres. In the north-east a drive towards Warsaw was mounted, while in the south French forces in Dalmatia and northern Italy were pushed back. The most impressive success was gained in the centre, though, where the main Austrian army, under Emperor Francis's younger brother, Archduke Charles, attacked the outnumbered Napoleonic forces in Bavaria and threw them back in confusion. This helped to inspire a serious revolt in the Tyrol, a former part of Austria bordering Switzerland and Italy, occupied since Austerlitz by France's Bavarian allies. The situation was fast becoming critical.

Characteristically, Napoleon proved equal to the challenge. Arriving in Bavaria in mid-April, he swiftly reorganized his battered forces there and in a skilful seven-day campaign of rapid manoeuvre, defence and attack, which he later judged one of his finest, turned the tide of the war. After driving the Austrians from his Bavarian allies' territory, Bonaparte advanced down the Danube on Vienna, hoping that, with their capital in peril, the Austrians would sue for peace. Spirits were certainly wavering among the Habsburg leadership following the recent reversal in their fortunes, but they were not quite ready yet to throw in the towel. Although Vienna was surrendered to save it from destruction in mid-May, no armistice was sought. Instead, the Austrians withdrew north of the Danube, burning all the bridges as they went, and prepared to fight on.

As in 1805, Napoleon's forces had grown weaker the further east they had come, and the Austrians now outnumbered the French in the area around Vienna. The Emperor, though, felt supremely confident in the wake of his recent successes and determined to attack in the hope of winning a major battle which might end the war. The result was the two-day battle of Aspern-Essling, fought on 21–22 May. In his impatience to get to grips with the enemy, Napoleon failed to ensure that the crossing he had his men build over the Danube a few miles to the east of Vienna was as secure as it should have been. Consequently, the Austrians were able to smash the French bridge on both days of the battle by releasing a range of floating battering rams downriver. This left Napoleon's army divided by the Danube with the part of it which had crossed to the northern bank put under intense pressure by Archduke Charles's much larger force. Marshals Lannes and Masséna had to summon all their skill as commanders to save their corps from destruction near the villages of Aspern and Essling on the 21st, while on the 22nd, against the odds, the Emperor almost managed to conjure up an improbable victory. In the end, however, Napoleon's inability to bring all his force to bear proved decisive. His attacks repelled, he had little choice but to order a fighting withdrawal from the Danube's northern bank.

Far from achieving the decisive victory he had hoped would end the war, Bonaparte suffered his first clear battlefield reverse at Aspern-Essling. Although total losses for each side were roughly equal, in spite of the heavy numerical advantage enjoyed by the Austrians, the fact that the French had been compelled to abandon the field allowed Archduke Charles to claim that he had beaten the Emperor. Adding to Napoleon's woes was the fact that among the 25,000 casualties suffered by his army was his good friend Lannes, who lost both legs to a cannonball towards the end of the fighting on 22 May. At first, it seemed that the courageous marshal would survive, but then gangrene set in and he died before the month was out. Napoleon had not been so personally touched by a death since Desaix's at Marengo nine years earlier.

In reacting to the adversity of personal loss and defeat, the Emperor showed himself at his best. Instead of retreating, he began preparations for a second attempt at crossing the Danube and getting to grips with the Austrian army. This time, he was methodical and thorough. Turning a large island in the middle of the river into a fortress bristling with artillery, he ensured that much more solid bridges were constructed between there and the south bank of the Danube and that obstacles were placed upriver to prevent anything being sent hurtling into the structures by the Austrians. To redress Archduke Charles's numerical advantage, meanwhile, he ordered up reinforcements from Spain and instructed French forces in northern Italy and Dalmatia, where, as in Bavaria, the initial

Austrian attacks had been stopped and subsequently thrown back, to march to join him as well.

By early July, Napoleon was ready. Feigning that he intended to cross once more near Aspern and Essling, he instead traversed the Danube a little way further east. By the time the Austrians realized what was going on, it was too late to prevent the French from getting the whole of their army across to the northern bank. Archduke Charles, encouraged by his victory in May, offered battle on 5–6 July nonetheless, but the result this time would be different.

The battle of Wagram started well enough for the Austrians. A French attack on their centre, on the afternoon of 5 July, was a bungled affair, the result predominantly of an inept display as a corps commander by Marshal Bernadotte, who was subsequently dismissed from his command following an angry altercation with the Emperor. Next day, however, the French did better. After resisting a strong Austrian attack on his left in the morning, Napoleon bludgeoned the centre of Archduke Charles's line with a massive artillery battery, while the ever-dependable Marshal Davout drove back the Austrian left. As the pressure mounted, Bonaparte ordered forward the corps of General Jacques Macdonald, a dour Frenchman of Scots descent whose father had fought for Bonnie Prince Charlie in the 1740s, to break the enemy centre. Despite the mauling they had taken from the French guns, the Austrians in this area showed remarkable resilience, inflicting heavy casualties on Macdonald's men, but by early afternoon the French were threatening to tear a hole in the middle of their adversaries' position. With Davout also beginning to turn his left flank, Archduke Charles realized the battle was lost and ordered a withdrawal before things got any worse.

Wagram was undoubtedly a French victory, but it was no Austerlitz, Jena-Auerstädt or Friedland. Not only were the Austrians able to extricate themselves from the field in good order, but they did so having inflicted a similar number of casualties upon the French as they had themselves sustained; around 35,000. Archduke Charles, however, had had enough. Within a few days he requested an armistice that Napoleon, his army as battered as that of his foes, was only too happy to grant.

Unlike in 1805, peace did not follow on swiftly from an armistice. The Austrian government remained hopeful of major assistance in the struggle against France from elsewhere, and so dragged out the peace negotiations, to which Archduke Charles had effectively committed them, until well into the autumn. The help Vienna hoped for, though, never came. There was no large-scale revolt in Germany against French domination of the Continent, the war in the Peninsula did not require the Emperor to divert forces there from central Europe, and the Prussians never seriously entertained the prospect of going to war after

Napoleon overturned the initial Austrian success in Bavaria. The British also proved a disappointment to the Austrians. Although they despatched a sizeable expeditionary force to the island of Walcheren in Belgium in late July, it was easily bottled up and ignominiously forced to withdraw a few months later having taken heavy losses, mostly from disease.

That left Russia as Austria's last hope of support if she were to fight on against Napoleon. Contrary to expectations in Vienna, however, the Russians had, following the Austrian attacks in April, honoured the alliance with France and gone to war against the Habsburgs. Or at least they kind of had. The Austrian assault on the French Empire in southern Germany, northern Italy, Dalmatia and Poland put St Petersburg in an unenviable position. Having been unwilling to damage Austro-Russian relations by mobilizing forces on the border to warn the Habsburgs against going to war, Alexander was even less keen actually to commit Russian soldiers to fighting the Austrians once war had started. The Tsar was well aware, however, that Napoleon would expect Russia to come to his assistance militarily. Indeed, vaguely worded as the secret treaty agreed at Erfurt had been on the subject of Russia fighting Austria, the alliance signed at Tilsit expressly committed Alexander to go to war with any power that attacked the French. Not to act against Austria in 1809, therefore, would effectively kill the Franco-Russian alliance and neither the Tsar nor his foreign minister were yet ready to do that. Both men felt that, disappointing as the alliance had in many ways so far been, it was still the best diplomatic framework within which to operate for the moment.

When the Austrians invaded various parts of the French Empire in April, therefore, Alexander grudgingly ordered a small army to assemble on the Austrian border under the command of General Gallitzin. Thanks to a combination of the Russian military's habitual slowness in mobilizing and the general reticence about fighting the Habsburgs, it was 18 May, five days after Napoleon had captured Vienna, before orders were sent to Gallitzin instructing him to enter Galicia, the Austrian-held area of the former Kingdom of Poland. Even then, Gallitzin did not advance until early June and did so with the intention of doing as little fighting as possible. Indeed, the Russian commander met an Austrian envoy shortly after crossing the border and promised him that his men would not cross to the west bank of the Vistula nor go south of its tributary, the Visloka. Nor was this in contravention of the Tsar's wishes, for Alexander himself had secretly informed Vienna that his troops would do all they could to avoid confrontation with Habsburg forces. Nothing better illustrates the farcical nature of the Russian involvement in the war of 1809 than the fact that Gallitzin's men suffered just two casualties in the whole campaign.

Contrasting sharply with the lacklustre efforts of the Russians, Napoleon's Polish allies shone brightly in the war against Austria. Although the initial

Habsburg assault threw the Grand Duchy of Warsaw's defenders back, resulting in the fall of Warsaw in early May, the Poles soon rallied under the inspired leadership of their Minister of War, General Josef Anton Poniatowski. A nephew of independent Poland's last king, Poniatowski showed great daring and imagination by opting for an offensive strategy to counter the Austrian invasion. Instead of trying to recapture Warsaw directly, he marched his army south into Galicia to threaten the invading force's line of communications, calling upon all Poles in the area to rise up against the Habsburgs as he did so. It turned out to be a tremendously successful ploy. The Galician Poles welcomed Poniatowski's men fulsomely, panicking the Austrians and compelling them to evacuate Warsaw and retreat precipitately from the Grand Duchy. Building on this success, and exploiting the fact that Napoleon's presence around Vienna prevented the Austrian army on the Polish front from receiving reinforcements, Poniatowski crowned his campaign by capturing the medieval Polish capital of Cracow before the armistice following Wagram brought active hostilities to an end.

The starkly contrasting performances of his Polish and Russian allies in spring and summer 1809 naturally shaped Napoleon's thinking as he considered the peace terms he would offer the Habsburgs. Technically, according to the terms of the alliance treaty signed at Tilsit, Alexander was entitled to join the Emperor in formulating a settlement, as Russia had taken part, albeit minimally, in the war. The Tsar was as unwilling to take a hand in imposing punitive terms on Austria as he had been to fight her soldiers, however, so he wrote to Napoleon over the summer 'graciously' ceding full responsibility for the settlement to him. Alexander was certainly not prepared to ignore Russian interests entirely, though, and was keen to point out to the Emperor in his letter that Russia had gone to war with Austria as a good and loyal ally of France, despite already being at war with three other powers (the Ottoman Empire, Britain and Sweden), thereby implying that St Petersburg should get a decent share of any territory that was to be taken from the Habsburgs.

Strictly speaking, the Tsar's claim that Russia had come to France's assistance – if such is an appropriate word to describe the activities of Gallitzin's army – while at war with three other powers was accurate, but the reality of Russia's military situation in spring and summer 1809 was considerably less grave than Alexander tried to make it sound. The war with Britain certainly involved economic difficulties for the Russians, but placed very little pressure on the Tsar's armed forces. The struggle with the Turks, on the other hand, did impose a military burden upon St Petersburg, but hardly a crippling one. That still left the war with the Swedes, of course, which, as we have seen, had proved trickier than the Russians had expected in 1808. By the end of March 1809, however, that conflict had all but ended in any meaningful sense after a dramatic and successful Russian offensive over the icebound Baltic into northern Sweden and the overthrow and assassination of the unbalanced Swedish king, Gustavus IV. Fighting did go on into the summer, but it was sporadic and posed no real threat to Russia. The truth, then, was that it placed no great strain on the Russians to go to war with Austria in 1809. Alexander was, therefore, to some extent trying to play Napoleon for a fool by exaggerating the sacrifice Russia had made to fulfil her alliance obligations. It was unlikely to dispose the Emperor favourably towards his ally.

Over the summer of 1809, Napoleon toyed with an idea that would have sent shivers down the spine of the Russians: partitioning the Austrian Empire into its three constituent kingdoms of Bohemia, Hungary and Austria. Such a draconian settlement could only have been imposed following the utter destruction of the Habsburg's armies, however, and that had not been achieved. The Austrians may have been beaten but they had not been annihilated. Bonaparte soon dropped the notion, but then raised the idea of deposing Emperor Francis and replacing him with a minor member of the Habsburg clan, Grand Duke Ferdinand of Würzburg, a pliable ally of France. How seriously Napoleon took this scheme is unclear, but it certainly terrified Francis and inclined him to accept the other terms the Emperor lay before him to end the War of the Fifth Coalition.

The treaty of Schönbrunn, signed on 14 October 1809, was a harsh settlement designed to convince Vienna once and for all that resistance to French domination of the Continent was not only futile but highly dangerous and costly. Alongside a large indemnity of 85 million francs, Austria was forced to restrict its army to 150,000 men. Vienna was compelled to rejoin the Continental Blockade and also to recognize Joseph's regime in Spain. The Habsburgs lost further territory to Bavaria (the Salzburg area) and parts of Bohemia to Saxony. Their remaining small foothold in what today constitutes north-eastern Italy, as well as large areas of modern Slovenia and Croatia, were also ceded and subsequently combined by the Emperor with Dalmatia to form a French satellite state named the Illyrian Provinces. Finally, Napoleon stripped the Austrians of the parts of Galicia that they had taken from the Poles in 1795, though he allowed them to retain the more extensive Polish lands they had annexed in the first partition of Poland in 1772. In all, Emperor Francis lost well over three million subjects, or around a fifth of the population of the Austrian Empire, and his realm was left landlocked.

Napoleon's relative charity over Galicia was less on account of any regard for the Habsburgs than concern for the sensitivities of his Russian allies, for the obvious beneficiaries of the redistribution of Galician territory were either the Grand Duchy of Warsaw or Russia. Given the less than distinguished performance of Gallitzin's army in the recent war, Bonaparte was strongly disinclined to give the Russians such a handsome reward, while to allow the Grand Duchy to extend too much would create a furore in St Petersburg and most likely win the Emperor the enduring enmity of the Russians. He settled, therefore, for giving the Poles four-fifths of the Galician lands that he did force the Habsburgs to cede and handing the remaining portion to the Russians, privately complaining as he did so that it was 'more than they earned'.

In light of the all but irrelevant contribution of Russian forces to the defeat of Austria in 1809, it is hard to disagree with Napoleon's comment. He gave them a fifth of the Galician lands, though, as a sop to the Russo-French alliance, judging that he needed to gift the Tsar something if he were to prevent him from breaking with France and colluding with her enemies once more. It was a purely Machiavellian decision, however, motivated not in the slightest by any sense of gratitude or good feeling toward Alexander or Russia. The Russian failure to support him properly in the Austrian war had a profound effect upon the emperor, undermining his faith in the Russian alliance. Of course, the main reason the Tsar had not supported the French more staunchly was because of his own doubts about his relations with France which had been raised by Napoleon's less than helpful attitude over issues such as Prussia and the Ottoman Empire. Had Alexander been made to feel more sure in 1807–8 that the French alliance was clearly the most beneficial diplomatic framework within which Russia could operate both now and in the future, he might have been less reticent about taking a much firmer line against Austria. As it was, his concerns about the Napoleonic alliance made him loath to weaken any possibility of collaborating with the Habsburgs in coming years should such a development turn out to be highly desirable (in the event that Napoleon endeavoured to secure all the Ottoman Empire for himself or resurrected the Kingdom of Poland, for example). The Russians did prove questionable allies to the French in 1809, but arguably no more so than the French had to them in the couple of years before.

Much as he did not want to see the Russian alliance collapse entirely in the wake of the defeat of Austria, Napoleon could not resist the urge to protest at the meagre assistance his allies had given him. The Russians could hardly deny the charge levelled at them, but they certainly were not going to apologize for their behaviour. Instead, they engaged in diplomatic tit-for-tat, retorting that the French had done even less to help them in their recent war with Sweden. It was not an altogether invalid point, but it did ignore one or two important facts. For a start, it would have been much harder for the French to have contributed effectively to the defeat of the Swedes than it would for the Russians to have helped beat the Austrians, as the French Empire was divided from Sweden by the British-dominated Baltic Sea whereas Russia and Austria shared a land border. Even more pertinent, St Petersburg had not wanted French assistance in the Swedish war as that would have reduced the prestige gained by the Russian armed forces from victory and might have complicated the reaching of a post-war settlement. As it was, it took six months from the effective defeat of Sweden in

March 1809 for the Russians to get the Swedes to agree to a peace treaty by which Stockholm agreed not only to cede Finland and the Baltic Åland islands to Russia, but also to enter into peace negotiations with St Petersburg's allies and, the real sticking point, jeopardize their relations with Britain by joining the Continental Blockade. Given that the last two measures were designed to benefit France more than Russia (a good sign that, despite the difficulties, the Tsar had not given up on the French alliance entirely yet), it was ungenerous of Napoleon to grumble that the Russians had let him down again by failing to force the Swedes to agree to fight the British.

If the Russo-Swedish peace treaty of September 1809 did little to improve the Emperor's opinion of his Russian allies, however, the Franco-Austrian settlement signed at Schönbrunn a month later did even greater damage to the Russo-French alliance in the eyes of the Russians. Despite the feeble efforts of Gallitzin's army, there was general disappointment in St Petersburg that Russia had not been given a greater share of the Galician territory handed out by Napoleon. The French gains in what became the Illyrian Provinces also worried the Russians, for they greatly bolstered France's position in south-east Europe and gave her direct access to Serbia. What really angered and alarmed the Tsar and other prominent Russians, though, was the granting to the Grand Duchy of Warsaw of four-fifths of the Galician lands taken from the Habsburgs. Not only was it viewed as an affront in St Petersburg that a small nation should received four times the reward that Russia did, but there was enormous anxiety and fear that such a generous donation indicated that Napoleon had decided to encourage Polish nationalism and might well soon resurrect the Kingdom of Poland. At the very least, it seemed to denote strong approval of the Grand Duchy's recent conduct, which, as well as urging Poles in Galicia to rebel against the Austrians had encouraged inhabitants of Russia's former Polish territories to rise up. The war of 1809 and the treaty of Schönbrunn, then, had at last brought to the fore what was potentially the most explosive issue in Franco-Russian relations; the Polish question.

Just as Russia's relations with the British were the most important gauge of the value and validity of the Franco-Russian alliance for Napoleon, the relationship between France and the Poles was the ultimate test of its worth as far as St Petersburg was concerned. Vital as issues such as the future of the Ottoman Empire, Prussia and Scandinavia were to the Russians, the Polish question was the most crucial of all. Russia had risen to prominence as a great power thanks to the demise of other, former great powers – Sweden, the Ottoman Empire and, especially Poland. The lands she had taken from the Poles in the eighteenth century were vast, comprising modern Lithuania and Belorussia as well as much of Latvia and Ukraine. In total, the Russians had annexed over 180,000 square miles of Polish territory, home to seven million inhabitants. The danger was that the Grand Duchy of Warsaw, fired by ardent nationalism and backed by the might of the Napoleonic Empire, might be able to win those lands back, thereby striking a crippling blow to Russian power. If the Russians were hypersensitive about the Polish question – and they were – it was because it contained such immense pontential peril.

For the first couple of years following Tilsit, the Polish question had remained in relative abeyance. The Russians did not like the existence of the Grand Duchy of Warsaw, and liked even less the creation of a small Polish army under French auspices, but they seemed broadly prepared to tolerate its existence, in the short term at least. As Franco-Russian relations had started to deteriorate in 1808, the Grand Duchy had begun to appear more problematical and threatening to St Petersburg, for it raised the prospect that Napoleon might switch allegiance from Russia to the Poles, but it was the events and outcome of the war of 1809 that really set the alarm bells ringing in the Russian capital. The activities of General Poniatowski, in trying to stir up Polish nationalism in Galicia and especially Russia, provoked uproar in St Petersburg, and prompted the Tsar to issue a formal complaint to the Emperor. Napoleon tried to reassure Alexander that there was nothing to worry about, but the publication in a Hamburg newspaper in August 1809 of an article claiming, falsely as it turned out, that Poniatowski was to be made viceroy of the Grand Duchy of Warsaw caused a fresh wave of panic in Russia. This was as nothing, however, to the furore that greeted news that the Poles were to receive four-fifths of the Galician lands Napoleon was stripping from the Habsburgs. To many Russians the message was clear; Napoleon was intent on recreating the Kingdom of Poland and this was the first step.

The Emperor was aware that, in giving the Poles what was, after all, no more than they deserved for their considerable efforts in the recent Austrian war, he was risking his relations with Russia, so he took the trouble to write to Alexander to reassure him that he would in no way aid the resurrection of former Poland and to promise that even the very name would disappear from history. As we have seen, though, the Tsar was no longer prepared to accept mere words from France's ruler and so replied by demanding that Napoleon commit his pledge not to recreate Poland to a binding treaty to be signed by all four Continental great powers and which would also delimit the Grand Duchy of Warsaw's borders. Napoleon duly authorized Caulaincourt to enter into discussions with Rumiantsev for a convention and by early January 1810 the two men had agreed upon the wording of a draft which was sent back to Paris for the Emperor's approval.

When Napoleon's reply arrived the following month, it caused profound shock and consternation in the Russian capital. He could not accept the draft convention, he claimed, because he could not pledge to prevent an event (the recreation of the Kingdom of Poland) that might come about as a result of conditions beyond his control. As excuses went, it was completely unconvincing and the Russians were appalled. In an effort to limit their horror at his rejection of the proposed Polish treaty, Napoleon suggested that an alternative, much more vague agreement be negotiated and that it be kept secret, but St Petersburg was wedded to the tightly worded convention negotiated by Caulaincourt and Rumiantsev, and insisted that it be made public so as to deliver a clear hammer blow to Polish national aspirations.

Caulaincourt tried desperately to get his master to reverse his decision over the Polish treaty, warning him time and again that its rejection had done enormous damage to the French alliance in St Petersburg, where wild rumours of Franco-Polish plots to undermine the Russian Empire had begun to fill the air. The Emperor would not change his mind, though, naively hoping to satisfy the Tsar over the Polish question by simply claiming that, if he really wanted to recreate the Kingdom of Poland, he would have done it in 1807 or 1809 following his victories in the wars of the fourth and fifth coalitions. Alexander was no more impressed by this reasoning than he had been by Napoleon's feeble excuse for rejecting the Polish treaty in the first place.

With hindsight, it is clear that Napoleon's rejection of the draft convention on Poland, and subsequent refusal to reverse his decision, was the final and decisive nail in the coffin of the French alliance as far as the Tsar was concerned. From the spring of 1810 onwards, Alexander effectively gave up on his relationship with the Emperor, officially maintaining the alliance solely in order to prevent Napoleon moving against Russia before she was ready either to defend herself or, indeed, to move against France. Over the next two years, relations between St Petersburg and Paris deteriorated steadily until the sham nature of the alliance, apparent to almost everyone by then anyway, was formally exposed by the French invasion of Russia.

Before moving on from Polish affairs, two questions need to be considered. First, could Napoleon realistically have followed a different policy towards the Poles, one that would have prevented the Tsar from abandoning the French alliance in the long term as well as the short? Second, were the Russians wildly overreacting by assuming that Bonaparte's rejection of the Polish treaty indicated that he had a secret and dangerous agenda for Poland, or was there some validity to their fears?

Clearly, the Emperor could very easily have agreed to the draft convention on the Polish question negotiated by Caulaincourt and Rumiantsev. Moreover, he could certainly have prevented the Grand Duchy of Warsaw from ever becoming the Kingdom of Poland. He could also have acted to suppress any Polish nationalism perceived to be a threat to Russia, either by brute force or by a simple threat that unless the Poles in the Grand Duchy accepted their fate they could always be handed over to their archenemy, the Tsar. Whether this alone would have been enough to save the Franco-Russian alliance in any meaningful sense *in the long term*, however, is debatable. The existence of any form of Polish state not under their own auspices was always likely to prove unacceptable to the Russians because of the potential threat it would pose to Russia's internal stability. Could Napoleon, therefore, realistically have sacrificed the Poles of the Grand Duchy in the interests of his broader foreign policy? The answer must surely be that he could have done so, although it would not have been without its cost. The sacrifice of the Poles of the Grand Duchy, either by returning them to Prussian rule or handing them over to the Russians, would not, of course, have looked, or been, very honourable or moral, but then, in the final analysis, diplomacy is not about morality but about power and what suits the biggest nations. Territories, and indeed whole states, regularly changed hands at this time on the basis of the desires of the most dominant powers, so there can be little doubt that the Emperor could have abandoned the Grand Duchy of Warsaw had he wanted to. The Poles would have been appalled, but there was little they could have done to harm Napoleon or his empire. The vast majority of Frenchmen, meanwhile, would hardly have raised a murmur at the loss of an eastern European state that had only been brought into existence in 1807 and seemed to be of slight importance to France's security or other vital interests. There was thus no insurmountable practical obstacle to Bonaparte sacrificing the Poles in the interests of the Franco-Russian alliance, although there were, admittedly, arguments against it. The moral issue was one, though it could be ignored easily enough. Harder to disregard, perhaps, was the Emperor's cherished self-image as a hero to the Polish nation, complicated possibly by his ongoing relationship with his mistress, Marie Walewska, but Napoleon was certainly not incapable of making personal sacrifices if he felt it to be in the interests of his policy. That still left more hard-nosed power-political considerations. Giving the Prussians back their former Polish territory, for example, would be potentially dangerous in that it would augment the power of a state whose rulers retained a fierce hostility towards the Emperor and France, but then it would not have increased Prussian might that much and the gift might have gone some way towards improving Prusso-French relations. Similarly, granting the Tsar control over the Grand Duchy of Warsaw's lands would have boosted Russian power, although this would surely have been offset by a consequent strengthening of the Franco-Russian alliance.

It seems hard to dispute that Napoleon could have abandoned the Poles had he judged it necessary in the interests of his foreign policy. Why he didn't do so when such a move would have done so much to resuscitate the Russian alliance, a cornerstone of the long-term maintenance of the Bonaparte dynasty and France's hegemony in western and central Europe, is thus a key question. Perhaps his affection for Marie Walewska and his fondness for being seen as a hero by the Poles played a part after all. They should certainly not be discarded out of hand as contributory factors, given the Emperor's often romantic nature. He also often commented that to abandon the Poles would be unconscionably dishonourable. Napoleon, however, almost always needed a hard-headed reason to back up an emotional one before committing himself to a particular course of action: the head had to support the heart. As regards the Polish question, that reason was provided by Napoleon's developing thoughts, in 1809–10, on his foreign policy in general and the place of the Poles within it.

The plain fact is that, hypersensitive as the Russians were about a possible secret Napoleonic agenda for Poland, the Emperor does seem from mid-1809 on to have been contemplating changing the basis of his foreign policy from the alliance with Russia to one with, among others, the Poles. As we have seen, the failure of the Russians to support him properly during his war with Austria made a profound impact upon Napoleon. Indeed, he went so far at one point in the summer of 1809 as to inform Caulaincourt bluntly that he no longer believed in the Russian alliance, but added that his ambassador in St Petersburg should carry on as usual lest France's enemies get wind of the deterioration in Franco-Russian relations and seek to exploit it. The fact that Napoleon tried to win the hand of a Russian bride in late 1809 and early 1810 indicates that, at that time anyway, he was keeping the option of maintaining the Russo-French alliance as the basis of his foreign policy very much open, but at the same time, he began to explore alternatives. The most important such, as we shall see shortly, was making Austria a key ally, but he was also interested in the possibility of how the Poles might help him maintain France's European hegemony. In this light, it is extremely interesting to find him repeatedly hinting to Vienna after the conclusion of peace at Schönbrunn that he would be willing to hand back the Illyrian Provinces to Austria in return for the cession of the Habsburgs' remaining Galician lands, which he would give to the Poles. Also intriguing is the fact that, in July 1810, the Emperor ordered his minister of war to have a large quantity of weapons kept ready in case he decided to arm the Polish population. This was essentially a precautionary, defensive measure designed to protect the Grand Duchy against a possible Russian attack, but it is not inconceivable that Bonaparte was at least toying with the possibility of one day using the Poles as an offensive weapon against Russia.

By the time Napoleon issued this order to his minister of war, his thoughts on the future direction of his foreign policy had become somewhat clearer, for just as the Tsar had effectively washed his hands once and for all of the Franco-Russian alliance as a meaningful arrangement in early 1810, the Emperor had also decided at around the same time to dispense with any real idea of relations with Russia having special significance or forming the cornerstone of his plans. Whereas the cause of Alexander's effective abandonment of the system established at Tilsit was the Polish question, for Napoleon, the straw which finally broke the camel's back was that tricky human convention called marriage.

The Emperor was always a keen student of history and his studies of great empires, such as those of Alexander and Charlemagne, taught him that his own empire was likely to be split up, or might not even survive at all, unless he could pass it on to an indisputable male heir upon his death. As things stood in 1809, his heir was his elder brother, Joseph, but he was not at all the kind of man likely to be able to hold the Napoleonic Empire together, as his precipitous flight from Madrid in summer 1808 had highlighted. Napoleon's other brothers were no better suited to the role of Emperor either, although his stepson, Eugène de Beauharnais, was a young man of very great promise. He was doing a sterling job ruling the Kingdom of Italy as Bonaparte's viceroy and had served with distinction in the war of 1809 at the head of Napoleon's forces in northern Italy. Eugène would probably have made an excellent emperor and was certainly greatly liked and admired by his stepfather-in-law, but Napoleon was not prepared to make him his official heir. The trouble was that he lacked either the royal blood which might make him acceptable to the established crowned heads of Europe or the Bonaparte blood that might allow his accession to the throne of France to go unchallenged following the Emperor's death. Napoleon's sister Caroline and her equally ambitious husband, Joachim Murat, for example, would be highly likely to seek to swap their Neapolitan thrones for the much greater French ones, claiming a closer blood link to the Emperor than Eugène, especially as all the female members of the Bonaparte clan detested Josephine and, by implication, her offspring with a passion. In order to secure a trouble-free succession to a man whom Napoleon himself could groom to continue his legacy from birth, the Emperor needed a legitimate son of his own.

The trouble was, of course, that after more than a decade of marriage, Josephine had shown that she could not provide him with one. As late as 1806, Napoleon had good reason to believe that responsibility for the couple's child-lessness lay with him rather than his wife. After all, she had had two children by her first marriage whereas he had so far had none, even with one of his many mistresses. But then, in December 1806, one of those mistresses gave birth to a son. Unfortunately, the Emperor could not be sure that the child was his as he was only one of the mother's partners at the time the boy was conceived, but his birth gave Napoleon hope that he might well be able to father an heir after all. He therefore started to play with the idea of divorcing Josephine and remarrying – hence his unsuccessful bid for the hand of the elder of the Tsar's sisters at Erfurt – but his retention of a genuinely deep affection for his wife, whom he also saw as a lucky talisman, made him reluctant to pursue the matter with much vigour. An event in the autumn of 1809, however, finally made him decide to act.

The young Pole, Marie Walewska, was the one mistress for whom Napoleon entertained real fondness, even love. Following their affair in Poland in early 1807, the Emperor had encouraged her to come to Paris, which she eventually did at the start of 1808, staying there and resuming their intimate relationship for several months before returning once more to Poland. Then, in late summer 1809, while Bonaparte was working out the peace settlement with Austria, he invited her to join him at Vienna. By the end of September, to both their surprise, Marie was pregnant. This time there could only be one father.

Marie Walewska's pregnancy was important for two reasons. First, it seemed to increase Napoleon's affection for the Poles. Before the child was even born, the Emperor was claiming, though out of earshot of the Russians, that one day it would be King of Poland.* Whether he was serious in this bold claim, we simply do not know, but there seems little reason to dismiss it out of hand as nothing more than the excited declaration of a new father.

The second, and more immediate, repercussion of Marie Walewska's pregnancy was that the conclusive proof of his ability to father a child finally convinced Napoleon to ditch Josephine and seek a new wife who might bear him the legitimate son and heir he craved. At the end of November 1809, therefore, following his return from central Europe, Napoleon told Josephine of his intention to divorce her. Her initial reaction was hysterical, with fits of sobbing and wailing, but when she realized that her husband was resolved, she accepted it with admirable forbearance. To his credit, Napoleon made sure that Josephine was looked after very well after the divorce, which took place in mid-December 1809, and remained on good terms with both her and her children thereafter. Nevertheless, the die had been cast and the Emperor's job now was to make sure that the pain he had caused his ex-wife (as well as himself) in the interests of his dynasty was not for nothing.

The prospect of producing a son and heir was certainly the most important benefit of the Emperor's decision to remarry, but it was not the only one. It also provided him with an opportunity to pursue diplomatic objectives. As he explained to his brother Joseph, 'I must look for ways to further the interests of France through my next union', which effectively meant that Napoleon must marry a member of one of Europe's leading established ruling families. More specifically, Bonaparte targeted a marriage to the younger of the Tsar's sisters, the Grand Duchess Anna, as a final test of the value and validity of the ailing Franco-Russian alliance. Should the Romanovs prove willing to form a dynastic link with Napoleon, there would be hope yet for the partnership between Russia and France; but should they refuse, the Emperor would consider the alliance truly moribund.

At the end of December 1809, Caulaincourt, following instructions from

---

* The child, born in May 1810 and named Alexandre, was a boy. Although he never became ruler of his mother's country, he did serve his father's nation as both an ambassador and, ultimately, foreign minister under the emperorship of Bonaparte's nephew, Napoleon III.

Paris, raised the issue with Alexander of his newly-divorced master marrying the Tsar's sister, Anna. As at Erfurt, the Russian ruler prevaricated, repeating that the final decision rested with his mother. Predictably, when the Tsar asked her, the stridently anti-French Dowager Empress was not at all supportive of the proposal, describing Napoleon as 'a man of vile character'. She allowed her son, however, as ruler of Russia and arbiter of his country's fate, the right to make the final choice whether to accept or decline. Probably she knew he would turn the offer down, for the Tsar had already confessed to his favourite sister, Catherine, that Bonaparte's marriage proposal was 'one of the most disagreeable plights in which I have ever found myself' and that, 'My own view is that because of all the trouble, annoyance, bad-feeling and hatred aroused by that person [Napoleon] it is easier to deny him his wishes than accept with a bad grace'. The affection Alexander had felt for the Emperor at, and for many months after, Tilsit had now clearly all but disappeared.

The Tsar put off rejecting the bid for Anna's hand as long as he could, hoping that the Emperor would agree to the draft convention on Poland, which Bonaparte was scrutinizing in Paris at this time, before he had to turn down the marriage proposal. Caulaincourt pressed Alexander repeatedly, though, in the first weeks of 1810 for an answer until finally, following an ultimatum from Napoleon in early February demanding a straight 'yes' or 'no', the Tsar was forced to stop prevaricating. He was flattered by the proposal, he claimed, but had to decline it on the grounds that Anna, at just fifteen, was too young to marry. To soften the blow, most particularly in the hope that it would encourage the Emperor not to reject the draft Polish treaty, the Tsar suggested that the offer might be more favourably received in a couple of years' time when Anna was more mature.

Napoleon, as Alexander must have guessed from the impatience with which Caulaincourt had demanded an answer, was not prepared to wait so long to find his new bride. Indeed, even before the Tsar's formal rejection of his bid for Anna's hand had been received, the Emperor had lost patience with the Russian's dithering, deciding that 'To adjourn is to refuse'. When news of the official rejection finally reached Paris, it hardly came as a surprise, but it infuriated Napoleon nonetheless. He considered the excuse of Anna's youth a pathetic one and took his supposed ally's refusal as proof of Alexander's bad faith. This was not an inaccurate reading of the situation, for although there was some genuine concern about Anna's age, this would certainly not have been an insurmountable obstacle to the marriage had that been what the Tsar wanted. Thus the rejection was a snub to the Emperor and indicated Alexander's lack of confidence in the French alliance. With his personal affection for Napoleon all but gone, and the thought in his mind that Russia and France might in the near future move from being allies to rivals or even enemies, the last thing the Tsar wanted was to make Bonaparte his brother-in-law.

The failure of the Russian marriage proposal – the second time, indeed, that the Emperor had been snubbed by the Romanovs on the issue – had a profound effect upon Napoleon. Coming on top of the disappointment of Russia's feeble performance during the war against Austria, it persuaded him, if not to break with Alexander forthwith – there was no point in driving him into the arms of France's enemies – then at least to look elsewhere for the basis of his future foreign policy. As St Petersburg could not be relied upon to support him, Napoleon decided, he would take steps to build relationships with other states that would enable him to contain any potential Russian threat to the security of his empire.

One such state, as we have seen, was the Grand Duchy of Warsaw, and it is interesting to note that Bonaparte's rejection of the draft Polish convention came almost immediately after the Tsar's refusal of his bid to marry Grand Duchess Anna. Partly perhaps this was pique at the rebuff he had received from Alexander, but, more importantly, it denoted a definite shift in the Emperor's thinking regarding his foreign policy. If the Russians were turning their back on the French alliance by rejecting his marriage proposal, then Napoleon would keep open his options to expand the Grand Duchy in future and turn it into a powerful bulwark against Russia should that become desirable or necessary.

The key state that Bonaparte sought to court, as his foreign policy evolved in early 1810, was his four-time enemy, Austria. Following their defeat in the war of 1809, the Habsburgs had appointed their ambassador in Paris, Count Metternich, foreign minister, and the new incumbent's chief policy was to pursue as good relations with Napoleonic France as possible. The motivation for this was not any affection for either the Emperor or his country, nor did it mark the end of Austrian desires to reclaim their lost territories or former position of dominance in Germany and Italy, although hope of actually achieving this had all but evaporated. Rather, Metternich's new approach signalled an appreciation of the realities of European politics as they stood in late 1809. The recent war had taught Vienna that the French Empire was too powerful to defeat and that to oppose it risked grave misfortune. By getting in Napoleon's good books, by 'adapting to the triumphant French system', as Metternich himself put it, the new Habsburg foreign minister hoped to achieve the security for the Austrian Empire and its elite that resistance to Bonaparte had failed to win. It was a stark measure of just how successful the Emperor's policy of cowing his defeated enemies could be.

The means Metternich chose to try to improve Austro-French relations was to promote the idea of a marriage with the daughter of Emperor Francis, the twenty-year-old Marie Louise. The Habsburg princess was not especially beautiful, afflicted, as she was, with the prominent chin prevalent among members of her family, but she had a good figure and, what was most important, her immediate female ancestors had all proved remarkably fecund. The notion of marrying her attracted Napoleon when it was put to him, and he even ordered negotiations exploring the possibility of the union to begin while he was still awaiting Alexander's response to his bid for Grand Duchess Anna's hand, a mark of how convinced he was that the eventual answer from Russia would be negative.

As soon as the Tsar's formal rejection had been received, Bonaparte pressed ahead vigorously with plans to marry Marie Louise. Francis was not keen to see his daughter wed a man he personally despised, but he was made to appreciate the sense in it by Metternich. The Austrian people too, as far as we can tell, seem to have broadly approved of the match as it offered the prospect of lasting peace with the mighty French. The marriage contract was duly signed as early as 9 March in Vienna, Archduke Charles ironically standing in for Napoleon, who remained in Paris. Marie Louise then travelled to France for her formal wedding at the start of April. It was noticeable, and portentous, that at the service the Austrian ambassador replaced his Russian counterpart as the foremost foreign emissary.

The marriage of Napoleon to Marie Louise, and the upturn in Franco-Austrian relations, cemented the shift in the Emperor's foreign policy away from Russia. Indeed, in the spring of 1810, his foreign minister, Champagny, even began to formulate plans for building an anti-Russian coalition. These were certainly not pursued with any vigour at this time, but the fact that the possibility of war with Russia was being seriously considered once again in Paris highlights just how far the Russo-French alliance had declined.

The potential threat stronger relations between France and Austria posed to Russia was not lost on the Tsar. The announcement of the betrothal of Napoleon and Marie Louise so soon after the bid for Grand Duchess Anna's hand had been rejected had provoked an indignant protest from Alexander at what he claimed was a slight to his family, but what had really upset him was the imminent union of the Bonaparte and Habsburg dynasties. Given that he could have prevented this union simply by agreeing to the Emperor's request to marry his sister, who was always Napoleon's first choice, it was a bit rich of the Tsar to make such a song and dance about the alleged affront to his family's honour; but then he wouldn't have been Alexander Pavlovich Romanov if he hadn't.

Once the Franco-Austrian knot had been tied, the Tsar remained both piqued and worried, behaving, in fact, rather as a spurned lover might when their former flame finds a new partner. Typically – although, to be fair, it was also in Russia's national interest – he soon tried to break up the new, improved relationship between Paris and Vienna by sending a special envoy to the Austrian capital to encourage the Habsburgs to resume an active policy of trying to restore their former position in Germany and Italy that the French had taken over. The Austrians, not wishing to offend the Russians, listened politely to the envoy's pleas but, when they were offered an alliance in mid-1810, Metternich made it absolutely clear that he was not interested and that Vienna's course had been set.

The course of Paris and of St Petersburg also appeared to have been set by mid-1810, and they ran in opposite directions. Disappointment over the Ottoman Empire, Prussia and the Polish question had destroyed Alexander's faith in the Franco-Russian alliance, while Russia's failure to support him properly in his war with Austria, or provide him with a Romanov bride, had shattered Napoleon's. The alliance made at Tilsit was, to most intents and purposes, dead, though it suited both sides to maintain the illusion of partnership for the time being – the French benefited from St Petersburg's continued hostility towards Britain and adherence to the Continental Blockade, while Russia gained time to build up her forces in preparation for a possible, perhaps even probable, renewal of war with France. As 1810 progressed, however, yet more points of dispute would surface between the Russians and the French which would make it hard to maintain even the illusion of an alliance.

Although Napoleon's formal acknowledgement at the Erfurt conference of Russian control of Moldavia and Wallachia had gone a little way towards mending some of the damage done to Russo-French relations by the Turkish question, that thorny problem remained a serious cause of friction between St Petersburg and Paris over the next few years. Russia, of course, remained at war with the Ottoman Empire following her deliberate sabotage of French-led peace moves in summer 1807, but by early 1809 the Tsar and his government were keen to end the conflict with the Turks. The struggle had become stalemated after the Russians had re-established control over the Principalities in winter 1807–8 and St Petersburg wanted to disengage, with its conquests acknowledged by Constantinople. To Russian dismay, however, the Turks refused point blank to agree to peace on the basis of their accepting the loss of Moldavia and Wallachia, so the war dragged on. Unwilling to recognize that their Turkish adversaries might have rather more gumption than they believed, most Russians put this rebuff of their peace initiative down to French intrigues at Constantinople, an incorrect assessment but one that highlights the intense suspicion felt in Russia towards France when it came to south-east Europe.

In late summer 1809, that suspicion surfaced again, although this time it was the relationship between the French and the Serbs that was the focus. Disappointed by the ineffectiveness of the support their rebellion against Ottoman rule had so far received from Russia, the Serbs appealed in August 1809 for backing from France. Napoleon was unwilling to destroy his relations with the Turks by answering the rebels' call, but the fact that an appeal had been made greatly alarmed and riled the Russians, who viewed themselves as the Serbs' rightful protectors. The Emperor's negative response to the appeal for help notwithstanding, Russian concern was heightened further that autumn, when the French took control of Habsburg lands bordering Serbia. Suddenly, France rather than Russia seemed to have become the favourite to lead any possible mass revolt by the Turks' European subjects.

The improvement of Franco-Austrian relations in early 1810 brought Russian anxiety over south-east Europe to fever pitch, with the emergence of the fear that Napoleon might seek to partition the Ottoman lands with the Habsburgs rather than the Romanovs. Such apprehensions were unfounded, however, for Bonaparte still favoured the continued existence of the Ottoman Empire in as complete a state as possible. Indeed, from 1810 onwards, Paris once again looked, as it had in 1806, to building as good a relationship with Constantinople as it could on the basis that the Turks might prove valuable diplomatic and, if necessary, military partners against Russia. The Tsar and his ministers were duly alarmed by the resumption of vigorous French efforts to court an empire against which they were at war, although fears that a close Franco-Turkish axis would result soon proved groundless. Napoleon was unwilling, at this stage at least, to seek anything so provocative as an alliance with Constantinople, while the Turks, having made peace with the British in early 1809 following two and a half years of mostly desultory war, had no desire to reignite hostilities with London by drawing too close to the French.

The Turkish question thus continued to exercise a baleful influence upon Franco-Russian relations in 1809–10 in a variety of ways. Much of the damage it wreaked upon the alliance was the result of largely unfounded Russian suspicion – one might even call it paranoia – though that suspicion was in turn at least partly caused by the disappointing attitude displayed by the French over Turkish affairs in 1807–8. St Petersburg's concern over the renewed French wooing of Constantinople from spring 1810 onwards, however, was certainly not baseless, for it was a move which clearly had a strong anti-Russian element. It conformed, moreover, with the Emperor's evolving foreign policy, which saw him courting the Austrians, the Poles and the Persians as well as the Turks. Good relations between France and these nations might not only replace the Russian alliance as a means of helping secure the longevity of French hegemony on the Continent, Napoleon believed, but could also provide the basis of a coalition to keep Russia in check should she seek to cause problems. In the first half of 1810, then, it seemed to the Russians that Napoleon was trying to encircle them, a not entirely inaccurate reading of events. Only among the Swedes, of all Russia's traditional enemies, did the French seem to have or seek no particular influence. By the autumn, though, to St Petersburg's horror and incredulity, one of the Emperor's marshals would be in charge at Stockholm.

It will be remembered that one of the conditions of the treaty of September 1809 terminating the Russo-Swedish war was that the Swedes would also make peace with Russia's ally, France. There had been no serious fighting between the

French and the Swedes since Napoleon's forces had expelled the Scandinavians from their possessions on the southern side of the Baltic in summer 1807, and in order to expedite peace talks in late 1809–early 1810, the Emperor agreed to hand back to Stockholm Swedish Pomerania and the island of Rügen as part of the settlement. In return, the Swedes broke with Britain and formally joined the Continental Blockade, as they had promised the Russians they would.

Franco-Swedish relations thus improved over the winter of 1809–10, but they did not suddenly bloom into close friendship. The problem was Sweden's adherence to the Continental Blockade. The great bulk of Swedish trade was seaborne and so severing commercial links with the world's foremost maritime power (Britain) threatened to inflict even more damage upon the Swedes' economy than it did upon those of other states. For this reason, Sweden's observance of the Blockade was less stringent than it might have been, though not so loose that the Swedes did not feel the pinch. This created a situation in which Napoleon complained that greater efforts should be made to sever trade with Britain, while Swedish merchants and consumers protested that the embargo should be lifted or at least relaxed.

The prospects of France and Sweden developing a close relationship did not, therefore, look good, but the sudden death of the heir to the Swedish throne, in June 1810, opened the way to a surprising development. Following the overthrow and assassination of King Gustavus IV in March 1809, the Swedes had placed his only blood relative, his uncle, on the throne as Charles XIII. The new king was not only old and childless, but also declining mentally, so a minor German royal had been elected Sweden's Crown Prince to ensure a peaceful succession and to provide leadership to the government. His abrupt death in summer 1810 necessitated a search for a replacement and, in a Europe dominated by France, the Swedes decided that it would be in their best interests this time to approach a Frenchman, preferably a relative of Napoleon. Having one of the Emperor's close associates in charge in Stockholm, the Swedes calculated, offered several advantages. The Emperor might, for example, prove willing to allow Sweden to loosen her observation of the Continental Blockade. The French connection could also be expected to provide security against the possibility of further Russian aggression. Indeed, if Franco-Russian relations continued to deteriorate, France might even be persuaded to help the Swedes win back Finland.

The Swedes' first choice was Napoleon's stepson, Eugène de Beauharnais, but this excellent young man was not prepared to renounce his Catholicism and become a Swedish Lutheran, and so ruled himself out. Other obvious candidates, such as one of the Emperor's brothers or brothers-in-law, were either deemed unsuitable or unlikely to accept as they already had a kingdom, so attention turned to Marshal Jean-Baptiste Bernadotte, who was related to Napoleon via his wife, Désirée, the sister of Joseph Bonaparte's wife and an old flame of the emperor. The Swedes had first come across the Gascon marshal during the War of the Fourth Coalition, when he had shown great courtesy to the officers of a Swedish division that had surrendered to him. Now, in late June 1810, that courteousness was repaid with interest by the offer of becoming Crown Prince of Sweden.

Unlike Eugéne, Bernadotte had no qualms about changing religion in order to secure a throne, but as a Frenchman and a Marshal of France, he needed the sanction of the Emperor before accepting the Swedes' offer. It was by no means certain that he would get it. Relations between the two men had always been difficult, thanks largely to the marshal's fierce jealousy of his master, and in 1810 Bernadotte was still in semi-disgrace following his dismissal from command of a corps during the battle of Wagram for incompetence and insubordination. Nevertheless, Napoleon raised no objection to the marshal accepting the Swedish offer. It might be useful having a Frenchman in charge in Stockholm after all, although Bonaparte rightly had reservations about just how pro-French Bernadotte would prove in his new role.

On 21 August 1810, the Swedish ruling elite duly elected Jean-Baptiste Bernadotte, a former Jacobin republican and bearer of a tattoo proclaiming 'Death to kings', Crown Prince of their country. The Russians were horrified. Tsar Alexander believed that at Tilsit Napoleon had ceded the dominant influence on the northern shores of the Baltic to Russia, yet here was a Frenchman being installed as heir to the Swedish throne and effective head of government. It now seemed that Bonaparte controlled the entrance to the Baltic entirely, Denmark having, of course, been driven into France's arms by the British attack on Copenhagen in 1807. Not only was this a potential menace to Russian trade, it raised the grim spectre of a northern front being opened should France and Russia ever go to war again.

That the Emperor was well aware of how Bernadotte's election would be received in St Petersburg is highlighted by his instructions to Caulaincourt to assure the Tsar that he had had nothing to do with the marshal's elevation and that it had been an entirely Swedish initiative. Technically, this was true, but it did not wash with the Russians. They knew that Napoleon could have blocked Bernadotte's election if he had wanted to and saw the fact that he hadn't as a provocative betrayal of what they understood to be the spirit of the agreements reached at Tilsit. Bonaparte had frustrated and upset the Russians over the Ottoman Empire, over Prussia, and over Poland; now he was adding Sweden to the list. In the event, as we shall see, Bernadotte would prove much less loyal to his former master than St Petersburg expected, but that would take time to become apparent. From the perspective of late summer 1810, it seemed to the Russians that by allowing one of his marshals to become Crown Prince of Sweden, the emperor was not only insulting them, but conspiring to injure them as well.

It is often claimed (in books written in English at any rate) that the key factor in the death of the Franco-Russian alliance was the Continental Blockade. This is false. By the time the Blockade became a real issue of dispute between the two powers, the alliance was already all but dead, mortally wounded, from Alexander's point of view, by the Emperor's attitude over the Turkish and Polish questions, and, from Napoleon's perspective, by the Tsar's failure to support him properly against Austria in 1809 or to provide him with a Romanov bride. Problems over the Continental Blockade did, however, deliver the *coup de grâce* to the moribund Russo-French relationship and also, as we shall see, played a role in fomenting Bonaparte's invasion of Russia in 1812.

The simple fact is that Russia's severance of commercial links with Britain did not become a major issue in Franco-Russian relations until the second half of 1810. True, it had caused some difficulty for the Tsar domestically, but this had not generated any real threat to his position or compelled him to relax the measures he had ordered against trading with the British. For two and a half years from late 1807, when Russia broke with Britain, the Blockade was enforced rigorously, in spite of the protests of many Russian merchants, in the hope that it would force Britain to make peace and loosen her maritime control as well as facilitate Russia's own commercial expansion. In mid-1810, however, Alexander quietly ordered the Blockade to be relaxed against neutral ships, thereby allowing British goods, and indeed some British ships flying neutral flags, to enter Russia via that route. This step did not by any means restore Russo-British commercial relations fully, but it did punch quite a major hole in Russia's adherence to the Continental Blockade.

The reasons for the Tsar's move, which is ignored by most historians who mention only his more dramatic public decree, or *ukaz*, of December 1810 (see below), are complicated. Certainly, the fact that none of the main objectives of Russian membership of the Continental Blockade had been achieved by summer 1810 contributed to the change. So too did the fact that Russia's adherence to the Blockade demonstrably damaged the Russian economy. Comparing the period 1802–6 to 1808–12, average annual exports from Russia fell from 54.1 million silver roubles to 34.1 million (largely the result of the loss of use to Russian exporters of British ships, which had hitherto carried over 60 per cent of Russia's export goods), while her imports declined from 40.8 million silver roubles to 20.6 million. This naturally had serious repercussions. Many export trades, such as grain, wood, hemp, flax and furs, suffered a major decline, while the price of luxury imports from overseas, a trade dominated by the British, shot up dramatically (between 1807–11, for example, the price of coffee more than doubled, while that of sugar more than trebled). Nor was the harm restricted to merchants and consumers, for government income from customs duties collapsed after Russia joined the Continental Blockade, from 9.1 million

silver roubles in 1805 to just 2.9 million in 1808, before recovering somewhat in subsequent years. In short, Russia suffered a significant economic decline after 1807, with both exports and imports dwindling, the cost of overseas goods rising, the value of the rouble decreasing, and government budget deficits increasing.*
Yet, strong as the economic pressure to relax observation of the Blockade by mid-1810 was, it would be overstating the case to argue that it forced Alexander's hand. Ailing as the Russian economy was, it was certainly not on the verge of collapse and could thus have continued to bear the burden of close observation of the Continental Blockade for some time yet. That did not, of course, mean that there were not a good many Russians who urged Alexander to authorize some form of relaxation all the same, but their pressure in summer 1810 was not so intense that it compelled him to act for fear of serious political upheaval or even the loss of his throne. The chief reason why the Tsar chose to relax observation of the Blockade was in response to the international, rather than the domestic, situation.

The disadvantages Russia endured as a consequence of observing the Continental Blockade required some form of recompense, but it had become patently clear by mid-1810 that she was not going to get any. The refusal of the British to make peace or to relax their maritime stranglehold, and the failure of Russian trade to expand are certainly relevant here, but the greatest compensation should have come from Napoleon in the form of an agreement to partition the Ottoman Empire, acknowledgement of Russian dominance on the northern shores of the Baltic and satisfaction over the Polish question. The Emperor frustrated the Russians over each of these, so it is little wonder that the Tsar decided in mid-1810 to reduce the damage being done to his country's economy by relaxing observation of the Blockade. The timing was crucial. Only once Alexander had become convinced that the French alliance was effectively a dead letter did he act in regard to the Continental Blockade. His action, moreover, was not mere retaliation, but a response to what he saw as an increasingly dangerous international situation for Russia. Bonaparte's refusal to rule out Polish expansion, his improving relations with Austria, and his courting of the Turks and the Persians were all perceived as serious threats in St Petersburg and so encouraged a massive increase in military spending, including, interestingly, the beginning of work that summer on the construction of a major series of fortifications along the Dvina and upper Dnieper rivers some way inside Russia. This expenditure had, of course, to be paid for: hence the relaxation of the Blockade in an attempt to lift the Russian economy and boost customs revenues.

---

* In truth, administrative mismanagement and heavy military expenditure also contributed to Russia's economic woes, but this did not prevent them generally all being blamed on her adherence to the Blockade.

The key reasons for Alexander's move in summer 1810 were thus bitter disappointment with the French alliance, and concern about the Emperor's activities and possible plans in the international sphere. Predictably, however, that did not prevent Napoleon from complaining irritably about the change in Russia's observation of the Blockade. Throughout the second half of 1810, Bonaparte protested both frequently and strongly about Russia's slack handling of neutral ships which both he and the Russians well knew often carried British goods. In mid-October, for example, he instructed Caulaincourt to 'insist strongly on the confiscation of all ships carrying colonial [British] merchandise', and to tell the Tsar that such seizures would not only yield Russia tens of millions of francs worth of goods but also push Britain towards peace. He returned to the latter theme the following month when he claimed to Alexander that if only Russia would 'seriously prevent the commerce in colonial products, England will make peace in a year'. None of this made the slightest difference to the Tsar's attitude. Indeed, if anything, it hardened over the late summer and autumn of 1810 as Napoleon, while vigorously exhorting everyone else to tighten the Blockade, began himself to undermine it.

From early 1810, the French economy, along with that of the rest of Europe, went into the doldrums, partly as a result of the intense economic warfare being waged, partly because of the general economic cycle, and partly due to the huge cost of all the wars that had been fought in recent years. Suddenly, the French treasury was faced with a shortage of cash to pay for the Emperor's great public works and huge military expenses, but Napoleon found a cunning solution. From August 1810, he introduced a system of licences authorizing the importation into France of a limited amount of British goods upon payment to the French treasury of a very large tariff.

This move had several important effects. First, by providing a lucrative new source of income, it helped solve France's cash-flow crisis. Indeed, part of the reason Bonaparte was so keen for the Tsar to act more vigorously against neutral ships in the second half of 1810 was that re-export to continental Europe from Russia of British goods threatened his own system of re-exporting such merchandise imported under the new licence arrangement. Secondly, the new system dealt a heavy blow to the thriving Europeon black market that had grown up since the introduction of the Continental Blockade by establishing a flow of British goods into Europe via France that sold, despite the high tariffs, for slightly less than they cost when they had been smuggled into the Continent. Thirdly, Napoleon's limited authorization to import British goods undermined his own Continental System, though, thanks to the concurrent decline in the black market, the damage was less severe than it might have been. Finally, there was the impact of the move upon European opinion. Whereas hitherto Bonaparte could claim that France endured the same hardships as every other part of his empire as a result of the Continental Blockade, now the French (or at least their government) were benefiting from the situation in a way that understandably stuck in the craw of other Europeans. This was only exacerbated, of course, by the intense pressure the Emperor put on others to enforce the Blockade as stringently as possible – and his willingness to engage in *ad hoc* exchanges of goods with the British in order to meet each country's particular short-term needs (for instance, French grain went to Britain in return for boots from Northampton and greatcoats from Lancashire) unsurprisingly didn't help either.

Napoleon's policy in regard to the Continental System was indeed becoming a confused and contradictory mess in the second half of 1810. By addressing short-term financial and material needs, he undermined his long-term objective of bringing the British to their knees by ruining their economy. To be fair, he was probably right to do so, but then it would most likely also have been in his best interests to have relaxed, or even abandoned, the Blockade as a whole at this time. He could not, however, quite shake the belief that if only he could get others to tighten the economic noose a bit further, London would cave in. This encouraged him at the end of 1810 to take a step that was to sour Franco-Russian relations even further.

On 13 December, the Emperor announced that he was annexing to France both Holland, from whose throne Louis Bonaparte had resigned in July following a series of bitter rows with his brother over his running of the country, and the north German coast between there and Denmark. There were two main reasons for this move. First, Napoleon decided that he could govern these areas more efficiently and effectively than their present rulers, particularly in regard to preparing for any possible British descent from across the North Sea and producing troops, ships and material for his ongoing wars. Secondly, and most important, observance of the Continental Blockade in both Holland and the north German coastal region was considerably less rigorous than the Emperor wanted. Enormous amounts of British merchandise seeped into the Continent across the North Sea and Napoleon believed that, if he could just stem that flow, Britain's economy might collapse at last. In order to achieve the level of stringency required, however, he decided – probably correctly – that he needed to impose direct rule on these areas (observance of the Continental Blockade was tightest in those parts of Europe which the Emperor ruled directly – except, of course, for the limited importation of British commodities allowed under licence and the occasional authorized exchange of goods between France and Britain).

The French takeover in Holland and north Germany was achieved smoothly enough in the areas themselves, and direct rule did indeed enable the Blockade to be tightened considerably, helping to make the period from early 1811 through to mid-1812 one of the worst for the British economy. The move was not, however, without its costs for Napoleon. For a start, it increased concern throughout Europe that no ruler was safe from the arbitrary actions of the Emperor, a fact which would help persuade many sovereigns to abandon him when the opportunity arose. Napoleon's latest extension of France's borders also created yet further friction with St Petersburg. The Russians were upset by French annexation of two places in particular. The first was the city of Lübeck, on the north German coast just to the east of Denmark. Its occupation gave France her first directly-controlled foothold in the Baltic, a region Russia liked to think of as one she should dominate. The second bone of contention was the Duchy of Oldenburg, a small enclave in north-western Germany which happened to be ruled by the Tsar's wife's uncle and whose heir was married to Alexander's favourite sister, Catherine. As such, the Duke's rule of the duchy had been formally guaranteed by the terms of the peace treaty signed at Tilsit, which pledged France and Russia to respect the territorial possessions of all members of the extended Bonaparte and Romanov families. The abrupt annexation therefore not only deeply affronted a tsar sensitive to any slight, real or imagined, to his family's honour, but also breached the agreement that had restored peace between Paris and St Petersburg in 1807.

Napoleon's decision to annex Oldenburg is often cited as the immediate cause of the momentous public decree, or *ukaz*, Alexander issued on the very last day of 1810. This is incorrect, as news of the annexations did not reach St Petersburg until early 1811. Before examining the real causes of the *ukaz*, however, it is necessary to explain exactly what it was.

The Tsar's decree did not, as again is sometimes claimed, formally withdraw Russia from the Continental Blockade. What it did do, though, was encourage the British and neutrals to circumvent the Blockade while placing major impediments in the way of French merchants looking to export goods to Russia. Specifically, the *ukaz* reduced tariffs on imports brought by sea in neutral ships, sharply increased tariffs on certain luxury imports provided predominantly by the French, and maintained the embargo on *direct* trade with British goods or vessels. In terms of its economic impact upon the effectiveness of Russia's adherence to the Continental Blockade, it was arguably less significant than Alexander's more subtle relaxation in mid 1810 of the rules regarding the treatment of neutral ships, but its political impact was greater. Partly this was due to the very public nature of the decree's issue, partly it was because everyone realized that it was largely an anti-French move.

That Russia might take some form of action hostile to French interests in late 1810 was anticipated in Paris. Indeed, Napoleon had instructed Caulaincourt at the start of December to tell the Tsar that, should he make so bold a gesture as to restore relations with Britain, the Emperor would consider it a *casus belli*. In the event, Alexander did not go quite that far, but the fact that Napoleon issued such a stark warning to his supposed ally speaks volumes about the state of the Russo-French alliance by this time.

Whether the Emperor's message made the Tsar think twice before going ahead and issuing his *ukaz* we do not know, but certainly Rumiantsev opposed the decree on the grounds that it might lead to a resumption of war with France, a development which he felt would be absolutely disastrous for Russia. His passionate pleading with Alexander to rethink fell on deaf ears, however, for the Tsar was determined to make a bold gesture.

If Napoleon's annexation of Oldenburg was not the cause of the *ukaz*, what was? In large part, it was designed simply to build on the earlier relaxation of rules regarding neutral ships in boosting the Russian economy. There was also a powerful personal and moral element to Alexander's decree. The Tsar was appalled that the Emperor could insist upon Russia observing the Blockade stringently while at the same time authorizing the direct importation of British goods into France, many of which were then re-exported, to the great profit of French merchants and the French treasury, to a European mainland deprived of such products except via the black market. It simply did not seem fair that Napoleon's government should benefit from the attempt to force Britain to make peace and relinquish her stranglehold on the seas while Russia and others suffered. It made Alexander furious and determined not to play Napoleon's game. His *ukaz* was intended to be a deliberate strike against both French trade with Russia and, by encouraging an alternative Russian route for British goods to reach the Continent, the Emperor's efforts to control European access to overseas merchandise. It also, of course, threatened to undermine the overall effectiveness of the Continental Blockade at a time when Napoleon was trying to make adherence to it outside France as tight as possible.

The Tsar's *ukaz* of 31 December 1810 is thus an appropriate point at which to declare the moribund Franco-Russian alliance finally dead. Indeed, by making such a public anti-French gesture, Alexander was effectively announcing its demise to the rest of Europe. In Paris, the Emperor was livid at the Russian move. He feared that it might cripple the Continental Blockade (both by opening a large gap in it and encouraging others to follow suit in undermining it), worried that it would seriously damage French finances by denying France a monopoly over the distribution of overseas goods throughout Europe, and was apprehensive that Russia might soon rejoin the ranks of his enemies. In St Petersburg, meanwhile, the Tsar was no happier with his erstwhile ally than the Emperor was with him. As 1811 opened, the stage was set for the death of a potent alliance to become the birth of a cataclysmic war.

13

War or Peace?

At Christmas 1810, just a few days before Alexander issued his momentous *ukaz* undermining Russia's participation in the Continental Blockade, the Tsar wrote to his favourite sister, Catherine. Commenting on the state of Russo-French relations, he remarked candidly, 'It seems that blood must flow again'. In part, of course, this sombre judgement reflected Alexander's expectation that Napoleon would react hostilely to his imminent decree, that the French emperor might even mobilize for war. More than that, however, the Russian ruler's comment betrayed belligerent ideas that were beginning to circulate in his own mind. In the event, the next war between France and Russia would be initiated in mid-1812 by a French invasion of the Tsar's lands, but as 1811 opened, Alexander was seriously considering instigating conflict with Napoleon that year by invading the French Empire.

The reason why the Tsar was thinking about starting a war with his erstwhile ally was a mixture of fear, ambition, frustration and envy. There was no automatic reason for Russia and France to go to war because their alliance had died. One of the factors that had played a critical role in killing the alliance, however, was certainly a major source of Alexander's belligerency. That issue was Poland. It would be hard to exaggerate the impact upon Russian opinion of Napoleon's refusal, in early 1810, to guarantee that the Kingdom of Poland would not be resurrected. Beyond destroying any remaining faith the Tsar had in the French alliance, it convinced many Russians that Bonaparte was not just a poor friend but actually a latent enemy. Throughout 1810 the impression grew in St Petersburg that the Emperor intended to recreate the old Kingdom of Poland at Russia's expense. At that time, Napoleon seems to have had no firm plans to take such a dramatic step, but he did show an interest in strengthening the Grand Duchy of Warsaw as a bulwark against Russia. What his *ultimate* policy towards the Polish question might be, moreover, was unresolved, and an effort to resurrect the old kingdom cannot be ruled out. In any case, whatever his possible intentions, many Russians, including the Tsar, had become convinced by the start of 1811 that the combination of the existence of a Polish state under Napoleon's protection and French mastery of most of Europe posed an imminent and potent threat to Russia. The idea was therefore born of launching a pre-emptive war to bring the Grand Duchy of Warsaw within the Russian Empire and to reduce France's awesome power.

There was more to the Russian movement for a pre-emptive war with Napoleon, however, than fear of what the Grand Duchy might become and ambition to extend Russian influence at that state's expense. There was also genuine concern that Russian backsliding over participation in the Continental Blockade might goad the Emperor into invasion, and the general opinion in St Petersburg in early 1811 was that, if there were to be a war, better that it should be fought on the territory of the French Empire rather than the Russian. Then there were those other Russian concerns about France's links with the Austrians, the Turks, the Persians and the Swedes. In early 1811 they were still relatively undeveloped but, given time, they might become strong. If Russia were to fight the French again, it might be better to do so sooner rather than later. Finally, in this age of autocratic rulers, one must not ignore the emotions of Alexander himself. By the end of 1810, the Tsar's former distaste for and jealousy of Napoleon was beginning to return as a result of the manner in which the French alliance had met its demise. Alexander had stuck his neck out for the special relationship struck up at Tilsit, especially by maintaining strict Russian adherence to the Continental Blockade for two and a half years, yet the Emperor had effectively humiliated him by consistently failing to give him what he and other Russians wanted from their ally. The Tsar's frustration was intense and French annexation of the Duchy of Oldenburg in December 1810 only served to add insult to injury. It is possible too that the birth on 20 March 1811 of Napoleon François Charles Joseph Bonaparte to the Emperor and his new Habsburg wife increased Alexander's resurgent personal antipathy further still, for it presented yet another sphere in which Bonaparte had outdone his Russian counterpart; the production of a male heir. For Alexander, there was definitely a return after 1810 to the resentment and envy of the French emperor that he had felt when constructing the Third Coalition or over the winter of 1806–7 (he would refer to Napoleon in a letter to his sister in December 1811 as 'that infernal creature who is the curse of all the human race', for example). Thus, although the Tsar's aspiration to reduce Bonaparte's power and influence was largely a question of Russian national interest and security, it also owed something to both Alexander's desire to vent his irritation at the bitter disappointment of the French alliance and his resurrected longing to usurp Napoleon as Europe's leading figure.

The plan formulated in the war ministry in St Petersburg to achieve the Tsar's aims was a simple and highly optimistic one. Russia would invade the Grand Duchy of Warsaw and Prussia, hoping that initial success in these operations would induce Austria to ally with her and spark risings throughout the French Empire and perhaps even within France herself. Unfortunately for the Russians, in reality neither the French nor the vast bulk of the peoples of French-dominated Europe were at all inclined to rise up *en masse* against Napoleon in 1811, while the Habsburgs would only consider risking a fifth war against France if Napoleon endured a quite staggering reversal of fortune. Even the downtrodden Prussians were most unlikely to support the Russians openly for fear that the Emperor would destroy Prussia utterly should she be defeated by him again. That only left the Poles of the Grand Duchy, hardly a likely source of cooperation for Russia, but, surprisingly, Alexander seems initially to have viewed the issue of whether he could garner Polish support as the key one in determining whether the pre-emptive war should go ahead. Should the Poles side with Russia, the Tsar reasoned, the balance of forces in northern Europe would swing against Napoleon (the wholehearted support of Prussia from the start was, rather naively, taken for granted in these calculations). Polish assistance would also facilitate the advance of the Russian armies into central Europe, whereas their opposition would either slow it or leave the invading forces' flanks vulnerable should they try to bypass the Grand Duchy. The attitude of the Poles, Alexander therefore decided, was critical.

Winning support for Russia in Warsaw, though, was a predictably tall order. To his credit, the Tsar at least appreciated this fact and shaped his policy accordingly. Back in spring 1809, while General Gallitzin's small Russian army was tardily mustering on the borders of Austrian Galicia, an envoy had arrived at the commander's headquarters. He was the representative of a small but wealthy group of Polish aristocrats from within the Grand Duchy of Warsaw who, impatient with Napoleon's failure so far to resurrect a fully independent kingdom of Poland, had decided to explore an alternative venue. Should Alexander be prepared to restore Poland to its former extensive boundaries and make it an independent state, the envoy had told Gallitzin, the Poles would recognize the Tsar as their king. The general had duly informed his master of this unexpected approach, but Alexander had been unwilling to follow it up, instructing Gallitzin only to inform the envoy that efforts should be made to build support among the Grand Duchy's nobles for a link to be made with Russia rather than France. Then, a year later, following Napoleon's refusal to ratify the draft treaty concerning the future of Poland, the Tsar had instructed his old Polish friend, Prince Adam Czartoryski, to draw up a plan for the reconstitution of a Polish kingdom under Russian rule. The Pole had produced a memorandum for Alexander's perusal, only to see him shelve it for the moment. Now, however, in early 1811, Russia's ruler turned to the idea and Czartoryski again. The Kingdom of Poland would be restored, excepting the sizeable Belorussian areas, and would be granted a constitution allowing it a measure of independence, the Tsar told the Polish prince, provided the Grand Duchy of Warsaw sided with Russia in the proposed war against Napoleon and accepted Alexander as king of the resurrected Polish state. Czartoryski was to spend the spring travelling throughout the Grand Duchy calling upon important noble families to inform them of the Tsar's offer and try to win support for it. Meanwhile, Prussia, Austria and Sweden would be approached regarding

Russian plans, and efforts would be made to establish closer links with influential Frenchmen who it was hoped might foment revolt against the Emperor.

That Alexander was confident in early spring 1811 that Russian plans for a pre-emptive war against France would receive widespread support was highlighted by his decision in March to move a sizeable force of five divisions to the border with the Grand Duchy to form the core of a projected army which would advance towards central Europe. Inevitably, news of this menacing troop movement soon reached the ear of Napoleon, along with word of Russian efforts to build an anti-French coalition including Prussia, Austria and the Poles. The Emperor immediately issued orders calling up more conscripts throughout the French Empire, and Napoleonic forces in Germany and Poland were reinforced. He also drew up a contingency plan of war, ordering the Grand Duchy of Warsaw's army to withdraw to the line of the Oder river in Prussia in the event of a Russian attack. Once there, the Polish force would be joined by Marshal Davout's army, which was stationed in northern Germany, and together they were to defend this line while Bonaparte planned and executed a counterthrust. It was a typically vigorous and forceful response from Napoleon to the crisis, but as he himself told Davout at this time, 'I do not want a war with Russia'. His response was intended solely to deter the Russians from attacking, not to provoke them nor in preparation for an attack of his own. Indeed, the Poles of the Grand Duchy, who, the Emperor feared, might try to exploit the situation to ignite a Russo-French conflict they hoped ultimately to benefit from, were explicitly instructed to keep all the extra ammunition and weaponry they were being sent away from the Russian border.

As Europe held its breath in the spring of 1811, everything depended upon the response of various nationalities to Russian efforts to win support; efforts which the Tsar expected to be successful. It did not take long, however, for Alexander's hopes of constructing a sixth anti-French coalition to be shattered. Both Prussia and Sweden, while polite, extremely hesitant to give any kind of encouragement or backing to Russia. The Austrians, meanwhile, ruled out any possibility of siding with the Russians and flatly rejected a proposal to cede their remaining Galician lands to the envisaged new Kingdom of Poland in return for Moldavia and Wallachia (which the Turks had not yet even formally yielded to Russia). Efforts to forge links with anti-Napoleonic groups in France proved predictably unproductive as well, and, in some ways most frustrating of all for the Tsar, Czartoryski reported that he was having almost no success in winning support for Russia among the Polish nobility of the Grand Duchy of Warsaw. Faced with such overwhelming rejection, Alexander bowed to the inevitable and ruled out the possibility of a pre-emptive war against France. By summer, the crisis had passed and the prospect of a new Russo-French conflict seemed to have faded. Four years of peace between Paris and St Petersburg would be celebrated that

July after all – though whether a half decade of tranquillity would be reached the following year was very much open to question.

Despite the preparations for war that both Russia and France made in the first few months of 1811, diplomatic relations between the two countries continued, albeit. Two issues dominated Franco-Russian exchanges during the first half of 1811: the Tsar's modification of his adherence to the Continental Blockade and Napoleon's annexation of the Duchy of Oldenburg.

The Emperor's initial response to Alexander's *ukaz* of 31 December 1810 was certainly not to invade Russia to compel him to reverse it. Napoleon was, however keen that the Russians should return to observing the Blockade stringently and devoted considerable diplomatic activity in early 1811 to trying to persuade them to do so. Russia's lenient treatment of neutral ships blew a major hole in the Blockade, and with each week that passed more and more British goods entered Europe via the Tsar's ports. Not only did this undermine the attempt to strangulate British trade with the Continent, it also challenged Napoleon's attempt to control (and profit from) the limited import of merchandise from Britain that he was allowing under his licence system. These were serious enough problems, but perhaps just as important was the psychological issue of the Russians defying the Emperor's wishes by tacitly re-engaging in trade with his British enemies. This set a potentially dangerous precedent that Napoleon was eager to expunge. St Petersburg was therefore bombarded with French protests in the weeks following the Tsar's *ukaz*, expressing bitter disappointment at the Russian attitude and pleading for it to be changed. None of them had any discernible effect upon Alexander, who, having set his course, was determined to stick to it, especially as he was planning to go to war with France soon. Until allies had been won, however, the Tsar and his subordinates maintained their outwardly courteous manner in dealing with the French remonstrances while at the same time showing no inclination to budge an inch over the lenient treatment of neutral ships.

Frustrated by the failure of his diplomats to win the Russians round, Napoleon himself wrote a letter to Alexander in late February 1811. It was a polite, mostly humble missive in which the Emperor bemoaned the dramatic decline in Russo-French relations and expressed a fervent wish for them to be repaired. Crucial to that was the rescinding of the Tsar's *ukaz*, the imposition of which had compelled Napoleon to conclude 'that Your Majesty is no longer friendly to me'. Indeed, it seemed to France and the rest of Europe that Russia was abandoning the French alliance and preparing to go over to Britain, a move which, Napoleon warned Alexander, would inevitably mean that 'war would sooner or later follow'.

Napoleon's letter had no more impact upon the Tsar's attitude than the protestations of his minions. Alexander replied politely enough, claiming to be still devoted both to the French alliance and to the Emperor personally, but this was just hollow platitude from a man who was preparing to order his armies to march into the French Empire. The Tsar professed surprise at the hostile reaction in France to his *ukaz*, disingenuously claiming that it had not been intended as an anti-French measure and pointing out that tariffs had been increased on all land-borne goods, not just French ones, even though he knew full well that the great bulk of merchandise entering Russia by land came from France. The decree had been a purely domestic decision aimed at boosting Russian trade, Alexander asserted, and signalled no fundamental shift in Russia's international position. The fact that Russian troops were advancing towards the Grand Duchy of Warsaw's borders as he made this claim called its validity into question.

Napoleon was less than satisfied with this response from his erstwhile ally, and his anger mounted when he heard of Russian officials burning French goods that had been smuggled into the Tsar's territories without paying the tariffs imposed by Alexander's *ukaz*. Given that French officials had been burning smuggled British goods throughout his own empire for some time, the Emperor's rage had a touch of hypocrisy about it, but was genuine enough nonetheless. Talking to a Russian envoy on 10 April, he railed, 'as I can only reply to an affront by an affront, I have given the order, in all the ports that are in my power, to burn everything that may come from Russia. Here is a charming alliance, a very edifying friendship.'

Just as Napoleon was frustrated by his notorious ally's attitude towards trade issues in the first few months of 1811, Alexander was similarly vexed by the Emperor's stance over the Duchy of Oldenburg. As soon as word reached St Petersburg of Napoleon's actions, the Tsar instructed his ambassador in Paris to deliver a strongly worded note of protest to the French foreign ministry, but when Kurakin went to see Champagny, the foreign minister refused even to accept the note, let alone read it. Eventually, the Russians did manage to make their feelings known and demanded that the French withdraw from the annexed duchy, but Napoleon was not prepared to do any such thing. All he would do to assuage Alexander's injured family honour was to offer to compensate the Tsar's uncle for his loss. The proposal that the deposed duke be given Erfurt and its environs, though, a territory barely a sixth the size of Oldenburg, seemed more a further snub to Alexander's wounded pride than a serious attempt to make amends.

Alarmed by the damage the Oldenburg affair was doing to the already tenuous Franco-Russian relationship, Rumiantsev, who remained vigorously opposed to the idea of war with France, came up with a scheme in the early spring of 1811 that he hoped might repair much of the harm done in recent months. The Duke of Oldenburg might be compensated for his loss, the Russian foreign minister suggested, by the cession of a roughly equal-sized slice of the Grand Duchy of Warsaw. The plan was intended to kill two birds with one stone. If Napoleon agreed to it, not only would the Oldenburg issue be resolved, but Russian paranoia about the Emperor's intentions over Poland would be quelled by the demonstration that Napoleon was prepared to sacrifice Polish interests. For some months, Alexander had been drifting ever further apart from Rumiantsev as they disagreed over questions such as the *ukaz* and plans for a pre-emptive war. Indeed, the Tsar practically became his own foreign minister from early 1811, bypassing Rumiantsev almost entirely, for example, in his efforts to garner allies for his projected invasion of the French Empire. Nevertheless, Alexander deemed this latest scheme worth a try and so it was suggested to Napoleon. Realizing that agreeing to it would cost him the loyalty of the Poles while by no means guaranteeing a full Russian return to the French fold, the Emperor rejected Rumiantsev's idea out of hand.

Throughout the spring of 1811, and indeed well into the summer, the Russians continued to complain about the Oldenburg affair, just as the French maintained their protestations at Russia's lenient treatment of neutral ships and punitive tariffs against French goods. Paris agreed to enter talks concerning compensation for the Duke of Oldenburg while St Petersburg consented to discuss the possibility of lowering the tariffs on land-borne merchandise, but on neither issue was progress made. Napoleon repeatedly suggested that Alexander should send a plenipotentiary to France to discuss the range of difficulties dividing their two nations, but the Tsar refused, fearing that an envoy that came under the Emperor's spell, as he had at Tilsit, might agree to proposals that would subsequently have to be disavowed.

Franco-Russian relations thus stagnated in the spring and summer of 1811, but there were notable changes within the French diplomatic service. In April, Jean-Baptiste Champagny was replaced as foreign minister by Hugues Maret. A diplomat of some experience but little skill, Maret was the archetypal 'yes-man' and served in his new post more as a chief clerk than a free-thinking head of foreign policy. Then, in late spring, Armand de Caulaincourt was withdrawn from the embassy in St Petersburg. The ambassador had fallen out of favour with the Tsar in recent months following the deepening rift with France, although Alexander retained a personal affection for him. Indeed, it was the good personal relations between the two men that explains Caulaincourt's recall, for Napoleon was concerned that his representative was becoming too favourable towards Russia and her ruler. As a replacement, the Emperor sent General Jacques Lauriston. A tough soldier rather than a natural diplomat, Lauriston had made his name in seizing the small Adriatic state of Ragusa in 1806 before the Russians could occupy it and then defending it over the following year against the attacks of the Tsar's forces. Whether this record of military success against the Russians played any part in his selection is unclear, although it would have been in fitting with Napoleon's character to choose a man whose presence in St Petersburg might remind his hosts of past failures at defeating the French.

Certainly, Lauriston's tact, or rather lack of it, could not have recommended him for the job, for he got off on the wrong foot with Alexander immediately when he gauchely criticized Russian drills at a military parade. Relations between the two men did not improve over the rest of Lauriston's ambassadorship, though it is unlikely in the grand scheme of things that this was important. Russo-French relations were in too deep a trough for even a man of Caulaincourt's charm and discretion to have done much to improve the situation.

Almost as soon as he returned to Paris in June 1811, Caulaincourt was summoned to report to the Emperor. When asked if the Tsar intended to make war against France, the former ambassador replied that Alexander fervently wanted to maintain peaceful relations with Napoleon. By this time, following the dismal failure of Russian efforts to build an anti-French coalition that spring, such an opinion might well have been accurate, but Bonaparte refused to countenance it and insisted that the recent war scare proved that the Tsar ultimately intended to fight him again. Grilled as to the main cause of Russian discontent with France, Caulaincourt repeated what he had been saying in despatches for month after month before he was recalled: it was the Polish question. The Emperor could either, the ex-ambassador claimed, sacrifice the Poles and resurrect the Russian alliance or stand by them and face interminable friction with St Petersburg. Seizing upon this, Napoleon asked whether satisfying the Russians over Poland would be enough to get them to implement the Continental Blockade stringently again, but then Caulaincourt changed tack and stated that 'The issue is no longer only about Poland'. Napoleon became exasperated with his former representative in Russia, chiding him for his personal affection for the Tsar and dismissing his criticisms of French actions that had undermined the alliance by asserting that it had been killed when the Russians had failed to support France properly against Austria in 1809. The lengthy interview eventually concluded with the Emperor frustrated at not having been offered the means to reverse the recent trend of Franco-Russian relations that he had hoped it might provide. The one thing it does seem finally to have persuaded Napoleon of, though, was the vital significance of the Polish question, for in August he unexpectedly offered St Petersburg a guarantee against the restoration of Poland. By this stage, however, words were not enough for the Russians, and the proposal got nowhere.

As summer 1811 neared its end, Napoleon's patience with Russia was running out. He seems to have genuinely wanted to patch up his differences with the Tsar up to this point, but he was not prepared to make the major sacrifices that might have induced Alexander to return to the French fold. No serious thought was given, for example, to ceding Constantinople and the Straits to Russia or to allowing her to absorb the Grand Duchy of Warsaw. Instead, the Emperor had angered the Tsar over his attitude to the Oldenburg affair, had shown no sympathy for the genuine distress the Blockade had caused Russian trade, and had only made an offer over Poland when it was far too late for such a move to be received with anything but suspicion and derision in St Petersburg.

All that having been said, it is clear that Napoleon made greater efforts in 1811 to restore decent relations between France and Russia than did Alexander. At a diplomatic reception held in Paris on the Emperor's forty-second birthday, 15 August, Bonaparte's frustration with the situation came to the surface in an encounter with the Russian ambassador. In front of the assembled dignitaries, he harangued Kurakin over Russia's policies and attitude over the past year. Accusing St Petersburg of bad faith and of aiming to annex the Grand Duchy of Warsaw, Napoleon vehemently asserted, 'even if your armies were camped on the heights of Montmartre, I would not yield an inch of Warsaw territory! I have guaranteed its integrity ... You will not have a single village, you will not have one mill! I am not thinking of reconstituting Poland ... but if you force me into war, I will use Poland as a weapon against you.' He then threatened to raise more soldiers if the crisis in Franco-Russian relations had not eased by the end of the autumn and warned that he would strip Russia of her Polish possessions if it came to war. He concluded on a more pacific note. If only Alexander would send a plenipotentiary to Paris, or simply grant Kurakin full power to negotiate on his behalf, the problems dividing the nominal allies might be sorted out and a new treaty of alliance drawn up.

Whether the confrontation with the Russian ambassador was pre-planned to convince the Tsar to adopt a more conciliatory tone towards France or an impromptu outburst of frustration is unclear, but the way Kurakin reported it back to St Petersburg made Alexander even less inclined to make serious efforts to mend fences with the French than before. The spectre of Russia being stripped of her Polish territories made a particularly forcible impression upon both the ambassador and his master, and served further to persuade them that this was the Emperor's ultimate intention.

With hindsight, Napoleon's birthday tirade can be viewed as the last chance he gave to the Russians to mend their ways (as Napoleon saw it) before he began to gear the French Empire up for war. If the outburst had indeed been pre-planned and intended as a final warning, though, it failed to have the desired impact in St Petersburg. Alexander was no more inclined that autumn to despatch a plenipotentiary to Paris or to compromise on Russia's lenient treatment of neutral ships than he had been all year. The Emperor's threats fell on deaf ears, so it only remained to be seen if he was prepared to carry them through.

It is impossible to pinpoint the exact moment when Napoleon decided to invade Russia, but an important step towards that fateful decision was taken the day after his confrontation with Kurakin. On 16 August 1811, the Emperor summoned his foreign minister and proceeded to dictate to him a memorandum on the Russian situation as a means of clarifying his own thoughts. There was no possibility, he reconfirmed, of trying to improve relations with the Tsar by compensating the Duke of Oldenburg at the expense of the Grand Duchy of Warsaw, as this would undermine that state and destroy Franco-Polish relations. Nor could the Grand Duchy be abandoned to St Petersburg in the hope of resurrecting the dead Russian alliance as, according to Napoleon, its possession would make Russia the greatest power in Europe.* The prospects for a significant improvement in Russo-French relations thus seemed poor. If Russia continued to drift towards the camp of France's enemies, a preventative war would have to be launched, the Emperor concluded, in order to arrest that dangerous development. The next few months would reveal Russian intentions. If they made serious efforts to patch up their differences with the French, which for Napoleon essentially meant accepting limited compensation for the Duke of Oldenburg and a return to a more stringent application of the Blockade, then a conflict might be averted. Otherwise, Russian enmity would have to be assumed and war would be launched the following summer. In preparation for this eventuality, Napoleonic forces in Germany and Poland would be built up from the autumn onwards.

Although he did not commit himself irrevocably to an offensive war against Russia, on 16 August 1811, Bonaparte did pave the way for the invasion that would take place the following summer. Nevertheless, he seems to have meant what he said in the memorandum about monitoring Russian policy and attitudes for a few months longer before putting his war machine into gear. It was as late as November 1811, for example, before Kurakin confirmed to St Petersburg that Napoleon was seriously preparing for war and that 'The time is fast approaching when, with courage and resolution, we must preserve our national heritage and the present limits of our frontiers'. Moreover, only on 16 December did Bonaparte order the recall of all his key Imperial Guard units serving in Spain, and it was three days after that before the Emperor's librarian was instructed to send him books on Russian topography and the history of Charles XII of Sweden's ill-fated invasion of Russia.[†]

---

* This was extraordinary reasoning not dissimilar to his exaggeration of the significance of Constantinople. Again, perhaps the most convincing explanation for it is that Napoleon wished to provide some kind of concrete argument not to yield something which for emotional reasons he was disinclined to give up anyway – in this case, his desire to maintain his role as Poland's saviour and maybe also to see his son by Marie Walewska one day become the Poles' king.

† In 1708, Charles XII had invaded the Russia of Peter the Great from Poland and penetrated as far as the Dnieper before the Russians, unable to match him militarily, adopted a strategy of refusing battle. Charles's army had then proceeded to wander around Russia and the Ukraine in search of enemies before enduring a terrible winter which savaged his forces. The following summer, at Poltava, some 600 or so miles south of Moscow, Peter smashed Charles's by now heavily outnumbered army and forced the Swedish king to flee with just 1,500 horsemen to Turkish Europe.

By the start of 1812, however, there was no mistaking the probability of a French invasion of Russia that year. This is therefore a good time to examine two fundamental questions concerning that momentous operation. First, why did Napoleon decide to invade, and secondly, was that decision as poor a one, without the benefit of hindsight, as it is almost always portrayed?

Several theories have been put forward as to why the Emperor eventually decided to invade Russia, some more bizarre than others. Sigmund Freud, for example, opined that Bonaparte marched into Russia in the subconscious hope of being defeated so as to punish himself for having divorced Josephine. Others have suggested that the invasion was merely a preliminary step towards the even more ambitious project of marching on British India via European Russia and the vast central Asian steppe. It seems unlikely that one would be adopting too remiss a position to discard both these theories out of hand.

A more serious hypothesis is that Napoleon launched a war against Russia in 1812 to divert the French people's attention from other concerns that the Emperor felt could not easily be dealt with. Certainly, the Europe-wide economic slump of the early 1810s, which was partly caused and certainly exacerbated by the fierce Anglo-French economic warfare, created much discontent within France, and a poor harvest in 1811, which pushed up bread prices, added to the prevailing gloom. This despondency was intensified further still by the failure of French forces to put an end to the Peninsular War, a conflict which claimed a mounting toll of lives and money that could only be made good by increased conscription and taxation. As a consequence of these factors, support for the Bonapartist regime was undoubtedly waning by late 1811 and early 1812 when the Russian invasion was being prepared. Dejected as many Frenchmen were, however, there was no serious threat of major unrest or revolt within France at this time, a fact which severely undermines the argument that the invasion of Russia was primarily a distraction. The sheer scale of the operation and the risks it entailed surely mean that it would only have been undertaken as a diversion if the threat to the Napoleonic regime in France was critical.

Another interesting but ultimately unconvincing theory as to why the Emperor decided to invade Russia was that it was an attempt finally to bring Britain to the peace table. This premise operates on two levels. The first is that the only hope Napoleon had of forcing the British to accept a European settlement highly favourable to France was through the Continental Blockade. Russia's lenient treatment of neutral ships was seriously weakening this effort and so the Tsar had to be compelled to adhere to the Blockade stringently once more. The second level of the theory is that by defeating Russia on her own ground, Bonaparte would destroy any hope London had of building another anti-French coalition, thereby forcing the British to bow to the inevitable and make peace. There are elements of validity to both branches of the thesis. The Emperor himself, for example, occasionally talked of a successful invasion of Russia forcing the British to the peace table for want of viable Continental allies, and we have already seen how important it was for him that the Russian gap in the Blockade be sealed. In the final analysis, however, the notion that Napoleon invaded Russia *primarily* in order to force Britain to make peace seems too Anglocentric. Napoleon may have hoped, perhaps even expected, that defeating the Russians would end the war with the British too, and it seems highly likely that a return to a stringent observation of the Blockade would have featured among his peace terms to the Tsar, but these were very much secondary issues in the Emperor's decision to invade. For a start, arguing that Napoleon invaded Russia in order to defeat the British is surely putting the cart before the horse. He invaded Russia in order to defeat the Russians. Any repercussions, as far as the struggle with London was concerned, were significant but ultimately coincidental. As regards the Blockade, strict Russian adherence to it was not as important an issue in terms of bringing the British to heel as it is sometimes made out to be. Napoleon never relied solely on economic warfare as a means of beating the British, but always retained the idea of invading Britain as an option; indeed he devoted much money and effort to the project in the years up to 1812. Moreover, Napoleon had already tacitly acknowledged that the Continental Blockade was unlikely to achieve the desired effect *vis-à-vis* the British, in summer 1810, when he had introduced his licence system for the import of British goods, a system which he in fact greatly extended in early 1812, just a few months before the invasion of Russia. It seems reasonable to conclude, therefore, that the main reason strict Russian observance of the Blockade was so important to the Emperor was not the goal of bringing Britain to her knees. Instead, the key reasons were the issue of Napoleon's credibility (see below) and the fact that the influx into Europe via Russia of British merchandise was undermining his efforts to make money from controlling the Continent's access to such goods. Insofar as thoughts of defeating Britain were a factor in the decision to invade Russia, then, they were only a minor one.

The issue of French honour, or, perhaps more precisely, credibility, was more significant in persuading Napoleon to invade. Indeed, in his proclamation to the *Grande Armée* on the cusp of the invasion, the Emperor highlighted Russia's breaking of the terms and spirit of the alliance made at Tilsit as a major cause of the war, arguing that they left France with the choice of either fighting or being dishonoured. Of course, commanders have always tried to stir their soldiers to greater efforts by appealing to their sense of honour, but Napoleon's words were not just hot air – or at least they weren't if one interprets them the way he did. By dishonour, what he really meant was loss of credibility. Russia and her Tsar had openly defied the Emperor, to some extent even humiliated him, and he was determined that this should not stand. By issuing his public *ukaz* and then trying to organize an anti-French war in such a way that the whole of Europe ·

soon became aware of it, Alexander had thrown down a gauntlet to Napoleonic authority. Were Napoleon to fail to pick it up, he might look weak or fearful, and this might encourage those rulers who opposed French dominance of the Continent, especially the monarchs of the other great powers, to unite against him. This was why he was so concerned that the Tsar should rescind his *ukaz*, for it would show Russia abandoning her independent stance and returning to a position of inferiority to France. In truth, Napoleon probably exaggerated the potential repercussions of failing to respond to the challenge head-on, but the importance he attached to the issue of credibility was real enough as is shown by the fact that he often used it to justify the Russian invasion.

Credibility, however, is not an entirely sufficient explanation for the Emperor's decision to invade Russia. Another, even more powerful factor was at work and it was related to that old thorn in the side of Russo-French relations; the Polish question. Napoleon certainly feared in 1811–12 that the Russians intended, as soon as a decent opportunity arose, to annex the Grand Duchy of Warsaw. Indeed, he openly accused St Petersburg of such an aim in his stormy encounter with Kurakin on 15 August 1811 and, in justifying the large demands of manpower he was making of his German allies in early 1812, he argued that 'the territory of the Confederation [by which he principally meant the Grand Duchy] is endangered'. Napoleon did not launch an invasion of Russia merely to forestall a Russian assault on Warsaw though. His plans were much greater than that. A clue to his intentions is provided by the fact that he referred to the invasion as the Second Polish War (the first having being fought in 1806–7). An even clearer hint was given in his proclamation to the *Grande Armée* on the eve of the attack: he concluded by claiming that 'the peace treaty we shall conclude this time will carry its own guarantee; it will put an end to the fatal influence which Russia has exercised over Europe for the past fifty years'. How was that to be achieved? The answer was contained in a memorandum dictated by Napoleon in April 1812: 'The object which the Emperor has in view is the organization of Poland, with the whole or a portion of her old territory.' In other words, Napoleon intended his Russian invasion to result in the resurrection of a much greater Polish state akin to, and perhaps called, the Kingdom of Poland. True, he never *publicly* proclaimed this as an aim of the war but it seems clear that this was his ideal goal. The alliance treaty he made with Austria in early 1812 even explicitly envisaged the Habsburgs' remaining Galician possessions being ceded to the Poles in return for compensation elsewhere. The Franco-Russian war of 1812 would clearly have more at stake than simply whether the Russians returned to observing the Continental Blockade strictly.

If the resurrection of a greater Poland was the ultimate aim of the invasion, what was the reason behind such a goal? Certainly it was no longing to satisfy Polish nationalist aspirations that most fired Napoleon, though the thought of making himself an even greater hero to the Poles may have provided an element of his motivation. Rather the key to the idea of building a stronger Poland was the desire to achieve the long-term security for both the Bonaparte dynasty and France's European dominance that the death of the Russian alliance had once again imperilled. Alexander's efforts to construct an anti-French coalition in the first third of 1811, and his consistent refusal throughout the year to budge over the issue of his *ukaz*, convinced the Emperor, not unreasonably, that St Petersburg was committed to making war on France as soon as it felt it could win. That clearly was not the case in 1811, but, as Napoleon confided to Marshal Davout, over time, and especially once their ongoing war with the Turks was resolved, the Russians 'could become more exacting'. It was to prevent this from happening, to stop the Russians from posing a serious threat to the French Empire in future, and to create a strong and loyal bulwark against them, that Bonaparte decided to try to roll back Russia's borders. The idea was most succinctly expressed by the Emperor himself shortly after the invasion had begun. 'It is time to finish with the Northern Colossus,' he told a group of his closest aides, 'to push him back and to place Poland between him and civilization.'

Before moving on from consideration of why Napoleon decided to invade Russia, there is one more point to be made. Even though the Emperor was right to take Russian hostility to France, from the end of 1810 on, for granted, there was no guarantee that St Petersburg would ever consider itself to be in a strong enough position to risk war with the French, especially so long as the Poles remained loyal to France and the Prussians and Austrians continued to be unwilling to take on the might of the French Empire. Napoleon could thus have chosen to wait on events. There were, however, two powerful reasons not to do so. First, as Russia was only likely to initiate a war when she felt she could win, the logic of waiting for that moment to arrive could easily be called into question. Second was the issue of the Emperor's age. There can be no doubting that Bonaparte's own abilities and character had played a key role in the building and maintenance of French dominance in Europe. He was a uniquely gifted individual and was aware of his own importance, especially on the battlefield. If there were to be a conflict with Russia in the future, it was better that he should be around to lead the French war effort. By late 1811, though, Napoleon was in physical and, some have argued, mental decline. He had begun to put on a good deal of weight, which undermined his general fitness, while his powers of concentration and energy were showing signs of diminishing, possibly the result of a failure of his pituitary gland. That he himself was aware of, and concerned about, a possible deterioration in his abilities is shown by a comment he made to General Vandamme shortly before the invasion. 'We are both getting old, my dear Vandamme,' he said, 'and I don't want to find myself in old age in a position in which people can kick me in the backside, so I am determined to bring things to a finish one way or the other.' In the wake of his triumph at Austerlitz, the Emperor had remarked, 'We are granted only a limited time for making war. I give myself another six years, after which even I ought to come to a stop.' The invasion of Russia took place six and a half years after this statement was made. Is it fanciful to imagine that Napoleon decided to invade when he did for fear that to put off a conflict he was convinced was inevitable would mean that he would have to fight it when he was some way past his prime?

Whatever reasons historians have chosen to explain Bonaparte's decision to invade Russia, almost all have condemned that choice as a foolish one. Given what happened, it is easy to see why, but is it possible that such judgements rely predominantly on hindsight? To counter this notion, a string of names can be trotted out of people who advised Napoleon against invading Russia before he actually did so. Fouché, the Emperor's ex-minister of police, Cambacérès, the archchancellor of the Empire, and Jerome Bonaparte all counselled against an invasion, for example, though as none of them was a man of particular understanding or experience in military or foreign affairs, the value one should place on their judgement must be open to question. Of more significance, perhaps, was the opposition of the former foreign minister Jean-Baptiste Champagny, who, instead of an invasion, advocated countering the Russian threat by partitioning Prussia and using much of Frederick William's territory to create a greater Polish state still ruled by the King of Saxony, a cynical idea but one not entirely without merit in power-political terms. Similarly noteworthy, the former captain that was ordered to prepare a demographic and statistical analysis of Russia, Leclerc, stopped short of advising against the invasion entirely but did warn that 'if the Emperor were to have his army penetrate into the interior of Russia, it would be annihilated, as was that of Charles XII at Poltava, or forced into precipitate retreat'.

The most famous and frequently cited opponent of the Russian invasion, though, was the former ambassador to St Petersburg, General Armand de Caulaincourt, a man of considerable military and diplomatic experience. According to his memoirs, he consistently argued against the invasion, suggesting instead that Napoleon should concentrate on building up an Austro-Polish-Swedish buffer zone to contain the Russian threat. Perhaps the key argument he deployed, or at least the one most often cited by historians, is a remarkably prophetic warning the Tsar allegedly gave him shortly before he left Russia and which Caulaincourt supposedly repeated to Bonaparte at their lengthy meeting in June 1811:

If Emperor Napoleon wages war against me, it is possible, even probable, that he will defeat us if we accept combat, but this will not give him peace. The Spaniards have often been defeated, and they are neither vanquished nor subdued ... Were the fortunes of war to prove contrary to me, I would rather withdraw to Kamchatka [the easternmost province of Asian Russia] than yield provinces and sign treaties in my capital that are no more than truces. The Frenchman is brave, but prolonged privations and a bad climate wear him down and discourage him. Our climate, our winter will wage the war for us.

It is just possible that Caulaincourt faithfully repeated in his memoirs exactly what Alexander said, and indeed likely that the Tsar tried to give him some kind of admonitory message to take back with him to Paris in late spring 1811, but the passage above smacks a little too much of wisdom after the event. At the time it was alleged to have been said, the Russians had spent the previous few months futilely trying to win allies in order to avoid fighting the French on their own soil. The calmness with which the Tsar allegedly discussed the prospect of an invasion seems somewhat suspicious. It is odd also that Alexander would have admitted quite so plainly to Napoleon's representative that he did not think his forces were a match for the French. Most dubious of all is the reference to the winter, which does not feature prominently in what we know of other Russian plans to counter an invasion up to the eve of the war. Although some of the passage quoted above rings true (the Tsar was certainly impressed by the example of the conflict in Iberia, for example), it seems not unreasonable to conclude that it was embellished by Caulaincourt after the invasion in order to strengthen his case that the Emperor should have heeded his advice before committing himself to the operation.

In any case, much as there were those who argued against the invasion before it took place, what historians have tended to ignore is that there was a more general opinion that Napoleon would in fact defeat the Russians. The wily Austrian statesman Metternich, for instance, expected the French to win, as indeed did most senior military and diplomatic figures throughout Europe (in this regard, there is a striking similarity with majority European opinion on the eve of the Nazi invasion of the Soviet Union in 1941). As far as most observers at the time were concerned, the imminent war was fraught with far greater peril for Russia and the Tsar than for France and the Emperor. Not only was the Russian Army weaker in numbers and quality of leadership than the mighty *Grande Armée*, but if the conflict started to go badly for Russia there was the possibility either of a peasants' revolt or a coup by the nobility. When a comet appeared in the night sky over Europe in late 1811 it was widely viewed in Russia as a portent of imminent disaster. In the event, of course, disaster befell the French and their allies, but most Russians in late 1811 and early 1812 feared that it would befall them.

The evidence, therefore, suggests that a great deal of the criticism of Napoleon's decision to invade Russia does indeed stem from hindsight. It is certainly a startling fact that the invasions of Charles XII in the eighteenth century, Bonaparte in the nineteenth and Hitler in the twentieth all ended in ruin for the invader, but, on each occasion, the fundamental problem was not so much the decision to invade *per se* as bad errors of judgement that were made in either planning or conducting the invasion. Charles XII, for example, did not need to march aimlessly into the Ukraine, and Hitler was actually offered peace terms by Stalin in 1941 that would have seen the Soviets cede vast territories to the Nazis, only for Hitler to turn them down as he hoped for the complete destruction rather than just the severe weakening of the Soviet regime. In Napoleon's case, the argument holds true also. As we shall see, he might have forced the Russians into an early decisive battle near the frontier that could have ended the war. Even failing this, he had strategic options other than the ill-starred one he did adopt that could have paved the way for a successful conclusion to the struggle. Few things are inevitable in history and the calamitous end to the Emperor's invasion of Russia was not one of them.

Nevertheless, the crossing of the Niemen and the fighting of a conflict on Russian soil was never going to be an easy operation, a fact of which Napoleon himself was well aware. Indeed, shortly before leaving Paris for eastern Europe in 1812, he confided to his prefect of police, 'I am embarking on the greatest and most difficult enterprise that I have so far attempted'. The invasion, he knew, would be a gamble – war always is – but his decision to invade Russia was not as irrational or foolish a one as it is generally portrayed. It was, though, the product of an avoidable and, with hindsight, disastrous failure on Bonaparte's behalf to keep the Russians as allies. For this error, the Emperor would end up paying far more than he, or anyone else in early 1812, imagined.

14

The Greatest Enterprise

A key part of Napoleon's preparations for the invasion of Russia from autumn 1811 on, and of Russian efforts to meet that assault, was the search for allies for the looming conflict. There was never really any doubt which side the Poles of the Grand Duchy of Warsaw would take, so French and Russian diplomatic activity focused on Prussia, Austria, Sweden and the Ottoman Empire.*

The imminent Russo-French struggle placed the Prussians in a most unenviable predicament. Having rejected Russian attempts to make them an ally earlier in the year, by autumn 1811 they were reconsidering their position. If Napoleon was going to invade Russia, it seemed probable that he would wish to use Prussia as a staging ground and the prospect of vast numbers of Napoleonic troops being quartered on Prussian soil and provided for largely at Prussian expense understandably filled Berlin with horror. It therefore decided to approach St Petersburg for an alliance.

The Russians, naturally, were delighted to have the Prussians come to them and responded positively to the approach. A secret military cooperation convention was swiftly signed in the Russian capital in October 1811, but it offered Berlin a future scarcely preferable to becoming a staging post for the *Grande Armée*. Although Russia pledged to come to Prussia's aid if she were invaded following a refusal to cooperate with Napoleon, this promise was given only on the understanding that the great majority of Prussian territory would be yielded to the French with a stand only being made behind the Vistula. This left Frederick William wavering as to his intentions, and when, in late 1811, a Prussian approach to Vienna for a military alliance was rejected and the Emperor made it clear to the Prussian king that unless he and his marshals received full cooperation in their preparations for war his realm would be abolished, the unfortunate monarch lost what little spirit he had managed to summon to resist the French. The culmination of the climbdown came on 24 February 1812 with the signing of a Franco-Prussian alliance which effectively made Frederick William's state

---

* Just before the invasion, Alexander did secretly send an emissary to General Poniatowski, commander of the Polish forces, with the extraordinary offer of the crown of Poland should he defect with his troops to the Russians, but this was very much a last-ditch act of desperation by an anxious Tsar and it was predictably rebuffed.

a French puppet. By this one-sided agreement, not only did Prussia undertake to bear the matin burden of quartering and supplying the *Grande Armée* as it gathered for the invasion of Russia, she also pledged to take part in that operation, contributing a force of 20,000 men, almost half the standing army she was allowed by the Franco-Prussian treaty of 1808. Unsurprisingly, some leading Prussians advocated fighting instead of agreeing to such terms, and a quarter of the Prussian army's officers resigned their commissions and left the country, many going to Russia, after the King put pen to paper, but the fact that Frederick William signed nonetheless showed just how successful Napoleon's policy of cowing the Prussians was.

The loss of Prussia as an ally was a blow to the Russians, but they were even more dejected the following month when Austria also signed a treaty of alliance with France. The agreement of March 1812 between Paris and Vienna was much more even-handed than the earlier pact with Berlin. In return for pledging 30,000 men to the invasion of Russia, the Habsburgs obtained a promise from Bonaparte that they would receive territorial gains should he defeat the Russians and also a guarantee that they would not be stripped of their Galician lands were a Polish kingdom to be recreated except in exchange for the return of what had become France's Illyrian Provinces. The fact that Emperor Francis secretly informed St Petersburg after signing the treaty that the Austrian troops would try to avoid combat with Russian forces during the forthcoming campaign suggested that his commitment to the French was hardly heartfelt or indissoluble, but the more critical point was that Austria was clearly not prepared to side with Russia unless Russia could defeat Napoleon's invasion on her own.

In the Franco-Russian contest for the support, no matter how desultory, of the two great powers of central Europe, then, the French clearly came out on top. Given the recent history of Europe, this outcome could be seen as surprising, but it is testament to the extent to which the Emperor had succeeded by this stage in cowing his former Prussian and Austrian adversaries. Looking at the past again, it must have seemed odds-on that the Swedes and Turks would both side with Bonaparte in 1812 as well, but here too events were to take a different course.

When Marshal Jean-Baptiste Bernadotte had become Crown Prince of Sweden almost everyone in Europe had expected Stockholm to gravitate towards Paris, especially as a few months before the Frenchman's elevation Napoleon had removed a major stumbling block to improved Franco-Swedish relations by returning Swedish Pomerania as part of the peace treaty signed in early 1810. Also part of the treaty, however, had been Sweden's agreement to join the Continental Blockade. With a former Marshal of France as heir to their throne and effective head of government, the Swedes hoped that the Emperor would prove willing to allow them to relax their observation of the Blockade, strict adherence to which was crippling Sweden's predominantly maritime commerce, but Bonaparte proved unshakable in his insistence that Stockholm continue to apply its measures against British trade as strenuously as possible. To be fair to him, Napoleon could hardly allow the Swedes to relax the Blockade whilst trying to ensure that everyone else adhered to it closely, but that only suggests that the Emperor should perhaps have had a rethink about the Continental System in general. In any case, the upshot of his uncompromising stance was a severe deterioration in Franco-Swedish relations, a development by which the new Crown Prince, a man fiercely jealous of his former master, was none too troubled.

When, therefore, in late 1811, Bonaparte approached the Swedes for their support in his impending invasion of Russia, he found them less receptive than he might have hoped for a nation which was a traditional enemy of the tsars and had been at war with the Russians as recently as 1809. The deal was simple: if Sweden helped the French against Russia, Napoleon would guarantee the return to Stockholm of their recently lost Finnish provinces. The reply the Emperor received surprised him. The Swedes claimed not to be bothered about Finland but did want Norway, then ruled by France's ally Denmark, so any agreement was made conditional upon Bonaparte agreeing to promise them that country. Napoleon, irritated by the failure of Bernadotte to prove more forthcoming in his dealings with his former homeland, rejected the Swedish proposal, commenting in private, 'There is nothing to be gained by sacrificing a loyal friend [Denmark] in order to gain an untrustworthy ally'. Efforts to forge a Franco-Swedish alliance consequently foundered, although this did not bother the Emperor too much. He was convinced that, as soon as the invasion got underway, Sweden would not be able to resist the temptation to exploit Russia's preoccupation and would attempt to reoccupy Finland.

What Napoleon did not expect the Swedes to do was come to an arrangement with St Petersburg, yet that is exactly what they did in spring 1812. This was partly, though not entirely – Sweden had put out feelers for a possible alliance with Russia in late 1811 – the result of the crass reannexation by Napoleon in January 1812 of Swedish Pomerania, a move designed to ensure that the whole of the southern coast of the Baltic was under French control prior to the invasion and perhaps also to warn Stockholm against seeking an accommodation with the Russians. In this latter aim it failed, for on 5 April Sweden and Russia signed a secret military and diplomatic accord. By its terms the two countries agreed to mount a joint descent upon the north German coast, with 25–30,000 Swedes and 15–20,000 Russians, but only after Sweden had occupied Norway and, if she felt it necessary, invaded Denmark to defeat her as well. Once peace was restored to Europe, both sides pledged to guarantee whatever conquests the other might have made. Seeing as no time frame was put upon the envisaged Swedish occupation of Norway and subsequent joint descent on French-occupied Germany, the treaty provided the Russians with no help in facing the imminent Napoleonic invasion; except, of course, the valuable knowledge that Sweden would not join in the attack. That alone would probably have been enough to make it worth St Petersburg's while to sign the accord, but a useful bonus for the Russians was that Stockholm agreed to act as an intermediary in efforts to bring about a formal Russo-British rapprochement. This resulted in mid-July 1812 in Britain and Russia making peace, and later helped pave the way for the eventual formation of a sixth anti-French coalition.

The Swedes, then, slipped through Napoleon's net, yet surely the Turks would not do the same? After all, the Ottoman Empire had been at war with Russia since the end of 1806 over possession of Moldavia and Wallachia, a conflict that in late 1811 and early 1812 remained unresolved. When, therefore, in February 1812 the Emperor approached Constantinople proposing an alliance whereby the Turks would muster a large army to invade southern Russia at the same time as he advanced further north and then, after the war, receive the whole northern shore of the Black Sea as a reward for their efforts, he must have expected it would be favourably received. As with the Swedes, however, the Turks proved surprisingly reticent. The truth is that they were exhausted by years of war and did not consider Napoleon's expectations of their military capabilities realistic (he envisaged them mustering and maintaining an army of at least 100,000 men for the proposed campaign in southern Russia). Besides, Turkish trust of the French had been undermined by the Emperor becoming an ally of their mutual Russian enemy in 1807.

If Napoleon underestimated Turkish war-weariness and overestimated their military capabilities, the Russians misjudged the other way round. In the summer and autumn of 1810, they had enjoyed a successful campaigning season against the Turks in south-eastern Europe, advancing from Wallachia into what is now Bulgaria. Confidently expecting Constantinople to agree to yield the Principalities formally before much longer, the Tsar had authorized the withdrawal of troops from this front in early 1811 in preparation for the pre-emptive war he was then hoping to fight against Napoleon. Instead of making peace with the Russians in the spring and summer of 1811, however, the Turks had exploited the weakening of enemy forces facing them to launch an offensive that drove Alexander's armies back into Wallachia. By autumn, with the prospect of a French invasion growing, the Russian commander in south-east Europe was ordered to try to make peace on the basis of Russia abandoning Wallachia but retaining Moldavia. To St Petersburg's chagrin, the Turks rejected this offer and insisted upon full restoration of both provinces. Eager for peace Constantinople may have been, but it had been watching developments in Europe closely and judged that it could afford to take a hard line with the Russians. This belief was justified in early 1812 when the Tsar's Minister of War pleaded with him to agree to the Turkish conditions, so desperate was the need for Russia to pool all her resources to meet the imminent French invasion. Reluctantly, Alexander acquiesced, and on 28 May the Treaty of Bucharest was signed, returning the Principalities to Ottoman rule and allowing the Russians to pull back tens of thousands of troops from south-east Europe.

Peace between Russia and the Turks was swiftly followed by a Russo-Persian agreement that ceded the Russians small gains in the Caucasus and allowed them to withdraw further soldiers to confront Napoleon's armies. The Emperor did not learn of either peace treaty until after he had invaded Russia and, although annoyed by them, dismissed them as unlikely to prove significant. This was a similar response to his failure to win the Swedes as allies; but was his nonchalant attitude in all three cases justified? Militarily, the troops freed up by the conclusion of peace with the Turks and Persians did not, in the event, play a decisive role in determining the outcome of the 1812 campaign. The availability of soldiers that might otherwise have been tied down guarding against the Swedish threat in Finland was more significant, as they were able to play a fuller part in the year's momentous events, but even here their part was far from crucial, as Russia's ultimate success did not depend on numbers. Had Napoleon fought a different, longer-term campaign, then the absence of the Swedes, Turks and Persians as co-combatants might have proved more important militarily, but he did not. Psychologically, however, the fact that the Russians did not have to think about wars on three other fronts when Bonaparte crossed the Niemen must surely have contributed to them adopting the dogged approach to resisting the invaders that they did. That is not to say that had the Russians remained embroiled with the Ottoman Empire, Persia and Sweden when the Emperor invaded they would have collapsed and surrendered, but it seems logical that it would have made it harder to maintain a resolute stand. In this regard, then, St Petersburg's success in coming to an arrangement with three of her traditional enemies in the weeks before the French invasion may have been rather more important than Napoleon supposed.

Although the Russians proved able to secure peaceful relations with most of their traditional enemies in the build-up to the 1812 campaign, the French failed in a belated effort to reach a settlement with the British. In mid-April, Paris approached London for a peace treaty. The basis upon which the Emperor announced he was willing to negotiate was, from the French point of view, not unreasonable. In return for agreeing to the restoration of the expelled royal family in Portugal and acknowledging the control over Sicily of the former rulers of Naples, Napoleon wanted Britain to accept Murat as the new king of Naples and Joseph as monarch in Spain. All other issues were to be resolved on the principle of *uti possedetis* (each side retaining what they currently held).

London summarily dismissed the French peace tentative. The Royal Navy's dominance of the Mediterranean Sea and the presence on the island of thousands of British soldiers were judged better guarantees of Sicily not falling to France than Napoleon's pledged word, and, by the spring of 1812, Portugal, though not yet restored to its former rulers, had been successfully cleared of the French on no fewer than three occasions since 1807, the most recent being the previous year. Nor was the Emperor's offer, through the principle of *uti possedetis*, to recognize the colonial conquests Britain had made at France's (and others') expense particularly attractive, as there was little the French could do to reverse them in the near future due to the supremacy of the Royal Navy. Indeed, *uti possedetis* was anathema to the British government as it would have meant accepting France's hegemony on the Continent, and her control of Belgium, Holland and the north German coast, both of which were considered intolerable threats to Britain's long-term security (as well, it must be said, as to her efforts to become the leading world power by keeping continental Europe divided and therefore unable to challenge her domination of the seas). Nor was London at all keen to give the French a helping hand in Spain, where resistance to Joseph's rule remained very much alive, by acknowledging the eldest Bonaparte brother as king and withdrawing British forces from the Peninsula.

It had been the situation in Iberia, and the desire to improve it before embarking upon a war against Russia, that had primarily prompted Napoleon's approach to the British. We left our account of events there in early 1809, following the Emperor's brief Spanish campaign and the expulsion of British forces from the Peninsula, Napoleon's departure to fight the Austrians at this critical juncture soon proved costly. The British returned to the Peninsula that spring, this time under the command of Sir Arthur Wellesley, better known by his title when elevated to the peerage that summer; Wellington. An excellent general, perhaps second only to Napoleon himself during this period, Wellesley promptly drove the French from Portugal and successfully maintained an Anglo-Portuguese army in Iberia over the following years. Lack of numbers meant he spent much of his time on the defensive, but he was able on occasion to mount thrusts into Spain.

Wellington's success was in contrast to the fate of the Spanish army, which had been all but annihilated by the French by the end of 1809. Fortunately for Wellington, though, the guerrilla menace in Spain grew as the threat from Spanish regular forces diminished. The *partidas*, as the guerrilla bands were called in Spain, exercised an influence way beyond their size, tying down far more French troops in trying to quash them than they themselves numbered. They played havoc with French communications, butchered tens of thousands of French soldiers (as well as many thousands of Spaniards), and made the imposition of law, order and effective government exceedingly difficult, thereby severely hindering any chance Joseph's regime had of winning the support of a sizeable percentage of the Spanish population. Far from being the freedom fighters of legend, the great majority of guerrillas were essentially little more than bandits who lived off whatever they could take from the invaders or, failing that, the local population. Nevertheless, their contribution to the eventual French defeat in the Peninsula was highly significant. Without them, the regular forces fighting Napoleon's armies would simply have been overwhelmed by sheer numbers.

Conversely, the inability of the French to master the guerrilla menace owed much to the continued presence of regular forces in Iberia, most especially the Anglo-Portuguese army of Wellington. If the British commander proved impossible to drive from the Peninsula, however, he did not on the other hand seem likely ever to be able to push the French back over the Pyrenees. Although another major effort at reconquering Portugal was defeated in early 1811, Wellington was unable to build upon his success throughout the rest of the year by advancing far into Spain.

As 1812 opened, the Peninsular War was thus a stalemate. To win it, the French would need to pour more troops than ever before into Iberia, but they could not safely do that until Russia had been dealt with. Indeed, in the short term, the removal of soldiers from the Peninsula for the Russian campaign presented Wellington with opportunities he was quick to take advantage of, capturing two key fortress towns on the Portuguese-Spanish border in the first four months of 1812. Still, the French retained large numbers of men south of the Pyrenees, sufficient to hold their ground, provided serious errors were not made, if not to do much more.

The fate of Iberia, then, looked set to be decided in Russia. A quick and easy French victory there would make it possible for Bonaparte to send more soldiers than ever before into the Peninsula, as well, perhaps, as at last encouraging the British to make peace. A defeat for the Emperor, on the other hand, especially a costly one, might lead to further withdrawals from Iberia that would make it impossible for the French to hold on to all, maybe even any, of Spain. The key campaign in deciding the outcome of the Peninsular War would not, therefore, be waged south of the Pyrenees but many hundreds of miles to the north-east in the vast expanse of the Tsar's empire.

The Russian Army that prepared to meet the French invasion in 1812 had been improved since Tilsit, but still retained serious weaknesses. During the tenure at the ministry of war from 1808–10 of General Alexei Arakcheev, an expert on cannon and a tough disciplinarian who had earned himself the nickname 'the Bulldog', Russian artillery had been the only arm to receive proper attention, but improvements were undoubtedly made in this area. Technologically, Russian cannon design and manufacture was modernized, leading to better quality and quantity of pieces. Russian howitzers were a particular success, being widely acknowledged as the best in Europe by 1812. Equally important, Russian artillery tactics were modified to incorporate greater use of the massed battery, employment of which had played a major role in bringing the French so many military triumphs. The standard of artillery officers (indeed of officers throughout the army), however, was little improved by 1812.

Arakcheev's successor at the war ministry was Mikhail Bogdanovich, Baron Barclay de Tolly, generally known just as Barclay. As his name suggests, his ancestry was partly Scottish, but he had been born in 1761 in the Tsar's Baltic territories to a relatively obscure aristocratic family of Lutheran Protestants. His non-Russian religion and nationality helped to make him unpopular with Orthodox Russian officers – the Russian Army was riven during this period by tension between what were called the 'Russian' and 'German' factions, 'German' here applying to anyone or anything that wasn't explicitly Russian – but Alexander liked his organized and efficient manner, and this was enough to secure him the position of minister of war in 1810. It proved a good appointment. Barclay was a thoughtful man who recognized the need for change within the Russian Army. One of his main targets was the lot of the average soldier. He advocated less severe punishment, a better diet, and generally more humane treatment for the Tsar's rank and file. Reactionaries among the Russian officer class (of whom there were many) viewed this with deep suspicion and continued to treat their troops as if they were little more than animals, but more enlightened officers accepted Barclay's recommendations and saw the morale and effectiveness of their men improve as a result. It was a similar story when the Minister of War promoted increased musketry training and less drill in the hope of boosting the Russian infantry's firepower. Conservative officers remained wedded to the cold steel of the bayonet as the more 'Russian' weapon, while more progressive commanders acted upon Barclay's wishes and improved their units' skill with the musket. Barclay also showed that he appreciated the advantage of more flexible military organization and oversaw both a slimming down of the cumbersome Russian infantry divisions and, shortly before the invasion, the introduction of the corps system. In January 1812, frustrated by the generally lackadaisical attitude of many Russian officers, Barclay tried to inculcate a more professional spirit into the army by introducing a manual entitled 'Code on the Conduct of Major Military Operations'. This defined the tasks and responsibilities of different officers and units, and gave guidelines for conduct in the field. Most Russian officers, though, simply dismissed it as either patronizing or overly Germanic in its quest for uniformity. The success of Barclays' reforms, then, was limited, and there were parts of the army that in 1812 remained as backward as ever, such as the transport and medical services, but the Baltic baron had unquestionably had a positive impact overall on the effectiveness of the Tsar's military.

The Russian Army was not just better than it had ever been in 1812, it was also bigger. At vast expense, Alexander had built up his regular land forces by the eve of the invasion to an unprecedented (in Russia) 409,000 men. In addition to these, the Tsar could call upon the services of the militia (*opolchenie*), although the few militia units that took part in battles or played any other kind of active military role in 1812 were invariably extremely poor quality, dreadfully equipped (weapons were usually no more than modified farm implements), and consequently next to useless. Even discounting the *opolchenie* altogether, though, Alexander still had over 400,000 soldiers with which to defend his lands. This, however, is a potentially misleading statistic. Of the 409,000 men in the army, only a little over half were ready (or nearly ready) to operate against the invaders. Well over a third were either scattered in distant garrisons or in reserve formations. For the first weeks of the invasion, therefore, Napoleon would have to contend with no more than 225,000 men. Subsequently, Russian numbers could be expected to grow as reserves were called up and troops recalled from other parts of the Tsar's empire, but even then the size of frontline forces was likely to remain limited to maybe 250–300,000 men by the difficulty the underdeveloped Russian economy and administration were bound to have in effectively equipping and maintaining more than that number of soldiers on active operations.

The roughly 225,000 troops the Emperor would have to contend with in the opening phase of the invasion were deployed in three main armies near Russia's western borders. The largest of these was the First Army of the West and consisted of a little under 130,000 front-line troops, 19,000 of them cavalry, and nearly 600 cannon. This force was stationed in an arc a little way to the east of the Niemen River with its headquarters at Vilna. Command of this army was given to the Minister of War, Barclay, but this appointment displeased several Russian generals who had held that rank longer than the Baltic baron. There was also some reason to doubt if Barclay was up to the job of such a senior field command. He had done well in leading much smaller forces both at Eylau and in the audacious crossing of the frozen Baltic Sea in early 1809, but was unproven in such a large, independent command. Nor was he a natural leader, most officers and men finding him laconic and diffident. Many Russian generals feared that the tall, sombre Lutheran would prove too cautious in directing the Tsar's largest army.

The Second Army of the West, at around 50,000 men, 11,000 of whom were cavalry, was rather less than half the size of Barclay's force. Positioned south of the First Army, between the Niemen and the huge expanse of all but impassable wetland known as the Pripet Marshes, the Second Army was commanded by General Prince Peter Ivanovich Bagration, the one Russian hero of the débâcle at Austerlitz. Bagration could scarcely have been more different from the minister of war. Where Barclay was pale, bald, stern and cautious, Bagration was swarthy, hirsute, lively and bold. Unsurprisingly, the two men did not get on, and this was made worse in 1812 by envy. Barclay was jealous of the prince's popularity with the army, both officers and men, while Bagration resented the Baltic baron's appointment to command the much larger First Army, especially as, despite being four years younger, the Second Army commander was a general of longer standing than the war minister.

The Third Army of the West contained around 45,000 frontline soldiers, and thus was almost as large as Bagration's force, but it was still forming south of the Pripet Marshes and east of Russia's frontier with Austria when Napoleon invaded. Command of this army, which was largely made up of troops who until recently had been fighting the Turks in south-east Europe, was given to General Count Alexander Petrovich Tormasov, a man most famed for his strict approach to discipline.

To confront the Russians, the Emperor mustered the largest army Europe had ever seen. The call for troops went out in 1811–12 to all parts of the French Empire. By the time of the invasion, Bonaparte had gathered more than 600,000 first- and second-line soldiers, 80,000 of them cavalry, and almost 1,500 cannon, in north-eastern Europe. Only around half the men in this force came from what was then France. The 300,000 'French' therefore included Belgians, Dutch, north-western Italians, and Germans from the left bank of the Rhine and near the North Sea coast. Perhaps as few as one in three of the soldiers who invaded Russia in 1812 was what we would today call French. Napoleon's various German allies within the Confederation of the Rhine contributed around 125,000 men, the largest contingents coming from Bavaria, Saxony and Westphalia, and the Austrians and Prussians provided a further 50,000 between them. The Poles of the Grand Duchy made up over a tenth of the force's total strength, thereby forming the largest single non-French national grouping, while the Kingdom of Italy supplied 30,000 soldiers. The remainder of the Emperor's army was made up of a mix of Swiss, Neapolitan, Danish, Illyrian and even Spanish and Portuguese units. One would be hard-pressed to think of a more nationally varied force in all of history.

The army Bonaparte mustered for the invasion of Russia was certainly immense, but its overall quality was not as good as that of previous Napoleonic forces. Much of the blame for this is often put on the relative lack of Frenchmen in the army, the argument being that other nationalities did not fight particularly well for the Emperor, but, in fact, most non-French units acquitted themselves as well as the French. Only the Prussians, Iberians and Dutch (whose country had been annexed in 1810) seem to have performed less well than they might, but together these made up less than 10 per cent of the total force.

The key reason why the army of 1812 was not as high quality, man for man, as Napoleon's previous forces was simply that such a large percentage of the troops were inexperienced conscripts fighting their first campaign. These men, of all nationalities, were often reluctant soldiers and many would prove unable to cope with the demands that the particularly tough conditions of 1812 were to make of them. The greenness of many of the troops was exacerbated, moreover, by the decline in quality of the Napoleonic officer class. The huge expansion in the rank and file inevitably created an increased demand for officers and led to many inexperienced or incompetent men being given commissions as well as to numerous officers being promoted beyond their abilities. Of course, the army that gathered in north-eastern Europe in 1812 contained as many, if not more, veterans and talented officers as any previous force Bonaparte had commanded, but their quality was diluted by sheer numbers.

Of the more than 600,000 men deployed in eastern Prussia and the Grand Duchy of Warsaw by the summer of 1812, around 450,000 were initially ordered to cross the Niemen into Russia, the rest being held back to protect supply lines, provide reserves and guard against any possible recalcitrance from the Emperor's allies. The invasion force proper was divided into five parts. By far the largest of these was the main army under Napoleon himself, consisting of three standard corps, two cavalry corps and the Imperial Guard. In keeping with the inflated scale of the whole enterprise, each of these formations was much larger than in previous years. The Imperial Guard now numbered almost 50,000; the two cavalry corps, commanded by Marshal Murat, came to over 20,000; the corps of Marshals Ney and Nicolas Charles Oudinot, a tough, fearless brewer's son raised to the marshalate in 1809, totalled just under 40,000 men each; and Davout's corps included over 70,000 soldiers. This mighty force was predominantly French and contained the bulk of the veterans who fought in 1812. It gathered in the weeks before the invasion west of the Niemen, roughly opposite Barclay's headquarters at Vilna.

To the main army's right rear (to its south-west) congregated an auxiliary army just over 80,000 strong, mostly Italians and Bavarians with a leavening of French, commanded by the Emperor's ex-stepson, Eugène de Beauharnais, Viceroy of Italy. To this force's right mustered another auxiliary army, again around 80,000 strong, this time a mix of Poles, Saxons and Westphalians, led by Jerome Bonaparte, King of Westphalia. Together, the main army and these two auxiliary armies formed Central Army Group, and thus constituted a whole new level of military organization. The choice of Eugène and Jerome to command the two auxiliary armies was an odd and, as it proved, unhelpful one. Both men lacked the military experience of other available commanders and, in Jerome's case, the skill too. Eugène at least had shown considerable promise, though perhaps not enough to warrant such a senior appointment, but Jerome's selection was entirely political. Napoleon wished to boost his brother's prestige as he was thinking of making him king of a resurrected Poland. That would have been a poor move on the Emperor's part, but maybe no worse than appointing the ineffectual and vain Jerome to command an army in the greatest campaign of the age.

The final parts of Bonaparte's invasion force were the flank armies, each comprised of a single corps. The left, or northern, of these, was commanded by Marshal Macdonald and gathered along the Baltic coast near Königsberg. Most of its 32,500 troops were Prussian, but there were a good many Poles, Bavarians and Westphalians in the corps as well. The right, or southern, flank of Central Army Group was guarded by the 34,000 men of Prince Schwarzenberg's Austrian corps.

The enormous size of the army Napoleon gathered for the 1812 campaign created a number of major difficulties. Perhaps the most daunting was simply maintaining such an immense force in the field. Contrary to the impression given by some studies, Napoleon was far from unaware or negligent of the problems of feeding and equipping his men in a part of Europe in which it was not practical for so many soldiers to live off the land for long. As he specifically told Davout, 'We can hope for nothing from the countryside and accordingly must take everything with us'. The efforts the Emperor made to procure sufficient supplies for his campaign were truly monumental. Thousands of tons of wheat and rye, a million bushels of oats, millions of bottles of wine and a couple of million bottles of brandy were stockpiled in the months before the invasion in key cities such as Danzig and Warsaw, as well as at a number of other bases in north-eastern Europe. Great herds of cattle and oxen were gathered to follow behind the invading armies to provide fresh meat, while Napoleon ensured that every soldier who was to cross the Niemen started the campaign with four days' rations in his knapsack and twenty more days' worth of food on carts that were to accompany the advancing troops. It was a similar story with more specifically military provisions, such as cartridges for muskets, shot and powder for cannon, and items of uniform. Individual soldiers and units were each given a generous initial supply, while huge amounts of additional stores were stockpiled in the Grand Duchy and Prussia.

It was not just a question of procuring enormous quantities of supplies, however, but also of getting them to the troops as they advanced into Russia and used up their initial quotas. Again, Napoleon was well aware of this, informing his former stepson, Eugène, that 'without adequate transportation, everything will be useless'. As much thought and effort went into sorting out transport for provisions as it did into gathering those provisions in the first place. A gigantic supply train, numbering 25,000 vehicles, excluding ammunition caissons, forges and ambulances, was assembled, providing the invading army with a massive lift capacity of 7,000 tonnes per day. To limit the amount of supplies that had to be carried, moreover, Bonaparte made sure that huge numbers of sickles and scythes were issued so that fodder could be cut for horses in Russia. Indeed, he planned the invasion for June, rather than May, so that crops in the fields would be ripe enough for cavalry mounts and draft animals to eat.

It is difficult to imagine what more Napoleon could have done to try to ensure that his vast army was adequately supplied in 1812, yet even before the Niemen was crossed problems were emerging. To preserve stockpiled food for after the operation began, the Emperor ordered his men to live off the land in the weeks before the invasion began. This not only created severe friction with the local population in Prussia and the Grand Duchy, but also meant that most troops were reduced to a less than adequate diet, due to the inability of the poor land of north-eastern Europe to provide for such great numbers. This in turn encouraged the spread of diseases such as diphtheria, dysentery and typhus, and perhaps as much as a tenth of Bonaparte's army had fallen sick with such ailments by the time the invasion commenced.

The simple fact is that the vast army Napoleon gathered in 1812 was simply too large to be adequately provisioned in a pre-industrial age. True, there were other factors behind the failure to supply the army effectively, but the most important was its sheer size. The enormity of the invading force also made it more cumbersome and slow-moving than a smaller army would have been, and this sluggishness would prove costly. Then there was the impossibility of one man effectively commanding and coordinating such a huge force over such a large theatre of operations, at least before the invention of the telegraph or radio communications. Bonaparte's style of leadership was always centralized upon himself, but even an individual of his phenomenal abilities could not direct and synchronize the movements of almost half a million men. This inevitably placed greater emphasis upon the initiative and skill of the Emperor's subordinates, but many of them proved to be men of relatively limited capabilities, at least in independent or semi-independent roles, who were hesitant in obeying instructions given by anyone but Napoleon himself. Perhaps the most harmful consequence of the enormity of the force the Emperor led across the Niemen, though, was the impact this had on Russian strategy. As we shall see, the Russians had no clear-cut plan for confronting the French invasion in summer 1812, merely a variety of options, any one of which might have been chosen. The vast size of Napoleon's army persuaded them to adopt the one that would prove least conducive to hopes for a swift French triumph.

Given that the immensity of the Imperial force that invaded Russia caused so many difficulties, one is left wondering why the Emperor chose to muster such a large army in the first place. At one level, the answer is simply that, until he invaded, he could not know for sure that the size of his force would cause such serious supply, movement, and command and control problems, or that it would convince the Russians to adopt the strategy they did. A man of his intelligence and insight could, however, have anticipated the severity of these difficulties.

Perhaps he just underestimated the acuteness of the problems he would face as a result of his army's size. Certainly, the Russians' response to his attack would confound him and he would be surprised by the difficulty of both controlling and supplying his force effectively.

The other key reason for mustering such a large army was that numbers count in war. Napoleon hoped to deliver a crushing blow to the Russians and having an overwhelming numerical advantage might help bring that about. In this, though, Bonaparte miscalculated badly. Instead of enabling him to smash the Russians in battle, the enormous size of his force would encourage them to avoid a showdown they felt they would lose. What is more, the slowness with which his vast horde moved would prevent the Emperor from forcing his reluctant enemy to fight him. In any case, as we have seen, the quality of many of the troops and officers in the invading army was dubious, so just how necessary the presence of huge numbers of such men was to inflicting an overwhelming defeat on the Russians is questionable. After all, the crushing French victory at Austerlitz had been won not by the weight of a mass of inexperienced conscripts but by the skill of an outnumbered army mostly composed of highly proficient veterans.

The gathering of such an immense army in 1812 would, however, have made sense in two circumstances. The first is that Napoleon was preparing for a long, hard war in which both sides would need to call upon vast reserves of manpower in order to try to defeat the other. Certainly, the conflict might well have become just such a draining, drawn out struggle had it been fought differently, but the Emperor does not seem to have expected this to happen. His plans and the way he conducted the campaign both indicate that he intended to reach a resolution within a few months or even weeks. Besides, even if he had expected a longer conflict, he could still have invaded with a smaller force than he did, dispersing the rest of his troops more widely around eastern and central Europe, where they could be properly fed and trained, and calling them to Russia as and when they were needed.

The other way in which the assembly of such a great army would have been more reasonable is if Napoleon hoped that the sheer size of the force he gathered near Russia's borders would cow the Tsar and persuade him to seek terms before the Niemen was even crossed. On the face of it, it seems unlikely that the Emperor would have gone to all the trouble and expense he did if he hoped or expected not to have to invade, but the idea that he may have hoped that the Russians would be intimidated into backing down should not be dismissed. In a letter from Foreign Minister Maret to Lauriston in late February 1812, for example, the ambassador was informed that Napoleon 'places no confidence in any kind of negotiation, unless the 450,000 men [sic] whom His Majesty has put into motion … should move the St Petersburg cabinet to serious rethinking [and] bring it back sincerely to the system that was established at Tilsit'. It is just possible, then, that Napoleon was playing a double game in 1812, preparing for an invasion that he hoped would not prove necessary. Of course, Alexander was never going to cede territory to enable the Emperor to create a greater Polish kingdom without recourse to arms first, but that was Napoleon's maximum aim, one that he would ideally like to have achieved but which he was aware would involve the greatest risk and expense. On the other hand, it was just possible that the Tsar might be cowed into returning to a more pro-French, anti-British policy by the massing of a vast horde on his borders, and in this case the key French goal of dealing with the Russian threat would have been achieved at minimum peril and cost.

If Napoleon *was* hoping that assembling such a huge army on Russia's borders would mean he would not actually have to invade, however, he was inadvertently creating serious problems for himself should the Russians not prove amenable to intimidation. In the final analysis, it is hard to avoid the conclusion that Napoleon would have been much better off marching into Russia at the head of a considerably smaller force, perhaps one two-thirds or even half the size of the unwieldy mass he did take across the Niemen. This would have been easier to supply, faster moving, and easier to command and coordinate. It would have contained a much higher concentration of veterans, and would not have overawed the Russians to the extent that they would have felt compelled to avoid battle. Such an army might well have enabled the Emperor to inflict the devastating battlefield defeat on the Russians he hoped for, even if this did not end the war, it would have provided an excellent first step towards eventual victory. Instead, Napoleon opted for overwhelming numbers as the route to triumph in 1812. In so doing, he not only hamstrung his own plans for beating his enemies, but also created the conditions for a French defeat in Russia to prove truly devastating.

Napoleon's original strategy to defeat Russia and bring Alexander to the peace table in 1812 was certainly not to march all the way to Moscow, but to inflict a shattering defeat on the Tsar's armies as far west as possible. To this end, he determined to thrust with his main army and Eugène's auxiliary force at the heart of Barclay's First Army of the West at Vilna, thereby splitting it in two. Marshal Macdonald's corps, which was to advance in the direction of Riga, would then, with the aid of part of the main army, keep the northern half of the Russian First Army occupied while the bulk of that force and Eugène's men destroyed the southern half. Meanwhile, Jerome's auxiliary army and Schwarzenberg's corps were to hold Bagration's Second Army in place so that it too could be annihilated when Bonaparte, having dealt with Barclay, swept down behind it and closed the trap. If all went well, Bonaparte calculated that the campaign could be over in just three weeks, before Tormasov's Third Army south of the Pripet Marshes could do anything to prevent the catastrophe. It was a typically bold and brilliant Napoleonic plan; on paper at least.

Of course, the Emperor was not so naive as to believe that the Russians would inevitably stand still as he advanced (although such strategic paralysis was not impossible), so he considered how he would react in the event of the enemy responding more proactively to his initial moves. There were three main possibilities open to the Russians as Napoleon saw it. They might respond to the invasion by ordering a mass retreat to a defensive line deeper inside Russia. The rivers Dvina, Berezina and Dnieper form a colossal arc some 150–200 miles east of the Niemen along which the Russians had been constructing fortifications since mid-1810. Should their adversaries retreat towards this line, Napoleon's forces would pursue them, hoping to catch up with them and bring them to battle before they could reach it, but, failing that, crushing them where they eventually turned to fight. The second proactive response the Russians might adopt, Napoleon thought, was for Barclay to move his army south to unite with Bagration. Then, the Emperor would march to outflank the combining armies with his own main army and Eugène's auxiliary force, trap the enemy between these and the armies of Jerome and Schwarzenberg, and destroy the ensnared Russian forces together. Finally, the Emperor judged that Barclay and Bagration might adopt different responses to the invasion based upon their personalities, the cautious Baltic baron pulling back in the face of the oncoming French while the fiery Russian hero of Austerlitz ordered a thrust at Warsaw aimed at throwing the invasion off balance. This was the scenario Napoleon considered most likely and was an astute reading of his adversaries' characters. If this was indeed what happened, Napoleon planned to obliterate Bagration using the auxiliary armies of Eugène and Jerome as well as a contingent of his main army, and then to turn the whole invasion force's attention towards catching up with and smashing Barclay, Tormasov's men being kept at bay by a flank force should they seek to interfere.

In contrast to the decisiveness with which the Emperor formulated his plans for the 1812 campaign, the Russians remained divided over strategy right up to, and even beyond, the start of the invasion. Essentially, four plans were on the table, with an additional supplementary scheme being considered as well. Bagration, just as Napoleon suspected he would, favoured responding to a French crossing of the Niemen by launching a thrust towards Warsaw aimed at threatening the enemy's lines of supply and communication. Barclay, meanwhile, suggested two alternative plans. The first was to make a stand near the frontier with the combined forces available, the second to withdraw east before turning and confronting Napoleon's army at whatever point such action seemed advisable or desirable. Belying his generally cautious nature, he seems to have favoured the former of these strategies until the vast size of the force the Emperor was intending to invade with became apparent. The fourth option was a scheme devised by an aged *émigré* Prussian general, von Phüll, who had gained the Tsar's confidence through the bizarre expedient of being able to talk about ancient battles as if he had actually fought in them. Phüll's plan was for Barclay's First Army to retreat to an entrenched camp near the Dvina river at Drissa, a town almost 200 miles east of the Niemen which overlooked the main roads to both St Petersburg and Moscow, and await a French assault there. Meanwhile, Bagration's Second Army would manoeuvre to attack the enemy's right flank as he advanced towards Drissa and then either join the First Army in the entrenched camp or remain outside and continue to harass Napoleon's flanks depending upon circumstances. Tormasov's Third Army could ultimately join up with either Barclay or Bagration.

The final decision as to which strategy to adopt rested with the Tsar (although he might devolve the choice). The foreign officers who had access to Alexander in the weeks before the invasion, most of them Prussians, felt confident that he would opt for Phüll's plan. There is good evidence to support this claim. In 1811, for example, the Tsar had written to King Frederick William, 'The system which has made Wellington victorious in Spain, and exhausted the French enemies, is what I intend to follow – avoid pitched battles and organize long lines of communication for retreat, leading to entrenched camps.'* Much effort and money had been put into building an entrenched camp at Drissa in the two years before the invasion, so it seemed only logical that the Russians would seek to use it. That said, the Drissa scheme had many enemies. Most Russian generals considered it cowardly and inglorious, while others felt it was courting disaster, a theory with which many subsequent commentators have concurred. Certainly, Drissa might easily have been outflanked, so it is perfectly possible that the camp would have become a trap rather than a sanctuary. Although Phüll's plan was thus perhaps foremost in Alexander's mind in early summer 1812, it was by no means certain that he would force his commanders to follow it.

Bagration's popularity within the army and his heroic status meant that his preferred strategy of thrusting at Warsaw had to be seriously considered. Indeed, had he been chosen as senior commander in 1812 instead of Barclay, as he felt he should have been and as many Russian generals had hoped he would be, it seems highly likely that some form of this scheme would have been adopted. It was extremely fortunate for the Russians, therefore, that he was not chosen, for his plan would have played straight into Napoleon's hands and almost certainly have resulted in disaster.

Instead, it was Barclay who carried most weight with the Tsar in early summer 1812 and, seeing the enormity of the army mustering on the other side of the

---

* Alexander was referring here to Wellington's use of the Lines of Torres Vedras, a mighty system of fortifications and earthworks north of Lisbon which were used to defend the Portuguese capital in the winter of 1810–11.

Niemen, he pressed Alexander to authorize a policy of retreat on the grounds that, as the enemy advanced further west, the size of his effective fighting force would be reduced by attrition and the need to leave troops to guard supply lines. The withdrawal was not, however, to be indefinite. The Russians would stand and fight somewhere, most likely behind the Dvina, Berezina or Dnieper, though not necessarily at Drissa. Even this was too much for some Russian generals and statesmen, such as State Secretary (roughly speaking, the Tsar's chief minister) Alexander Shishkov, who felt that it was ignominious, craven and defeatist to cede large tracts of territory to the enemy.

The Russian high command, therefore, was divided in 1812 between those who advocated some form of strategy of retreat and those who wished to yield as little ground as possible to the French, perhaps even to launch a counter-offensive into the Grand Duchy of Warsaw. This division was also apparent in consideration of a supplementary scheme for dealing with the imminent invasion. Admiral Chichagov, the navy minister, proposed to Alexander that the Russian troops stationed in south-east Europe, rather than being withdrawn, should march on the kingdom of Italy via Serbia and the Illyrian Provinces, raising rebellion among the Slavs of the region as they went. The idea was that a thrust at the Illyrian Provinces and Italy would force the French to divert troops to defend their position there, while provoking a Slavic revolt would alarm both the Turks and the Austrians, encouraging the latter to withdraw their contingent from the Emperor's invasion force and persuading the former not to seek to exploit Napoleon's attack on Russia. The uprising would also, it was hoped, pave the way for the establishment of a Russian-dominated pan-Slav state. Rumiantsev, who was still foreign minister, though increasingly redundant in the role, was appalled by Chichagov's plan, arguing that it was dangerous and impractical nonsense, and that it made no sense to antagonize the Turks and Austrians at a time when Russia wanted them to be as well-disposed towards her as possible. In response, Chichagov accused Rumiantsev of treason, a gauge of the fevered atmosphere in St Petersburg in the weeks before the invasion. For his part, the Tsar was initially favourable to the plan, a sure sign that he was not totally committed to a passive strategy in 1812, but was prepared to countenance more aggressive means of dealing with the threat Russia faced. By the end of spring, however, the scheme was dead. What killed it was simply the sheer size of the invasion force Napoleon had mustered in north-eastern Europe. With so many soldiers preparing to cross the Niemen, it was decided that all available troops were needed to help defend Mother Russia and that aggressive ploys such as Chichagov's were too risky.

It was the immensity of the Emperor's invasion force that ultimately resolved the dispute in Russia, at least temporarily, between the advocates of retreat and those who favoured yielding as little ground as possible to the enemy. Napoleon's army was simply too large to fight near the frontier, so the Tsar's troops would have to withdraw in the face of its advance and make a stand somewhere deeper inside Russia. The decision dismayed a good many Russian generals, among them Bagration. In spite of the size of the enemy force, these men would maintain pressure on Alexander and Barclay in the first weeks of the invasion to halt what they saw as a humiliating and dishonourable retreat. If only the Emperor had marched into Russia at the head of an army half or two-thirds the size, it seems all but certain that his enemies would have offered him the major battle near the border that he desired and hoped would bring the campaign to a speedy conclusion. How such a confrontation would have turned out is, of course, open to speculation, but the likelihood would surely have been a victory for the invaders. True, this might not have ended the war as Napoleon hoped it would, but it would certainly have been preferable to what actually happened.

Even as late as spring 1812, neither Paris nor St Petersburg had given up entirely on the prospect of a peaceful resolution to their differences. Unfortunately, however, each side's minimum conditions for a settlement proved incompatible with those of the other. Although both Alexander and Napoleon were aware of the risks of war, they preferred to adopt an uncompromising attitude that made conflict almost certain rather than backing down over the key issues that divided them.

The Russian position was made clear in April. The only real concession they were prepared to make to France's grievances was to modify the tariffs on land-borne goods that punished French traders. In return for this, St Petersburg wanted compensation for the Duke of Oldenburg and demanded that the French evacuate Prussia and Swedish Pomerania. Indeed, the concentration of Napoleonic troops east of the Oder was declared to be tantamount to an act of war. On the issue of observance of the Continental Blockade, the Russians were prepared to maintain their embargo on British ships entering their ports, although they suggested that they might introduce a licence system similar to the one Napoleon had introduced in French-controlled Europe, a proposal that was unlikely to go down well with the Emperor. As far as the key matter of neutral ships was concerned, Russia adopted a hard-line stance, insisting upon recognition of her right to receive them.

There was nothing there to make Napoleon even remotely inclined to call off the invasion. He took affront at the demand that he withdraw from Prussia, a move which he felt would leave the Grand Duchy of Warsaw isolated and vulnerable to a Russian attack, and was irritated by the refusal of St Petersburg to drop the Oldenburg matter. Most important, though, was the Russian attitude towards the Blockade. Had the Russians agreed to return to its stringent observation, it is possible that war could have been averted. Such a climbdown by the Tsar might have convinced the Emperor that Russia could be cowed and did not need to be invaded or stripped of territory in order to remove the potential threat she posed to French interests, allies and hegemony within Europe. Essentially, Napoleon's price for peace in 1812 was, as Foreign Minister Maret explained in a letter to Lauriston in late February, that Russia, like Austria since late 1809, should accept a 'situation of inferiority' *vis-à-vis* France, the prime test of which would be an agreement to return to a strict adherence to the Continental Blockade. This was simply too much for Alexander, who, despite not wishing to provoke Napoleon (Lauriston was disingenuously assured in April 1812, for example, that the Tsar remained 'a friend and loyal ally' to France), preferred to fight rather than undergo the humiliation of altering Russian policy in response to the threat of invasion. His failure to win Austria or Prussia as an ally in the forthcoming conflict troubled the Tsar, but it did not make him any more inclined to submit meekly to the Emperor's demand that he return to a stringent observation of the Blockade. Instead, and in stark contrast to Rumiantsev, who was so traumatized by the imminent French invasion that he suffered an apoplectic stroke in late spring 1812, Alexander became stoical, ready to accept whatever might come of the looming struggle. His attitude is perhaps best exemplified in a letter he wrote to his old friend Czartoryski in April. 'There is no longer that swagger which caused one to scorn the foe. On the contrary, one appreciates his full strength, one feels that reverses are quite possible, but in spite of that one is disposed to uphold the honour of the empire to the bitter end.'

The Tsar left St Petersburg on 20 April and headed for Vilna, the headquarters of Barclay's First Army of the West, where, to most of his generals' disquiet, he announced that he intended to play an active role as head of his country's armed forces during the impending war. Following his arrival at Vilna, though, Alexander also seemed more interested in social affairs than military ones, embarking upon a lively round of parties, balls and receptions aimed at courting the local, non-Russian aristocracy. His efforts seem to have been appreciated, but just how loyal the nobility, much less the general population, of the Tsar's north-western provinces would prove once Russian forces retreated from the region remained open to question.

While Alexander was at Vilna, on 18 May to be precise, a French emissary arrived. Count Louis de Narbonne was a dashing nobleman in his late fifties who had attached himself to the Bonapartist regime in France and won the Emperor's confidence. Napoleon sent Narbonne to Vilna for two reasons: to gather what information he could about the mood at Russian headquarters and to see if there was any hope of resolving the crisis between France and Russia short of war. In relation to the latter, Bonaparte gave his emissary a letter to hand over to the Tsar. In it the Emperor expressed a desire for peace with Alexander, claimed that he held Russia's ruler in the highest regard, declared that he wished to resurrect 'the sentiments of Tilsit and Erfurt', and stated that all the Tsar had to do to avert war was to ensure that his ports were closed to all British trade once more. In light of the clear statement of the Russian position given in April, it is surprising to find Napoleon bothering even to suggest that Russia return to a strict observation of the Continental Blockade. Perhaps, therefore, it was merely a ruse intended to provide cover for Narbonne to gather what information he could at Vilna. On the other hand, it may have been a genuine, if rather forlorn, effort to seek a peaceful settlement that the Emperor considered acceptable, in which case one must conclude that he had reservations about the imminent invasion. Evidence to support this theory can be found in the words of Napoleon himself shortly after the end of his most recent battle, that of Wagram in 1809: 'Battle should only be offered when there is no other turn of fortune to be hoped for, as from its nature the fate of a battle is always dubious.' It was a most unusual thing for a man who had gained so much from war to have said, but one must not forget that the struggle with Austria in 1809 had been a tough affair, including his first battlefield defeat at Aspern-Essling. Moreover, the Emperor turned forty in 1809 and middle age tends to make one less bold, less inclined to take risks. It was suggested in the previous chapter that part of the reason Napoleon decided to prepare for a showdown with Russia in 1812 was that he was concerned about deterioration in his physical (and maybe intellectual) state. Perhaps fear that his decline might already have gone too far made him think twice about whether he was doing the right thing on the eve of the invasion.

Whatever Napoleon's reasons for suggesting a peaceful solution to Alexander, the Tsar's response was predictably negative. At a meeting with Narbonne on the same day the Frenchman arrived at Vilna, Alexander angrily accused Napoleon of 'ranging all Europe against Russia', and defiantly asserted that 'the Russian nation is not one which recoils before danger. All the bayonets in Europe on my frontiers will not make me alter my language.' His reply to Napoleon's peace offer was unequivocal: 'having done all I could to preserve peace honourably and uphold a political system which might lead to universal peace, I will do nothing to besmirch the honour of the nation over which I rule.' Narbonne was allowed to remain in Vilna only until a formal written response to the Emperor's letter had been drafted and was then politely forced to leave in order to prevent him gathering much information about the situation at Russian headquarters.

Napoleon's emissary returned to his master at the same city from which he had been despatched; Dresden. Bonaparte had arrived at the Saxon capital on 16 May, a week after leaving Paris, and summoned there all the crowned heads of French-controlled or allied Europe. For the next fortnight, the Emperor was fêted by a swathe of dignitaries and royals, including the rulers of both Austria and Prussia, an experience which greatly amused a man who had once been a mere artillery lieutenant born with none of the advantages enjoyed by those who now fawned over him. Of course, there was a more serious purpose to the glittering gathering at Dresden than just Napoleon's entertainment. As at Erfurt three and half years earlier, Bonaparte hoped to awe the Russians through a display of French power ahead of the looming conflict or even induce them to cave in before a shot was fired and agree to his conditions for peace. The failure of Narbonne's mission proved the futility of the latter hope, while the Tsar and his generals did not need an extravagant spectacle to appreciate just how powerful the Empire they were about to take on was. The hundreds of thousands of soldiers mustering in north-eastern Europe already made that perfectly clear.

Napoleon left Dresden at the end of May, travelling into the Grand Duchy of Warsaw at the start of a period of inspections of supply depots, transport arrangements and troop formations. Everywhere he went he was passionately greeted, being lionised even, by the Poles, whose hopes for what the imminent war might bring were unsurprisingly high. Despite this enthusiastic acclamation, the Emperor refused to utter the words the inhabitants of the Grand Duchy wished to hear. On the issue of resurrecting the Kingdom of Poland, he maintained a frustrating but resolute public silence.

This poses an important question. If the formation of a greater Polish kingdom was an aim of the war, why did Napoleon not announce the recreation of such a state on the eve of the conflict? It has often been argued that this would have facilitated the invasion by winning the Emperor the wholehearted support not only of the Poles of the Grand Duchy of Warsaw but also that of the bulk of Alexander's predominantly non-Russian subjects who lived in the western provinces of the Tsar's empire. Indeed, one Russian officer, who fought as chief of staff of a cavalry division in 1812 and went on to become a general, later opined that had Napoleon announced the resurrection of a Polish kingdom, 'Russia would have been irretrievably lost. Poland could without excessive effort have raised an army of 200,000, would have done so with pleasure, and many of our Polish provinces would have risen in revolt against us if Napoleon had only promised this conceited nation that it would be formed into a separate kingdom and would have its own king.' Just how accurate this dramatic prediction would have proved is, however, open to question. For a start, it implies that the Poles did not contribute much to the campaign, whereas, in fact, the forces provided by the Grand Duchy of Warsaw not only formed the largest contingent relative to population of any of the contributing states, but also fought with an effort probably not even surpassed by the French elements within the invading army. Of course, more Poles lived outside the Grand Duchy's borders in 1812 than within, but the idea that they would have risen in revolt and formed an army many tens of thousands strong the moment Napoleon declared the resurrection of the kingdom of Poland is a little far-fetched. Russia was so immense, her communications so primitive, and the bulk of her people so uneducated that widespread, coordinated rebellion was never likely, especially while fear of Russian reprisals should events turn out unfavourably remained. In any case, the Russians abandoned their western provinces once the campaign got underway, so a major Polish rebellion would probably not have been that helpful to the invaders. From a longer perspective, the declaration of a resurrected Polish kingdom might well have aided recruitment of troops for Napoleon's armies, but this would only have been an important factor if the Emperor had fought a different, more protracted kind of war. Perhaps he should have done this, but as he did not, there were limits to how much assistance the peoples of the Tsar's western provinces could give the invaders in the few months the campaign lasted.

It is unlikely, then, that a formal pledge to resurrect the kingdom of Poland would made much difference to the course or outcome of the war in 1812; at least given the kind of campaign Napoleon decided to fight. There was thus little advantage to be gained from Napoleon's point of view in publicly committing himself to forming a greater Polish kingdom. Conversely, there would have been several drawbacks to making such a commitment. First, placing the Polish question so openly at the heart of the campaign might have created the unfortunate impression within both France and the multinational *Grande Armée* that the war was being fought solely for the Poles. There was a feeling to this effect anyway it did not help to make the conflict popular outside the Grand Duchy. In contrast, a Napoleonic promise to resurrect an enlarged Poland would have made it easier for the Tsar to sell the imminent war to his people as a struggle for Russia's survival as a great power and would thereby have strengthened the Russians' determination to resist come what may. Better to defeat the Russian armies and get Alexander to the peace table before presenting him with draconian terms for a settlement. Then there were the possible diplomatic repercussions among Bonaparte's allies of publicly pledging to recreate a greater Polish kingdom. How might the King of Saxony have reacted to the prospect of being stripped of his title as ruler of the Grand Duchy of Warsaw? More importantly, how might the Austrians or Prussians have reacted to the prospect of a major Polish state being recreated on their doorstep, especially one that would seek the restoration of the Habsburgs' remaining Galician provinces and perhaps also the wealthy Prussian territory of Silesia, annexation of which would provide a continuous land link between Warsaw and Paris via the German states of the Confederation of the Rhine? Of course, the rulers of Saxony, Austria and Prussia were all concerned about what the Emperor had in mind for the Poles anyway, but there is a big difference between an unsubstantiated worry and a confirmed one. The key reason why Napoleon did not pledge himself overtly to creating a greater Polish kingdom, though, was the wish, typical of him, to keep his options open. If the war went very well and the Russian armies were smashed, the creation of an enlarged Polish state would be feasible and the Emperor, flushed with victory, could ignore any rumblings of discontent from his allies. If, however, the conflict did not go so well, it might be desirable to make a compromise peace with St Petersburg that would be rendered extremely difficult by a public commitment to resurrect the Kingdom of Poland. Despite the creation of a greater Polish state being his ultimate aim in 1812, therefore Napoleon decided to keep his cards close to his chest and to leave as many avenues as possible open. One can argue that it was a devious policy and less than the Poles deserved, but it is hard to deny its wisdom.

The Emperor might have launched his invasion in early June, but he chose to delay for a couple of weeks, a decision that would prove costly later in the year. Two main reasons have been advanced for the delay. Partly, it seems that Napoleon decided that more time was needed to improve the medical provision for his armies, with more surgeons, ambulances and supplies being ordered up. Still, the standard of medical provision for the forces that invaded Russia was far from ideal, although it was considerably better than that of the Russians. The postponement was also called in order to give grass and crops in the Russian fields more time to ripen so that the 200,000 horses and tens of thousands of other beasts that would cross the Niemen with Napoleon's armies would be able to live off the land as far as possible. In this, the invaders were victims of the seasons, summer arriving atypically late in north-eastern Europe in 1812. It would not be the last time that year that they would have cause to bewail the Russian climate.

There was perhaps one more reason why the Emperor delayed the invasion. Despite the abject failure of Narbonne's mission to Vilna in mid-May, in June, Lauriston, who was still in St Petersburg, was instructed to leave the city and travel to see the Tsar in a last-ditch effort for a peaceful resolution – on French terms, of course – to the crisis. The ambassador's task was abruptly thwarted, though, by the military governor of the Russian capital, who denied the Frenchman permission to depart. On hearing the news, Napoleon simply commented, 'So that is that'.

The Emperor's efforts for peace in May and June 1812, significantly made privately rather than publicly, certainly do not suggest a man desperate to fight the Russians. Instead they imply that he would have preferred to achieve his minimum aim (a Russian return to strict observation of the Continental Blockade as a symbol of St Peterburg's acceptance of French dominance in Europe) without conflict rather than risking war to try to obtain his maximum aim (the creation of a greater Polish kingdom). This is not to insinuate that he considered it likely that he would lose if it came to a trial of arms – he told his secretary shortly before the invasion, 'Never has an expedition against them [the Russians] been more certain of success' – but it does indicate that he was well aware of the potential difficulties of waging war on Russian soil and of the perils to which his campaign might give rise.

Napoleon arrived at the frontier between the Grand Duchy of Warsaw and Russia on 22 June. Four days earlier, the United States Congress had voted to declare war on Britain in response to the Royal Navy's continuous interference with American ships on the high seas and forcible impressment of British sailors found serving on US vessels. The War of 1812, as it became known, lasted two and a half years and ended with a stalemate peace at Christmas 1814. Britain's embroilment with the Americans would do less to impinge upon London's prosecution of the war against France than the Emperor hoped it might. Bonaparte's conflict with Russia, on the other hand, the real war of 1812, would have the most profound repercussions.

On the evening of 22 June, Napoleon wrote the proclamation to be read to his invading soldiers at dawn on the 24th, by which time the campaign would finally be underway. It was typically stirring stuff:

> Soldiers! The second Polish war has begun; the first ended at Friedland and Tilsit. At Tilsit, Russia swore eternal friendship with France and war against England. Today she has broken her promises! She will give no further explanation of her strange behaviour until the French eagles have again withdrawn behind the Rhine, leaving our distant allies at her mercy. She will learn to her cost that her destiny must be fulfilled. Does she think us degenerate? Are we no longer the soldiers of Austerlitz? She places us between dishonour and war; there can be no doubt which course we shall choose. Forward then, let us cross the Niemen, so that we can carry the war into her own territory. The second Polish war will bring as much glory to French arms as did the first. But the peace treaty which we shall conclude this time will carry its own guarantee; it will put an end to the fatal influence which Russia has exercised over Europe for the past fifty years.

The day after drafting the proclamation, the Emperor made a reconnaissance of part of the Polish bank of the Niemen to decide exactly where the pontoon bridges for his main army were to be constructed, a classic example of his painstaking attention to detail as well as his tendency to take too much upon himself. He had already decided that his main army would cross roughly opposite the town of Kovno so that supplies for the force could be borne down the Niemen River and its tributary the Vilia as far as Vilna. Eugène's auxiliary army was to cross in the same area, with Jerome's force traversing seventy miles to the south. Schwarzenberg's flank army would cross south of Jerome while Marshal Macdonald's corps to the main army's left (north) was poignantly to bridge the Niemen near Tilsit.

Inspecting the western bank of the Niemen potentially exposed Napoleon to cannon fire from the opposite shore, so rather than donning his usual uniform of a colonel of the *chasseurs à cheval* of the Imperial Guard and his distinctive black hat, he and his small entourage instead dressed as Polish lancers and so were ignored by any Russians to the east who might have seen them. Eventually, the disguised Emperor found what he deemed the perfect spot for several bridges to be constructed and gave orders for them to be erected after dark that same day.

Heading back to camp that afternoon, a hare darted between his horse's legs, causing it to rear and throwing its illustrious rider from the saddle. Bonaparte was unharmed, but news of the fall soon spread and was inevitably interpreted by superstitious types as a bad omen. Napoleon was not immune to superstition himself, so it was perhaps as much for his own benefit as for that of his former ambassador to St Petersburg that he assured Caulaincourt, accompanying him as part of his inner staff, 'Russia will sue for peace in less than two months. The big landowners will be terrified and some of them ruined. Tsar Alexander will be in a very awkward position.' It was to prove a less than accurate prediction.

The invasion began shortly after 8 p.m. on 23 June, the first French soldiers to step upon Russian soil being a force of light infantry ferried across the Niemen to establish a protective screen for the construction of the pontoon bridges for the main army. This work began at 10 p.m. and it was a testament to the skill of the engineers of the *Grande Armée* that three crossings were ready by dawn. Eerily, the only opposition from the eastern bank came from a lone Cossack officer who rode down to the river's edge shortly after the light infantry landed and asked, 'What do you want? Why do you come to Russia?' Supposedly, the Emperor's troops bullishly replied, 'To make war on you! To take Vilna and set Poland free!' The Cossack simply rode back whence he had come, disappearing into a nearby wood. A brief exchange of wild shots between some Russians hidden by the trees and the soldiers by the river bank followed in which neither side took any casualties. It was a bloodless, almost comical start to what would turn into one of the costliest and most tragic campaigns in history.

1. A classic Napoleonic pose, with hand inserted into his waistcoat. In his forty-third year, middle-age, overwork and stress were beginning to take their toll on a once lean physique. The Emperor's physical deterioration proceeded apace after the disaster of the Russian campaign later that year. *Napoleon Bonaparte in his Study, 1812*, oil on canvas by Jacques Louis David (*Bridgeman Art Library*).

2. Tsar Alexander, depicted here in his thirties, had an imposing physical presence and was widely considered handsome. With the exception of Napoleon, perhaps no other man had a greater influence upon the history of the early nineteenth century than Russia's young ruler. *Alexander I of Russia*, oil on canvas by François Pascal Simon Gerard (*Bridgeman Art Library*).

3. Austerlitz was not only arguably Napoleon's finest battlefield victory, but also a magnificent personal triumph for the Emperor over his rival, Tsar Alexander. Neither man ever forgot the dramatic events of that fateful day. *The Battle of Austerlitz in Moravia, 2 December 1805*, engraving by Antonio Verico after a painting by Antoine Charles Horace Vernet (*Bridgeman Art Library*).

4. Eylau was one of Napoleon's most brutal engagements against the Russians. Depicted here is Marshal Murat's famous mass cavalry charge, a bold gambit which saved the French from almost certain defeat. *The Battle of Eylau, 8 February 1807*, watercolour on paper by Jean Antoine Simeon Fort (*Bridgeman Art Library*).

5. The meeting between Napoleon and Alexander on a raft floating on the River Niemen was one of the most memorable and significant moments in the history of the Napoleonic Era. Contrary to the impression given by this French image, the Russian ruler in fact towered over his counterpart. *The Meeting between Napoleon I and Tsar Alexander I at Niemen, 25 June 1807*, engraving by nineteenth-century French School (*Bridgeman Art Library*).

6. The ghastliness of the retreat from Moscow in 1812 has become legendary. Here, just a couple of the hardships which confronted the soldiers are shown in the form of the bitter weather, and the dead horse being butchered for food to stave off starvation. *The Miseries of the French Grand Army in their Retreat from Moscow, bivouacking, 1812*, print published by Edward Orme (*Bridgeman Art Library*).

7. The capture of Smolensk, one of Russia's holiest cities, was a major coup for Napoleon in 1812, but more important ultimately was the opportunity he missed there to crush the defeated Russian army. *The Battle of Smolensk, 17 August 1812*, oil on canvas by Jean Charles Langlois (*Bridgeman Art Library*).

8. The confrontation which took place between Napoleon and his enemies at Leipzig in autumn 1813 was a truly colossal affair which in some ways presaged the huge battles which would come to typify the warfare of the two world wars. *The Battle of Leipzig, 18 October 1813, detail of Napoleon in the foreground*, gouache on paper by nineteenth-century French School (*Bridgeman Art Library*).

9. Marshal Davout was a prickly, stern character who did not make friends easily, but Napoleon never had a more loyal nor more highly skilled subordinate. No enemy of France could feel secure while the brilliant, bald-headed disciplinarian was opposite them on the field of battle. *Portrait of Louis Nicolas Davout, Prince of Eckmühl*, oil on canvas by Tito Marzocchi de Belluci (*Bridgeman Art Library*).

10. Though neither as famous as the likes of Kutuzov and Bagration, nor as militarily accomplished as the best French commanders, Barclay was probably the best Russian general of his generation. Without him, the 1812 campaign might have proved to be a catastrophe for the Russians rather than the French. *Portrait of Mikhail Barclay de Tolly*, oil on canvas by George Dawe (*Bridgeman Art Library*).

15

Invasion

The Emperor of the French crossed the Niemen for the first time at 5 a.m. on 24 June, mounted poignantly, upon a horse named Friedland. This first foray into the Tsar's territory only lasted long enough for a brief exploration of the ground between the river and the town of Kovno (modern Kaunas), the first significant settlement on the Russian side of the border. That accomplished, Napoleon and his entourage recrossed the Niemen and breakfasted on its western bank. He spent the rest of the morning watching troops file past his temporary command post on their way towards the pontoon bridges constructed the previous night. It would be well into the next day before the whole of the Emperor's main army, almost quarter of a million strong, had traversed the river which demarcated the western border of Russia, but during the few hours that Bonaparte stood and watched, thousands upon thousands of soldiers of many nationalities and in a wide array of uniforms filed past their commander. They were accompanied by an assortment of civilians – wives, mistresses, prostitutes, servants, traders and so on – whose presence was always a feature of any army on campaign in this period. Their numbers reflected the enormous size of the force they marched with: at least 50,000 non-combatants accompanied the 450,000 Imperial troops who invaded Russia that summer.

As he gazed upon the passing multitude that morning, Napoleon seemed lost in thought, absent-mindedly tapping his riding crop against his boot and occasionally humming the tune to *Malbrouck s'enva-t-en guerre* (Marlborough goes to war), an odd choice given that Marlborough was a famous British general of the early eighteenth century who made his name defeating the French. At noon, content that things were proceeding satisfactorily, he crossed to the Niemen's eastern bank once more. After lunch, the Old Guard, the elite of the *Grande Armée*, assembled around their emperor and then, in late afternoon, accompanied him into Kovno. The town, indeed this whole region, was predominantly populated by Lithuanians and Poles, but any pleasure the locals felt in the arrival of a man who might liberate them from Russian overlordship was more than tempered by anxiety about the damage the hordes of invading soldiers might do as they passed through. It was perhaps partly out of frustration that he had not been welcomed more heartily that Napoleon chose to spend his first night in Russia not in Kovno but three-quarters of a mile outside it in a monastery.

The biggest disappointment for the Emperor of the first full day of the Russian campaign, though, was not so much the apprehensive attitude of the local population as the almost total lack of opposition his forces encountered. Not only had Kovno fallen without resistance of any kind being put up by the Tsar's soldiers, but even the advance guard of the invading force, which had pushed on beyond the town, had seen next to nothing of General Barclay's First Army of the West. Of course, this made things much easier for the invaders in many ways, but the priority was not to advance as far as possible as effortlessly as possible, but to come to grips with and destroy the Tsar's armies as soon and as near to the border as he could. The first indications of Russian intentions were not encouraging.

It was not until the evening of 24 June, some twenty-four hours after the first enemy troops landed on the eastern bank of the Niemen, that Tsar Alexander learned that his empire had been invaded. He was attending a ball outside Vilna, some sixty miles to the south east of Kovno, and was apprised of the news by his chief of police, General Balashov, during the dancing after supper. His reaction was calm and controlled, retiring from the gathering as unobtrusively as he could and encouraging others to continue to enjoy the evening's entertainment.

Alexander returned immediately to his headquarters in Vilna and, in his role as commander-in-chief of Russia's armies, convened a conference with his senior subordinates in the vicinity for the early hours of 25 June. Information was now coming in thick and fast from scouts and local people loyal to the Tsar, and it did not paint a pleasant picture. Before the invasion, the Russians had realized that Napoleon was gathering a very large army in Prussia and the Grand Duchy of Warsaw, but these initial reports of the size of the invading force suggested that previous guesses had been underestimates. Right up to this point, a good number of Alexander's key subordinates had been urging him to order Barclay to advance to meet any French invasion at the border and then drive it back beyond Warsaw, but revelation of the enormous size of the Emperor's forces temporarily silenced such aggressive counsel. Barclay himself, whose estimate of the size of enemy forces had been closer than most, had been inclined towards a policy of withdrawal behind the Dvina, around 150 miles from the frontier, for some weeks, but no definite decision as to the general strategy to be followed had been made when the first Napoleonic troops entered Russia. Intelligence as to the massive size of the invading army seemed to make it inevitable that Barclay's preferred approach would win out over the more aggressive designs of others, yet at the conference in the early hours of 25 June a definite decision as to general strategy was, incredibly, still not given by the Tsar, who wished to await further information about the invaders before authorizing what would in effect be a headlong flight to the Russian interior. Consequently, the main result of the meeting was the drafting of two proclamations, one for the army and one for civilians. In the first, Alexander called down the wrath of God upon Napoleon and assured his troops that the invaders would be repulsed, while in the second, despatched to St Petersburg and other major population centres, the Tsar pledged, 'I will not make peace so long as a single enemy soldier remains armed within my empire'.

Alexander was keen to appear resolved to resist the invaders come what may, though there is some reason to question just how wholeheartedly resolute he really was at this point. On the evening of the 25th, the Tsar summoned General Balashov to him. Encouraged by Foreign Minister Rumiantsev, Alexander had written a letter which he instructed his chief of police to deliver to Napoleon. It was by no means a craven, fearful epistle – indeed it repeated the pledge made to the Russian people that the Tsar would not negotiate while enemy troops remained in Russia – but one sentence did suggest that Alexander's resolution might be shakeable. 'If Your Majesty will order a withdrawal of your troops from Russian territory,' he wrote, 'I am prepared to regard what has happened as though it had never happened, and an agreement between us is still possible.' Surely not even the Tsar could have seriously believed that the Emperor would order his soldiers back across the Niemen without having first secured a settlement acceptable to him, so one is left to wonder what moved him to raise the idea of a negotiated agreement with Napoleon at all. Shocked by the vastness of the Emperor's forces, did the Tsar perhaps fear that the invaders would smash his armies if they caught them near the frontier and hope that Napoleon would agree to negotiate before that happened (and before his pledge not to make peace while the enemy remained on Russian soil could be made public in St Petersburg and elsewhere)? It is impossible to say, although Alexander's subsequent display of resolution during the invasion argues against such an interpretation. In the event, his armies were not smashed so what actually happened in 1812 is not the best guide to how resolute the Tsar would have remained had his forces suffered a crushing defeat. This is all, of course, hypothetical, but the key point is that it is by no means certain that Alexander, and others who were seemingly steadfast in their determination to resist the invaders to the bitter end in 1812, would not have been willing to make peace with Napoleon had he succeeded in delivering a shattering blow to Russia's armies.

Whatever the intention of the Tsar's letter – and perhaps all he was trying to do was absolve himself in his own mind of responsibility for the death and destruction that would result from the war – when the Emperor eventually received and read it on 1 July, events had moved on. The Russian First Army had successfully managed to evade the advancing enemy and, despite gaining territory, Napoleon's armies were already encountering serious difficulties. Balashov had actually reached French lines with the Tsar's letter shortly after being despatched with it, but the Emperor had refused to receive him for several days. Initially, he interpreted news that a Russian emissary had arrived with a missive from Alexander as indicative of a major weakening of resolve of the part of his fellow ruler and only delayed seeing Balashov so that his armies would have time to capture the city of Vilna, thereby putting him in a stronger position should peace talks open in the near future. When he actually read the letter, Napoleon was frustrated by it, as he had hoped that it would be more faint-hearted than it was. The serious difficulties that his armies were already facing in Russia also irritated him and these made him keen to encourage Alexander along the path towards a negotiated settlement that would favour the French. In his reply to the Tsar's letter, therefore, despite firmly blaming Russia for the war, Napoleon assured his fellow ruler that 'My private feelings towards you remain unaffected by these events' and declared, 'Should Your Majesty wish to end hostilities, you will find me ready to do so'. By the time Alexander received the letter, the campaign, though hardly going brilliantly for the Russians, had at least not developed into the early disaster it might have done, so the Tsar did not deign to respond. There would be no further communication between the two emperors before Napoleon occupied Moscow.

In tracing the story of this correspondence, we have moved a little way ahead of the story of the invasion. Back on the evening of 25 June, the Tsar finally made a major decision regarding his response to the invasion. With alarming reports coming in of a lightning French advance towards Vilna, Russia's ruler became jittery and decided that he must flee the city lest he be captured. By the early hours of the 26th, all was ready for the departure of the Tsar and his entourage, and they duly left. The critical question of whether to defend Russia's third largest city or to retreat to the interior was devolved by the commander-in-chief to General Barclay, a sensible but weak-willed decision that displayed a potentially alarming shirking of responsibility on the Tsar's part.

Unsurprisingly, Barclay ordered a general withdrawal towards the Dvina shortly after Alexander left Vilna, though it did not begin until the next day. It was conducted in good order and so avoided any real danger of the invading hordes catching the First Army. Russian spirits, however, were undeniably knocked by the decision to retreat, and there was much displeasure and concern at the abandonment of such a major city as Vilna. Those who opposed the First Army's commander and his preference for flight over fight began to sharpen their knives.

Napoleon concluded from the lack of contact between his forces and those of the enemy during the first days of the invasion that Barclay was planning to withdraw his First Army deeper into Russia before turning to fight. This suggested that the invaders should press on as fast as they could in the hope of catching up with at least a part of the main Russian army before they pulled too far away, and certainly some of the marshals, particularly the fiery Murat and Oudinot, endeavoured to drive their men on as hard as possible. The Emperor, though, was more cautious. Before the invasion, he had expected the Russians to defend Vilna, which had, after all, been the Tsar's headquarters for several weeks, and he was wary that to allow his subordinates to advance too quickly could lead to them becoming vulnerable to a sudden Russian counter-attack. He therefore ordered his more aggressive subordinates to slow their progress. Until he had more concrete information regarding the enemy's dispositions and intentions, the Emperor seemed determined to proceed warily.

Given the centrality to Napoleon's strategy of bringing the Russians to combat as near to the frontier as possible, his caution in these early days of the campaign can easily be called into question. Certainly, there was some sense in seeking to avoid reverses, but it was only by risking a setback that the Emperor would have had any real chance in this opening phase of catching up with and destroying at least part of Russia's First Army of the West. Napoleon blamed his caution upon the commanders of the two auxiliary armies that were to cross the Niemen to the south of the main force, his former stepson Eugène de Beauharnais and his brother Jerome. Although the two flank forces, Marshal Macdonald's largely Prussian corps in the north and Prince Schwarzenberg's Austrians away to the south, succeeded in advancing into Russian territory without difficulties, both Eugène and Jerome fell behind schedule from the start, the former by two days, the latter by almost a week. Both attributed their tardiness to problems of finding enough transport to bring forward supplies, although in Jerome's case personal incompetence was an issue as well. According to Napoleon's plan, Eugène's force was needed to support the main army as it advanced on Barclay while Jerome's was to press Bagration's Second Army and prevent it from joining up with the much larger First. With both men falling behind, the Emperor's caution seems more justified. Even so, one can question just how seriously Bonaparte really did need Eugène to support him given that he already had almost a quarter of a million troops in his main army. One can even dispute the significance of Jerome's slowness in light of intelligence Napoleon received shortly after invading that Bagration, far from advancing or holding his position, from where he might be able to thrust at the main Imperial army's rear as it moved forward, was in headlong retreat. The real reason for the Emperor's caution, therefore, was perhaps less the tardiness of his subordinates than his own changed military approach; no longer the bold, risk-taking commander in the field of his younger years but a more wary, middle-aged general more concerned to avoid any reverse himself than to inflict one on the enemy.

In spite of Napoleon's caution, his advance guard reached Vilna on 28 June, just over four days after the first troops had crossed the Niemen some sixty or so miles to the north-west, a decent if not lightning rate of progress. The only resistance the Russians offered was a brief artillery bombardment delivered at very long range as the invaders approached the city. To all intents and purposes, Russia's third largest urban centre was undefended, although the bridges over the Vilia and such supplies as the retreating First Army could not carry had been destroyed. With political expediency to the fore, the first soldiers into the city were a unit of Polish lancers from the Grand Duchy who received a hearty welcome from the locals. Subsequent non-Polish units were also cheered as they entered Vilna that day and the Emperor himself was greeted cordially if not as rapturously as he had been in Warsaw almost six years earlier. On the face of it, the capture of such a major city less than a week into the campaign seemed a triumph for the invaders, but all was far from rosy.

For a start, the transport problems of which Eugène and Jerome complained were anything but illusory. Although Napoleon's main army advanced along a major route into Russia, Eugène's and Jerome's auxiliary armies both had to advance, at least initially, along poor Polish roads which became easily congested. Moreover, as the main army had priority for such transport as was available, the auxiliary forces were left to cope as best they could with less adequate provision. Already, the detailed preparations Napoleon had made for supplying his forces were beginning to break down and things were only going to get worse the further into Russia the invaders advanced.

To alleviate the supply situation, the Emperor had instructed his cavalry and wagoneers to feed the tens of thousands of horses that accompanied the invasion off the land. He had even delayed the invasion partly to give extra time for crops to ripen in the fields. As fate would have it, though, spring and summer both came uncommonly late to eastern Europe in 1812, and the rye and wheat upon which horses fed in this opening phase of the campaign was not yet ready for consumption. Consequently, horses either ate what was available and then generally developed stomach disorders that could incapacitate or even kill them, or they made do with such limited supplies as could be got forward. Of course, the hungrier the horses got, the more prone to exhaustion they became. The result was an equine calamity, with thousands of beasts dying from hunger, exhaustion or illness in the opening days and weeks of the war.

If the horses fared particularly badly, the men of the invading armies had serious problems of their own. For the first few days of the campaign, the sun shone down mercilessly, baking the soldiers as they advanced during the day. At night, though, temperatures plummeted, a sharp contrast, a feature of eastern European summers, that came as a shock to the system to the great majority of Napoleon's troops. The nocturnal cold, moreover, created further problems for the Emperor by creating a demand for firewood among the invading soldiers. This was procured in the form of planks from hundreds of huts and other buildings in the vicinity of wherever men stopped for the night. The result was a swathe of destruction that severely undermined any warmth the populace of the Tsar's western provinces felt towards their supposed liberators.

Nor did the carnage wrought by the invaders end with the destruction of buildings. Soldiers being what they were in the early nineteenth century, pillage and, in extreme cases, more serious misdemeanours accompanied armies wherever they went. Napoleon tried to prevent his troops from committing acts which would damage relations with the Poles and Lithuanians through whose lands his forces were passing by ordering that any man caught engaging in looting (or more serious acts) was to be summarily tried and executed, but this did little to prevent it becoming a major problem. Soldiers were certainly hanged when they were caught, but too few were caught for the draconian punishment to be that much of a deterrent. There were just 520 *gendarmes*, or military police, for the entire *Grande Armée*. Given the failure to control his troops' transgressions, Napoleon and his men soon found that the locals adopted, at best, an ambivalent attitude towards their presence beyond the Niemen, leaving the Emperor to complain shortly after the fall of Vilna that 'These Poles are not like those in the Duchy of Warsaw'. Indeed, it was perhaps fortunate for the invaders that the Russian armies proved every bit as much a burden to the inhabitants of the Tsar's western provinces, plundering, and worse, as they retreated. This at least meant that the unlucky locals had reason to dislike both sides.

The first few days of the 1812 campaign were only a superficial success for Napoleon. To be sure, the fall of Vilna was a blow to Russian pride and morale, but more important than that was the failure to come to grips with the Tsar's armies, whose defeat would do far more to incline the enemy towards accepting peace terms favourable to the French than the capture of what was not really a Russian city. With serious difficulties already emerging, it was now imperative that a victory over Russia's forces came as soon as possible. First, though, they would have to be caught.

Shortly after Napoleon arrived in Vilna the weather broke and the searing heat of the past week was replaced by several days of torrential rain. This was not only miserable for the soldiers in the field, it also increased the already alarming rate of sickness among the troops and greatly complicated the Emperor's efforts to bring the enemy to battle by turning most roads in this part of Europe to mud, making the transport situation even worse and slowing movement yet further. In these circumstances, any hope of catching Barclay's retreating First Army in the immediate future seemed slim, but then reports arrived at Vilna suggesting that Bagration was marching his men north-east in an effort to link up with Barclay, a move which put them within striking range of the invaders. Here, perhaps, was an opportunity to annihilate Russia's Second Army of the West.

Tasking the corps of Murat, Ney and Oudinot, plus a couple of divisions from

Davout's corps, to shadow Barclay, Napoleon ordered Marshal Davout to take the rest of his massive corps (some 50,000 troops) down the Vilia, east of Vilna, to secure any crossings and prevent Bagration from effecting a junction with the First Army. Jerome, meanwhile, who finally had 55,000 of his 80,000-strong auxiliary army on Russian soil, was commanded to press forward against Bagration as quickly as possible from the west. As the Emperor's brother pinned the Russian Second Army down, Davout would sweep down on the enemy's flank and rear from the north, supported by up to 30,000 of Eugène's men, who were currently pressing on towards Vilna from Kovno. Bagration's army would be crushed by an Imperial force almost three times as large. It was an excellent plan.

Unfortunately for Napoleon, however, plans rarely go completely smoothly, and this was no exception. Eugène's slowness in moving his auxiliary army forward to Vilna led the Emperor to delay releasing Davout down the Vilia lest a gap appear in the invaders' lines which the enemy might exploit. Again, Napoleon was being overly cautious, and it reduced the likelihood of his soldiers being able to catch the retreating Russians. Even more serious was Jerome's continued tardiness in moving his army forward. There is no denying that his men had had an arduous advance through tough country with poor roads, but the fact is that it was hard going for everybody and everyone else managed to perform better. Compounding his incompetence, Jerome dismissed the one corps commander in his army, General Dominique Vandamme, who, thanks to his impetuous nature, was pressing on in the fashion Napoleon intended. The charge was embezzlement, although it was probably more pertinent that the King of Westphalia simply didn't like the brusque Vandamme. When he heard of the dismissal, the Emperor was furious but he refused to reinstate the general lest it offend and undermine his brother. This sensitivity to his sibling's feelings and position would soon, as Napoleon himself came to realize, prove mistaken.

On 5 July, with Napoleon wondering why neither Jerome nor Davout had yet come into contact with Bagration's army, one of his brother's aides arrived in Vilna with a report. It stated that scouts from the Westphalian king's force had concluded that the Russian Second Army was not, as originally thought, retreating north-east towards Barclay, but south-east towards Minsk. The news was frustrating enough, but the fact that Jerome had known about it on 3 July yet had apparently seen no need to inform the Emperor for two days sent Napoleon into a rage. He immediately dictated a stinging reply, attacking his brother's slowness both in advancing his army and in reporting vital information: 'it would be impossible to manoeuvre in worse fashion'. Thanks to his 'singular failure to appreciate the first notions about warfare' Jerome had 'robbed me of the fruit of my manoeuvres and of the best opportunity ever presented in war'. Finally realizing the gross error he had made in appointing Jerome to such a senior position in the first place, Napoleon authorized Marshal Davout to take overall charge should his force and that of the Emperor's brother draw close enough together to make unity of command sensible, though he failed to inform Jerome himself of the arrangement. When Davout invoked the order, therefore, on 13 July, the King of Westphalia, still fuming from the dressing down his elder sibling had given him a week earlier, erupted in a fit of pique and promptly resigned from his command, returning to his German realm in a huff and throwing his army into temporary chaos.

Once again, however, we have got slightly ahead of ourselves. Napoleon responded to Jerome's report of 5 July by ordering his brother and Davout to chase Bagration south in the hope of catching him. Davout's men reached Minsk just three days later, an impressive advance given the conditions and one which showed what could be done under competent command. They found the city abandoned, but their frustration at not finding the enemy was at least partly offset by the capture of large quantities of stores. Jerome, meanwhile, should already have found Bagration, for the Russian commander rested his men on 7 July near a town where the Emperor's brother's troops were supposed to be the same day. Instead, they were miles away, their advance being little less tardy than it had been before Napoleon had taken Jerome to task. Consequently, Bagration and his Second Army escaped the net, and with Davout's soldiers exhausted after their efforts and badly in need of a rest, the Emperor sullenly called a halt to the vigorous pursuit of the enemy. Napoleon would not get the crushing victory near the frontier that he wanted.

There seems little doubt that, whereas the odds were probably always against the invaders bringing Barclay's First Army to battle near the border in summer 1812, there was a definite opportunity to force Bagration into an engagement. Responsibility for the failure to do so has generally been laid, understandably, at Jerome's door, but one must remember that he was only in a position to lead his army so poorly because his brother put him there. Better men were available. Davout would probably have been the best choice and his large corps could have been entrusted to the wily Masséna, whose talents were imprudently unemployed by Napoleon in 1812.

Less valid a criticism of the Emperor than his poor choice of commander for his second auxiliary army, however, is his decision to remain at Vilna while the hunt for Bagration was in progress. This has sometimes been put down to lethargy on his part, the result of good living and middle age, but this is not fair. He was far from idle at Vilna. With elements of his *Grande Armée* as far apart as the Baltic in the north and the Pripet Marshes in the south, Vilna was a sensible temporary headquarters for the invasion force where he could both contact and be contacted easily. The city also needed to be organized as a massive supply depot and Napoleon's administrative and organizational skills were invaluable in this. The transport arrangements for the invading armies needed attention after the difficulties of the first week as well, and the Emperor's efforts here, while far from solving the problems entirely, at least served to keep the system functioning.

The other main task Napoleon carried out while at Vilna was to organize a provisional government for this part of the Tsar's empire which he linked to that of the Grand Duchy of Warsaw. If anything proves that Napoleon's ideal goal in 1812 was to strip Russia of her north-western provinces, this is surely it. Wherever he had organized provisional governments in the past, more permanent French satellite states had soon emerged. For the Poles, it seemed like the resurrection of their old kingdom was at hand and a delegation was duly sent to the Emperor at Vilna to plead with him to take that crucial step forthwith. He listened sympathetically to their appeal but then rejected it. The arguments for and against a public commitment to the recreation of the Kingdom of Poland were essentially the same a fortnight into the invasion as they had been before it; indeed, the failure to bring the Russians to battle and the difficulties the invading armies were already experiencing militated against taking a step that would have removed the possibility of any kind of compromise peace. The Poles, naturally, were bitterly disappointed, but they realized that Napoleon was still their best hope if their dream was to be achieved. For the moment, they would simply have to remain patient and hope that the Emperor could catch and crush Russia's retreating armies.

Some accounts of the 1812 campaign give the impression that the Russians coolly followed a brilliant preconceived strategy of luring the invaders to their doom ever deeper inside the Tsar's enormous realm. This is nonsense. The Russians were never as sanguine about the invasion as they have sometimes been portrayed – the loss of Vilna and Minsk so early and without a fight, for example, hit morale and led to defeatist talk in St Petersburg – while Russian strategy was not skilfully predetermined and universally accepted but largely made up on the spot and subject to much controversy. Barclay's decision to withdraw behind the River Dvina, for instance, was abhorred by many senior Russian commanders, most especially Prince Bagration. In early July, he wrote to Alexander pleading, 'The First Army should advance on Vilna at once without fail. What is there to fear? ... I implore you to advance ... It ill suits Russians to run ... One feels ashamed.' The Georgian general had many friends in high places in the Russian Army, including Barclay's chief of staff. His advice could not simply be ignored and it is certainly not beyond the bounds of possibility that the Tsar might have decided to follow the course of action advocated by the popular Bagration instead of that favoured by the widely disliked Barclay.

Again, it was the sheer size of Napoleon's army that persuaded Alexander to maintain the retreat; at least as far as the Dvina. The Tsar reached Drissa on the river's eastern bank shortly before Barclay's First Army, which arrived on 10–11 July, and he determined that here his forces would turn and fight. Drissa, of course, was the site of a major fortified camp in which it had been envisaged before the invasion that a stand might be made, but once Barclay and his subordinates arrived there, they immediately began to revise their plans. The camp was not only too cramped to accommodate all the First Army's troops, it lacked defences along a whole side and could easily be outflanked. As Karl von Clausewitz, the great military thinker who actually saw the camp at Drissa in July 1812, later wrote: 'If the Russians had not abandoned this position of their own accord, they would have been attacked from the rear ... driven into the semi-circle of trenches, and forced to surrender.' Drissa was a disaster waiting to happen. When the militarily ignorant Alexander informed his generals that he wanted the army to make a stand there, even most of those who opposed the policy of retreat were horrified and frantically endeavoured to persuade him to change his mind. At this critical juncture, the Tsar might have asserted his authority as commander-in-chief and ignored the objections of his subordinates, as he had ignored Kutuzov before Austerlitz, but the memory of that earlier débâcle perhaps persuaded Russia's ruler to yield this time. The warnings of possible catastrophe had the desired effect and Alexander agreed to the urgent appeals to abandon the fortified camp. Tactfully, Barclay explained to the Tsar that he would have followed his wishes to fight at Drissa without question but for the absence of Bagration and the Second Army, who were still some way off to the south and without whom the Russians simply would not have the manpower to win. This soothed Alexander's *amour propre* and inclined him towards the First Army commander's new strategy, a further retreat, this time of around a hundred miles, south-east to the town of Vitebsk, where it was hoped Bagration would finally be able to link up with the larger Russian force. Then, the combined armies would turn and fight.

Despatching 14,000 troops north-east to defend the Baltic city of Riga against the advancing corps of Marshal Macdonald, and leaving a further 25,000 under General Ludwig Wittgenstein to protect the First Army's northern flank, Barclay led his men out of Drissa shortly after they had arrived there. With a healthy lead on the invaders, the withdrawal was unmolested and the First Army reached Vitebsk on 20 July, where it stopped, began to throw up defensive earthworks and awaited the arrival of Bagration's Second Army.

With a key moment in the campaign now seemingly drawing near, a group of leading Russians, led by State Secretary Shishkov, decided to address the thorny issue of the Tsar's exercise of supreme command over the armies in the field. His initial desire to make a stand at Drissa had shocked many and convinced them that it was only a matter of time before one of Alexander's interventions in military affairs proved calamitous. As the retreat got under way once more,

Shishkov, Balashov and Arakcheev, the former minister of war who was now serving as the Tsar's personal military adviser, wrote a letter pleading with Alexander to relinquish his active role in the field and return to St Petersburg, where, as they diplomatically put it, his skills would be better used in steadying morale, raising troops and money, and overseeing the war effort in general. Despite the tactful tone of the letter, the Tsar was not pleased to receive it, but it is to his credit that he seems to have realized his own military limitations and that he agreed to leave the generals to get on with their job. In mid-July, without appointing anyone to take overall responsibility for the various Russian armies in the field and thus leaving the command potentially dangerously divided, Alexander set off to return to his capital. First, though, he decided to visit that other great Russian city, the old capital, Moscow. Few can have imagined that barely two months later it would be in enemy hands.

Following the failure to trap Bagration's army near the frontier in early July, Napoleon ordered Davout to march his corps parallel to and a little way to the south of the main invasion force as it advanced east, his task being to prevent the Second Army from taking a direct route to join up with Barclay. The rest of the main army and the two auxiliary armies, meanwhile, apart from the ever-growing number of units detached to garrison captured towns or protect the elongating supply lines, were to press on towards the Dvina in the hope of bringing the Russian First Army to battle.

The Emperor initially expected Barclay to make a stand at Drissa and so formulated a strategy to outflank the camp and force the Russians into an engagement in which they would be at a severe disadvantage. Learning in mid-July that Drissa had been abandoned, Bonaparte had to alter his plans, as well, thanks to Jerome's piqued departure for Westphalia, as the structure of his invasion force. The latter problem was effectively solved by the auxiliary armies being disbanded as an entity and the Emperor taking their various units into his main army, a change which demoted his former stepson Eugène from an army to a corps commander, a role to which he was better suited. The other regular corps which had formed part of Eugène's auxiliary army, that of the cultured General Gouvion St Cyr, was now despatched by Napoleon north of the Dvina along with Marshal Oudinot's corps, the two men being ordered to prevent the 25,000 soldiers Barclay had detached under Wittgenstein from attacking the main army's northern flank or supply lines. The rest of the units under Napoleon's immediate control remained south of the river and continued their advance east in pursuit of the retreating First Army.

During this advance from the Vilna area to Vitebsk the invaders' problems became even more serious than hitherto. The days got even hotter – veterans of the Egyptian campaign complained that the heat in Russia was comparable to that they had experienced in 1798–99 – while the nights mostly remained cold. The sun parched the poor Russian roads so that huge dust clouds were thrown up by the advancing troops, blinding and choking those who followed. Some soldiers endeavoured to lessen the effects of the dust by making crude goggles from whatever glass they could find or, despite the heat, wrapping their heads in cloth. The only real relief, though, came when the heavens opened, but that brought problems of its own, turning the roads into quagmires through which it was physically exhausting to march after each downpour.

The other major disadvantage to the occasional rainstorms was that they slowed the movement of supplies as well as men. Napoleon may have patched up the *Grande Armée*'s logistics during his stay in Vilna, but he could not make them function perfectly. The further east his armies went, the more difficult it became to provision them. It would be overstating the case to say that the system broke down entirely, at least at this stage, but it is certainly true that most soldiers failed to receive as much food or other supplies as they were supposed to. Hunger, of course, increased the troops' vulnerability to illness and exhaustion, and ever greater numbers began to fall out of their units, especially new recruits. It has been estimated that three weeks and 200 miles into the campaign, the total number of effectives in the main invasion force had dropped from near 400,000 to just under 300,000, due primarily to sickness, fatigue and straggling. Some of the tens of thousands of soldiers not fit for duty subsequently returned to their units, but many, through desertion, debilitation or death, did not.

In an effort to remedy the supply problem, foraging, authorized or not, became more and more widespread, but the country between the Niemen and the upper Dvina and Dnieper rivers had little to offer. Sparsely populated, with most of the terrain forest, marsh or lake instead of arable farmland, there was little food to be had, particularly as the retreating Russian armies did what they could to prevent any provisions they could not carry away themselves from falling into enemy hands. Fortunately for the invaders, sometimes the Russian scorched earth policy missed things, for example at the town of Orsha, where a huge quantity of flour was captured, although the joy this particular prize brought was limited. With the bricks required to build field ovens held up many miles to the rear, the soldiers were forced to turn the captured flour into a kind of gruel instead of baking it as bread. Still, that was preferable to what many troops resorted to when they struggled to find enough drinking water – imbibing horses' urine. Indeed, the unfortunate horses that accompanied the invasion of Russia in 1812 provided not just liquid but food as well, those which succumbed to illness or exhaustion being swiftly butchered, cooked and eaten by famished men.[*]

---

[*] Indeed there is an apocryphal story that the French predilection for horsemeat dates to the Russian campaign.

Despite not suffering the worst hardships of the campaign himself, Napoleon, who generally travelled in Russia in a closed carriage from which he could conduct the business of running an empire as well as a war, was aware of the suffering his men were undergoing, which only made it more imperative that the Russians be brought to battle as soon as possible in the hope that a decisive victory might pave the way for peace. It was with evident exhilaration, therefore, that on 24 July reports from his advance guard confirmed that the Russian First Army was within striking distance near Vitebsk. Fierce skirmishing between Imperial troops and elements of Barclay's force at Ostronovo, around a dozen miles west of Vitebsk, over the next two days convinced Napoleon that, at last, the enemy was preparing to fight. Excitedly, the Emperor wrote to his foreign minister at Vilna proclaiming, 'We are on the eve of great events'.

The skirmishing was renewed for a third day on the morning of the 27th, but then Napoleon unexpectedly ordered his troops to break off until the morrow. He wished for a lull of twenty-four hours in which to reorganize the forces he had to hand and await the arrival of further units still a little way off. Convinced that the major battle he so desperately wanted was imminent, he intended to use this hiatus to ensure that he would achieve a crushing victory. The Russians, however, found an even better use for the pause their foe gave them.

As the Emperor prepared to smash Barclay's First Army of the West, his Russian counterpart arrived in Moscow, over 300 miles to the east. Alexander feared that the constant retreats of his armed forces would have tarnished him in the eyes of the people, so he was extremely gratified to receive a warm welcome from large crowds of Muscovites. The fact seems to be that Russians, or at least those in this part of the empire, had become infected with a peculiar spirit in 1812 which no one has ever quite managed to pin down exactly. Many have called it nationalism or patriotism, akin perhaps to the spirit that had infused France during the dark days of 1793–94, but a better definition would perhaps be virulent xenophobia with a large dose of religious hatred thrown in. Certainly, there was much animosity directed at the invaders, and the Tsar was pleased to find the merchants and nobles of Moscow only too willing to make voluntary contributions of hundreds of thousands of roubles and thousands of serfs to aid the war effort. If that was the positive side of the spirit of 1812, however, there was a dark side too. The hatred of foreigners whipped up by many leading Russians, such as the governor of Moscow, was also directed at non-Russians in the Tsar's service, those of Alexander's subjects who did not have a Russian name, and those of non-Orthodox religion (something not helped by the Tsar portraying the conflict during his time in Moscow as a religious struggle, a pseudo-crusade). Anyone who was not authentically 'Russian' came under immediate suspicion, no matter what their record. The most notable victim of this paranoia was General

Barclay, against whom many Russians turned violently, blaming him for the igno-minious retreats. It was a gross injustice, for without those ignominious retreats, which Barclay had ensured were conducted effectively and efficiently, the Russian armies would have been annihilated. Indeed, it would not be overstating the case to argue that the dour, Protestant, Baltic baron, of German and Scots ancestry, did more than any other individual in 1812 to save Russia from disaster, yet he would receive no thanks for his efforts from the people who most owed it to him.

The ingratitude shown to Barclay was just the tip of the iceberg of Russian xenophobia and religious hatred in 1812. Anyone French (or to some extent any other nationality in common with the invading soldiery) who happened to live in Moscow, St Petersburg or any other Russian city might find themselves or their property threatened or attacked, even if they were no friends of Napoleon and his regime. It was towards the invaders themselves, however, that the real venom was directed, the fact that the bulk of them were conscripts who would rather not have come to Russia in the first place not being taken into consideration. Of course, it would be naive in the extreme to expect the Russians to have treated the invading troops with anything but hostility, but the savagery meted out by the Russian peasantry to any individual or small group of Napoleonic soldiers unfortunate enough to be caught by them went far beyond the pale.

It is sometimes suggested that Napoleon could have averted this hatred, could even have won the Russian peasantry to his side, by pledging to abolish serfdom in the Tsar's lands. This is simplistic. For a start, a promise to free the serfs would have been completely impractical; the invading armies could hardly have gone to every village liberating oppressed peasants as they went. It would, moreover, have been a flagrant interference in Russian domestic policies which, no matter how noble, would have complicated the achievement of peace enormously. True, it would have been more feasible to have abolished serfdom in the Polish and Lithuanian provinces through which the invaders advanced in the opening phase of the campaign and over which the Emperor established a provisional government, but the peasants in this region were not a problem for the Imperial armies anyway. Besides, freeing the serfs here would have alienated the local nobility and perhaps inclined many of them towards supporting Alexander, something which would not have aided the Napoleonic cause.

The Tsar left Moscow at the end of July and arrived back in St Petersburg on 3 August. He soon observed, 'Here I have found a worse frame of mind than at Moscow or in the interior'. There was a definite whiff of anxiety and defeatism in the air which news of a disaster for Barclay's First Army at Vitebsk would have strengthened considerably. Fortunately for Alexander, though, such shattering news would never arrive.

There was an engagement worthy of being called a battle in Russia in late July, but it was not fought by the Russian First Army. On the 23rd, around a hundred miles south of Vitebsk near a town called Mohilev on the mighty Dnieper river, Prince Bagration's Second Army attacked Marshal Davout's corps. Following his instruction to prevent Bagration from leading his men towards a union with the First Army via the most direct route, Davout had established a defensive position astride the main road north along the western bank of the Dnieper. For most of the day, the Russians tested the strength of the defenders with piecemeal assaults (their losses of 3,000 were relatively small) before deciding that Davout's force was too strong to be brushed aside and might indeed inflict a more serious defeat upon the Second Army should it press its attack hard. Bagration therefore decided to disengage and continue his retreat along a less direct route. Davout, his men weary from almost constant marching since they had crossed the Niemen, was in no position to launch a vigorous pursuit against his bruised but by no means crippled adversary.

Barclay learned of Bagration's repulse a few days later. By this time, those who favoured a bolder strategy than one of continual retreat included virtually every senior officer in the First Army, but the army commander, who had had some reservations about fighting at Vitebsk anyway, was now convinced that it would be courting disaster to make a stand knowing that there was no possibility of support from the Second Army. The long retreat had taken a heavy toll on the Russians, with thousands of troops deserting and others falling sick or dropping out of their units due to exhaustion. Indeed, the First Army shrank by around a sixth during the first few weeks of the campaign. Barclay therefore ignored the complaints of many of his subordinates and determined that a further withdrawal was necessary, this time one of around eighty miles to the ancient and holy Russian city of Smolensk, which stood astride the upper Dnieper. Bagration should, he felt, be able to join the First Army there, and then the long-awaited stand would be made.

The problem was that, having waited at Vitebsk for the Second Army, Napoleon's main body had caught up with Barclay's men and any retreat might be severely disrupted, even turned into a rout, should the enemy fall on the dispirited Russian columns as they made yet another withdrawal. Barclay realized that discipline and order were essential if disaster was to be avoided but it would take time to organize an army that had been expecting to fight a battle to conduct an efficient, well-ordered retreat.

The Emperor's decision to suspend hostilities for twenty-four hours on the morning of 27 July gave the First Army and its commander the time they needed. Hoping the pause would ensure the enemy's annihilation, instead it facilitated his escape. Finding no sign of the First Army in front of Vitebsk on the morning of the 28th, Napoleon's first thought was that Barclay was planning a gigantic ambush and had hidden all his troops among the woods and valleys in the area.

He therefore ordered a cautious advance only to discover after a little while that the enemy had gone. Murat was swiftly instructed to launch a pursuit with his cavalry, but when he eventually caught up with the well-organized Russian rearguard his horses were exhausted and his attack was easily, and bloodily, repulsed.

The First Army had quietly slipped away towards Smolensk on the night of 27–28 July, leaving campfires burning to maintain the illusion that they still intended to make a stand. It was a skilfully planned and conducted withdrawal that put a good distance between the Russians and the invaders and for which most of the credit must go to Barclay, whose forte was always organization and administration. It is very difficult to say, of course, exactly what would have happened had Napoleon not called that fateful halt on the 27th, but there seems little doubt that events would have turned out less favourably for the Russians. Had the advance guard of the Imperial army, which could have been reinforced throughout the day, been instructed to continue to press the enemy as it had on the 25th–26th, it is probable that Barclay would have had either to sacrifice his rearguard in order to give the rest of his men a chance to escape or to reinforce it with the rest of the First Army in the hope that the invaders could be given a bloody enough nose to discourage them from pursuing a subsequent retreat vigorously. Either way, the Russians would have been flirting with disaster. Bonaparte's halt, then, can only be seen as ill-judged, a blunder even, and one that it is hard to imagine the Napoleon of earlier years making. In his effort to guarantee victory absolutely, another sign of his new-found caution as a military commander, the Emperor had thrown away what had already been a near-certain triumph.

The Russian First Army's escape from Vitebsk was a bitter disappointment to Napoleon. When his subordinates tried to look on the positive side of things by rejoicing at the fall of another significant Russian town, the Emperor angrily snapped, 'Do you think I have come all this way just to conquer these huts?' Adding to his frustration was the knowledge that a vigorous pursuit of Barclay's retreating men was out of the question. The Russians were relatively fresh after a good period of rest at Vitebsk while the invading forces had been almost constantly on the march since Vilna. To drive them on too hard would risk breaking all cohesion and might bring about the collapse of the already creaking supply system. Thwarted, Napoleon called a halt to operations and ordered his weary units to reorganize and consolidate.

The key question confronting the Emperor now was how long this halt in operations should last. When the bold Murat, unfazed by his repulse at the hands of the First Army's rearguard, pressed him to push on after the Russians, Napoleon gave a surprising reply. 'The first campaign of Russia is over,' he said. 'Let us here plant our eagles where two great rivers [the upper Dvina and Dnieper] mark out our position ... 1813 will see us at Moscow: 1814 in Petersburg. The Russian war is a war of three years.' It seemed that the Emperor was radically changing his strategy. Hitherto, his prime aim had been to bring the Russians to battle, crush their armies and force Alexander to sue for peace, the nature of which would depend upon the extent of the defeat of the Tsar's armed forces, the state of Russian morale and wider European affairs. Now, he seemed to be accepting that he was in for a much longer conflict which would involve attempting to capture Russia's two greatest cities.

As July passed into August, many stragglers returned to their units, convoys of supplies caught up with the army, and the Imperial troops enjoyed a well-earned rest. This all made the situation seem less bleak. Reports also arrived confirming that the Russian First Army had halted at Smolensk, where it was joined in early August by Bagration's Second Army. (Davout had been ordered in late July to abandon his shadowing of that force and close up with the main army.) The combination of an improved situation in the affairs of his own troops and the presence of the enemy only a few days' march away soon proved too strong for Napoleon to resist. In the first week of August, he suddenly called a council of war and declared to his subordinates that European affairs demanded that he end the war in Russia in 1812. To achieve this, a decisive battle was needed and that could be achieved by pushing on to Smolensk and even, if the Russians retreated still further, Moscow, before which they would surely make a stand. Many of those present, most especially his chief of staff, Marshal Berthier, his former stepson, Eugène, and the ex-ambassador to St Petersburg, Armand de Caulaincourt, now serving as one of the Emperor's closest personal aides, were disquieted by this new-found determination to push on and alarmed by the thought of the army advancing as far as Moscow. When they tried to object, however, raising pertinent issues such as whether the supply system could stand the added strain of a further advance east, Napoleon remained adamant and accused them of having got too used to a soft life.

The next day, Berthier tried to dissuade the Emperor again, this time by bringing Count Daru, the man responsible for overseeing the *Grande Armée*'s logistics, to plead with him. Napoleon listened politely as Daru raised a list of concerns. The supply system might break down entirely, he warned, if it extended much further east. Certainly, there was a limit beyond which it could not go, for the beasts of burden which pulled the wagons needed to bring their fodder with them and if the distances grew too great they would have to bring so much fodder that there would be no room for other supplies on the wagons. That problem could be solved, or at least partially remedied, by living off the land, but it was not clear how much the countryside between Vitebsk and Moscow could provide, either for men or animals. The experience in Russia so far had not been encouraging. If the supply system did break down and living off the land proved unfeasible, the repercussions, Daru warned, would be disastrous. Already, he pointed out, the army was down by perhaps as much as a third on its effectives due to disease, exhaustion, hunger and desertion, all of which were largely attributable to the difficulties of supplying such a large force.

Napoleon has often been accused of ignoring these logistical problems in deciding to advance east of Vitebsk in 1812. He did not. As he told Daru, he was well aware of the potential hazards of the situation, but he was also aware of the difficulties that would attend a policy of halting. The supply system might indeed prove incapable of sustaining an advance on Moscow that year, but was it any more likely to be able to provide for the army over the long Russian winter if it halted at Vitebsk? Even if it was able, could the army successfully defend such long supply lines against Russian attack? The risk of the army being cut off at Vitebsk was great enough for it to be wiser to retreat all the way back to the Vistula, but that would be tantamount to admitting defeat, which the Emperor was not willing to do while there was a chance that a further advance, and possibly only a short one, might bring the decisive battlefield victory that he was sure would bring the Tsar to the peace table. Besides, a retreat would make all the suffering endured so far seem worthless. There was also a possibility that the discipline and morale of the *Grande Armée* would break down entirely if it was ordered to trudge all the way back beyond the Niemen.

Such was the unenviable predicament facing Napoleon in early August 1812; whatever he chose to do – advance, halt or retreat – would carry great risks. Ideally, the Russians would advance from their position at Smolensk and attack the invaders, but that seemed highly improbable given the course of events during the campaign so far and the fact that Barclay and Bagration, even together, were still heavily outnumbered. But then, on 8 August, unexpected and exhilarating news arrived at Imperial headquarters.

Bagration's Second Army had finally united with Barclay's First Army near Smolensk on 4 August. The combined Russian force numbered around 125,000, though that was still much lower than the 185,000 Napoleon had under his direct command near Vitebsk (one must remember that both sides, especially the invaders, had made significant detachments during the campaign to protect their flanks and supply lines, and to garrison towns). Of course, the Russians did not know exactly how many soldiers the Emperor had at his immediate disposal, but they were aware that it was far fewer than at the start of the campaign. Barclay therefore found it impossible to resist pleas for a change of strategy. He had intended, in any case, to make a stand at Smolensk, should the invaders advance towards him; but now the enemy had halted, at least temporarily, the more aggressive individuals among the Russian leadership pressed vigorously for a counter-attack against Napoleon's dispersed formations near Vitebsk. At a council of war held on 6 August, the First Army commander agreed, with some reluctance, to lead the bulk of his force west in an attempt to catch the invaders off guard and destroy part of their army.

The first Napoleon sensed of the nascent counter-offensive was news of a major cavalry skirmish between a large force of Cossacks and a detachment of French cavalry at Inkovo, north-west of Smolensk, on 8 August. The Russian force had been too big for it merely to be a scouting party, even a strong one, and the Emperor jumped to the conclusion that a Russian attack was afoot. He was delighted and immediately issued orders for his units to concentrate in preparation for a major battle near Vitebsk.

Had there been a realistic chance of the Russians catching the enemy scattered and unawares, their counter-offensive might have been a reasonable strategy, but Napoleon was not a man who was easily caught off guard. Hoping to ambush the invaders, the Russians were instead marching into immense peril themselves. Had they conducted the counter-offensive as efficiently as they had their retreats, it seems highly probable that they would have been soundly thrashed by the Emperor, who would have enjoyed a fifty per cent numerical advantage as well as choice of ground for the battle. It was to Napoleon's great misfortune, therefore, that the Russians proved considerably less adept at advancing than they had at withdrawing.

The key factor which stymied the Russian counter-offensive of early August was the distrust, animosity and suspicion that existed between Barclay and Bagration. We have already seen how their widely differing personalities and rivalry for the role of commander of the First Army had set them apart, and the bad blood between them had only got worse over recent weeks with the Second Army commander waging what can only be described as a concerted campaign against the Baltic baron and his policy of retreat. Now that Bagration had seemingly got his way and the Russians were moving forward instead of back, one might have expected things to have improved, but, extraordinarily, it seems that the Georgian deliberately tried to engineer a reverse for Barclay by failing to advance his troops as fast as he should have, thereby potentially leaving the First Army exposed. That, at least, was Barclay's own interpretation of Bagration's conduct, his suspicion being that the Georgian hoped that a setback for the First Army commander would encourage Alexander to remove him from command of Russia's largest force and hand over control to Bagration. Had he been less cautious an individual or more personally committed to the new strategy of a counter-attack, Barclay might well have driven his men on to possible disaster, but instead he advanced with extreme hesitancy before calling a complete halt for six days. The envisaged counter-offensive simply never materialized.

Back at Vitebsk, meanwhile, Napoleon swiftly interpreted the lack of action in the couple of days following the clash at Inkovo as a sign that the Russians had thought better of attacking after all. He was determined, however, to have a battle and so formulated an offensive plan of his own. The bulk of the forces under his immediate command would head south from Vitebsk towards Rosasna near the bend of the Dnieper river, their movement being masked by the heavily wooded terrain between the Dvina and Dnieper rivers and a large cavalry screen. They would then cross the Dnieper some seventy or so miles west of Smolensk and advance along the southern bank towards the ancient city, thereby threatening the enemy's lines of communication back to Moscow and hopefully forcing him to fight. It was a splendid plan, but, as always, its success would depend upon its execution.

The manoeuvre began on 11 August, and three days later, a force 175,000 strong was on the southern bank of the Dnieper without the enemy having any idea about what was happening. It was mid-afternoon on the 14th before the first Russian resistance was encountered. The advance guard under Murat ran into a body of 8,000 infantry and 1,500 horsemen under General Neveroski at Krasny, some thirty miles south-west of Smolensk. This small Russian force had been placed here by Barclay to guard the approach to the ancient city along the Dnieper's southern bank, but its size indicates that an attack was not seriously expected from this direction. Despite having only cavalry to hand, Murat, as was his impetuous wont, hurled them at the enemy, only to see the Russian foot soldiers form into a huge square, the best defence against horsemen. A little later, Marshal Ney arrived with some infantry and suggested that he be allowed to take over the attack as his men could inflict severe damage on the tightly packed Russians with their musketry. Foolishly, Murat refused and continued to throw his cavalry at the enemy, who was by now retreating slowly down the road towards Smolensk. By the time the combat ended with nightfall, Neveroski's force had been reduced to fewer than 4,000, but the fact is that it should have been annihilated. More important than that, though, the stout Russian resistance had slowed the invaders' advance on Smolensk and bought valuable time for Barclay and Bagration, who were by now becoming aware of what was unfolding, to respond to the threat.

With Russia's second holiest city and their line of communication to Moscow under threat, the two army commanders swiftly ordered all available forces to concentrate at Smolensk. Bagration's men, having advanced less far than Barclay's during the recent abortive counter-offensive, were nearest to the city and mostly managed to reach it during 15 August. It was evening on the 16th, however, before the First Army commander and most of his soldiers arrived. Nevertheless, it would prove time enough, for Napoleon, rather than commanding his army to march on to Smolensk with all despatch on the 15th, his forty-third birthday, instead called a one day halt to regroup in anticipation of battle. He even spent part of the day reviewing the troops as if he were in Paris. It seemed an extraordinary and unnecessary delay for which the Emperor has been much censured and for which historians have struggled to find a good reason. The most obvious is that it was caution again, the desire to make sure that units were rested and in good order before the critical battle. It is possible, though, that he had decided he did not want to capture Smolensk too soon lest its fall encourage the Russians to retreat before he had had a chance to get to grips with them properly. The city would act as a magnet so long as it was in Russian hands, and if the whole of Barclay's and Bagration's armies could be drawn towards it the potential scale of a Napoleonic victory would be that much greater. Almost eight weeks into the war, the Emperor was at last preparing to fight the battle that he hoped would end it.

In 1812, the bulk of Smolensk lay on the southern bank of the Dnieper river. The heart of the town was the Old City around which ran a four mile long medieval wall, eighteen feet thick and thirty to forty feet high, with twenty-nine towers dotted along its length. In front of the wall were a ditch and a glacis, although both were in poor repair. Beyond that stretched Smolensk's southern suburbs, a tangle of mostly wooden buildings interspersed with the odd open space or orchard and among which, to the south-east, nestled an old earthen fort grandly named the Royal Citadel. Entrusted with defending this southern part of the city on 15–16 August while the rest of the Russian armies mustered on the Dnieper's northern bank was General Nikolai Raevski with 20,000 men and seventy-two guns. Deploying his meagre artillery in small batteries on the old towers, he pushed most of his soldiers out into the suburbs from where he intended them to conduct a fighting withdrawal to the Old City, thereby buying time for the bulk of the First and Second Armies to reach the area.

To Raevski's surprise, the invaders did not come into view until early on the 16th, and even then Murat and Ney, the marshals whose troops were spearheading the advance, did not seek to engage the Russians but instead waited for the Emperor himself to arrive. Napoleon finally appeared around lunchtime, having spent the morning awaiting confirmation that all the bridges over the Dnieper between Smolensk and Orsha had been destroyed so that the Russians could not outflank his army to the west. Rather than ordering an all-out assault on the Old City that afternoon, however, he authorized only limited attacks – some cavalry skirmishes and a narrowly unsuccessful attempt to capture the Royal Citadel – while allowing the rest of both his and the Russian armies to mass on either side of the Dnieper.

By the following morning, 17 August, the invaders had surrounded the southern section of Smolensk with a semicircle of troops, while Raevski and his men had been replaced south of the river by General Dmitri Dokhturov and his corps, the bulk of the Russian armies remaining on the Dnieper's northern bank. At his disposal, Napoleon had three strong regular corps – those of Marshals Ney and Davout as well as General Poniatowski's Poles (formerly part of Jerome's auxiliary army) – three cavalry corps under the irrepressible Murat, the bulk of the Imperial Guard, and 500 guns. It was a formidable force, but it would still prove no easy task to smash the Russians. The defences of Smolensk, though old, were sturdy, but that was not the greatest of the Emperor's concerns. More problematic was how to ensure that the enemy was not merely beaten but annihilated. With the Dnieper dividing the bulk of the Russians from the invaders, the only way Barclay and Bagration could be forced to commit their entire armies to battle would be for part of the Imperial force to cross the river upstream. Dividing the army in the face of the enemy while he still controlled the bridges over the Dnieper at Smolensk, though, would run the risk of defeat for the smaller section of Napoleon's force. Again, caution took hold of the Emperor. First, he delayed a major attack on the 17th until early afternoon in the vain hope that the Russians might sally forth and attack his positions, thereby easing his predicament. Then, when an all-out assault was finally launched, its sole objective was the capture of southern Smolensk. No troops were despatched east to cross the Dnieper upstream to try to get to grips with the Russians on the northern bank.

Most of the fighting that afternoon was left to the infantry as they slowly pressed their Russian counterparts ever closer back towards the walls of the Old City. It was bloody work clearing the suburbs street by street, building by building, but sheer weight of numbers eventually told. Poniatowski's Poles acquitted themselves particularly well, showing a desperate bravery in their quest to be first to reach the city walls. This resulted in no fewer than eighty-six soldiers being rewarded after the battle with the coveted cross of the *Légion d'Honneur*. As evening began to fall, the remnants of Dokhturov's heavily outnumbered corps finally retreated within the sanctuary of the Old City, whose stout walls had managed to resist a long and fearsome bombardment from the massed artillery of the enemy. Napoleon's gunners, tired of pounding away to no real effect against the medieval masonry, now elevated their barrels and fired over the walls into the Old City itself, turning the ancient heart of Smolensk into a desolate wreck of burning wood, crumbling stone, and charred or crushed flesh. When at last the barrage died down around 8 p.m., the Russians somehow still retained their foothold on the southern bank of the Dnieper, though at a hefty cost. Losses during the two days of fighting at Smolensk on 16–17 August are uncertain, with all manner of figures being suggested by various sources, but it seems likely that total casualties were around 20,000, with the Russians sustaining a couple of thousand more losses than their adversaries.

On the northern bank of the Dnieper, Bagration and most of his fellow senior officers in the Russian armies were inclined to view the fighting so far as a triumph – despite taking heavier losses, the outnumbered Russians had, after all, successfully managed to hold on to the Old City – and they looked forward to continuing the struggle on the morrow. Barclay, however, was of a different mind. As commander of the largest of the Tsar's armies deployed at Smolensk, he was effectively in a position to dictate strategy, and on the evening of 17 August, fearing that Napoleon would cut off the armies' line of retreat to Moscow if they stayed put, he decided that the Russians must abandon the city to the enemy and withdraw. Bagration, indeed almost all the senior officers, were appalled, General Bennigsen and the Grand Duke Constantine, Alexander's younger brother, even going to far as to accuse the First Army commander outright of cowardice. In a fury, Constantine outlandishly ranted at Barclay, 'You German, you sausagemaker, you traitor, you scoundrel; you are selling Russia.' Having finally made the stand that so many Russians had yearned for for so long, it was the bitterest of disappointments to these men to have the commander of the largest body of troops determine to give up a fight that had so far gone quite well and to yield a major city whose loss, old prophecies foretold, would signal that disaster was about to befall the entire realm.

Despite the hail of abuse and protest, Barclay stuck by his decision, ordering his subordinate, General Dokhturov, to pull what was left of his corps back across the river under cover of darkness, torching any supplies they could not bring with them and destroying the bridges behind them. With the First Army committed to a policy of withdrawal, Bagration had little choice but to retreat with his smaller Second Army too. In fact, Barclay arranged for his Georgian counterpart to withdraw east along the northern bank of the Dnieper first, that very night, but asked him to leave detachments to guard fords over the river so that the enemy could not intercept the First Army's subsequent retreat. In his rage, Bagration would fail to do this, with potentially disastrous consequences.

On the southern bank of the Dnieper, meanwhile, Napoleon, though disappointed not to have captured Smolensk that day, was arranging for Marshal Davout to lead a major assault to storm the Old City the following morning. There seems little doubt that this attack would have been successful, for, by nightfall on the 17th, the Emperor's gunners had made two key discoveries. First, although Smolensk's medieval walls were too thick to breach with the guns available, the towers along their length were less strong and could be brought down, and second, batteries could be established along the Dnieper's southern bank that would enable artillery to fire on the bridges that linked the two parts of the city, putting the invaders in a position either to cut off the garrison from the northern bank or wreak havoc as soldiers tried to cross from one side of the river to the other. It would probably have been another bloody fight, but the Old City would have fallen and any Russian troops sent to defend it would most likely have ended up dead or as prisoners.

Of course, Dokhturov's withdrawal on the night of 17–18 August meant that Davout never had to lead the assault. Instead, the marshal's corps entered the Old City at dawn unopposed. The sight that greeted them was not a pleasant one, as an eyewitness later wrote.

> Never, since the start of operations, had we encountered such a sight. Preceded by our musicians, proud but frowning, we passed these ruins where wounded Russians lay covered in blood and dirt … How many men were burned and asphyxiated! … On the thresholds of spared dwellings the wounded beseeched us to help them … The dead, the dying, the wounded, the living, men, bearded ancients, women, and children filled the cathedral. Entire families clad in rags, their terror-stricken faces streaked with tears, were clustered around the altars, weakened, famished, worn out. Everyone trembled at our approach.

Inevitably, the invaders ransacked the city for any supplies or booty that could be found, but behaviour towards the Russians themselves appears to have been generally good. Indeed, over the following days, the *Grande Armée*'s surgeons worked feverishly in improvised hospitals with largely makeshift medical supplies treating many thousands of soldiers of all nationalities as well as civilians.

There remained a war to be fought, however, and on 18 August, the key task for Napoleon's men was to get across the Dnieper and maintain contact with the enemy. It would prove a tricky undertaking, for Barclay decided to contest the enemy's efforts to cross before leading his First Army away east after nightfall. At first, the invaders focused on rebuilding the bridges Dokhturov's men had destroyed, but that resulted in a bitter firefight between Russian infantry on the northern bank and men of Davout's corps in the Old City (surprisingly, the marshal himself grabbed a musket and joined in the skirmish despite being notoriously short-sighted). Eventually, Davout's soldiers won this localized battle, enabling the engineers to proceed with their work, but the first Imperial troops across the Dnieper were units of Württembergers and Portuguese who found a ford downriver from the city. The Russians moved quickly to counter this threat and another fierce firefight developed. Again, Napoleon's men eventually emerged triumphant, but it was early evening before the first pontoon bridge over the river was complete.

Thus the 18th was another day of frustration for the Emperor, but at least it ended with his army in a position to cross the Dnieper in force next morning. Whether it would find anyone to fight once it got there, however, was another question, for on the night of 18–19 August Barclay led his First Army after Bagration. Unlike at Vitebsk, though, the withdrawal from Smolensk did not go like clockwork. Heading north before turning east in the hope of confusing the enemy, the bulk of Barclay's men got lost in the darkness and by dawn had made relatively little progress away from the invaders.

Napoleon hoped to use the 19th to destroy at least a part of the retreating First Army. To this end, he despatched General Junot and his corps (formerly that of the dismissed General Vandamme) along the southern bank of the Dnieper, ordering him to ford the river and place his force in the enemy's path. Junot was chosen because his corps was relatively fresh, having missed the fighting on the 17th thanks to its commander misreading his map and consequently only arriving at Smolensk in the evening. That error should perhaps have warned the Emperor to choose someone else to conduct such a crucial task, but, fortunately for the Russians, it didn't. Junot, then, was to form the anvil with Murat and Ney instructed to take the role of hammer, pursuing Barclay's men along the northern bank of the Dnieper. It was unclear at this stage how much of the First Army might be caught in the trap Napoleon was preparing, but it seemed that there was a decent chance of at least the rearguard being ensnared.

Barclay's rearguard was commanded on 19 August by General Pavel Tuchkov and he performed his task excellently. It did not take too long for Murat and Ney to catch up with the back end of the retreating First Army, but Tuchkov managed to hold them at bay as he covered the withdrawal. Using the terrain expertly, the Russian general defended a succession of ridges that ran north–south and deployed his men in ravines and woods from which it proved hard for the pursuers to evict them. The pressure from Murat and Ney was intense, though, and slowed the bulk of the First Army to a crawl, for Barclay was unwilling to pull too far away from his valiant rearguard and leave it to its fate.

A little way to the south-east, meanwhile, the hapless Junot finally got his corps across the Dnieper having taken longer than he should have to find a ford. Thanks to the sterling efforts of Ney and Murat, he was not too late to advance north and cut off the retreat of the bulk of Barclay's army, but instead he halted. Even when the fiery Murat himself arrived in person to urge the general to stir himself, Junot demurred and stayed put. Why he did so has never satisfactorily been explained. It is possible that he was fearful of being ambushed in the wooded country through which he would have to advance, or that he wished to give his men a rest, or that he suffered a crisis of confidence and, convinced that he would lose any battle he had to fight, chose to avoid one. Whatever the reason, it was incompetence of the grossest sort. By late afternoon, the pressure on the Russians was reaching its climax, as exemplified by the wounding and capture of the heroic General Tuchkov. Barclay was now forced to commit almost all the troops he had to hand to hold the enemy off. Had Junot attacked the First Army's flank or rear at this point, the result would in all probability have been decisive. Instead, the Russians were able to fend off Ney and Murat until nightfall and then use the cover of darkness to put a healthy distance between themselves and their pursuers. Barclay's losses on 19 August, at almost 10,000, a couple of thousand more than the invaders, were serious enough, but they might have been much worse.

Needless to say, when he heard of Junot's ineptitude, Napoleon exploded with fury. 'Junot has let the Russians escape,' he raged. 'He is losing the campaign for me.' The Emperor was so livid that he refused even to see his subordinate, censuring him severely in a letter instead (although, surprisingly, he did not remove Junot from his command). Murat was even more forthright when he spoke to the bungling general following his abysmal failure. 'You are not worthy to be the last dragoon in Napoleon's army,' the hot-blooded King of Naples scathingly declared. Junot, who had perhaps been suffering from mental problems, never recovered from the opprobrium heaped upon him following his failure. A few months later he went mad and in 1813 took his own life.

Harsh as it may sound, given his subsequent personal tragedy, the criticism levelled at Junot was justified. His performance was dismal. At least part of the blame for the failure to smash the bulk of Barclay's First Army east of Smolensk, however, must go to Napoleon. It was he, after all, who gave Junot the critical role for which he proved so ill-suited. True, his corps was fresh and the Emperor could surely not have expected its commander to perform quite as badly as he did, but Junot was not one recognized as one of the Empire's best generals (he had been criticized for his performance in Iberia) and had given recent proof of his ineffectiveness in arriving late for the fighting at Smolensk. Even more significant perhaps were the Emperor's own failings on 19 August. It is notable that Napoleon essentially left the fighting on the 19th to his subordinates; indeed he retired to Smolensk at 5 p.m., around the most critical time in the struggle between Murat and Ney and the Russians. Had he taken a more active role, it might have been he rather than Murat who had gone to plead with Junot to move his corps forward, and it is hard to see how the general could then have remained inactive. In his defence, it must be said that the French believed they were dealing only with a rearguard until very late in the day (which also explains why both Davout's and Poniatowski's corps were allowed to rest and reorganize at Smolensk on the 19th). Even so, one might have expected the Emperor to have made a greater personal effort to ensure that as many Russians as possible were killed or captured. While there were certainly things for Napoleon to sort out in Smolensk, such as provision for the wounded and the ever-present issue of supply, these did not necessarily need his personal attention just yet. The most likely explanation for his early retirement to the city is simply that the events of recent days had taken their toll on him physically and he felt exhausted and unwell.

Beyond the question of responsibility for the failure to smash the majority of Barclay's First Army on 19 August, there is the issue of whether the Emperor might have done rather better at Smolensk before this. Many commentators have criticized him for his slowness in advancing to the city on the 15th and even more for his strategy once he arrived there. Instead of assaulting Smolensk directly, it has been suggested, Napoleon should have left a smallish force (a corps or so) to mask the city and taken the rest of his army east, crossed the Dnieper where Junot did, and advanced against the Russians along the northern bank. Then, he would still have had a numerical advantage and might have smashed Barclay and Bagration in the open field or even have trapped them in Smolensk itself. This is all hypothetical, of course, although convincing enough in theory. Such a plan would not have been without risks, however. Barclay's biggest concern at Smolensk was that Napoleon would do pretty much what was outlined below, but that suggests that, had the Emperor done it, the First Army, and, by default, the Second Army too, would have withdrawn before the invaders could have closed with them on the northern bank. Whether the Russians would then have escaped entirely is anyone's guess. Alternatively, Barclay and Bagration might have been bolder and have sought to exploit any division of the enemy army by launching a forceful attack on the smaller part left to mask Smolensk. How such a scenario would have played out is, again, uncertain, but it is not impossible that the invaders would have put the masking force to flight and moved the whole of their armies to the southern bank of the Dnieper, thereby making Napoleon's strategic predicament worse than it actually turned out to be.

Perhaps then, the Emperor was not so misguided in proceeding as he did before 19 August. He did, after all, force the Russians to abandon their second holiest city and then, having secured the crossings over the Dnieper, created the opportunity to deliver a crushing blow to a large part of the combined armies which faced him. Had he succeeded in delivering that blow, who knows what impact it might have had on Russian morale and willingness to fight on? Instead, as we have seen, another chance to gain a critical triumph over the Tsar's armed forces went begging. It was becoming a bad habit.

Following Barclay's escape on 19 August, Napoleon was again faced with the question of whether to continue to advance after the retreating enemy or to call a halt around Smolensk until next spring. Before the campaign, he had mooted the possibility, should he not win the war in the first few months, of wintering near Smolensk and organizing the liberated Polish and Lithuanian lands to his rear. Now the army was actually here, almost all his key subordinates advocated calling an operational halt. Initially, it seemed that he agreed with them. According to Caulaincourt, the Emperor said to him:

> By abandoning Smolensk, which is one of their Holy Cities, the Russian generals are dishonouring their arms in the eyes of their own people. That will put me in a strong position. We will drive them a little further back for our own comfort. I will dig myself in. We will rest the troops; the country will shape up around this pivot – and we'll see how Alexander likes that ... I will establish headquarters at Vitebsk. I will raise Poland in arms, and later on I will choose, if necessary, between Moscow and St Petersburg.

As at Vitebsk a little over a fortnight earlier, though, it was not long before Napoleon, who was always psychologically disposed towards taking the offensive in preference to sitting on the defensive, was reconsidering his position. This was partly helped by positive news from the various corps operating in Russia outside the Emperor's direct control. Away to the south-west, near the border with the Grand Duchy of Warsaw, the Russian Third Army under General Tormasov had thrust at Brest-Litovsk, west of the Pripet Marshes, in an effort to threaten Warsaw and the invading armies' supply lines. The danger had been easily dealt with, however, as Napoleon learned in mid-August, by Schwarzenberg's Austrian corps and General Reynier's Saxon corps, which had been detached from Jerome's auxiliary army early in the campaign specifically in order to help check any move by Tormasov. In the north, meanwhile, Marshal Macdonald had made good progress along the Baltic with his corps and the Prussians under his command had now put the port of Riga at the mouth of the Dvina under siege. Finally, further down the Dvina in the area to the north-west of Vitebsk, the corps of Marshal Oudinot and General Gouvion St Cyr finally emerged triumphant in a running fight with Wittgenstein's Russians that had been going on since late July when they won the battle of Polotsk on 18 August, a victory which secured the main army's northern flank and for which St Cyr was promoted to the marshalate.

All these successes meant that, should he want to, Napoleon could advance east of Smolensk with the main army without having to worry overly about possible threats to his flanks or supply lines. Of course, the difficulties of provisioning the army were only likely to get worse the further east it went, the factor which perhaps more than any other weighed on the minds of those who opposed another advance, but initial indications were that the countryside between Smolensk and Moscow was richer and more fertile than that through which the invaders had so far marched. This inclined the Emperor to push on.

There were also several factors in the Emperor's mind militating against halting near Smolensk. Militarily, he was loath to give up the initiative while the Russians still had time to reorganize and mount a counter-attack upon his stretched forces before winter arrived and made campaigning extremely difficult. Momentum, he realized, is often critical in war, and at the moment, despite their problems, the invaders had it. Then there was the issue of domestic politics. Napoleon's centralizing tendencies made him vital to the effective running of an empire that now covered a huge part of Europe. His absence from its heart at Paris for a prolonged period could not but have a deleterious effect. The longer he was away, moreover, the greater the risk of a coup by discontented factions within French society upset by the ailing economy and increased taxation and conscription. Finally, there was the international situation. If the Russian war dragged on into 1813, might there be risings within the Empire or, even more serious, Prussia or Austria, both reluctant allies in the first place, defect? In Spain as well, the sooner French forces could be reinforced the better. Finally, there were the British to be considered. The longer Napoleon was occupied in dealing with Russia, the easier it would be for London to foment trouble in Europe for France and the further away it would push the day when the French might turn their full attention to settling accounts with the islanders once and for all.

There were thus many good reasons for wishing to terminate the conflict with Russia as swiftly as possible, but the only way that was likely to be achieved was if the invaders could gain a decisive victory in the near future. The key question was whether a further advance might genuinely create an opportunity to obtain such a success; for if it did not, the invaders' predicament was only likely to get worse and Napoleon might find himself at Moscow, some 600 miles from the Niemen, contemplating whether to winter there, advance still further in whatever time was left before the weather made active campaigning impossible, or retreat. The Emperor though, was certain that the Russians would fight for Moscow, confident that this would enable him to crush their armies, and convinced that if that did not bring peace then the capture of Russia's former capital would. In the event, he was proved correct on only the first of those convictions, but there is a danger in using hindsight to condemn him. Although the Russian armies were not smashed in defence of Moscow, the possibility that they might have been cannot be ruled out. Nor was it entirely fanciful for the Emperor to imagine that the loss of Moscow would bring Alexander to the peace table. Almost all of the solemn occasions of state, including the coronation of the tsars, took place in the former capital. It was also a major trading centre, and although Russia's head, in the form of her government, had moved to St Petersburg, the heart of the country remained in Moscow, the hub of the old realm of Muscovy from which the Russian Empire had emerged. Its loss was bound to be a massive blow to Russian morale, which was not as steadfast in late summer 1812 as is often portrayed. When news of the fall of Smolensk reached Moscow, for example, people began to flee the city in their droves, fearing that the old capital would be next. Even in St Petersburg, which Napoleon's main army was nowhere near, treasures began to be packed up for removal to the interior in early September. True, most of the army's senior figures, it seems, remained ill-disposed to seeking peace, and that inevitably would have made it very difficult for the Tsar, whose personal resolution has already been questioned, to have negotiated with the invaders had he been inclined. The crucial point, however, is that the invaders never managed to inflict the crushing defeat of Russia's armed forces that the Emperor had always sought. Had they done so, the Russian generals' resolve might have cracked as it had in 1807 after Friedland.

On St Helena, with the benefit of hindsight, Napoleon would call his decision to press on from Smolensk in late summer 1812 the biggest mistake of his life.

Given what happened, it is not hard to see why. He always insisted, however, that the decision he made at the time was a reasonable one, and that there were powerful arguments against halting operations in late summer, a view with which the most talented of his senior subordinates, Marshal Davout, agreed.

With the Emperor thus preparing to lead his army further east just a few days after the fall of Smolensk, General Poniatowki came to him with an interesting suggestion. The Pole pleaded with Napoleon to let him lead his corps south-west into the Ukraine and march on Kiev. The area near there had been part of the old kingdom of Poland and Poniatowski was confident that the locals would rise up against the Tsar's overlordship as his Polish troops advanced. The region could then be secured for the invaders and its bounty of food, fodder and horses would become available to them instead of the enemy. It was an intriguing plan, though how successful it would have been in practice is open to question. In any case, the Emperor was not inclined to sanction it. It was in moving into the Ukraine that Charles XII's Russian campaign had gone disastrously wrong, he reminded the Pole, but more significant was the matter of how Vienna might react should he allow Poniatowski to fan the flames of revolt in a part of the Russian Empire which bordered on the predominantly Polish-populated Austrian province of Galicia. Besides, having all but decided to press on after Barclay and Bagration, Napoleon needed as many troops as he could muster and that certainly included the hard-fighting Poles and their skilful commander. Poniatowski, though, would not take no for an answer (he had urged Napoleon to invade the Ukraine as early as summer 1811 so it was clearly a pet project of his) until the Emperor finally tired of the Pole's importuning and snapped, 'No, you are not going to Kiev, and if you dare make any such move, I shall not hesitate to have you shot!'

On the morning of 24 August, Napoleon received a report from Murat that the Russian armies had halted some sixty miles to the east at Dorogobuzh. It was just the kind of news he had hoped for in order to persuade his unwilling subordinates that it was worth making a further advance. With the enemy so near, it made sense to make one more effort to gain the decisive victory that had so far eluded them, especially as the troops had had a few days rest. Nonetheless, disquiet predominated among the army's leadership as the invaders took to the road again. The Emperor, in contrast, was in a positive frame of mind, remarking to Caulaincourt, 'Before a month is out, we shall be in Moscow; in six weeks we shall have peace'. He was to be proved only half right.

On the same day as General Dokhturov's corps fought valiantly to hold on to Smolensk, 17 August, a messenger arrived in St Petersburg bearing an important letter for the Tsar. Prince Volkonsky was an aide to General Count Shuvalov, a corps commander in the First Army of the West, and the letter he bore had been written by his master five days earlier as the abortive Russian counter-offensive towards Vitebsk had been grinding to a halt. The main objective of the letter was to plead with Alexander to appoint a single commander to take responsibility for all Russia's armies. Shuvalov had witnessed the bitter rivalry between Barclay and Bagration, and was aware of its deleterious effects. Unfairly, he blamed the First Army commander for all the problems, even going so far as to warn, 'Another commander is essential, and Your Majesty must appoint him without losing a minute or Russia will be lost'.

Shuvalov's letter was just the tip of an iceberg – the clamour for Barclay's removal had been growing throughout Russia, largely out of frustration with his continual retreats, but partly also simply because he was not a real Russian – but it finally prompted the Tsar to take action. He called a meeting of his senior military subordinates that very evening to discuss who should be given command of Russia's armed forces. Their advice was unanimous and accorded with the strong preference of the bulk of Russians, so far as it can be discerned.

The man Alexander's aides recommended be made commander-in-chief was Mikhail Ilarionovich Golenischev-Kutuzov. Sixty-seven years old in 1812, Kutuzov was a member of an old noble Russian family, making him suitable to politically significant Russians on grounds of both class and nationality. Since the debacle of Austerlitz, his only post of any real importance had been a short stint as commander of Russian forces in south-east Europe from autumn 1811 until the end of the war against the Turks the following spring. Upon his return from that posting, Alexander had given him only the minor position of general in charge of the St Petersburg militia, for the truth is that the Tsar did not like Kutuzov as an individual, regarding him as 'a hatcher of intrigues and an immoral and thoroughly dangerous character'. This was not an unfair judgement, although it doubtless owed much to the fact that Kutuzov reminded Alexander of his lowest ebb as ruler of Russia, the humiliating defeat of 2 December 1805 for which the Tsar was largely to blame having overruled the general's advice not to offer battle. Certainly, Kutuzov, despite his advancing years, was a louche personality who indulged his passion for good food, fine wine and loose women at every opportunity, even on campaign. His extravagance had made him grossly fat and physically unfit. Indeed he was so large by 1812 that he could not mount a horse without help and therefore mostly travelled in a carriage, even when inspecting troops. As a commander, he had a tendency towards laziness and his reluctance to commit his orders to paper could lead to confusion, but he could be determined and cunning. He was also, and this was a definite benefit when facing Napoleon, a naturally cautious general inclined to pay plenty of respect to an enemy's strengths.

Despite the unanimous recommendation of his senior military subordinates, Alexander delayed three days before summoning Kutuzov to him on 20 August and offering him supreme command of Russia's armed forces in the field. The old, half-blind warrior graciously accepted the offer, despite being personally ill-disposed towards the young Tsar as he was towards him. Barclay and Bagration were to retain their positions as commanders of the First and Second Armies for the moment but would now be subordinate to Kutuzov. The xenophobes, nationalists and opponents of retreat were thus handed a victory of sorts, though how far the new commander-in-chief would live up to their expectations was yet to be seen.

Napoleon's army resumed its advance on the morning of 25 August. The Emperor went forward with 124,000 infantry, 32,000 cavalry and 587 guns, a powerful force but one much reduced from the vast horde that had crossed the Niemen nine weeks earlier by a combination of disease, desertion, exhaustion, battle losses, and the need to protect supply lines and garrison captured towns. The weather was initially poor with heavy rain turning the roads to mud yet again, and when the army reached Dorogobuzh to find the Russians long gone, Bonaparte briefly considered turning back. Next day, though, the rain stopped and he decided to march on towards Moscow after all.

During the advance east from Smolensk, the invaders had to contend with a menace that until now had been little noticed; the Cossacks. These light horsemen buzzed around the advancing enemy columns like flies, failing to inflict many casualties (at this stage) but disrupting efforts to forage and scout other than in force. The regular Russian troops, meanwhile, continued to destroy whatever might be of use to the invaders that they could not carry off themselves, a policy which devastated the countryside through which they passed but for which Napoleon's men were blamed by a deeply embittered peasantry. Despite this scorched earth tactic and increased attention from the Cossacks, it seems that Imperial soldiers managed to plunder more during this leg of their advance than at any other comparable time during the campaign. This was just as well, for the supply system was being stretched to breaking point by this latest push.

Nor was that the only thing being severely strained. Relations among Napoleon's senior subordinates, rarely placid at the best of times, showed signs of serious deterioration, most particularly when Murat threatened to go after Davout with a sword when the later criticized (quite rightly) the former's reckless treatment of his cavalry's mounts. Then there was the Emperor's health. This latest war was taking a heavy physical toll on a middle-aged man whose well-being had already been eroded by years of hard campaigning and running an empire during which eighteen-hour days were not unusual. By late August, he was suffering from irritation of the bladder, an irregular pulse, a persistent dry cough, swollen legs, acute dysuria, and, a common problem for him, painful haemorrhoids. It is little wonder that his aides found him short-tempered and irritable.

One thing that lifted Napoleon's spirits was the thought of bringing the Russians to battle, so he was encouraged when his advance guard ran into the enemy rearguard near Gzhatsk, a little over halfway between Smolensk and Moscow, at the start of September. The forces clashed briefly again soon after at Gridnevo, a dozen miles nearer the former Russian capital, and once more near the huge Kolotskoi monastery a similar distance further on. This last encounter took place on the morning of 5 September and, coming so quickly after the other two, strongly suggested that a much bigger clash might not be far off. Sure enough, just a handful of miles to the east the entire Russian First and Second Armies were digging in for battle.

Leaving St Petersburg shortly after his appointment as commander-in-chief, Kutuzov joined the armies of Barclay and Bagration on 29 August at Tsarevo, a short way south-west of Gzhatsk. They were down to under 100,000 men following their recent battles and retreats, although they were expecting reinforcements from Moscow soon. Kutuzov's arrival lifted morale among the weary troops, especially when word got round of how he had exclaimed upon arrival, 'How could anyone think of retreating with such lads!' In fact, Barclay and Bagration had decided to make a stand at Tsarevo in the hope of turning the invaders back from Moscow and had ordered the men to dig in. Initially, the new commander-in-chief concurred with their choice of battlefield, but he soon changed his mind when aides, playing on his vanity, pressed him to choose a battlefield of his own so he would not have to share the glory of the victory they expected him to win with others. On the night of 30–31 August, therefore, the Russians retreated a little way east to the village of Ivashkovo near Gzhatsk, where they were joined by 15,600 recruits from Moscow under General Mikhail Miloradovich. As the soldiers began to dig in here, Kutuzov wrote the Tsar a letter which reveals considerable doubt in his ability to prevent Russia's holiest city from falling to the enemy. 'Things being as they are,' he wrote, 'I shall give battle to save Moscow, though I shall undertake the combat with every precaution demanded by the issue at stake.' Kutuzov knew that Russia and her ruler would never forgive him if he did not make a bold stand in defence of the old capital, but he was also canny enough to realize that it was ultimately more important for him to save the army rather than Moscow, so it seems that his carefully worded letter may at some level have been intended to prepare Alexander psychologically for the city's loss.

There proved to be one more small retreat before battle was offered, however. As the Russians prepared to fight at Ivashkovo, General Bennigsen, the Russian commander at Eylau and Friedland, now Kutuzov's chief of staff, suggested to his leader that there was a better site for a defensive stand a couple of days' march to the east. Impressed by what he was told, Kutuzov ordered his men to pull back once more. The army, whose rearguard now became embroiled in the running battle with the invaders' advance guard described above, reached Bennigsen's position on the morning of 3 September. There was decent defensive terrain sure enough, though whether it was really any better than that at Ivashkovo or Tsarevo was debatable. Still, they were here now and no one seemed to think that anywhere else along the seventy-five mile route to Moscow was there a location more suited to fighting a defensive battle. Besides, when Kutuzov toured the area that afternoon a large eagle was seen hovering above him everywhere he went, a traditional omen of good fortune in Russia. For the third time in the space of a week, therefore, the soldiers were ordered to dig in, this time near a village whose moment in history had arrived. It was called Borodino.

16

Moscow

The battle of Borodino was fought some seventy-five miles west of Moscow in an area of low hills and valleys set with a patchwork of woodland, farmland and heath. Bisecting the battlefield's northern half and running east–west was the new Moscow–Smolensk road along which, roughly speaking, both armies marched to reach the area. Borodino itself straddled this major highway, as did, around a mile to the east, the village of Gorki, which served as Russian headquarters. Just east of Borodino, the New Road crossed another main feature of the area, the Kolocha river. This waterway was difficult to traverse unless bridged. West of Borodino it flowed more or less parallel to the New Road, half to a quarter of a mile to the south, while east of the village the Kolocha snaked its way north-east where, after a few miles, it emptied into the mighty Moskva river. This lower stretch of the Kolocha could only easily be crossed by a ford at Maloe, around a mile north-east of Gorki, and its eastern bank was noticeably steeper than its western. The Kolocha had several tributaries, but the only one of any real significance in the battle was the Semenovka. This stream entered the Kolocha on its southern side around half a mile to the west of Borodino. The Semenovka was only a mile and a half long and the valley through which it flowed ran south from the Kolocha for half its course before turning south-east. Where the stream turned, an even smaller waterway, the Kamenka, joined the Semenovka. The Kamenka valley was shallow and ran south-west to north-east. Both the Kamenka and the upper Semenovka were little more than trickles, and even the lower Semenovka could be traversed with ease.

To the east of the lower Semenovka, around half a mile south of Borodino, the ground rose through an area of scrubby woodland until it reached a low but prominent hill. On top of this mound, the Russians built what became known as the Great Redoubt, an earthwork fortification that overlooked both the Kolocha and the New Road to the north-west and which dominated the entire lower Semenovka. Half a mile to the south of the redoubt, near the eastern crest of the upper Semenovka valley, lay the hamlet of Semenovskaya which was flattened by the Russians to provide firewood and materials for the construction of defensive earthworks. East of here, the land fanned out into a large and open plateau. Half a mile south-west of Semenovskaya, in the area south of where the Kamenka trickled into the Semenovka, the Russians built three more crude fortifications on the summits of three hillocks. Facing roughly north-west, these were smaller than the Great Redoubt and, thanks to their broadly arrowhead shape, were called the *flèches* (the French for arrows). Directly south of these earthworks was a sizeable area of dense brushwood, to the south of which in turn lay the village of Utitsa. This settlement, roughly two miles south of Borodino, stood astride the old Moscow–Smolensk road, which ran east–west along the southern fringe of the battlefield. Around three-quarters of a mile to the east of Utitsa, on the southern side of the Old Road, stood another low but prominent hill known to posterity as the Utitsa Mound.

Almost all the fighting at the battle of Borodino took place along the two-mile front running from the village after which the clash would be named, in the north, to Utitsa and its mound, in the south. Before the invaders could attack that line, however, they had to deal with yet another Russian earthwork. This one, a pentagonal redoubt some sixty yards wide, stood on a low hill a mile and a half south-west of Borodino and a similar distance north-west of Utitsa near the hamlet of Shevardino. It mounted a dozen heavy field-cannon and was defended by a full division from Bagration's Second Army under General Prince Gorchakov.

Napoleon arrived north-west of the Shevardino Redoubt along the New Road on the afternoon of 5 September, some time ahead of the greater part of his army, which caught up with him throughout that evening and the following day. Before him, a couple of miles to the east, he could see the mass of Kutuzov's force drawn up for battle. The Russians certainly looked like they were preparing to fight, encouraging news to the Emperor, but before he could think about tackling the bulk of the enemy army, he realized he would have to reduce the Shevardino Redoubt and chase off its defenders, for they stood in the middle of where he had already decided he would initially position his own army for the imminent battle. Not wishing to lose time, he ordered an assault to be mounted that very afternoon.

The attack, which commenced around 4 p.m., was led by the division of General Compans, part of Marshal Davout's corps. To begin with, all went well. Pockets of Russian troops posted in advance of the redoubt were pushed back easily enough and the Imperial guns were able to knock out the cannon within the earthwork, which did not turn out to be as formidably constructed as it might have been. Then, shortly after 5 p.m., the redoubt was stormed and captured by Compans's triumphant soldiers, but the engagement did not end there. As Gorchakov's men fell back, they were reinforced by more of Bagration's troops (eventually some 18,000 Russians took part in the struggle for the Shevardino Redoubt) and the enemy advance was checked. For the next hour or so, the two sides exchanged fire before, with daylight fading fast, Gorchakov launched a powerful counter-attack that swept Compans's men from the redoubt. Over the next few hours, until 10 p.m., when the fighting finally stopped, the disputed earthwork changed hands several times following charges and countercharges involving ever greater numbers of infantry, cavalry and guns on each side. It was a fierce and confused struggle fought in the meagre light provided by the moon and the intermittent flashes of cannon and muskets. Finally, with the Polish corps of General Poniatowski approaching the combat from the south-west and threatening to cut off the Russians' retreat, Bagration ordered Gorchakov to fall back and rejoin the rest of the Second Army a mile or so to the east. The redoubt and the hill upon which it stood belonged to Napoleon.

According to General Barclay, the Russians lost 6–7,000 men in a struggle that he considered utterly futile. Certainly, it is hard to imagine how the Shevardino Redoubt could have been held in the long term, given its isolation from Kutuzov's main line over a mile to the east. Nor did the valiant soldiers who fell trying to defend or recapture it on 5 September managed to make enemy efforts to defeat them prohibitively expensive. The Imperial army's losses were probably around 4,000, no more than two-thirds those of the Russians. This prelude to the Battle of Borodino can therefore only be seen as a clear triumph for the invaders, though few of the victors felt overly inclined to celebrate as the enemy finally fell back. The experience of the past few hours had been a sobering one. If the Russians fought as tenaciously when the main bodies of the two sides met, it threatened to be a bloodbath.

As day dawned the morning after the fall of the Shevardino Redoubt, Kutuzov's army awaited a Napoleonic onslaught. Before long, however, it became clear that the Emperor had no intention of attacking the main Russian line that day. This can hardly have come as much of a relief to soldiers who would probably rather have got the battle over and done with as soon as possible, instead of enduring a prolonged, tense wait. The delay at least gave the Russians time to improve the defences of the Great Redoubt and the *flèches*. These earthworks, begun on 4 September rather than the 3rd, and at the instigation of Barclay and Bagration rather than Kutuzov himself, were incomplete, but every day more that could be spent on them would make them more formidable. The work was predominantly done not by regular soldiers but by militia. Desperate for reinforcements, Kutuzov had urgently demanded that the governor of Moscow send him as many men as possible. Over 15,000 new recruits enlisted in the Moscow area had joined the army at the end of August, and, on 3 September, a ragged but large band of 15,000 *opolchenie* or militia, peasants armed with pikes, farm implements and an assortment of similar improvised weaponry, reached the battlefield to swell Russian numbers further. These 'troops' were of limited value in combating the enemy directly, but they could be used to build and repair earthworks, fetch materials, carry the wounded to the rear, and intercept any regular soldiers who tried to leave the line of battle. Only in desperate circumstances were they expected to fight.

The onus of stopping the invaders and saving Moscow would thus fall squarely on the regular soldiers of Kutuzov's force. These amounted on 6 September to 72,000 infantry, 17,000 cavalry and 14,500 gunners manning a massive 640 cannon, around a quarter of which were lethal twelve-pounders.* The real strength of the Russian army thus appeared to lie with its artillery, especially as the guns were of a high quality. Although the gunners would play a crucial role in the forthcoming battle, however, the Russian cannon were not as effectively deployed as they might have been, many guns barely firing a shot due to poor positioning on the field and lack of coordinated control to remedy the problem. A greater burden than was necessary would therefore be placed upon the infantry and cavalry, but, fortunately for the Russians, both were well prepared for the imminent clash. For the Tsar's foot soldiers, Borodino would be the kind of battle that suited them best, a defensive struggle of attrition, while the regular Russian cavalry enjoyed an important advantage over their foes in the quality and condition of their horses, which helped counter the generally superior ability of Napoleon's riders. Kutuzov's horsemen could also expect at least some assistance from the 7,000 Cossacks, led by General Platov, who were with the army, bringing the total number of men under the old general's command to about 125,000.†

Numerically, the Russians were only at a slight disadvantage to the invaders, but the way in which Kutuzov deployed his forces threatened to exaggerate the enemy's advantage. For a start, he positioned almost all his troops, even the reserves, within potential range and full view of the invaders' artillery, and then compounded the error by insisting that the infantry be drawn up in columns, a deep formation ideal for close combat but which made each enemy cannonball likely to kill or wound more soldiers than it would were it to hit a unit in line. (Much of Wellington's success in Iberia was down to his deployment of men in line and, as far as possible, out of sight of enemy guns.) Potentially even worse than this, Kutuzov strung his troops out over too great a distance and left parts of his line perilously weak. Even though he must (or at least should) have known that the lower Kolocha was difficult to cross, and that its steep eastern bank between Borodino and the Moskva river presented a formidable obstacle to any attacker, the Russian commander naively expected Napoleon to focus his assault along, and to the north of, the New Road (indeed, several earthworks not

---

* They fired a cannonball which weighed twelve pounds.
† It is possible that Kutuzov may have had nearer 150,000 men with him at Borodino, the bulk of the additional 'troops' being militia, but it is ultimately something of an exercise in guesswork trying to establish Russian strength and I have favoured the more common conservative estimate.

hitherto mentioned were constructed a little way east of the lower Kolocha to help repel such an attack). Consequently, almost all of Barclay's First Army – three regular corps (those of Generals Baggavout, Ostermann-Tolstoi, and Dokhturov) and three cavalry corps – as well as the bulk of the Cossacks under their leader Platov, were deployed behind the lower Kolocha between the confluence with the Moskva and the Great Redoubt. The Redoubt itself was packed with twenty mighty twelve-pounder cannon and the area from the hill on which it stood to Semenovskaya was entrusted to the corps of General Raevski from Bagration's Second Army (which is why the Great Redoubt is sometimes called the Raevski Redoubt). The area south of Semenovskaya, which included the *flèches*, was defended by the second of Bagration's corps, that of General Borozdin, and a cavalry corps was deployed behind the Second Army's regular corps to act as a kind of reserve. The only troops Kutuzov initially posted south of the *flèches* were 7,000 militia and 1,500 Cossacks, a woefully inadequate force to prop up the left wing of the army. Fortunately for the Russians, the fall of the Shevardino Redoubt seems to have increased the commander's concern about his southern flank and he moved the fourth of Barclay's regular corps, that of General Nikolai Tuchkov (a brother of the man who had been captured commanding the First Army's rearguard during the retreat from Smolensk), from the north of the battlefield to the area around Utitsa on the night of 5–6 September. The main Russian reserve was formed by a corps of the Imperial Guard, commanded in Grand Duke Constantine's absence by the aged General Lavrov. It was positioned south of Russian headquarters at Gorki. Light infantry from the Imperial Guard also held Borodino, while the *opolchenie* not deployed on the left wing were mostly spread out behind the main Russian line, where they could assist the regular forces by repairing earthworks, fetching ammunition, evacuating the wounded and returning shirkers to the fight.

It was obvious to most of Kutuzov's chief subordinates that, even after the movement of Tuchkov's corps south, the Russian left wing remained highly vulnerable, while the right seemed overly strong. Barclay therefore pressed the commander-in-chief on 6 September to move the whole line southwards, but Kutuzov did nothing, even though Napoleon's deployments that day increased the improbability of him concentrating his attack north of the New Road. The First Army commander also urged his superior to abandon Borodino as he felt the soldiers posted there in front of the main Russian line were too vulnerable to the enemy. Again, Kutuzov took no action. It seems incredible that the man most Russians view as the great hero of 1812 could have been quite so remiss in preparing for the battle that would determine the fate of Russia's holiest city, but the simple fact is that he was. One can only assume that he remained convinced, in spite of its unlikelihood, that Napoleon would launch his main thrust against the Russian right.

Whatever the potential hazards of Kutuzov's dispositions, however, the Russian rank-and-file enjoyed high morale as the great battle approached. They were rested and fed, had confidence (misplaced though it may have been) in their commander, who exhorted them to 'Serve loyally and honourably to the last drop of your blood!', and felt sure that God was on their side. On the afternoon of 6 September, the Black Virgin of Smolensk, a holy ikon salvaged from the city by the corps of General Dokhturov, was paraded around the whole Russian host while clerics sprayed holy water over both regimental banners and the heads of the Tsarist soldiery. A rationalist Frenchman in Napoleon's retinue who observed the affair from a distance later commented of it, 'Credulous from ignorance, they worshipped their images, fancying themselves devoted by God to the defence of Heaven and their consecrated soil', but, idolatrous and deluded as he believed the enemy to be, it seems that such spiritual activity did have an impact in making Kutuzov's men more willing to fight and die the next day. Infused with religious fervour, Russia's peasant sons were ready to take on the might of the Napoleonic war machine.

Examining the Russian lines in the early morning of 6 September, Napoleon seems to have been reassured that the enemy was still determined to make a stand, despite losing the Shevardino Redoubt the previous evening. He therefore felt he could afford to postpone the battle until the morrow, giving his men time to rest and allowing a cavalry corps and, more importantly, the bulk of the reserve artillery to join the army before the main hostilities commenced. Obviously, this would also give the Russians more time to strengthen the earthworks they were throwing up, but this does not seem to have concerned the Emperor very much.

Napoleon had at his disposal for the approaching battle almost 90,000 infantry, nigh on 30,000 cavalry, and 16,000 gunners and engineers, the former manning 587 cannon. His total strength of around 135,000 was a little greater than the Russians' 125,000, 30,000 of whom, it must be remembered were either raw recruits or militia, giving the Emperor an overall qualitative as well as quantitative advantage over his adversaries, especially as many of the best and most experienced troops with whom he had crossed the Niemen were with him. In fact, the only area in which Imperial forces appeared to be at a disadvantage was in terms of the weight of their artillery. Not only did they have fewer guns, but only one in ten of their cannon were twelve-pounders, Napoleon's *belles filles* (beautiful daughters) as he called them. The rest were a mixture of four- or eight-pounders or 6-inch howitzers, potentially lethal, of course, and relatively mobile, but with less hitting power, especially at longer ranges, than the big guns. Fortunately for the invaders, though, the level of ability of the gunnery officers was higher in their army than in that of the enemy, and Napoleon's cannon would be wielded with considerably greater skill than Kutuzov's, thereby evening the artillery odds.

Despite these advantages, however, the reconnaissance that Napoleon and his chief subordinates did on 6 September gave them some pause for thought. The difficulty of crossing the lower Kolocha and the steepness of its eastern bank effectively ruled out a major attack on the right of the Russian position (as almost everyone but Kutuzov appears to have appreciated), but the earthworks the Russians were constructing in the centre and left-centre of their line threatened to make a direct assault on these areas potentially awkward, especially as the broken terrain in this part of the field would hinder attacking movements. Nevertheless, the Emperor determined upon a direct frontal assault on the enemy centre and left-centre as the linchpin of his battle plan, gambling that his men would be able to break Bagration's Second Army and capture the Great Redoubt and *flèches* before Barclay's First Army could save them. With a gaping hole smashed in their line, the Russian left could be easily finished off before the rest of Kutuzov's force was overwhelmed by the victorious Imperial army. To achieve this triumph, Napoleon deployed his forces as follows: in the north, Eugène's corps, strengthened by a division from Davout's corps as well as by General Grouchy's cavalry corps, would capture Borodino before crossing the Kolocha and storming the Great Redoubt; south of them, Ney's corps, also reinforced by one of Davout's divisions, would advance to capture the ruined hamlet of Semenovskaya, but only after Davout's remaining three divisions had captured the *flèches*; in the south, meanwhile, General Poniatowski's Polish corps, much reduced by detachments and the fierce fighting at Smolensk, would march on Utitsa, pinning down the Russian left and threatening to outflank Kutuzov's line; in reserve near Shevardino, the Imperial Guard, Junot's corps and three cavalry corps under Murat would await orders from the Emperor to move into action as the situation demanded.

Napoleon's basic strategy for the battle of Borodino was not as crude and maladroit as it is sometimes portrayed, but it did have a major flaw. He seems to have imagined that the Russian centre and left-centre would put up less of a fight than they in fact did. This part of Kutuzov's line was undoubtedly weaker than it should have been, but that is not to say that it could be easily overrun. The Russians were doughty fighters, especially on the defensive, had a lot of artillery to back them up, enjoyed high morale, and were determined to prevent their holiest city from falling into the hands of the invaders. Any direct assault on them in prepared positions was likely to prove tough, bloody and protracted. If the Emperor did not fully appreciate this, in spite of the lesson of the attack on the Shevardino Redoubt, Marshal Davout certainly did and he pressed his master to adopt a different strategy. Emphasizing the vulnerability of the Russian left to an outflanking manoeuvre, Napoleon's most gifted subordinate pleaded to be allowed to take 40,000 men on an overnight march around the enemy's southern wing, so that he could irrupt into their rear as the following morning dawned and the rest of the Imperial army advanced to pin the Russians in place. Such a move would throw Kutuzov completely, Davout argued, and compel him to withdraw as much of his force as he could into the angle formed by the lower Kolocha and Moskva rivers, where they would be trapped and at the invaders' mercy. It was a bold plan which might well have worked, but the Emperor was feeling cautious. 'Ah, you are always for turning the enemy,' he told the marshal. 'It is too dangerous a manoeuvre!' It was a remarkable attitude for a man who had made his reputation as a general by outflanking his opponents and taking risks. To be sure, dividing his army in the face of the enemy would have been perilous, but only if the Russians abandoned their positions to go over to the offensive and Davout's flanking force arrived late on the battlefield, neither of which was likely. The other objections Napoleon made to the plan were contradictory. If the Russians got wind of Davout's manoeuvre, he suggested to the marshal, they would retreat overnight and refuse to give battle, as they had before; but he then undermined his own argument by claiming that his study of military history had led him to conclude that large Russian armies were not worried by the prospect of being outflanked in major battles.

The Imperial army, then, would fight on 7 September in accordance with a flawed strategy. Instead of focusing on exploiting the main Russian weakness, the vulnerability of their southern flank, tens of thousands of troops would be committed to frontal assaults upon prepared positions defended by tough, dogged, and highly motivated Russian soldiers backed by a formidable weight of artillery. Napoleon might well still win, but the prospects of him achieving a victory sufficiently crushing to end the war were less than they could have been.

The night of 6–7 September was a cold one. While most of the Imperial and Russian armies tried to snatch whatever sleep they could, some men on both sides continued to work long after dark. On the Russian side of the field, efforts to make the earthworks that Napoleon's men would assault on the morrow as strong as possible carried on, while French engineers constructed five bridges over the Kolocha, west of where the Semenovka stream flowed into it, and threw up three large bulwarks east of Shevardino to hold 120 of the Imperial army's cannon.

Perhaps those with work to do were the fortunate ones, for they at least did not have much time to reflect upon what might happen when the sun came up. A Westphalian captain later recalled what must have been emotions shared by many that night:

> I could not escape the feeling that something huge and destructive was hanging over all of us. This mood led me to look at my men. There they were, sleeping around me on

the cold, hard ground. I knew them all very well … and I was aware that many of these brave troops would not survive until tomorrow evening, but would be lying torn and bloody on the field of battle. For a moment it was all too easy to wish that the Russians would simply steal away again during the night, but then I remembered how we had suffered over the last few weeks. Better an horrific end than a horror without end! Our only salvation lay in battle and victory!

The Emperor too was in an anxious frame of mind that night, waking repeatedly to check that the Russians were still there. He helped pass the time by finalizing a proclamation to be read to the army shortly before the battle commenced. It read:

> Soldiers! Here is the battle you have so long desired! Henceforward, victory depends on you: we have need of it. We will win ourselves abundance of supplies, good winter quarters, and a prompt return to our Motherland. Conduct yourselves as you did at Austerlitz, Friedland, Vitebsk and Smolensk, so that posterity will for ever acclaim with pride your conduct on this day. Let them say to each one of you: 'He took part in the great battle beneath the walls of Moscow!'

It was a typically rousing proclamation, if rather liberal in its geographical exactitude, appealing to the men's sense of glory and honour as well as the material issues that had been of such concern to them in recent weeks.

Napoleon's own mood that night, however, was rather less optimistic than the words he wrote. At one point, unable to sleep, he turned to an aide and mournfully said, 'What is war? It is a barbaric trade in which everything comes down to being the stronger at a given point', before going on to bemoan the vagaries of fortune. It was not the best frame of mind for a commander about to fight a crucial battle to be in. This melancholy pensiveness was doubtless a reflection of the acute physical discomfort he was experiencing. He had a heavy cold and a hacking cough that he could not shift, and his bladder problems were causing him considerable pain. The arrival of a new portrait of his son in the late afternoon of 6 September had temporarily lifted his spirits and he had enthusiastically put it on display for his retinue and the soldiers of the Guard to see. The joy that brought, though, had been more than a little dented by news which also arrived that afternoon of a major defeat for French forces in the Peninsula. Following the fall to the British of the border fortresses of Ciudad Rodrigo and Badajoz, in January and April respectively, Wellington had led an invasion of Spain, but by midsummer, this offensive had looked to be petering out in indecisive manoeuvring west of Madrid. Indeed, the British had begun to retreat back towards Portugal in the face of superior forces under Marshal Auguste Marmont, one of Napoleon's oldest associates. But then the Frenchman had made an egregious error. Stretching his army too thin in an attempt to get between Wellington and the border, Marmont had presented Wellington with a glorious opportunity to crush part of the superior French force. On 22 July, at Salamanca, Wellington had gratefully taken it, sending the sections of the enemy army that escaped annihilation reeling back in headlong retreat and opening the way for Madrid to fall to the British. Marmont's defeat did not yet spell the end of Bonapartist rule in Spain, but it did make a swift end to the war in Russia even more imperative, so that forces in the Peninsula could be reinforced as soon as possible in order to reverse the marshal's blunder.

In contrast to Napoleon, Kutuzov appears to have had no problem sleeping on the night before Borodino, his rest aided, one suspects, by a healthy dose of drink. For both men, the morning would bring danger and opportunity; for the two huge armies they commanded would clash in a titanic battle that would potentially determine the fate not only of Moscow, but of the entire war.

An hour before dawn on 7 September 1812, the units of the Imperial army began to move into their assigned positions for the start of battle. After the anxiety of the past few hours, Napoleon himself seemed to be in good spirits. 'We have them at last!' he confidently proclaimed to his entourage. 'We are going to break open the gates of Moscow!' Arriving at his command post for the coming engagement near the captured Shevardino Redoubt, the Emperor sat on a reversed chair and espied the land in front of him as first light began to flood over it. 'It is a trifle cold,' he commented, 'but the sun is bright.' Then he added, referring to that propitious moment almost seven years ago when French troops marching to victory over another Russian army had been suddenly illuminated, 'It is the sun of Austerlitz!'

An indication that this day might not go as well as the great triumph of December 1805 was not long in surfacing. As light spread over the battlefield, it became clear that, incredibly, the earthworks that the Imperial engineers had constructed east of Shevardino the previous night to protect 120 of the army's cannon had been sited too far back for the guns to be able to bombard the enemy positions effectively. Something had obviously gone wrong between the Emperor deciding that the earthworks should be built and the engineers being told where to build them, though exactly who was to blame is not clear. There was no choice but to abandon the hastily constructed defences and move the guns further forward to a more exposed position.

By 6 a.m. the artillery was ready and, shortly afterwards, the battle commenced with a huge explosion of cannon fire that filled the air with smoke and noise. When the Russians responded in kind, the din intensified. For the next twelve hours, the guns of both sides kept up an almost continuous fire that shrouded the field in an artificial fog, created so much noise that officers were barely able to make themselves heard, and caused the earth for a dozen miles around to shake. More men had fought at Wagram in 1809, but never before had so many cannon been massed in one place. Borodino truly was the dawn of the age of artillery.

Devastating as artillery can be to life and limb, however, it is a military truism that only infantry can take and hold ground, and this was highlighted by the first clear success of the day for the Imperial army. Shortly after the rival batteries had opened fire, the men of Eugène's corps, many of them Italians rather than Frenchmen, stormed the village of Borodino, their approach masked by a thick mist that covered this part of the field. It has already been seen how Barclay unsuccessfully pleaded with Kutuzov on the 6th to abandon the village, and on the morning of the battle, the First Army commander took matters into his own hands by sending an aide forward to Borodino to order the Imperial Guard troops there to fall back to the eastern bank of the Kolocha. The messenger arrived too late. Eugène's men attacked with speed and vigour, destroying half the defending force within just quarter of an hour as they swept through the village. Buoyed by their success, the leading regiment in the attack recklessly marched on down the New Road and over the Kolocha towards Gorki, only to be abruptly and bloodily halted by units from Dokhturov's corps before being sent reeling back over the river in tattered confusion. These Russians of the First Army had no intention of trying to recapture Borodino, however, and settled for burning the bridge over which the repulsed Imperial troops had imprudently advanced.

A little over a mile to the south, meanwhile, two of Davout's divisions advanced at around 6.30 a.m. to attack the two westernmost *flèches* (at this stage, the nature of the terrain had hidden the third *flèche* from the invaders' sight). Marching over broken terrain and in the face of deadly Russian cannon fire, the assault developed slowly, but eventually the attackers closed to within a couple of hundred yards of the *flèches*. Then the guns of General Borozdin's corps switched to canister. As a Russian artillery general, who observed the work his gunners did in defending the *flèches* that morning, later wrote, 'the execution wrought by our batteries was frightful, and the enemy columns faded away perceptibly despite the continual reinforcements which arrived. The more effort the enemy put into the attack the more their casualties piled up.' Around 7.30, General Compans, hero of the capture of the Shevardino Redoubt, was hit in the shoulder and had to leave the field. Their commander down, the division assaulting the southernmost *flèche* faltered until Marshal Davout, a man as courageous as he was intelligent, rode forward to urge Compans's men on. He too was soon injured when his horse was killed under him and his fall left him badly concussed and bruised. Nevertheless, the brave soldiers of Compans's division finally managed to storm the southernmost *flèche*. Their success was short-lived. The Russians had deliberately left the rear of the *flèches* open to facilitate counter-attacking them should they fall, so the exhausted and battered Frenchmen had little defence against the fierce assault of Borozdin's troops, who, in typical Russian fashion, bellowed '*Oorah!*' as they charged. Forced to abandon their hard-won prize, Compans's men were soon being driven further back by Russian cavalry and Napoleon had to send Junot's corps, as well as some of Murat's cavalry, forward some time after 8.00 to stabilize his own right-centre. Clearly, the men of Bagration's Second Army were not going to crack as readily as the Emperor had hoped.

Although there is some dispute among military historians as to whether Napoleon was right to reject Davout's bold outflanking strategy, it is widely agreed that he should have given greater emphasis at Borodino to attacking the Russian left and achieving at least a tactical outflanking success. Instead, this task was entrusted solely to General Poniatowski's understrength Polish corps. That said, the Pole has been criticized for advancing too cautiously during the battle and it is certainly likely that, had he been more aggressive, he might have pushed back the Russian left wing further than he did. Without support, however, a successful advance would have left his corps vulnerable to a Russian counter-attack, which might have overwhelmed it. The truth is that Poniatowski was probably sensible not to push too hard against the Russian left until the Imperial troops on *his* left were also driving the enemy before them back. He simply did not have the numbers to achieve what a much stronger force might have.

In any event, it was 8 a.m. before the Poles first engaged the soldiers of Tuchkov's corps near Utitsa. Weakened by calls to send soldiers to help defend the *flèches*, Tuchkov realized he could not hope to hold the village long and so ordered his men to retreat from it, setting buildings ablaze as they did so. For the next couple of hours, the fighting in this southern end of the line degenerated into a series of running skirmishes in which the Poles slowly pushed the Russians further back.

It was half past ten before Poniatowski was ready to launch an assault on the Utitsa mound, which had now become the linchpin of the Russian left wing. Bombarding the hillock with a large battery of twenty-two guns to soften the enemy up, his men advanced and soon captured the crucial mound. By now, however, the Russians had begun to reinforce their vulnerable southern flank with units from General Baggovout's corps. Some time between nine and ten, a messenger had informed Baggovout that the situation on the Russian left and left-centre was becoming desperate and had implored him to move south with his men as fast as he could. 'We are finished if you don't hurry up,' the messenger had exclaimed. 'Bagration's army has been pounded into the ground and it's a miracle that Tuchkov is still hanging on.' On its long march from the north of the Russian line to the south, Baggovout's corps came under heavy bombardment from batteries massed behind Napoleon's centre and right-centre, but arrived to reinforce Kutuzov's left and left-centre just in time. The units which marched to join Tuchkov could not prevent the Utitsa mound from falling, but they did enable a powerful counter-attack to be launched around noon which swept the Poles from the hillock and all the way back to Utitsa itself. General Tuchkov fell mortally wounded during this advance, leaving Baggovout to assume command of the left wing for the remainder of the battle. Without reinforcement or progress along some other part of the line, Poniatowski and his valiant Poles were going nowhere.

Following the bloody repulse of the regiment that had been foolhardy enough to charge east along the New Road across the Kolocha, Eugène's corps had settled down near Borodino to regroup and prepare for the next part of their job: the capture of the Great Redoubt. Around 7.30, the Viceroy of Italy had begun to move most of his troops west and then south across the bridges constructed over the Kolocha the previous night by Imperial engineers, leaving just one division and some cavalry to guard Borodino itself. By nine, Eugène's men were ready to cross the lower Semenovka and advance towards their objective.

If the *flèches* three-quarters of a mile to the south were daunting obstacles, the Great Redoubt was an even more formidable barrier. Protected on all sides from attack, the 20 large cannon it accommodated could each fire a solid twelve-pound ball with fearsome force towards any unit unfortunate enough to come within their considerable range. It does not take too much imagination to envisage what such a projectile might do to ranks of tightly packed men, and the guns were potentially even more deadly at close range, when the crew would switch to canister. Add to that the men of Raevski's corps defending the low hill upon which the Redoubt stood, as well as units from Dokhturov's corps posted nearby to the north-east and free to come to their comrades' assistance, and it is not hard to see what an unenviable task confronted Eugéne's troops.

The Viceroy's men came under fire as soon as they began their advance, but they traversed the Semenovka without too much difficulty and proceeded up the slope that led to the Redoubt. The light brushwood here provided some cover, but it also hid pits that the Russians had dug to trap unsuspecting attackers and to which a number of soldiers duly fell victim. It was a long, slow but mercifully gentle climb up the shallow incline on what was fast becoming an unusually hot September's day, and as more and more units became embroiled with the enemy, they at least knew that the fearsome guns of the Redoubt would have to look elsewhere for victims of their murderous fire. Those cannon took a heavy toll on the attackers, but the more they fired, the thicker became the huge pall of smoke that surrounded them, making it harder for them to shoot accurately or even to see their adversaries. Indeed, Frenchmen were clambering through the gun embrasures before General Raevski realized the Redoubt was in danger, and it was only thanks to the fury with which the Russian gunners defended their position against this sudden assault that he was able to avoid capture or death.

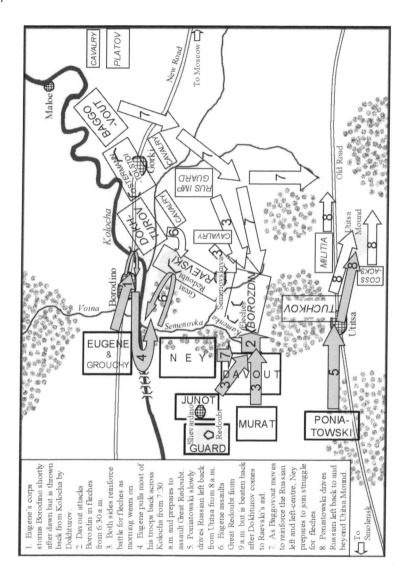

Battle of Borodino: Phase One

Nevertheless, the artillerymen could not hold out long against experienced foot soldiers and the Redoubt, to great Imperial rejoicing, fell.

French joy did not last long. As they had done earlier when the southernmost *flèche* had fallen, the Russians launched a swift and powerful counter-attack that overwhelmed their temporarily victorious enemies. General Bonamy, the commander of the regiment who had stormed the Redoubt, was less fortunate than Raevski and was captured as his men were driven back down the hill. He had received over a dozen wounds in the fighting, testimony to the bravery of Napoleon's officers. Eugène's soldiers mounted a counter-attack of their own, but Raevski's men, reinforced by troops from Dokhturov's corps, were too strong for them. The invaders were beaten back across the Semenovka. The Russian line had yet again proved more resilient than the Emperor had expected.

By mid-morning, the stoutness of Russian resistance was unmistakable and it was causing Napoleon much consternation. 'These Russians let themselves be killed as if they were not human beings at all but machines,' he exclaimed to Berthier and Caulaincourt. 'They are not taken prisoner … this is not helping us. They are citadels which only cannonballs can demolish.' Clearly, it was going to take a monumental effort to break the Russian line frontally, so that is what the Emperor ordered. By 10 a.m., a massive force had been gathered opposite the Russian left-centre comprising three regular corps (those of Davout, Ney and Junot), two of Murat's cavalry corps, and about 400 cannon. Their task was to break through the enemy line between the hamlet of Semenovskaya and the *flèches*, an area defended by Borozdin's battered corps, part of Baggovout's corps, some of Tuchkov's men, Bagration's single cavalry corps, the bulk of the Russian Imperial Guard, which had to be sent forward from its position in reserve to bolster the line, and around 300 guns.

The assault began with an enormous exchange of cannon fire that pounded each side's troops mercilessly. Then several divisions of Ney's and Davout's corps moved forward against the two westernmost *flèches*. Despite the weight of shot fired at them, as well as a taxing flanking fire from men of Tuchkov's corps positioned in the dense brushwood to the south of the *flèches*, they successfully stormed their objectives, only to discover for the first time that there was a third *flèche* hitherto hidden by the terrain. Before they could think about assaulting it, however, the Russians launched a mighty counter-attack which drove the Imperial troops back and recaptured the lost earthworks. The invaders rallied and, before long, another powerful attack, this time organized and led by Marshal Murat, had taken the southernmost *flèche* once more. Inevitably, the Russians counter-attacked and the flamboyant Murat had to take shelter among a unit of Württembergers to avoid capture. Despite his limited German, Murat tried to chivvy these soldiers along by telling them to shoot (*schiess*) but, to the troops' amusement, what he said sounded more like *scheiss* (shit). Nevertheless, the Württembergers managed to hold the earthwork. To secure the gain, Junot's men chased the troublesome infantrymen of Tuchkov's corps from the woods to the south, while Ney and Davout turned their attention to taking the remaining two *flèches*. It was a veritable maelstrom of death, destruction, choking smoke and deafening noise in that triangle of land formed by the Kamenka, the upper Semenovka and the woods to the north of Utitsa, with charge and countercharge conducted by soldiers on both sides with an astonishing courage that General Bagration could only watch and applaud. Slowly, the invaders began to gain the upper hand thanks to their numerical advantage, and they were given an unexpected boost when a random musketball struck the commander of the Russian Second Army in the leg as he bravely tried to rally the defenders of one of the *flèches*. With remarkable self-control, Bagration tried to hide the fact that he had been hit, but he was unable to prevent himself from slumping forward in the saddle. He was caught by an aide as he tumbled from his horse in the sight of hundreds of his men. Although the Georgian did not die from his injury for over a fortnight, the rumour spread like wildfire that he had been killed as he was carried from the field. To the soldiers of the Second Army, who adored their commander, it was devastating news and their morale was severely hit. The second *flèche* soon fell, followed by the third, and by noon the Russians had finally been pushed back beyond the upper Semenovka.

Immediately to the north, meanwhile, more fierce fighting had been going on near Semenovskaya. The assault on this area was spearheaded by the cavalry corps of Generals Latour-Maubourg and Nansouty, the former attacking to the north of the flattened hamlet, the latter to the south. Initially, Latour's men had very much the better of things, for, having crossed the upper Semenovka and scrambled up its steeper than expected eastern bank, they had caught infantry of Borozdin's corps largely unprepared and, so, inflicted heavy damage upon them. Nansouty's troopers to the south came up against the more skilled soldiers of the Russian Imperial Guard, who rapidly formed squares against which little impression could be made. As these disciplined infantrymen began to whittle away at the horsemen that swarmed around them with their muskets, Russian cavalry charged Latour's men near Semenovskaya and a lengthy running battle developed. When further Russian cavalry engaged Nansouty's troopers and forced them to retreat, it seemed that the invaders might soon lose their foothold near the hamlet entirely, but the timely arrival of an infantry division stabilized the situation. With the two sides now evenly balanced, it was the outcome of the struggle for the *flèches* that effectively decided the result of the fighting near Semenovskaya too. As their comrades to the south fell back, the Russians in the vicinity of the hamlet had little choice but to do the same or risk being overwhelmed.

By midday then, Napoleon's men had finally managed to buckle the Russian left-centre. The soldiers who had achieved this feat, however, had themselves been badly battered and needed reinforcement if their success was to be exploited and a large hole punched in the enemy line. Murat, Ney and Davout all sent messages back to the Emperor's command post near Shevardino, pleading with him to commit the Imperial Guard to the battle. Initially, he ordered part of it forward but quickly changed his mind and ordered it to halt. In previous years, Napoleon would at least have ridden forward himself to observe the situation closely, but today he stayed put, trying to follow the course of the battle from over a mile to the rear and nursing his heavy cold and other physical ailments. Further pleas for him to commit the Guard arrived, but he ignored them, refusing to believe that the Russian line, which had proved so resilient so far, could be quite as vulnerable as his subordinates were suggesting and fearful that his precious Guard would be badly mauled if he committed it. Caution, as so often on this campaign, held sway in the Emperor's mind.

Ney, who had sustained four minor injuries that morning, was incensed by his master's rejection of his and his fellow marshals' appeals for reinforcement. 'Why is the Emperor in the rear of the army?' he cried angrily. 'If ... he is no longer a general ... then he should go back to the Tuileries and let us be generals for him.' With the benefit of hindsight, many historians have sympathized with the fiery marshal's ire, arguing that, by deciding to withhold the Guard, Napoleon missed his chance to shatter the Russian army. It is, of course, impossible to prove the validity of this argument, but it certainly does not seem implausible. The Russian left-centre had taken a fearsome battering after six hours of combat, the degree of which is highlighted by the fact that almost half of Bagration's regimental and brigade commanders had been killed or wounded. Moreover, almost all Kutuzov's reserve, the Russian Imperial Guard, had already been committed to the fray, so the only substantial body of troops he had available to stabilize the faltering part of his line was Ostermann-Tolstoi's corps. In the event, this proved enough against the weary and depleted soldiers of Davout, Ney and Murat, but whether it could have stopped the might of Napoleon's Guard as well is doubtful. The balance of probability, then, is that, had he committed the Guard, the Emperor would have smashed a hole in Kutuzov's left-centre that would have won him the battle and created the opportunity for him to turn his victory into a rout. It was the chance to inflict a devastating defeat upon the Tsar's armies that he had been longing for ever since he crossed the Niemen, and he let it slip.

Napoleon did not have his finest day as a commander at Borodino, but at least some justification for his blunder in refusing to send in the Guard was provided by events in the northern part of the battlefield. Watching the morning's proceedings from the Russian right wing, General Platov, commander of the

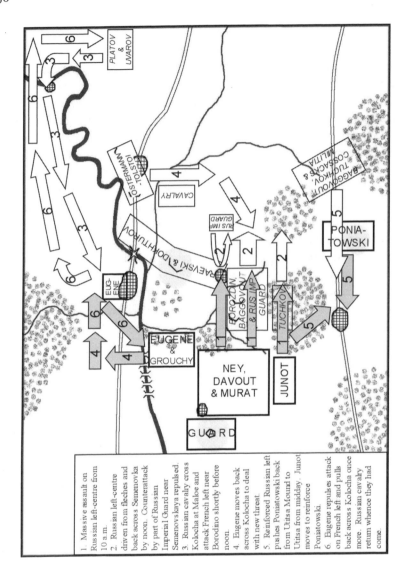

Battle of Borodino: Phase Two

Cossack forces, had observed the bulk of Eugène's corps moving south of the Kolocha and began to think about the possibility of launching a counter-attack against the invaders' left wing. An aide was duly sent south to Gorki to find the commander-in-chief and request permission for Platov's plan.

Kutuzov should have been busy overseeing the defence of the Russian line, but instead he spent most of the day eating and drinking, leaving the task of running the battle to his subordinates. The great military commentator, Karl von Clausewitz, who was present at Russian headquarters that day, later scornfully wrote of Kutuzov that at Borodino, 'He appeared destitute of inward activity, of any clear view of surrounding occurrences, of any liveliness of perception, or independence of action'. The only role the Russian commander-in-chief played was to approve or reject his generals' suggestions and requests, usually without thinking them over too deeply and speaking, ironically enough, in French. Platov's plan he approved, and some time after 11 a.m. a force of 5,500 Cossacks, 2,500 regular cavalry under General Uvarov, and 36 pieces of horse artillery began to move towards the ford near Maloe. Crossing the Kolocha, Platov's unruly horsemen swept west while Uvarov led his troopers south-west towards Borodino. Soon, the regular cavalry ran into a screen of light horsemen posted north of the village and made short work of putting the outnumbered enemy to flight.

Napoleon learned of the defeat of his cavalry near Borodino at around the same time as Murat, Ney and Davout were pleading with him to send forward the Imperial Guard. He had been preparing to unleash another attack against the Great Redoubt, but the news from his left wing worried him. What if the Russian horsemen were merely the vanguard of a major counter-attack by a large part of Barclay's First Army? Immediately, the second assault on the Great Redoubt was postponed and orders were sent out for Eugène to recross the Kolocha with a sizeable part of his corps to deal with the enemy cavalry. The Guard, meanwhile, so urgently requested to punch through the Russian left-centre, was instead instructed to prepare for a possible march north.

With hindsight, it is easy to condemn the Emperor for excessive caution. In the event, Uvarov's cavalry were checked by the division Eugène had left to guard Borodino and then sent packing by the other units that recrossed the Kolocha with the Viceroy, while Platov's Cossacks milled around to no discernible effect west and north of the village before joining Uvarov's men in withdrawing whence they had come. Yet this largely unimpressive attack on the Imperial left flank had a critical psychological impact upon Napoleon. It seems to have persuaded him that, as the Russians were able and willing to launch a counter-attack in the north, they were probably not as vulnerable as his marshals were telling him in the centre and south. Of course, he might not have committed the Guard even without the sudden Russian cavalry attack – he was always reluctant to use these elite troops – but that attack killed off any hope there might have been of the Emperor acceding to the pleas of Murat, Ney and Davout to send forward his reserve to reinforce the assault on the Russian left-centre. Inadvertently, the Platov–Uvarov raid may have saved Kutuzov's army from catastrophe.

By the time the Russian horsemen north of the Kolocha had been seen off by Eugène and his troops, the left-centre of Kutuzov's line had been successfully stabilized and new defensive positions adopted to the east of the upper Semenovka. The Great Redoubt thus now jutted out and Napoleon's attention turned to the capture of this mighty earthwork.

By 2 p.m. the forces for the assault were ready. Eugène was back south of the Kolocha with the bulk of his corps, and his three infantry divisions would be supported by two cavalry corps, with a third in reserve, as well as the firepower of hundreds of cannon. The plan was simple: the guns would soften up both the Redoubt and the Russian units positioned nearby before two cavalry corps attacked to north and south of the fortification and the infantry advanced against it frontally.

Yet another ferocious exchange of cannon fire marked the beginning of the assault, and as the cavalry corps started their advance, the one to the north commanded by Caulaincourt's younger brother, the one to the south led by Latour-Maubourg, the hooves of thousands of horses threw up a mighty dust cloud which, mingling with the smoke of the guns, obscured the invaders' approach from the enemy. Unperturbed, the heavy cannon in the Great Redoubt continued to belch forth their deadly missiles, giving the low hill upon which the earthwork stood the appearance, according to one eyewitness, of 'a volcano in the midst of the army'.

Even deadlier than the twelve-pounders in the Redoubt, though, were the massed cannon of the *Grande Armée*, whose pummelling fire forced Russian regiments either side of the fortification to pull back lest they be obliterated. As the Imperial cavalry swept past the Redoubt, most units ploughed on into these retreating enemy troops, but some swung their horses round to attack the earthwork from the rear. Overwhelmed and lacking support, the Redoubt's defenders were annihilated almost to a man as Polish and Saxon horsemen, soon joined by French infantrymen, stormed the ramparts.

With the fall of the Great Redoubt around 3 p.m., the second crisis point in the battle had been reached. Away to the south, Poniatowski reacted to news of the success by launching a two-pronged attack, with the help of Junot's men, against Baggovout's positions on and around the Utitsa mound. Slowly, the Russians were forced back, but it took two hours for the Poles and Westphalians to gain undisputed control of the mound, and even then the enemy was able to retire in good order.

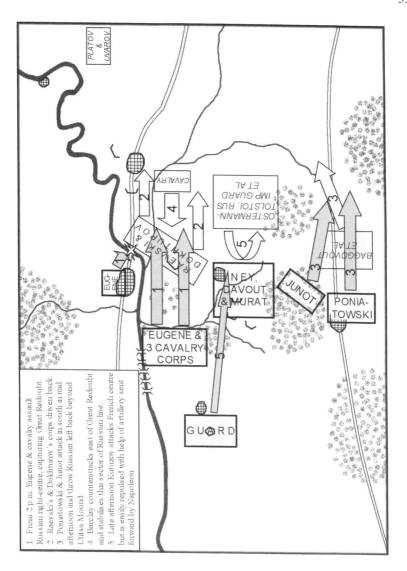

Battle of Borodino: Phase Three

The resistance of Kutuzov's left wing might have counted for nought, however, had his centre caved in following the loss of the Redoubt. That it did not, owed little, if anything to the Russian commander-in-chief, and much to General Barclay. Eugène sought to exploit the success in capturing the Great Redoubt by throwing everything he had at the enemy formations to its rear. The onslaught was led by three cavalry corps and initially it looked as if a gaping hole might be ripped in the Russian line. At this moment, Barclay came to his army's rescue. Keeping a cool head while most of those around him were on the verge of panic, he mustered together the First Army's cavalry corps and led them in a desperate counter-attack. It proved just enough. The invaders' advance was checked 500 yards east of the Redoubt and for the next hour and a half a frenetic cavalry battle took place in which neither side was able to gain a decisive advantage. At some point, Caulaincourt's brother was mortally wounded in action, and Barclay himself only narrowly avoided a similar fate. He had no fewer than three horses killed under him, and his groom shot dead a French horseman who was about to cleave his master's bald head in two.

Early in the cavalry battle, Eugène sent an appeal to his former stepfather to send in the Guard, but again Napoleon refused. 'I will not have my Guard destroyed,' he exclaimed. 'When you are eight hundred leagues from France you do not wreck your last reserve.' Would the Guard have been wrecked? It seems unlikely. More probably it would have tilted the balance decisively in the invaders' favour and smashed a hole in the Russian line, although it would undoubtedly have been a risk to commit them – and risks, as we have seen, were not something the Emperor had shown himself inclined to take so far. The fact is, though, that the only way Napoleon could hope to achieve the kind of crushing victory he needed was to gamble. Three times on 6–7 September he might have taken a chance that could have delivered a devastating triumph, but by rejecting Davout's bold battle plan and then twice refusing to commit the Imperial Guard he effectively ensured that he would win a marginal victory at best.

The combination of Barclay's gallant cavalry attack and the Emperor's holding back of his reserve bought the Russians the precious time they needed to stabilize their line east of the fallen Great Redoubt. Around 5 p.m., the exhausted horsemen on both sides broke off their prolonged struggle and retired. The artillery soon resumed an exchange of fire, but it was less fierce than earlier in the day. Still, Eugène felt it prudent to command his soldiers to lie down in order to minimize casualties.

The last attack of the day came from the Russians, as if to show that they were not a spent force. Kutuzov gathered troops on his left-centre to strike at the exhausted men of Davout's and Ney's corps. Davout saw the assault being prepared, and requested that Napoleon send forward the Guard to help check it. Predictably, the Emperor refused, but he did at least despatch eighty guns from the artillery reserve, and these made quick and bloody work of Kutuzov's ill-advised assault. By 6 p.m., with light fading, the battle effectively came to an end. It had been a truly terrible day.

As the fighting ceased and darkness descended, mist and drizzle fell over the battlefield. Both armies pulled back a little, the invaders even abandoning the Great Redoubt lest the Russians decided to subject it to a massive bombardment the following dawn. While many soldiers tried to build fires to stave off the growing cold, others ransacked the corpses of friends and enemies searching for food or booty. On neither side of the field was there any sign of joy, although both commanders claimed a victory of sorts: Napoleon because his men had captured key enemy positions and pushed the Russian line back some 1,000–1,500 yards; Kutuzov because his army still blocked the road to Moscow as night fell. The Emperor's claim was stronger, but few of his soldiers felt that they had achieved much of a triumph. The mood among the Imperial army that night, according to one member of Bonaparte's entourage, was one of 'gloomy taciturnity'. No songs, no jokes, no cheer, just a sullen reflection on the horrors of the day just passed and of the incredible tenacity of the Russian soldiers.

In exile, Napoleon would refer to Borodino as 'the most terrible of all my battles', while Kutuzov dubbed it the 'most bloody battle of modern times'. For a young Russian officer on the commander-in-chief's staff, Borodino was his first major combat and, looking back on a long career in later years, he would comment that, compared to the events of 7 September 1812, all the other battles he witnessed were 'like war manoeuvres'. Another participant remarked simply that 'anyone who saw this battle has a fair idea of what hell must be like'.

As striking as the verbal testimony are the statistics relating to Borodino. It has been calculated that Imperial forces fired a staggering 90,000 artillery rounds and almost two million musketballs in the twelve hours of fighting (stark proof, incidentally, that, contrary to the impression given by some accounts of the invasion, the Napoleonic supply system had far from broken down entirely by this stage). Figures for the Russians are harder to gauge reliably, but it seems that although they were lower than the astounding numbers for the invaders, they were still extraordinarily high.

The butcher's bill, predictably, was horrendous. A total of around 45,000 dead and wounded is generally accepted for Kutuzov's armies, equivalent to thirty-five per cent of all Russians present at the battle. This was the highest loss recorded in a single day's fighting by any European army since Hannibal's annihilation of the Roman force at Cannae over two millennia before, and it would not be surpassed in the modern era for a further hundred years, when the deadly technology of machine guns and mammoth artillery pieces turned the first day of the Somme into a massacre. Whole Russian regiments, and even divisions, were all but wiped out at Borodino.

Napoleon's losses are more controversial. The Russians have tried to claim that the invaders suffered nigh on 60,000 casualties, but this seems more than a little excessive given the size of the force which occupied Moscow shortly after the battle. Most likely, the *Grande Armée* sustained something like 30,000 killed and wounded at Borodino, about two-thirds the Russians' losses. Again, to put this figure in some sort of context, Napoleon's army lost about the same number of men in one day's fighting as the Allied Fifth Army lost between landing at Salerno in southern Italy in September 1943 and capturing Rome nine months later.

Compounding the already appalling casualty figures was the fact that few of the tens of thousands of wounded at Borodino suffered only minor wounds. Thousands upon thousands who sustained injuries during the battle succumbed to them shortly afterwards. Even for those with less directly mortal wounds, the fatality rate proved unusually high in the days and weeks following the titanic clash. The wounded in the Imperial army were generally rather better treated than those in the Russian force, but the scarcity of food and the difficulties of supply meant that many did not receive the level of care and sustenance required to prevent their less serious injuries from becoming more deadly. Less than a fortnight after the battle, fully three-quarters of the Imperial troops recorded as wounded at Borodino were dead. The situation for the Russian wounded, most of whom were abandoned by their comrades in the town of Mozhaisk, is predictably less clear, but it seems highly probable that it was even worse.

There is no doubt that the major killer at Borodino was artillery, and the fact that, despite having fewer and, on average, less heavy guns, the *Grande Armée* fired perhaps fifty per cent more rounds than the Russians, thanks to their more skilful deployment of this arm, largely explains why Kutuzov's armies sustained greater losses than their opponents. Thousands upon thousands of soldiers of both sides were simply torn apart by cannonballs, exploding shells or canister. If the fields of France and Flanders in 1914–18 saw the high point of the age of artillery, then Borodino was its grim dawn.

The other notable fact about losses at Borodino was the remarkably low number of prisoners and guns the invaders captured, despite occupying the Russian positions; just 700–800 and twenty respectively. Kutuzov's men had, quite literally, chosen to die rather than surrender. The tenacity, bravery and sheer doggedness of the Russian troops on 7 September 1812 had been as astonishing as the courage, determination and fortitude of their adversaries.

What had decided the battle in the end had been the superior skill of the Imperial leadership. Napoleon's battle plan may have been crude and based on a miscalculation of the enemy's resilience, and he certainly did not have one of his great days as a commander, but at least he outperformed his counterpart, whose initial dispositions were awful and who effectively left the running of the battle to his subordinates. With the advantage of the terrain, with a marked superiority in artillery, with an army of highly motivated and fanatically brave soldiers, and with an adversary who was far from at the peak of his form as a general, Kutuzov should arguably have defeated the Emperor at Borodino and forced him to retreat back down the road towards Smolensk. Instead, his failings led to a defeat that opened Napoleon's route to Moscow. Indeed, but for the heroism of his men and the mistakes of his opponent, Kutuzov might well have suffered a reverse comparable to, even greater than, those of Austerlitz, Jena-Auerstädt or Friedland. It had not been the most propitious start for the man to whom the salvation of the Russian Empire had been entrusted.

As the sun rose on the morning of 8 September, it illuminated a scene of utter carnage. As one eyewitness described it, 'the few places that were not encumbered with the slain were covered with broken lances, muskets, helmets and cuirasses, or with canister and bullets, as numerous as hailstones after a violent storm'. The Russians had vacated the field in the early hours. Extraordinarily, some generals had urged Kutuzov to stand and fight a second day, but as the full scale of the damage the First and especially Second Armies had sustained became apparent, it had been clear that retreat east towards Moscow was the only sensible option. The withdrawal was conducted in good order and with as many of the wounded as were able to be carried or could march unaided. The advance guard of the Imperial army did not follow them until the afternoon and then received a sharp check outside the town of Mozhaisk that showed that the Russians were not a broken force for all that they were severely battered. A vigorous Napoleonic pursuit, such as had followed the victories of Jena-Auerstädt or Friedland, was simply not an option. The *Grande Armée* had been far too badly pummelled itself.

The Emperor toured the battlefield around noon. The weather was cold, gloomy, wet and windy to accompany what was a miserable excursion. Napoleon tried to put as positive a gloss on things as he could, suggesting that the enemy had sustained several times as many dead as his own army, but an aide sarcastically remarked of the comment in his memoirs that Napoleon must have been including with the Russians the many thousands of Germans and other non-Frenchmen that had died fighting on the invaders' side. The truth was that there was simply no way of hiding the magnitude of the losses suffered by both armies and it is interesting that in a letter to his young wife Marie-Louise the Emperor uncharacteristically admitted to having taken a great many casualties in the battle.

As the bulk of the Imperial army's soldiers moved off after the retreating Russians on 9 September, the key question was whether Kutuzov would make another stand in defence of Moscow. Most of his officers and men certainly expected and wanted him to, as did Moscow's governor, Count Fyodor Rostopchin. The man who in 1800 had strongly urged Tsar Paul to seek a close friendship with Napoleonic France, Rostopchin was now almost fifty, though he looked older, and had become a rabid Francophobe. A Muscovite by birth, he had only become governor that spring, and then only thanks to the support of Alexander's sister Catherine (the Tsar himself did not much care for him). In his first weeks in office, he had seemed bent on making himself unpopular with the citizens of Moscow by harrying the various forms of vice, from brothels to drinking dens to gaming houses, which served to entertain the masses. Once the invasion had started, however, his stock had risen dramatically as he had caught and directed the xenophobic mood, encouraging the dissemination of violently anti-French propaganda and even parading French prisoners of war on the streets of Moscow with insulting placards around their necks. Now, in the wake of the reverse at Borodino and with the Russian armies' retreat drawing disturbingly close to the city walls, Rostopchin issued a defiant proclamation calling on the citizens to help fight the invaders and asserting that Kutuzov had pledged to 'defend Moscow to the last drop of my blood'.

It seems likely that the governor's claim regarding the commander-in-chief's position was fabricated. Certainly, Kutuzov talked of fighting another battle to save Moscow, and he and his generals did inspect the ground west of Moscow to assess its suitably as a battlefield, but the probability is that this was just for show and that all along he intended to abandon the city to its fate. This at least was the clear line he took in a fateful meeting with his subordinates held in a log hut at Fili, just west of Moscow, on the afternoon of 13 September. Kutuzov had met Rostopchin that morning and the governor had strongly urged him to make a stand on the hills outside the city. His chief of staff, Bennigsen, also advocated offering battle again, as did Barclay's chief of staff. The First Army commander himself, though, strongly opposed renewing the fight, arguing that not only were Russian forces too weak at present to win a decisive victory that might turn Napoleon back, but also that, were they to suffer a second defeat, the entire army would be 'annihilated down to the last man'. Many of Kutuzov's subordinates were unwilling to accept this pessimistic prognosis, either because they believed that the Emperor's army must have taken an even greater battering than their own at Borodino or simply because they could not face the thought of abandoning Moscow while the army was still able to fight for it. For an hour the arguments went back and forth, the meeting of generals split fairly evenly between those who advocated making a second stand and those who felt that it would be wiser to keep retreating and leave the former capital to the enemy. The impasse was broken by Kutuzov. 'Napoleon is a torrent which as yet we are unable to stem,' he declared. 'Moscow will be the sponge that will suck him dry ... I order a retreat.' He then lifted his bulky frame from his chair and left the hut.

When he heard of the commander-in-chief's decision, Rostopchin was livid, but he had no authority to overrule it. News that the retreat would continue beyond Moscow also caused a great deal of consternation among the officers and men of the First and Second Armies. If Russia's holiest city were to be given up without a fight, did that mean that the war was lost? Kutuzov knew that his order to retreat was controversial, that it would provoke much anxiety and alarm, and that it would hit morale in both the army and the country hard, but he himself remained confident that the invaders could ultimately be defeated. He wrote to the Tsar explaining his decision. 'I dare humbly to submit,' he wrote, 'that the entry of the enemy into Moscow is still far from entailing the fall of Russia ... The loss of Moscow can be atoned: it does not imply the loss of the country.' Only the next few weeks would tell, however, whether Alexander would prove as resolute in the face of adversity as Kutuzov.

Moscow in 1812 was a city of over 250,000 souls, making it one of the most populous in Europe, although in summer its population typically fell by around thirty per cent as a result of a mass exodus of wealthy citizens (with most of their households) to the countryside to escape the stifling heat. As the invaders approached in mid-September, tens of thousands of poorer Muscovites made an impromptu mass exodus of their own, reducing the city's population to just a third of its normal level. It was an extraordinary and almost entirely voluntary migration. One can only assume that many Muscovites had taken the torrent of Francophobic propaganda fed to them by their governor and others to heart, and expected the invaders to commit all manner of atrocities once they entered the city.

Those invaders first caught sight of Russia's former capital on the morning of 14 September. It had taken twelve gruelling weeks and almost 600 arduous miles to reach this point, but as the first Imperial soldiers beheld Moscow's famous onion domes and cupolas, they dared to hope that the war would soon be over. There was relief too that they would not have to fight again for the city, for the Russians had contacted Napoleon's advance guard offering to cede Moscow freely so long as they were allowed to retreat unhindered. The Emperor was only too pleased to accept the suggestion, confident that the fact that Kutuzov was unwilling to make another stand in defence of Russia's holiest city was proof that his army was a broken reed after its mauling at Borodino and would offer no resistance for the rest of the year. Had he been in a more ruthless mood, Napoleon could almost certainly have inflicted a very severe mauling on Kutuzov's men, many thousands of whom had become detached from their units and might have been captured in Moscow's streets. Indeed, so dispirited and disorganized was the Russian army in the immediate wake of the decision to abandon the former capital that it is not inconceivable that it might have been smashed as a force.

Instead, to its great fortune, it was allowed to withdraw unmolested. Napoleon, like the bulk of his soldiers, believed that simply occupying Moscow would be enough to force the Tsar to the peace table and that any further fighting would be an unnecessary and senseless waste of life. This humane attitude was to their credit, but it would not turn out to be in their interests.

The first Imperial troops entered the city on the afternoon of 14 September. It was like a ghost town, eerily quiet and with few faces to be seen. As they approached the Kremlin, the famous citadel at Moscow's heart, the soldiers encountered limited resistance from a small number of individuals, but these were easily dealt with and the fortress compound occupied. Among the first to enter were a unit of Polish cavalry. What a poignant moment it must have been for these men whose country Russia had played the leading role in carving up.

Napoleon himself, meanwhile, arrived with the Imperial Guard at the Dragomilov Gate on the western side of Moscow at 3 p.m. Expecting a deputation of the city's leading dignitaries to come to him and formally hand over control, the customary procedure in these circumstances in the early nineteenth century, he waited. When no delegation came, he sent some aides into the city to find individuals of standing, but by the time they returned empty-handed evening was falling and, rather than stealing into Moscow like a thief in the night, a furious Emperor decided to postpone his entry until the morrow. Accommodation was swiftly found in a large tavern near the Dragomilov Gate and Napoleon retired to bed frustrated, angry and a little perplexed.

That night a spate of fires sprang up in the city. It was initially assumed that they were accidental, started by careless soldiers eager for warmth, and by the time the Emperor rode into Moscow the following morning and took up residence in the Kremlin, they had been brought under control. Napoleon's main concern on 15 September, therefore, was the deployment of the roughly 100,000 men now under his immediate control. Unsure exactly where Kutuzov intended to halt his retreat, Napoleon decided to ring the city with troops. Eugène was stationed to the north, Ney to the east, Davout to the west, and Murat and Poniatowki to the south, while the Imperial Guard remained in Moscow proper with their master (Junot's small corps had been left near Borodino to protect the wounded and the supply line to Smolensk). As usual, there was much grumbling about the Guard getting the best of it, but central Moscow soon proved to be a less comfortable cantonment than expected.

On the night of the 15th, a rash of fires erupted in the bazaar quarter of Moscow to the east of the Kremlin. Soon after, blazes broke out elsewhere in the former Russian capital, the great majority of whose buildings were constructed of wood rather than stone or brick. It was incredible but unmistakable what was happening. The Muscovites were trying to torch their own city. Fanned by a strong wind and with more conflagrations being started all the time, an inferno was raging through Moscow by the morning of the 16th. A shocked Napoleon climbed the tallest tower in the Kremlin to observe the enormous blaze and was horrified. 'The barbarians, the savages,' he cried, 'to burn their city like this!' When the Kremlin stables and, even more dangerously, the arsenal narrowly avoided going up in flames that day, it was considered sensible for the Emperor to move his headquarters elsewhere until the fire could be brought under control. The Petrovsky Palace a couple of miles north of Moscow was chosen and just how intense the inferno was by the evening of 16 September is shown by the fact that one could easily read by its light in the grounds of the new Imperial HQ.

The fire burned furiously until late on the 17th (indeed, it was not extinguished entirely until the 20th, when a rainstorm doused the few remaining blazes). For the forty-eight hours that it gripped the city, the Moscow firestorm created havoc. As more and more soldiers were drafted in to fight the conflagration and save as much of the former capital as possible, discipline broke down. Troops roamed the streets searching for booty that could be 'rescued' from the fire. Furs, silks, silver, wine, food; all manner of goods were seized by the marauding men in what became known to them as 'the Moscow Fair'. Napoleon's soldiers, however, did not just loot. They did fight fires, or at least tried to, and they did catch a good number of arsonists in the act, who were promptly hanged as an example to others. Proper order was only restored to the army, though, after the Emperor returned to the Kremlin on the morning of 18 September.

Ultimate responsibility for the Moscow inferno rests with one man, Fyodor Rostopchin. Maddened by Kutuzov's refusal to defend the former capital, the governor had made it his mission to try to destroy the city he was being forced to yield. On his own initiative, with no orders from the Tsar or anyone else, he released all Moscow's dangerous criminals and promised them pardons if they would torch the city once the invaders occupied it. He even handed out explosive fuses to help them, had all firefighting equipment removed or destroyed, and made no effort to evacuate Moscow's huge stockpiles of gunpowder and munitions in the hope that they would explode in the fire.

The conflagration that Rostopchin organized has often been justified as an attempt to deny the enemy supplies and shelter, and there was certainly an element of this to it, but fundamentally it was an irrational act arranged by a man who appears to have been less than entirely sane at this time (indeed, he later admitted that he had 'acted as though I were a demon or an Asiatic drugged with opium'). There are no accurate figures, but many thousands of Russians, particularly the sick, wounded or infirm, must have perished in the blaze, and it was only thanks to the extraordinary efforts of French soldiers that Moscow's largest orphanage, a little way east of the Kremlin, did not burn down killing scores of children. The damage done to homes, churches and other historic buildings was catastrophic.

What really marked the deliberate burning of Moscow as a senseless act of wanton destruction, though, was the fact that, although two-thirds of the ancient city was devastated by the fire, the invaders still managed to save more than enough shelter for the troops and huge quantities of supplies of all kinds. By way of example, the invaders captured 150 cannon, 60,000 new muskets, two million musket cartridges, tons of gunpowder, and thousands of cannonballs, all of which Rostopchin had hoped would go up in flames. To be sure, the indiscipline of the soldiers during the inferno had depleted stocks of food, but not in any significant way. The great fire of Moscow was not the heroic gesture of defiance it is sometimes portrayed as, but the mad, futile act of a bunch of half-crazed fanatics and criminals.

It had been a hectic first few days in the Imperial occupation of Russia's former capital, but, by 20 September, order had been restored to the ravaged city and Napoleon was free to turn his mind to other affairs. With Kutuzov's army battered and in retreat, and with Moscow, the sacred heart of old Muscovy, in his hands, the Emperor was sure that it would only be a matter of days before a messenger arrived from St Petersburg requesting peace talks. All he had to do was wait.

The obvious direction for Kutuzov to lead his men in after the abandonment of Moscow was north in order to cover any enemy thrust towards St Petersburg, but considering such a move on Napoleon's part unlikely at this time of year, the Russian commander instead headed first south-east and then due west in order to position himself south of the former capital. This placed his armies astride the invaders' route towards both the fertile lands of the Ukraine and the important arms manufacturing centre of Tula, thereby shielding them and enabling his own forces to draw on the food, fodder and weaponry they could provide.

Kutuzov's move foxed the Emperor, who had not expected him to leave his armies so close to his own. When he discovered on 21 September that the Russians were within striking distance to the south of Moscow, he briefly considered leading his force after them in search of another battle. He swiftly discarded the idea, however, confident that he would not require another victory to secure peace.

In the Russian camp too, some thought was given to seeking a further showdown, although not by the commander-in-chief. General Bennigsen led those who advocated attacking the invaders in late September, and his aggressive spirit had many supporters among officers and men who felt ashamed and disconsolate at having abandoned Moscow. Kutuzov, though, would not brook such offensive notions, instead ordering that his soldiers march to Tarutino, a town fifty-five miles south-west of the former capital, where they would bide their time. Bennigsen and his followers were frustrated and disheartened by what they saw as a cowardly strategy, and the commander-in-chief did not help himself by refusing to explain either his overall plan or the reasoning behind it to any but his closest confidants. Unsurprisingly, many of his subordinates began to suspect that their chief was afraid of confronting Napoleon again and had no idea how to deal with him.

Kutuzov did, however, have a strategy, and a cunning one at that. At its heart was the idea of playing for time. As things stood at the end of September, when his armies arrived at Tarutino, he commanded around 80,000 men, a good many of them either militia or new recruits. This, he deemed, quite rightly, was an insufficient force with which to inflict a defeat upon the invaders and drive them from Moscow. While Napoleon was unlikely to see his main army increase in strength so long as it remained at the end of hugely extended supply lines, whose protection severely drained Imperial manpower, though, Kutuzov could expect his own force to grow over the coming weeks with the arrival of more new recruits and soldiers from other fronts, such as the Caucasus. The key, then, was to keep the Emperor holed up in Moscow for as long as possible, and that meant making no attempt to seek battle until the Russians had secured a decisive numerical advantage. Indeed it went further. In order to discourage the enemy from seeking battle themselves, Kutuzov instructed his pickets to fraternize with their imperial counterparts and generally give the impression that they were just waiting for the war to end officially. This policy of deception and delay was not perhaps heroic, but it was undeniably sensible in the circumstances.

One man who would have agreed wholeheartedly with Kutuzov's plan, had the commander-in-chief bothered to explain it fully to his subordinates, was General Barclay, but his key role in the tumultuous events of 1812 was drawing to an end. The dour Barclay and his louche Russian superior never got on personally and the First Army commander felt increasingly marginalized and undervalued. Nor was this paranoia. We have already seen how Barclay was resented and criticized by many Russians, largely for being what they called 'German', and Kutuzov felt no compunction to defend the beleaguered general, even in spite of his gallant efforts at Borodino. Indeed, in a letter to the Tsar, the commander-in-chief as good as blamed Barclay for the fall of Moscow by deceitfully writing, 'Your Imperial and Most Gracious Majesty will allow that these consequences are indivisibly bound up with the loss of Smolensk and with that thoroughly disordered state of the armies in which I found them.' When, therefore, in early October Kutuzov decided to merge the First Army with the Second Army of the dead Bagration, an exasperated Barclay used the opportunity this provided to resign his field command and return to St Petersburg to focus on his duties as Minister of War. Thus his Russian enemies finally got what they wanted, but their celebration was shameful. But for Barclay, the Tsar's armies would almost certainly have suffered a calamitous defeat in 1812; either near the border, where his colleague Bagration had wanted to fight; or at Smolensk, where he had sensibly decided to withdraw before Napoleon could trap both his and Bagration's forces; or at Borodino, where he had saved his side by organizing the vital cavalry counter-attack after the fall of the Great Redoubt. Thanks to xenophobia and, later, Tolstoy's novel *War and Peace*, the Russians elevated Kutuzov to the status of the great hero of 1812. They should have chosen Barclay instead.

Keen as Kutuzov was to lull the invaders into a false sense of security regarding his regular army, he had more immediately aggressive plans for his irregular forces. It was clear to even a military novice that by mid-September the supply lines for Napoleon's main army were highly vulnerable. Now that that army was some way inside Russia proper and the Emperor had called a halt to operations, the time for attacking them seriously had come.

Inevitably, a leading role in the assault on the invaders' lines of communication was taken by Russia's irregular cavalry *par excellence*, the Cossacks. Encouraged to volunteer for Kutuzov's army by the promise of being able to loot at the *Grande Armée*'s expense, the numbers serving near Moscow had swollen to around 20,000 by mid-October. They typically operated in fairly small bands, often in collaboration with locals, but occasionally came together for bigger operations. One such instance came on 24 September, when a large force of Cossacks succeeded in cutting the main Moscow–Smolensk road near Mozhaisk. Mildly alarmed, the Emperor despatched some cavalry of his own to chase them off, but the Russians cunningly laid an ambush and took them all prisoner. A subsequent, much stronger Imperial force succeeded where the other had failed so spectacularly, but a point had been made.

The Cossacks, though, were only part of the problem. As had happened in Spain, a peasantry fuelled by hatred stirred up by xenophobes and religious extremists now started to play an ugly role in the drama that was the 1812 campaign. A few days before the battle of Borodino had been fought, a Lieutenant-Colonel Denis Davidov had come to see Kutuzov to persuade him to harness the seething fury of the Russian serfs for their cause. The commander-in-chief had granted him a force of fifty hussars and eighty Cossacks with which to scour the countryside west of Moscow, encouraging the peasants to join him in attacking enemy supply convoys and any small groups of Imperial troops they could find. When Davidov proved that he could harness the serfs to the army's ends (in spite of the fact that they arguably had as much reason to be furious with Kutuzov's men as with Napoleon's), others copied him until the former Russian capital was surrounded by bands of partisans. Many of the leaders of these bands became national heroes, and they certainly included colourful characters. Ermolai Chetvertakov, for example, was a dragoon private in the regular army who was taken prisoner but managed to escape. With the help of a friend, he killed two French stragglers and stole their weapons and uniforms. Armed and in disguise, Chetvertakov and his accomplice next targeted an unfortunate pair of Imperial cavalrymen whom they duly murdered and relieved of their horses. Over the next few weeks, the former dragoon private managed to recruit almost fifty angry serfs into a small, personal army. Finding an isolated group of a dozen French heavy cavalrymen, Chetvertakov's band ambushed and killed them. Soon after, his force swollen by his growing fame, he oversaw the brutal elimination of a group of almost sixty Imperial soldiers. Eventually, his band grew to over three hundred operating near the town of Gzhatsk.

Often depicted as valiant Russian nationalists doing their bit to defend their beloved motherland, the partisans who plagued Napoleon's men and supply lines, like their counterparts in Iberia, were generally nothing of the sort. Most were driven by hatred of the invaders rather than love of Russia or her tsar, and this was reflected in the typically appalling treatment meted out to Imperial soldiers unlucky enough to be captured by them. Torture was commonplace, savage murder almost inevitable. The Emperor was horrified by the serfs' brutality and strongly appealed to Kutuzov to do something to curb their atrocious behaviour. The Russian commander-in-chief's response was unhelpful to say the least. While he was able to restrain the conduct of the soldiers in his army, he argued (conveniently ignoring the participation of some Cossacks and even, on occasion, regular troops in the atrocities), 'It is difficult to control a people who for three hundred years have never known war within their frontiers [*not true*], who are ready to immolate themselves for their country [*a highly dubious assertion*], and who are not susceptible to the distinction between what is and what is not the usage of civilized warfare.' Napoleon was extremely disappointed with this reply, but the fact is that not only was Kutuzov unwilling to take any action to curb the excesses, he actually approved of them. As we have seen, he provided Davidov, as well as other partisan leaders, with men and supplies, and even turned a blind eye to the fact that some officers under his command, usually Cossacks, gave or sold enemy prisoners to the peasants knowing full well what fate would befall them. His general attitude towards men who committed atrocities was neatly summed up in a comment he made to one of their leaders: 'It does not matter to me that these people wear caps rather than military shakos, or that they are clad in peasant smocks instead of proper uniforms.' War is always unpleasant, of course, but in taking the attitude he did, Kutuzov helped to make it darker and more cruel than it need have been.

Justification for the behaviour of the partisans is often proffered in the form of the simple fact that their country had been invaded, but this is spurious. That fact could certainly be used to justify the direct involvement of civilians in the struggle against Napoleon, but it does not validate the brutal torture and murder of men who had surrendered. Besides, the violence was not primarily politically motivated. It was a violence born of ignorance, xenophobic hatred and religious extremism. Key to the savagery, as in Spain, were the clergy. As one of Napoleon's aides later commented, Russian priests taught the serfs to view the invaders as a 'legion of devils commanded by the Antichrist, infernal spirits, horrible to look upon, and whose very touch defiled'. In short, they were encouraged by men they believed to be God's representatives on Earth to see fellow peasants from other parts of Europe as inhuman and evil.

The serfs' savagery can also be partly explained by the fact that some of the invaders committed acts of brutality against Russian peasants, but this was never that widespread, nor was it done systematically or with the consent, tacit or otherwise, of the army's commanders. In fact, the serfs probably suffered as much at the hands of Russian soldiers who crossed their lands, requisitioning and burning as they went, as they did at those of the invaders. The partisan activity of autumn 1812 was not the reasonable response of a nationalistic people who had been systematically brutalized by the invaders, but a deeply regrettable outburst of primal violence largely organized and directed by men, especially Kutuzov, who should have been horrified by it.

A final point to be made about the partisan activity, and one which further undermines its justification, is that it was of relatively little impact, at least at this stage. True, supply convoys from Smolensk to Moscow had now to be escorted by 1,500 troops in order to secure their safe passage, but this was not a particularly serious inconvenience. More telling is the fact that in the whole time Napoleon was at Moscow, over a month, only two couriers were captured as they rode between that city and Vilna. Similarly, partisans were unable during that period to capture a single relay-post garrison between the former capital and Smolensk. The real threat to Imperial communications came from proper military forces operating under direct command and following a humane code of conduct (within the context of war). The partisans were mostly an unnecessary and undesirable stain on a conflict that, so long as Barclay rather than Kutuzov had been Russia's chief general, had been conducted with relative humanity and decency.

That Napoleon was eager, desperate even, for peace once he occupied Moscow was shown by the way in which he responded to the great fire. He was extremely concerned that the Tsar might assume that Imperial forces had torched the holy city and that this would make a settlement all but unattainable. He therefore found practically the only nobleman left in the former capital, a man called Yakovlev, charmed him, and persuaded him to carry a letter to Alexander. The main thrust of the missive was to express the Emperor's personal anguish at the destruction done to life and property by the inferno and to place the blame for it firmly on the shoulders of Rostopchin, but it also had another purpose. Although he stopped short of suggesting talks or making firm peace proposals, Napoleon assured the Tsar that he felt no personal animosity towards him and added that 'A single note from Your Majesty would have stopped my campaign, either before or after the last battle'. An olive branch was unmistakeably being extended.

Yakovlev left Moscow with the Emperor's letter on 20 September. For the next fortnight, Napoleon awaited a response that never came. Of course there was always the possibility that Yakovlev had decided to abandon his mission or even that he had been waylaid and the letter lost (in fact, he was detained by Russian officials opposed to peace and his epistle was not forwarded to the Tsar), but even so Napoleon was more than a little surprised that a messenger did not arrive from St Petersburg. After all, Alexander must surely have heard of the defeat at Borodino and the fall of Moscow by now, and everything the Emperor knew, or thought he knew, about the Tsar suggested that his nerve should have broken and that he should be keen to make peace.

By early October, Napoleon decided that he needed to try to push things forward. He would despatch an emissary to Kutuzov to ask for a formal armistice and safe passage for an Imperial representative to St Petersburg, where Alexander would be presented with a letter from the Emperor explicitly proposing peace negotiations. The first choice for this mission was Armand de Caulaincourt, former ambassador to Russia and a man who had enjoyed close relations with the Tsar, but he not only refused to go, claiming that the confidence he had once enjoyed with Alexander would be of no use now, but even urged Napoleon to drop the whole idea, arguing that the Russians would interpret an approach for peace talks as a sign of weakness that could only make them more inclined to continue the struggle. Frustrated by this rejection, the Emperor turned to Caulaincourt's successor in St Petersburg, General Lauriston, but he too initially refused to go and only agreed when Bonaparte directly ordered him. The growing desperation of Napoleon's position was shown all too clearly in his plea to the unwilling ambassador: 'I wish for peace. I must have it. I need it at all costs except my honour.'

Lauriston set off from Moscow at the head of an Imperial delegation on 5 October. His first destination was Kutuzov's camp at Tarutino and he arrived there that afternoon, asking to be escorted to the commander-in-chief's head-quarters. Kutuzov, though, was unwilling to let him come too close to the Russian army's encampments, rightly fearing that part of the reason for his request to see him was to gather military intelligence about numbers and mood. He therefore kept Lauriston waiting some distance from Tarutino until midnight before riding out to meet him. The first Imperial request, that for a formal armistice around Moscow, Kutuzov rejected on the grounds that he did not have the authority to conclude such a truce. He did not wish Lauriston, and thus Napoleon, to interpret this as a bellicose refusal, however, lest it stir the Emperor and his army from their relative inactivity in and around the former capital, so the wily Russian craftily argued that a *de facto* armistice was already in operation anyway along the line where his and Marshal Murat's pickets met to the north-east of Tarutino.

There was a similarly mixed response to the second of Lauriston's requests; that he be granted safe passage to St Petersburg to deliver a letter from the Emperor to the Tsar. Kutuzov politely refused to allow Napoleon's emissary to proceed to the Russian capital in person but offered to forward Napoleon's message for him. Having little choice but to accept this suggestion, Lauriston handed the missive over and returned to Moscow. Later that day, the Emperor's letter did indeed begin its journey north to St Petersburg, but accompanying it was another letter from the commander-in-chief to the Tsar playing up Russia's prospects in the war and strongly urging him not to agree to peace talks.

Despite the less than total success of Lauriston's mission, Napoleon was extremely pleased to hear upon his emissary's return that his request for negotiations would shortly be winging its way to Alexander. 'When they receive my letter in Petersburg,' he assured Lauriston, 'they will celebrate with bonfires.' The war, he was convinced, would shortly be over, and he and his men would return home happy and victorious. Rarely can he have been more wrong.

News of the battle of Borodino first reached St Petersburg on 11 September and it was less than accurate. Prematurely, the Tsar announced to the congregation in the Nevsky Cathedral that evening that Kutuzov had won a great victory and that, as a reward, he was promoting the general to the rank of field marshal and granting him a huge cash donation. That night, the people of St Petersburg celebrated until dawn, dancing in the streets, ringing church bells and setting off fireworks. Rumours spread like wildfire about the 'victory', and there was even speculation that Napoleon would soon be brought to the capital in an iron cage (not the last time that such a prophecy would be made and subsequently proved false).

One can imagine the confusion and alarm the following evening, therefore, when more accurate reports started to arrive in St Petersburg which suggested that the battle had not been quite the triumph proclaimed by Alexander. Mozhaisk, a town east of Borodino, was said to be in enemy hands. Kutuzov was rumoured to be retreating towards Moscow, not advancing on Smolensk. There were tales of Russian losses on a scale never before experienced. The Tsar and his ministers shortly learnt the painful truth, but rather than issuing an official proclamation they simply maintained a silence and refused to deny the worrying reports and rumours that were arriving in the capital. On 18 September, Alexander was informed of the fall of Moscow, but still no official pronouncement was made until the end of the month, by which time everyone in St Petersburg already knew and most of them imagined that the situation was even worse than it was. The city sank into a deep gloom and much resentment was directed towards the

Tsar himself. As Russia's ruler was driven to the cathedral on the 27th to mark the eleventh anniversary of his coronation, streets that would normally have been thronging with revellers were much emptier than usual and those who had come out to see the procession pass stood in silence. Even when he reached the cathedral, descended from his carriage and climbed the stairs, there was not a single cheer. Nor was Alexander's popularity at its nadir just in St Petersburg. His sister wrote to him from north-east of Moscow a few days after that city had fallen to say, 'You are openly blamed for the misfortunes of your Empire, for ruin general and particular, in fact for having lost your country's honour and your own. All classes combine to accuse you.'

It was in these circumstances that the Tsar had to decide between entering peace talks or continuing the war. Many in St Petersburg high society advocated the former, as did both Alexander's mother and brother, the Dowager Empress Maria Feodorovna and Grand Duke Constantine. Of the large diplomatic corps in the Russian capital, drawn from a wide array of states, most anticipated a negotiated settlement with the French at best.

It was perhaps Napoleon's worst stroke of bad luck in a campaign in which Fortune had rarely shone on him that the Tsar, a man whose character was generally marked more by vacillation than resolution, ignored the mood and advice of many of those around him and set his face against making peace with the Emperor. Although some of his pronouncements on the issue suggest that he was trying to convince himself as much as others of his determination to fight on – for example, he exaggeratedly claimed at one point that, rather than make peace with Napoleon, he would prefer to 'let my beard grow to the waist and eat potatoes in Siberia' – he at no point in September or October 1812 seemed inclined to terminate the war. The simple fact appears to be that, like Kutuzov, he remained hopeful that the invaders could be defeated when others were in despair. A meeting he had held in Finland with Crown Prince Bernadotte of Sweden at the end of August, at which the former French marshal had reiterated his adopted country's pledge not to side with Napoleon, doubtless helped with this, for it allowed more troops to be freed from guarding the recently acquired Finnish provinces. The continued neutrality of the Ottoman Empire was similarly encouraging and enabled still further soldiers to march to join the forces committed to combating the *Grande Armée*. The key factor, though, was Napoleon's failure to inflict a truly crushing defeat on the Russian armies. Borodino, bloodbath as it had been, had damaged the Imperial army almost as much as Kutuzov's. Had the outcome been more one-sided, had the Russians been routed rather than merely defeated, it is far from improbable that Alexander would have decided to seek peace. Instead, Kutuzov had managed to retain a large army in being and this gave the Tsar a lifeline to which to cling. When he received Napoleon's letter of early October, Alexander, as Caulaincourt had predicted, was heartened by the Emperor's evident desire for peace and more than ever inclined to believe those who argued that Russia could win this war if only she stuck it out. Indeed, he now formally forbade his subordinates to receive any further communications from the invaders. Needless to say, Napoleon's suggestion of peace talks went unanswered. His bluff had been well and truly called.

As early as 3 October, the Emperor issued orders instructing his various corps to be ready to move on from Moscow at short notice. For two more weeks, though, he delayed giving the order to leave, clinging stubbornly to the hope that a messenger would arrive from St Petersburg with a positive reply from the Tsar to his offer of peace talks. He passed the time working, attending military parades, reading novels, playing pontoon with his former stepson Eugène, or going to see the plays that he arranged to be put on in Moscow to entertain the troops, but nearly always, according to his valet, his demeanour was 'moody and taciturn'. News from Spain, where Madrid had fallen to Wellington on 12 August and French forces had evacuated the whole of the south of the country in order to consolidate in the north, certainly did not help his disposition, but the main cause of Napoleon's glumness was the unexpected silence of the Tsar.

Inevitably, Napoleon had to begin considering what to do if Alexander refused to make peace, but none of the options available held much appeal. His initial idea was to march on St Petersburg, some 400 miles from Moscow, but that was quickly ruled out as impractical. By the time the army got there, winter would have set in and, in any case, it was extremely unlikely that the men could be provisioned on such an advance.

The Emperor's thoughts therefore switched to a less ambitious but still partially offensive move; concentrating his main army near Velikiye-Luki. This town was around a hundred miles north-east of Vitebsk and thus relatively close to the area in which the detached corps of Marshals Oudinot and Gouvion St Cyr were operating. Ostensibly, then, a move to Velikiye-Luki would strengthen Bonaparte's main striking force and, by shortening its lines of communication, simplify the ongoing supply problem. Napoleon also hoped that it would establish a clear threat to St Petersburg that might induce the Tsar to make peace. This scheme, however, was soon dropped. Once at Velikiye-Luki, the army would have to go into winter quarters, but the area was much less well suited to maintaining a large force for several cold and snowy months than, say, the Smolensk area. It was highly unlikely, moreover, that the Russians would interpret the move as constituting a serious threat to their capital, which would still be over 250 miles away.

Another option briefly considered but swiftly ruled out was remaining in Moscow over the winter. A survey of provisions available in the city suggested that there were enough to supply the approximately 100,000 men under the

Emperor's immediate control for up to six months, but other problems could not be so easily dealt with. Moscow itself was not readily defensible and it was almost certain that the main Imperial army would be cut off by the enemy if it stayed there. It might survive such an ordeal, of course, but the severance of links with the rest of Napoleon's forces and the Empire would be very problematical. The Emperor would effectively lose control not only of the majority of Imperial troops, but also of the Imperial government, and he feared that that might open the way for major military reverses and possibly even a coup in Paris.

Against his will, the Emperor was inexorably being drawn towards an unpalatable conclusion. He had to retreat. The question, though, was where to. Davout suggested that the army should head south-west from Moscow, capture the major Russian arms manufacturing centre at Tula, and then head for the fertile lands of the Ukraine, where it could winter before resuming offensive campaigning the following year. If Kutuzov tried to stand in the invaders' way, Davout was confident he could be dealt with. Indeed, a second victory over the old Russian field marshal might even cause the Tsar to consider making peace. Napoleon, however, had reassessed his earlier dismissal of the capabilities of Kutuzov's army in the light of the Russians' unexpected refusal to end the war and was consequently less confident of the outcome of another major battle than his subordinate. He was mindful, moreover, that a defeat for an army in retreat could prove catastrophic. Caution again was beginning to dominate his mind.

The rejection of Davout's suggestion left only two places to which the army might sensibly retreat: Smolensk or the border. The latter of these was anathema to Napoleon at this point, for even if a limited foothold were maintained within the Tsar's empire, at say Vilna, it would still look as if the Russian campaign had been a serious defeat. The Smolensk area it was to be, then, even though it would undoubtedly be harder to supply his men over the winter there than it would near the frontier.

The route to be taken in getting to Smolensk, however, had still to be decided. There were two obvious alternatives. The army could always return the way it had come. The advantages of this were that the invaders knew the way and would benefit from using one of the few good roads in Russia, the new Moscow–Smolensk road. The land through which they would pass, though, would be stripped bare, complicating the supply problem. Alternatively, Bonaparte's main force might retreat on a course parallel but some way to the south of the one by which they had come. There would be a good chance of procuring a fair amount of food and fodder on this route (by contrast, the land to the north of the route the army had taken in advancing to Moscow was much less rich and hospitable), but taking this more southerly path would increase the possibility of running into Kutuzov, which, as we have seen, the Emperor felt was not a desirable thing. Nevertheless, it was this route that he eventually chose.

Orders for a withdrawal to Smolensk via a route to the south of that by which the army had come were finally issued to the corps and other commanders on 18 October, the move to begin two days later. With the benefit of hindsight, Napoleon has frequently been severely criticized for delaying the decision so long, and, given what subsequently happened, it is certainly true that the deferral of the departure was unfortunate.

There were several reasons why Bonaparte put the fateful moment off longer than he might have. First, the weather did not seem likely to prove the difficulty that Caulaincourt and others with experience of Russia insisted that it would. Early October in Moscow was unseasonably warm, and even when snow suddenly fell on the 13th, it did not settle and the following days were very mild. Besides, the Emperor had ordered a study to be made of the Muscovite weather over the past two decades and that showed that temperatures rarely dropped below freezing until mid-November, by which time he expected his army to be in winter quarters near Smolensk.

The second reason for delay was the continuing hope that the Tsar might at the last moment agree to peace talks. On 14 October, aware that time was running short, Napoleon desperately despatched a second delegation to Kutuzov's headquarters hoping to secure safe passage to St Petersburg for an emissary. The Russian commander-in-chief kept the deputation hanging on for a couple of days, and then refused to accede to their wishes. There is more than coincidence in the return of the delegation to Moscow on 17 October and the issuing of the orders to retreat the following day.

The final reason for the delay in issuing the withdrawal orders was a personal, psychological one. It seems that the Emperor sensed that he was at a crossroads in October 1812, that his campaign might be on the verge of defeat, that the retreat he realized he was going to have to make from Moscow might continue longer than he hoped. This made him reluctant to take the fateful step. As one of his aides eloquently put it, 'Having reached the peak of his glory, he doubtless foresaw that from this moment would date his decline; and this is why he remained immobile, holding himself back and clinging for a few more instants to this summit.'

Nevertheless, by mid-October he could hesitate no longer. He wrote to his Foreign Minister, Maret, at Vilna to inform him of his intention to retreat to Smolensk. He tried to sound as positive as he could about what would undoubtedly be generally perceived throughout Europe as a reverse. The main army would reach their destination before the end of the first week of November, Napoleon confidently predicted, and it would then go into winter quarters from which it would emerge the following spring to march on and capture St Petersburg. Fate, however, had a rather different course of events in store.

17

Retreat

The same day that Napoleon issued the orders to leave Moscow, 18 October, the Russians launched a surprise attack some forty-five miles south-west of the city. Although reinforcements, mostly in the form of new recruits, had strengthened Kutuzov's badly battered army to around 110,000 by this time, giving him more men near Moscow than the Emperor, the Russian commander-in-chief had been reluctant to make any aggressive move. For some time, however, pressure had been mounting from many of his subordinates for something positive to be done against the invaders. Kutuzov resisted all such pleas until he was presented with a plan that had such support that it would have strained his relationship with his generals to breaking point had he rejected it. It had become apparent by mid-October that the enemy troops nearest the Russian HQ at Tarutino – Murat's cavalry – had grown dangerously lax about security. A scheme was formulated to take advantage of this fact and deliver a much desired triumph of arms.

On the morning of 18 October, a swarm of Russian horsemen fell upon the unsuspecting soldiers of General Sébastiani's cavalry corps near the village of Vinkovo. Meanwhile, a strong infantry force tried to drive through French lines and capture a defile which straddled the line of retreat towards Moscow for almost all of Murat's troops as well as Poniatowski's Polish corps. Had this objective fallen into Russian hands, it is probable that few Imperial horsemen or Poles would have escaped, and it is to the King of Naples's credit that he recognized the danger straightaway. Mustering what soldiers were available to him, Murat led a fierce counter-attack which, despite odds of perhaps as much as five to one in the Russians' favour, succeeded in driving the attackers back and enabled the bulk of his and Poniatowski's men to withdraw safely to Voronovo.

The heroics of the Imperial cavalry and their leader notwithstanding, the battle of Vinkovo, as it became known, had nearly been a disaster for the invaders. When he heard how his units had been caught napping by the enemy, Napoleon was rightly furious. His negligent subordinates only avoided the severest of censures thanks to their bravery and skill in extricating themselves from a situation into which they should not have allowed themselves to fall in the first place. The truth was, though, that even with a courageous and adept recovery from the initial surprise, Imperial losses should have been far worse than the 4,500 men (almost half of them captured) and thirty-eight cannon they did sustain. Fortunately for the invaders, the Russians bungled their attack at Vinkovo badly, largely due to the fractiousness and poor organization of their leaders, one of whom, General Baggovout, was killed by a cannonball during the battle. Nevertheless, there were hearty celebrations back at Kutuzov's headquarters at Tarutino that night. If the attack had failed to deliver the resounding victory that its architects had promised, and had cost several thousand casualties, at least some pleasure could be taken from giving the enemy a bloody nose and forcing him to retreat.

It was not just at Russian headquarters, though, that the fight at Vinkovo was accorded an inflated significance. For no reason better than that he simply lost his nerve, Napoleon reacted to the news of the reverse by bringing forward the date for departure from Moscow by twenty-four hours to 19 October. The abrupt change of departure date, which halved the time available to make final preparations for leaving, threw the army into even greater chaos than it was already in and led to bad mistakes being made. Huge quantities of oats for the horses, for example, ended up being left behind in the confusion and other important provisions earmarked to supply the men were also abandoned or even mistakenly destroyed.

Regardless of the somewhat panicky bringing forward of the departure date, Napoleon endeavoured to disguise the fact that he was retreating, to his own army as well as the enemy. Negotiators were despatched to Tarutino once more to ask for a formal armistice as if the Emperor planned to winter in Moscow, while the Imperial army was told that it was resuming the offensive and manoeuvring to attack Kutuzov's left flank in order to end the war. Only the corps commanders knew at this stage that their destination was Smolensk, a sure sign of how psychologically vulnerable the Emperor felt his army was. To Europe at large, Napoleon explained in a bulletin that his abandonment of Russia's former capital was being made purely on the grounds that it was 'an unhealthy and impure cesspool' which was unfit to shelter his troops for a prolonged period.

The Emperor left Moscow on 19 October at the head of an army of 95,000 men and 500 guns. Marshal Mortier, at the head of several thousand members of the Imperial Guard and tens of cannon, was instructed to wait behind until the 23rd and then blow up the Kremlin, a rather petty order on Napoleon's part that fortunately was largely unsuccessfully carried out thanks to rain dampening the fuses. Accompanying the soldiers were several tens of thousands of non-combatants, a mixture of camp followers, foreigners (particularly French) who had been living in Moscow, and even a fair number of Russian girls who had found lovers among the invading army. There were also thousands upon thousands of conveyances of every kind – wagons, carriages, carts, artillery caissons, the list goes on. Those that were big enough carried, by Imperial decree, at least two wounded soldiers, but most noticeable was the vast quantity of booty that they carried. Gold, silver, jewellery, paintings, religious artefacts, furs, silks, wines, even furniture; Moscow was stripped of practically everything of value by the departing army. The huge column that filed out of Russia's holiest city in mid-October 1812 presented a peculiar sight. As one French eyewitness later memorably wrote, 'It looked like a caravan, a wandering nation, or rather one of those armies of antiquity returning with slaves and spoil after a great devastation'.

In the event, the plundering of Moscow cost the invaders more than it did the Russians. Not only were more important but less financially valuable commodities, such as food, removed from transports or knapsacks in order to accommodate booty, but the sheer volume of loot and the thousands upon thousands of conveyances needed to carry it slowed the army's rate of march, especially as many of the transports overturned or broke, clogging the road. In the first five days out of Moscow, heading south-west, Napoleon's force travelled just sixty miles. To be sure, heavy rain on the 19–20 October did not help, but the army, untroubled as it was by Russians at this stage, should have been able to move more quickly than that. Ultimate responsibility must, of course, rest with the Emperor. The bringing forward of the departure date had not facilitated an organized exodus, and he failed to lay down clear and strict orders regarding the removal of booty. It is naive to suggest that he should have banned his men from carrying any loot at all – plunder was one of the key attractions of the military life at this time and to deny the soldiers what they saw as their right would have created tremendous disciplinary problems – but he certainly should have placed restrictions upon the quantity taken away, much of which was taken simply for the sake of taking it and soon ended up abandoned by the roadside.

The slowness of the Imperial army's march during those first days set in motion a chain of events that would have profound consequences. Having decided to retreat to Smolensk via a route roughly parallel to, but some way south of, that by which he had advanced to Moscow, Napoleon should have pressed on towards his objective with all possible speed. Had he done so, it is quite possible that his force would have evaded the bulk of Kutuzov's army entirely and arrived at Smolensk relatively intact and before the weather became especially bitter. Instead, his army's tardiness would prove the start of its destruction.

News that there was a substantial body of troops on the road south-west of Moscow was not long in reaching Kutuzov's headquarters at Tarutino. Initially, however, it was believed that the invaders had sent out no more than a corps in search of supplies. Therefore the Russian commander-in-chief only despatched a force of 12,000 infantry, 3,000 cavalry and eighty-four guns under General Dokhturov to investigate the enemy movement, ordering him 'on no account to engage in a combat which might require further aid from the main army'. Having gained a small victory at Vinkovo, Kutuzov was not keen to seek any further battles in the near future.

Dokhturov duly set off in search of the foe but received a rude shock when he found them. This was not a single corps on the march but practically the whole of the army under Napoleon's immediate control. The Russian general now took a fateful decision. Rather than retreating back towards the main body of Kutuzov's force, he ordered his men to race towards the small town of Maloyaroslavets which stood astride the road down which the enemy was advancing. Messengers were sent back towards Tarutino to inform the commander-in-chief of the discovery and of the bold action Dokhturov was taking in response. Once he was made aware that the great bulk of Napoleon's army in Moscow was on the move, Kutuzov set his own force in motion to shadow it and to re-establish contact with Dokhturov's detached corps. Exactly what he intended to do is unclear – indeed, it is likely that even he was unsure – but the fact remained that two large armies were now converging upon a small Russian town.

Maloyaroslavets, a settlement of some 10,000 souls built upon a hill overlooking the River Lusha around seventy-five miles south-west of Moscow, was reached on the evening of 23 October by General Delzons's division of Prince Eugène's corps. Crossing the river to the north of the town by a lone bridge, Delzons's men encountered only a few Cossacks, whom they swiftly chased off in order to take possession of the settlement and its hill. Unaware that those irregular horsemen were not the only enemies in the vicinity, the divisional commander pulled most of his troops back towards the river in order to cover the vital bridge more closely, a sensible enough decision but one which left the minority of soldiers in Maloyaroslavets out on a limb.

Dokhturov, meanwhile, was closing on the town that evening. When he learnt of the presence of a French division on the southern side of the Lusha, he determined to attack that very night. Approaching with great stealth under cover of darkness, the Russians caught the enemy completely by surprise in the early hours of the 24th. Maloyaroslavets was quickly taken and its French occupiers sent reeling down the hill towards the river in confusion. Delzons now made up for his earlier error by organizing his numerically inferior forces and holding the Russian assault on the southern side of the river where a number of buildings provided a handy defensive position. It was a potentially crucial achievement for it kept the Lusha crossing in French hands and paved the way for reinforcements to attack Dokhturov's corps after dawn and sweep the obstructing Russians aside.

During the remaining hours of darkness, Dokhturov set about organizing his forces to resist the expected enemy assault at first light. Maloyaroslavets itself was fortified, while the bulk of his eighty-four guns were placed upon a ridge to the rear of the town from where they could bombard any troops that crossed the

Lusha or advanced up the hill. On the northern bank of the river, meanwhile, Prince Eugène gathered his other two divisions in readiness to go to Delzons's aid at dawn.

As the sun rose on 24 October, the Imperial forces attacked. The battle between Dokhturov's and Eugène's corps was an even one numerically, but the Russians enjoyed the stronger position. Their cannon took a heavy toll of those attempting to cross the river before the Viceroy of Italy's own artillery managed to silence the enemy batteries sufficiently for the bulk of his men to get across the Lusha. Once there, a vigorous assault was mounted on Maloyaroslavets itself. Despite the many hazards of attacking a fortified position uphill, Delzons's division succeeded in recapturing the town, though their commander fell with a bullet in his head early in the attack.

The French success was short-lived. Dokhturov ordered an immediate counter-attack and it was not long before Delzons's exhausted and leaderless troops were streaming back down the hill again towards the river. Over the next few hours, the battle raged back and forth, Maloyaroslavets changing hands no fewer than seven times that morning in fierce fighting in which no quarter was asked for or given. The town itself was unsurprisingly wrecked by the conflict, yet as buildings were smashed soldiers simply took cover among the rubble and fought on. The level of courage on both sides was staggering, the Italian division of General Pino particularly distinguishing themselves with their heroics.

As the morning wore on, Davout's corps began to arrive in support of Eugène and two of his crack divisions were gradually committed to the struggle, while on the Russian side, troops from Raevski's corps, the lead element of Kutuzov's main army, reinforced Dokhturov's weary soldiers just in the nick of time to prevent them being overwhelmed by their ever-growing number of enemies. Nevertheless, the battle was unmistakably swinging in favour of the invaders by midday when the Russians took the decision to give up Maloyaroslavets as lost and withdraw to the ridge behind the town.

The Russian withdrawal, conducted in good order and to another strong defensive position, which dominated the road along which the Emperor was hoping to march, effectively signalled the end of the battle. By 1 p.m., Napoleon and the bulk of his army were present on the northern bank of the Lusha, but the Emperor decided against ordering an attack on the Russian-held ridge or even a large-scale crossing of the river for fear of the damage the well-sited enemy guns might wreak on his densely-packed ranks of men. Instead, he merely ordered his men on the southern bank of the Lusha to hold their positions. It was yet another cautious decision. To be sure, there was a danger that the rest of Kutuzov's army might appear as he ordered a major attack or crossing and catch him with his forces divided by a river spanned by a single bridge, but, if that was his main concern, he should arguably have pulled all his forces back to the northern bank, for the five divisions which had crossed were highly vulnerable to a potential attack by the bulk of the Russian army. Even when Dokhturov and Raevski were ordered to make a further withdrawal that afternoon to draw nearer to Kutuzov's main body away to the south, the Emperor refused to send many more troops over the Lusha. It seemed that both commanders-in-chief were unsure what to do. Kutuzov, rather than reinforcing his subordinates in their defensive position and determining to fight a major battle in order to protect the road towards the richer lands to the south-west, was holding back and leaving the initiative to the enemy, while Napoleon failed singularly to exploit this situation and, in his turn, appeared to be waiting for the Russians to make the decisive move.

In the fighting at Maloyaroslavets, the Imperial army had lost around 6,000 casualties, compared to 6,700 for the Russians. As at Borodino, very few prisoners had been taken. It had been a heavy sacrifice, relative to the limited number of troops engaged. The Russians having withdrawn, the Emperor claimed a victory for his army, but strategically the situation on the morning of 25 October was mixed. The successes of the previous day had opened up one main route from Maloyaroslavets to Smolensk, that which ran roughly west via the towns of Medyn and Yelna, but Kutuzov's army still apparently guarded the other, which ran south-west to Kaluga before turning west. Of the two, the Kaluga route would lead through the richest territory, although the Medyn–Yelna route also passed through relatively abundant lands.

Napoleon thus had a decision to make. Should he press on down his preferred road towards Kaluga at the risk of having to fight a major battle with Kutuzov or should he head towards Medyn and hope that he could keep the Russians at bay until he reached Smolensk? Of course, there was a third option, a retreat north towards the main Moscow–Smolensk road by which the invaders had advanced in the summer, but that hardly seemed a likely choice for the great French Emperor, especially after a victory for his army. If only he had ensured that his force left Moscow less encumbered by loot and in better order, it would have made faster progress and reached Maloyaroslavets, and quite possibly Kaluga too, well ahead of the Russians. Instead, its tardiness had resulted in the fierce engagement on 23–24 October and allowed Kutuzov to place his main body astride the invaders' preferred route.

On the morning of 25 October, Napoleon decided to conduct a brief personal reconnaissance south of Maloyaroslavets to see if there was any sign of the enemy deploying for battle astride the Kaluga road. He had not progressed far when suddenly a sizeable group of Russian light horsemen burst from a nearby wood a little way ahead and charged towards him. The Emperor's only immediate escort was two squadrons of cavalry and they were hard pressed to keep the enemy at bay. At one point, the Russians got within a few dozen yards of the world's most powerful man before the timely arrival of elements of the Imperial Guard persuaded Kutuzov's cavalrymen to flee. Napoleon had probably never been closer to capture in his life.

There seems little doubt that, despite his efforts to laugh off the incident, the Emperor's brush with the Russian horsemen left him deeply shaken, as is shown by the fact that from this day on he always wore a vial of poison around his neck to consume in case he were captured. Whether his close shave affected his thinking on the 25th, however, is less clear. What is certain is that he abruptly abandoned all scouting efforts and called a council of war with his senior subordinates to discuss what course of action the army should take.

If ever there was a man who passionately believed that it was a leader's job to lead, it was Napoleon, so the calling of a council of war highlighted just how awkward he found his current predicament. He knew that a tough decision had to be made and, unusually for him, he wanted the security of the support of others before making it. It became clear almost as soon as the meeting started that the Emperor favoured retreating back north and then heading west along the Moscow–Smolensk road. His nerve had gone. The bold Murat was the only marshal to push strongly for an advance down the Kaluga road and he endeavoured to convince Napoleon that, if it came to a battle, the hardened Imperial army would surely defeat Kutuzov's force with the latter's substantial leavening of raw recruits. He had to admit, though, that the weakened state of the Imperial cavalry would preclude a pursuit to destroy the enemy and that, therefore, there could be no guarantee of the Russians being shaken off entirely if the army took Murat's preferred route. For his part, Marshal Davout forcefully advocated the Medyn–Yelna route leading west from Maloyaroslavets. This would take the army, he claimed, through a 'fat, fertile, nourishing' countryside, whereas the old route along the Moscow–Smolensk road by which the invaders had advanced would offer nothing but 'sand and cinders'. The bulk of Napoleon's subordinates, however, agreed with their emperor. Their priority seemed to be avoiding contact with Kutuzov's army. If the best chance of doing that was to head back north and then return the way they had come, then so be it. Later that day, Bonaparte issued the orders for a withdrawal halfway back to Moscow from where the road for Mozhaisk would be taken and then the Moscow–Smolensk road rejoined.

The decision to turn back at Maloyaroslavets is often described as one of the worst Napoleon ever made. By retracing his steps and heading back north, he effectively ended up losing perhaps a week of reasonably good weather on the march to Smolensk compared to if he had struck out west from Maloyaroslavets or headed directly west from Moscow in the first place, a loss that would prove very costly during the last few days before the army reached its destination. Compounding the error, it seems that Kutuzov had no intention in late October of offering battle against the mass of the Imperial army, even if they had pushed on down the Kaluga road. Murat was right to point out that much of the Russian army opposing them was made up of raw recruits, a fact of which Kutuzov himself was all too aware. We have already seen how he instructed Dokhturov not to do anything that might result in a major battle and then ordered his subordinate to withdraw from a good defensive position behind Maloyaroslavets on the afternoon of 24 October. That night, he pulled all but a few cavalry units, such as the one that nearly captured Napoleon, further south and then, the following night, withdrew still further in the belief that the invaders would press on towards Kaluga. The simple fact is that Kutuzov did not want to fight another large-scale pitched battle against the Imperial army because, like Murat, he was sure, at this point anyway, that the Russians would lose. Of course, there was no way Napoleon could know his counterpart's mind, but if he had only ordered a proper reconnaissance south along the Kaluga road on the morning of 25 October, instead of the limited and abandoned effort that was made, he would have found the way all but unblocked. The routes to Smolensk via Medyn and even Kaluga would probably not have been as hazardous as Napoleon and most of his marshals believed.

In electing to turn back at Maloyaroslavets, the Emperor and those who supported his decision were effectively declaring that they were more concerned about the Russian army than they were about the Russian landscape or weather, for by heading back towards the Moscow–Smolensk road the army was prolonging its retreat as winter approached and channelling it through countryside that had been devastated in the summer. We cannot be sure, of course, how things would have turned out had Napoleon's men pushed on south or turned west on 25 October instead, but it seems highly unlikely that they would have gone as badly as they in actuality did. The decision to retreat back north taken at Maloyaroslavets was to prove calamitous. One member of the Emperor's entourage later wrote grandiloquently of Maloyaroslavets as 'this fatal field which put a halt to the conquest of the world, where twenty victories were thrown to the wind, and where our great empire began to crumble to the ground'. The Russians were less flamboyant in their analysis. When they rebuilt the shattered town after the invasion they put up a small plaque commemorating the battle which had been fought there. It commented simply, 'End of offensive, beginning of rout and ruin of the enemy'.

In explaining his decision to march on from Smolensk towards Moscow back in August, Napoleon had told his subordinates, 'this army cannot now stop … One may advance at the head of it, but not stop to go back'. Now, however, in late October, the withdrawal from Maloyaroslavets tore away the veil: the army was in full retreat, perhaps even flight.

What happened in the six or seven weeks following the fateful council of war has gone down in legend. Practically the entire Imperial army in Russia, already seriously depleted, it must be said, by disease, desertion, exhaustion and combat casualties, disintegrated. The stories of men freezing or starving to death and of Cossacks and partisans extracting a bloody revenge on the invaders are well-known, but what is less widely appreciated is the shattering psychological decline of much of the *Grande Armée*. To be sure, cold, hunger and the enemy all played their part in undermining the cohesion and discipline of the retreating forces, but even before these factors took hold, Napoleon's once proud and seemingly indomitable army was beginning to collapse. And it started with the withdrawal from Maloyaroslavets.

Almost all participants who left a record agree that, slow and slightly shambolic as the march from Moscow to Maloyaroslavets was, spirits remained fairly high and there were few major difficulties. As the army began to trudge back north following Eugène's apparent victory, however, it did so, as one eyewitness commented, 'with downcast eyes, as if ashamed and humbled'. In ordering the withdrawal, the Emperor and most of his marshals had given way to fear and doubt. It was as if they no longer believed that the war could be won, as if they now saw themselves not as conquerors but fugitives. That gnawing feeling now began to seep through the army at large, with disastrous consequences.

Before the army even rejoined the Moscow–Smolensk road, discipline and order had begun to break down. More and more men fell out of their units, preferring to take their chances in small bands of stragglers rather then remain under strict military control. And at this stage, it should be stressed, straggling or desertion was very much a choice. The weather had not yet turned bitter, nor were the men starving, nor were the Russians pressing hard on the army as it retreated. What ate away at Napoleon's forces at this point was a psychological cancer, the feeling that the invaders were a spent force, that all they had endured since late June had been for nought, that, stuck hundreds of miles inside hostile territory that offered little succour, their fate might already be sealed. It was not long before the retreating column stretched fully fifty miles due to the sheer number of stragglers who clogged the roads and held up units behind them.

On 29 October, the leading elements of the Imperial army recrossed the Borodino battlefield, followed over the next few days by the rest of the force. One can only imagine the trauma such an experience must have caused. There they saw a 'multitude of dead bodies which, deprived of burial fifty-two days, scarcely retained the human form ... The whole plain was entirely covered with them ... In one place were to be seen garments still red with blood and bones gnawed by dogs and birds of prey'.

From the end of October, hunger began to take a grip on the *Grande Armée*. It affected the horses first, victims of the administrative chaos that had resulted in huge quantities of oats being left behind in Moscow. As increasing numbers of horses began to collapse, more and more booty and other provisions had to be abandoned by the roadside, although at least the unfortunate beasts could be carved up to feed the men (dogs and cats were eaten too when the chance presented itself). Still, food was in ever shorter supply, and this only undermined discipline even further. The situation was perhaps best summed up by Sergeant Bourgogne of the Imperial Guard, a unit not noted for its indiscipline, when he confessed to a friend: 'If I met anyone in the woods with a loaf of bread I would force him to give me half; no, I would kill him and take it all.' Fights among Imperial troops became commonplace over those three basic commodities, food, clothing and shelter, none of which were readily available in the devastated landscape through which the army had been condemned to march.

On 31 October, one week after the battle at Maloyaroslavets, the Emperor and the Guard, marching near the front of the elongated column, reached the town of Viazma, still a hundred miles short of Smolensk. Already, Napoleon knew that his army was in a dreadful state and that all attempts to restore order were having little impact. If only those soldiers still with the colours (a majority, though a shrinking one, of his force) could be persuaded to stay with their units until they reached the Smolensk area, Napoleon remained hopeful that he would then be able to halt the retreat, gather the bulk of his widely dispersed army there, and return to the offensive in 1813. How realistic this ambition was, we shall never know, for now two other factors began to play an increasing part in the retreat from Moscow: the weather and the Russians.

It is a sign of how desperate the Emperor was becoming by the end of October 1812 that he asked his former ambassador in St Petersburg, Armand de Caulaincourt, whether he thought there was any chance of Alexander making peace if Imperial troops were to abandon the properly Russian areas of the Tsar's realm and withdraw to the provinces dominated by non-Russians. 'No more than at Moscow', was Caulaincourt's harshly realistic assessment of the odds. 'The news of our retreat will have made everyone exultant.'

It was learnt in St Petersburg that Moscow had been retaken by Russian forces on 27 October. The city erupted with joy. The great conqueror and his invincible army were in retreat, the Antichrist and his satanic minions were falling back. Alexander ordered a celebration in the capital's largest cathedral, and this time, a sharp contrast to the events of a month earlier, the people on the streets cheered him enthusiastically.

Now it was the Russians' turn to go over to the offensive and a bold plan was swiftly formulated for the complete eradication of the invading army. Thanks to the continuing neutrality of both Sweden and the Ottoman Empire, tens of thousands of troops had been freed from Russia's north-western and south-western frontiers, and had been sent to reinforce the armies of General Wittgenstein in the north and General Tormasov in the south. These strengthened forces were now to press forward towards the Berezina river, which flows north–south roughly 150 miles west of Smolensk, driving back anyone that stood in their way. They would then link up near the town of Borisov, thereby cutting off Napoleon's line of communications back to the Grand Duchy of Warsaw, Prussia and Austria. Meanwhile, Kutuzov, with the largest Russian army, was to harry the main Imperial force as it retreated and eventually form the third side of a trap that would ensnare the enemy deep inside Russian territory and force its capitulation or destruction.

The main problem with the Russian plan, what was to prove in some ways its fatal flaw, was the character and attitude of the man the Tsar had reluctantly appointed commander-in-chief of Russia's armed forces, but that is a story for later. We left the commander-in-chief and his army withdrawing south towards Kaluga following the battle of Maloyaroslavets, and just how far he pulled back was highlighted by the fact that he did not learn that Napoleon had retreated north towards Mozhaisk until 28 October. When it finally arrived, however, the news both surprised and delighted the old field marshal. Immediately, he appreciated its significance. The enemy was withdrawing via a route which had already been stripped of practically everything which might be used to feed, shelter or clothe the Emperor's men. It was a dream come true for the cautious Kutuzov. He would not have to risk a major battle to defeat the retreating invaders; the landscape and, soon, the weather would do it for him. Of course, with an army of 100,000, Kutuzov could not simply sit back and do nothing against the enemy, but he remained determined to avoid a large-scale pitched battle. Instead, his thousands of Cossacks would harry the flanks and rear of the retreating Imperial column, while the peasantry would be encouraged to pick off any small groups of Napoleonic troops who became isolated. The bulk of the regular troops at his disposal, meanwhile, would shadow the retreating enemy column some way to the south – in the event they used the Medyn–Yelna route – so that they could procure supplies from the lands they passed through and act as a barrier between the Imperial army and Russia's more fertile areas. Only the corps of the audacious General Miloradovich, dubbed by many the Russian Murat, would seek to get within striking distance of the enemy, yet even that limited force would prove more than a handful for the retreating invaders.

The more constant menace for Napoleon's men once they had rejoined the Moscow–Smolensk road, though, was that of the Cossacks and partisans. Another of the great disadvantages of returning the way they had come in the summer was that the invaders had to march through areas which had already been devastated and so contained an exceptionally livid peasantry. The local serf population seethed with a rage that they directed against Imperial troops whenever they could. Had the entire retreating army retained its discipline and order, there would have been little the partisans could have done against it, but large parts of it did not. The Russian peasantry became the nemesis of those who fell out of their units on this leg of the retreat, taking a huge toll upon those who straggled too far from the protection of those who retained their discipline. There are no accurate figures, but as Napoleon's forces fell back through Russian territory untold thousands perished at the hands of the serfs. The manner of these unfortunate soldiers' deaths makes grim reading. Some were impaled on stakes, some thrown into vats of boiling water. Others had their eyes pulled out, their limbs severed, nails hammered into their bodies or wooden stakes driven down their throats. Some were burned alive, others buried alive in huge pits. Vicious beatings with hammers, sticks, stones, farm implements, almost anything that came to hand, were commonplace. One eyewitness saw a group of peasants repeatedly dropping men from a height to the ground until their bodies were nothing but pulp. Another band of serfs was seen beating the brains out of a line of prisoners to the tune of a song. It beggars belief that people who did such things could ever be considered heroes, yet too often the Russian peasantry has been seen in this light. Whatever excuses one endeavours to make for them, their conduct was not heroic, but barbaric.

Appalling as the fate of anyone who fell into the hands of the partisans was likely to be, it seems probable that a higher toll was taken on the retreating army by the Cossacks. These irregular horsemen, many thousands strong, operated on the flanks and rear of Napoleon's main force as well as against the many isolated detachments of Imperial troops. As with the partisans, soldiers who remained disciplined and with their units generally had little to fear from the Cossacks, although they could overwhelm small groups of organized men provided the numerical odds were sufficiently heavily stacked in their favour. Their real forte, though, was falling upon bands of stragglers or deserters. Mostly, such unfortunate groups would simply be cut down where they stood, but occasionally they were allowed to surrender. If captured, Imperial soldiers typically faced one of two fates. Often, Cossack (and even some regular army) leaders gave or sold prisoners to the enraged and savage peasantry. Those soldiers fortunate enough to avoid being handed over to the serfs nevertheless generally faced severe mistreatment at the hands of their captors. All were robbed, most were savagely beaten, many were stripped naked, a good number were subsequently killed, while others were given no form of sustenance on their forced marches to detention camps. It is little wonder that no more than one in five of those who fell into the hands of the Cossacks, or of the Russian regular army, in 1812 survived. To be fair, Russian soldiers taken prisoner by the invaders also died in their droves during that autumn and winter of starvation, exposure or disease – indeed a high mortality rate among captives was inevitable in the circumstances – but it was only on the Russian side that deliberate and malicious maltreatment of prisoners was typical and tacitly accepted, even encouraged at times, by those in command. To his credit, the Tsar ordered Kutuzov to ensure that captured Napoleonic troops were treated humanely, but the commander-in-chief simply ignored his complaints. When one learns that even Alexander's own brother, Grand Duke Constantine, was witnessed personally executing a French prisoner, one realises the extent of the problem the Tsar was trying to address.

The heavy losses inflicted by the Cossacks and the partisans notwithstanding, the greatest threat to Napoleon's main force remained Kutuzov's regular army. In its dramatically weakened state, the collection of corps under Bonaparte's immediate control would have been very hard-pressed to resist a coordinated, well-organized and committed Russian onslaught. It was fortunate, therefore, that one did not come. What did happen on 3 November, though, is that General Miloradovich launched an attack aimed at isolating and destroying the Imperial rearguard under Marshal Davout.

Davout was castigated by the Emperor, and has subsequently been criticized by many historians, for losing contact with the corps ahead of him by early November, but this is harsh. As the rearguard, Davout's corps not only faced the greatest degree of Cossack attention, but also had to wade through the sea of stragglers who had fallen out of units ahead of it. This inevitably slowed its rate of advance, and the fact that, as the last part of the army to traverse any area, it found nothing to sustain it from the countryside, meant that it suffered especially seriously from hunger, malnutrition, exhaustion and disease. The figures speak for themselves. In the fortnight since leaving Moscow, Davout's corps had been reduced from 28,000 effectives to just 15,000. This depleted corps Miloradovich, with 20,000 regular cavalry and good infantry support, suddenly attacked and surrounded on 3 November a little way east of the town of Viazma. Had the Russian commander been supported by other parts of Kutuzov's army, there seems little doubt but that Davout's corps would have been forced to surrender, but he was not. Instead, the bald-headed marshal received invaluable support in the form of, first, two divisions of Eugène's corps, sent hastily back by the Viceroy of Italy as soon as he heard of his comrade's predicament, and then one of Ney's divisions. After prolonged fierce fighting, Miloradovich's snare was broken and Davout's corps was able to break through to Viazma and link up once more with the middle section of the retreating army. Even so, it had been a costly day. The invaders lost 6,000 dead and wounded and a further 2,500 prisoners. Russian losses are uncertain, but it is likely, given the trend of battles during the 1812 campaign, that their casualties were not dissimilar.

For several days following the engagement east of Viazma, the pressure on the invaders from Cossacks, partisans and regular troops eased, though the *Grande Armée*'s suffering did not. If anything, in fact, it got worse, for on 4 November the Russian winter arrived with a vengeance. To be sure, the cold at night had been a problem, and even claimed lives, since late October, but it was as nothing compared to the weather that set in for a week or so in early November. The blizzards that blew in then led to almost all contact between Imperial forces and the Russians being temporarily broken off as both sides focused all their efforts on coping with the bitter conditions. The greatest victims of the freezing cold, the snow and the ice were the remaining horses of Napoleon's main army. These beasts, drawn predominantly from central and western Europe, were simply unable to cope with the savage Russian winter and perished in their droves. Those that did not die of cold often fell prey to ice (for which only a small percentage of them had been shod), slipping and breaking limbs. By the time the army finally reached Smolensk from 9 November onwards, the cavalry had been reduced from thousands to hundreds and most of the beasts of burden were also dead.

Of course, General Winter, as the Russians dubbed it, attacked men as well as horses. Soldiers did whatever they could to stave off the elements, but all too often it was not enough. During the day, they marched wrapped in anything they could find, but still frostbite was rife from this time on. At night, they slept huddled close to roaring fires, but even this had its dangers: those who lay down too close to the blaze often developed gangrene in their extremities the following day, when they returned to the bitter cold. Troops unfortunate enough not to find shelter or warm clothing or who slept too far from a source of heat frequently died. One survivor of the campaign claimed that during the night of 8–9 November, the coldest of this particular period of especially bitter weather, as many as 10,000 men and horses perished. Another later wrote of the scenes by the roadside on the last leg of the retreat to Smolensk that 'Never did a battlefield present so much horror'. For many, the savage cold and snow of early November proved the last straw, draining their final reserves of willpower. Hundreds of men simply lost the spirit to go on, collapsed to the ground, and awaited death's embrace.

As Napoleon's hugely depleted main army trudged into Smolensk from 9 November onwards, the savage wintry weather thankfully eased. It remained bitingly cold and snowy, but it was not as remorselessly vicious as it had been for the previous few days. Back in Moscow, the Emperor had envisaged halting the retreat in the Smolensk area and settling down for the winter before resuming the offensive the following spring. Any realistic hope he had of doing that had probably vanished the moment he turned back from Maloyaroslavets and his force started to disintegrate, but the bitter weather of early November, which might not have caught the army still on the march had they not lost so much time in retracing their steps after the battle of 24 October, killed off all thought of stopping the retreat this far east. The invaders' travails were far from over yet.

The Imperial army that trailed into Smolensk over the handful of days after 9 November amounted to no more than 45,000 men and 220 guns. This was less than half the force with which Napoleon had set out from Moscow, but losses had been even heavier than that suggests, for many units that had been detached during the advance were picked up on the way back. Junot's corps near Borodino, several thousand strong, had been the largest such group, but there were others elsewhere, such as at Viazma. It is impossible to ascertain exact losses between Moscow and Smolensk, but they clearly ran to many tens of thousands, especially if one includes the non-combatants who accompanied the army.

Those soldiers fortunate enough to have survived the three-week journey back from Moscow hoped fervently that Smolensk would provide them with the basics they had been lacking, but most were to be cruelly disappointed. Stores accumulated in the city were much lower than expected. Partly this was because of the perennial difficulties of transporting goods forward – plenty of provisions did exist but it had not been possible to bring the bulk of them this far east, a situation only exacerbated by the advent of winter – but also it was the result of troops already stationed in this part of Russia, or those retiring ahead of the main army, depleting the stocks. Still, enough food remained, if husbanded carefully, to provide for Napoleon's 45,000 men for a fortnight, but this was almost all used up or stolen within three days of the first soldiers arriving, as all semblance of discipline was lost in an orgy of looting. Slowly order was restored, but that still left the last units to arrive in Smolensk empty-handed. To add insult to injury, these unlucky troops also struggled to find decent shelter, for the city had been so damaged by the battle in August that there was not enough good, warm accommodation for the whole of even the dramatically reduced force.

The lack of supplies and good shelter was far from the only concern troubling Napoleon at Smolensk. A few days before he had reached the city, the Emperor had received some worrying news from Paris. On 22 October, General Malet, a psychologically disturbed individual who had been receiving attention at a mental institution, had escaped supervision and then, incredibly, tried to seize power by announcing that Napoleon had been killed in Russia and that the Republic would be restored. With the help of members of the Paris garrison, whom he duped, Malet and his gaggle of co-conspirators had succeeded in arresting the Minister of Police and several other important figures before other people in the government had woken up to what was going on and swiftly suppressed the coup. It had all lasted no more than twelve hours and the plotters had soon been executed for their actions, but the Malet conspiracy nevertheless alarmed the Emperor. What would have happened had any really significant figures, like Talleyrand or Fouché, the former foreign and police ministers, been involved in the coup? Was his position as France's ruler less secure than he had thought? For some time, Bonaparte had been thinking of returning to Paris once the army was safely ensconced in defensible winter quarters in order to reassert firm control over the running of the Empire before rejoining his forces in Russia in time for the start of campaigning in 1813. News of the Malet conspiracy convinced him that he had to go back as soon as he sensibly could.

Before he could leave the army, though, Napoleon needed to ensure that it was safe, but achieving that was being rendered harder by events on his northern flank. He had entrusted this theatre in the summer to Marshals Oudinot and St Cyr, who had initially had considerable success in pushing back the Russian force, under General Wittgenstein, confronting them. By mid-autumn, however, the tables had begun to turn and Wittgenstein, with a now considerably strengthened army, had begun to put his foes under severe pressure. On 19 October, the Russians had succeeded in recapturing the key town of Polotsk on the Dvina following a two-day battle against St Cyr's corps, news which the Emperor did not receive until the start of November. (By contrast, Wittgenstein's success was known of in St Petersburg a week earlier and brought about, according to the American ambassador there, a 'change from despondency to confidence' in the capital, a transformation greatly strengthened shortly afterwards when word of Napoleon's retreat from Moscow arrived.) Although St Cyr's men had inflicted twice as many casualties on the Russians as they had themselves sustained, 12,000 to 6,000, the attack had left the marshal so seriously wounded that he had to return to France. It also shattered his corps, and left Oudinot and his 20,000 men little choice but to fall back in the face of superior numbers. To remedy the situation, the Emperor ordered Marshal Victor, who had crossed the Niemen on 3 September at the head of a corps of 34,000 reinforcements and advanced to Smolensk, to lead most of his force north-west to counter the threat from Wittgenstein. Absorbing part of St Cyr's shattered corps (the rest, several thousand strong, withdrew west under the Bavarian General Wrede to screen the approaches to Vilna), Victor joined Oudinot and succeeded in steadying Napoleon's northern flank, though not in time to save the city of Vitebsk, along with its garrison and large stores of supplies, from falling into Russian hands on 7 November.

With most of Victor's men committed to holding off Wittgenstein instead of reinforcing the main Imperial army against the threat posed by Kutuzov's regular troops and Cossacks, the last thing Napoleon needed was the news which reached him soon after he arrived in Smolensk. A division of soldiers, which had been despatched south-east from the city in anticipation of the main army approaching via the more southerly route initially favoured by the Emperor, was surprised on the morning of 9 November by elements of Kutuzov's force. Had he shown more spirit, the division's commander would soon have realized that his position was far from irretrievable and that he could have conducted a fighting withdrawal towards Smolensk. Instead, he tamely surrendered, denying Napoleon at a stroke the support of several thousand desperately needed, relatively fresh troops.

The loss of a fresh division and the fall of Vitebsk made it imperative for the Emperor's army to leave Smolensk as soon as possible. The men needed rest, however, and little could be done until order was restored following the almost total breakdown of discipline that had marked the troops' arrival at the city. It was 12 November, therefore, before the head of the Imperial column set out west on the southern side of the Dnieper and headed for Orsha. Napoleon himself left with the Guard at dawn on the 14th, the corps of Eugène, Davout and Ney, now in charge of the rearguard, scheduled to follow. Victor's and Oudinot's troops, meanwhile, were to fall back slowly in front of Wittgenstein and join the main army between Orsha and the Berezina. Still, the Emperor did not intend to withdraw from the Russian Empire entirely. His plan now was to reach the Belorussian city of Minsk, which was packed with supplies and where he expected to be joined by his southern flank corps of Schwarzenberg and Reynier as well as by a substantial body of Polish cavalry that he believed was being raised in the Grand Duchy.

While the invaders rested and reorganized at Smolensk, Kutuzov's army manoeuvred around the city's southern flank and prepared to launch an attack on the enemy as they renewed their retreat. The blow fell on 15 November, when General Miloradovich struck at a gap that had developed between the Imperial Guard and Prince Eugène's corps near the town of Krasny. The following day, the Viceroy's greatly outnumbered units managed to fight their way past the Russians and rejoin the Emperor, although they suffered heavy casualties in the process. That still left Napoleon's army divided though, with the corps of Davout and Ney in severe danger of being cut off and forced to capitulate. It was almost a rerun of events east of Viazma around a fortnight earlier, only this time Miloradovich received reinforcements from the rest of Kutuzov's army. By 17 November, there were 35,000 Russians blocking the road near Krasny.

With the situation at crisis point, Napoleon finally decided to commit his finest troops, the Imperial Guard, to battle. With 16,000 elite soldiers, the Emperor attacked Miloradovich's force from the west while Davout attempted to break through from the east. The westerly assault took the Russians by surprise, and one eyewitness, the partisan leader Davidov, later recorded that the Guard cut through the enemy 'like a hundred-gun warship through fishing boats'. Miloradovich's men fell back, and for the next few hours, the Emperor's finest men held their ground in order to allow Davout's battered corps to pass through and rejoin the bulk of the army. Despite their initial repulse, the Russians arguably enjoyed a sufficient numerical advantage, at least if Kutuzov sent up more troops, to smash the Imperial Guard, but their commander-in-chief and most of his subordinates were wary of closing with Napoleon's legendary warriors. Instead, Miloradovich held back and contented himself with bombarding the Napoleonic elite with a mass of cannon, a tactic that ensured that although the Guard would be able to retreat from Krasny, it would do so having sustained heavy losses.

The victory at Krasny was a great one in that it was achieved very much against the odds, but it was also a Pyrrhic one. Although he saved several thousand of Davout's troops from capture, the Emperor lost at least as many in doing so, most of them crack Guardsmen. Moreover, Ney's corps had to be abandoned to its fate following the battle, for it was nowhere to be seen as darkness fell on the 17th and Napoleon took the difficult but sensible decision to resume his retreat westwards with the rest of his army lest Kutuzov finally decide to attack in strength the next day.

The withdrawal from Krasny to Orsha can really only be described as a flight. Desperate to reach the crossing over the Dnieper before Kutuzov or Wittgenstein, Napoleon ordered the men to march fourteen hours a day, much of it done in the dark due to the time of year. The sixty or so miles were covered in just two days and, with little intervention from the enemy, the Dnieper was crossed and the town reached on 19 November. At Orsha, the troops found sizeable stocks of rations and other goods, which were distributed with rather more order than at Smolensk. The population from here westwards, mostly non-Russian ethnically, also proved to be, if not exactly friendly to the invaders, at least not fanatically hostile. Napoleon's force could take further comfort from the fact that the corps of Victor and Oudinot, somewhat battered from their running fight against Wittgenstein's army but certainly in much better shape than most of the units that had retreated from Moscow, were now close at hand.

Perhaps the greatest boost to Imperial morale at Orsha, however, came on the evening of 21 November when, against all expectations, Marshal Ney and the remnants of his corps rejoined the army. Ney and his rearguard had not left Smolensk until the 17th, the same day on which the Imperial Guard was engaged at Krasny. This was in accordance with Napoleon's original instructions, but these had been superseded and the marshal had been supposed to leave on the 16th. Somehow, it seems that Ney did not get a copy of the new orders. As Davout had left the city, he had urged his fellow marshal to hasten his retreat, but Ney, pig-headed character that he was, had refused to heed sound advice from a man with whom he had recently quarrelled bitterly over accusations that his troops had engaged in wanton looting and had denied Davout's soldiers much needed supplies. It was this obstinacy more than anything else that resulted in Ney's 6,000 infantry, single squadron of cavalry and twelve cannon being cut off and abandoned.

If Ney was as stubborn, at times asinine, he was also an extremely doughty fighter. Few other commanders, when confronted with a vastly superior force, as he was on 18 November near Krasny, would have responded to Miloradovich's demand for his capitulation with the brusque reply, 'A Marshal never surrenders', and then proceeded to launch a series of attacks in the hope of breaking through the enemy's lines. Almost inevitably, none of Ney's assaults succeeded in breaching the Russian position, but nor had Miloradovich destroyed his corps by nightfall. Ordering his men to light camp fires to make the Russians believe they were staying where they were, the marshal used the cover of darkness to lead his troops northwards towards the Dnieper. Only at dawn on the 19th did the enemy discover his ruse. Miloradovich responded to it by sending a swarm of Cossacks, strengthened by horse artillery, after him. When these horsemen duly caught up with the retreating soldiers later that day, Ney simply ordered his troops to form square and continue to withdraw, even taking up a musket himself. The Dnieper was finally reached at midnight and what was left of the fugitive corps risked life and limb to cross the mighty barrier over its precarious covering of ice. By dawn, a couple of thousand men had made it across, but their guns and some of their comrades had to be abandoned on the southern bank. For much of the 20th, Ney's ragged band made good progress westwards along the north side of the Dnieper, but their Cossack pursuers eventually found a way across and renewed their attacks, mounting some of their guns on sleighs in order to prevent them becoming bogged down in the snow. As the heroic retreat continued into the 21st, with Ney's corps being harried all the time by the Cossacks, it must have begun to seem as if there was no escape after all. Then, in the nick of time, troops from Prince Eugène's corps, responding to a plea for help which Ney had sent ahead with a Polish officer the previous evening, arrived to cover the last stages of the withdrawal to Orsha. It had been a quite remarkable escapade.

Ney rejoined Napoleon's army with just 900 of his men, but that was 900 more than the Emperor had ever expected to see again. Ignoring the fact that but for the marshal's pig-headedness the daring acts of the past few days might not have been necessary, and realizing that the army needed heroes at this stage rather than villains, Bonaparte showered Ney with praise, dubbing him 'the bravest of the brave' and subsequently bestowing upon him the title of Prince of the Moscowa. In all, Napoleon had lost at least 20,000 troops to enemy action in the past week (many thousands of the non-combatants with the army had been killed, wounded or captured as well), but it could have been much worse. The bulk of his main force had survived the hundred or so miles from Smolensk to Orsha. Still, though, safety remained some way off for the Emperor and his soldiers.

The day before he reached Orsha, Napoleon had received a dire piece of news. Two days earlier, on 16 November, Minsk, with its two million rations and piles of other provisions, had fallen to the Russians. Much of its garrison of several thousand largely Polish troops had managed to escape and was falling back north-east towards the Berezina, but 5,000 wounded Imperial troops recuperating within the city's walls had been captured by the enemy. The loss of Minsk meant the invaders now had little choice but to retire at least as far as Vilna, if not across the Niemen entirely. With more than a touch of understatement, the Emperor remarked to Caulaincourt, 'This is beginning to be very serious'.

Bonaparte had hoped that Minsk would be protected by the corps on his southern flank, those of Generals Schwarzenberg and Reynier, but they had clearly failed in this. Partly, this was because by autumn 1812 they were outnumbered in their area of operations east of the Russian border with the Grand Duchy and Austria. Thanks to the Turks' continuing neutrality, General Tormasov's Third Army of the West had been absorbed by the Army of Moldavia from south-east Europe under Admiral Pavel Chichagov. This gave the Russians around 65,000 men by mid-October, whereas Schwarzenberg and Reynier had only 34,000 Austrians and Saxons at their disposal and, as Vienna made perfectly clear to their general, no hope of reinforcement, at least from that quarter. When the Russians advanced, therefore, the Austro-Saxon forces prudently chose to retire, but instead of falling back north-east towards Minsk and the retreating main Imperial army, as the Emperor had hoped and expected them to, Schwarzenberg, who with a much larger corps than Reynier was in a position to dictate strategy, elected to withdraw north-west in the direction of the frontier. Whether, as Napoleon suspected, there was an element of treachery in Schwarzenberg's actions is uncertain. Anyhow, the move opened the way not only to Minsk, but, beyond that, to the town of Borisov on the Berezina, the place where the two Russian flank armies were scheduled to meet to cut off the Emperor's route out of Russia. Despite the Russians' numerical advantage, there seems little reason to doubt that, with more than 30,000 men, Schwarzenberg could have held the perfectly defensible city of Minsk for several weeks at least, so one can easily imagine Chichagov's joy at the golden opportunity with which he had been presented. Detaching 27,000 troops under General Sacken to shadow the retreating Austrians and Saxons, the admiral swiftly advanced on and captured the valuable prize with the rest of his force.

As soon as he heard that Minsk had fallen, Napoleon focused all his attention upon Borisov, the only major crossing point along the upper stretches of the Berezina. If Chichagov reached the area first, he might destroy the bridge over the river, leaving the main Imperial army and the northern flank corps of Oudinot and Victor trapped between the three Russian armies converging upon them. On 19 November, therefore, he ordered Oudinot, whose corps was closest to Borisov, to march with all haste to the key town, while Victor was instructed to close up with the main army as it retreated west towards the Berezina. Until Oudinot arrived, the only troops the Emperor would have to protect the vital Borisov crossing were the Polish division of General Dombrowski, which had been detached from Poniatowski's now all but non-existent corps back in the summer. They were good soldiers, but were unlikely to prove a match for Chichagov's far larger army.

It was thus a race to the Berezina, and on 21 November, the same day that Ney and the remnants of his corps rejoined the main Imperial army, the Russians won it. Three divisions, the spearhead of Chichagov's force, fell upon Dombrowski's troops on the western bank of the Berezina and, despite the Poles putting up stern resistance in a long, hard fight, succeeded in pushing them back across the river and capturing Borisov. Two days later, on the afternoon of the 23rd, Oudinot's corps fell upon elements of Chichagov's army east of the town, scattered them and even managed to recapture the settlement, but the Russians were able to withdraw to the western bank of the Berezina, destroying the crucial bridge over the river as they went.

In most years, the loss of the only bridge over the upper Berezina would not have been the calamity it was for Napoleon's army in 1812, for the river would typically have been sufficiently frozen in late November for cavalry and even guns to cross almost anywhere. In a stroke of extreme bad luck, however, this year an unusual thaw suddenly set in in this part of Russia. This not only melted the Berezina's surface but, in so doing, caused the river to burst its banks and thus present an even more formidable obstacle to the Imperial troops' safe retreat.

The Emperor's position now seemed truly grim. He had resumed the retreat from Orsha with 25,000 effectives, 110 guns and a militarily useless horde of 40,000 stragglers, camp followers and other civilians. Even with the addition of Victor's and Oudinot's corps, he remained at a serious numerical disadvantage to the combined force of the three Russian armies closing on him from the west, north and east. His only hope was to find some way out of the trap, but how and where?

The obvious escape route was to head south, but that would mean abandoning the city of Vilna, which Napoleon still hoped to retain as an advanced base over the winter, and, assuming the Russians could be evaded, heading towards the border of an unreliable ally (Austria) rather than a reliable one (the Grand Duchy of Warsaw). This would put Vienna in potentially an altogether too powerful position for comfort (what if the Austrians suddenly changed sides?) and so such a move was discounted. That only seemed to leave one option: for the army to head north and try to fight its way past Wittgenstein. Given Wittgenstein's success over the past few weeks, however, this was not an especially pleasant prospect. He would doubtless do all he could to slow the Imperial advance while Kutuzov and Chichagov closed from behind to overwhelm Napoleon's forces. What the Emperor really wanted, and why he had been so keen to hold the crossing at Borisov, was to place a barrier between his army and those of Wittgenstein and Kutuzov. If only he could get across the Berezina, he was confident he could deal with Chichagov without too much difficulty and then reach the relative safety of Vilna or, if necessary, the Niemen. With the bridge at Borisov destroyed, however, escape via this route did not seem feasible.

Then, on 24 November, Napoleon was given an unexpected but extremely welcome glimmer of hope that his preferred course of action might still just be possible. A messenger arrived in the Imperial camp from Vilna with a story of how he had crossed the Berezina via a ford near the village of Studienka, around a dozen miles north of Borisov. It was only a small ford, unsuitable for getting the whole army across, but it would allow a limited force to be placed on the western bank to act as a bridgehead while Imperial engineers constructed pontoon bridges over the river.

Two problems remained, however. First, Chichagov had deployed his men in an extended line along the Berezina's western bank running from opposite Studienka in the north to the town of Usha in the south, some twenty-five miles past Borisov, for the express purpose of countering any attempt by the enemy to effect a crossing. As soon as he discovered where the invaders were attempting to cross, he would concentrate his force and prevent it. Secondly, in his desperation to get his forces marching as quickly as possible, Napoleon had issued a draconian order at Orsha that anything that might slow the army's rate of march and that was not utterly essential should be destroyed. In the spree of destruction that followed, the army's pontoon bridging equipment had been inadvertently demolished.

While the first of these difficulties might be resolved by making diversionary thrusts to the south of Borisov to draw Chichagov's men away from Studienka, the second seemed more intractable. Sufficient wood for a couple of bridges might be obtained by knocking down the dwellings of Studienka and other nearby villages, but the engineers would still need forges, tools and nails to construct pontoons capable of conveying an army to the other side of a river. It was a stroke of great fortune, therefore, and of great foresight on his part, that General Jean-Baptiste Eblé, the man in charge of the *Grande Armée*'s bridging operations, had salvaged from the destruction at Orsha a pair of field forges, charcoal to fuel them, and a supply of tools and nails. The crossing of the Berezina was feasible.

On 25 November, Napoleon duly arranged for diversionary thrusts to be made some way south of Borisov. The Russian response delighted him. Chichagov drew his entire force south to counter them. Once the enemy had disappeared from opposite Studienka, the invaders began to play their hand. A small advance guard was sent across the river via the ford and established a flimsy bridgehead. Then, at dusk, Eblé and his 400 mostly Dutch pontoneers began the construction of two makeshift bridges to span the hundred yards that separated the Berezina's two banks.

Working through the night, the Imperial sappers endured the freezing cold of the water as well as strong currents to complete their task. Many of them died of exposure or drowning, but their surviving comrades laboured on stoically. (Eblé himself would survive the crossing and even make it out of Russia only to die tragically of disease in East Prussia before the year was out.) By 1 p.m. on the 26th, the first of the two bridges, the infantry bridge, had been completed and

Oudinot's corps, supported by Dombrowski's division, crossed to form a serious front should Chichagov realize his error and return north in force. By 3 p.m., the second bridge, this one capable of bearing artillery, was finished and Oudinot's guns, as well as those of the Imperial Guard, were sent across to establish a formidable battery to help defend the vital crossing. As darkness fell, there was still, thankfully, no sign of any of the three Russian armies.

That changed the next day. Chichagov had finally realized his error in concentrating his army south of Borisov late on 26 November and promptly began to march north. On the morning of the 27th, advance elements of his force came into contact with Oudinot's corps and a running fight ensued which lasted the rest of the day. Slowly, the Imperial units drew back under the increasing Russian pressure, but they held firm and the crossing never came under serious threat.

Wittgenstein also began to make his presence felt on the 27th, attacking the corps of Victor, which had been ordered to keep his army at bay on the eastern bank. Again, weight of numbers compelled the Imperial troops to conduct a fighting withdrawal, but like Oudinot's corps on the western side of the river, Victor's men remained solid in the face of adversity and shielded the crossing effectively.

Meanwhile, throughout 27 November, the Imperial army continued to cross the Berezina via the makeshift bridges. Repairs had to be made frequently to the structures, often by sappers standing up to their necks in icy water, but they generally held well, at least until 4 p.m., when a section of the larger, artillery bridge collapsed. Eblé's amazing troops would prove able to mend the damage within a few hours, but at the moment the timbers broke, plunging scores of unfortunates into the freezing river below where many of them drowned, it seemed to the tens of thousands of stragglers and camp followers still on the eastern bank that it was only a matter of time before the other pontoon collapsed too, leaving them stranded. There consequently followed a stampede for the smaller bridge in which hundreds were trampled to death or pushed from the structure into the Berezina. Remarkably, the infantry pontoon did not break under the strain, and as order was slowly restored and the stragglers and camp followers were assured that the other bridge would be repaired, the soldiers of Eugène and Davout were able, once they had cleared a way through the corpses that now littered the approach to the crossing, to make it over to the western bank, leaving Victor's corps the only organized body on the eastern side of the river (the Emperor and the Guard had crossed around lunchtime).

Only a few thousand non-combatants had been able or had been allowed to cross the Berezina to this point, but once Davout's and Eugène's men were safely across, General Eblé did his best to try to persuade the horde of stragglers and camp followers to make their way over the bridges. Now that darkness had fallen, and with it the temperature, however, this mass of humanity chose instead to remain huddled around their fires, believing that they would be able to cross more safely the next day.

Next morning, the 28th, Chichagov renewed his attack on the western bank. Again Oudinot's and Dombrowski's men put up sterling resistance, aided by the remaining men of Ney's corps. The Russian assault was better coordinated than on the previous day, though, and when Oudinot was injured and had to retire, the Imperial line almost buckled until Ney stepped into the breach and took overall responsibility for dealing with the threat. The 'bravest of the brave' successfully steadied the eclectic mix of Polish, French, Swiss, Croat, Italian, Dutch and Portuguese troops under his command, and when Napoleon committed what was left of the army's heavy cavalry (now hundreds rather than thousands strong) to a bold charge, it not only accounted for around 2,000 Russians but persuaded Chichagov to break off his attacks for the rest of the day.

On the eastern bank on 28 November, meanwhile, Marshal Victor faced an even more menacing attack from the 30,000 strong army of General Wittgenstein. Launching a powerful, well-orchestrated attack at 8 a.m., the Russian commander drove his foes relentlessly back towards the river. Victor's line held as it withdrew, but he was not helped by the fact that one of his divisions, which comprised 4,000 infantry and 500 cavalry and had been marching to join the others overnight, had got lost, taken the wrong road, and ended up walking straight into the heart of Wittgenstein's army, where it promptly surrendered. Napoleon was furious when he heard of the blunder and was compelled to send some units back across the Berezina to strengthen the position on the eastern bank.

With the pressure from Wittgenstein mounting, it was touch and go whether Victor would be able to hold out until darkness descended and he could withdraw safely under its cover. Events reached crisis point around midday, when the Russians began to outflank the marshal's left and established a battery of guns within range of the vital bridges. As they opened fire on the structures, which were crowded with stragglers trying to make it to the western bank, the second major panic within two days erupted. Again, hordes of non-combatants rushed the pontoons and hundreds more died by being trampled or drowned, many when a section of the artillery bridge, weakened by enemy fire, collapsed under the weight of people trying to cross. The situation was only salvaged when Napoleon established a large battery on the western bank which bombarded the Russian troops trying to outflank Victor and forced them to withdraw their guns out of range of the bridges.

Victor's ordeal was not yet over, however, for by now the advance guard of Kutuzov's army, the corps of General Miloradovich, had joined Wittgenstein in attacking the marshal's battered corps. The numerical odds were something like five to one in the Russians' favour, yet, with their backs to the wall and fighting literally for their lives, Victor's predominantly German and Polish soldiers managed to hold the enemy off until nightfall. At 9 p.m., he finally got the order to withdraw to the western bank, a move which was completed around 1 a.m. on the 29th. Once again, General Eblé endeavoured to persuade the many thousands of non-combatants still on the eastern bank to cross, but still they were unwilling to leave the warmth of their fires and go over while it was dark.

The following morning, Eblé delayed torching the bridges in the vain hope of getting as many of the stragglers and camp followers across as possible, but finally he could wait no longer. As they saw their avenue of escape go up in flames, the mob left on the eastern side of the Berezina panicked for a third time in three days. Again there was a mad rush for the bridges and again hundreds died, either trampled to death, drowned or consumed by fire, until both structures collapsed into the Berezina's icy waters. No one knows exactly how many perished in their frantic attempts to cross the river, but it was choked with corpses for weeks to come.

Whilst it would be absurd to refer to those non-combatants who died in trying to get to the Berezina's western bank as the lucky ones, the fate which awaited the many thousands of stragglers and camp followers left on the eastern side of the river was scarcely better. In a shameful act of brutality, Cossacks butchered many of these people in cold blood. Those who survived became prisoners, but with winter having arrived and food in short supply, almost all died of exposure or starvation over the coming days and weeks. In all, at least 30,000 stragglers or civilians perished either in trying to cross the Berezina or as a result of being stranded on its eastern bank.

Losses among combatants in late November were heavy too. The Russians lost upwards of 10,000 killed and many more wounded, while the invaders sustained casualties of around 20,000, the bulk of them from the corps of Oudinot and Victor, whose extraordinary courage and fortitude resulted in the loss of over half their effective strength but saved the army from complete disaster.

In the wake of the Berezina crossing, Napoleon was left with a force of around 40,000 soldiers and 200 guns, while some 10–15,000 stragglers and civilians had also made it to the river's western bank. Although losses had been horrendous, it was nonetheless a tremendous achievement in extremely difficult and unpropitious circumstances to get so many out of a deadly trap.

The question remains, however, whether, even allowing for the bravery and magnificent efforts of Bonaparte's men, the Russians ought not to have brought about the utter destruction of the Emperor's force on the banks of the Berezina. Certainly, Tsar Alexander was bitterly disappointed that his armies did not fulfil the overall strategy formulated in St Petersburg and force Napoleon to capitulate with his force east of the Berezina. In his mind, there was only one culprit for the Russian failure; Kutuzov. Unquestionably, the commander-in-chief's pursuit of the Imperial army throughout the retreat, but particularly after Krasny, might have been more dynamic. Only Miloradovich's corps, of the regular forces under Kutuzov's immediate command, conducted operations with anything approaching vigour, and it is revealing that his were the only troops from the old field marshal's army to engage the enemy at the Berezina (and then only on part of one day).

Why, though, did Kutuzov's troops move so apparently sluggishly? After all, they marched through more fertile lands than Napoleon's men, at least as far as Smolensk, and so were better fed than the enemy. They were also more familiar with the climate and terrain, had better winter clothing than the invaders, were not operating in hostile country, were not slowed by swarms of Cossacks on their flanks and rear, and had a lot more cavalry than their adversaries. By these measures, it should not have been too difficult for Kutuzov's army to have outpaced the retreating Imperial forces, yet, by and large, it did not. Indeed, at times, the commander-in-chief seemed to move at a veritable snail's pace, particularly in advancing from Krasny towards the Berezina, which he and the bulk of his army only reached two days after the bridges over the river had been destroyed.

Several reasons have been suggested to account for Kutuzov's slowness. His undoubted natural tendency towards laziness is one, and it has often been argued that he simply did not stir himself enough to ensure that the army he led did all it could to bring about the ensnarement and capitulation of the enemy. More flatteringly, it has been contended by the Russian commander-in-chief's supporters that he was following a cunning and skilful plan in the last few months of 1812. According to this theory, Kutuzov knew that the bulk of the Imperial army would be destroyed by a combination of the weather, starvation, disease, the Cossacks and the partisans, and so contented himself with shadowing the enemy, unwilling to risk unnecessary losses to his army either from marching them too hard or committing them to engagements against what was still, as battles like Maloyaroslavets and Krasny showed, a formidable adversary. If Kutuzov was indeed trying to minimize casualties to his own side, however, he was not terribly successful. By mid-November, at least 30,000 of the 90,000 or so regular troops with which he had set out from Tarutino a month earlier had died, while a similar number had either deserted or become stragglers. Given that his own army was so reduced and battered, it is likely that part of the reason for Kutuzov's slowness, at least in advancing towards the Berezina, was that he was scared of fighting another major battle against the invaders and their leader. Indeed, all three Russian commanders, Wittgenstein and Chichagov as well as Kutuzov, appear to have been reluctant to engage the main Imperial force under Napoleon. They all overestimated the effective strength of the Imperial army; the Emperor's reputation in battle remained fearsome, and we have already seen how even the bold Miloradovich was loath to close with the Imperial Guard.

The most interesting interpretation of Kutuzov's failure to ensnare and force the capitulation of the Emperor and his army, though, is that, unlike the Tsar, the old field marshal did not want to destroy Napoleon and his forces entirely, merely to weaken them considerably and drive them from Russian soil. It is intriguing to note that, as well as advancing painfully slowly towards the Berezina himself, the commander-in-chief sent instructions to both Wittgenstein and Chichagov in November 1812 that proved deleterious to their efforts to prevent the Imperial army from escaping. Wittgenstein slowed his march towards the Berezina after Kutuzov warned him that, now Minsk had fallen, Napoleon would probably seek to head north-west from Orsha instead of west towards the river. Chichagov, meanwhile, was ordered to be especially careful to prevent the enemy from moving south towards the Ukraine, an instruction which at least partly explains why the admiral was so badly duped by the invaders' diversionary moves on the 25th. Of course, both warnings, contradictory as they are, do not necessarily prove that Kutuzov was actively trying to facilitate Napoleon's escape. It does seem, however, that the old field marshal was more than a little unsure of the wisdom of crushing the Imperial forces entirely. He is intriguingly recorded as having commented in late 1812: 'I am by no means sure that the total destruction of the Emperor Napoleon and his army would be such a benefit to the world. His succession would not fall to Russia or any other continental power, but to that which already commands the sea [Britain] and whose domination would then be intolerable.' It would prove a prophetic statement.

Whatever the reason for Kutuzov's failure to engage the retreating enemy more effectively and bring about the complete capitulation or destruction of Bonaparte and his forces, the fact remains that, by the end of November 1812, Imperial strength in Russia had fallen from hundreds of thousands to tens of thousands. Probably no more than a quarter of the total number of soldiers who had crossed the Niemen during the campaign remained with their units. Already, Napoleon's losses had become catastrophic, but in some ways the worst leg of the retreat was still to come.

The vicious cold snap that had suddenly hit the Emperor's forces in early November and killed untold thousands of men and horses had thankfully been relatively short-lived. Since then, the weather had certainly been wintry and had continued to claim lives, albeit if at a less dramatic rate, but it had not been as bitter as during those final days of the march to Smolensk. Indeed, there had even been something of a thaw in mid- to late November which, as we have seen, unfroze the Berezina and almost trapped Napoleon and his army. In early December, however, as those Imperial troops who had made it across the river alive retreated west towards their new destination, Vilna, the Russian winter turned remorselessly savage once more.

Temperatures suddenly plummeted and remained bitterly cold during both day and night. The constant glacial chill made even the most basic of functions difficult. Men could barely speak, for example, as vocal cords froze, shrouding this leg of the retreat in an unsettling quiet. As one survivor later wrote, 'The dull, monotonous sound of our footsteps, the crunching of the snow and the faint groans of the dying were all that interrupted this vast and lugubrious taciturnity.' The relentless cold also made many men dizzy, almost as if they were drunk. Those that fell down usually did not get up again. If the unyielding icy cold now became the biggest killer, the next most frequent cause of death in early December was the result of efforts to stave off the polar chill. At night, men built fires and huddled round them, often sitting so close that they were scorched by the flames. Yet the heavenly relief of warmth came with an even higher price than singed faces or burnt hands, for gangrene became rife, claiming the lives of thousands.

Nor should we forget the horses' suffering. The few thousand horses remaining with the army, a fraction of the tens of thousands which had crossed the Niemen that year, were all but wiped out by this second vicious cold snap. It is a sign of how desperate things became that almost all officers who had somehow managed to keep their mounts alive to this point were ordered to give them up so that four companies of 160 men each could be formed to provide the army with at least a skeletal cavalry arm.

The positive side of the death of so many horses was that the carcases provided food, but, with the rations obtained in Smolensk and Orsha having long since been consumed, and with very meagre pickings to be had from the wintry landscape, it was almost inevitable that cannibalism would rear its ugly head on this final stage of the retreat. No one knows for sure how widespread it became, but it seems grimly logical to assume that if people who were starving could not get horse flesh, many must have indulged in the ultimate taboo in order to stave off the Reaper.

Given the horrendous problems of cold and hunger that Napoleon's forces faced in early December, it was fortunate that the pressure from the enemy eased. The Russians did follow them west of the Berezina, the armies of Wittgenstein and Kutuzov helped by the refreezing of the river, but did not really pursue them, largely because the dire climatic conditions caused them severe difficulties as well. Several thousand Cossacks, though, did attempt to catch up with and attack the retreating invaders, largely in the hope of claiming any booty they still carried, and Imperial forces had to fight a fairly sharp action near the town of Molodetchno on 3 December. That night, even more alarmingly (for Napoleon himself at any rate), a group of Cossacks, several hundred strong, nearly captured the Emperor as he rested at a country house. As they approached his temporary base, however, many fell through the ice covering a river, thereby disrupting their attack and losing the element of surprise.

Two days later, Imperial headquarters was at the town of Smorgoni, around forty miles south-east of Vilna and less than a hundred miles from the frontier. That evening Napoleon called a conference with his chief subordinates. With some distance put between the retreating army and the main Russian forces, and with richly stocked Vilna and the Niemen now close at hand, the Emperor had decided that it was time for him to return to Paris. Bonaparte haters have often lambasted him for 'abandoning' his army, the second such time he had done so (the first was in Egypt) as they love to comment, but as in 1799, Napoleon had good cause to head for France. There was no hope of disguising the fact that he and his forces had suffered a very heavy defeat in Russia and the Emperor's presence in Paris would do much to help quell alarm as news of the disaster spread. Bonaparte himself was also best able to raise new armies to counter any threat to France or the Empire in 1813, and his presence at the heart of his Europe-wide domain might make reluctant allies like Austria and Prussia think twice before deciding to take up arms against him once more. Bad news from Spain was also a factor. The latest information Napoleon had was that Wellington was besieging the key northern Spanish city of Burgos. If that fell, the way to the Pyrenees would be open and an invasion of southern France would become a distinct possibility.* There was a nascent sense in late 1812 that the future of the Napoleonic Empire was in the balance and, as the Emperor explained to Caulaincourt, 'In the existing state of affairs, I can only maintain my grip on Europe from the Tuileries'.

For these reasons, and because they realized that Napoleon's continuing presence with the army was unlikely to make much difference to its fate at this stage, his chief subordinates agreed that it was sensible for the Emperor to return to France as soon as possible. There was less accord over his choice of man to succeed him in overall command of Imperial forces in Russia; Marshal Murat. In many ways the best figure to have taken over from the Emperor would have been Marshal Davout, easily the most militarily accomplished of those available and certainly the best able to operate in an independent role, but he was a notoriously prickly character who had argued bitterly with too many of the men he would have had to command, including Murat and Ney. Prince Eugène was another possible candidate and was initially favoured by Napoleon, but the Emperor soon realized that the young Viceroy would struggle to gain the unquestioning loyalty of many of the fractious marshals and generals. That still left the 'the bravest of the brave', but courageous as Ney was and much as he was the current darling of the army after his exploits between Smolensk and Orsha, there were doubts

---

* In fact, Wellington had been forced by early December to retreat all the way back to the Portuguese border after French forces in the Peninsula had reorganized and cooperated against the British threat, but Napoleon did not learn this until later.

over his ability to operate effectively as a commander-in-chief without direct supervision. The same could probably have been said about Napoleon's choice, Murat, but the Emperor seems, rather naïvely, to have hoped that his status as King of Naples would give him the authority necessary for him to accomplish the task of handling the remaining leg of the retreat successfully.

Napoleon left Smorgoni at 10 p.m. on 5 December with a handful of companions and a small Polish cavalry escort. He travelled incognito, pretending to be Caulaincourt's secretary. Two days later, he crossed the Niemen not far from where he had entered Russia back in late June, and on the 10th he reached Warsaw. He took time there to upbraid his ambassador extraordinary, the Abbé de Pradt, for failing to raise more troops in the Grand Duchy, especially the cavalry that he had hoped would reinforce his retreating army near Minsk. He also met a group of Polish ministers and urged them to raise more units and prepare to defend the Grand Duchy, pledging that he would return at the head of a new army in the spring. On 12 December, the Emperor stayed in Posen, and forty-eight hours later he was in Dresden, capital of Saxony. From there, he despatched two letters, one to Emperor Francis of Austria, the other to King Frederick William of Prussia. The message was simple and the threat implicit. Napoleon expected both men to maintain their alliances with France. Finally, just before midnight on the 18th, Bonaparte arrived back at the Tuileries palace in the heart of Paris.

His return came none too soon, for two days earlier, a bulletin he had written shortly before he had left the army had been published in the capital. It was a more honest account of the recent campaign than some the Emperor had written in his career, although it understandably dwelt more on the successes the army had enjoyed than on its sufferings and reverses. Nonetheless, the fact that the invasion had ended in disaster could not be hidden entirely and it is interesting that Napoleon chose to end the bulletin with the initially odd-seeming remark, 'His Majesty's health has never been better'. Not a callous, egocentric comment as Bonaparte haters have often tried to depict it, this was a strongly political statement intended to counter rumours that he had been killed, captured or lost his mind, and to remind those who might think about acting against him both in France and the rest of Europe that the Emperor was alive, well and remained a force to be reckoned with. Certainly, when he suddenly and unexpectedly returned to Paris a week before Christmas, it caused a great stir and did much to counteract talk of defeatism or political change.

Back in Russia meanwhile, the army struggled on towards Vilna, reaching the city on 8 December. The Emperor's departure had inevitably led to some perturbation and grumbling among the troops, but the fact is that very few soldiers of any nationality seem to have developed real animosity towards Napoleon at any stage of the awful retreat. Indeed, most appear to have continued to idolize him. Even men captured by the Russians generally remained strikingly loyal. For example, very few German prisoners volunteered to join the German Legion the Russians set up to fight Napoleon, even though it would have got them out of the terrible conditions of their captivity. On the contrary, the majority of those German captives still alive in August 1813 celebrated the Emperor's birthday in their Russian detention camps. It can, and has, been argued that Napoleon did not deserve such remarkable loyalty, but this is largely based on the contention that he was indifferent to the suffering and death of his troops. He was not. As he confided to General Rapp at one particularly tough part of the retreat, 'Those poor soldiers make my heart bleed, yet I can do nothing for them'. In fact, he did what he could, and his leadership and military skill were invaluable to the army at several points during late 1812, particularly at Krasny and in crossing the Berezina. True, some, perhaps most, of the responsibility for the suffering of the *Grande Armée* in Russia must ultimately be laid at Napoleon's door, but, as his troops realized, the errors he made, such as lingering too long in Moscow or turning back from Maloyaroslavets, were genuine miscalculations, not careless decisions made with no concern for the consequences for his men. If the Emperoro could at times seem unmoved by the human tragedy of his campaigns, that was more a reflection of his position than his personality. As a war leader, he simply could not give way to open outpourings of grief or remorse. Few, if any, great war leaders have.

Fewer than 15,000 of the troops who had made it across the Berezina remained with their units by the time they reached Vilna. Many of their comrades had died, others had joined the ever-growing swarm of stragglers. To those who made it to Vilna, whether with the colours or not, the city seemed like something out of a dream. Its warehouses were packed with four million rations of biscuit and almost as many of meat. There was clothing in abundance as well as thousands of gallons of drink. The armouries were well stocked too, though that was of little concern to the vast majority. Had the army been in better shape, it is not inconceivable that, with such bountiful supplies, a surfeit of good accommodation available, and the city walls in a good state of repair, Vilna might have withstood a siege at least until the spring.

Sensibly, the Emperor had left the final decision whether to stop the retreat there or continue over the Niemen to the commanders who remained with the army, although he hoped that the city might yet be held. What happened as Imperial forces reached Vilna, though, ruled out any possibility of any prolonged defence of the place being mounted. There was a breakdown of discipline and order comparable only to that which had occurred at Smolensk a month earlier. General van Hogendorp, the Dutch governor of the city, had made detailed and effective arrangements for the army's arrival, including allocating shelter and distributing food, but these arrangements were simply ignored. Instead, hundreds died in a massive crush at the city gates as desperate men, mindful of what had happened at Smolensk, rushed to get to Vilna's bounty first, an especially senseless waste of life given that there was more than enough to go around. Those frozen and famished soldiers who escaped the crush took what they wanted from warehouses, a good number glutting themselves so severely on food and drink that they subsequently collapsed in the streets and died of exposure. Many officers, all thought of duty and responsibility gone, joined the soldiers under their command in an anarchic free-for-all, greatly complicating efforts to restore order. Sorrowfully, Marshal Berthier, the Emperor's emotional chief of staff, who had been close to tears at not being chosen to accompany his master back to Paris, felt compelled to write to Napoleon to inform him of the situation. 'Sire, I must tell you the whole truth,' he wrote. 'The army is in a complete state of chaos.'

Even the anarchy that prevailed in Vilna did not really justify Murat's response to the sudden approach of a small force of Cossacks on 9 December, though. The King of Naples, his nerve broken by the trauma of the retreat, simply panicked. Rather than organizing what troops remained with their units to chase the enemy off, or at least to prepare to meet any possible attack, he issued hurried orders for the retreat to resume next day. As a result, huge stocks of supplies, as well as 30,000 sick and wounded men convalescing in the city, soon fell into Russian hands for want of time to organize their evacuation. Almost all the captured invalids subsequently died, many as a result of Cossack brutality, others through denial of food or care, or from exposure as they were thrown onto the streets. It took weeks to clear the city of dead bodies and hundreds of labourers to dig huge ditches to bury them.

A small Imperial army left Vilna in good order on 10 December, made up of several thousand soldiers from the main army who had stayed with their units, a similar number from the city's garrison, and the disciplined remnants of that part of St Cyr's corps which had fallen back west following the defeat at Polotsk in October. They were accompanied by a horde of stragglers and other non-combatants. All thoughts were now focused fixedly on survival and escape from Russia, although that did not prevent a chaotic rush from developing when the wagon carrying the army's treasury had to be abandoned at the bottom of a steep, icy hill. Scores of people died in the ensuing riot.

The hero of this final stage of the long, ghastly retreat was Marshal Ney. It was he who commanded the rearguard, beating off Cossack attacks near Kovno on 13–14 December, and he that effectively took over responsibility for what remained of the army in the absence of any real leadership on the part of Murat. Ney was even allegedly the last Frenchman to leave Russian soil on the 14th. That any Imperial soldiers from Napoleon's main army made it back over the Niemen still with their colours was largely down to the fiery, flame-haired Alsatian.

So the terrible retreat from Russia ended. Although the coming months would see further long withdrawals, they would be as nothing compared to the ordeal of late 1812. Never again would Imperial troops experience such glacial cold or such abject hunger. Never again would a force commanded by the Emperor come so close to complete and utter destruction. Never before had an army suffered such staggering losses. And never before had an empire as great as Napoleon's collapsed as quickly as would his over the next sixteen months.

Field Marshal Kutuzov informed the Tsar on 22 December that 'the war has finished with the complete destruction of the enemy'. This was not quite true, but nor was it entirely misleading. It is impossible to be precise, but it seems that, in all, perhaps 550,000 imperial troops crossed the Niemen in 1812, the great majority in late June. Of these, some 85,000 belonged to corps which made up the flank armies of Macdonald and of Schwarzenberg and Reynier. Having beaten off the Russian force under General Sacken, the latter of these had retired by mid-December to Austria, Reynier continuing the retreat with the remnant of his Saxon corps to his troops' homeland. Some 20,000 Austrians survived, only a few thousand Saxons. In the north, Macdonald began to fall back from the port city of Riga in mid-December, but the Russian force which followed him succeeded in isolating the Prussian bulk of his command on Christmas Day. Five days later, the Prussian commander, General Yorck, agreed to the Convention of Tauroggen, by which he and his 17,000 surviving soldiers became neutrals. The rest of Macdonald corps, meanwhile, continued their south-westwards march towards Yorck's fatherland. Around 9,000 reached it safely in early January.

Thus only about 50,000, or just under sixty per cent, of the soldiers of the flank armies are known to have survived the 1812 campaign, the bulk of them either Austrians or Prussians whose services it was highly unlikely Napoleon would be able to call upon again. A casualty rate in excess of forty per cent can only be considered very heavy, but it pales in comparison with the losses endured by the main body of troops which operated between the two flanking armies. From this central group, it seems that just 25,000 men recrossed the Niemen in December 1812, the majority of them as stragglers rather than with their units. Only a few thousand had been all the way to Moscow and back. The bulk had joined the main army's retreat west of the Dnieper, many west of the Berezina.

In all, then, the *Grande Armée* appears to have lost something in the region of 475,000 soldiers in Russia, or around eighty-five per cent of those that crossed the Niemen. Thankfully, not all of those 475,000 died. Some 30,000 troops are known to have left Russia early in the campaign either as sick, wounded or to form cadres for new units in western Europe. A great many of the 50,000 or so men who deserted from the army in the first weeks of the campaign probably managed to get back across the Niemen too. Then there were at least a few thousand deserters who ended up settling in the Tsar's western provinces. Indeed, there remain inhabitants of these areas today with French and other non-Slavic surnames that date from 1812. Finally, around 20,000 of the maybe 100,000 troops taken prisoner by the Russians eventually returned home in 1814 following the end of hostilities in Europe.

The likelihood nevertheless remains that something not far short of 400,000 Imperial soldiers perished in Russia. They succumbed to a variety of factors. There are no totally reliable figures for causes of death in Russia, but it is clear that tens of thousands of Imperial troops died as a direct result of clashes with the Russian armies, either on the battlefield or from their wounds shortly afterwards. A quick run through of the casualty figures for the main engagements of the campaign, however, makes it clear that battle can only have accounted for a relatively limited portion of total deaths (probably around a quarter of total casualties). The bulk of those who perished in Russia, which includes the great majority of those who were captured by Russian forces, were victims of a variety of other causes, including disease, starvation, the weather, the Cossacks and partisan atrocities. Exactly how many men died as a result of each is impossible to gauge accurately, especially as there is no way of knowing the ultimate fate of most of the vast number of troops who deserted or straggled at various points during the campaign but there can be little doubt that each of the five main factors listed above accounted for a sizeable portion of total deaths.

In addition to the military losses, the bulk of the host of civilians who accompanied the *Grande Armée* during the campaign also perished in Russia. It really is anyone's guess exactly how many people died, but it certainly ran to several tens of thousands.

As well as being an immense human tragedy, the sheer scale of Imperial losses in Russia massively weakened Napoleon's military power. Somehow, he would manage over the next sixteen months to find tens of thousands of new troops to replace at least partially those lost in 1812, but these raw recruits were not a match individually for the many thousands of veteran soldiers who never returned from Alexander's realm. Similarly, although Imperial manufacturers would prove capable of replacing the more than a thousand cannon lost in Russia, it was impossible suddenly to conjure up equally skilled replacements for the thousands of experienced gunners who had died. It was the cavalry, though, that was worst hit. As well as tens of thousands of veteran horsemen dying, practically every one of the 200,000 horses which crossed the Niemen in 1812 perished. Fewer than half these animals were cavalry mounts (the majority were beasts of burden), but it was these steeds that it would prove most difficult to replace. The Imperial cavalry arm would never be more than a poor shadow of its former self after the disastrous Russian campaign, a fact which was to have crucial military significance.

It was not just the French and their allies who sustained horrendous losses in 1812. Reliable figures for Russian casualties are even rarer than those for their opponents, but it is certain that the Tsar's forces suffered hugely. For a start, given the outcome of most engagements, more Russian soldiers than Imperial troops died as a result of battle. But again, such military losses are only part of the story. It was not just Napoleon's men who suffered from hunger or disease or bad weather (although, admittedly, the invaders did suffer worse). Up to the fall of Moscow, the Russians deployed somewhere between 250–300,000 men against the invaders, yet barely 150,000 remained with the colours by mid-September (85,000 with Kutuzov, almost 15,000 at Riga, perhaps 20,000 under Wittgenstein, and 30,000 or so under Tormasov). A month later, when the retreat from Moscow commenced, all these forces had been strengthened with new recruits or soldiers freed from other theatres. Kutuzov now had at least 110,000 men, there were around 25,000 at Riga, Wittgenstein's command had more than doubled in strength, and Tormasov's army had been incorporated into Chichagov's 65,000-strong force. In other words, the Russians had rebuilt to around a quarter of a million men. By the end of the year, though, the numbers of troops still with their units had been dramatically reduced once more. Kutuzov reached Vilna in mid-December with fewer than 30,000 effectives, Chichagov and Wittgenstein commanded a similar number between them by this time, Tormasov was at Minsk with 10,000, and the flank armies (the former garrison of Riga in the north and Sacken's force in the south) together amounted to around 35,000. The reconstituted Russian armies of autumn 1812 had thus lost well over half their effective strength by the end of the campaign.

In total, Russian military casualties in 1812 were probably between 250,000 and 300,000. How many of these were fatal is impossible to say, but as with the Imperial side, although some Russian stragglers or deserters will have survived, the great majority, especially in the winter, must have died. Sharing their fate were thousands of Russian civilians. Some certainly died at the hands of the invading troops, but far more perished simply as a result of being caught up in a war zone, or from the hunger and exposure that followed when they fled or were evicted from the many settlements that stood in the path of the armies.

During the six years of the Second World War, the bloodiest conflict of all time, some 105 million soldiers were mobilized by all sides, of whom fifteen million, around fourteen per cent, perished. By far the heaviest losses, both in total and as a percentage of troops mobilized, were endured by the Soviet Union: seven and a half million dead out of twenty-five million deployed, a death rate of thirty per cent that has rightly become legendary. In 1812, almost a million soldiers took part in the six-month campaign east of the Niemen: 550,000 Imperial troops and 350–400,000 Russians. Something in the region of 600–650,000 – roughly two out of every three – died. Such figures do not need the elaboration of words.

The Russian campaign of 1812 was an overwhelming disaster, militarily and politically, for Napoleon, and in humanitarian terms for both sides. It is little wonder, then, that much ink has been spilt over the years in seeking to explain where it all went wrong. The most famous, and commonly believed, reason for the Imperial calamity is the one upon which the Emperor himself focused in his bulletin of December 1812. It was all down to the Russian winter.

Although many Russians and most Imperial troops at the time, as well as figures as prominent as the military theorist Clausewitz and the Austrian general Schwarzenberg, essentially agreed with Napoleon's explanation, it is unsatisfactory. It was not just the winter that defeated Napoleon's armies in Russia. General Winter was only a major factor from early November onwards, by which time the Emperor's main army had already begun to disintegrate and his forces were struggling to cope with the Russians on all fronts. That said, it is probable that, but for the winter, the Emperor's armies would have retained enough fighting power and discipline to have been able to halt their retreat somewhere inside the Tsar's realm. It is certain, moreover, that without the winter many tens of thousands of Imperial troops who died would not have. Thus, although it is wrong to put the Imperial rout down solely, or even primarily, to the winter, it may well have been the factor that, coming on top of others, ensured Napoleon's total defeat and prevented his forces from continuing the war in Russia into 1813.

With the diminution in significance generally accorded the Russian winter by historians nowadays, some have focused instead upon the hardships experienced during the Russian summer as a key factor in the Emperor's defeat, but these in turn have sometimes been given too much weight. There is no doubt that the draining heat, disease and supply problems of the first months of the invasion cost Napoleon the services of tens of thousands of troops through death, illness, desertion and straggling, but the rate of attrition can easily be exaggerated. Too often in studying the 1812 campaign the mistake is made of only considering the main army under the Emperor's direct control. Thus one occasionally gets the impression that, having crossed the Niemen with 450,000 men, Napoleon had just 100,000 left by the time he entered Moscow. The tens of thousands of troops under Schwarzenberg, Reynier, Oudinot, St Cyr and Macdonald are ignored, as are the many thousands of others detached in smaller units throughout the Tsar's realm in places like Vilna, Minsk and Smolensk or along the main army's lines of communication back to the Grand Duchy of Warsaw and Prussia. Still, even when these factors are taken into account, it seems likely that the *Grande Armée* overall had lost as much as a third of its effective strength to non-military causes – primarily desertion, straggling and sickness – by the time Moscow was captured. The vast majority of these losses, however, was in raw recruits, so the actual damage done to Napoleon's war-making potential was not as great as mere numbers would suggest. Indeed, given the difficulties of trying to supply his army, it could even be argued that the desertion or straggling of a large number of inexperienced troops was something of a blessing in disguise.

No explanation of the Napoleonic catastrophe in 1812 would, of course, be complete without reference to the role played by the Russians. In this regard, two champions have historically been lauded most vociferously: Field Marshal Kutuzov and the Russian people. Much has already been said about Kutuzov and the severe doubts that may be raised as to whether the heroic stature granted him is deserved. His role, though not insignificant, was essentially a passive rather than an active one. He did not win the war for Russia – indeed, he was arguably the man most responsible for Russia's victory being less absolute than it might have been – but he did avoid committing errors that might have lost it, such as making a stand outside the gates of Moscow after Borodino. That said, of course, at Borodino itself his leadership was so lacklustre that the Russians were fortunate not to have been beaten considerably more gravely than they were.

The Russian people do not really merit being considered the key cause of Napoleon's defeat either, least of all in the sense that Marxist or Soviet historians have referred to them. Their attention has focused on the supposed 'people's war' that erupted in 1812, but this is a dubious analysis of the conduct of the Russian peasantry. In general, the Russian people did not voluntarily rally to the defence of their country, much less to that of the Tsar, but took part in the campaign either as conscripted soldiers or as partisans stirred by xenophobia, religious hatred and a passion for vengeance rather than by patriotism. Of course, whatever their motivation, the partisans still killed a great number of Imperial troops, but most of those unfortunates would have died of other causes, including exposure or starvation, anyway. In similar vein, although Russia's peasant soldiers made a much more substantial contribution to their country's ultimate victory, it should not be exaggerated. Rather like Kutuzov, their key role was to do what they could to prevent the invaders from smashing the Tsar's armies rather than to crush those of the enemy. Right to the end, the Russians typically came off worse in engagements with disciplined Imperial soldiers. None of this is to demean the often exemplary courage that tens of thousands of Russian troops displayed, nor to deny that without such fortitude Russia would have been lost, but it is to point out that there were limits to the role the men who made up the Russian armies played in 1812. Napoleon's defeat was not primarily brought about by his adversaries on the field of battle.

One factor often overlooked or underplayed by the historians of all campaigns is luck. Napoleon, on the other hand, never underestimated its importance and clearly felt that it played a major role in Russia in 1812. As he said to General Rapp on the morning of Borodino, 'Fortune is a fickle courtesan. I have always said so, and now I am beginning to experience it.' Certainly, it is hard to deny that he did not have a terribly lucky campaign. He was unfortunate that Barclay rather than Bagration was given command of the Russian First Army, that his brother Jerome proved quite so incompetent as a commander, that Junot let him down so badly near Smolensk, that the Russians did not make a second stand in front of Moscow, that neither the Swedes nor the Turks chose to exploit the difficulties of their traditional Russian foe in 1812, that Dokhturov decided to make a stand at Maloyaroslavets, that Schwarzenberg chose to abandon Minsk, and that the Berezina unfroze in late November. Most of all, Napoleon was unfortunate that the Russians effectively stumbled upon the best strategy to deal with his invasion and that Alexander did not lose his nerve and sue for peace. Of course, there were moments of good luck for Napoleon too, but these were heavily outweighed by the bad. In the final analysis, though, it is neither very satisfying nor convincing to put the Emperor's defeat in 1812 primarily down to ill fortune.

If one is to identify a prime cause of the disastrous defeat sustained by the *Grande Armée* in Russia, one needs to focus upon its leader, Napoleon himself. His conduct of the campaign, though not entirely devoid of his earlier brilliance, was characterized by a series of crucial blunders. As General Compans commented in a letter to his wife following his escape from Russia, 'the calculations of [the Emperor's] brain were not as successful in this campaign as in others'. He invaded Russia with far too large and unwieldy an army, one that could not be adequately provisioned nor move swiftly enough to force the enemy to stand and fight. He then failed to take any of the opportunities, some better than others, that the Russians presented him with to bring them to battle, allowing his adversaries to escape from near the frontier, from Vitebsk and from Smolensk. He drove on from Smolensk towards Moscow when the great majority of his key subordinates opposed such a move. Having done so, he lost his chance to inflict a crushing defeat on the Russians at Borodino through uninspired generalship. At this point, if he could no longer have won the war in 1812, defeat was not by any means yet certain. A reasonably well-ordered withdrawal to the Smolensk area, or Minsk and Vilna, followed by a prolongation of the war into 1813 was not an impossibility, but further blunders wrecked any chance there was of such an outcome. The Emperor should have left Moscow sooner than he did, in less of a rush, and with greater control over what his men took with them, a fact that he freely admitted in exile on St Helena when he ruefully commented, 'I ought only to have stayed two weeks there'. Had he departed at the start of October, he would in all probability have swept past Kutuzov's army towards the fertile lands south-west of Moscow and have reached Smolensk within three weeks, Minsk and Vilna, had he gone on, within five, thereby beating the advent of the really bad weather from early November on. The chances are as well that such a retreat would have been conducted in good order as there would have been food, relatively good weather, and, above all, no overriding sense of impending doom like that which infected the army after it turned back from Maloyaroslavets. With hindsight, it was at Maloyaroslavets that Napoleon threw away his last chance of salvaging the war in Russia. By ordering a withdrawal back north from there, he shattered his army's morale and slowed its retreat to possible safety by perhaps a week. Without such a delay, the bitter cold snap of early November might not have caused such carnage (the army might have been able to shelter in Smolensk and Vitebsk), Chichagov's force might have been beaten not only to the Berezina but perhaps also to Minsk, and, had the retreat continued to Vilna or the frontier, a week of awful weather in December might have been avoided.

Of course, there have always been those who have argued that the Russian campaign was fundamentally unwinnable, that the problems of time and space were insurmountable before the industrial era and that Napoleon was predestined to fail. Such a view perhaps lacks imagination, however. It was certainly not inconceivable that Napoleon could have inflicted a crushing defeat on the Tsar's armies, perhaps more than one, and we simply do not know how Alexander and the rest of the Russian government would have reacted to this. Even without another Austerlitz or Friedland, the Russian war was not necessarily unwinnable. Napoleon might have endeavoured to achieve victory by taking and trying to hold the Russian lands which had once belonged to the kingdom of Poland. If the Austrian chancellor, Klemens von Metternich is to be believed, this was more or less what the Emperor was considering shortly before the invasion. 'My undertaking', he apparently informed Metternich in May 1812,

> is of the kind that is solved by patience; triumph will come to the most patient. I am going to open the campaign by crossing the Niemen and will terminate it at Smolensk and Minsk. There I will halt. I will fortify these two places, and from Vilna, where I will establish the General Headquarters during the next winter, I will organise Lithuania … We will see who will get tired of it first, I to let my army live at the expense of Russia, or Alexander to feed my army at the expense of his country.

Whether such a strategy would have succeeded it is impossible to say. Certainly there would have been serious difficulties, not least in supplying a large army in a less than abundant part of Europe. Given the superior sophistication of the Napoleonic administrative system compared to that of Russia, however, as well as the greater resources available to the Emperor, the odds in a more prolonged war would probably have favoured the invaders at least, unless French mastery of Europe had begun to crumble from within.

In the final analysis, of course, all considerations of what might have been, fascinating as it may be, is hypothetical. What matters most is what actually happened. The plain fact is that in Russia in the second half of 1812 the forces of the greatest European empire since the Romans suffered a truly cataclysmic defeat, thereby both shattering the notion of Napoleonic invincibility and devastating the military potential at the Emperor's disposal. The crucial question now was whether Europe's colossus, having been knocked so brutally to the ground, would be able to get back on his feet.

18

The Russians March West

Speeding up the last leg of his army's advance so as to give the impression that he was driving the enemy from Russian territory at the tips of his men's bayonets, Field Marshal Kutuzov reached Vilna in mid-December 1812. A few days later, a triumphant Tsar Alexander left his capital at St Petersburg, where he had been since late summer, and rode to join his armed forces. He arrived in Vilna in the early hours of the 23rd, where, despite his feelings of dislike towards Kutuzov and disappointment in his conduct of the recent campaign, he made a display of embracing the Russian commander-in-chief and congratulating him on the defeat of Napoleon's forces. Next day, Alexander's thirty-fifth birthday, the field marshal reciprocated the Tsar's insincere but conspicuous praise by throwing a lavish celebratory ball in his ruler's honour.

The artificial but enthusiastic thanksgiving and mutual appreciation of Christmas 1812 hid more than just personal animosity between Russia's monarch and his chief military commander, however. There was also a fundamental divergence of opinion over what Russia should do next. As far as Kutuzov was concerned, the war against Napoleon was over. He was the prime advocate of the isolationist branch of Russian thought at this time, which also included men as important as State Chancellor Shishkov and Foreign Minister Rumiantsev. The isolationists felt that Russia had suffered more than enough already from wars with Napoleonic France and pressed for a peace that would largely leave the French Empire intact. For men like Kutuzov, the establishment of a new Russian border along the Vistula and a free hand against the Turks were the rewards the Russians should seek from the defeat of the invasion. The isolationists were not overly concerned with the fate of central and western Europe, provided, of course, that Russia's western border was not threatened. Napoleon's disastrous reverse in 1812 seemed to guarantee that, and the advancing of the frontier west to the Vistula would also help further. That achieved, the Russians should concentrate on expanding at the expense of the Ottoman Empire. To continue the war with France for any other aim, such as the 'liberation' of Germany or the overthrow of the Emperor, seemed ill advised. On one hand, there was no guarantee of success. True, Napoleon's catastrophic losses in Russia, and anti-French rumblings in Austria and Prussia, boded well for a major campaign west of the Niemen, but the battered state of Russian forces presented severe problems. Kutuzov's army alone had sustained almost 50,000 casualties in the final weeks of the campaign, and by the end of the year just one in three of his soldiers would be fit for active service. Alternatively, a campaign in central Europe might prove more successful than many isolationists felt desirable. If Napoleon were to sustain further heavy defeats, his empire, and quite possibly his regime, might crumble, a development that Kutuzov and others were far from sure was necessarily in Russia's best interests, as it would leave Austria and Britain in a much better position to resist Russian expansion at the Turks' expense and the British free to monopolize European as well as overseas trade.

Opposing the isolationists were what might be termed the interventionists. These argued that, having driven the French from their own soil, the Russians should now endeavour to expel them from most of the rest of Europe, particularly Germany, both to increase Russian security and to remove the dangerous influence of Revolutionary ideas and laws from as much of the Continent as possible. Many interventionists already envisaged the complete dismantling of the Napoleonic Empire and the overthrow of the Bonapartist regime as the ultimate goals. Among them was a young German, Count Karl Robert Nesselrode, who from late 1812 effectively became Russia's foreign minister, a post he would hold for the next half century.

Born in Westphalia to a family of minor nobility, Nesselrode had arrived in Russia in 1796 at the age of sixteen. A little later, he had followed his father into a career within the Russian foreign ministry, serving as the clerk responsible for writing out the Russian drafts of the Tilsit treaties and then as a member of staff in the Paris embassy during the brief period of Russo-French alliance. Far from being a friend of France or her emperor though, the young German, who had married into the upper echelons of the Russian aristocracy in 1811, was a staunch anti-Bonapartist and arch-conservative who advocated Russia's intervention in the affairs of central and western Europe as the champion of *ancien régime* ideas and chief agent of turning back the Continent's political clock to before 1789.

However, Nesselrode, as well as many other interventionists close to the Tsar, only had or gained influence in late 1812 because Alexander already broadly shared their views. Indeed, far from taking the lead in shaping Russian foreign policy, Nesselrode effectively acted as a mere functionary charged with implementing his master's will, in a way not dissimilar to the French foreign minister, Hugues Maret. That is not to say that Nesselrode had no real influence in determining the line St Petersburg took in international affairs, but it is to point out that it was a limited, suggestive one rather than a wide-ranging, formative one. It was Nesselrode's obedience and bureaucratic skills rather than any ability or predilection for independent thought that most recommended him to a tsar determined to take personal charge of Russian foreign policy.

Even before he arrived in Vilna and conferred with Kutuzov, Alexander had decided to pursue the war against Napoleon beyond the Niemen. Indeed, while large numbers of invading troops were still on Russian soil, albeit in retreat, he had written to his ambassador in London confidently asserting, 'When, with the aid of Providence, I have repulsed the enemy beyond our frontiers, I will not stop there, and it is only then that I will reach agreement with England on the most effective assistance that I can ask for to succeed in liberating Europe from the French yoke'. As well as indicating the Tsar's desire to continue the war west of the Niemen, this letter hints at two key reasons that drove him towards his momentous decision. The first was his growing sense of divine purpose. Always a religious man, Alexander became, in the second half of 1812, a zealot. Having turned to the Bible for inspiration and succour in the dark days of the invasion, he ascribed Napoleon's defeat to the will of God and began to see himself as a divine instrument. What God wanted, Alexander seems to have decided in late 1812, was for the Emperor of the French to be overthrown, or at least to have his power severely curtailed. Over and over again, the Tsar read the eleventh chapter of the Old Testament Book of Daniel in which the King of the North brings down the hitherto all-conquering King of the South, while Alexander's friends and allies were frequently informed that he was doing God's work and that Providence was on his side.

The second factor behind the Tsar's decision to prosecute the war beyond the Niemen was his desire to play the role of Europe's 'liberator' and to supplant Napoleon as the Continent's leading figure; the same aspirations he had had in leading his country to war in 1805. Shrewd associates exploited this Alexandrian yearning to be seen as a European hero by assuring the Tsar that he would be lauded to the skies if only he took it upon himself to lead an anti-Napoleonic crusade. Enemies of France and her ruler from throughout Europe, but especially from Prussia and Britain, struggled to outdo each other in their extravagant praise of a man whom, just a few years earlier, they had despised for allying himself with the Emperor. Perhaps the most important of these flatterers was the former Prussian chief minister Baron von Stein who, in ridiculously exaggerated language, pleaded with Alexander 'to deliver the human race from the most absurd and degrading of tyrannies'.

Alongside a powerful sense of divine mission and personal ambition, Alexander's desire to continue the war into central Europe stemmed from practical considerations too. He shared the view held by other interventionists that the security of Russia's western frontier would be best served by ejecting the French from Germany and generally weakening their position in Europe. He was also keen to expand Russian territory and saw the battlefield as a more certain way of achieving this than the conference table. The Vistula had already been claimed as Russia's rightful western border in the agreement reached with the Swedes earlier in 1812, and by the end of the year the Tsar was being urged, particularly by his old friend Adam Czartoryski, to bring all Polish lands, including those currently and formerly owned by Austria and Prussia, under his rule as a self-proclaimed King of Poland. Nesselrode warned against such a bold policy, viewing it as morally damaging to any hope of Austro-Russian cooperation against Napoleon, this helped persuade Alexander to proceed with more circumspection. Still, the Tsar's aim remained to gain control over as much Polish territory as possible whilst avoiding alienating Vienna.

A final factor behind Alexander's decision to send his forces across the Niemen was the crucial but easily overlooked one of the Tsar's supreme confidence that he could defeat the Emperor in central Europe. Although Kutuzov warned him of the dire state of much of the Russian army and pleaded with him at least to rest the troops until the spring, Alexander was convinced that his forces should strike while the iron was hot. After all, the enemy was in an even worse state than the Russians, the Cossacks had shown themselves to be able to cope well with harsh winter conditions, and almost every German who had the Tsar's ear assured him with the utmost confidence that all Germany would rise up against the French at the mere approach of Russian soldiers. To a monarch who already felt that God was on his side, it seemed that advancing beyond the frontier might turn into little more than a cakewalk.

Alexander's decision to send his armies across the Niemen was arguably as important as his decision not to make peace during the dark days of the French invasion. Had the Tsar sought a settlement with Napoleon, as his chief military adviser (Kutuzov), his prime domestic minister (Shishkov) and his nominal foreign minister (Rumiantsev) all advocated, it is hard to see how the French Empire would have been brought down in 1813–14. Spain might have had to be abandoned, but the British and their Iberian allies could not have hoped to cross the Pyrenees unless the French were massively embroiled in central Europe. Without Russian involvement, though, the chances of France getting heavily bogged down in Germany were slim. Prussia might just conceivably still have rebelled against her hated French ally, but a rebellion lacking Russian support would probably have been easily crushed, while both Austria and the other German states remained hesitant to take up arms against Napoleon even after the Russian disaster. As for the prospect of widespread popular anti-French risings throughout the Empire, there was none. In the event, Napoleonic hegemony in Europe would not be ended solely by Russian armies, but by the formidable forces of a coalition of four major powers joined by a number of lesser European states. Without both the catastrophe endured by the *Grande Armée* in Russia and Alexander's subsequent decision to continue the war into central Europe, however, that coalition would never have existed. Russia and her ruler would truly prove to be the Emperor's nemesis.

Despite the horrendous losses sustained by the *Grande Armée* in Russia, the Imperial position in north-eastern Europe at the start of 1813 was not quite so hopeless as subsequent events would make it seem. True, of the 75,000 or so survivors who had crossed the Niemen in late 1812, around half were either Austrian or Prussian and would never fight for Napoleon again, while many of the rest were in no fit state to resist a Russian advance, at least until they had been rested and reorganized. There remained, however, sizeable bodies of troops that had never crossed into Russia but had stayed in Prussia or the Grand Duchy of Warsaw. Unfortunately, most of these were of poor quality, being either inexperienced conscripts or soldiers deemed more fit for rear area duties than front-line fighting, but there was a leavening of units of a higher standard. In the hands of a highly skilled commander, Imperial forces might have been able to slow, if not halt a Russian advance. Unhappily for the Emperor, his troops were not to receive such sufficiently skilled guidance in the opening months of 1813.

Marshal Joachim Murat, King of Naples, had served Napoleon loyally and with frequent aplomb as the commander of his cavalry for many years, but in 1813 he spoilt his record in spectacular fashion. We have already seen how the man entrusted with command of the remainder of the Emperor's forces in north-east Europe had panicked in December 1812 when a small force of Cossacks had approached Vilna and how he had failed to provide any kind of leadership to those fleeing the Tsar's realm, but he soon surpassed even these failings. Reaching the Prussian city of Königsberg shortly before Christmas, Murat had ordered the remnants of the invasion force to rest here, but when news of the defection of General Yorck's Prussian troops reached him early in the new year, he immediately ordered a renewed withdrawal behind the Vistula. Though essentially a prudent act, the sense of panic engendered by the abrupt resumption of the retreat did little to encourage Imperial soldiers and much to give the local inhabitants the impression that now was an opportune time to rise up against the French. Even less to Murat's credit than his infectious jitteriness was his extraordinary decision, once the army had withdrawn behind the Vistula in mid-January, to hand over command to the young and relatively inexperienced Eugène and return to his southern European kingdom. Napoleon, whose decision it had been to appoint the King of Naples as his replacement as commander-in-chief in early December 1812, took his subordinate's abrupt abandonment of his command with surprising composure, realizing perhaps that it was for the best. He simply commented, 'I find Murat's conduct very extravagant – I can think of nothing similar. This is a brave man in battle, but he lacks intelligence and moral courage.' The Emperor would doubtless have been more irate had he sensed at this stage which way the political wind was beginning to blow in Naples, where his own sister, Queen Caroline, began plotting in early 1813 for her and her husband's survival by contacting Vienna and offering to keep their kingdom neutral in the forthcoming campaigns, provided Austria was prepared to guarantee the Murats their throne.

With Murat gone, one of the major obstacles to the outstanding Marshal Davout being appointed commander-in-chief of Imperial forces in north-eastern Europe was removed, but rather than give this key role to his most skilled and loyal subordinate, Napoleon bizarrely decided to acquiesce in Murat's handing over command to Eugène. The loyalty of the Viceroy of Italy was not in question, nor his competence as a corps commander, but skilled control of an entire army was still a little beyond this gifted young man. Some of what he did once he assumed command was astute, such as sending most of the survivors of the invasion back to central Germany to rest and help organize new units, but his overall conduct of what was admittedly a very difficult campaign to fight in early 1813 was not as adept as it might have been. Though nowhere nearly as inclined to panic as Murat, Eugène was willing to yield ground too easily at times by overestimating the size and condition of enemy forces. He also placed too much emphasis on holding a number of towns at the expense of maintaining as large a field army as possible. Danzig, Glogau, Küstrin, Modlin, Posen, Stettin and Thorn were all left with large garrisons and smaller ones were placed elsewhere. Perhaps as many as 100,000 Imperial soldiers ended up tied down in towns and cities in north-eastern Europe. None of these troops were available to the Emperor once he resumed command of the army in the field, although they tied down large numbers of the enemy.

The Russian advance over the Niemen, which began in mid-January, was divided into two main thrusts, one of 48,000 men into the heart of the Grand Duchy of Warsaw led by Generals Miloradovich, Tormasov and Sacken, the other of 55,000 men under Wittgenstein, Chichagov (soon to be replaced by Barclay) and Platov into north-eastern Prussia. As commander-in-chief, it was Kutuzov's responsibility to coordinate the various Russian corps, a task he performed with only limited success. Accompanying the old field marshal and his headquarters staff was the Tsar, eager for the military glory that had evaded him when he had taken the field in previous campaigns. In an effort to rouse his forces, Alexander issued a bold proclamation calling upon them 'to liberate from oppression and misery even those nations who have taken up arms against Russia'. Among Prussians, who had rather suffered from French hegemony in Europe, the approach of Russian troops was generally welcomed, but the Poles of the Grand Duchy were considerably less happy. With Polish units having sustained calamitous casualties in Russia and replacements not properly organized, the defence of the Grand Duchy depended largely upon Schwarzenberg's Austrian corps. Unfortunately, even before the Russians advanced, Vienna had ordered their general to ignore any instructions to defend Warsaw and instead to pull back behind the Vistula. By the end of January, Schwarzenberg had copied

Yorck's act of neutralizing his troops, leaving the Polish capital without adequate protection against the approaching Russians. The city was abandoned in early February to save it from destruction, leaving General Miloradovich free to march in unopposed on the 8th.

Further north, the Russian advance was similarly easy. An early show of resistance by Imperial troops at Elbing was swiftly overcome, with fifteen cannon and several hundred prisoners being captured in the process. Thereafter, the campaign largely developed into one in which Eugène's forces constantly retreated in the face of approaching Russian units. Town after town was put under siege as the Tsar's soldiers reached them. This slowed the Russian advance and reduced the number of troops available for mobile operations, yet by mid-February elements of Wittgenstein's corps had crossed the River Oder and the bulk of the Grand Duchy had been overrun.*

A month into the Russian campaign, a bolder, more experienced French commander than Eugène might have launched a counter-attack, catching the Russian field forces by surprise and strung out, but in fairness to the Viceroy it must be pointed out that the intelligence reaching him about the state, size and location of enemy units was at best hazy thanks to the dearth of Imperial cavalry. Even without a French counterthrust, however, the Russian advance seemed to have pretty much stopped, at least temporarily, by mid-February when Kutuzov called a halt to forward operations in order to reorganize, sort out the lengthening supply lines and, most important of all, await a decision from Prussia on whether or not she was going to join them in the war against Napoleon. The Russians had begun the dismemberment of the French Empire. It was up to others now to unite with them and take it further.

As news of the cataclysmic scale of the disaster suffered by the *Grande Armée* in Russia reached the various states within the French Empire in early 1813, rulers inevitably began to reappraise their countries' position. Almost all decided, for the moment at least, to remain loyal to Napoleon. Doubtless this was largely occasioned by fear of the possible consequences of breaking openly with the Emperor, but one must not forget that the power of Napoleon to awe those who might resist him was severely weakened not only by the catastrophe in Russia but by the huge Russian advance of January–February 1813. Moreover, the Tsar was not averse to issuing vague threats of his own, publicly warning those German

---

* General Poniatowski managed to keep a small Polish force in the field until mid-May, when the city of Cracow fell to the Russians and he was forced to abandon his homeland and retreat into Austria with around 10,000 fellow Poles. Amazingly, Napoleon successfully negotiated with Vienna for these troops to be allowed to join him and fight once more under his command later that year.

rulers who did not rally to his side that they might end up being destroyed 'through the strength of public opinion and [more pertinently] the power of righteous arms'. Still, of the minor German states, only Mecklenburg deserted Napoleon outright in spring 1813, and her ruler was related to Alexander. True, Bavaria and Saxony both toyed with neutrality, the latter even adopting it for a while, but both eventually reaffirmed their loyalty to the Emperor.

Even in Prussia, the path to war with France was far from straightforward, despite a concerted effort by the Tsar to win her over. Throughout the invasion of 1812, the Russians had maintained limited contact with Berlin. As the war had turned in their favour, they had promised Prussia that they would not seek revenge for the participation of some of her troops in Napoleon's campaign, if she now defected from the Emperor. This had had no immediate effect, but Alexander persevered, writing to General Yorck shortly before he signed the Convention of Tauroggen informing him that it was his intention to restore to Prussia her lost territories. This time, the approach seemed to bear fruit (although Yorck would almost certainly have agreed to neutralize his force anyway). The Tsar was so encouraged by news of Tauroggen that in early January 1813 he sent General von Boyen, one of the many Prussians who had come to Russia in spring 1812, back to Berlin to offer Frederick William a military alliance. Baron von Stein, meanwhile, was urged to appeal to his former master to break with Napoleon and also to travel to north-eastern Prussia and try to incite the locals to join the Russian troops in marching against the French. Finally, in crossing the Niemen into Prussian territory in mid-January, Alexander issued a proclamation pledging 'to give back to the kingdom of Frederick the Great its former frontiers and lustre'.

The Tsar's efforts to woo Frederick William and his nation had only limited success initially. Although many Prussians welcomed the advancing Russians and efforts began to be made to raise units to fight the French in areas behind the front line, the results of this unauthorized recruitment drive were unimpressive. It seemed that, while most Prussians were happy to be rid of Napoleon's troops, few were keen to take up arms against them. Even more disappointing was the attitude of the Prussian King. Rather than declaring himself on Russia's side straight away, Frederick William played a very cagey game in early 1813. Indeed, upon hearing of the Convention of Tauroggen, he immediately publicly disavowed it and issued orders for Yorck's arrest and court-martial (orders which were never carried out, as Yorck sensibly remained behind Russian lines until the political situation had changed). By mid-February, however, the pressure upon the King to declare his hand against Napoleon was becoming acute. Nationalistic feeling among small pockets of the Prussian population and widespread anti-French sentiment throughout the country were certainly creating a strong impetus for war, but more important than that were practical considerations.

The Russians seemed to be winning their fight against the French easily in early 1813 and many among the Prussian elite feared that, if Frederick William did not join the Tsar soon, Prussia would be in no position to wield any influence at the eventual peace conference. With Berlin still in French hands, however, Frederick William continued to hesitate. Then something happened which finally made him commit himself. On 20 February, a force of Cossacks made a thrust towards the Prussian capital. They had no intention of attacking the city and were insufficiently strong to have done so successfully anyway, but the move alarmed Eugène. In his biggest error of the campaign, the Viceroy ordered Imperial forces to abandon Berlin and pull back behind the River Elbe. Before the month was out, Prussia had signed a formal military alliance with Russia and shortly afterwards she would declare war on France.

The terms of the Treaty of Kalisch (a Polish town that was serving as Russian headquarters in late February) were essentially dictated by the Russians and agreed to by the Prussians. The two countries pledged to cooperate militarily and swore not to make a separate peace with Napoleon. To win the war, each promised to endeavour to induce Austria to join them and to persuade Britain to provide them with financial subsidies. The Russians undertook to maintain at least 150,000 men in the field, the Prussians 80,000. This, of course, was still almost double the 42,000 Prussia's army had been restricted to since 1808, yet by April the Prussians would be able more than to meet their quota. Partly this was the result of Napoleon having unwisely authorized Prussia to raise more troops in late 1812 in the hope that they would fight for rather than against him; partly it was down to a massive wave of conscription unleashed in spring 1813 by the Prussian government; but mainly, it was due to a system whereby Prussia had partially obviated the restriction placed upon the size of her army by releasing a certain number of soldiers every year and recruiting others to replace them so that, by 1813, there were over 30,000 trained reservists ready to join the colours at short notice. What would these Prussian soldiers be fighting for? The Treaty of Kalisch carefully pledged to restore Prussia to her former status rather than specifically to her former boundaries, for the Russians were determined to absorb the Polish lands that had once belonged to Frederick William within their own empire and envisaged compensating Berlin for the loss with Saxony, a deal which was more than satisfactory to the Prussians.

Units from Wittgenstein's corps triumphantly entered Berlin on 4 March, where they were warmly received by large crowds. A few days later, the Tsar joined his new ally, the King of Prussia, at Breslau (modern Wroclaw) in Silesia, where the two men greeted and embraced each other like old friends, which, despite recent difficulties, they essentially were. On the 16th, Prussia at last officially declared war on France. When he heard the news, Napoleon's response was stoical. 'Better a declared enemy than a doubtful ally,' he tersely commented.

If Prussia was now at last committed to the anti-Napoleonic cause, the position of others remained less satisfactory as far as the Russians were concerned. Now that the French were on the retreat across central Europe, the Tsar hoped to see the Swedes land a force in northern Germany in accordance with agreements reached in 1812, but Crown Prince Bernadotte was slow to act. It was mid-May before a force of 24,000 soldiers was finally sent to Swedish Pomerania on the southern side of the Baltic and some weeks after that before Bernadotte fully committed Sweden to war against his country of birth.

With the Swedes proving recalcitrant, St Petersburg tried to coax the Danes into the war on their side. Alexander offered Denmark control over several north German cities currently held by the French, including Hamburg and Lübeck, in return for abandoning Napoleon, and even suggested that she might be allowed to occupy Holland if she accepted the loss of Norway to Sweden. The Danes told the Russians bluntly that they could not consent to any agreement that did not confirm Danish possession of Norway. Prevented from agreeing to this by his prior treaty with Stockholm, the Tsar had to abandon his efforts to win the Danes over.

As frustrating as Sweden's hesitation and Denmark's rejection of the bribes offered her were, the Russians' greatest disappointment of the first few months of 1813 was the refusal of Austria to join the anti-French coalition. Vienna was furiously courted not just by Russia, but by Britain and Prussia too (as well as by France), yet the Austrians refused to commit themselves. True, they declared themselves neutral shortly after Schwarzenberg copied Yorck's lead, thereby technically effecting a break of sorts with Napoleon, but they went no further than that, despite Alexander pledging to return Austria to her borders of 1805 if only she took the extra step. The Austrian Chancellor, Klemens von Metternich, was as disquieted by the prospect of Russian expansion in Europe as he was by France's current hegemony, and both Austria's finances and army were in need of further attention before the country could sensibly go to war. Besides, Metternich also had a scheme for restoring Austria's position and securing her foreign policy goals that he hoped might not necessitate a costly and risky recourse to arms.

Even though Austria chose to remain on the sidelines for the moment, the entry of Prussia into the war was enough to give renewed impetus to the Russian, or as it now became, Allied campaign. Shortly after the Prussians declared war, Hamburg unexpectedly fell to part of Wittgenstein's corps which made a lunge towards the lower Elbe, followed not long thereafter by another great north German port, Lübeck. Rather than being greeted warmly as they generally had been in Prussia, the Russians were given a tepid or even hostile welcome in these cities. Still, the success of their thrust in the north led Napoleon to order his best marshal, Davout, to the lower Elbe in order to prevent the enemy from pushing on into Holland and turning the Empire's flank. True to form,

Davout would perform expertly in his new job, but in doing so he would not be available for other, arguably more important battles elsewhere in Europe that year.

At the same time as the Allies pressed forward in the north, Russian forces along the middle stretch of the Elbe closed in on the fortress city of Magdeburg, putting it under a siege that would last many months. The main Allied effort in the early spring of 1813, though, was directed towards the invasion of Saxony and push towards the upper Elbe. Rather than resisting the attack as a loyal Imperial ally or declaring himself for Napoleon's enemies, the King of Saxony tried to steer a middle course by adopting a neutral stance, a position which frustrated both sides. The Saxon capital, Dresden, fell on 27 March, the Allies again receiving an at best apathetic reception, but the loss of the city persuaded Eugène to abandon the line of the upper Elbe and withdraw behind the River Saale. Here, the Viceroy was ordered by Napoleon to halt his long retreat. He had around 35,000 men close to hand with a further 20,000 in reserve, enough to hold the line until the Emperor arrived in late April at the head of a new army he was busy recruiting in France.

Having reached the Elbe, an impressive advance by anyone's standards, the Russians and their new Prussian allies had in early April to decide what to do next. Wittgenstein launched an attack across the lower Elbe near Hamburg, but the arrival of reinforcements, as well as the inimitable Davout, had greatly stiffened French resistance in this theatre and the assault was bloodily repulsed. The Allies therefore decided simply to hold the line of the lower Elbe for the moment and summoned Wittgenstein to Saxony to join the main Allied army.

In Saxony, opinion was divided at Allied headquarters between those who wanted to push on towards the Saale and keep up the pressure on Eugène, and those who thought it more prudent to fortify the line of the upper Elbe and wait for Napoleon and the new army he was raising to attack them. The cautious Kutuzov championed the latter strategy, warning the Tsar, 'We can cross the Elbe all right, but before long we shall cross it again with a bloody nose'. Alexander, however, was supremely confident and had the support of the fiery senior Prussian commander, General Gebhard Leberecht von Blücher, an aggressive, Francophobic, nationalist septuagenarian with a handsome moustache and a lust to avenge the humiliation his country had suffered in recent years. To halt now would look cowardly and discourage others from joining them, the Tsar and his supporters argued. Besides, Napoleon had endured such horrendous losses in Russia that there was surely no way he would be able to advance at the head of a new army before the summer, and even then it would be a ragtag assortment of conscripts. If only the Allies maintained their forward momentum, the Rhine and maybe even Paris could be reached in the coming weeks.

As news of the disastrous outcome of the campaign in Russia began to reach France in late 1812 it caused severe consternation, partly because, as Napoleon remarked, 'A people who have been brought up on victories often do not know how to accept defeat'. With the Emperor back in Paris, however, the mood in the country started to change from one of disbelief and despair to one of grim determination. When Napoleon called upon France to rebuild her army and stem the Russian tide, the country responded. Caulaincourt later commented of early 1813, 'The entire French nation overlooked his reverses and vied with one another in displaying zeal and devotion ... It was a personal triumph for the Emperor, who with amazing energy directed all the resources of which his genius was capable into organizing the great national endeavour.'

In fact, the construction of the French army of 1813 had begun as early as September 1812, when, from Moscow, Napoleon had issued orders for the calling up of 137,000 fresh conscripts a year ahead of schedule. Many of these men were in training by the time the Emperor returned to Paris, but he swiftly realized that he would need yet more soldiers. In February 1813, therefore, the class of 1814 was called up some eighteen months sooner than planned, although these troops would not be ready to fight before the summer. Nor did the gargantuan effort stop there. Thousands more men who had avoided conscription in earlier years were drafted into the army, many members of the *gendarmerie* (a paramilitary police force established by the Emperor) and of the National Guard (a militia) were called up, and the navy was milked of large numbers of sailors, especially gunners, who were retrained to fight on land. The fact that many of those who had survived the Russian campaign were officers or NCOs helped in the training of the new army, but Napoleon still felt compelled to withdraw many thousands of experienced troops, particularly veteran NCOs, from his already depleted forces in Spain to help provide a stiffer backbone to his fresh units. Meanwhile, the manufactories of France busied themselves producing uniforms, muskets, ammunition, cannon and other military necessities so that the new soldiers could go into battle armed and equipped.

Despite widespread resistance to the latest wave of conscription, by mid-April Napoleon had some 226,000 men and 457 cannon available west of the Elbe for operations in Germany, the great bulk of which had joined the army in recent months. By August, despite heavy losses in the intervening months, the Emperor would have over 400,000 troops and 1300 guns at his disposal. It was a staggering administrative achievement, the scale of which amazed Europe. Central to its success was the figure of Napoleon himself, who worked tirelessly to rebuild his armies and, with them, his and France's fortunes. His subordinates laboured like Trojans too, although they sometimes could not match their master's phenomenal energy. On one occasion, Count Daru, the army's head of logistics, could not prevent himself from falling asleep as the Emperor dictated orders to him. He awoke later to find that Napoleon had finished writing the orders himself.

If Napoleon's call for new troops was largely answered within France, the response elsewhere was unsurprisingly less impressive. Demands were made of the Emperor's allies throughout Europe for fresh soldiers to save civilization from the advancing Russian barbarians, as Napoleon put it, but all too few were either inclined or able to meet the request. Rather naïvely, the Emperor had hoped in late 1812 that the Austrians and even the Prussians would remain loyal to their alliance with France and raise new units to fight the Tsar's forces should they cross the Niemen. Swiftly disabused of this, he nevertheless continued to hope that Austria at least could be persuaded to stand by him. This was partly based upon his marriage to the Austrian Emperor's daughter, but he recognized that it would take more than that to win Vienna over. Initially, he concentrated on trying to convince his father-in-law that he would emerge victorious from the struggle against Alexander in the hope that this would persuade him into thinking that it might be in Austria's best interests to back the winning side, but the impressive Russian advance in the early months of 1813 undermined this. In early April, therefore, Napoleon changed tack, sending Count Narbonne to Vienna to offer the Habsburgs Silesia, a wealthy Prussian province which Frederick the Great had taken from Austria in the mid-eighteenth century, in return for 100,000 Austrian troops. The proposal was politely rejected.

Elsewhere in Europe, the Emperor generally had greater, if far from total, success. In Italy, for example, the kingdom in the north presided over by Eugène responded well to Napoleon's call, although, in the event, the Italian troops would end up fighting in their homeland against Austrians rather than in Germany against Russians. Further south in the peninsula, in the Kingdom of Naples, the incipient treachery of the Murats meant that the Emperor would receive no assistance from that quarter in 1813. In Germany, meanwhile, the states of the Confederation of the Rhine did manage to provide tens of thousands of fresh troops by late summer, but their recruitment efforts were nowhere near as impressive as those within France. In part, this was the result of disaffection with the French alliance, but there were other factors at work as well. The machinery of conscription was never as efficient or effective within the Confederation as it was within France and it must be remembered that the German states allied to Napoleon had also suffered horrendous losses in 1812 which had drained the available manpower pool. There was also, of course, considerable doubt in Germany as to the eventual outcome of the war in 1813, so it is hardly surprising that states like Bavaria were unwilling to commit themselves wholeheartedly to the Napoleonic cause.

Despite the failure of most of his allies to live up to his hopes, by mid-spring 1813 Napoleon still had a formidable army, in terms of numbers and morale at any rate, with which to confront the Russians and Prussians in central Europe. These new forces, however, had considerable weaknesses. For a start, they were predominantly made up of raw recruits who, due to pressures of time and lack of veterans, were given rather less formal training than was desirable. The average French infantryman of 1813 could neither march as fast nor fight as well as his predecessors of previous campaigns, most artillerymen lacked the skill in handling guns which had been commonplace in the *Grande Armée* in former years, and the support units, such as the engineers, were weaker than they had ever been under Napoleon. Indeed, it is little wonder that Caulaincourt was to refer to the French armies of 1813 as 'an organized mob'. Of course, the Russians and the Prussians also had large numbers of inexperienced conscripts in their expanding armies, but they had a higher percentage of veterans and well-trained troops than the French.

It was among the cavalry, though, that the Emperor's forces were at a particular disadvantage. As cavalrymen had much more to learn than foot soldiers, the lack of time for thorough training in 1813 was particularly deleterious to their effectiveness. Even worse than this was the dearth of mounts available. Many of the horses used by the *Grande Armée* in previous years had come from Poland or Prussia, sources now denied to it, while much of western and central Europe had been practically emptied of horses in 1812 in order to provide the vast numbers Napoleon had demanded then. This dire lack of cavalry was to have a profound impact upon the events of 1813, and the problems caused by the shortage of horses did not stop there. The mobility of the French artillery was restricted by a deficiency of beasts to pull the guns, while the supply system, which would have a higher significance in 1813 than in previous Napoleonic campaigns in central Europe due to the inability of the raw recruits to live off the land effectively, would find it extremely hard to provision the armies on the move without sufficient horses to move the many supply carts.

The Emperor finally left Paris on 15 April. Two days later he arrived at Mainz on the Rhine, where he stayed for a week planning his imminent campaign. He was determined to adopt an offensive strategy, partly because he was always happier on the attack, partly because he felt that an aggressive attitude would show the rest of Europe that he and France were far from a spent force. Earlier in the year, he had envisaged driving on Berlin via northern Germany, then marching on to relieve the tens of thousands of Imperial troops bottled up in Danzig and pushing the enemy back beyond the Vistula. Now, however, he judged that he would need many more soldiers than he had in order for such a bold plan to work, so he adjusted his strategy. Retaining the line of the Vistula as his ultimate goal, Napoleon now looked to win an early success in Saxony, where the confident Russians and Prussians had pushed over the upper Elbe. After detaching units to strengthen his forces near the key fortress city of Magdeburg on the middle Elbe, the bulk of the newly-raised French army would advance to join Eugène on the Saale before thrusting via Leipzig to Dresden, a move which Napoleon anticipated would cut the main Russo-Prussian force's lines of communication back to Prussia and Poland. He would then close on the stranded enemy and crush him. It was another visionary Napoleonic plan.

On 25 April, the Emperor arrived in Erfurt, just a few dozen miles west of the Saale River. Less than five years earlier, he and the Tsar had met in the town as allies. Now it would serve as the springboard for a campaign, the ultimate goal of which was to throw the Russians back across the Vistula in bloody ruin. Once again, the fate of Europe was set to be decided upon the battlefield.

Just as Napoleon's campaign got underway, fate struck down his Russian military counterpart. On 28 April, years of over-indulgence and the strain of recent months finally caught up with Kutuzov. At Bunzlau in Silesia, the sixty-seven-year-old field marshal suffered a massive stroke and died. The Russian army mourned his passing, but Alexander saw in it the chance to promote to supreme command a man who had increasingly become a favourite over the past year. Affecting that a leader such as Kutuzov could never truly be replaced, the Tsar nevertheless offered the position of commander-in-chief of Allied forces to General Ludwig Wittgenstein. As his name suggests, Wittgenstein was of German origin (his father had been a general in the Prussian army). At just forty-three, he was younger and a commander of less seniority than several other possible candidates for the vacant post. Two such rivals, Generals Miloradovich and Tormasov, were so incensed by the promotion of a German who was junior to them that they refused point blank to serve under him. Although this was gross insubordination, Alexander was unwilling to crack down on his generals at this critical time. Instead, he suggested a poor compromise whereby Wittgenstein became commander-in-chief but the corps of Miloradovich and Tormasov were only answerable to the Tsar himself. This not only sowed confusion within the Allied high command but gave the militarily inexperienced and inept Alexander a potentially dangerous role in Russo-Prussian strategy.

Saxony, the region where the lion's share of the key engagements of 1813 were to be fought, was a largely pastoral land, fertile and relatively flat. In other words, it was ideal cavalry country, and the Allies endeavoured to exploit their considerable advantage in this arm from the start. On 29 April, a large force of 10,000 veteran Russian horsemen fell upon the advance guard of Marshal Ney's corps near Weissenfels, a town on the Saale around twenty miles south-west of Leipzig. For the great majority of Frenchmen attacked, it was the first time they had seen combat. They also had no cavalry support of their own, so dire was the shortage in Napoleon's army. The odds therefore seemed to favour a French defeat, but in a warning of what was to come, Ney's raw recruits fought like tigers, sending the Russians packing. It was most encouraging start for the Emperor.

Just two days later, however, Napoleon suffered a cruel personal blow. As the leading units of the army pushed on towards Leipzig that day, they stumbled across stiff Allied resistance. In the ensuing combat, Marshal Jean-Baptiste Bessières, commander of the Imperial Guard cavalry and a close friend of the Emperor since the early days, was hit in the chest by a cannonball, becoming the second of the Marshalate to die as a result of battle (Lannes had been the first in 1809). Napoleon was bitterly upset by the loss, but Ney reflected the increasingly stoical attitude of many of the Emperor's subordinates when he commented impassively of Bessières's demise, 'It's our lot. It's a fine way to die.'

Bessières's death highlighted the weakness of French intelligence regarding enemy positions or strength, the inevitable product of the army's dearth of cavalry, its principal information gatherers. Despite being able to muster over 140,000 men and 372 cannon for the thrust towards Leipzig in spring 1813, just 7,500 of Napoleon's soldiers were horsemen. By way of comparison, the Allies in Saxony had around four times as much cavalry, the bulk of it Russian, as well as a marked advantage in guns. Perhaps surprisingly, though, they were at an overall numerical disadvantage, a fact which they failed to appreciate in spite of their wealth of horsemen. Perhaps they simply could not believe that Napoleon could have gathered such a large force so soon.

Despite the Russian cavalry's unexpected reverse at Weissenfels, and oblivious of their overall inferiority in numbers, the Allies remained confident. As the sun set on 1 May, they planned to strike at the advancing French army. A dozen or so miles south-west of Leipzig lies the town of Lützen. That evening, Ney encamped three of the five divisions that made up his 45,000-strong corps in and around the town, pushing the remaining two a few miles south-east to shelter among a cluster of five villages named Starsiedl, Rahna, Kaja, Klein Görschen and Gross Görschen. Poor intelligence gathering now betrayed the Allies again, for they took Ney's force to be much smaller than it was and proceeded to base their planning upon this error. Under cover of darkness, the bulk of Allied forces in the Leipzig area would gather behind a range of low hills to the south of the five villages and then sweep down upon Ney's troops, catching them by surprise and crushing them. That achieved, the Russo-Prussian army would drive north into the flank of the rest of Napoleon's force, pushing it back against the River Elster, which flowed west from Leipzig. There, the Allies confidently predicted, the Emperor and his raw new army would meet their fate.

On the morning of 2 May 1813, Napoleon's attention was fixed upon capturing the city of Leipzig. Unaware of Allied plans, he expected the main fighting that day to take place there rather than near Lützen, so most of his army was ordered to close on the city, Ney's corps being ordered to protect the southern flank of the

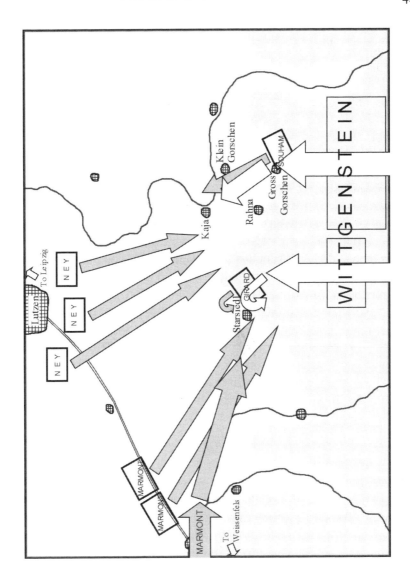

Battle of Lützen: The Allied Attack

advance against possible enemy manoeuvres. By early afternoon, leading elements of the army under Eugène were in position to attack their objective, but then, a dozen miles to the south-west, the Allies unleashed an assault of their own.

Caution was never a strength of Marshal Ney, but he was being especially lackadaisical in his attitude on this particular spring day. In contravention of general orders to keep his corps concentrated, he had left his divisions divided by the few miles of countryside between Lützen and the five villages to the south-east of the town. He had also failed to post pickets or to order a sweep of the land around his position for signs of the enemy. Instead, he let his men rest and relax, not expecting for one moment that they would be disturbed. Around noon, he was given a rude shock. A good number of Ney's soldiers were engaged in digging up potatoes from fields around the five villages when a large Allied army began to pour over the low hills to their south. Some 39,000 Russians with 314 guns, supported by 33,000 Prussians and 136 guns, had taken their enemy by complete surprise.

Ney and his corps were fortunate that the orders for the Allied attack prepared by Wittgenstein and his staff were overly complex, for this led to confusion and slowed the Russo-Prussian advance. Generals Souham and Girard, the commanders of the two divisions posted around the five villages, made full use of this, hurriedly organizing a sound defensive line centred upon Gross Görschen and Starsiedl, while Ney's other three divisions camped near Lützen began to march to their aid. When it finally hit, the weight of the Allied onslaught fell mostly upon Souham's troops at Gross Görschen (the name given to the battle in Germany) and compelled them to abandon the village and withdraw past Rahna and Klein Görschen towards Kaja, where the arrival of Ney's other divisions helped stabilize the line. A little way to the west at Starsiedl, meanwhile, Girard's soldiers held their ground well against an enemy assault before they too were reinforced by two divisions of Marshal Marmont's corps that had been nearing Lützen on their way towards Leipzig when the Allies attacked.

Despite the timely arrival of Marmont's troops, as well as Ney's other three divisions, the French remained at a serious disadvantage. They had fewer men, fewer cannon, almost no cavalry, and the great bulk of their soldiers were inexperienced conscripts. Nonetheless, they fought with tremendous courage to hold a line running from Starsiedl east to Kaja and a little way beyond. By 2.30 p.m., though, it seemed only a matter of time before the French line broke and the Allies achieved a victory. It was then, with impeccable timing, that Napoleon arrived on the field.

The Emperor had, of course, known of the fighting south-east of Lützen for some time, but his arrival on the scene was delayed by the need to ascertain whether it was a major assault or merely a diversionary attack designed to draw troops away from Leipzig. As more and more information reached him, he realized that his presence was demanded, so he quickly formulated a plan of battle. Ney and Marmont were to hold their position, supported, upon its arrival, by the Imperial Guard. Meanwhile, two other corps, those of Marshal Macdonald and General Henri-Gratien Bertrand, were to manoeuvre to attack the Allied right and left respectively. If all went perfectly, the enemy army would be enveloped and smashed.

In order for Macdonald and Bertrand to encircle the Allies, however, the French centre under Ney and Marmont would have to hold. When Napoleon reached the field at 2.30 p.m., followed over the next hour by the Guard, the prospect of this happening looked bleak. The troops of Marmont and Ney had been enduring a fearsome bombardment from the enemy artillery, and the Allies seemed poised to achieve a breakthrough. Appreciating the critical nature of the situation immediately and with no concern for his personal safety, the Emperor rode all along the French front line, giving advice and making his presence felt wherever he went. Raucous cries of 'Vive l'Empereur!' rent the air and the exhausted men of Ney's and Marmont's corps found the energy and the valour to hold their ground. By half past three, the greatest danger had passed and the Imperial Guard had arrived in force to stabilize the French line.

With the Guard's arrival, the overall numerical inferiority of Napoleon's army on the battlefield was reduced to just a few thousand, but then, around four o'clock, the Allies received substantial reinforcements themselves in the form of a sizeable reserve, largely comprised of Russian Guard units, which the Tsar had been holding back waiting for the ideal moment to lead them forward himself and win the battle. In truth, that moment had now come and gone, the fact that Alexander had missed it being testament to his military incompetence, but the arrival of thousands of fresh troops, many of them elite veterans, inevitably put the French line under severe pressure once more. Again the situation became critical and again the Emperor and his soldiers rose to the challenge. With the French compelled to yield ground between Starsiedl and Kaja by the force of the renewed Allied assault, Napoleon organized a brilliant counter-attack by elements of the Guard and Ney's corps which threw the enemy back.

By half past five, the Russo-Prussian onslaught was beginning to slacken, and with the corps of Macdonald and Bertrand at last in position on the Allied flanks, it was time for the French to go over to the offensive. Around 6 p.m., a battery of seventy cannon massed by the Emperor in the centre of his line opened fire at short range on the Allies opposite it, wreaking tremendous damage. Shortly after, Napoleon sent forward the Guard, supported by those of Ney's troops who were not entirely exhausted, against the centre of the enemy line, while Bertrand and Macdonald began to attack the Allied flanks. Realizing the peril in which his army now found itself, and with the middle of his line beginning to collapse, Wittgenstein swiftly ordered a retreat.

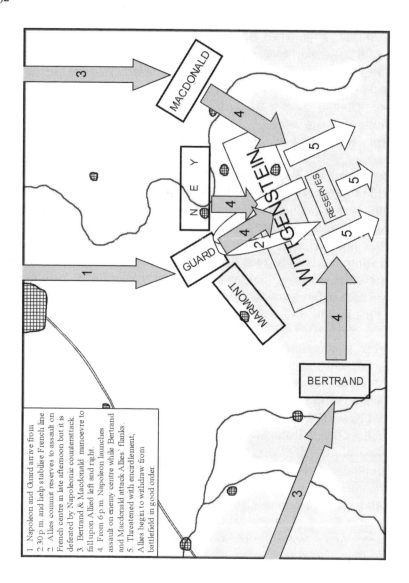

1. Napoleon and Guard arrive from
2.30 p.m. and help stabilise French line.
2. Allies commit reserves to assault on
French centre in late afternoon but it is
defeated by Napoleonic counterattack.
3. Bertrand & Macdonald manoeuvre to
fall upon Allied left and right.
4. From 6 p.m. Napoleon launches
assault on enemy centre while Bertrand
and Macdonald attack Allies' flanks.
5. Threatened with encirclement,
Allies begin to withdraw from
battlefield in good order.

Battle of Lützen: The French Attack

Three things prevented a hard-won French victory turning into a rout comparable to Austerlitz or Friedland. First, the Russian and Prussian troops were generally of a higher quality and better organized than in previous years. This meant that they were able to conduct a fighting withdrawal in good order and with some skill. Secondly, the French troops, despite their undoubted bravery, were mostly of a poorer quality than in previous years and were unable to outmarch or outmanoeuvre the retreating Allies. Had Macdonald's and Bertrand's corps been chiefly made up of veterans rather than raw conscripts, they would almost certainly have reached the battlefield earlier and might have succeeded in encircling the enemy. Finally, and perhaps most importantly, the French army lacked horses. Not only did this prevent the artillery from keeping up with the infantry as Napoleon's soldiers finally advanced, but, even worse, the dearth of cavalry prevented the Emperor from delivering a truly telling blow against his retreating foes. The Allies used their numerous horsemen to cover their withdrawal, their presence forcing the advancing French infantry continually to form square, thereby greatly slowing their progress and allowing the rest of the Russo-Prussian army to escape.

The French abandoned their attempt to pursue the Allies as night fell on the evening of 2 May. They had failed to win a decisive victory, but to have won at all was a tremendous achievement given the inexperience of the bulk of their troops, their inferiority in artillery, their dire lack of cavalry, and the fact that they had been taken by surprise. True, the Allies might have been led rather better than they were, but that does not detract from the remarkable courage and tenacity of the French, especially the corps of Ney and Marmont, which bore the brunt of the fighting. Napoleon too had had a good day, displaying outstanding bravery and no little skill. Although disappointed not to have achieved a more crushing victory, he was relieved at the same time to have avoided an all too possible defeat. Above all, he was delighted with the performance of his troops. In a letter to his old associate Cambacérès after the battle, he wrote, 'Nothing could equal the bravery, the determination and the passion that all these young soldiers are showing me; they are full of enthusiasm'. Less happily, he had also been impressed by his adversaries. He had grown frustratingly used to Russian doggedness over the past year, but their Prussian allies had surprised him. Frederick William's troops in 1813 were a different prospect than their predecessors of 1806.

Losses at Lützen were around 20,000 on each side. A rather lower figure is sometimes claimed for the Allies, but this seems unlikely given the course and outcome of the battle. A dozen miles to the north-east, meanwhile, Leipzig had fallen that afternoon to a force led by Eugène. The Russians and Prussians who had defended the city had been considerably outnumbered, but had managed to withdraw in good order and subsequently rejoined the main body of the Allied army. The Emperor immediately made Leipzig his forward base of operations and main supply dump for the next phase of the campaign. In a proclamation to his army the day after Lützen, he endeavoured to urge his men on to even greater triumphs, especially over the troublesome Russians. 'We shall throw these Tartars back to their dreadful country that they ought not to have left,' he boldly prophesied. 'Let them stay in their frozen deserts, home of slavery, barbarism and corruption where man is reduced to the level of the beast.' There was clearly a lot more fighting ahead for Napoleon's raw new army.

The French tried to keep up with the retreating Allies after Lützen, but it soon proved largely impossible. Brave as the new recruits were, they could not march as fast as the Emperor wanted them to, and straggling and disorder became increasingly common. With a higher ratio of experienced troops under his command than in most of the rest of the army, Eugène, leading the advance guard, did manage to catch up with the Russo-Prussian rearguard under Miloradovich near Colditz on 5 May, but the subsequent action only confirmed that it would be extremely difficult to bring the Allies to battle if they were unwilling.

Following the engagement at Colditz, Eugène was sent back to northern Italy to help raise more units and organize the defence of the region against a possible Austrian attack, tasks he fulfilled with aplomb. His departure left Ney as Napoleon's senior subordinate, so it was to him that the Emperor entrusted around a third of his army, with orders to march north-east towards Torgau on the Elbe so as to establish a threat to Berlin. The Emperor himself, meanwhile, would push on south-east towards Dresden, hoping that Ney's thrust would induce the Prussians to divide from their Russian allies and head north to defend their capital. If that happened, he would endeavour to smash the Tsar's forces before reuniting with Ney to batter Berlin's defenders. It was a sound enough plan, but it depended upon the Allies behaving exactly as Napoleon wanted them to.

In previous years, the Emperor's enemies might well have fallen into his trap, but bitter experience had taught them a crucial lesson: if they were to defeat the French they had to work together. Therefore, although the establishment of a threat to Berlin caused consternation among the Prussian contingent of the main Allied army in Saxony, Blücher and his subordinates stood by the Russian decision to withdraw east towards Silesia, through which the Tsar's army's line of communications ran all the way back to Russia. This left the Prussian capital vulnerable should Napoleon move against it in force, but, more important than that, it maintained Allied unity.

The French crossed the Elbe on 11 May. At Dresden, Miloradovich had made a limited effort to slow the passage over the river, but the Emperor's army was too large for him to make a serious stand without the support of the rest of the main Allied army; support which, to Napoleon's surprise, was not forthcoming.

The fact is that Lützen had temporarily shaken Allied morale and confidence, the nervous Frederick William even crying out at one point, 'God in Heaven, does this mean I must go back to Memel after all?'* Fortunately for the Allies, Alexander retained his composure in the face of disappointment and retreat better than his fellow monarch, although even his formerly unshakeable belief in the certainty of victory had been dented by recent events.

Further north, meanwhile, Ney crossed the Elbe at Torgau. His passage had been threatened less by the enemy than by the Emperor's nominal Saxon allies, who had initially barred the town's gates to the French on the grounds that Saxony was now a neutral state. Technically, this was correct, as King Frederick Augustus had signed a neutrality agreement sponsored by the Austrians in April, but Napoleon was in no mood to brook such dissension from a supposed ally. When he learnt of the obstruction being offered to Ney's troops, the Emperor quickly despatched an angry missive to the Saxon King threatening to strip him of his crown unless he started to live up to the responsibilities of his alliance with France. The warning worked, Frederick Augustus ordering Torgau to be handed over to Ney and instructing what was left of his armed forces to work with the French, but it was hardly a voluntary decision. Saxon loyalty to Napoleon was far from unswerving, as would be made clear later in the year.

Once the French were over the Elbe, the Allies had a critical decision to make. Should they continue their retreat over the next major river, the Oder, or should they make a stand somewhere in eastern Saxony? By mid-May, the Allied withdrawal had reached the town of Bautzen on the upper Spree just a few miles from the border with Austria. Here the main army was reinforced by 16,000 Russians under General Barclay and a further 11,000 Russians and Prussians under General Kleist. This greatly eased the anxiety within Allied headquarters that had accompanied the retreat from Lützen and the decision was swiftly reached to make a stand on the good defensive ground to the east of the town. Confidence in victory was not as firm as it had been before the battle of a fortnight ago, but it was deemed probable enough. Besides, to retreat any further might begin to look like cowardice and would most likely destroy any hope of Austria joining the coalition in the near future.

The Allies might have been less inclined to make a stand had they appreciated the magnitude of the forces at Napoleon's disposal by mid-May. Further waves of new recruits reached Saxony shortly after Lützen and these, plus the few thousand Saxon troops bullied out of Frederick Augustus, gave the Emperor and Ney a combined force around twice as large as the main Russo-Prussian army at Bautzen. Bonaparte now had around 120,000 men under his immediate

---

* Memel was the town near the Russian border to which Frederick William had been forced to flee in 1807.

command, while the marshal was in charge of almost 85,000. That said, the French still had rather fewer cannon than their adversaries, and their cavalry arm remained small; just 12,000 with Napoleon, fewer than 5,000 with Ney.

It was perhaps these weaknesses, and fear that they would prevent him winning a truly decisive victory on the battlefield, that led the Emperor in mid-May to make an attempt to initiate peace talks with the Tsar. He expressed his hopes to an aide: 'If the Emperor Alexander and I could have just one talk together, I am certain we would end up agreeing with each other ... A single conversation at Russian headquarters and we could divide the world between us!' It was a naive belief, based upon a misreading of the Tsar's character in 1813. Napoleon was mesmerized by the mistaken conviction that if only he could meet Alexander face-to-face he would be able to flatter him and restore the good personal relations of the Tilsit period. Although he appears to have been prepared to grant the Russians 'profitable concessions', as he put it to Caulaincourt, to back up his smooth talk, to imagine that it would be possible to turn the clock back to 1807 was unrealistic. After the bitter disappointment of the alliance with France and the experience of the invasion of 1812, the Tsar was in no mood to make friends with Napoleon again. His foreign policy agenda was altogether different now. When Alexander's old friend Caulaincourt arrived at Allied headquarters in mid-May requesting an audience with him, therefore, the response was unequivocal: he was told to return forthwith to his master. If the Emperor was to achieve the peace he wanted, he was going to have to force the Tsar to give it to him.

The advance guard of Napoleon's army discovered the Allies preparing to make a stand near Bautzen on 16 May, but no attack developed for several days in order to give Caulaincourt's mission a chance to succeed and to allow the Emperor time to develop a plan of battle in case it did not. The Allied position was a strong one. Their main line stretched for around seven miles approximately south–west to north–east along high ground which overlooked the River Spree to the west. At the southern, or left, end of the line, where the terrain was highest, was the village of Binnewitz, barely a handful of miles from the Austrian frontier. To the north, or right, was a network of ponds, bogs and causeways, to the rear of which was a village called Preititz. Bautzen itself stood on the eastern bank of the Spree opposite the left-centre of the Allied position. The main Allied line was covered by sporadic woods and hamlets and reinforced by several earthworks. In this formidable position, around 65,000 Russians and over 30,000 Prussians, backed by 472 Russian and 150 Prussian cannon, awaited a French attack.

Napoleon's army was in position to assault the Allied line from across the River Spree by 19 May, but he delayed. Rather than fight a straightforward frontal battle as he essentially had at Borodino, the Emperor's plan at Bautzen was more subtle and potentially more devastating. He would attack across the Spree, but with the key purpose of distracting and pinning down the Allies rather than breaking through their line. Ney and his army, meanwhile, would march so as to fall upon the enemy right-rear after the Allies had been fixed in place by Napoleon. Driving south through Preititz, the Marshal and his men would be in a position to cut off the enemy's retreat eastwards. The only avenue of escape for the Allies then would be south towards the mountainous Austrian border. If they stood and fought with their backs to the frontier they would be crushed by sheer weight of numbers, but if they crossed it they would be violating Austrian neutrality and Vienna would be compelled under international law to disarm any units which entered its territory. Either way, the largest Russo-Prussian army in central Europe would be removed from the equation and the road to Berlin and then the Vistula would be opened. It was an excellent plan, but it contained a fatal flaw in the person of Marshal Ney. He may have been the bravest of the brave but he was not the cleverest of the clever. Time and again, Ney would prove himself not up to the kind of semi-independent command with which he was now entrusted, at least when it required subtle and intelligent interpretation of a complicated strategy. Unfortunately for Napoleon, Ney never properly understood what was required of him; he simply lacked the strategic nous. That said, the flame-haired marshal was not helped by an order from the Emperor instructing him to detach two of the four corps under his command to guard against any possible threat from his rear as he advanced south-east towards Preititz. This was the product of confusion caused by lack of intelligence regarding enemy numbers and dispositions, and Napoleon subsequently revoked it, but by that time the two corps had been detached and would not rejoin Ney until after he had arrived on the battlefield.

The Allies, meanwhile, were suffering from intelligence failures of their own. Although they were aware of Ney's army, they greatly underestimated its size and so neglected to make any detailed plans to cope with the possibility of an attack from the north. On 19 May, while the Emperor was reconnoitring the Allied line, Wittgenstein sent Barclay and Yorck to explore to the north of the Russo-Prussian position. In so doing, they ran into an Italian division of General Bertrand's corps as it was marching to join the extreme left of the French line and gave it a severe mauling before being forced to withdraw back south by the arrival of the advance guard of Ney's army under General Lauriston, the former ambassador to Russia. The Allies lost around 2,000 men in the fighting, but inflicted almost 3,000 casualties on the enemy. This limited Russo-Prussian victory was not without its cost, however, for they mistook Lauriston's corps for the whole of Ney's force and assumed that it would join the main French battle line rather than form part of a separate attack on the Allied right-rear. As the sun set on the 19th, therefore, the Allies were dangerously ignorant of the scale of the peril mounting to their north.

Napoleon also knew by the evening of 19 May that the bulk of Ney's force would not be in position to assault the right-rear of the enemy line until the morning of the 21st, having advanced more slowly than the Emperor had envisaged. Rather than postpone his own pinning attack until then and risk having the Allies withdraw before the trap could be sprung, Napoleon decided to go ahead with an assault next day anyway, albeit a more restricted one than he had originally intended.

The French artillery opened fire on the Allies from the west bank of the Spree shortly after midday on 20 May. The Russians and Prussians responded in kind, but in spite of the hail of cannon fire directed at them, Napoleon's engineers succeeded in throwing pontoon bridges across the relatively narrow river to both the north and south of Bautzen. Oudinot's corps of three divisions on the right of the French line was the first over the Spree that afternoon and lost little time in pressing on towards Binnewitz, a key position on the Allied left. Despite the hilly ground, Oudinot's men, soon supported by part of Macdonald's corps after it had cleared Bautzen of its small Allied garrison, did so well against the Russians facing them that the Tsar insisted that a large part of the Allied reserve be committed to their southern flank in order to prop it up. Alexander was convinced that Napoleon would try to turn the Allied left in order to cut them off from Austria, a belief that betrayed his lack of military understanding. The more knowledgeable Wittgenstein thought such a manoeuvre improbable, but he was powerless to prevent his political master from committing ever more of his reserves to the left. Meanwhile, to the north of Bautzen, the rest of Macdonald's troops supported by Marmont's corps pushed back the Allied centre, while on the French left Bertrand's corps made it over the Spree in the face of stiff resistance from Blücher's Prussians and Barclay's Russians.

By the time the fighting died out that evening, the whole of Napoleon's army had succeeded in getting across the Spree, although the Allies remained in possession of their main line, which ran along the high ground and was fortified by earthworks. Progress had been particularly impressive in the south, despite the increasing numbers of Russians committed to the battle there, while the Allies had been most successful in checking Bertrand's advance in the north. In short, everything had gone pretty much as Napoleon had hoped and intended. His thrust on the right had drawn Allied attention to the south in preparation for Ney's arrival in the north next morning, without being so successful as to persuade the Allies to withdraw overnight. It was all set up perfectly for the *coup de grâce* to be delivered the following day. The Emperor and his army had fulfilled their part of the plan. Now it was down to Ney to finish the job.

Although Napoleon was determined to wait for Ney to arrive in the Allied right-rear before launching a major attack to their front on 21 May, fighting

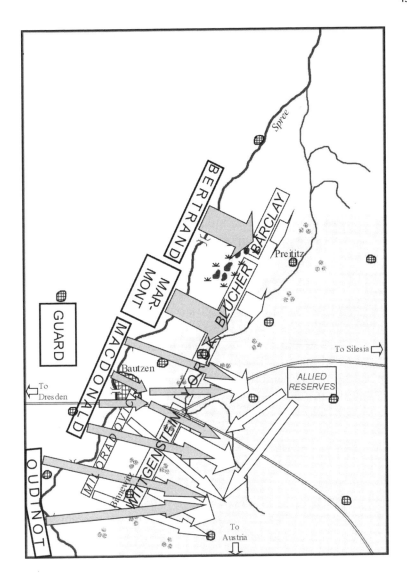

Battle of Bautzen: 20 May

nevertheless resumed shortly after dawn. Preoccupied still with the Allies' southern flank, Alexander ordered a vigorous attack to be made against the five divisions of Oudinot and Macdonald deployed on the French right to which practically all the Russians' reserves were committed. It was a powerful blow which drove the enemy divisions from the ground they had occupied the previous day but did not break them. As at Lützen, the Emperor's inexperienced troops were proving more resilient than expected.

Ney, meanwhile, hit the Allied right flank with his leading divisions as the Russians were busy assaulting Oudinot and Macdonald. Initially, the Tsar was convinced that this must be a diversionary attack, and this, plus the fact that almost all the Allied reserves had been committed to the struggle in the south, meant that Ney faced rather less opposition to his advance than he might have. By 10 a.m., an hour ahead of schedule, he had advanced as far as the village of Preititz, which Russian troops from Barclay's corps were busy turning into a stronghold.

Thus far, Ney had performed well enough in his semi-independent command, but now he began to show his limitations. His lack of strategic intelligence led him to obey the letter rather than the spirit of his instructions. As his orders had told him to be at Preititz by eleven, he decided to wait an hour before resuming his advance. Then, he allowed himself to become bogged down in a bitter fight for control of the village rather than masking the settlement with part of his force and continuing on with the bulk of his divisions. Preititz eventually fell in the early afternoon, but the battle for it had bought the Allies time to organize the defence of their right-rear. Ney now again became embroiled in a struggle of only secondary importance, this time an assault on some of Blücher's Prussians drawn up on high ground to the south-east of Preititz. Once more, these enemy units could have been masked and bypassed in the interests of advancing as far as possible in order to cut off the Allies' retreat.

Ney was without two of the four corps entrusted to him throughout the morning and part of the afternoon of 21 May. The two corps which Napoleon had ordered Ney to detach in the days before the battle were still some way behind the Marshal's leading divisions on the morning of the 21st, despite the Emperor's subsequent reversal of his detachment order, and so would not join the fight until the afternoon. Had they been with him from the start, it is possible that Ney would have been bolder in pushing on. That said, the two corps which the Marshal did have with him from the start together made up some two-thirds of his total command and certainly considerably outnumbered the force the Allies could muster to face him on their right flank. In the final analysis, there really is no escaping the fact that Ney bungled his crucial attack at Bautzen and that a superior commander could have done much better.

With Oudinot, Macdonald and Marmont pinning down the Allied left and centre, and Ney occupying much of their right, Napoleon ordered Bertrand's corps to assault the Prussian divisions opposite it around lunchtime. This should probably have broken the Allied line given how thinly stretched it was becoming, but, despite making initial progress, the attack faded in the face of stiff resistance from determined soldiers in strong defensive positions. It was therefore left up to the veterans of the Imperial Guard to breach the enemy line as they had at Lützen. In mid-afternoon, Bonaparte's finest warriors advanced resolutely against the Allied right-centre. Wittgenstein, Blücher, even Alexander all knew that they could hold no longer. Their men were exhausted and ammunition was beginning to run low. A general retreat eastwards towards Silesia was ordered.

Despite being heavily outnumbered, the Allies successfully managed to extricate themselves from the battlefield at Bautzen. As at Lützen, their superiority in cavalry was the key factor here, precluding any pursuit by the victorious French. Losses in the battle, at around 20,000 on each side, were perhaps rather lower than they might have been given the duration of the fighting. Certainly, Napoleon was bitterly disappointed not to have done much more damage to the Allied army. 'Not a gun, not a prisoner!', he griped after the battle. 'These people don't leave me so much as a nail!' The lion's share of the blame for this failure can only be laid at Ney's door, although credit should also be given to the heroic performance of many of the Allied troops, especially Blücher's Prussians and Barclay's Russians on the right. Indeed, given the heavy French superiority in numbers and the fact that Ney should probably have succeeded in cutting off the Allies' escape route east, it is tempting to see Bautzen less as a minor French victory than as a potentially decisive triumph thrown away.

In the days after the battle, a disconsolate Napoleon led the bulk of his army east after the retreating Allies. On 22 May, he suffered a loss that deepened his gloom still further. In a sharp clash with the Allied rearguard, General Duroc, one of Bonaparte's oldest and closest friends, and, for many years his Grand Marshal of the Palace in charge of the Imperial household, was mortally wounded. He lingered on long enough to receive a visit from his master, but there was nothing that could be done to save him. Six days later came some better news from Hoyerswerda, some way to the north of Bautzen. Oudinot had been sent to probe towards Berlin and on 28 May he bloodily repulsed an attack by a Prussian force under General von Bülow (although just over a week later the tables would be turned, Oudinot suffering a reverse at Luckau). On 29 May came even better news. The ever-reliable Davout had recaptured Hamburg, a city he would successfully defend for almost a year. The main army under Napoleon, meanwhile, made slow but steady progress eastwards. By 1 June, the advance guard had reached the Silesian city of Breslau on the Oder, while the Emperor himself was a little way further west at Neumarkt. Next day, seemingly out of the blue, the Emperor agreed to a thirty-six-hour armistice, extended on 4 June until 20 July. The war, for the moment at least, was over.

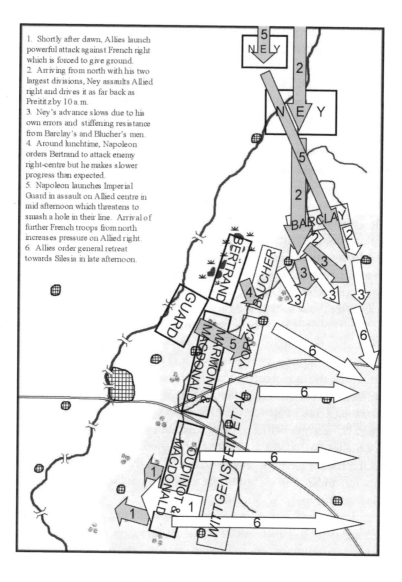

1. Shortly after dawn, Allies launch powerful attack against French right which is forced to give ground.
2. Arriving from north with his two largest divisions, Ney assaults Allied right and drives it as far back as Preititz by 10 a.m.
3. Ney's advance slows due to his own errors and stiffening resistance from Barclay's and Blucher's men.
4. Around lunchtime, Napoleon orders Bertrand to attack enemy right-centre but he makes slower progress than expected.
5. Napoleon launches Imperial Guard in assault on Allied centre in mid afternoon which threatens to smash a hole in their line. Arrival of further French troops from north increases pressure on Allied right.
6. Allies order general retreat towards Silesia in late afternoon.

Battle of Bautzen: 21 May

The armistice of summer 1813 was suggested and sponsored by Vienna, and the idea behind it was that it would create a breathing space in which a peace deal might be struck. The main reasons why both Napoleon and the Allies decided to accept the Austrian idea of a ceasefire, though, were military. In the wake of Bautzen, the Allies especially were somewhat in disarray. Their morale was low following a second defeat and withdrawal within the space of a few weeks, and serious tensions were developing among their high command. Wittgenstein used the French victory as an excuse to resign as commander-in-chief, the real reason for his stepping down being extreme irritation with the Tsar's unhelpful interference in military affairs. This gave Alexander the chance to appoint an old favourite, Barclay de Tolly, as Wittgenstein's successor, but he was still unpopular with most ethnic Russians among the higher echelons of the Tsar's army. More problematic than that, though, was the disagreement that erupted between Barclay and the senior Prussian commander, Blücher. Barclay's instinct after Bautzen was to retreat all the way into Poland, but this was anathema to the fiery old Prussian. Blücher, often more courageous than he was sensible, was all for making another stand shortly after the defeat at Bautzen in the hope of throwing the French back. In the end, they compromised on a retreat into Silesia, with the decision what to do then being deferred.

The Austrian suggestion of an armistice therefore came at a very opportune moment for the Allies and they agreed to it enthusiastically. The ceasefire would give them time to reorganize, raise more troops, and, perhaps most important, push hard for Vienna to join the coalition and tip the balance against Napoleon. Neither the Russians nor the Prussians seem to have believed, or even hoped, for one minute that the truce would actually lead to a peace settlement.

The need for the French to agree to an armistice was not as great as that of the Allies, but there were still pressing reasons for the Emperor to consent to a temporary cessation of hostilities. By early June, the rigours of the campaign were really beginning to take a toll on his predominantly raw new army. Straggling was reaching alarming levels and the sick list was growing daily. Cossacks were also beginning to disrupt the ever-lengthening French supply lines, and stocks of ammunition and food were starting to run low. A period of truce, moreover, would buy time for the Emperor's mostly inexperienced soldiers to be given further training to close the overall gap on the Allies in terms of troop quality.

Two issues above all, however, persuaded Napoleon to agree to a ceasefire. First was the desire to strengthen his cavalry arm. His weakness in this area had had profoundly deleterious effects upon his recent operations. Indeed, it would be perfectly reasonable to argue that, had he had a considerably stronger cavalry arm in spring 1813, he would already have smashed the Allies' main army and won the campaign. The Emperor therefore hoped that the temporary cessation in hostilities would give him time to build up a decent mounted force in central

Europe, largely from yet further withdrawals of French forces in Spain.

The second key issue persuading him to agree to a truce was concern about Austria. Although the Austrians did not openly threaten him with intervention should he refuse their suggestion of an armistice, Napoleon was becoming increasingly concerned that the Habsburgs were waiting for the most opportune time to declare war. With his lines of communication back to France becoming ever longer and his army experiencing more and more difficulties, the Emperor was seriously worried that to offend Vienna by rejecting its proposal might finally persuade the Austrian government to throw in its lot with the Russians and Prussians.

Thus Napoleon had a number of powerful reasons to agree to a ceasefire in early summer 1813. Furthermore, contrary to the impression given by many accounts of the events of the period, he was by no means averse to the prospect of a peace settlement at this point, provided that its terms were, from his point of view, acceptable (perhaps the loss of the Grand Duchy of Warsaw, minor modifications in Germany and cession of the Illyrian Provinces to Austria). He had after all tried to engineer peace talks with the Tsar shortly before Bautzen.

Despite all this, however, Bonaparte's decision to agree to the armistice of June 1813 has often been heralded as one of his greatest mistakes. As we shall see in the next chapter, any prospect of a peace acceptable to Napoleon swiftly disappeared, while it was the Allies rather than the French that most benefited militarily from the temporary cessation of hostilities. Of course, one cannot say with any degree of certainty what would have happened had the Emperor continued his campaign in early June, but it is undoubtedly possible that he might have inflicted a serious blow against the Allies. Despite his concerns, it seems unlikely that Austria would have committed herself to war before late summer, leaving Napoleon free to have another crack at the main Russo-Prussian army. In early June, this was at Schweidnitz in Silesia, to the south of Bonaparte's much larger force. In other words, the French were in a good position to fall upon their enemy's flank or rear and to have another go at bringing off the kind of envelopment that had been attempted at both Lützen and Bautzen. Making this even more possible, Blücher had effectively won his dispute with Barclay and the Allied high command had decided that it would make a stand at Schweidnitz if it were attacked there.

Had Napoleon had a better insight into Austrian intentions in early summer 1813, had he been more aware of the difficulties which beset the Allies and less concerned about those of his own army, perhaps simply had he been in a more confident mood in the wake of the disappointments of Bautzen and the death of Duroc, he might have rejected the suggestion of an armistice, at least until he had had another attempt at smashing the main Russo-Prussian army.

Whether history would then have followed a very different course we do not know; but it might have. Individual decisions can sometimes have a critical impact upon future events, and the Emperor's decision to accept the Austrian ceasefire proposal may well have been one of those occasions. He could not have known it in June 1813, but in agreeing to the armistice, Napoleon was doing much to seal his own fate.

19

Disaster in Germany

Contrary to subsequent French suspicions, Vienna's successful sponsoring of an armistice between Napoleon and the Russians and Prussians in early June 1813 was not just a desperate effort to save the Allies from impending doom. Since early in the year, Austria had been suggesting to each warring government that they agree to a ceasefire to be followed by peace talks which she offered to mediate. Her efforts had met with little success for a long time. Both sides were wary of Austrian motives, Napoleon because of Vienna's move from alliance with France to a position of alleged neutrality, the Russians and Prussians because Austria had until recently been a French ally and because her Chancellor, Klemens von Metternich, had played a central role in arranging the Emperor's dynastic marriage to the Habsburg ruler's eldest daughter, Marie-Louise. In any case, in the first half of 1813, Alexander, Frederick William and Napoleon had all been far more interested in winning Austria as a military partner than as a mediator. By early June, however, both sides were finally prepared to agree to an Austrian-sponsored armistice. The prospects of the truce turning into peace were never good, but that is not to say that none of the parties involved desired some kind of peaceful settlement. At least two of the powers concerned, Austria and France, were prepared to consider what they saw as a compromise peace in summer 1813. Unfortunately, their respective views of what constituted an acceptable settlement were poles apart.

Despite claiming to be neutral mediators, the Austrian government and its chief minister were in reality anything but. It is clear that from the start Metternich essentially positioned himself in the Allied camp. Indeed, in April, he had informed the Russians that 'if France does not accede to an arrangement based on the principles which His Imperial Majesty [Emperor Francis] believes necessary to the existence of his Empire and the well-being of Europe, His Majesty will use all the forces which Providence has put in his hands to cooperate in perfect accord with the Allied powers in the establishment of such an order of things.' The wording is elaborate but the meaning is clear enough: either Napoleon accepted what Vienna saw as an acceptable basis for peace or Austria would join the Allies.

It would be inaccurate, however, to view the Austrians as too intimately aligned with the Russians and Prussians. Their aims were significantly different to those of the Allies in a couple of ways. Although Vienna, like Berlin and St Petersburg, wanted to make substantial gains in both territory and influence at the expense of the Napoleonic Empire, it was much more prepared to consider non-military means to achieve those ends than the Allies. It was indeed more important for the Habsburgs in 1813 to achieve their minimum aims without recourse to war than to try to realize their maximum goals through conflict. Emperor Francis was terrified of the prospect of war with France, even in the wake of Napoleon's Russian disaster, and although Metternich was much less fearful, he preferred to avoid the messiness and uncertainty of conflict if possible. Nor were the Habsburgs or their chief minister as adamantly opposed to either Napoleon or a strong France as the Russians or Prussians (or, of course, the British). Indeed, the Austrian Government actually now favoured the French retaining at least some of the gains in territory and influence that they had made since the Revolution and were even happy for the Emperor to remain in power in Paris. There are two key reasons for this change of heart since earlier years. First, Vienna was becoming increasingly alarmed about Prussian and, especially, Russian expansionism in Germany, Poland and south-east Europe. Now that those two nations were bound closely together, the threat seemed even greater and Metternich saw a strong France as a natural ally for Austria in checking too great an extension of Russo-Prussian power. Secondly, it was not lost on Vienna that Napoleon's heir was the Austrian emperor's grandson, so the attraction of maintaining the Bonaparte dynasty was obvious.

As far as the Russian and Prussian governments are concerned, they were united in wanting Napoleon overthrown and France stripped of practically all her international gains since the Revolution, and they saw war as the only means of achieving those ends. There is not the slightest indication that either saw the Austrian-sponsored armistice as a genuine opportunity to try to make peace. Instead, they viewed Napoleon's willingness to accept a truce as evidence that, despite his victories at Lützen and Bautzen, he feared he would ultimately lose the war, a belief that only encouraged their bellicose attitude. True, they consented to Metternich putting peace proposals to the Emperor that fell short of their ultimate goals, but they did so on the strict understanding that they were not bound or restricted by them should the Emperor, against expectations, agree to them. Indeed, they specifically envisaged that if Napoleon were to agree to the proposals, further demands would be made of him at the peace table.*

In mid-June, Metternich met Tsar Alexander and the Prussian leadership

---

* The position of the British government in mid 1813 was, if anything, even more hard-line than that of Russia and Prussia, and it was prepared to offer huge subsidies to Tsar Alexander and King Frederick William if they undertook to maintain large armies in the field against France, an offer which both monarchs gladly accepted just a few days after the start of the armistice.

to thrash out a set of proposals which he could put to Napoleon as a basis for peace. Although there was apparent agreement that, ideally, the French should be expelled from Italy, Holland and Spain as well as Germany, Poland and south-east Europe, the Austrian Chancellor succeeded in getting the Russians and Prussians to agree to a more limited initial programme, albeit with the critical provisos mentioned above. This programme essentially reflected Vienna's (though not London's, Berlin's or St Petersburg's) absolute minimum terms for a settlement with France and comprised four key demands: (1) French withdrawal from the lands in northern Germany annexed in late 1810; (2) the formal dissolution of both the Confederation of the Rhine and the Grand Duchy of Warsaw; (3) the restitution to Prussia of the German lands she lost in 1807; and (4) the return to Austria of the territory now comprising the Illyrian Provinces.

Ignoring the hard-line policy of Russia and Prussia, many have firmly placed responsibility for the failure to reach a peaceful settlement in summer 1813 at the door of Napoleon, accusing him of seeing the armistice only as a chance to improve his armed forces before renewing hostilities. Certainly, the Emperor devoted much attention over the summer to organizing supplies, raising, equipping and training new troops, sorting out hospital arrangements and other military preparations, but it would have been remiss of him in the extreme not to have prepared for a resumption of war that might come whether he wanted it or not. The truth is that Napoleon was not averse to making peace in summer 1813 as is sometimes suggested. As he said to Caulaincourt in early June, 'If we did not intend to treat with a view to peace, we should not be so stupid as to treat for an armistice at the present time'. The key obstacle to peace was not his abhorrence of making a deal short of total victory, but the gulf which separated what he on the one hand and his enemies on the other saw as an acceptable settlement.

Much of the ammunition for those who blame Napoleon for the failure of peace efforts in mid-1813 is provided by Metternich's account of the stormy interview he had with the Emperor in Dresden on 26 June, at which he put forward the minimum proposals agreed with the Russians and Prussians. The Austrian Chancellor portrays Napoleon as utterly opposed to any concession. 'I shall never cede one inch of territory!' Metternich claimed Napoleon shouted at one point. 'A man such as I does not take much heed of the lives of a million men,' he allegedly snarled at another moment. Is this belligerent, uncompromising depiction of the Emperor accurate, though? There is good reason to believe it is not. The French version of the interview, the only other account, gives a different story, which, though undoubtedly biased, rings altogether more true than Metternich's report. According to the Austrian Chancellor, for example, he ended the meeting with the words, 'You are lost, Sire. I had the presentiment of it when I came: now, in going, I have the certainty.' This is surely far too neat, the kind of thing one wishes one had said at the conclusion of a tempestuous dialogue but which one does not think of until much later. If this is embellished, then perhaps other parts of the account are too? Would Napoleon really have said that he was not prepared to cede an inch of territory or that he did not care if a million men died in continued fighting? It seems highly unlikely that the Emperor would have wished to portray himself as so utterly intransigent or callous, especially as it seems that, at the very least, he was willing to write off the Grand Duchy of Warsaw and the Illyrian provinces as the price for peace. The loss of all French influence in Germany east of the Rhine, though, was too much for him to swallow following a victorious, if far from decisive, spring campaign in Saxony. That, according to Napoleon, 'would be only a vast capitulation', and if he grew furious with the Austrian Chancellor during their meeting, which the French account does not hide, then it was the understandable result of Metternich behaving as anything but the impartial, neutral mediator he claimed to be by making such a bold demand.

But were Metternich's proposals really as draconian as Napoleon claimed? The Emperor argued that, if he accepted them, it would severely, perhaps terminally, undermine his regime. As he put it to those around him, 'They offer me a doubtful permission to exist.' While the loss of influence in Germany would undoubtedly have been a major blow to French prestige and power, however, there is little reason to believe that that would necessarily have led to rebellion against his rule in France, as Napoleon claimed. He would remain in power, and indeed was welcomed back as ruler, following worse reverses. Almost all his key supporters also believed that the regime could survive a major concession, such as the loss of Germany, made in order to secure peace. Many of his marshals, including Berthier, Ney and Oudinot, most people in government in Paris, and many other key aides, such as Caulaincourt, all urged the Emperor to make a compromise if one were required to achieve a settlement. He ignored all their pleas.

Given what happened in the second half of 1813 and the first months of 1814, Napoleon's refusal to give up French influence in Germany seems reckless at best. This interpretation depends, however, upon two assumptions that were unclear in 1813. The first was that France was certain to lose the war if it resumed. This depends ultimately upon hindsight. While it was clear that France would struggle if Austria joined the list of her enemies, it was not so certain that she would necessarily be crushed. Complete victory was unlikely, to be sure, but it was not inconceivable that the French could have done enough to force her opponents to negotiate seriously for peace rather than trying to impose a settlement upon them. Certainly, Napoleon felt that victory of some kind, or at least the avoidance of total defeat, was possible, even probable, which is partly why he was so reluctant to make such a major compromise as ceding Germany without a fight.

The second assumption is that the Emperor could have achieved a lasting and tolerable peace by agreeing to the proposals put to him by Metternich. The truth, as Napoleon himself realized, was that he could not. He knew how desirable peace was for a France and Empire exhausted by war, but after the fateful Dresden meeting he did not believe that his enemies' demands would stop at the proposals put to him by the Austrian Chancellor as the minimum requirements for a settlement. If they were the minimum, what further ultimata awaited him should he agree to accept them? The Emperor was convinced that the rulers of the four other major European powers wanted him overthrown and the Empire dismantled entirely, which was not far from the truth in the case of Britain, Russia and Prussia. To agree to make a major concession such as withdrawing from Germany, would only serve to encourage France's foes to demand more, would convince the still (barely) neutral Austrians that the French were already half-beaten, and would severely undermine French morale and attempts to retain their position east of the Rhine should hostilities resume.*

The failure to make peace in summer 1813 was, therefore, more the fault of the Russians and Prussians (and British) than of Napoleon. If the Emperor was naive in hoping that the cession of the Grand Duchy of Warsaw and the Illyrian provinces would suffice to secure a settlement, at least he showed some interest in reaching peace, which was more than his enemies did. The real tragedy of the situation was that, looked at abstractly, the minimum proposals put to Napoleon by Metternich were perhaps a reasonable enough basis for peace. They would have involved a major compromise by France, which reflected the shifting balance of power against her, but would have left her with much of her Empire intact, which would have been an appropriate payoff for her ceding Germany without a fight. Sadly, though, such a peace was simply not feasible in mid-1813.

The day after his stormy meeting with the Emperor, Metternich signed a secret treaty with the Allies at Reichenbach in Silesia formally pledging that Austria would declare war on France unless she accepted the minimum demands put to Napoleon as a preliminary foundation for peace talks. Just a few days later, however, the elation this brought to the Russian and Prussian high commands was tempered by a not untypical piece of unilateral diplomacy by the Habsburg chief minister. Returning to Dresden after signing the Reichenbach treaty, Metternich agreed with the Emperor that a peace conference should be held at Prague and that the armistice, due to elapse on 20 July, should be extended to 10 August, ostensibly in order to provide more time for a possible peaceful

---

* One is tempted to make a comparison with Churchill's attitude to seeking peace talks with the Nazis in 1940. He argued against it on the basis that it was a slippery slope which would end up either with Britain giving away far more than was desirable or choosing to fight on but having severely undermined morale. There are, of course, differences in the two scenarios, but the similarities are striking. France's military chances looked better in 1813 than did Britain's in 1940, and whereas Napoleon's adversaries were determined to impose an extremely harsh settlement upon the French, it seems that Hitler was prepared to be relatively generous had the British sought a settlement.

solution to be reached. Both steps infuriated the Russians and Prussians, whom the Austrian Chancellor had not bothered to consult before agreeing upon the measures with Napoleon. According to Nesselrode, Alexander's foreign minister in all but name, the Allies were extremely irritated by 'the idea of a congress and the delay it would cause in the resumption of hostilities', but nevertheless went along with it so as to avoid offending their prospective partners in war. Russo-Prussian anger was also mitigated by Metternich's explanation of his actions: Austria simply needed more time to prepare fully for the looming conflict. The Chancellor was doubtless broadly telling the truth for once, and indeed it was the same reason of military preparedness that had primarily prompted Napoleon to share Metternich's desire for a congress and an extension to the armistice. Both men also still held out the faintest of hope that something might come out of the Prague conference: Bonaparte that the Austrians might waver if he agreed to talk and that the demands put to him might be reduced; the Austrian Chancellor that the Emperor might decide to accept his ultimata after all.

The congress at Prague was never realistically going to avert a resumption of hostilities, but by the time it finally convened, after a delay caused largely by the Russians and Prussians dragging their heels, the momentum for war in the Allied camp had reached its zenith. In early July, following Austria's effective accession to the anti-Napoleonic coalition with the signing of the treaty of Reichenbach, the Crown Prince of Sweden, Bernadotte, had finally agreed to commit his country fully to the struggle against his former master and homeland. Just as heartening to the Russian and Prussian hawks was the news that arrived from Spain around the same time. In the wake of the disaster in Russia, Napoleon had pulled sizeable numbers of troops out of the Peninsula in order to stiffen the backbone of his new armies in Germany. With their forces in Iberia already stretched dangerously thin by reductions made before the invasion of Russia, the French position south of the Pyrenees was now more vulnerable than ever. Recognizing this, the Emperor had authorized a withdrawal behind the Ebro, asking his commanders to hold just the north-east of Spain from now on. Even this limited task proved beyond his subordinates. Seeking to exploit the catastrophe in Russia, the British government had decided in late 1812 greatly to reinforce its army in the Peninsula, which had frustratingly been compelled to retreat to the Portuguese border following its great victory at Salamanca and the capture of Madrid in the summer. In spring 1813, it was a much more formidable force that moved forward under Wellington into Spain yet again. Over the following weeks, the British and their Portuguese allies totally outmanoeuvred the main French army, under the Emperor's brother Joseph and the elderly Marshal Jourdan, in what was arguably Wellington's finest campaign. His complex and brilliant plan reached its culmination at the battle of Vitoria on 21 June, where he routed the enemy, capturing over 150 cannon as well as the French baggage train, which was full of assorted treasures and money. Although the highly skilled Marshal Suchet in Catalonia continued to maintain a French presence south of the Pyrenees for some time, Wellington's victory at Vitoria all but ended the Peninsular War and paved the way for an invasion of south-western France. This induced Napoleon to send one of his better marshals, Nicolas Soult, to the area in order to rally the routed French forces and try to stop the British. Soult would do pretty well in the circumstances, but the absence that autumn of yet another highly skilled commander from the main French army in Saxony would prove costly.

The farcical Prague conference was played out in late July and early August, no one seriously expecting that it would achieve anything and many of its participants actively hoping it would not. None of the national leaders attended in person (unless one counts Metternich) and most sent less prestigious representatives than they might have. By 7 August, tiring of the charade, the Habsburgs' chief minister delivered a final ultimatum to the French, either to accept his demands expounded over a month ago at Dresden by the 10th or face war with Austria as well as the Allies. It was the evening of 9 August before Napoleon received the final ultimatum, but he decided to respond as positively to it as he felt he could. He agreed to the dissolution of the Grand Duchy of Warsaw, the cession of almost all the territory of the Illyrian Provinces to Austria, and the handing over of Danzig and its environs to the Prussians, but that was as much as he was prepared to cede without a further trial of strength. Metternich did not receive the Emperor's reply until the 11th, by which time the armistice had officially expired. Technically, there was still a week's grace during which hostilities should not recommence, but the Austrian Chancellor saw no reason to delay what he felt was unavoidable. The next day, 12 August 1813, he informed Caulaincourt, Napoleon's representative at Prague, that the Austrians were formally declaring war on France. For the first time since the beginning of the Revolutionary Wars over twenty years earlier, the French found themselves simultaneously embroiled against all four other major European powers.

The accession of Austria to the Sixth Coalition undeniably tilted the balance of forces against Napoleon, but his position was not yet hopeless at the resumption of hostilities in mid-August. Numerically, the French were not at as great a disadvantage as one might suspect. Further tremendous recruiting and manufacturing efforts, both in France and the Empire, had raised the size of the Emperor's field armies in Germany to over 400,000, around ten per cent of which were cavalry, backed by nearly 1,300 cannon. The bulk of these troops, almost 300,000 men, were deployed in mid-August in the general vicinity of Dresden and Bautzen under Napoleon's direct command, but 120,000 soldiers were ordered to operate further north against the Prussian heartland, a third of them under Davout at Hamburg, the bulk of the rest under Oudinot to the south of Berlin.

Also to be considered in calculating the balance of forces with the Allies were the great many troops still deployed in garrisons in north-east Europe and along the Elbe, as well as the predominantly Italian and Bavarian armies under Eugène and General Wrede which guarded against any Austrian threat to two of France's key allies. Altogether, these various forces amounted to perhaps as many as a quarter of a million men.

The Allied field armies that would confront those of Napoleon in the key German theatre of war numbered a little over half a million soldiers, supported by almost 1,400 guns, giving them an advantage of around a hundred thousand men and a hundred cannon. Of these, however, more than a tenth would not play an active role in the campaign until the end of September, meaning that the Emperor and his adversaries were relatively well matched numerically in late summer. The largest contingent of the Allied field armies that would fight in Germany, totalling almost 200,000, was Russian, while there were over 150,000 Prussians in the key theatre by this stage, 40,000 Swedes and more than 120,000 Austrians. The biggest Allied army began the campaign south of Saxony in the Austrian province of Bohemia. Almost a quarter of a million men strong, it was commanded by Prince Schwarzenberg, the same general who had led Napoleon's right wing during the invasion of Russia. Only half his troops were fellow Austrians, however, the rest being a mix of Russians and Prussians under the overall supervision of General Barclay de Tolly. As commander of the coalition's largest army, Schwarzenberg was appointed to the largely nominal role of commander-in-chief of all Allied forces in central Europe. Chosen more for his distinguished social background than any particular military aptitude, the Austrian would have to deal with the presence at his headquarters of the three crowned heads of Russia, Prussia and Austria, an unenviable task, especially as Alexander had almost vetoed his appointment as commander-in-chief at the last moment, as he toyed with the idea of demanding the position for himself. Horrified by this, Metternich had threatened to withdraw Austria from the coalition unless Schwarzenberg was confirmed in his role immediately, a drastic step which had compelled the Tsar to back down. To the north-east of Schwarzenberg's Army of Bohemia was the almost 100,000-strong Army of Silesia under Blücher. Again, his force was not entirely made up of fellow countrymen, well over a third of it being Russian rather than Prussian. Near Berlin was the Army of the North, 120,000 soldiers commanded by the Crown Prince of Sweden, who was appointed to the role ahead of a Russian because his allies feared he would otherwise focus more on fighting the Danes than the French. A large part of this army was, of course, Swedish, but there were even more Prussians and not too many fewer Russians under Bernadotte's command. Finally, slowly heading west through the Grand Duchy of Warsaw was the 60,000-strong, all-Russian Army of Poland under Bennigsen. Added to these field forces were another quarter million or more Allied soldiers deployed either against French garrisons in north-east Europe, or along the Austrian borders with Bavaria or the Kingdom of Italy, or held in reserve.

The bare numbers do not, then, suggest that the French cause was necessarily already a lost one, but there were other ways in which Napoleon and his men were at a disadvantage than simple figures. The Imperial cavalry, though greatly enlarged during the period of the armistice, remained considerably weaker than the Emperor would have liked, making up a significantly smaller proportion of his field forces than in the Allied armies. The artillery too, though roughly comparable in size to that of the Allies, still lacked mobility due to the general lack of horses, while the bulk of the infantry, as in the spring, were inexperienced conscripts.

The Allied armies also contained many green recruits, of course, especially in Austrian units, but their troops were, on average, more experienced or better trained than their adversaries. Cavalry, especially Russian and Prussian, was a particular Allied strength, although Napoleon's enemies would continue to prove themselves generally less adept at utilizing their artillery than the French.

In quality as well as quantity of their field armies, then, the Allies enjoyed a narrow advantage over the Emperor in summer 1813. They were also, crucially, likely to be able to replace any losses they sustained more readily than the French, whose manpower supplies had been severely depleted in recent years, most especially by the Russian catastrophe and the ongoing war in Spain. The odds thus seemed clearly on an Allied victory, but there remained the key factor of leadership. Napoleon was still the greatest captain of the age, while his enemies' best general was fighting in northern Spain against Soult rather than in central Europe against the Emperor himself. No commander the Russians, Austrians, Prussians or Swedes had to hand was anywhere near a match for Napoleon on the field of battle, and they knew it. If the Allies were to turn their advantages over the French into ultimate victory, therefore, they had to find some way of neutralizing the potent threat that was Napoleon.

The solution they proposed was inglorious, but proved highly effective. The Allies agreed at Trachenberg in Silesia in August 1813 that they would not fight an army commanded by the Emperor in person unless they enjoyed a considerable numerical superiority on the field of battle. Their various armies would endeavour to manoeuvre so as to bring this about and would readily fight a force commanded by one of Napoleon's subordinates even without a considerable advantage in numbers should the opportunity arise, but the Emperor himself was only to be taken on if the Allies had such a numerical superiority that victory was all but guaranteed. If the Emperor tried to bring one of the Allied armies to battle on terms less than highly favourable to his adversaries, it was to withdraw in the face of his advance while other Allied forces manoeuvred to threaten his base of operations or lines of communication and make him give up the chase. The Allies were aware that this was not necessarily a strategy that would bring about a speedy conclusion to the hostilities, but that did not overly worry them. Better a slow victory than a quick defeat, especially as they felt that time was on their side.

For his part, the Emperor knew that if he were to win the war, or at least compel his adversaries to allow him to end it without making too many major concessions, he needed to divide the Allies so that he could obviate his numerical disadvantage by concentrating on just part of their massive field force at a time. To achieve this, Oudinot, supported by Davout from Hamburg, was to advance against Berlin while Napoleon initially remained on the defensive near Dresden against the armies of Schwarzenberg and Blücher. The plan was that Oudinot would smash Bernadotte's Army of the North in battle, thereby possibly inducing Sweden to abandon the coalition, and capture the Prussian capital before advancing to the relief of the besieged French garrisons of Küstrin and Stettin. With their heartland thus invaded, the Prussians in the Armies of Silesia and Bohemia were then likely to rush north, as was a large part of the Russian contingent in each force, in order to defend the lines of communication back to Russia. That would leave the Austrians and any Russians left behind vulnerable to a strike by the Emperor's main army near Dresden. If Napoleon could then win a decisive victory over Schwarzenberg, Austria might be knocked out of the war, leaving him free to concentrate all his forces against the Russians and Prussians.

There were, of course, flaws in this plan. For a start, it was based upon an optimistic view of how events might work out. Bernadotte was certainly not much of a general, but it was not likely that a French army led by the less than outstanding Oudinot would manage to crush an enemy force of similar size. The thrust on Berlin needed to be larger and led by a better commander. Had the Emperor given Davout this key role, with Oudinot his subordinate, the brilliant marshal might have inflicted the kind of defeat on the Army of the North that the Emperor hoped for, but, foolishly, Napoleon left him in a secondary role on the lower Elbe instead of making him the commander of the vital thrust towards Berlin.* In any case, even if Bernadotte were heavily defeated and the Prussian

---

* It remains hard to fathom just why Napoleon did not utilize Davout more effectively in 1813. The Hamburg front was an important one, to be sure, but it was not the most crucial. Davout, in Oudinot's place in late summer 1813, or in Ney's back in May, would probably have altered the course of history, perhaps momentously. Obviously, the Emperor expected the subordinates who let him down in 1813 to perform better than they sometimes did, and in choosing commanders for different tasks he did not have the benefit of hindsight. Even allowing for that, one would have expected Napoleon to have given Davout a more significant role than he did. Maybe Napoleon's judgement was coloured by the retreat from Russia, in which Davout had not had his finest hour (although much of the criticism levelled at him was unfair, as we have seen). If so, this was yet another example of how the 1812 campaign helped to bring about the Emperor's demise.

capital fell, there was no guarantee that Sweden would abandon the coalition or that the Prussian and Russian forces in Silesia and Bohemia would rush north and leave the Austrians vulnerable.

Nevertheless, the basic tenets of the Emperor's latest plan were sound enough. The Army of the North might have been beaten by a similar-sized or larger force under one of Napoleon's better subordinates. Berlin might have fallen. The large garrisons of Küstrin and Stettin, perhaps even of Danzig might have been relieved. All these things could only have improved the French position in central Europe and there was always the chance, if Napoleon was patient, that Blücher or Schwarzenberg might make a bad error and leave themselves vulnerable to a heavy defeat by the main French army in Saxony. The war was not a foregone conclusion when it resumed in late summer 1813. It would, however, require the Emperor, his key subordinates and his troops all to perform well if eventual defeat were to be avoided.

Within days of the resumption of hostilities, Napoleon altered his strategy. News that Blücher was advancing west from Silesia towards Bautzen faster than Schwarzenberg was marching north from Bohemia towards Dresden seemed to throw up the possibility of the Emperor falling upon the Army of Silesia, smashing it, and returning to protect the Saxon capital before the Allied commander-in-chief and his troops could threaten the city seriously. It was a tempting prospect, and when Bonaparte learned on 17 August that a new army of Russians (Bennigsen's Army of Poland) was advancing west towards Silesia, he determined to go after Blücher before it could come to his aid.

Leaving 20,000 men under Marshal St Cyr in Dresden, the Emperor thrust east with the rest of the forces under his immediate command hoping to catch the impulsive Blücher and destroy his army. In conformity with the agreed Allied strategy, the Army of Silesia began to withdraw back east as soon as its commander became aware that the Emperor himself was at the head of the force moving towards him. Bonaparte, of course, pushed on in pursuit, but on 22 August came unwelcome news from Dresden. Schwarzenberg had moved faster than Napoleon had expected and would be in position to assault the Saxon capital with vastly superior forces than St Cyr had to hand in a matter of days. Over the next forty-eight hours, Napoleon's advance guard fought a running battle against the retreating Blücher's rearguard near Bunzlau in Silesia, a combat in which the French had the better of things, but message after message arrived from St Cyr underlining the danger in which he now found himself. Frustrated, the Emperor realized he had little choice but to turn back with most of his army before it was too late. Dresden was too important to lose, both politically, as the capital of one of his key German allies, and militarily, as his main base of operations and the site of masses of artillery and vast quantities of supplies. He therefore detached 120,000 men under the command of Marshal Macdonald with strict instructions that he was to continue to drive Blücher back as far as Jauer, around thirty miles to the south-east of Bunzlau, before retiring behind the Bobr river and going over to the defensive. Meanwhile, Napoleon would march with the bulk of his army to rescue St Cyr in Dresden.

It was a race against time. As Schwarzenberg's army began to gather to the south of the Saxon capital on 24 August, it must have seemed as if the Emperor would not make it. Boldly, St Cyr launched a surprise counter-attack on the 25th which startled the Allies and helped persuade them to delay their assault on the city until the next day when more of their units would be in a position to join in the attack.

The key reason for Allied hesitation, though, was the information reaching the high command by this time regarding enemy movements to the north-east of the Army of Bohemia. Following some prodigious marching, which brought back memories of the *Grande Armée*'s earlier feats, Napoleon's relief force was fast approaching the danger area, giving the Allies pause for thought. Of especial concern was a body of troops that was manoeuvring towards the right-rear of Schwarzenberg's army, threatening its lines of communication back to Bohemia. This was the 40,000-strong corps of General Vandamme, although but for a report of dubious accuracy from one of the Emperor's aides, it would have been the bulk of the Emperor's force. As he had advanced towards Dresden, Napoleon had begun to turn his plan to save the city into a strategy to smash the Army of Bohemia. If St Cyr could hold out with only limited direct reinforcement, then the Emperor would be free to use the majority of his relief force to drive into the right-rear of Schwarzenberg's army and sever its best line of retreat. The French would probably not have enough troops to prevent the enemy from escaping, but they might do a tremendous amount of damage to the Allies' largest field force. On 25 August, however, General Gourgaud, a loyal aide who would eventually follow his master into exile, painted such a gloomy picture of St Cyr's prospects at Dresden, upon his return to Napoleon's headquarters from a scouting mission to the city, that the Emperor felt compelled to adopt a more conservative plan. The outflanking attack against Schwarzenberg's right-rear would be carried out only by Vandamme, while the rest of the soldiers under Napoleon's immediate command would march directly to the relief of the Saxon capital. With the benefit of hindsight, it seems likely that Vandamme's 40,000 would have been enough to enable St Cyr to hold Dresden and that the bulk of Napoleon's force could have carried out his more aggressive strategy.

Reports of the approach of tens of thousands of French troops, quite possibly led by Napoleon himself, almost encouraged the cautious Schwarzenberg to fall back immediately towards Bohemia. The Tsar, however, would not entertain the idea that such a large army as the Allies had should not at least make an attempt to defeat the greatly outnumbered garrison of Dresden and strike a blow that would resonate throughout Germany. At dawn on 26 August, therefore, large detachments having been made to guard against the threat to the army's right-rear, 150,000 Allied troops prepared to attack the 20,000-strong corps of Marshal St Cyr.

The French position was tenuous, to be sure, but not as hopeless as the numbers made it seem. After capturing the Saxon capital in May, Napoleon had ordered its fortifications to be strengthened and they now posed a formidable obstacle to any attacker. St Cyr had further enhanced the city's defensive potential by barricading streets in the suburbs, turning buildings there into mini-fortresses and erecting impromptu palisades to shelter his soldiers. He had also thrown up five earthworks just outside the suburbs in which he placed some of his artillery. His first line of defence, though, was a line of villages that ran in a rough semi-circle to the south of Dresden a mile or two out, each end of the line protected by the Elbe river which flowed more or less east–west through the heart of the city. In short, it was a strong defensive position well protected by plentiful guns.

The Allied attack was slow in developing on the morning of the 26th. As ever, Napoleon's enemies struggled to organize an offensive effectively and there was the usual confusion and lack of decisiveness. It was, therefore, past nine before St Cyr was even forced to abandon his outer line, his men simply falling back to the redoubts and the suburbs. Following up, the Allies launched a series of ill-coordinated assaults on the French earthworks, each of which was beaten back without much difficulty. Sensibly, Schwarzenberg now ordered his units to regroup.

Whether the attack would be renewed, however, hung in the balance for a while. Around the same time as St Cyr withdrew from his first line of defence, Napoleon arrived in Dresden at the head of the first wave of reinforcements. It was not long before the city was ringing with cries of 'Vive l'Empereur!', making the great man's presence known to the enemy. Despite having been one of the key advocates of launching an attack on the 26th, the Tsar now seems to have lost his nerve and called for the army to withdraw in accordance with the Trachenberg plan. Unusually, it was the timid Frederick William who now became one of the most belligerent voices among the Allied high command. The French were still heavily outnumbered, he calmly pointed out, so the Allies should not be persuaded to break off an action in which they still held the advantage just because the Emperor had arrived. The Prussian King's counsel won more support than Alexander's and the Allies decided to press on with the battle.

For hour after hour, Russian, Prussian and Austrian troops endeavoured to force their way into Dresden, but despite their large numerical superiority, they had little success. The French, strengthened throughout the day by the arrival of further reinforcements until they eventually numbered 70,000, held their

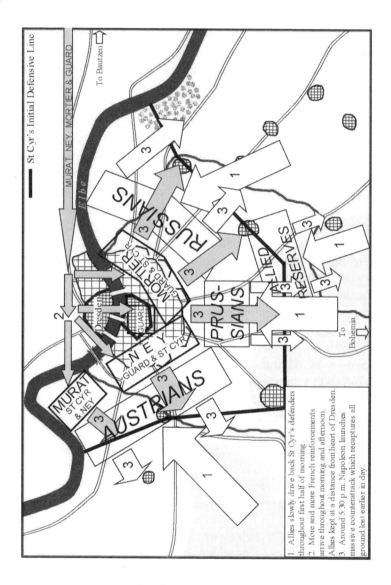

Battle of Dresden: 26 August

ground with relative ease. A couple of the redoubts fell temporarily, but the Allies never looked likely to be able to penetrate the defensive line of the suburbs. As at Lützen, Napoleon exposed himself to enemy fire in directing the French defence along with St Cyr. Then, around half past five, the Emperor unleashed a fierce counter-attack against the exhausted and demoralized Allied units. Three columns led by Marshals Ney, Mortier and Murat, back from Naples and loyal for the moment, assaulted the left, right and centre of the enemy line and drove it back on all fronts. The veterans of the Guard played a particularly vital role in the successful counter-attack, but many conscripts fighting their first battle also did well. By the time combat was broken off, the French had recovered all the ground they had earlier lost.

During the night of 26–27 August, the defenders of Dresden were further strengthened by the arrival of the corps of Marshals Marmont and Victor, bringing Napoleon's force up to 120,000 men. The Allies too were reinforced by units only now reaching the battle zone, giving Schwarzenberg an army of 170,000 with which to confront the Emperor on the 27th. It would have been more but for the need to detach tens of thousands of troops to protect his right-rear against the threat posed by Vandamme and the tardy marching of a further 20,000 Allied soldiers who were still some way to the south.

Despite the bitter disappointment of the 26th and the Tsar's continued anxiety to retreat, the Allied commander-in-chief determined to renew the attack on Dresden on the 27th. For this purpose, he massed two-thirds of his available force, including the bulk of his cavalry, in the centre, directly south of the city, with the remaining third split evenly between the two flanks. Napoleon, meanwhile, rather than planning to stay on the defensive, was formulating an offensive of his own that would exploit the uneven Allied dispositions to full effect. He left 50,000 men in the centre under St Cyr and Marmont to pin down the enemy masses there, but put 35,000 soldiers on each flank, the right, or western, one under Murat, the left, or eastern, under Ney, and charged them with doing as much damage to the forces opposite them as possible.

The Emperor's attacks pre-empted those of his opponent. Ney moved forward at 6 a.m., Murat half an hour later. Both were soon enjoying considerable success, while in the centre, despite their advantage of numbers, the Allies failed to make much headway against skilful French defence. It had been a wet and windy night, the bad weather continuing into the next day, and this was exploited by Napoleon to the full. Tributary streams of the Elbe to the west and east of Dresden had been engorged by the heavy rain, making communication between the centre and wings of the opposing lines difficult and preventing Schwarzenberg from doing much to help the forces on his flanks resist the onslaught of Ney and Murat. The wet conditions also made it harder for infantry to fire their muskets, which gave the strong cavalry forces posted by the Emperor on his two wings a notable

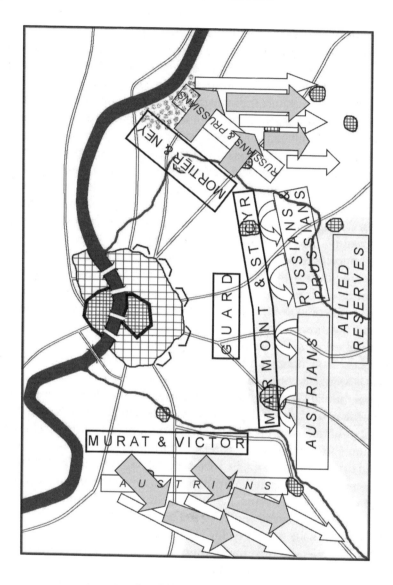

Battle of Dresden: 27 August

advantage over their predominantly unmounted foes who, unlike the French foot soldiers in the centre, did not have the benefit of prepared defensive positions.

With their flanks being pushed back and the centre making little progress, the Allied high command had a narrow personal escape in the early afternoon of the 27th. A battery of heavy French artillery noticed a group of important looking riders on a hill around a mile to the south and took aim. The distinguished band included not only Schwarzenberg and his staff, but the rulers of Russia and Prussia and their aides too. Suddenly, a volley of roundshot flew towards them, which, something of a fluke at the extreme range involved, proved alarmingly accurate. As the deadly missiles landed around and among them, it was sheer chance that neither the Allied commander-in-chief, the Tsar nor the King were hit. Alexander had the closest escape, a cannon ball narrowly missing him and mortally wounding General Moreau, the former hero of the French Republic who had been exiled to the United States following involvement in an attempt to assassinate the Emperor and whom the Tsar had only recently tempted, with large sums of money, to return to Europe and serve as a special military adviser in the war against his fellow countrymen. Whether their brush with death caused the Allied leaders to lose heart or not, it was clear by mid-afternoon that the battle was well and truly lost and that if they did not retreat soon, the triumphant forces of Ney and Murat working round the flanks might soon make it very difficult for the bulk of Allied troops in the centre to extricate themselves from the battlefield. A little way to the south-east as well, Vandamme and his corps were pressing hard against the forces detached to guard against them, further imperilling the Army of Bohemia's escape. By 3 p.m., Schwarzenberg's main body was in full, if well-ordered, retreat.

The French victory at Dresden was a remarkable achievement which showed what could be accomplished if the Emperor, his key subordinates and his troops all performed well against an enemy that, despite superior numbers and a greater proportion of cavalry and experienced troops, remained eminently beatable. For the loss of just 10,000 casualties, the French had inflicted almost four times as many losses on the Allies, capturing over 20,000 prisoners as well as twenty-six guns in the process. The Russian and Prussian troops under Schwarzenberg's command had fought tolerably well despite the defeat, but the commander-in-chief's fellow Austrians had done poorly, especially on the left flank on the second day of the battle where they had surrendered in droves. There could be no denying that Dresden had been a great triumph for Napoleon and his army, won against the odds. Another defeat like that and the Allies might just be ready to reconsider their position.

It was a singular misfortune for the French and their emperor that he was unable to lead the pursuit of the retreating Allied army in the days after the victory at

Dresden. Returning from the field of battle to the city in the late afternoon of a rainy 27 August, he looked, according to his valet, 'as if he had been dragged from the river'. Already he was beginning to suffer from a cold that, along with a bout of severe diarrhoea, would prevent him from leading the army as it sought to exploit its defeat of Schwarzenberg's force. Without Napoleon's guiding hand, the pursuit was not as coordinated, vigorous or effective as it might have been. To be sure, it was never likely, given the Army of Bohemia's great size and superiority in cavalry, that any pursuit could have inflicted sufficient destruction to make any of Napoleon's main enemies sue for peace, but it might have caused serious friction among the Allies had the Russians and Prussians sustained very heavy losses while fighting under Austrian command, and it could only have improved the French position to have battered Schwarzenberg's army as severely as possible. Instead, the aftermath of the great victory at Dresden proved a disappointment to the Emperor.

Shortly before Caulaincourt had left his post as ambassador in St Petersburg, the Tsar had apparently said to him, 'With you, marvels only take place where the Emperor is in personal attendance; and he cannot be everywhere'. The veracity of this comment seemed to be proved by the events of late August 1813. The day after his triumph at Dresden, Napoleon received two pieces of grim news. The first concerned events near Berlin, towards which, in accordance with the Emperor's strategy, Oudinot had been advancing. Initially, the marshal's progress had been good and his troops had easily dealt with any resistance they encountered. Indeed, the unimpressive Bernadotte had been seriously considering abandoning the Prussian capital until, on 23 August, one of Oudinot's corps ran into trouble less than ten miles south of the city near a village called Gross Beeren. The Prussian General Friedrich von Bülow, an altogether more competent commander than the Army of the North's actual leader, had noticed that the four corps under Oudinot's immediate command had become dangerously widely separated and exploited this to fall upon the isolated units of General Reynier on the 23rd. With 30,000 Prussians against Reynier's 23,000 French and Saxons, von Bülow did not have a great numerical advantage, but he soon proved himself more than a match for his adversary, throwing the enemy back in confusion, capturing thirteen cannon and inflicting 3,000 casualties for the loss of just a thousand of his own men. Reynier rallied his troops and Oudinot's other three corps remained intact, but the reverse at Gross Beeren seems to have shattered the marshal's nerve. Unnecessarily, he ordered an immediate withdrawal all the way back to the Elbe, a move which compelled Davout, who had been progressing east from Hamburg with the soldiers under his command, to also abandon his advance on Berlin. Thus a minor Prussian victory turned into a significant strategic setback for the French.

Reports of Oudinot's timid withdrawal in the wake of Reynier's defeat at Gross

Beeren, though, was a mere irritation to the Emperor in comparison with the other news he received on 28 August. Following his abandonment of the pursuit of Blücher, the force Napoleon had left to keep an eye on the Army of Silesia under Marshal Macdonald had initially done well in chasing the retreating Allies towards Jauer as instructed. Indeed, between the Bobr and Katzbach rivers, both tributaries of the Oder, Macdonald's advance guard under General Lauriston had severely battered Blücher's rearguard, inflicting 7,000 casualties for the loss of just 800 men. On 26 August, however, the first day of the battle of Dresden away to the west, it had all gone wrong. Reaching the left bank of the Katzbach with 75,000 of his 120,000-strong force, Macdonald chose to cross as swiftly as possible in order to maintain the pressure on the enemy. His motives were good, but his decision was soon shown to be reckless. Throwing pontoon bridges over the river, the marshal's troops rushed across and hurried on after the Allies. As the leading units breasted a ridge on the eastern bank of the Katzbach, they began to run into stiffening resistance and before long it was clear that Blücher had ordered his entire army to turn and fight. The French had blundered into a trap and the weather soon made it even worse. As at Dresden, it rained heavily in Silesia on 26 August, and by the afternoon the Katzbach had become so engorged that it washed away Macdonald's pontoon bridges, leaving his force divided. With the bulk of their artillery still on the western bank and with the outnumbered French infantry on the eastern bank struggling to fire their muskets in the wet, the Prussian and Russian cavalry were at a great advantage. The result of the battle was never really in doubt, only the extent of the damage that would be done to Macdonald's army. It was severe. Over 10,000 were killed or drowned trying to swim the Katzbach, while perhaps as many as 20,000, along with fifty cannon, were captured. As the army fell back towards the Bobr in disarray that night, Macdonald, to his credit, took responsibility for the disaster entirely upon himself.

On 30 August, two days after Napoleon learnt of the defeats at Gross Beeren and the Katzbach, the French sustained another serious reverse. In the wake of the Emperor's victory at Dresden, Vandamme, eager to win himself a marshal's baton, was at the forefront of the ill-coordinated French effort to pursue the retreating Allied army and impede its escape back into Bohemia. For three days, from 27–29 August, he fought a running battle against Russian forces, inflicting thousands of casualties but failing to rout the hardy soldiers from across the Niemen. Then, on the 30th, the Russians, promised the support of some Austrian units, turned to make a stand near the village of Kulm with the intention of forcing Vandamme to break off his pursuit. Just as the French closed to fight, a large column of Prussians stumbled, completely by chance, into their rear, leaving them surrounded and outnumbered almost two to one. Vandamme's men fought with remarkable valour and skill to extricate the majority of the corps, but

13,000 soldiers ended up being captured, including the general himself. He was subsequently taken to Allied headquarters, where the Tsar, ungraciously, accused him of looting. The straight-talking Frenchman calmly looked Alexander in the eye and retorted, 'At least I have never been accused of killing my father!', a riposte which cut the Tsar to the quick. Vandamme was promptly sent off to Russia, from where he would not return until 1814.

These three blows more than offset the Emperor's impressive victory at Dresden. French losses in late August at least matched those of their adversaries, and they could afford them less. Worse than that was the psychological impact. As the Allied high command had trudged away from the Saxon capital, it had done so with its tail between its legs and the disquieting worry in its mind that it might not be possible to defeat Napoleon after all. By the end of August, the mood had changed entirely. The French had given up their pursuit, the prestige of the Army of Bohemia had been restored by the lucky triumph at Kulm, Berlin was still in Allied hands, and a large French force had been severely mauled by Blücher's Prussians and Russians. The momentum of war, so crucial in deciding its outcome, had swung from the Allies to the Emperor and then back to the Allies in a matter of days. Now it was with them once more, Napoleon's enemies were determined not to lose it again.

At the end of August, the Emperor re-evaluated his strategy, toying with the idea of advancing into Bohemia and trying to capture Prague. Quickly, and correctly, he dismissed the notion. The political and military significance of Prague was not sufficiently high to merit the risks involved in stretching French communications over the mountains separating Saxony and Bohemia, and the advance would have left Dresden exposed as well. He therefore returned to his original plan, with a couple of modifications. First, Oudinot was replaced by Ney as overall commander of the various corps designated to tackle the Army of the North and capture Berlin. Napoleon was more than a little disappointed with the demoted marshal's performance, commenting to his chief of staff, Berthier, 'It is truly difficult to find anyone more scatterbrained than Oudinot'. Unfortunately, one possible candidate for such a distinction was the man who replaced him, but the Emperor seems to have hoped that the second modification to his plan would obviate the deficiencies of 'the bravest of the brave'. Bonaparte ordered Ney to press on towards Berlin in early September, informing him that he hoped to be able to join him in person with reinforcements around the 9th or 10th.

The Emperor's plans, however, were soon thrown awry by Blücher. It became clear to Napoleon by the start of September that the Prussian general was pressing Marshal Macdonald much harder in the wake of his victory at the Katzbach than he had expected. The Emperor therefore led the bulk of the troops under his immediate command near Dresden east in a fresh attempt to deal with the troublesome Army of Silesia. He joined Macdonald's demoralized force at Bautzen, only for Blücher to reverse his westwards advance the moment he learnt of the junction of the two French armies. Napoleon pursued for a while, infuriated that Blücher refused to stand and fight, but then news arrived that the Army of Bohemia, recovering more quickly from Dresden than the Emperor had expected, was once again closing on the Saxon capital. The pursuit of Blücher was promptly abandoned and the French army marched back west to deal with Schwarzenberg. As it drew near, he in turn halted his advance and withdrew back south towards Bohemia, thereby adding to Napoleon's growing frustration.

By the end of the first week of September, annoyed as he was by his failure to bring either Blücher or Schwarzenberg to battle, the Emperor was at least in a position to head north with part of his army near Dresden and reinforce Ney in his attempt to capture Berlin. But then yet more bad news arrived. On 6 September, the careless, flame-haired marshal had stumbled into an ambush laid for him by General von Bülow at Dennewitz, around forty miles south-west of the Prussian capital. Ney's failure to reconnoitre effectively ahead allowed the enemy to spring a trap, but it was his poor performance during the subsequent battle, and after, that turned it into a major French reverse. The engagement itself was an even affair, Ney's troops fighting every bit as well as their adversaries, but two failures on the part of the French leadership decided the outcome. First, Ney behaved more like a corps or even divisional commander than the commander of an army, throwing himself into the heart of the action at a time when he should have stayed back and directed the battle from the rear. Secondly, and even worse, lacking a proper overview of the entire engagement, Ney ordered Oudinot to march his corps from the left side of the field to the right just at the moment when such a move might lead to the collapse of the French left. It appears that Oudinot realized this fact but disgracefully obeyed the order without question, knowing that it would lead to defeat for the man who had replaced him as army commander. In the days following the battle, the Allies pursued the vanquished French as they fell back towards the Elbe in disarray, and it was now that the real damage was done to Ney's force. Losses at Dennewitz itself had been fairly even, at around 10,000 to 7,000, but by the time the pursuit had been broken off Ney had lost some 22,000 men in total, a great many of them prisoners, as well as over fifty cannon: in all, more than a third of the army which had fought von Bülow on the 6th.

Napoleon took the news of Ney's misadventures with surprising equanimity. It was as if he was becoming resigned to his subordinates letting him down. He simply ordered the marshal to halt his retreat on the Elbe at Torgau and hold his position there. Davout, meanwhile, led his forces once more back to Hamburg, having advanced east towards Berlin at the same time as Ney had pushed north. Despite the second abject failure of a thrust towards the Prussian capital, the

French strategy remained viable, although mounting French losses were making things more difficult. Napoleon badly needed a victory to turn the recent tide of the war, but instead of reinforcing Ney and marching on Berlin, still probably his best chance of forcing one of the enemy armies to fight him, he spent the whole of the middle part of September marching to and fro after Blücher and Schwarzenberg, both of whom continued to withdraw whenever he came near and then advance to threaten Dresden whenever he moved against the other.

It soon became clear to the Emperor that he could not continue marching back and forth indefinitely. Not only were his men growing increasingly tired and disheartened, they were beginning to go hungry by late September. The countryside of Saxony had been picked clean of provisions and efforts to bring forward food from further west were hampered by heavy autumnal rains and Cossack attacks on French supply lines. Napoleon therefore took the decision to transfer his main base of operations a little nearer France, to Leipzig.

At the same time as the Emperor altered his strategy, the Allies changed theirs. The arrival in late September, between the Armies of Silesia and Bohemia, of Bennigsen's 60,000 Russians, as well as a growing sense that things were going their way, encouraged the Allied high command to conduct their campaign more aggressively. Blücher started to lead his army north-west in order to join up with the bulk of Bernadotte's force, which was beginning to establish bridgeheads across the Elbe north-east of Leipzig, while Schwarzenberg, with Bennigsen to his right, prepared to advance through western Saxony. The general aim was to catch the French in a vice.

Napoleon, of course, was not the kind of man to leave the initiative to his opponents, so, when he learnt in the first week of October of Blücher's movement towards Bernadotte, he decided to go after the two northernmost Allied armies. It was at this point that he had to make a crucial decision that he had been putting off for over a week: whether to abandon Dresden entirely or leave it with a garrison. Militarily, the obvious thing to do was to leave the city in order to maximize the number of troops the Emperor had to hand for fighting a pitched battle against the Allied armies, but Napoleon had to think politically as well. Saxony was, for the moment at least, a French ally, so to abandon her capital would send out a potentially dangerous message to the rest of Germany. Exacerbating the problem, a great stir was already being caused throughout the Confederation of the Rhine by the temporary fall of Kassel, the capital of Jerome Bonaparte's Kingdom of Westphalia. A small Russian band from the Army of the North under General Chernyshev had made a dash for the city on its commander's initiative. Its initial attack had been easily repulsed but Jerome, not much of a soldier at the best of times, then panicked and fled, fearing that a much larger Allied force must be close behind. The following day, 1 October, Chernyshev walked into the city. He and his troops left just two days later to rejoin the Army of the North on the Elbe, but profound damage had been done to the French cause nonetheless. In these circumstances, political considerations won out over military ones regarding Dresden. Napoleon left two corps under the supervision of Marshal St Cyr to hold the city until such time as the Emperor could throw the Allies out of Saxony. It would prove a critical decision.

Active French field forces in Germany at the end of September numbered around 270,000, about 150,000 down on the start of the campaign in mid-August. Around two-thirds of the casualties were victims of combat, either killed, wounded or captured, but the rest were on the sick list. The demands of marching during a predominantly wet, cold autumn, often with less sustenance than was desirable, inevitably took their toll on the inexperienced conscripts who made up the bulk of Napoleon's army. Disease spread and exhaustion was common. The two corps that the Emperor left in Dresden, then, represented about an eighth of his remaining available field force, another eighth or so being with Davout on the lower Elbe. Of the rest, almost 50,000 were under the command of Marshal Murat south of Leipzig, charged with guarding the city against any threat from Schwarzenberg and Bennigsen, which left Bonaparte himself with around 150,000 soldiers with which to try to bring Blücher and Bernadotte to battle. Between them, the two Allied commanders had around 140,000 troops north-east of Leipzig in early October, a sizeable part of the Army of the North being on the lower Elbe confronting Davout's force. Napoleon would thus enjoy a narrow numerical advantage if he could bring Blücher and Bernadotte to battle, but he would have to do so before Murat was overwhelmed by the quarter of a million or so Allied soldiers under Schwarzenberg and Bennigsen.

The Emperor made his lunge northwards at the end of the first week of October but his men advanced slowly in the wet, muddy conditions, giving the Allies plenty of notice of the threat. In accordance with the Trachenberg plan, Blücher and Bernadotte agreed that they should manoeuvre to avoid battle, but the two men fell out bitterly over which direction to move in. The Crown Prince would only countenance a withdrawal back across the Elbe, but the Prussian had had enough of such timidity. Instead, he argued that the Allies should thrust westwards so as to stay on the left bank of the Elbe and in a position to descend upon Leipzig in conjunction with Schwarzenberg and Bennigsen coming up from the south. Unable to agree, the two commanders divided their forces, each going his preferred way. This left Napoleon clutching at nothing once more and confused as to where his enemy had gone to boot.

To the Emperor's frustration at yet again failing to bring his adversaries to battle was soon added the vexation of an ally's defection. Early October was a good period for Austrian diplomacy. On the 3rd, she concluded a treaty of alliance with Britain, securing her £1,000,000 per annum for putting at least 150,000 men in the field against France. In some ways more significant than that, though, was the accord Vienna reached with Bavaria five days later. Disquiet had been growing throughout the Confederation of the Rhine at Napoleon's failure to strike a truly telling blow against the Allies, and the Austrians skilfully exploited the situation to start to unravel France's system of German alliances. Rather than bullying the Bavarians into abandoning the French, Metternich deftly coaxed them, pledging that they would be independent after the war and promising to compensate them for any former Austrian territories given them by the Emperor that Vienna wished to take back. With the tide of war flowing against Napoleon, the terms on offer from Metternich generous ones, and Bonaparte unable to guarantee that he would be able to come to Bavaria's assistance should she be invaded by the Austrian army on her borders, King Max Joseph decided, not without some remorse, that it was time to change sides. On 8 October, he signed a pact with Vienna whereby his kingdom left the Confederation of the Rhine and committed itself to providing at least 36,000 troops to fight the French.

Bavaria's defection was undoubtedly a major blow to Napoleon, tilting the balance of forces still further against him, creating a new threat to his lines of communication back to France, and setting a dangerous precedent that his other allies, not just in Germany but elsewhere, might follow. Although it did not quite yet assure the end of French predominance in Germany, much less the demise of the entire Napoleonic Empire and regime, it did make it imperative for the Emperor to win some kind of victory against the Allies as soon as possible. As the second week of October neared its end, however, Bonaparte had to abandon any thought of pursuing either Bernadotte or Blücher. News from Murat indicated that Schwarzenberg was drawing dangerously close to Leipzig. Napoleon therefore rushed south to join the King of Naples and defend his base of operations.

The Emperor reached the city on the afternoon of 14 October. Just a few miles to the south-east he could hear the sounds of a great clash being fought between Murat's cavalry and Russian horsemen from Schwarzenberg's army, an encounter in which the French prevailed. With the Army of Bohemia and the bulk of his own force now so close, Napoleon sensed the opportunity for the major battle that had eluded him since Dresden. Instead of leading his men south on the 15th, though, Bonaparte chose to wait for Schwarzenberg to attack him, fearing that if he advanced the Allies would simply retreat as usual. Whether he was right or whether by delaying he committed a bad error, we shall never know. Either way, by nightfall on 15 October, not only was Schwarzenberg positioned to the south-east of Leipzig ready to attack, but Blücher had arrived to the north of the city eager to crush the French army caught between himself and his ally. The scene was set for the greatest confrontation of the entire Napoleonic Wars.

Ask most people, in the English-speaking world at least, what was Napoleon's most serious battlefield defeat, the one that, more than any other, spelt his doom, and the answer almost inevitably given will be Waterloo. Ironically, however, the truth of the matter is that the Emperor did not 'meet his Waterloo' at Waterloo in summer 1815, but at Leipzig in autumn 1813. Waterloo was certainly one of the most intriguing military clashes of all time, and it was not without some significance, but ultimately it was a closing act of an epilogue rather than a key part of the main story. What transpired at Leipzig in mid-October 1813 was the real denouement of the Napoleonic era.

Yet the momentous battle was possibly almost averted at the eleventh hour. On the evening of 15 October, Tsar Alexander, King Frederick William and some of their closest advisers were scouting towards enemy lines and, in the darkness, came into dangerously close proximity to a unit of French light cavalry. Napoleon's horsemen heard and identified the Allied monarchs and tried to surround their band silently in order to capture them and carry them back to the Emperor. As the troopers began to edge round their prey, however, one soldier dropped his sabre, while another fired his carbine in alarm. The illustrious group immediately fled at full speed back towards their lines, hotly pursued by the French, but the swift arrival on the scene of a strong force of Allied cavalry soon compelled them to break off the chase. It had been Alexander's second close shave of the campaign.

Leipzig in 1813 sat near the confluence of four rivers. The largest of these was the Elster, which flowed from south of the city before bending west as it passed it. Running south–north to the east of the Elster was the Pleisse, which joined the larger river just west of Leipzig. Just north of that confluence, the Parthe flowed into the Elster from a north-easterly direction. Finally, tracing a course similar to the Elster as it ran west from Leipzig, but to the south of the larger river, was the Luppe. The two rivers joined near a village called Lindenau, a little way south-west of the confluence of the Elster and Pleisse. What all this meant for the imminent battle was that it would be difficult for the Allies to launch major attacks from the west or south-west of Leipzig as that would mean crossing two rivers in each case. Besides, the ground near the city between the Elster and Pleisse and Elster and Luppe was marshy. Between the Pleisse and the Parthe, however (to the east and south-east of Leipzig), the terrain was undulating and relatively open, making it decent cavalry country, but the presence of a number of ridges, hamlets and small woods also provided succour for defenders. North-west, north and north-east of the city, the land between the Elster and the Parthe was flatter and more open, the easiest ground for an attacker. Although efforts had been made to fortify Leipzig and its suburbs, Napoleon intended to hold Schwarzenberg and Blücher away from the city, using outlying villages as defensive strongholds, before launching a counter-attack that he hoped would smash the larger of the two Allied armies confronting him.

Notwithstanding the Trachenberg plan, Schwarzenberg, under intense pressure from a once again confident and bellicose Tsar, and the ever-belligerent Blücher, decided to attack the Emperor on 16 October despite only having a fairly slim numerical advantage. The French had nearly 180,000 men and almost 700 guns at Leipzig by the morning of the 16th, while the Allies had just over 200,000 soldiers and 900 cannon, around three-quarters of the troops and two-thirds of the artillery belonging to Schwarzenberg's army. Mirroring the Allied dispositions, Napoleon deployed the bulk of his force, the corps of Victor, Macdonald, Lauriston, Poniatowski, Augereau and Murat, as well as the Imperial Guard, to the south-east of the city against the Army of Bohemia, and even planned to draw south some of the troops who were stationed to the north of Leipzig to counter Blücher (the corps of Ney, Marmont and Bertrand) when he was ready to launch the counterstroke that he hoped would shatter Schwarzenberg's force.

The Allied plan was simple enough: essentially to drive the French back into Leipzig inflicting as much damage upon them as possible in the process. In the north, Blücher, in characteristically aggressive fashion, chose to attack the enemy directly, but Schwarzenberg to the south-east planned to try to outflank the French as well as assault them frontally. A corps of 19,000 Austrians under General Gyulai were to work their way across the Pleisse and Elster before marching north to attack Lindenau, west of Leipzig, while a further 28,000 under General Meerveldt were to cross the Pleisse and advance up the marshy stretch of land between that river and the Elster before recrossing and falling upon the French right flank. That left a little over 100,000 troops, many of them Russian, under the supervision of General Barclay de Tolly to conduct a frontal assault on the French line south-east of Leipzig. The Russians pleaded with Schwarzenberg not to send so many soldiers across the Pleisse, believing that they would be slowed by the marshes and that it would be better to try to outflank the French on the firmer ground to the east of Leipzig, but the commander-in-chief would not be moved.

Barclay began his attack early in the morning of 16 October. Conditions were misty and it was drizzling, which did not help, but it was not a well-coordinated assault in any case. Rather than hitting the French line simultaneously, the various Allied divisions went into action piecemeal, making it easier for Napoleon's men to repel them. Still, for hour after hour, waves of Barclay's troops broke against the French, forcing the Emperor to commit much of his Guard to help prevent the enemy from making significant progress. Between the Pleisse and the Elster, Meerveldt's attempted outflanking manoeuvre bogged down, as the Russians had warned it would, in the marshy terrain, leaving his almost 30,000 men having less impact on the morning's fighting than they might have done. Although they did manage to attack Poniatowski's corps on the French right, the assault was fairly easily rebuffed, especially after Napoleon despatched Augereau's corps to support the valiant Poles. General Gyulai, advancing west of the Elster, did better than his compatriot Meerveldt, reaching and attacking the village of Lindenau to the rear of Leipzig by mid-morning. Indeed, Gyulai's troops even succeeded in capturing the settlement, thereby severing Napoleon's army's line of retreat, but they could not hold it for long. Alerted to the emerging danger, Marshal Ney, given overall responsibility by the Emperor for the northern part of the battlefield in spite of his blundering at Bautzen and Dennewitz, despatched General Bertrand's corps to deal with the threat. By midday, Bertrand had driven the Austrians from Lindenau and firmly re-established French control over both the village and the route west from Leipzig.

Meanwhile, to the south-east of the city, Barclay's frontal assaults had petered out around 11 a.m. Now was the perfect time for the counter-attack Napoleon had planned, with the Allies exhausted and disorganized, but the units he had hoped to bring down from the north to give his assault real power were unavailable. One corps, Bertrand's, had been sent to Lindenau, while the other, that of Marshal Marmont, was heavily engaged with Blücher north of Leipzig. The Emperor therefore chose to delay his counter-attack, asking Ney if there were any other units he could afford to send south. In the meantime, Napoleon organized a massive battery of 150 cannon in the centre of his line to bombard the Allies opposite until he was ready to go over to the offensive.

By the time the great counter-attack was eventually launched, however, the Emperor was not there to direct it. He had moved instead to the north of the vast battlefield where the soldiers under Ney's overall command were coming under increasing pressure from Blücher's Army of Silesia. Throughout the morning, the old general had been surprisingly cautious in probing the French line north of Leipzig, but once he was sure it was not too strong he began to attack it more vigorously. The fiercest fighting in the early afternoon was between the corps of Marmont and Yorck for control of the village of Möckern to the north-west of the city, but east of there, there was an intriguing clash between Russian units under the French émigré general Count Langeron and Dombrowski's Polish division of Ney's corps. Both Marmont's and Dombrowski's men fought with great skill and courage, but after a couple of hours Prussian and Russian numbers were beginning to tell and it looked like the Franco-Polish line might crack. It was in these circumstances that unfortunately, if understandably, Ney made a poor decision. A little while earlier, the Marshal had responded to the Emperor's plea for more troops to deliver his counter-attack in the south by despatching one of the two divisions from his own corps that he had to hand, that of General Souham. Now, Ney abruptly recalled Souham, thereby preventing him from taking part in the crucial French assault on Schwarzenberg's Army of Bohemia.

By the time Souham made it back to the French line in the north his services were no longer so desperately needed in that sector. Indeed, an angry Napoleon immediately despatched him back south again to take part in the fighting there. Two things had helped stabilize the French position north of Leipzig by mid-afternoon. One was the timely arrival from the north-east of the third division of Ney's corps, the 4,700 men of General Delmas. The other was the arrival in the sector of the Emperor himself. His presence, as ever, lifted the men and his skilful guidance helped Marmont's and Ney's troops make the most of their limited numbers.

Shortly before Napoleon had headed off to help steady the French line in the north, he had launched his crucial counter-attack on Schwarzenberg's army to the south-east. The point had simply been reached by early afternoon where it could be held back no longer, regardless of the failure of units from the north to arrive to reinforce it. Lacking those extra soldiers, though, the Emperor had had to abandon his original intention of enveloping Schwarzenberg's right flank, a move which, had it come off, might well have resulted in a decisive victory.

Even without reinforcements, the French counter-attack made good progress initially. Battered by artillery, the Allies under Barclay's command began to yield under pressure from enemy infantry, but it was left to the massed cavalry of Marshal Murat, 10,000-strong, to deliver the *coup de grâce*. Around 2.30 p.m., they started to roll forward. Soon they were cutting a swathe through the Allied ranks, driving towards the command post occupied by the Tsar. Had the Emperor still been in the southern sector of the battlefield at this point, he would certainly have done all in his power to make sure that the cavalry was adequately supported by infantry and artillery, and there is a chance that much of the Army of Bohemia would then have broken and fled. Without his masterful guiding hand, though, the moment was lost and Alexander had time to muster the Allied reserves, led by Russian cavalry, for a massive counter-attack which drove the French back to their original line.

The momentum now threatened to swing in the Allies favour, for by late afternoon General Meerveldt was finally in position to launch a vigorous attack across the Pleisse against the French right flank. The Polish troops of General Poniatowski, who, supported by Augereau's men, had fought superbly in this section of the line all day, held the Austrians as best they could, but without further reinforcement Napoleon's right was in danger of giving way. Thankfully, help soon arrived in the form of General Souham's division, at last taking a part in the proceedings, followed by soldiers of the Guard. The Austrians proved incapable of dealing with the assaults of the fresh Frenchmen. A good number were taken prisoner, including Meerveldt himself, while the rest were thrown back across the Pleisse.

The repulse of the Austrian outflanking attack effectively marked the end of the fighting in the southern sector on 16 October, leaving both armies more or less occupying the positions they had held at dawn. In the north, however,

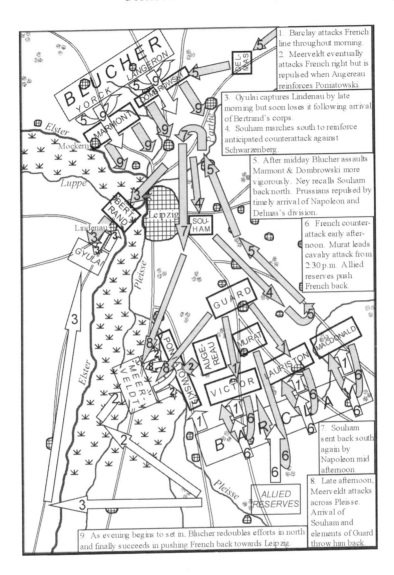

1 Barclay attacks French line throughout morning.

2 Meerveldt eventually attacks French right but is repulsed when Augereau reinforces Poniatowski.

3. Gyulai captures Lindenau by late morning but soon loses it following arrival of Bertrand's corps.

4. Souham marches south to reinforce anticipated counterattack against Schwarzenberg.

5. After midday Blucher assaults Marmont & Dombrowski more vigorously. Ney recalls Souham back north. Prussians repulsed by timely arrival of Napoleon and Delmas's division.

6. French counter-attack early after-noon. Murat leads cavalry attack from 2:30 p.m. Allied reserves push French back.

7. Souham sent back south again by Napoleon mid afternoon.

8. Late afternoon, Meerveldt attacks across Pleisse. Arrival of Souham and elements of Guard throw him back.

9. As evening begins to set in, Blucher redoubles efforts in north and finally succeeds in pushing French back towards Leipzig.

Battle of Leipzig: 16 October

the Allies finally succeeded in pushing the French back. Shortly after 5 p.m., it had seemed as if Marmont was about to win an unlikely victory against the Prussians confronting him at Möckern when his men put a division of Yorck's corps to flight. The hesitation of the Marshal's Württemberg cavalry to charge and exploit the success, though, helped the Prussians to rally; soon afterwards Blücher redoubled his efforts, throwing in all available troops in a last-ditch effort to drive the enemy back. As the sun was setting, the French and Polish line finally gave way, retreating in good order to Leipzig's northern suburbs.

Overall, the battle of 16 October ended as a draw. The French were compelled to abandon their original defensive line in the north, but they held it in the south and inflicted slightly heavier casualties on the Allies than they themselves sustained (30,000 to 25,000). In a broader sense, though, Napoleon's failure to defeat his adversaries effectively turned the day's fighting into an Allied victory. Had he smashed Schwarzenberg's army as he had hoped to do, the whole course of the campaign would surely have been changed. Whether that would have significantly altered the eventual outcome of the war is impossible to say, but it cannot be ruled out. Nor was it by any means inconceivable, moreover, that the Emperor *could* have smashed the Army of Bohemia on 16 October. Had Blücher not pressured Marmont so heavily in the north or had Gyulai's Austrians not drawn Bertrand over to Lindenau, for example, Napoleon might well have been able to muster a corps to undertake the enveloping move against Schwarzenberg's right that he had planned. Even without this manoeuvre, the French came close to routing a large part of the Army of Bohemia, which was only saved by Napoleon's absence at the critical time and the Tsar's, for once, skilled leadership in organizing and launching the crucial counter-charge of the Russian cavalry. The biggest imponderable of the battle, though, is the absence of the two corps the Emperor had left behind in Dresden. Had they been with him on the 16th, he would certainly have been able to launch his enveloping move and the likelihood is that Schwarzenberg's army would have received a severe beating. Instead, the Army of Bohemia, battered as it undoubtedly was, was in a position on the evening of 16 October to renew the fight at Leipzig in the immediate future, aided by Blücher's Army of Silesia.

The failure to smash Schwarzenberg's army on 16 October left the Emperor unsure what to do next. He could always try again on the 17th, but he knew that the Allies had other forces in the region that would surely now be hurrying to Leipzig. It was unclear whether it would be sensible with a tired and largely inexperienced army to press the issue once more against a foe that might grow considerably stronger as the fight progressed. On the other hand, Schwarzenberg and Blücher might not be greatly reinforced next day, so to retreat from Leipzig might be premature, as well as damaging to French morale and a great fillip to Napoleon's enemies throughout Europe. In the end, Napoleon effectively followed a middle course. He decided to rest and reorganize his forces on the 17th, making no aggressive move, but not withdrawing either, and only fighting if he were attacked. The immediate decision about whether to renew the fight was left to the Allies. It was as if the Emperor no longer really believed that he could win at Leipzig but was not yet prepared to accept defeat.

Napoleon's atypically uncertain, almost befuddled, state of mind was reflected in a peace initiative he made on the night of 16 October. Summoning the captured Austrian General Meerveldt to him, Napoleon told his distinguished prisoner that he was prepared to cede the Illyrian Provinces, the Grand Duchy of Warsaw and what was left of French-controlled Spain, as well as restore the independence of Holland and the areas of north Germany annexed to France at the end of 1810, as part of a peace deal. Meerveldt was then returned to Schwarzenberg's headquarters, where he informed the Allied high command of the Emperor's offer. Just how seriously the Emperor took this peace effort is unclear, but awaiting a reply to it does seem to have been one of the reasons he did not attack or retreat on 17 October. In the event, no response came, not even an acknowledgement of the message. The Allies, already aware that massive reinforcements would soon join them, were encouraged by Napoleon's apparent pusillanimity. If the Emperor stayed where he was throughout the 17th, on the 18th the strengthened Allied hordes would crush him.

After the chaos and carnage of the previous day, 17 October was a peculiar contrast. There was some fighting, but no more than sporadic skirmishing between French and Prussian soldiers to the north of Leipzig. To lift morale, as well as reward success, there were notable promotions on both sides of the lines. King Frederick William elevated Blücher to the rank of field marshal, ostensibly for his capture of Möckern on the 16th, but really more for his sound overall performance since Prussia had joined the war back in March, including his victory over Macdonald at the Katzbach. Napoleon, meanwhile, made General Poniatowski the first (and only) non-French member of his marshalate in recognition of his and his Polish troops' sterling service to the imperial cause.

The key development of 17 October was the arrival of reinforcements. The Emperor was pleased to be joined by the 14,000-strong French and Saxon corps of General Reynier, bringing his total strength once more to over 170,000, but this increase in numbers paled into insignificance next to the vastly greater growth of Allied forces. From the south-east, General Colloredo joined Schwarzenberg's army with his corps of nearly 20,000 Austrians and over a hundred guns. From the east came General Bennigsen with over 30,000 Russians and another 134 cannon, the rest of his Army of Poland having been left to cover St Cyr's forces in Dresden. Finally, from the north-east, Bernadotte arrived at the head of almost 70,000 Prussians, Russians and Swedes and 226 pieces of artillery of the Army of the North. Total Allied strength thus leapt from around 175,000 men and 900 guns at dawn on the 17th to almost 300,000 soldiers and over 1,350 cannon at sunrise on the 18th, giving them roughly a five to three superiority in troops and a two to one advantage in guns. At long last, Napoleon's enemies were in a position to beat him on the battlefield.

Faced by such overwhelming odds, retreat must have appeared an obvious option for the French, yet at first light on 18 October they remained at Leipzig ready to offer battle. This was not necessarily, however, the folly it might at first seem. The Emperor realized from late on the 17th, when the slow-marching Bernadotte, bringing more than half the Allies' reinforcements, finally arrived, that a withdrawal westwards was now highly advisable, but he sensibly wanted to conduct such a retreat with as little interference from the enemy as possible. The best way to do that was to give the Allies a bloody nose before pulling back, something which might also soften the blow to French morale that would result from withdrawing and make France's German and other allies think twice before following Bavaria's lead. A few weeks earlier at Dresden, another fortified Saxon city, the French had managed to hold and indeed then throw back an Allied army that greatly outnumbered them. True, the situation now was even less favourable than it had been in late August – Leipzig's defences were less formidable than those of Dresden, the French could expect no further reinforcements to help swing the contest, and it was almost inconceivable that the Allied high command would conduct the battle as maladroitly as they had the one at Dresden – but still the Emperor had reason to hope that he could at least make the Allies pay such a heavy price for ejecting him from Saxony that they would not attempt to hinder his withdrawal.

At 2 a.m. on 18 October Napoleon ordered his forces to the south and east of Leipzig to pull back a couple of miles in order to establish a shorter, more continuous line of defence closer to the city. Running from the right bank of the Elster in the north-west to the eastern bank of the Pleisse in the south, the new French line was essentially a tighter version of the huge arc of Allied troops with which it found itself confronted at dawn. To the north-west and north was Blücher's Army of Silesia, to the north-east Bernadotte's Army of the North. East of Leipzig were Bennigsen's Russians, while to the south-east and south lay Schwarzenberg's Army of Bohemia. General Gyulai and his corps remained on the left bank of the Elster, the only threat to the French army's line of retreat via Lindenau towards Erfurt. The Allied plan was basic in order to avoid confusion that might lead to localized disasters. The combined armies would attack the French line from all directions and seek to drive it back into Leipzig. At 7 a.m., the Allies began to roll forward.

The story of the second phase of the great battle of Leipzig was not one of skilful manoeuvres or daring attacks that only narrowly failed to bring spectacular success. Rather it was a tale of attrition, of grinding away, of slow but inexorable Allied pressure. In the south and south-east, Schwarzenberg's army launched attack after attack, only to be repeatedly beaten back. Poniatowski's Poles particularly distinguished themselves once more in this sector, but the Army of Bohemia did not press its assaults as vigorously as it might have. The French were in decent, if not especially formidable, defensive positions and there was always the chance that an attack pushed too hard might result in the kind of losses that could break units. To the north, Blücher was more aggressive, but his progress was slow and limited in the face of stiff, well-organized resistance. In the west, Gyulai tried to dislodge Bertrand from Lindenau in the morning but was easily repulsed and remained unable to pose any serious threat to the French line of retreat throughout the rest of the day.

Back to the east of Leipzig, the best Allied progress was made by Bennigsen's Russians, supported on their left by their countrymen in Schwarzenberg's army. To their amazement, some of the French troops in this sector found themselves undergoing an attack that would have been more familiar to their medieval ancestors when they were subjected to volley after volley of arrows from bands of Bashkirs, horsed warriors not too dissimilar from the Cossacks. Fortunately, the Bashkir weapons were rather less effective than the mighty longbows wielded by the English at Crecy and Agincourt and caused more surprise than harm. Most Russians, of course, were armed with muskets, and it was these soldiers whose steady pressure threatened to puncture the French line until the Emperor sent in the Guard to rescue the situation, a task the veterans carried out with their ususal aplomb.

Perhaps the most alarming episode for the French, however, came in the north-east. Throughout the morning of the 18th, Bernadotte was dilatory in organizing attacks against his former countrymen, a reflection of his limitations as a commander as much as anything else. The most interesting thing to happen on this front for most of the day was the occasional firing of some rockets by a small group of British soldiers attached to the Crown Prince's army. A new weapon, rockets, which were little more than large fireworks packed with musket balls, did even less physical damage to Napoleon's men than the Bashkir arrows, but the noise as they flew randomly overhead and the bang when they eventually exploded (hardly ever where they were supposed to) caused confusion and consternation. Again, it was the more conventionally armed soldiers of the Army of the North, particularly the Russians and Prussians, who finally began to make progress as the afternoon wore on. Then, around half past four, the Saxon units in Reynier's corps, part of the French line in this sector, suddenly defected to the Allies, leaving a dangerous hole where they had been. It is almost certain that the defection was prearranged with Bernadotte, who had commanded a Saxon corps when still with the *Grande Armée*, but the ex-marshal failed to exploit the situation as effectively as he might have. His troops advanced to penetrate the sudden gap, but without the alacrity required, giving the Emperor time to direct the Guard to the vulnerable point, launch a successful counter-attack and reorganize his line.

As dusk fell on 18 October, neither side was in a position to claim a great victory. The Allies had pushed the French back a little, in the north and east anyway, but they had also sustained heavier casualties than their opponents and had not broken their line at any point. Napoleon, meanwhile, had bloodied the Allies' nose, but not enough to make them unwilling to engage in yet another day's fighting on the morrow.

The Emperor had already decided to retreat by the time the firing ceased on the evening of the 18th, but he would have had to withdraw anyway whatever he decided. In the past few days, the French had fired a staggering 220,000 rounds of artillery, leaving them with just 16,000. Again, had Napoleon evacuated Dresden entirely, he would have had more ammunition available at Leipzig, but as it was, he needed to pull back to Erfurt in order to replenish his stocks.

The initial phases of the withdrawal went well. In the early hours of the morning of 19 October, French forces started quietly to pull back from their positions around Leipzig into the city, leaving camp fires burning to fool the enemy into thinking they were staying put. By the time the sun rose and the Allies became aware of what was happening, some of Bonaparte's men were already across the Elster to the west and heading off in the direction of Erfurt, while the rest were either in the city proper or its suburbs.

As soon as they realized the French were retreating, the Allies rushed forward to attack, hoping to turn the withdrawal into a rout. Napoleon had designated around 30,000 men drawn mostly from three corps, those of Reynier, Poniatowski and Macdonald, to act as the rearguard and hold the enemy back as long as possible. These men now faced odds of something like eight or nine to one, but they fought magnificently, the Poles and Germans among their numbers every bit as heroically as the French. For five or six hours, they made the Allies fight for every street, house and garden while their comrades made their way over the one surviving bridge linking Leipzig with the western bank of the Elster and escape. The Emperor himself crossed around mid-morning, rejecting uncivilized suggestions that his forces should set fire to the city to cover their retreat.

Shortly before 1 p.m., with the bulk of the army safely over the river, the rearguard finally began to buckle under the intense Allied pressure. It was now their turn to escape and, understandably, their withdrawal became something of a flight. Once they were across the bridge, however, it would be blown up and the enemy left impotent on the eastern bank until they could find or build some other way over the Elster. At least that was the plan. Tragically, the bridge was blasted while most of the rearguard was still on the wrong side of the river.

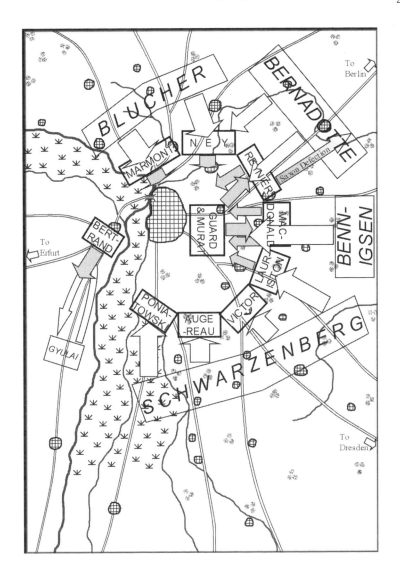

Battle of Leipzig: 18 October

Exactly what happened and why is somewhat shrouded in confusion, but the outline is known. Responsibility for blowing the bridge was delegated by Napoleon to General Dulauloy of the Guard. For some reason, Dulauloy passed on the responsibility sometime before one o'clock to a Colonel Montfort, possibly so that he could go off to try to ascertain how many more troops had still to cross the river. When Allied troops appeared on the eastern bank of the Elster and started firing across the water, Montfort disgracefully fled west, leaving a corporal to decide when to set off the explosives. Whether the corporal then panicked or decided that as the Allies had reached the eastern bank the French rearguard must either have crossed already or been captured, he lost little time in ordering the bridge blown up. All those who had been crossing the bridge at the time were killed, but their fate was arguably preferable to the hundreds of soldiers of the rearguard who drowned trying to swim the Elster. The most notable such casualty was Poniatowski. A member of the marshalate for just a couple of days, he only succumbed to the river because of the four wounds he had sustained fighting in Leipzig. Many men who attempted to swim across survived, however, including Marshal Macdonald, but most of those left stranded on the Elster's eastern bank did not wish to risk the current and had little choice but to surrender. As well as the 15,000 sick and wounded in Leipzig's hospitals, a further 15,000 fit soldiers of Napoleon's rearguard became prisoners as a direct result of the premature destruction of the bridge. Among their number were two eminent generals, Lauriston, the former ambassador in St Petersburg, and Reynier. The former was brought before the Tsar, but Alexander, fearing a repeat of his antagonistic brush with Vandamme at the end of August, was gracious to his captive despite never having liked him previously.

Unsurprisingly, given what happened on 19 October, Napoleon has been much criticized for failing to ensure that there was more than one bridge over the Elster for the retreat. Few have put it more pithily than Marshal Augereau, who exclaimed at one point on the day of the withdrawal, 'Does the bugger know what he's doing?' The truth is, though, that there was good reason to only have the one bridge, as it reduced the chances of the Allies capturing a crossing over the Elster intact, something which would have greatly speeded up the pursuit of the Emperor's retreating forces. Besides, the withdrawal was going well despite there only being one crossing right up until the fateful moment when the explosives were set off prematurely. Had those given responsibility for the crucial task performed it as they could and should have, the Battle of Leipzig would not have terminated in the disastrous manner it did for the French.

Nothing shaped perceptions of what had happened at Leipzig as much as the way the battle ended. The Allies, despite having suffered heavy casualties, were ecstatic, none more so than the Tsar. In a by now characteristic effusion of pompous religiosity, he wrote to a friend, 'Almighty God has granted us a glorious victory over the renowned Napoleon after a four day battle beneath the walls of Leipzig. The Almighty has demonstrated that in His eyes nobody in this world is strong or great except those whom He Himself exalts.' If God had indeed seen fit to decide the outcome of the battle, however. He had also clearly resolved that the Allies should pay dearly for their triumph. Over the four days from 16–19 October, the French lost 38,000 dead and wounded, a heavy toll, but only a few thousand more than they had lost in a single day against a much smaller army at Borodino. Allied killed and injured at Leipzig, meanwhile, amounted to more than 54,000, almost fifty per cent more than their foes. The distribution of these casualties among the various Allied nationalities who fought at what is often called the Battle of the Nations says much about the relative contribution of each to victory. The Swedes lost only a few hundred men, while the 15,000 casualties suffered by the Austrians in Schwarzenberg's army seem relatively light compared to the 16,000 lost by the Prussians, who made up a considerably smaller proportion of the total forces engaged, or the 22,500 that the Russians, roughly equal to the Austrians in numbers, sustained.

The capture of half of Napoleon's rearguard was crucial, therefore, to the perception of Leipzig as a stunning Allied triumph, though also significant was the seizure of over 300 French cannon, many of which would still have been lost even had the bridge not been blown prematurely. What might have been seen throughout Europe as a hard-fought, even contest from which the French made a strategic withdrawal in good order to regroup and fight another day became perceived as a decisive Allied victory that sent the Emperor and his army reeling from Saxony in confusion and alarm. It was this even more than the losses sustained by the French that made the battle of Leipzig such a critical engagement.

Napoleon, however, did not head westwards on 19 October believing that the struggle for central Europe was over. Orders were written and despatched to St Cyr instructing him to break out of Dresden, march north along the Elbe gathering the garrisons of Torgau, Wittenberg, Magdeburg and Hamburg as he went, and then menace the Allies' rear and lines of communication with the 150,000 strong force he would have assembled. The Emperor himself, meanwhile, planned to restock at Erfurt before taking any opportunity that might present itself to strike at one of the Allied armies with the more than 130,000 troops he still commanded. There was undoubtedly at least a whiff of fantasy to these schemes, though they were not entirely unrealistic. In the event, neither came anywhere near fruition. The orders for St Cyr were intercepted, leaving him awaiting his fate in Dresden, while news which Napoleon received soon after arriving in Erfurt on 23 October led him to abandon all thought of willingly fighting the Allies again east of the Rhine.

That news was that Württemberg, hitherto one of France's staunchest German allies, was about to defect to the Allies. The writing had been on the wall even before Leipzig, with the defection of Bavaria and the temporary capture of Kassel, but Napoleon's defeat at the great battle proved to be the catalyst that shattered French dominance east of the Rhine. It would be hard to exaggerate the psychological impact throughout Europe of the fact that the Emperor himself had been beaten on the battlefield. Even in Russia in 1812 he had won every battle he had fought, despite losing the campaign. The defeat at Leipzig, therefore, seemed to be the death knell of the Napoleonic Empire. In the days and weeks following it, there was a veritable stampede of German states abandoning the French and joining the Allies. Most were welcomed and allowed to sign agreements similar to that made between Bavaria and Austria, but there were a couple of exceptions. Westphalia, ruled by Jerome Bonaparte until he fled in the wake of Leipzig, was to be broken up and its territory redistributed roughly as it had been before Napoleon had created the kingdom in 1807. Saxony, meanwhile, though a state long before the advent of the Emperor, was prevented from defecting to the Allies in spite of its king's wishes to do so. Instead, the Prussians and Russians simply decided to occupy the territory, determined that it should be annexed to Prussia as compensation for Russia taking over the former Prussian lands in Poland that made up the Grand Duchy of Warsaw.

With his German allies all abandoning him, Napoleon had little choice but to retreat behind the Rhine lest he find himself cut off from France. It was 200 miles from Leipzig to the river that marked the French frontier, however, and the Emperor expected to be pursued all the way. In some ways, the retreat of 1813 can be seen as a reprise of the more famous withdrawal of a year earlier, but the flight to France went very much better than had the flight from Moscow. That said, rain, mud and an outbreak of typhus combined to make it a far from enjoyable experience for all concerned, though at least the Allies posed less of a menace than Napoleon had feared they might. Of the main enemy armies, only Blücher's really tried to catch up with and intercept the retreating French. Schwarzenberg followed on more slowly, as was his wont, Bennigsen concentrated on mopping up any remaining resistance in Saxony, and Bernadotte headed north-west, ostensibly to 'liberate' Holland but really to invade Denmark and secure the cession of Norway to Sweden. Still, the French had to fight several sharp engagements against elements of Blücher's pursuing force. A more constant threat was presented by the packs of prowling Cossacks which, as in Russia, fell on stragglers or small groups of soldiers, taking them prisoner or, in some cases, butchering them. Despite these difficulties, the Emperor showed remarkable good grace during the retreat by allowing the thousands of Germans still serving with the army to return home. The same offer was made to the Poles, but they turned it down, preferring to stay on and fight.

The great crisis of the retreat, at least potentially, came towards the end of October near Hanau, a town not far from the city of Frankfurt-am-Main. Here, a Bavarian army, 30,000-strong with fifty-eight cannon, was deployed by its commander, Napoleon's former subordinate, General Wrede, across the main road leading to Mainz, the main French base on the Rhine. Wrede's aim was to slow Napoleon's retreat sufficiently to allow Blücher and Schwarzenberg to catch up, but he did not position his forces well. They had a river to their rear, impeding any possible withdrawal, and woods to their front, obscuring the movements of any approaching units. When he arrived on the scene on 30 October and surveyed the Bavarian dispositions, the Emperor commented wryly that although he had been able to make Wrede a count, he had clearly failed to make him much of a general. He then ordered the forces he had immediately to hand, just 17,000 soldiers and a few dozen guns, to attack. The ensuing engagement was an easy victory for the French, the Bavarians struggling to escape and losing almost 10,000 men killed, wounded or captured during the battle and on the day after when Marshal Marmont captured the town of Hanau itself. Much of the responsibility for the debacle must be put down to Wrede's poor generalship, but it would not be unreasonable to suggest that most of his troops might not have been keen to fight against men whom until recently they had fought alongside.

Napoleon crossed the Rhine and entered Mainz two days after the battle. He stayed in the city for almost a week, arranging defences along the frontier and resting and reorganizing the army. Some 70–80,000 soldiers had remained with their units throughout the retreat and perhaps another 40,000 straggled over the Rhine and rejoined the colours during early November. Losses on the withdrawal through Germany had been relatively light, thousands rather than tens of thousands, and many of those who did not cross the Rhine had been released voluntarily by the Emperor. Indeed, given the inexperience of most of the army, the wet weather and the, albeit relatively limited, attentions of the Allies, the retreat from Leipzig was arguably something of a triumph. Still, Napoleon was fortunate that his enemies were in a poor position in November to attempt to cross the frontier and invade France herself. Their supply situation had got worse the further west they had advanced and the whole logistics system needed a major overhaul before the Rhine could be crossed.

If the war in the key theatre went into abeyance for a while, from early November the Allies continued to push France nearer towards ultimate defeat elsewhere. In the north, mainly under Russian forces from Bernadotte's army under Counts Stroganov and Vorontsov, they put Hamburg under siege, bottling up thousands of French troops under Marshal Davout for the rest of the war. The Crown Prince himself, meanwhile, prepared to invade Denmark to the irritation of his allies who felt he should instead be concentrating on expelling the French from Holland. That happened soon enough anyway. On 12 November, a band of Cossacks captured the Dutch town of Zwolle, creating something of a panic among French forces in the country. Three days later, they abandoned

Amsterdam, which prompted the Dutch to rise up, establish a provisional government, and invite William VI of Orange to become their sovereign.

The last two months of 1813 also saw the surrender of almost every French garrison throughout central and north-eastern Europe. With Napoleon withdrawing behind the Rhine, all hope of relief seemed lost and capitulation became an obvious course to follow. It must be stressed, however, that several of the garrisons only surrendered on the basis of terms upon which the Allies then dishonourably reneged. This was certainly the case at Dresden, where St Cyr agreed to submit as early as 11 November on the understanding that he and his men would be allowed to retain their arms and would be exchanged for Allied prisoners held by the French. Once they had him outside the defences of the Saxon capital, however, the Allies insisted that his men surrender their weapons and refused to consider allowing them to return to France. Something similar happened at Stettin on 30 November and Danzig on 2 December. Küstrin, Modlin, Wittenberg and Torgau all fell to the Allies too, leaving just Magdeburg and Hamburg in French hands at the end of the year. The loss of these garrisons did not necessarily free that many more Allied troops for the imminent invasion of France, as there were limits on the number of men that could be supplied that far west, but how Napoleon must have wished that he had not allowed so many of his soldiers – tens of thousands of them – to become pinned down in 1813 in defending towns.

In southern Europe, the Austrians swiftly overran the sparsely defended Illyrian Provinces and then invaded the kingdom of Italy. Defence of the realm was entrusted to its viceroy and Napoleon's former stepson, Eugène de Beauharnais, who proved himself a fiercely loyal and competent. Outnumbered in the ratio three to two, he sensibly abandoned the north-eastern part of the kingdom and established a defensive line along the Adige river. Here, he managed to hold the Austrians with his mostly Italian troops until the end of 1813, resisting in the process the importunate blandishments of his father-in-law, the King of Bavaria, to join the Allies. As he explained to his mother, the former Empress Josephine, 'The Emperor's star fades, but that is simply a further reason to remain faithful to him'.

Perhaps the most momentous event of late 1813 outside the main theatre of war, though, came in the Pyrenees. Following the spectacular victory at Vitoria in the summer, Wellington's campaign had become rather bogged down for a couple months in trying to capture the two Spanish towns of Pamplona and San Sebastian. He needed to take at least one of them to enable him to establish a secure line of communications for an invasion of south-west France. At the very end of August, San Sebastian had successfully been stormed, and in early October Wellington's army made its first tentative sortie onto French soil. By the end of that month, Pamplona had surrendered too, but the most important event of these weeks, as far as the British general was concerned, was the Allied victory at Leipzig. Only when he heard of this, and of Napoleon's move to retreat behind the Rhine, was Wellington prepared to commit himself fully to an invasion of France, secure in the knowledge that the bulk of French forces, and their emperor, would be kept occupied by the Russians, Prussians and Austrians in the north.

In the late summer of 1813, there had been something like three-quarters of a million French and French-allied troops throughout Europe, the Confederation of the Rhine had been more or less intact, Holland, the Illyrian Provinces and the whole of Italy all remained in French hands, and France herself had not been invaded for almost twenty years. By the end of the autumn, barely a quarter of a million soldiers remained with the French colours, the *Rheinbund* had collapsed and its states had defected to the Allies, Holland had been invaded and risen in revolt, the Illyrian Provinces had been overrun, the Kingdom of Italy was under attack, the Murats in Naples were about to defect, and Wellington had penetrated the Pyrenean frontier. It had been a spectacular swing in fortune and, for France and Napoleon, things were only going to get worse.

20

On to Paris!

Shortly after Napoleon crossed the Rhine at Mainz in early November 1813, the rulers of his principal Continental enemies arrived at Frankfurt-am-Main, barely twenty miles from the great river which had marked the French frontier for the past two decades. In the wake of Leipzig, the tide of war was flowing so strongly in the Allies' favour that it threatened to become a torrent that would sweep Napoleon not just from his empire but even from France herself. Yet the tide could still perhaps be stemmed. Hope remained that all was not yet lost.

Napoleon's greatest hope was that the Allies would fall out, that the alliance against him would splinter. Of course, all the previous coalitions against Republican and Imperial France had crumbled, to a greater or lesser extent, as a result of notable French military success, something which was clearly absent in the wake of the retreat from Leipzig, yet the prospect of this latest, sixth, coalition fracturing was not inconceivable. As the Continental rulers gathered at Frankfurt, there were significant differences of opinion between them concerning the next step in the war and the aims to be pursued.

Alexander and Frederick William, the latter now so in thrall to the Tsar that a French observer of the period commented that the Prussian gave the impression of being his Russian counterpart's aide-de-camp, both wished to push straight on into France, a position strongly supported by that fiery Francophobe Blücher. Emperor Francis, his chief minister Metternich, the Allied commander-in-chief Schwarzenberg, and Crown Prince Bernadotte, however, were all reluctant to cross the Rhine, especially in late autumn 1813. To a great extent, this less aggressive stance was based upon practical military considerations. The Allied armies' supply lines had become stretched to breaking point, the troops were exhausted, and there was genuine concern among much of the Allied high command that an invasion of France would be furiously resisted as it had been in the 1790s, resulting in very heavy Allied casualties at best or a costly and embarrassing defeat at worst.

The respective positions of the leading Allied figures also reflected personal and political considerations, though. There is no doubt that Alexander, like Frederick William and Blücher, wanted revenge on the man and, at least in the Prussians' case, the country that had heaped humiliations upon them in the past. All three burned with a passionate desire to capture Paris and overthrow the Emperor.

Indeed, Metternich believed that the Tsar was bent on destroying the French capital in revenge for the destruction of Moscow (notwithstanding the fact that that was brought about by Russians). The Austrian was wrong in thinking this – Alexander would fortunately prove himself a better man than that – but the Tsar certainly wanted Paris to fall and Napoleon to be removed from power, justifying his bellicose stance as a mission to 'free' the French people from their 'tyrant'. Once that was achieved, Alexander at this time was considering installing Bernadotte as the new French emperor or king, though his motives for this are unclear. Perhaps he believed that the former marshal would be acceptable to the French people, a consideration which was important to the Tsar, although it is highly improbable that Alexander was not taking Russian interests into account as well. Maybe he thought Bernadotte would be little more than a Russian puppet or at least that placing him upon the throne of France would open the way for Russia to dominate Sweden and the Baltic. Certainly the other major Allies feared such developments and none of them was consequently prepared to countenance a France ruled by Bernadotte. The Austrians still favoured Napoleon retaining the throne so that it would pass to his half-Habsburg son one day, while the British wanted to see the Bourbons restored and were supported in this by the Prussians, who had seen more than enough of Bernadotte in autumn 1813 to wish him not to become France's ruler. Only Bernadotte himself agreed with Alexander's aim, though unlike the Tsar he did not wish to see France invaded, recognizing that any chance he had of being accepted by the French people would be ruined should he be placed on the throne following an Allied capture of Paris. Instead, he hoped that an internal rebellion would remove Napoleon and that he would then be able to fill the power vacuum.

Just as the question of who should rule France divided the Allies, the issue of the future of Europe remained to be settled and there was much disagreement here too. Poland, Saxony, Germany, Italy and the Low Countries were all potential flashpoints that might create a major rupture in the coalition should any of the powers press their case too hard before Napoleon had been finally defeated. The fate of France herself was another thorny problem on which there was division. The Russians and Prussians agreed that she should be restricted to the borders of 1791 (those she had before the start of the French Revolutionary wars), the British felt that the settlement should go at least that far, while the Austrians and the Swedes were prepared, indeed keen, to allow France to retain the 'natural frontiers' of the Pyrenees, the Alps and the Rhine to enable her better to balance the power of Britain and Russia.

It was partly to try to end the war before all these divisions could tear the coalition asunder and partly in pursuit of Austrian aims that Metternich launched a peace initiative in mid-November 1813. The Austrians had already dug their heels in at Frankfurt and had effectively refused to advance into France until their troops had been rested and the Allied supply situation sorted out, a move which forced the more belligerent Russians and Prussians to delay crossing the Rhine for fear of wrecking the coalition and allowing Napoleon to campaign against weakened Allied forces. This gave the wily Chancellor a narrow window in which to endeavour to end the conflict on terms favourable to Vienna.

Exactly what transpired between the devious Metternich and the rest of the Allies in late autumn 1813 is unclear. He seems to have discussed with them the possibility of approaching Napoleon with a peace offer, although it is unlikely that he received formal approval, at the highest level at least, to propose the terms he did. If he did receive such approval, it would have been given only to conciliate the Austrians and in anticipation that the offer would be rejected, leaving the Habsburgs duty-bound to play a full part in the invasion of France. The terms Metternich offered the Emperor were, in the circumstances, generous. He would retain his throne and France would keep the 'natural frontiers', though lose those other parts of the Empire that still remained, such as Italy. The offer was delivered, significantly orally rather than in writing, on 14 November by Baron de St Aignan, a French diplomat captured at Leipzig and the brother-in-law of Napoleon's friend and aide, Caulaincourt.

One finds in many accounts of this period Napoleon being censured for failing to snap up this offer and save Europe from several more months of bloodshed, but such views are flawed. True, he was initially reluctant to accept the terms, but by the end of November, Caulaincourt, whom he had appointed his new foreign minister, largely in the hope that it would appease Tsar Alexander and make it easier to reach a settlement, had persuaded him to agree to Metternich's terms. If the Allies as a whole had been prepared to accept peace on the basis of Napoleon remaining in power and France retaining the 'natural frontiers', there is little reason to doubt that peace could and would have been made. That it was not was due to Austria's allies. Hardenberg, the Prussian chief minister, is on record as calling Metternich's peace proposals 'a mad business' and did not approve of them, while Castlereagh, the British Foreign Secretary, remarked in typically understated diplomatic language in the autumn of 1813 that Britain was 'likely to view with disfavour any peace which does not confine France within her ancient limits' and even threatened to withdraw British subsidies to their Continental allies should they agree to allow the French the Rhine frontier. The appointment of his old friend Caulaincourt as French Foreign Minister notwithstanding, Alexander was no more inclined to agree to Metternich's proposals than the British or Prussians. He remained committed to removing Napoleon from power and restricting France to the frontiers of 1791. Indeed, any kind of agreed settlement was anathema to him. He wanted complete victory and the fall of Paris. As he ominously commented at this time, 'The sword alone can and must decide the course of events'.

The plain truth is that there was never any realistic prospect of peace on the basis of Metternich's offer in autumn 1813; in fact probably no possibility of peace at this time on any basis other than the complete defeat of Napoleonic France. Caulaincourt replied to the Austrian proposals on 1 December, accepting them and calling for a European congress to be established as soon as possible to work the final settlement out. Metternich was encouraged by the French response but knew that it would be an uphill task trying to persuade his allies to agree to a peace conference on the basis accepted by Napoleon. His reply to Caulaincourt was therefore non-committal, appreciating the Emperor's willingness to compromise but stating that he had to confer with the other members of the coalition before the proposed congress could be arranged (a sure indication that they had not agreed to the Chancellor's peace tentative in the first place). In the event, the Habsburgs' allies would agree to a peace conference, though only after severe hectoring from the Austrians, with no intention of offering the French the 'natural frontiers', and with some question as to how seriously at least some of them took it. By the time that congress convened, moreover, active hostilities had been renewed, the Rhine had been crossed and Napoleonic France was in dire peril. The sword, it seemed, would indeed decide the course of events.

By mid-December 1813, the Allies in north-west Europe had approaching half a million front-line troops ready to reduce the last couple of French fortresses in Germany and invade France, with yet more soldiers available in reserve. Schwarzenberg's Army of Bohemia remained the largest force, numbering around 200,000, while Blücher's Army of Silesia was 100,000-strong, the Army of the North under Bernadotte mustered 120,000, and Bennigsen's Army of Poland amounted to a further few tens of thousands. The largest national contingent remained the Russians. They made up around a third of Schwarzenberg's force (half was Austrian and the rest German), a little over half of Blücher's army (the remainder being Prussian), around a third of Bernadotte's host (half of which was Prussian and only a sixth Swedish), and all of Bennigsen's force. There was thus some justification for Alexander viewing himself as the unofficial leader of the coalition, although this irritated both the British, who had been fighting Napoleonic France continuously since 1803 and whose best general commanded 125,000 British and Iberian troops near the Franco-Spanish border, and the Austrians, who, in addition to providing around 100,000 men on France's Rhine frontier, fielded another army of 75,000 in northern Italy which prevented Napoleon from withdrawing his forces from this theatre to help defend the French heartland.

 Despite France having already been invaded from Spain in October, Napoleon recognized that it was the armies on the other side of the Rhine that posed by far the greatest threat in late 1813. Soult in south-west France and Suchet in

Catalonia, between them commanding around 100,000 men, seemed likely to be able to prevent Wellington from making any dramatic advance in the next few months, while Eugène's 50,000-strong army in Italy appeared to have the measure of its Austrian opponents despite being heavily outnumbered. It would therefore be the struggle in northern France that would be critical, but if he were to have any chance of winning it, or at least preventing his enemies from winning, Napoleon needed far more troops than he had to hand.

Over the winter of 1813–14, the Emperor tried to conscript almost a million men to defend the homeland, to repeat the incredible feat of 1793–94. Barely 100,000 of these in the end served with the colours in any capacity, and it was this fact, ultimately, that decided the campaign. There are several reasons why Napoleon's call to save *la Patrie* elicited such a muted response. For a start, Napoleon himself had lost a great deal of support since the heyday of 1807, and particularly since 1812. With so many French families having lost members in wars in Iberia, Russia and central Europe, few were willing, understandably, to send further sons or brothers to fight. Even those families which had not been touched by personal loss usually knew friends who had, and all were subject to the increasingly heavy taxes of recent years levied to fund the mammoth conflicts the Emperor had waged. If the bulk of the French people were not necessarily desperate to be rid of Napoleon by late 1813 – there were, for example, no major uprisings – neither were they prepared to continue to make major sacrifices to sustain his regime, an attitude that was encouraged by skilful Allied propaganda which repeatedly stressed over the winter of 1813–14 that the coalition powers were waging war against Napoleon rather than the French people and that they wished to see France 'great, strong and happy'.

Another reason for the failure of Napoleon to recruit anywhere near as many new soldiers as he hoped was the fact that his nation was physically and psychologically shattered by late 1813. Over twenty years of almost continuous war had taken their toll. Theoretically, the million men the Emperor called-up were available and could be clothed and armed – France had not been so ruined that she could not potentially produce and equip a million troops from a population of around 30,000,000 – but it was a titanic ask of a pre-industrial nation that had endured so much for so long. Had the Allies played their hand less adeptly and descended upon France as avenging angels, determined to wreck the country and make its people suffer, an attitude some Russians and Prussians advocated, it is probable that there would have been an upsurge in recruiting and certainly in partisan activity, either of which might have prevented or at least hindered an Allied victory. By and large, though, the coalition soldiers behaved relatively well, especially the British in the south. There were certainly instances of atrocities being committed by Russian and Prussian troops, which did elicit localized responses in the form of attacks on Allied convoys or small detachments of men, but never enough to have a significant impact upon the overall course of events. The parts of France which were not directly affected by the Allied invasion, which, of course, constituted the great majority of the country, generally wished to have nothing to do with the conflict, and because the French people were typically less xenophobic, and the Church in France less powerful and more enlightened, than in Russia or Spain, there was no prospect of whipping up resistance to the invaders through hatred of foreigners or religious bigotry.

Perhaps most important in explaining why so few French were prepared to fight for their emperor and country in 1814, however, was the pervasive feeling of defeatism which gripped the nation. Almost everyone seemed to believe that the campaign was lost before it began and so were unwilling to make sacrifices for a cause which seemed doomed. Partly this was the result of a concerted effort by Royalist agents throughout France, aided by treacherous individuals like former foreign minister, Talleyrand, to spread defeatist rumours, but mostly it was the consequence of a string of disastrous defeats in recent years in Russia, Germany and Spain. Crucially, the feeling that France was fighting a lost cause even spread to the upper echelons of the Napoleonic regime, with calamitous effects for the Emperor. Many prefects, for example, believing that Napoleon's days were numbered and looking to curry favour with whoever might replace him, obstructed efforts to recruit soldiers or form partisan bands, while the performance of General Henri Clarke as Minister of War, the man ultimately responsible for overseeing the raising of troops and production of military equipment, was so poor as to have invited the suspicion of many a historian that he was actively working to undermine the regime he served.

The failure of Napoleon to raise more than a fraction of the new troops he hoped for in winter 1813–14 left him facing highly unfavourable odds. French forces were not quite as hopelessly weak as is often made out – the several tens of thousands of men holding out in Hamburg and Magdeburg would tie down large numbers of Allied soldiers, a force of 25,000 was gathering at Lyon under Augereau, many tens of thousands of troops guarded the Rhine frontier from Switzerland to the coast (15,000 at Mainz alone), and a sizeable, if not huge, reserve was being built up near Paris – but it was clear that Napoleon's most important forces, those in northern France, would be both heavily outnumbered and sorely lacking in well-trained or experienced troops. To remedy the latter problem, at least partially, the Emperor exchanged 25,000 veterans from the armies of Soult and Suchet with an equal number of raw recruits, but his plan to withdraw part of Eugène's army to help defend France was destroyed in early 1814 when it became apparent that Murat was going to renege on his promise, given to Napoleon upon leaving him during the retreat from Leipzig, that he would provide 30,000 Neapolitan troops to help fight the Austrians in northern Italy.

Facing adverse odds, Napoleon looked to diplomacy to help ease his predicament. In late 1813, he belatedly attempted to make peace with Spain. The French still held Catalonia, many thousands of Spanish prisoners of war and, perhaps most importantly, Ferdinand, the 'legitimate' Spanish king, so their bargaining position was not entirely hopeless. Indeed in December, to Napoleon's delight, Ferdinand agreed to the treaty of Valençay, which would have seen him restored to the throne along with peace between France and Spain. Had this subsequently come into effect, Wellington's army would have had to withdraw from the Franco-Spanish border area for lack of a major base from which to operate and be supplied. The British troops maybe could have been redeployed in the Low Countries, though it would have taken some time for them to do so, and the huge numbers of Allied soldiers already operating between the North Sea and Switzerland were stretching the supply situation taut as it was. In the meantime, the 100,000 men of Soult and Suchet could have made a major difference to the strategic situation in northern France. It was fortunate for Wellington and the Allies in general, therefore, that the Cortès, Spain's effective government in the absence of the captive king, rejected the Valençay Treaty out of hand.

Napoleon nevertheless remained hopeful in late 1813 that he could still retain both his throne and the 'natural frontiers'. His plan to defend northern France was imaginative and typically unconventional. Instead of fighting an exclusively defensive campaign, holding fast near Paris and waiting for the Allies to grind him down with their superior numbers, he intended to adopt a strategy which incorporated rapid manoeuvre by smallish forces aimed at chipping away at enemy strength and morale without draining that of the French too much. Although the majority of his troops would fight defensively, either holding fortresses near the border that would prevent the Allies from sending their full strength deep inside France or seeking to shield Paris from the advancing foe, the key formations would operate under the Emperor himself and would move to attack the enemy armies' flanks as they approached the French capital, jabbing at them rather than seeking to trade body blows. In this way, Napoleon hoped to be able to inflict a series of local defeats on the Allies which, while unlikely to be decisive individually, might together persuade his adversaries to grant him acceptable peace terms. Whatever else happened, though, Paris had to remain in French hands. Not only did the city have tremendous symbolic psychological significance, greater than that of Moscow or Berlin, for example, but it was also the hub of the centralized Napoleonic state and the army's principal arsenal and supply depot. The position of Governor of Paris, the man responsible for improving its fortifications and raising forces to defend them, was obviously a critical one, therefore, but Napoleon made a disastrous choice in appointing his ineffectual elder brother, Joseph. Although aware of his sibling's limitations, the Emperor believed that he at least could be relied upon to remain totally loyal to him and to do all he could to help defend the country and regime. As it turned out, Joseph would let him down even on this score.

Just as Napoleon made the defence of Paris the crux of his strategy, the Allies put its capture at the heart of their own. Their forces would operate in four main groups. In Germany, Bennigsen's Russians and about half of Bernadotte's Army of the North would initially concentrate upon reducing the French-held cities of Hamburg and Magdeburg, and, in the latter case, invading Denmark, an ally of France but, more importantly, possessor of Norway which the Swedes were determined to force Copenhagen to hand over. Once these tasks were achieved, these coalition troops were supposed to support the invasion of France, but although the Danes would yield quickly, Magdeburg and especially Hamburg, held by the indomitable Davout, would hold out for months. The second half of Bernadotte's army, Prussians under Bülow and Russians under General Ferdinand Winzingerode, meanwhile, were to operate in the Low Countries, completing the conquest of Holland before invading Belgium and, once that region had been overrun, continuing into France proper. There, they would operate alongside Blücher's Army of Silesia, which was charged with crossing the Rhine in the general vicinity of Mainz and driving towards Paris from the north-east. Finally, Schwarzenberg's host was to invade France from the east via Switzerland, even though the Swiss had, in agreement with Napoleon, recently declared themselves neutral. Militarily, such a move would outflank the French forces guarding the Rhine frontier north of Switzerland, and this was considered more important than observing Swiss neutrality. Once Schwarzenberg's force had penetrated deeper into France, the bulk of it would march on Paris, joining up with Blücher's army a little way to the east of the city for the final push. The remainder would head south-west towards Lyon, France's second city, where it was envisaged it would link up with the Austrian army currently fighting Eugène in northern Italy and deny Napoleon an obvious escape route should he decide to fight on after the fall of Paris. Overall, the Allied plan was a sound one, and dividing their forces so that the Rhine would be crossed in three areas (the Low Countries, Germany and Switzerland) had the advantage of making it easier to provision the troops by opening up a number of supply routes. It also, however, gave the Emperor the opportunity of operating against just part of the Allied host at any one time, the very situation he hoped to exploit.

The Army of Bohemia crossed into Switzerland near Basel on 20 December 1813. It was neither greeted nor resisted, the Swiss sullenly allowing it to pass through on its march towards France. At New Year, as Schwarzenberg was emerging onto French territory, Blücher started his campaign by crossing the Rhine. With a smaller army and facing many more troops than his Austrian ally, the Prussian might have expected a stiff fight, but he did not get one. French forces before him either retreated inside fortified towns, like Mainz, or fell back in the face of the enemy advance. Napoleon had never anticipated a major struggle for the border area – he didn't have the men to make such a strategy sensible – but nor did he expect Marshal Victor, who had been given responsibility for the sector, to put up quite as little resistance as he did. The result was that Victor lost his command and Blücher advanced more quickly than the Emperor had hoped. The Russians and Prussians of Winzingerode and Bülow certainly had a tougher time in the Low Countries, where the commanders, including the old stalwart of the Republic and hero of 1793–94, Lazare Carnot, at Antwerp, conducted a skilful defensive campaign with limited resources.

By late January, with Bülow and Winzingerode still embroiled in Belgium, both Blücher and Schwarzenberg were barely 150 miles from Paris to the east and east south-east respectively. By now, the forces under their immediate command had been reduced to around 50,000 and 150,000, due mostly to the need to detach units either to protect supply lines or mask French fortress towns, a large number of which were being held in the north-east of the country. This was still many more troops than Napoleon had between them and his capital. His field forces to the east of Paris, an area of predominantly flat countryside dissected by three major rivers all flowing roughly east–west, the Aisne in the north, the Marne in the centre, and the Seine in the south, numbered just 85,000, but so long as he could prevent the two Allied armies from uniting he had a chance of inflicting defeats upon them, especially Blücher. On 25 January, therefore, he said goodbye to his wife and son and left for the front. He would never see either again.

French resistance east of Paris began to stiffen in late January, even before the Emperor reached the front, especially against Blücher's Army of Silesia, which was predictably proving the more energetic of the two Allied forces marching towards the capital. There were skirmishes at Bar-le-Duc and St Dizier in the final week of the month, but the most notable clash came on the 29th at Brienne, a little over a hundred miles east south-east of Paris, where Napoleon had spent several often unhappy years at school. Both Allied and French armies had become dispersed, the former on the march, the latter because of the need to shield the capital against possible enemy thrusts in a number of directions. Still, the Emperor managed to gather together around 30,000 troops, mostly raw conscripts, with which to attack the 25,000 or so Russians and Prussians who were at Brienne. From late morning until after dark, battle raged for possession of the town and its castle, during which both army commanders had narrow escapes. Napoleon was suddenly charged at one point by a couple of Cossacks who were shot uncomfortably close to him, while Blücher fled the castle literally as it fell to the French, taking flight via the rear entrance as Napoleon's men burst in through the front. The struggle finished with the Allies defeated and retreating south-east in the direction of the village of La Rothière. They had lost 4,000 men to the French 3,000. It was a modestly encouraging start to the Emperor's campaign.

In the wake of Brienne, the two opposing forces lost contact. It was bitterly cold and windy, and snow fell heavily. Conditions were nowhere near as bad as they had been in Russia in late 1812, but they were unfriendly enough to make the French inclined to enjoy the shelter of Brienne and the handful of villages a few miles south-east of the town. Blücher, however, was determined to gain revenge for his defeat, regardless of the weather. By the start of February, he had gathered all his immediately available forces, some 53,000 in all, to the south-east of La Rothière, where he was joined by 25,000 Germans under General Wrede and 33,000 Russians under Barclay, the advance units of Schwarzenberg's Army of Bohemia. Napoleon, whose own forces south-east of Brienne had risen to around 40,000, had no idea how strong Blücher now was. He did not expect any of the slow-moving Schwarzenberg's army to be in a position to support the Prussian commander just yet, and the Allied build-up was masked by snowstorms and that by now perennial French handicap, lack of intelligence thanks to a weak cavalry arm.

It was with a massive numerical advantage of almost three to one, therefore, that Blücher fell upon the French forces deployed a few miles south-east of Brienne on 1 February. Napoleon needed to be at the top of his form to avoid a disaster, but fortunately for his men he was. Using a string of villages as strongpoints in his line, at the centre of which stood La Rothière, the Emperor conducted a skilful defensive stand against the odds in blizzard conditions that were reminiscent of Eylau. Through superb marshalling and direction of his limited forces to the key points, he and his troops managed to repel attack after attack and held their position pretty much intact until nightfall. The crisis of the fight came when Barclay's Russians stormed La Rothière, almost expelling the French from the village entirely and threatening to rupture the centre of Napoleon's position, but a well-timed and expertly led counter-attack saved the day. After dark, the battle ended, enabling the Emperor to disengage and withdraw in good order.

In some ways, La Rothière was something of a moral victory for the heavily outnumbered and largely inexperienced French, with losses being even at around 6,000 each (although Bonaparte's army did also lose fifty cannon). The Allies, though, treated it as a major triumph, proof that they could defeat the 'Ogre' on his own soil – even if they needed odds of almost three to one to do it. Conversely, the French reaction to the battle was as pessimistic as their enemies' was optimistic. Several thousand conscripts, convinced that the war was lost, deserted on the road from Brienne via Troyes to Nogent-sur-Seine, just sixty miles south-east of Paris, while the Emperor was in a despondent mood, aware that, now that the Armies of Silesia and Bohemia had successfully linked up, the military situation was bleaker than ever. Surprisingly, one of the few men who did not give way to extremes of emotion was the Tsar. After his at times painful experiences in 1813, he was cautious not to assume that victory was assured just yet. Upon reaching the town of Troyes, less than thirty miles south-east of the Emperor's new headquarters at Nogent, a few days after the battle, he was besieged by a deputation of Royalists who pleaded with him to restore the Bourbons once Napoleon and Paris fell. Flattered that they should come to him first, of all the Allied monarchs, Alexander nevertheless retained an even disposition. 'Gentlemen,' he said, 'you are a little premature.'

A few days after the Allied victory at La Rothière, on 5 February to be precise, a peace conference opened at Châtillon-sur-Seine, 120 miles south-east of Paris. This was the upshot of Metternich's peace offer of the previous November and Napoleon's positive response to it, but it only came about after some severe Austrian badgering of their coalition partners.

With no progress having been made towards the establishment of a congress to discuss a settlement by early January, the Emperor had sent Caulaincourt to Allied headquarters in an effort to move things along. It was as clear a sign as any of the prevailing mood there that Napoleon's Foreign Minister was not even allowed access to the Allied high command. Metternich, though, was determined that the conference should take place, that peace should be secured as soon as possible lest the divisions among the coalition deepen, and that it should be made on terms as close as possible to those which best suited Vienna. Once again, the attitude of Austria's allies towards a negotiated, compromise peace was highlighted by the fact that the Habsburgs' chief minister had to go as far as threatening to withdraw from the war unless they agreed to a congress taking place. Faced with such an ultimatum, the Russians, Prussians and British grudgingly consented, but they refused point blank to entertain any thought of an armistice while the talks took place.

Napoleon, by contrast, was eager to reach a settlement. Indeed, he explicitly informed Caulaincourt in January 1814 that, despite doubting that most of his enemies wanted peace at that time, 'for myself, I certainly desire it', although he continued, 'but it must be solid and honourable. France without her natural frontiers, without Ostend or Antwerp, would no longer be able to take her place among the States of Europe.' This was the key for him, what, alongside survival, he was prepared to continue fighting for, despite the unenviable odds against him. Given the diminished position of France *vis-à-vis* Britain, Russia, Germany and others in the nineteenth and much of the twentieth centuries, it is hard to deny that he had a point.

Unfortunately for the Emperor, of the major powers confronting him, only Austria favoured granting the French their 'natural frontiers'. The other three were committed to restricting them to the borders of 1791. They would not shift on this in early 1814 and Metternich had to accept that the best he could offer Napoleon territorially was a return to the situation before the Revolutionary Wars had started. The Austrian Chancellor had more success, however, in gaining some support, albeit tepid, for the Habsburg goal of the Bonaparte dynasty remaining in place. The issue of who should rule France at the end of the war was a particularly tricky one. Each of the major powers had their own preferences, as we have seen, but the divergence of opinion meant that at least two of them would end up disappointed. A crucial consideration, as each of the Allies, to varying degrees, had by now come to appreciate, was that the future government of France should be acceptable to the bulk of the French people; if it were not, there might be further revolution, civil war, even that anathema of the established ruling elites, a return to Jacobinism. This factor weighed in the Emperor's favour, as it seemed there was no real pressure from within France to remove him from power. A Bourbon restoration or the imposition of Bernadotte, on the other hand, could not be guaranteed to receive the acceptance of the majority of Frenchmen. This was one reason why the British Foreign Secretary, Lord Castlereagh, a devotee of the late William Pitt and an inveterate opponent of the Emperor, appears to have modified his position in early 1814 and become prepared to countenance Napoleon's retention of the throne provided France was reduced to her frontiers of 1791.

There were other reasons for this unexpected shift too. Like Metternich, Castlereagh was concerned for the future of the coalition should the war not end soon. The last thing he wanted to see was the grand alliance collapse on the brink of victory, allowing Napoleon to retain the 'natural frontiers' or possibly even more. Indeed, he was determined that the coalition should remain in existence long after the peace, with the prime goal of preventing any potential French revanchism; or, in more cynical words, keeping France down so that Britain was free to dominate the world's oceans and trade. Then there was Castlereagh's alarm at Russia's growing power and influence. Not only did the Russians seem determined to dominate the Baltic (their annexation of Finland), south-east Europe (their wars against the Turks), the Middle East (their expansion at Persia's expense), and Poland (their occupation of the Grand Duchy of Warsaw), but they also seemed to be establishing a powerful position in central Europe via their dominant partnership with Prussia. This made Castlereagh, like the Austrian Chancellor, resolutely determined to prevent Bernadotte, whom they saw as Alexander's stooge, from ascending the French throne. Realizing that that could best be done by forming a united front with the Austrians regarding France's future ruler further helped the British Foreign Secretary stomach his personal distaste at the prospect of Napoleon retaining power.

The Tsar, however, remained determined that Napoleon must be removed and that Paris should fall before peace was imposed. He was supported in this stance, predictably enough, by the Prussians. Having agreed only with extreme reluctance and under severe pressure to the establishment of a congress to discuss peace at Châtillon, Alexander did everything in his power to sabotage it. He ensured that both the Russians and Prussians sent representatives to the conference who were renowned opponents of Napoleon (although the Austrian and British delegates were not particularly well disposed towards him either), and then instructed his delegate, Count Razumovsky, to do all he could to hinder the proceedings. The obstruction commenced with the congress itself, the Tsar's representative insisting that it be immediately adjourned as his papers of accreditation were not in order, a patent excuse for delay.

Despite Alexander's hostility to the peace talks, the demands of coalition politics and, above all, the expectation that it would be rejected led the Tsar grudgingly to allow an offer of the frontiers of 1791 and Napoleon's retention of power to be put to Caulaincourt on 8 February. This was obviously less than the Emperor had hoped for, especially as France was to have no say in how the territories she would lose were to be carved up and as the British refused categorically even to discuss the issue of freedom of the seas, a request the French had tabled in the hope of gaining some kind of compensation for the sacrifices they were prepared to make. Unsurprisingly, Caulaincourt asked for time to confer with his master.

Needless to say, the terms offered bitterly disappointed Napoleon, but he was at such a low ebb in early February 1814 that, contrary to the Tsar's expectations and desires, he was prepared to consider them seriously. News from all fronts at this time was depressing. In the Low Countries, Brussels fell to Bülow's Prussians; in the south, Wellington was making slow but steady progress towards the port city of Bayonne; while in Italy Murat, egged on by his wife, Bonaparte's own sister, finally betrayed France and her emperor by joining the Sixth Coalition. Napoleon's reaction to this egregious act of treachery, once he had got over the shock, was understandably incensed: 'The conduct of the King of Naples and that of the Queen is quite unspeakable. I hope to live long enough to avenge for myself and for France such an outrage and such horrible ingratitude.'

It was the military situation east of Paris, though, that most concerned the Emperor. With the armies of Blücher and Schwarzenberg united, it seemed that Napoleon's preferred strategy, to chip away at sections of each force, was in ruins. The capital was by no means yet lost, but there equally seemed to Napoleon at this time to be little prospect of inflicting reverses on the Allies sufficient to make them consider improving their peace terms. Caulaincourt could try his best to win better conditions diplomatically, but at the end of the day, the Emperor was prepared to accept what the Allies offered him.

Two things prevented peace from being made in mid-February. The first was the attitude of the Tsar. When Caulaincourt returned to Châtillon following his discussions with Napoleon it soon became apparent that the French were basically willing to accept the offer put to them. A horrified Alexander responded by breaking off all talks, thereby confronting his allies with a choice between following suit or rupturing the coalition. They followed suit, but Metternich and Castlereagh did their best to try to persuade the Tsar to change his mind. He simply would not, bluntly telling the British Foreign Secretary in language that shocked and offended him, 'Understand once and for all that I shall not always be ready to have my troops make marches of four hundred leagues to come to your aid. I will not make peace so long as Napoleon remains on the throne.' This left Metternich and Castlereagh with a straight choice between fighting on or making a separate peace with France. The latter would not only tear the coalition they both valued so highly in two, but would leave Russia and Prussia free to continue a struggle which they might yet win on their own, rendering any Austro-British agreement with the Emperor worthless and leaving Alexander in a position to determine the fate of most of Europe unchecked. There was never really any doubt as to what they would do.

In the event, however, they did not have to make such a choice, for Napoleon suddenly decided to reject the Allied offer for the moment and try once more to win more favourable terms on the battlefield. What occasioned this sudden change of heart were the actions of the Army of Silesia. In the wake of his victory at La Rothière, Blücher became infused with a dangerously bloated sense of confidence. Instead of remaining in close contact with Schwarzenberg, which would have been the sensible thing to do, the Prussian field marshal abruptly decided to lead his army on a dramatic march on Paris down the valley of the Marne. He was doubtless largely motivated in this reckless act by fear that the peace conference at Châtillon might end the war before he could capture Paris and ensure Napoleon's fall, goals he shared with the Tsar and held with comparable passion. This also perhaps partly explains why, in his haste, he allowed his forces to become dangerously stretched out. It was this, the vulnerability of the Army of Silesia to a sudden counter-attack which might even lead to its utter destruction, that persuaded the Emperor to give war another chance. Telling Caulaincourt to stall at Châtillon and casually reassuring him, 'There will always be time to make such a peace as they are proposing to us', Napoleon roused his troops for another crack at Blücher's Russians and Prussians. Perhaps all hope of retaining the 'natural frontiers' was not yet lost after all.

The mini campaign fought by Napoleon east of Paris in mid-February 1814 is often lauded as one of his finest, a return to his imperious best as a commander. This is a fair assessment, but the Emperor's dazzling brilliance carried with it a dangerous consequence, for it would temporarily blind him to the reality of his overall predicament and lead him to spurn the last hope he had of possibly saving his regime.

Blücher had many positive qualities as a general. He was determined, aggressive, courageous and an inspiration to his men. He was also, however, prone to incaution, even recklessness, and in February 1814 this almost cost him his army. By the 10th of that month, his forces were strung out in the most perilous fashion in his haste to close on Paris. Napoleon could not believe his good fortune. Having failed to prevent Schwarzenberg and Blücher from uniting, they had willingly divided once more and the latter had left himself vulnerable to a major reverse.

The blow fell first on the small, isolated Russian corps of General Olsufiev near Champaubert, a village around sixty miles due east of Paris. Despite being in the middle of Blücher's strung out line of march, Olsufiev's 5,000-strong force was beyond immediate aid when 30,000 Frenchmen led by the Emperor in person descended upon it on 10 February. Given the odds, the issue was never in doubt, although the difficult conditions – the ground was so muddy following a thaw that the French had to enlist the support of local villagers to help drag their cannon into position – enabled around a thousand Russians to escape. Still, 4,000 were killed or taken prisoner for the loss of just 200 of Napoleon's soldiers. Olsufiev himself was captured in a wood by a nineteen-year-old private.

Next day, leaving part of his force to guard against the threat from Blücher's units east of Champaubert, Napoleon marched west. After about ten miles, he came across the Russian corps of General Sacken at the village of Montmirail. Despite having barely 11,000 men and just thirty-six guns to Sacken's 18,000 troops and ninety cannon, Napoleon determined to attack, confident that his soldiers, mostly units of the Guard, could at least keep the enemy pinned down until reinforcements arrived to win the day. The fighting was tough, but the Guardsmen as well as the couple of thousand conscripts he had under his command more than rewarded their commander's faith in them. The battle appeared to be in question when a few thousand Prussians of General Yorck's corps unexpectedly arrived to attack the French right, but the threat was comfortably dealt with, and, soon after, the battle was won with the entry into the fray of the reinforcements Napoleon had been waiting for. The arrival of Marshal Mortier with another 10,000 members of the fearsome Imperial Guard broke the Allied will to resist and they withdrew from the battlefield, fleeing north. For the loss of 2,000 men, the French had inflicted 4,000 casualties on their foes and won a second battle in two days.

In the wake of their defeat at Montmirail, the corps of Sacken and Yorck were in dire peril. While they were pursued from behind by the Emperor, Marshal Macdonald, whose corps had been ordered to guard the approach to Paris down the Marne valley, was instructed by his master to race for Château-Thierry, hold or destroy the crossings over the Marne there, and thus cut off the enemy's escape route, forcing them to surrender *en masse*. In order to beat the Allies to the town, however, Macdonald had to take a route which traversed the Marne downriver from his objective. Unfortunately for the French, the bridge at this point had been recently demolished so as to slow the speedy advance of Blücher's army towards the capital. With no choice but to take a lengthy detour, Macdonald lost the crucial race.

Despite this stroke of good fortune, the corps of Sacken and Yorck still had a rough time of it. Reaching Château-Thierry ahead of Macdonald meant that at least part of their force could escape north of the Marne, destroying the bridges behind them to slow the pursuit, but the fight to hold the French under Napoleon back while they crossed the river cost them a good many dead, 3,000 prisoners, and the loss of twenty cannon and a huge number of wagons loaded with supplies. In all, the Allies lost around 6,000 men to the French 600 on 12–13 February.

Nor was it over yet for Blücher's army. The escape of Yorck and Sacken over the Marne gave them a valuable breathing space in their flight from the French, but the pursuit could in theory have been maintained. That it was not was due to news from further south that Napoleon received while chasing the enemy to Château-Thierry. Schwarzenberg, rarely one to stir himself to prompt action, had for once taken the bit between his teeth and exploited the Emperor's preoccupation with the threat from Blücher to drive towards Paris from the south-east along the valley of the Seine. The corps Bonaparte had left to shield the capital from any advance by the Army of Bohemia were only strong enough to slow it down, not turn it back, and he therefore realized that he had to abandon his pursuit of Sacken and Yorck and march fast to block Schwarzenberg. On the way, however, he would have one more chance to give the Army of Silesia a good drubbing.

Another of Blücher's strengths as a commander was that he was a steadfast ally, a fact that would save Wellington and his army at Waterloo. On 14 February 1814 it was Schwarzenberg whom he tried to help, launching an attack on the corps of Marshal Marmont near the village of Vauchamps, fifty-five miles east of Paris and about fifteen south-east of Château-Thierry, in the hope of distracting Napoleon and impeding his march south. Heavily outnumbered by the 22,000 men the old Prussian had under his command, Marmont had little choice but to give ground, but the Emperor was only too willing to divert his dash south temporarily in order to support his subordinate and teach Blücher a lesson. Lifting French strength to around 25,000 with his arrival, Napoleon made short work of throwing the Allies back, severely mauling them in the process. As at Champaubert just four days earlier, thick, cloying mud impeded the effective deployment of French guns, but that did not save Blücher entirely. He lost around 7,000 men, a third of his force, on 14 February, as well as 16 guns. French casualties were less than a thousand.

After Vauchamps, the Emperor raced south to deal with Schwarzenberg, confident that the threat to Paris from the Army of Silesia had been eliminated for the time being at least. There was a tinge of disappointment that he had been unable to destroy Blücher's force utterly, but the damage he had dealt had been serious enough, achieved at very little cost to his own army. His success would all be for naught, however, unless he could also turn back the advance of the Army of Bohemia.

By 17 February, Schwarzenberg's advance guard, the Russian corps of General Wittgenstein, was at Nangis, north of the Seine and less than forty miles from Paris. It was here that Napoleon began to throw back the second Allied lunge towards his capital. Outnumbered, outfought and caught by surprise, Wittgenstein's troops were swiftly put to flight, losing 6,000 prisoners in the process. Stunned by the Emperor's sudden descent – the French had covered the distance between the Marne and the Seine faster than Schwarzenberg had expected – the Allied commander-in-chief abruptly ordered his forces to withdraw south of the Seine. Anticipating this response, Napoleon ordered Marshal Victor to march his corps with all speed to Montereau on the Seine, to seize and hold the crossing there, and to hinder the escape of a large part of Schwarzenberg's army. Unlike Macdonald, Victor had no reasonable excuse for his failure to carry out his orders. Approaching Montereau late on the afternoon of 17 February, he halted short of his objective when he saw that the bridge there was defended by an Allied force. Had he attacked, the chances are that he would have defeated the enemy and taken control of the vital crossing. At the very least, he would have created a heightened sense of alarm within the Allied army which the Emperor, nearby at the head of an army now 60,000-strong, could have exploited the next day. When he heard of Victor's pusillanimity, Napoleon was livid and peremptorily dismissed him from his command. To his credit, the marshal begged to be allowed to stay with the army and do anything he could to help defend France, even offering to serve as a private. The Emperor's ire relented and he gave his wayward subordinate command of two divisions of the Guard, a post arguably more suited to his level of military competence.

The upshot of Victor's failure was that the Emperor and his men faced a more difficult task on 18 February and stood to earn a less crushing victory than they might have. Given time to improve their defensive positions covering the town of Montereau and its vital bridge, the Allies were able to put up a stiff fight and evacuate the great majority of their troops who had ventured north of the Seine to the relative safety of its southern bank. After six hours of combat, during which Napoleon dismounted at one point to aim one of his cannon, a reminder of his training as an artillery officer, the Allies lost 6,000 men and twenty-five guns compared to 2,500 French losses. There was no denying that the Emperor had won yet another clear victory; but as at Château-Thierry, it was marred by thoughts of what might have been.

Although the fighting south-east of Paris on 17–18 February damaged Schwarzenberg's army less severely than Bonaparte had hoped, it nevertheless greatly undermined the Allied commander-in-chief's confidence. Abandoning all thoughts of going forward, he ordered the Army of Bohemia to retreat eastwards. Napoleon followed with all the field forces he had to hand, hoping to compel the Austrian to fight a major battle which, after his recent run of victories, he was sure he would win, despite being outnumbered. Schwarzenberg was unwilling to oblige him. He had no stomach for a massive confrontation and, in any case, greatly overestimated the size of the Emperor's army, imagining it to be more than twice as large as it was. The retreat therefore continued past Troyes towards the plateau of Langres, over 120 miles south-east of Paris. Indeed, Schwarzenberg had half a mind to withdraw all the way back to the frontier. What prevented him from doing so was another failure by one of Napoleon's subordinates. As he chased the Army of Bohemia, the Emperor ordered Marshal Augereau at Lyon, south of the plateau of Langres, to march north-east to menace Schwarzenberg's lines of communication back to Switzerland. It was a threat to which the Allied commander-in-chief was particularly sensitive and, had that been exploited now, there is every chance he would not have halted his retreat short of the border. Fortunately for the Allies, though, Augereau held fast at Lyon, complaining to his master that his troops were useless and that he could do nothing with them. It brought a stinging rebuke from Napoleon: 'I am ordering you to take to the field within twelve hours after the receipt of this letter. If you are still the Augereau of Castiglione,* keep your command; if your sixty years are weighing on you, leave it and turn it over to your most senior general.' Belatedly, Augereau left Lyon, only to advance a paltry distance before retiring once more to the city upon discovering that Schwarzenberg had detached a small force to guard against the threat he and his army of 25,000 posed.

The upshot of the Emperor's fine victories of mid-February 1814 was a resurrection of the peace conference at Châtillon which the Tsar had done his best to kill. Convinced by the mauling handed out to Blücher's Army of Silesia that the war was unlikely to end any time soon, Metternich once more vigorously pressed the case for a compromise settlement. Yet again, Alexander was the chief obstacle, and it took the threat of Austria making a separate peace with Napoleon to get him to agree to the congress reconvening on 17 February. Still the Tsar was determined to wreck the talks, instructing his representative, Razumovsky, to resume the disruptive tactics that had hampered the initial meeting of the conference. Alexander remained focused firmly upon complete military victory, threatening to transfer all Russian forces in the Army of Bohemia to the Army of Silesia in an effort to put backbone into the timid Schwarzenberg and insisting

---

* A battle in northern Italy in 1796 at which Augereau had distinguished himself.

that the corps of Bülow and Winzingerode from Bernadotte's Army of the North be put under the command of the aggressive Blücher to enable him to mount another drive on Paris. Such brusque threats and demands inevitably strained Allied relations severely, but the Tsar got his way. Schwarzenberg halted his retreat and Bernadotte's two corps in the Low Countries were ordered to march to join the Army of Silesia as soon as circumstances permitted, much to the chagrin of Sweden's adopted Crown Prince.

If Alexander remained fixated upon achieving total military victory in the wake of the serious reverses of mid-February, Metternich and, to a lesser extent, Castlereagh became more determined to conclude a peace with Napoleon acceptable to them both. That meant the offer presented to Caulaincourt on the 8th: the frontiers of 1791 and Napoleon to retain the throne. Following the resumption of the Châtillon conference, therefore, the Tsar was once again pressured into agreeing to these terms being put forward, but a deadline for acceptance of 10 March was set. Metternich and Castlereagh had been dismayed by the Emperor's recent spate of victories, as well as by the failure of Allied armies to make much progress in south-west France or northern Italy (the latter in spite of the treachery of Marshal Murat), but they appreciated that the overall advantage still lay with the Allies.

Caulaincourt realized this too and so pressed his master to accept the repeated offer. Napoleon, though, was not interested. His caustic comment on the terms was, 'If I am to be flagellated let it at least be compulsorily inflicted'. His brilliant victories of mid-February had blinded him to the fundamental realities of his predicament. Having been prepared, albeit reluctantly, to accept the Allied terms a couple of weeks earlier, the Emperor was now thinking of driving the enemy back across the Rhine. When Schwarzenberg requested an armistice in the wake of his defeat at Montereau, Napoleon not only dismissed it, unless the Allies undertook to evacuate his territory forthwith, but demanded that they acknowledge France's right to the 'natural frontiers' as the basis for a settlement. Subsequently, he even introduced other proposals into the talks at Châtillon, such as that Eugène be allowed to retain rule over the kingdom of Italy as far east as the Adige river and that France be handed back most of the overseas colonies that the British had seized from them during their long war.

The Allied deadline for acceptance of their offer consequently came and went. Whether there was any real prospect of peace being made on the basis of its terms had Napoleon accepted them is open to debate, given the unyielding position adopted by the Tsar, but it is just possible that in the immediate wake of the brilliant French victories of mid-February Alexander could have been browbeaten into modifying his stance or that Austria, Britain, Sweden, and maybe even Prussia would have been prepared to make peace regardless of Russia's attitude. What is certain is that the Emperor's decision to demand more than the borders of 1791 played a key part in a general hardening of Allied attitudes towards him that helped seal his fate. It convinced Castlereagh, for example, that Napoleon would never truly accept the loss of Belgium and its strategically valuable port of Antwerp, and so made him determined that he had to be removed from power. Metternich too was no longer prepared to argue for Napoleon retaining the throne after his failure for a second time to accept an offer the Austrian Chancellor had gone to such lengths to put on the table.

The hardening of both statesmen's attitude also owed much to a sudden improvement in the Allied military position in late February and early March. In the south-west, Wellington's defeat of Soult at Orthez created the prospect of greater progress being made on this front, but more important was the easing of the peril Schwarzenberg believed himself to be in and the unexpectedly quick rallying of Blücher's badly battered Army of Silesia. (Indeed, the two were connected, for it was Blücher's resumption of an advance towards Paris, undertaken in the knowledge that he would shortly be reinforced by Winzingerode and Bülow from the north, that forced Napoleon to break off his pursuit of the Army of Bohemia.)

The first clear sign of the hardening Allied attitude came a day before the deadline for the Emperor's acceptance of their peace offer expired. On 9 March, the leading coalition powers signed the treaty of Chaumont (a town near the plateau of Langres then serving as Allied headquarters). This agreement formally laid out some of the Allies' aims, including independence for Holland, Switzerland and the German states, the return of Spain and lands in Italy to their former rulers, and the restriction of France to her pre-Revolutionary Wars frontiers. It also reconfirmed earlier promises given by each of the signatories not to conclude a separate peace with Napoleon, increased British subsidies to a massive £5 million per annum, to be divided equally among their coalition partners in return for fielding at least 150,000 troops each against the French, and pledged all the Allies to maintain the settlement eventually to be reached with France for twenty years. The treaty stopped short of insisting upon the removal of Napoleon from power, but given the rigidly hostile attitude of the Tsar, the other powers' willingness to recommit themselves at this time not to make a separate peace shows that they all now expected and wished for him to fall.

By the end of the month, this had been made explicit and public. The Châtillon conference was terminated by the Allies once and for all in mid-March, and less than a week later they issued a proclamation stating that peace could only be restored once Napoleon had been removed from power. The days might be lengthening as the spring of 1814 arrived, but night was falling upon Imperial France and her ruler.

Brilliant as Napoleon's victories against the Allies were in mid February 1814, they did not alter the overall military situation fundamentally. Within a fortnight of the string of defeats his army suffered, Blücher was back on the offensive, advancing back down the Marne valley towards Paris. With reinforcements coming south from Belgium to join the Army of Silesia, Napoleon could not afford to rely upon the corps he had left to guard against any threat from that force to hold the enemy back, so, to his great disappointment, he had to abandon the pursuit of Schwarzenberg in late February and march north to deal with the renewed Russo-Prussian menace.

Word of Napoleon advancing to meet him led Blücher to flee north towards the River Aisne. After the severe battering his army had taken in recent weeks, the Prussian knew that he could only hope to fight the Emperor with any hope of success once he had been joined by the troops heading south from Belgium. As he fled, though, Napoleon pursued, eager to smash the enemy army before it could be reinforced.

The key, as at Château-Thierry and Montereau, was control of a vital river crossing, this time the town of Soissons on the Aisne, around fifty-five miles north-east of Paris. As the pursuit began, it was in French hands but besieged by a Russo-Prussian force. Should the garrison hold out, Blücher would have to race for another crossing which he was highly unlikely to get to ahead of Napoleon's chasing army. The result would in all probability have been the destruction of the fiery field marshal's force. It was to his enormous relief, therefore, and the Emperor's acute frustration, that the defenders of Soissons yielded the town on 3 March, enabling Blücher to get his fleeing soldiers across the Aisne in safety.

Despite this lucky escape, the Army of Silesia continued to be pursued by the Emperor. Heading east from Soissons, it linked up with Winzingerode's Russian corps near the village of Craonne and there turned to fight. Blücher's plan was to hold the French frontally while Winzingerode outflanked them, but guessing the enemy design, Napoleon pre-empted it by attacking with 37,000 men on 7 March before the Allies were ready. Although now outnumbered, the Emperor hoped to inflict a serious reverse on his opponents, the key to his strategy being the successful execution of a flanking manoeuvre by Marshal Ney's corps. With what was now predictable ineptness, Ney bungled the crucial attack, sending in his men too early only to see them sharply rebuffed. Around 4 p.m., the five-hour battle of Craonne petered out in a draw. French losses, at 5,400, were marginally higher than the 5,000 of the Allies, but it was the Russians and Prussians who retreated north-west towards the city of Laon.

Denied a victory at Craonne, Napoleon determined to push on after the enemy and force them to fight again. Reaching Laon on 8 March, Blücher was further reinforced by Bülow's Prussian corps, bringing the strength of the Army of Silesia up to 85,000 men and 150 guns. The following morning, a thick fog hid the size of the Prusso-Russian army from the Emperor, so he remained determined to bring about a battle. Once more, he intended to hold the Allied line with the bulk of his force while outflanking it with one of his corps. The key manoeuvre this time was entrusted to Marshal Marmont, a more skilled commander than Ney, but one who was prone to making costly errors (it had been his mistake that had allowed Wellington to smash the French army at Salamanca in 1812, for example).

A hint of what was to come was provided by Marmont's sluggish advance with his 10,000-strong corps to take up a position to the east of Napoleon's main body of just under 40,000. It was afternoon on 9 March before he was in position and it was clear that the Emperor would have to wait until the morrow before launching his attack. Such fighting as there was on the 9th, therefore, was desultory. At least that was the case until the evening. By nightfall, Marmont, perhaps seeking to make up for his earlier tardiness, had advanced as far as the village of Athies, a few miles to the east of Laon. It was a hopelessly vulnerable position, as he soon found out. Allied scouts quickly confirmed the dangerous isolation and limited strength of Marmont's corps, and Blücher lost no time in ordering a night-time attack by units from four of his corps, two Russian, two Prussian. The marshal was put to flight in short order, losing a third of his men and forty-five guns in the process. Indeed, he was fortunate to escape his blunder with any of his command intact.

As the sun rose on 10 March, Marmont's corps was in headlong flight south with a much larger number of Russians and Prussians in pursuit, threatening to complete the work of the night just passed. Faced with a crisis, Napoleon responded with customary skill and composure. Despite now realizing just how much larger Blücher's army was than his own, the Emperor ordered the troops under his direct command to attack in order to draw the pressure being exerted against Marmont onto himself. It was a gambit that worked only too well, the Allies abandoning the pursuit of the marshal's corps and turning their attention to the Emperor's main body. In spite of the disparity in numbers, the French had rather the better of the fighting, inflicting more casualties on their opponents than they sustained themselves in this phase of the battle. Still, by the end of the two-day struggle at Laon, it was clear that the Allies had won. Not only did the Emperor retreat from the field, recrossing to the southern bank of the Aisne, but total French losses, at 6,000, were fifty per cent higher than those of the Russians and Prussians.

Napoleon had no doubt who was to blame for the defeat at Laon. He accused Marmont, justifiably if harshly, of 'crass stupidity' and remarked that the marshal had 'behaved like a second lieutenant'. In truth, though, there was never any real prospect of Napoleon winning the kind of victory he had hoped for once Bülow and Winzingerode had joined the Army of Silesia. The best he could probably have obtained was another drawn battle like Craonne, after which he would still have had to retreat in the face of markedly superior numbers.

Pyschologically, the impact of Laon was profound for both sides, leading some to brand it the most decisive engagement of the 1814 campaign. For the Allies, and especially Blücher's army, it gave a boost in morale following the disasters of mid-February and eased many doubts raised by those recent reverses. The effect on the French, meanwhile, was the opposite, crushing any hope that had been created a few weeks earlier and plunging the country back into a general mood of despair. Even Napoleon himself, though determined to fight on, was deflated by the defeat, ominously ordering his brother Joseph to ensure that redoubts were constructed in the northern Paris suburb of Montmartre.

The Emperor faced an unenviable strategic predicament following his retreat from Laon. Not only was Blücher still able to mount a drive towards the French capital from the north-east, but Schwarzenberg was once again advancing on the city, albeit slowly, from the south-east. Having failed to crush the Army of Silesia, Napoleon resolved to try his luck against the Army of Bohemia instead. Rather than marching directly to take on Schwarzenberg, however, he exploited an opportunity to restore morale following Laon. Learning that an isolated Russian corps had occupied Rheims, some eighty miles north-east of Paris, he fell upon the city with a superior force on 13 March and routed the enemy. For the loss of just 700 men, the French killed or captured 6,000 Russians, their commander being among the dead. The victory did much to lift spirits among those troops who had taken part in the engagement, but did depressingly little to offset the more widespread gloom that was gripping the country after Laon.

By the time the Emperor caught up with the vanguard of Schwarzenberg's army a week after his triumph at Rheims, it had advanced considerably less far west than it might have. The corps Napoleon had left to guard against any thrust from the Allied commander-in-chief had been doing what they could to hinder his advance, but the real reason for the slowness of his forward movement was that he continued greatly to overestimate the size of forces available to the French and so was determined to be cautious. It was as far east as the village of Arcis-sur-Aube, some eighty miles east-south-east of Paris, that Bonaparte attacked Schwarzenberg's vanguard on 20 March, driving it several miles back from the Aube's southern bank.

It is a sign of how slowly the Army of Bohemia had moved in recent weeks that Napoleon was sure it must be its rearguard rather than its advance guard that faced him at Arcis. Having pushed it back south-east on the 20th, therefore – away from where he believed the bulk of Schwarzenberg's army to be – he resolved to attack again next day in the hope of destroying it. In reality, the Emperor had driven the enemy vanguard back towards the rest of the Allied force, with the result that, by dawn on 21 March, some 80,000 Austrian, Russian and German troops were drawn up behind a range of low heights a few miles south of the Aube. Napoleon had fewer than 30,000 soldiers at hand.

Given the huge disparity in numbers, Arcis-sur-Aube was at best likely to resemble Laon in its outcome, although there would be no French blunder comparable to Marmont's at the previous battle. Napoleon swiftly realized from the reports of his scouts on the morning of the 21st that he was facing a force almost three times the size of his own and responded by ordering preparations to be made for a withdrawal back north of the Aube. The French were undoubtedly fortunate that the Allies did not attack until 3 p.m., after the withdrawal actually commenced, the result of Schwarzenberg yet again grossly overestimating the magnitude of the enemy army. For the next three hours, an ever-diminishing French rearguard under Marshal Oudinot fought an excellent defensive battle against increasing numbers of Allied troops until the vast majority of Napoleon's army had been successfully pulled back to the northern side of the Aube and the bridge over the river had been blown.

Casualties at Arcis favoured the French 3,000 to 4,000, although the Allies could absorb their losses more easily than their adversaries. More significant strategically than these numbers was the fact that it was the French who retreated following the battle. Inevitably, Schwarzenberg failed to pursue.

By late March 1814, the Emperor's military predicament was as bad as, if not worse than, it had been at the start of February. It was no coincidence that it was at this time that the Allies publicly committed themselves to his overthrow. With all hope of a settlement that allowed him to retain the throne gone, at least unless he could dramatically alter the present course of the campaign, Napoleon reconsidered his strategy. He could always pull all his forces back on Paris and make the Allies besiege him there. It might be many months before the city fell, but fall it surely would unless his enemies gave up the fight and withdrew, allowing him to remain in power. No, somehow he had to find a way to compel Blücher and Schwarzenberg to draw back from the capital without (and this was the really tricky part) sustaining inordinate losses to his own dwindling forces. Recent direct attacks on their armies having failed on both counts, the Emperor decided upon an imaginative scheme that, while risky, might achieve his objectives. Instead of tackling the Armies of Silesia and Bohemia head-on, he would leave part of his field force to slow their advance on Paris as best they could while he led the rest away from the city towards the frontier in order to menace the Allies' supply lines. In so doing, Napoleon hoped not only to induce the enemy to pull back to protect their vital communications, but also to swell his force by linking up with the many thousands of troops still holding out in a dozen or so towns in north-eastern France.

While this plan was desperate, it came close to succeeding nonetheless. On 22 March, a group of Russian Guards cavalry captured a French despatch rider carrying a letter from the Emperor to his wife, Marie-Louise. In it, Napoleon outlined his plan to attack the Allied supply lines and relieve the French garrisons.

This information did not, as many accounts of the period have it, encourage the Allies to quicken their advance on Paris. On the contrary, the revelation of the threat to his communications, as well as to the Allied forces besieging the French towns, led Schwarzenberg to halt his progress westwards and plan a march against Napoleon and his army, now to his north-east.

The Emperor's plan was working well when a band of Cossacks rode into Allied headquarters in the early hours of 24 March bearing a bundle of despatches from Paris that they had just captured. It was these papers, not Napoleon's letter to his wife, that were of critical significance. Intended for the Emperor, they described a capital that was not as well defended as it should have been, whose fortifications had barely been improved, and whose leadership was clearly lacking in fight. As soon as he had read them, the Tsar, supported by Frederick William, demanded that Schwarzenberg forget about Napoleon and order the Allied armies to march full speed on Paris. The Austrian was initially unwilling to comply with Alexander's plan, but the Tsar simply would not take no for an answer, browbeating the commander-in-chief into accepting his wishes. Leaving a single corps behind to impede Napoleon's progress should he head back west, Schwarzenberg ordered his and Blücher's armies to advance on the enemy capital as fast as they could. For the once all-conquering Emperor of the French, the game was at last very nearly up.

On 28 March, the Armies of Silesia and Bohemia linked up near Meaux, a town on the Marne just twenty-five miles east north-east of Paris. Late on the following afternoon, Tsar Alexander and King Frederick William saw the French capital for the first time from the heights of Clichy to the north of the city. Some 40,000 troops defended Paris at the end of March 1814, and although the Allies had four times as many soldiers to hand, any attempt to fight for the capital might prove horrifically costly. Indeed the next day, 30 March, the Allies lost 8,400 men, 6,000 of them Russians, fighting in the northern suburbs of Belleville and Montmartre.

Having bloodied the enemy's nose to salvage some kind of honour, the military and civil leadership in the city then threw in the towel, as the despatches intercepted a few days earlier had suggested they would. At 5 p.m. on the 30th, Marshal Marmont, the senior general in the area, requested an armistice. The Tsar, usurping Schwarzenberg's role as commander-in-chief, insisted that the capital must be handed over to the Allies first. Marmont agreed and discussions to work out the details were completed by 2 a.m. the following morning. French forces in Paris were to evacuate the city by 7 a.m. and withdraw to the south, leaving the Allies free to march in unopposed. It had taken them longer than they had originally envisaged – twenty-two years to be precise – but the established monarchies of Europe had finally managed to capture the heart of Revolutionary and Napoleonic France.

Marmont's actions had the full support of, indeed had been partly prompted by, Paris's civil authorities. Marie-Louise, who had been appointed Regent by Napoleon in his absence at the front, had been sent away from the capital with her son on 28 March, ostensibly to remove any possibility of them falling into enemy hands, while Joseph Bonaparte, the governor of the city, had fled two days later. This created a political vacuum which the treacherous and cunning Talleyrand was only too eager to fill. The former foreign minister set the tone for the civic authorities in late March 1814 and that tone was one of capitulation.

Could Paris have held out longer? The Emperor certainly believed so or else he would not have marched east following the battle at Arcis-sur-Aube. There was, after all, always the chance that the Allies would ignore his move to threaten their communications and march straight on the capital. If that happened Napoleon needed to feel confident that the city could hold out long enough for him to do enough damage to the enemy's supply lines to force them to pull back.

Why did Paris not hold out longer, then? The blame has often been attributed to Marshal Marmont, who has been accused of capitulating too easily in order to curry favour with the Allies and the Bourbons. His defenders, though, have argued that he capitulated after just one day's fighting in order to save the city, and country, from further suffering in what he now saw as a hopeless cause. This is perhaps closer to the truth. The fact is that Marmont did not have the necessary manpower resources or support from the civil authorities to be able to defend Paris for more than a few days if the Allies were determined to fight him resolutely, as the bitter struggles for Belleville and Montmartre suggested they were. The real blame for the failure of the capital to hold out as long as Napoleon had hoped thus lies with the Emperor's useless brother Joseph. Whether through incompetence, indolence, apathy or perhaps even treachery, Joseph failed utterly in his role as governor of Paris. He did almost nothing to improve the city's physical defences or to recruit troops to help man them from among the hundreds of thousands of souls who lived in the capital. He provided no leadership or spirit of resistance. And as soon as the Allies started to attack the suburbs he fled, clearing the way for Talleyrand to come to the fore politically.

The last time a foreign army had marched into Paris it had been led by Henry V of England almost four hundred years before. This time, the man everyone looked to as the conqueror of the French capital was Alexander I of Russia. Fittingly, the first Allied troops to enter the city on the late morning of 31 March were Russian cavalry. They were followed by the Tsar, the King of Prussia and Prince Schwarzenberg. Although the three men rode together in a line, Alexander was in the centre mounted on a magnificent white charger and with a permanent smile of ecstasy on his face. Entering Paris from the east, the procession rode through the heart of the capital, past the Hôtel de Ville, the Louvre, the Tuileries, and what is now the Place de la Concorde to the Champs-Élysées, at the end of which, ironically, the mighty Arc de Triomphe was being constructed. Many Parisians came out to watch the troops and their leaders pass, and there were even a few cries of '*Vivent les Alliés!*' or '*Vive Alexandre!*' from bitter opponents of the now moribund Napoleonic regime. The vast majority, though, watched in silence, perhaps still trying to come to terms with how things had come to this.

The Emperor was informed of the fall of his capital just hours after its capitulation had been agreed. Having learnt that the Allies were marching headlong towards the city on 27 March, his first reaction had been to continue east to threaten the enemy's communications, trusting that Paris would hold out long enough to force its attackers to retreat for want of supplies. His marshals, however, had practically revolted, demanding that they rush back to assist in the defence of the capital. It was a sign of how precarious Napoleon now felt his grip on power to be that he had acquiesced.

The race, of course, proved in vain. The single corps left behind by the Allies to hinder Napoleon's movements was brusquely swept aside with little delay to the French advance, but Blücher and Schwarzenberg simply had too big a lead. In the end, the Emperor sped ahead of his main body with a small force, but even then he ran out of time. He was informed of the capital's surrender at Essonnes, twenty miles south of the city. From there he retired another twenty miles south-east to the palace of Fontainebleau, where he waited for the bulk of his army to join him over the next couple of days.

News of the fall of Paris left Napoleon incredulous and appalled. How could a city of so many people, so well provisioned with food and military hardware, not be able to hold out for more than a day? In ranting against the incompetence, or worse, of Marmont, his brother Joseph, and the civil authorities of Paris he hit the nail on the head in at least two cases.

Once the shouting was over, the Emperor had to decide what to do next. Many of the troops assembling at Fontainebleau in early April, around 60,000 in all, cried '*Vive l'Empereur! À Paris! À Paris!*', and initially it seems that he was inclined to lead them in an effort to retake the capital, but on the 4th, common sense, in the form of what has become known as the Marshal's Revolt, asserted itself. A group of Napoleon's senior subordinates, led by Michel Ney, met their master and bluntly informed him that they would not lead their men in a futile assault on Paris. The war was over. Not only had the capital fallen, but France's second city, Lyon, had been captured by a section of the Army of Bohemia, Marshal Augereau not putting up any kind of fight. In the south-west, meanwhile, Bordeaux had gone over to the enemy and Wellington was fast closing on the city of Toulouse, where he was to fight and win a final battle against Marshal Soult on 10 April. In Italy too, it was surely now only a matter of time before the redoubtable Eugène, after months of fighting against the odds, was overwhelmed by the combination of an Austrian army to his east, a Neapolitan one to his south, and a British one which had recently landed at Genoa to his rear. All that was left to do was make peace.

The difficulty was that the Allies had publicly and expressly stated that they would not make peace until Napoleon had been removed from power. The marshals therefore had a request to make of the Emperor: abdicate, not unconditionally, but in favour of his son, to whom Ney and his companions pledged they would be loyal if their master consented. Would this be enough to satisfy the Allies? It was unlikely, but it was surely worth a try. On 4 April, in an effort to salvage something from the wreck of his empire, Bonaparte signed a decree of abdication in favour of his three-year-old son. Caulaincourt, Ney and Macdonald would take it to the Tsar in Paris and do their best to persuade him to accept it.

Alexander agreed to meet the three as soon as they arrived in the capital in the early hours of 5 April. The Frenchmen can hardly have been encouraged to find that the Tsar was staying at Talleyrand's house, but they were welcomed warmly by the Russian ruler nonetheless, who greeted Caulaincourt as an old friend and praised the two marshals on the valorous, if unsuccessful, defence of France. The trio in turn thanked Alexander for the moderation he had shown in occupying the French capital. For the next two hours, Napoleon's spokesmen argued the case for his conditional abdication and the succession of his son, the gist of which was that only the continuation of the Bonapartist regime could guarantee stability in France and that no other government would be acceptable to the French army. The Tsar listened politely and promised to give them an answer later in the day. Caulaincourt and the marshals left at 5 a.m. to kick their heels for a few anxious hours.

Bizarre as it may seem, there was just the glimmer of a possibility that Alexander might have accepted the succession of Napoleon's son. The fact is that he was undecided what should be done about the future government of France in early April. His former support for Bernadotte had all but disappeared following the Crown Prince's dismal showing in the recent campaign and his reluctance to play the role of faithful poodle to the Tsar, but he had no liking either for the solution proposed by the British, Prussians, and indeed his own Foreign Minister; a Bourbon restoration. Not only did he personally dislike the entire Bourbon clan, but he was worried that they might prove too close to the British, in whose country they had been staying for many years, as well as unacceptable to the French people and army, who might subsequently rebel against a restored Bourbon dynasty and put who knew what in its place. Moreover, accepting his bitter enemy's son as ruler of France was just the kind of grand, unexpected gesture that would appeal to Alexander's image of himself as a magnanimous victor and friend to all the peoples of Europe. Of course, a unilateral Russian declaration of support for Napoleon II would be sure to infuriate the British, but the Austrians might well find it an acceptable solution to the problem, and the Prussians were always likely to go along with whatever the Tsar decided. Besides, Alexander was the man on the spot in a rapidly developing situation, the Emperor Francis, Metternich and Castlereagh all being many miles away at Dijon in early April.

In the end, the Tsar decided not to accept Napoleon's son as ruler of France and demanded that the Emperor's abdication be made unconditional. As soon as he had learnt what Napoleon's representatives had come to suggest, Talleyrand did all he could to dissuade Alexander from agreeing to it. The oily, manipulative former foreign minister had so ingratiated himself with the Allies that he had won their blessing to form a provisional government on 1 April from members of the old Napoleonic administration that he was confident would now support his goal of bringing about a Royalist restoration. The Bourbon case was one that he pressed upon the Tsar throughout early April, doubly so after Caulaincourt, Ney and Macdonald suggested an alternative. Alexander need not worry about the Bourbons being too close to the British, Talleyrand reassured him. Royalist France and Britain had been traditional rivals. There was also, the ex-foreign minister claimed, a real groundswell of support for the old royal family, evinced by the fact that Bordeaux had fallen not to Wellington's army but to a pro-Bourbon rebellion. The restoration of France's 'legitimate' rulers, moreover, would bring stability to Europe, Talleyrand asserted, whereas placing the Emperor's son on the throne would only leave the way open for Napoleon to continue to dominate the French government to the misery of all. Most of what the unctuous Frenchman said was exaggerated or half-truths at best (support for the old monarchy was only strong in a few areas of France) but he had a manner of putting things that persuaded others and there seems little doubt that he did much to make the idea of a Bourbon restoration more acceptable to the Tsar.

Still, one thing gave Alexander pause for thought before ruling out the accession of Napoleon's son and granting his support, or at least acquiescence, to the Bourbons: the attitude of the French army. Ney and Macdonald had given the clear impression that that vital institution remained staunchly behind the Bonapartist regime, raising the spectre of the war dragging on if it were removed. And who could say how long such a struggle might continue? There were still tens of thousands of French troops under arms after all. Alternatively, the army might play a longer game, waiting for the Allied troops to leave France before launching a coup to overthrow the Bourbons and restore the Emperor.

What happened to the south of Paris on the morning of 5 April, therefore, was quite possibly crucial. For some days, Talleyrand had been working his charm not just on the Tsar but on Marshal Marmont. He praised him for his brave defence of Paris's northern suburbs, but even more so for his decision to spare the city further suffering by withdrawing. Sadly, that had not quite ended the war yet. Another gesture was needed. If the marshal would lead his corps into the Allied camp rather than joining up with Napoleon, that would send a powerful message that the struggle, and France's suffering, really was over. And, of course, it would make the victorious Allies and the Bourbons look very favourably upon Marmont himself. Whether thoughts for his own future or that of his country predominated we do not know, but on the morning of 5 April, shortly after the meeting between Alexander and the Emperor's delegation broke up, Marmont began to lead his corps towards the Allied lines. As they began to realize what was happening, his men became mutinous but their commander managed to retain their loyalty by arguing that, whether they liked it or not, the days of the Empire and the Emperor were finished and their duty now was to secure peace for France.

If Napoleon had been irate with Marmont for surrendering Paris, he was apopletic when he heard that he had taken his corps over to the enemy. The unquestioning loyalty of the army had been his trump card, the factor that might just allow him to secure the throne for his son. It had perhaps always been something of a bluff, but it was one that might have worked had Marmont not exposed it. It was for this act of treachery on 5 April, even more than his surrender of Paris five days earlier, that a new word soon entered the French language. Marmont's Imperial title was *Duc de Raguse*, in recognition of his defence of the city of Ragusa against the Russians in 1806–7, and from this was created the verb *raguser*, to betray.

Caulaincourt, Ney and Macdonald returned to Alexander's lodgings shortly after midday on the 5th. What the Tsar had to tell them was not to their liking, but he at least offered something to sugar the bitter pill. Napoleon's abdication must be unconditional, the men were informed, although Alexander gave them his personal assurance that their master would be given a small, independent state to rule as part of a settlement, suggesting that he was still concerned about the reaction in the army and the country to Bonaparte's removal. Realizing that there was nothing they could do to change the Tsar's mind, the delegation returned dejectedly to Fontainebleau.

Napoleon really had no choice. It was, finally, all over. On 6 April 1814, he signed an unconditional decree of abdication. The very same day, the rump of the old Imperial Senate, as much a tool in Talleyrand's hands as its larger incarnation had once been in the Emperor's, voted, with the approval of the Allies, to restore the Bourbon monarchy. Europe's colossus had fallen, the genius of the age, the man many looked to as the embodiment of meritocracy and modernity, had been toppled by the combined forces of the established crowned heads to be replaced by a fat oaf and his reactionary clique of mostly talentless cronies who owed everything in life to their elevated birth. As Hegel, the renowned German philosopher put it, 'There is nothing more tragic in Greek literature. The entire mass of mediocrity, with its irresistible leaden weight … has succeeded in bringing down the highest to the same level as itself.'

Once he had abdicated, the Allies still had to decide what to do with the former Emperor. He could hardly become a private citizen in France after all. The new King's brother, the Comte d'Artois, wanted him executed, as did a number of leading Prussians and Russians, although quite what legal charge could have been mustered is unclear, largely because there wasn't one. It was the Tsar, however, who, once again, was to play the key role in determining Napoleon's fate.

Given his strident opposition to Napoleon retaining his throne during the 1814 campaign, one might have expected Alexander to press for a particularly harsh settlement, perhaps even to support calls for an execution. Instead, he adopted a more charitable position than that favoured by many of the ex-Emperor's enemies. Partly this was a reflection of the Tsar's complex character, his desire to appear (relatively) magnanimous to a vanquished foe, but there was calculation behind his attitude as well. The French Army and people might accept Napoleon being removed from power, but enough of them were unlikely to view with equanimity any attempt to treat their former master with undue harshness to make it advisable not to be too draconian. Conversely, a comparatively generous-seeming settlement might make the many Bonapartists look favourably upon Alexander, thereby increasing Russian influence in France.

There was particular guile in the Tsar's suggestion of a kingdom for Napoleon to rule. Elba, an island of just ninety square miles off the coast of Tuscany, had been suggested by Alexander to Caulaincourt at their second meeting on 5 April, and Napoleon had at least not been totally averse to the idea of becoming its ruler. It would, after all, be close to duchies in central Italy which were being mooted as possible territories for his wife and son. The key for the Tsar, though, was Elba's proximity to the northern Italian lands of which Napoleon had been King until his abdication, but which would now revert to Habsburg overlordship. The idea was that the 'Corsican Ogre' would be close enough to the former kingdom of Italy to make it theoretically feasible for him to escape from Elba to the mainland and proclaim himself restored to his Italian crown. Fear of this would keep Vienna's attention fixed on southern Europe, giving Russia a freer hand in Poland. The problem with Elba, however, as the British and Austrians argued, was that it was also close to France, but Alexander was determined that the small Mediterranean island must be Napoleon's new realm, and it was officially confirmed with the treaty of Fontainebleau of April 1814. Elba would be given to him for life, as a prison as much as a kingdom, and he would be allowed to rule it under the title of Emperor. The central Italian duchies of Parma, Piacenza and Guastalla, meanwhile, would be granted to Marie-Louise and her heirs, Napoleon's siblings would be given pensions, paid for by the French government.

The Bourbon regime was also to provide two million francs a year to enable Napoleon to pay for a small court, miniature army-cum-personal bodyguard, and other administrative necessities on Elba. In return for all this, the former Emperor was to renounce for himself and his heirs all right of sovereignty over the lands of the French Empire or any other country.

All the Allied powers, except the British, signed the treaty on 11 April and it was taken to Fontainebleau for Napoleon to put his name to the next day. He had spent the past few days wondering whether he had done the right thing in abdicating or whether he should have fled to Italy to join Eugène, who did not surrender until the 17th, or even tried to lead a guerrilla war like the one which had done so much to drive the French from Spain. When he read the terms of the treaty, however, he decided they were acceptable and agreed to sign provided the British did so too. His hand forced, Castlereagh acquiesced in the interests of coalition unity.

Just how magnanimous the Tsar was to Bonaparte in spring 1814 is open to question, given that he had been the key obstacle to the Emperor's retention of power and that the 'generous' clauses of the treaty of Fontainebleau had largely been formulated either to appease Napoleon's supporters, further Russian foreign policy or irritate the Bourbons. Less debatable, though, is Alexander's magnanimity towards the French people. A few hours after entering Paris, he had written to a friend declaring, 'I have come as a conqueror who seeks no other honour than the happiness of the vanquished'. It was typical high-flown Alexandrian pomposity but contained a core of truth. The Tsar did show himself to be a friend to the people of France that spring.

It began immediately Marmont had agreed to yield the capital to the Allies. When a delegation of senior civilians came to see him on the morning of 31 March, he told them, 'I esteem France and the French, and I hope they will give me the opportunity to do good for them. Please tell the Parisians, gentlemen, that I am not entering their walls as an enemy, and it is for them to accept me as a friend.' Nor was this mere empty rhetoric. Alexander pledged that the policing of Paris would be left to the National Guard as far as possible, that Allied troops would not be housed in private residences, and that nothing would be taken from the city's inhabitants without recompense. These were noble as well as sensible gestures, and they did much to make the Allied occupation of the French capital relatively trouble-free. General Sacken, appointed military governor by the Tsar, ensuring not only that Russian troops behaved themselves within the city, but also that soldiers of other nationalities, especially the Prussians, did not engage in looting or worse either. Outside Paris and elsewhere in France, the behaviour of some Allied troops was less restrained, but that was the fault of local officers, not Alexander.

Gradually, the French began to respond to the magnanimity of their self-appointed protector. Many Parisians came to develop a genuine regard, even affection, for the Tsar, and he befriended a number of staunch Bonapartists, including Josephine and her children. Indeed, when the former Empress unexpectedly died that May from pneumonia (contracted after taking a stroll with her new companion on a chilly day), Alexander paid her the compliment of sending a band of Russian guardsmen to accompany her coffin to its resting place. It was a thoughtful and sincere act, and it mirrored a general respect shown by the Tsar that spring for symbols of France's recent past. When it was suggested to him, for example, that he should order his men to destroy the Pont d'Austerlitz, the bridge over the Seine built to commemorate the great Napoleonic victory achieved at his personal expense in 1805, he refused, commenting magnificently: 'There is no need for us to touch the bridge. It will be enough if history records that the Russian army once marched across it.'

Alexander also showed a sensibility towards the legacy of the French Revolution that most of his allies, and certainly the Bourbons, did not always, appreciate. He recognized that the clock could not be turned back to 1788 and that the restored monarchy would have to rule with at least some kind of nod to popular sovereignty if it were to survive. He therefore entrusted the provisional French government to draw up a draft constitution which would force the King to share power with some form of parliament. The document created by Talleyrand and his supporters was pretty conservative, granting the monarch wide, if not absolute powers, and restoring the old nobility, but even so it was too much for Louis XVIII and his brother, the Comte d'Artois. Their initial reaction upon returning to France, to a less than rapturous welcome, in late April was to reject the proposed constitution as injurious to the dignity of royalty. Horrified that with an attitude like that the Bourbon restoration would last no time at all, Talleyrand and the Tsar badgered the stubborn pair of reactionaries to be more yielding and to accept a constitutional form of rule. Grudgingly, Louis agreed to compromise. He rejected the draft constitution drawn up for him, but he consented to grant himself one based upon negotiations with the Senate.

Meanwhile, the war throughout Europe was slowly ending. An armistice was officially signed on 23 April, although the fighting had ceased almost everywhere by then anyway. Under the terms of the truce, the French agreed to surrender the few remaining fortresses they held in return for the Allies pledging to evacuate France in the near future. An official peace treaty would follow shortly. It should have come as no surprise that the last French commander to lay down his arms was the redoubtable Marshal Davout, still holding out at Hamburg three weeks after the Emperor had abdicated.

At Fontainebleau, Napoleon awaited the arrival of his wife and son before setting off to his new kingdom of Elba. They never came. Emperor Francis was determined not to let his daughter and her child rejoin their husband and father, packing them off to Vienna shortly after they gave themselves up to Austrian forces following Bonaparte's abdication. Marie-Louise soon fell for the charms of a Count Neipperg, a man chosen by Metternich specifically to seduce her, while Napoleon's son grew up having no contact with his father, as his Habsburg grandfather intended.

On 20 April, in the great courtyard at Fontainebleau Palace now known as the *Cour des Adieux*, the former Emperor said goodbye to his Imperial Guardsmen. It was an occasion full of emotion at which grizzled veterans of umpteen campaigns wept openly and without shame. Unable to embrace every one of 'his children', Napoleon instead kissed their flag.

The first part of the journey south to the Mediterranean coast went smoothly enough, but the poorly chosen route then veered into staunchly Royalist territory where many people came onto the streets to protest as the former Emperor passed. The nadir came at Avignon, where a mob had to be beaten back as they attempted to drag him from his coach and lynch him. On 29 April, Napoleon and his entourage reached Fréjus on the Mediterranean, the same town to which he had returned to France from Egypt in 1799. There, he boarded the British ship HMS *Undaunted* which was to carry him to Elba. It was a sign of his incredible personal magnetism that in no time at all he won over both the officers and crew, many of whom had been risking their lives in fighting Napoleonic France for years. Four days later, on 3 May, the former master of Europe set foot for the first time on the tiny island that was to be both his kingdom and his prison.

21

A New, Old Europe

With Napoleon despatched to Elba, the Allies wasted little time in converting the armistice agreed with the French in late April 1814 into peace. Of the four victorious great powers, there was most desire for a punitive settlement among the Prussians, with many Russians sharing their outlook. It was to France's fortune that the Tsar himself inclined towards the more conciliatory attitude of the leading Austrian and British negotiators, Metternich and Castlereagh.

The Allied statesmen of 1814 acted primarily as all statesmen act: out of their country's self-interest and in accordance with their prevailing views of how best to achieve their goals. Whereas Napoleon had operated on the basis of overturning the balance of power in Europe, the Allied statesmen of 1814 nearly all saw the restoration of some kind of balance as crucial. A France that was completely emasculated would ruin this so she was left strong enough to play a part in a restored European system founded upon no one power predominating over the rest (at least not militarily: the British emerged from the Napoleonic Wars with a naval and economic hegemony that was at least equal to the politico-military hegemony that Bonaparte had briefly enjoyed). There was also a feeling that the best way of persuading the French people to accept the peace settlement (and with it the restored Bourbon monarchy) in the long-term was to make it relatively mild.

The treaty of Paris, signed on 30 May 1814, was thus less harsh than it might have been. Gone were all of Napoleon's annexations and client states as well as the 'natural frontiers', with King Louis XVIII formally renouncing any claim to the lost lands, but some generosity was shown in returning France to her pre-Revolutionary Wars borders in that adjustments were made in the north and south-east which resulted in pockets of territory which had been beyond the frontiers of 1792 being incorporated in the country. The French also got some of their overseas colonies back from the British, although London was careful to hang on to the rich West Indian islands of Saint Lucia and Tobago and the strategically important Seychelles and Mauritius in the Indian Ocean. Further-more, to Prussian chagrin, there was to be no indemnity imposed upon France.

This settlement was only the start of the process of reshaping Europe, for it left a swathe of issues to be resolved concerning the redistribution of the lands of the former Napoleonic Empire and the nature of the regimes which were to rule them. The treaty of Paris therefore included a clause committing the victorious Allied powers to convene at Vienna to discuss all outstanding questions and, in resolving them, to re-establish 'a system of real and permanent Balance of Power in Europe'. The French would be allowed to attend, but the treaty explicitly stated that they would have little or no say in the proceedings.

Before the Congress of Vienna convened, Alexander decided to conduct a tour of northern Europe, beginning with England. Arriving in early June, he was the first reigning Russian ruler to visit the country,* and the reception he was given served to confirm his own belief that he and his country had played the key part in the overthrow of the 'Corsican Ogre'. Crowds cheered wildly, while numerous biographies were rushed out to meet the demand for knowledge about the Tsar, each one exalting him in terms such as 'a new Messiah from the East' or 'the agent appointed by Providence to restore Peace to the World'. Eminent institutions competed to bestow honours upon him. The University of Oxford, for example, granted him an honorary doctorate, while the Corporation of London, representing the all-powerful financial centre in the City, threw a lavish banquet for the man it lauded as a 'hero' and a 'Christian conqueror'.

Not everyone in England liked Alexander or was happy with the level of adulation accorded him, though. Indeed, the British government, recognizing the Tsar's lofty standing in the summer of 1814, had deliberately invited other Allied dignitaries, including King Frederick William, to accompany him on the visit in the hope of diluting the Russian ruler's status. It did not work, and the Tory Establishment, which felt that it had done at least as much as Alexander to bring the recent wars to a successful conclusion, was left fuming at the praise given to a foreign monarch. Relations between the Tsar and the British government were further strained during the visit by Alexander's courting of the more progressive Whig Opposition, all part of his liberal affectation. The deepest resentment at the Russian ruler's visit, however, was felt by the Prince Regent. Relations between the two men did not get off to a good start when Alexander chose to stay in a Piccadilly hotel rather than at St James's Palace, but the real cause of friction was the unpopular Prince's envy of the Tsar's rapturous reception and the fact that the Russian ruler had been with his armies as they had marched to victory, a privilege denied Britain's regent (although he often talked and behaved as if he had campaigned with Wellington, even to Wellington himself!). Soon, the relationship descended almost to the level of farce, each man deliberately trying to upstage or embarrass the other, as when Alexander mischievously bowed to the Prince's estranged wife in public, forcing the embittered Regent to do likewise.

It came as a great relief to both the Prince and the government, therefore, when

---

* When Peter the Great had visited England a little over a century earlier he had still been heir to the Russian throne.

the Tsar left England in late June. He spent the rest of the month and early July in Holland, where he was given a reception every bit as warm as that accorded him on the other side of the North Sea, before travelling back to his own capital via northern Germany, crowds and dignitaries coming out to cheer and greet him wherever he went. They cheered too in St Petersburg when he returned after an absence of more than a year and a half, though not quite as heartily as they had elsewhere.*

It was a matter of just a few weeks before Alexander was off again, this time to the Congress of Vienna. Arriving in late September, he immediately became the centre of attention as he had been throughout Europe that summer. Everyone wanted to see him and meet him, and he was the most sought-after guest to have at any of the multitude of balls and other engagements that made life in the Austrian capital for the next few months the frantic social whirl it became, at least for the European elite.

Fascinating as the hustle and bustle of high society was to many contemporaries, though, gossip of affairs and illicit liaisons attaching themselves to almost every senior figure at some time or another, the real reason why the Congress of Vienna had been convened was, of course, to discuss and resolve political issues. Although representatives from practically every European state and nation attended, there was little attempt to hide the fact that the great powers, excluding France, intended to make all the key decisions themselves. The ruler of each power appointed a small body of official representatives, the Tsar choosing his foreign minister, Nesselrode, his agent at the Châtillon conference, Razumovsky, and his ambassador in Vienna, Stackelberg, but there was also a host of special advisers who were often as important. Alexander brought with him a particularly eclectic delegation, hardly any of which were true Russians. Czartoryski was there to advise on Polish issues, while Stein, a Prussian by adoption, a moderate reformer by inclination and a German nationalist by conviction, was Alexander's key expert on German affairs (the fact that Stein remained with the Tsar rather than returning to Frederick William's service highlights the centrality everyone accorded to Russia and her ruler in international affairs at this time). A rising figure who advised Alexander at Vienna was Ionnes Capodistrias, a thirty-eight-year-old liberal aristocrat from Corfu who would shortly go on to share the role of Russian Foreign Minister with Nesselrode and, in 1827, become the first president of the Greek Republic. Although Capodistrias was to a large extent just another manifestation of the Tsar's desire to affect a kind of pseudo-liberalism, his growing status alarmed the other great powers who feared that it indicated a renewed interest in extending Russian influence in south-east Europe.

---

* It is interesting that rulers and statesmen are often praised more unreservedly outside their own country, where their failings are maybe less obvious.

The discussions which took place in Vienna from autumn 1814 to early summer 1815 covered the fate of most of the Continent of Europe. Scandinavia, the Low Countries, Switzerland, Germany, Poland, Italy, the former Illyrian Provinces; all were debated. Some issues were resolved easily, such as the Low Countries, others, like Germany, took much greater effort before a solution was reached. Only one question, or more accurately two closely connected ones, threatened to destroy the alliance which had defeated Napoleonic France: the fate of Saxony and Poland.

The Russians and Prussians arrived at Vienna determined to win approval for their annexation respectively of the Grand Duchy of Warsaw and Saxony. In return, they were prepared to allow Austria to aggrandize herself in Italy and Illyria, and to acquiesce in Britain's retention of the various colonial gains she had made in recent years. Both the British and the Austrians, however, were convinced that Russian annexation of the Grand Duchy would result in too great an expansion of the Tsar's power and influence. They preferred either that the Polish lands Napoleon had taken from Prussia and Austria be returned to them or, failing that, that a genuinely independent Polish state be established. Indeed, so important did they feel it was to block Alexander's plans for Poland that in the early weeks of the congress the Austrians tried to win Prussian support for their anti-Russian stand by promising them Saxony if they joined Britain and Austria in isolating Russia. This move understandably infuriated the Russians when they learnt of it. At the same time as they leant heavily, and successfully, upon Frederick William and his government to keep Prussia on their side, they adopted an increasingly strident tone over the Polish issue, Alexander menacingly commenting at one point in late 1814, 'I have two hundred thousand soldiers in the Duchy of Warsaw; let them try to drive me from it'.

This was, of course, the Russians' trump card. Slowly the Austrians and British began to realize that they could not hope to stop Alexander annexing at least part of the Grand Duchy unless they were prepared to go to war over the issue, which neither was. Towards the end of 1814, therefore, they changed tactics. If Russian control of the bulk of the Grand Duchy had to be conceded, then they would at least try to persuade the Tsar to give some of the territory back to Prussia and refuse to cede to him the Polish territories remaining in Habsburg hands which he had been endeavouring to persuade the Austrians to give up in return for lands in Italy. As the Prussians seemed to be little more than Russian puppets, moreover, the British and Austrians now determined that they should be denied Saxony. This predictably enraged the Prussians, who at the very end of the year suddenly demanded that their acquisition of Saxony be recognized forthwith. Refusal to comply, they warned, would be viewed as tantamount to a declaration of war.

Whereas the British and Austrians had responded to Russia's increasingly resolute attitude by giving way, they met Prussia's aggressive stand head-on. This was to the advantage of France and her representative in Vienna, the slippery Talleyrand, for Britain and Austria sought to strengthen their hand by inviting the French to join them in a tripartite pact. Seizing an opportunity to allow France to begin to play the role of a major power once more, Talleyrand responded positively. The subsequent secret accord pledged each country to take whatever measures were necessary, including war, to prevent Prussia from swallowing the whole of Saxony. Like the Prussian outburst which provoked it, the treaty was almost certainly a bluff, but as rumours of it were allowed to reach Prussian and Russian ears, it had the desired effect. Eager (not for the last time) to maintain his reputation as the man who had united Europe against Napoleon and become the continent's peacebringer and saviour, the Tsar leant on the Prussians to moderate their demands for Saxon territory to less than half of that kingdom. In return for this, Alexander agreed to give the westernmost part of the Grand Duchy of Warsaw back to Frederick William, while the city of Cracow and its environs were to become independent as a sop to Austria for agreeing to Prussia annexing part of Saxony.

By the end of February 1815, therefore the main threat to the alliance that had defeated Napoleonic France had been all but overcome. At times it had seemed unlikely that any kind of solution that was acceptable to all the great powers would be found, but the immense cost of the wars of the previous two decades and the Tsar's desire to be seen as Europe's pacifier, had proved decisive influences for compromise. There would be many who gained from this resolution of difficulties and some, particularly in Poland and Saxony, who lost, but arguably the biggest loser of all was Napoleon, for the Allies resolved their differences just as he desperately needed them to remain divided.

It is hard to envisage Napoleon living out the rest of his life as emperor of the tiny Mediterranean island of Elba. It was probably too small a realm to contain the energy and ambition of such a man. That said, the responsibility for his breaking the terms of the treaty of Fontainebleau, by returning to France in March 1815 and proclaiming his restoration, lies predominantly with the Bourbons and the Allies. The culpability of the former rests with the fact, as Napoleon himself was only too keen to point out, that they breached the terms of the treaty of Fontainebleau by refusing to provide him with the annuity of two million francs, even though they had been left 160 million francs worth of real estate and other property by the Emperor when he had left France. This left Napoleon on the verge of bankruptcy less than a year into his rule on Elba, unable to pay the several hundred troops he was allowed, and needed, to protect himself against possible assassination attempts. The responsibility of the Allies, meanwhile, lies in their response to warnings that Napoleon might try to return to the European mainland as a result of his financial difficulties. Instead of finding some way to force the Bourbons to pay up, or searching for another means of easing the Emperor's fiscal problems, they began to plan moving Napoleon somewhere else, such as the Azores or the remote island of St Helena in the South Atlantic.

It was when Bonaparte got wind of Allied intentions early in 1815 from agents loyal to him on the Continent that he made up his mind to flee Elba and gamble upon the French welcoming him back as their emperor. He was aware that the Bourbons were not popular in France and rumours of Allied divisions at Vienna gave hope that he might not face the united forces of old Europe should he seek restoration. On 26 February, he boarded one of seven ships that would form the force to 'invade' his former realm.

Landing in southern France with an 'army' of barely a thousand troops, Napoleon marched boldly north towards Paris, gathering ever more soldiers to him as they deserted the Bourbon cause, until King Louis was left with little choice but to flee the country. It is often said that Napoleon did not have the support of a good many Frenchmen in 1815 and that he owed his bloodless restoration predominantly to the loyalty of the army. While this is true, many French people, particularly peasants, did welcome his return and he was undeniably considerably more popular overall than the Bourbons. Had France been left to her own devices in 1815, there seems little doubt that Napoleon would have been easily able to hold onto his throne.

It should not have been a certainty that the Allies would respond to Napoleon's return by pledging to overthrow him a second time. The Emperor was at pains to pledge himself publicly to observe the terms of the treaty of Paris of May 1814, not to seek to expand French territory, and to maintain peace and stability in Europe. Even if his sincerity on this score could be doubted, the fact was that France, more shattered than any other power by two decades of war, was simply in no mood or position to embark upon an adventurous foreign policy. It was not inconceivable that a Bonapartist France could have coexisted peaceably with the rest of Europe, especially as the Allies could have eased their concerns by containing her with military alliances and strengthened buffer states (as in fact they would do with Bourbon France). It is hard to escape the conclusion that the response of the Allied powers to Napoleon's return was driven less by the need to remove an insurmountable obstacle to future peace than a mixture of personal desire for revenge against a man who had previously beaten and humiliated them and concern that allowing the 'Corsican upstart' to rule in France would undermine the Allies' attempt in 1814–15 to re-establish a more conservative Europe based upon the *ancien régime* ideas of monarchical 'legitimacy', social hierarchy and privilege through birth.

No European ruler was more determined to depose the Emperor once more than the Tsar. Embarrassed by the fact that Bonaparte had escaped from the island he had personally insisted upon him being exiled to, Alexander took a stridently anti-Napoleonic stand in spring 1815. He personally declared, 'No peace with Bonaparte! The first task must be to overthrow him', and offered to take supreme command of the Allied war effort, a proposition that was tactfully refused. His foreign minister, meanwhile, publicly pledged to field 400,000 troops to fight the 'Ogre'. Whether a Russia severely drained by war could afford to supply so many men on active campaign far from the homeland was open to question, but in pledging a vast subsidy to their Continental ally, the British showed that they were determined to do what they could to help.

Despite Napoleon's protestations of peaceful intentions and respect for the settlement the great powers were imposing upon Europe, the Allies officially declared him an outlaw on 13 March and then twelve days later formed the Seventh Coalition, each pledging to field an army of at least 150,000 men until the Emperor was overthrown.* Desperate to avoid a war he was all but certain ultimately to lose, Napoleon continued to make pacific overtures and pledges. The Allies were always going to turn a deaf ear anyway, but Napoleon's cause was far from helped by the activities of Joachim Murat in Italy. Clinging to the throne of Naples in the face of British and Bourbon opposition, Murat idiotically decided on his own initiative that Napoleon's return to France was a signal to begin to rebuild the lost Empire and so attacked the Austrians in Italy. The Emperor was almost as furious with his brother-in-law as he had been the previous year when he had betrayed the Bonapartist cause, and he did his best to distance himself and France from his former subordinate's actions. The Allies, though, insisted that Murat had acted as part of a grand Napoleonic design and highlighted his recklessness as 'proof' that Europe could not live at peace with the Emperor. With no support from the French, Murat was soon defeated and forced to flee Italy, a livid Napoleon refusing his offer to serve once more as a marshal of France.

If Napoleon's spurning of Murat was understandable, there was also little doubt that he could have done with the services of his experienced, if headstrong, former cavalry master. Facing war against the combined might of Europe's established monarchies, France needed every able commander she could find. By midsummer, all four of the Allies would be ready to invade from north and east with forces more than twice as numerous as those the French could hope to field. The situation was not perhaps as unpropitious as it had been in 1814, but the danger was that, if Napoleon fought a repeat of that campaign and allowed the Allies to occupy most of northern and eastern France, the heartland of his popular support, French morale and backing for the Bonapartist cause might

---

* The Allies' excuse for their legally dubious actions was that Napoleon had broken the terms of the treaty of Fontainebleau, but the spuriousness of this argument has already been shown in explaining how the Bourbons and Allies all but forced Bonaparte to take the action he did.

quickly evaporate. He therefore determined upon a more aggressive strategy that would lead to one of the most famous campaigns of all time.

By early June, two Allied armies, one Prussian under Field Marshal Blücher, one British (or more accurately British, Dutch, German and Belgian) under the Duke of Wellington, were in position in Belgium ready to invade France with around a quarter of a million troops. They were waiting, however, for the Austro-German and Russian armies of Schwarzenberg and Barclay de Tolly, who between them commanded approaching half a million men, to arrive on the upper Rhine before advancing. This gave the Emperor a slim chance of defeating Blücher and Wellington before the more numerous Russian and Austrian hordes could attack. Gathering an army of around 125,000 men and 360 cannon near his northern border, on 15 June he marched into Belgium.

It is highly probable, though admittedly not certain, that whatever happened over the next few days would not have altered the ultimate result of the war of the Seventh Coalition. Having expended vast amounts of lives and money to remove Napoleon once, the Allies were likely to do whatever it took to get rid of him again, yet still the Waterloo campaign and the battle after which it was named are often cited, in the English-speaking world particularly, as among the most decisive in history. They were not. Even had Napoleon won and, against the odds, secured the acceptance of the Allies to his keeping his throne, the result would not have been as significant as the huge, Russian-led campaigns of 1812 and 1813, which broke French hegemony in Europe, or even the 1814 campaign, which denied France the 'natural frontiers' and control over Italy and removed Napoleon from power for the first time. The most the Waterloo campaign could realistically have achieved was Allied recognition of the Emperor's rule over a France restricted to the borders of early 1792. That would not have been unimportant by any means, particularly for the French, but it is almost inconceivable that the events of 1815 could have paved the way for any kind of notable expansion of France, much less the restoration of Napoleonic hegemony in Europe. The Waterloo campaign was not an irrelevance, but neither was it anything like the key struggle of the Napoleonic Wars.

Catching both Blücher and Wellington by surprise, the Emperor thrust at the junction of their two armies, attempting to drive them apart and defeat them in detail. On 16 June, he went some way towards achieving this by seriously mauling the Prussians at Ligny with the bulk of his army, while Marshal Ney with the remainder of the army did just enough to prevent the British from coming to their aid several miles down the road at Quatre Bras. Blücher's defeat might have been even more severe than it was but for Ney's error in failing to release part of his command to assault the Prussian right, but it was nonetheless heavy enough to force him to retreat with some haste, leaving Wellington at the mercy of the French.

Three decisions on the following morning proved decisive. First, Napoleon failed to move with all speed against the Duke's army at Quatre Bras. Had he done so, there is little reason to doubt that it would have been smashed by a qualitatively and quantitatively superior French force. The delay gave Wellington time to withdraw from his perilous position and retreat towards the village of Waterloo, followed by the Emperor. The second critical decision of 17 June was taken by Blücher. Rather than retreating east towards Germany, the obvious direction for him to take, he withdrew north so as to remain in contact with Wellington. This meant that the Prussians would be able to march to the Duke's aid next day, providing him with the assistance without which he could not have won the battle of Waterloo. Finally, there was Napoleon's famous decision to divide his army, sending a third of it off under Marshal Grouchy to chase the Prussians. Though this need not have proved an error, Grouchy's performance turned it into one. Had he performed more competently, he could either have rejoined Napoleon at Waterloo next day or prevented the Prussians from arriving there in such force. Instead, his lack of vigour in pursuing Blücher's army and, even worse, his failure to march towards the sound of the guns on the 18th prevented him from playing a role of any real significance in the day's proceedings.

On 18 June 1815, Wellington fought a very good defensive battle based upon holding the line of a low ridge and a couple of strongpoints in front of it. Napoleon, conversely, had a poor day as a general, failing to ensure that French attacks were coordinated and allowing the rash Ney to throw away much of the cavalry in futile attacks upon well-formed infantry squares. Still, the numerical and qualitative advantages of the French over the British, Germans and Dutch would have been sufficient to win the battle had not Blücher's Prussians arrived to save the day. Within a couple of hours of the battle starting, and almost as soon as the first major French attack on the enemy-held ridge went in, the initial wave of Prussian reinforcements appeared to Napoleon's right, forcing him to divert troops to meet the new threat. As more and more of Blücher's soldiers arrived throughout the afternoon and early evening, all possibility of a French victory disappeared, and when the Emperor's final gamble of sending in his Guard failed, his army broke and fled back towards France.

Bad a defeat as Waterloo undoubtedly was, in the short campaign as a whole the Allies lost almost as many men as the French (55,000 to 60,000), though they could admittedly afford the losses more easily. The Napoleonic cause was thus not yet entirely hopeless, for in late June the Emperor had 117,000 men immediately available for the defence of Paris, a great many garrison troops in northern France, and more soldiers on the way (the brilliant Davout, appointed Minister of War and Governor of Paris upon Napoleon's return, was proving considerably more loyal and adept in those posts than his predecessors of the previous year). News from other fronts, moreover, was encouraging. The skilful Marshal Suchet had beaten an Austrian force in north-west Italy and the advance guard of Schwarzenberg's massive Austro-German army had been given a bloody nose on the Rhine by the redoubtable General Rapp. The Emperor arrived back in Paris on 21 June, however, with no real stomach for continuing the fight. The military situation was considerably better than it had been in 1814, but Napoleon seems to have had little doubt after Waterloo that the ultimate outcome would be the same.* On the 22nd, he abdicated in favour of his four-year-old son and a provisional government was set up, headed by the scheming Minister of Police, Joseph Fouché. The Emperor can have held little hope that his dynasty would be allowed to continue. His son was effectively held captive by his father-in-law, the Austrian Emperor, and the bulk of the army seemed unlikely to fight for Napoleon II without talismanic Napoleon I at its head (the ex-Emperor actually offered to serve Fouché's new government as a general, but was turned down – Fouché expected the Allies to insist upon a second Bourbon restoration and wanted to curry favour with King Louis by doing nothing that would obstruct his return).

Following his abdication, Napoelon left Paris, unsure what to do next. His former step-daughter, Hortense de Beauharnais, suggested that he surrender himself to the Tsar, who she improbably argued might grant him asylum in Russia, but Napoleon was not inclined to trust to the whims of the unpredictable Alexander. He eventually decided to try to flee to the United States and on 3 July arrived at the west coast port of Rochefort in search of a ship to carry him across the Atlantic.

That same day, Paris fell to the armies of Wellington and Blücher with little resistance being shown. Coming so quickly in the wake of the victory at Waterloo, it distorted perceptions, both at the time and since, of how and why the challenge of Napoleonic France had been defeated, seeming to diminish the role of Russia and boost that of Britain and Prussia. In fact, Russian troops did fight in 1815, reducing a few French fortresses in the north-east of the country, but their military contribution was undeniably pretty minimal.

Alexander himself rushed ahead of the bulk of his army to reach Paris on 10 July. A few days earlier, the Bourbons had been unilaterally restored by the British and Prussians, thereby preventing the Tsar, whose opinion of Louis XVIII and his clan had deteriorated even further when he had seen how easily they had been deposed in March, from taking any possible steps to block their return to the French throne. Still, Alexander's arrival was not without significance for, along with Wellington, he served to restrain a vengeful Blücher from destroying parts

---

* While it is true that Napoleon toyed with the idea of continuing the struggle, there was never any real conviction behind it. Far from being prepared to fight to the last Frenchman in a desperate attempt to salvage his crown, something he might well have done, he chose to spare France such agony.

of the French capital, such as the Pont d'Iéna. With the Francophobic Prussians in the ascendancy, however, the Tsar could do little to prevent the occupation of 1815 being more oppressive than the Russian-led one of the previous year.

Back at Rochefort, meanwhile, Napoleon found his path to the United States blocked by the Royal Navy. Unwilling to risk running the gauntlet of the British blockade (perhaps he feared that to be captured in flight as if a common criminal would encourage the Allies to treat him as such), he decided to appeal to the mercy of the English ruling elite. Boarding the frigate HMS *Bellerophon*, Bonaparte wrote a famous (and unanswered) letter to the Prince Regent, throwing himself 'on the hospitality of the English people' and putting himself 'under the protection of their laws'. Incredibly, Napoleon genuinely seems to have envisaged leading the rest of his life as an English country gentleman, but the British government was determined to punish the 'Corsican Ogre'. At the end of July, therefore, with their captive not having been allowed to set foot on English soil but being kept aboard ship in Plymouth sound, the government in London informed Napoleon that he was to be exiled to the remote island of St Helena, a decision formally approved by the other major European powers on 2 August. His detractors have often argued that Bonaparte was lucky, that he might have been handed over to the Bourbons or the Prussians for execution, but the man himself was furious. He angrily pleaded to know by what law he was a prisoner when he had boarded a British ship voluntarily, and demanded due and fair legal process rather than the arbitrary decision with which he was confronted. Given that peace had been restored between France and the Allies in early July, he could not legally be considered a prisoner of war, and it is certainly difficult to imagine what crime he could have been convicted of that would have justified the sentence of permanent exile (let alone one of execution), but his pleading was all, of course, in vain. The power and will of the English ruling elite, rather than legal or moral technicalities, were what counted in summer 1815. Thus, on 7 August, the man who had been master of Europe just a few years before began the long journey as a captive to a barren rock in the middle of the South Atlantic. This time, there would be no coming back.

Just as Napoleon's treatment by the victorious Allies was harsher in 1815 than it had been the year before, so too was the peace settlement imposed upon France. Having shown a preference for Napoleon over the Bourbons, the French populace, or at least sections of it, were viewed by the Allied leadership as incorrigible and the attitude of the victors was, as a result, generally more punitive than it had been in 1814. This was reflected not only in the revised settlement, but also in the turning of a blind eye to – even encouragement of – the so-called 'White Terror' that the returning Bourbons unleashed against groups they suspected of opposition to their regime: Bonapartists, Jacobins, even Protestants. Autocratic as his rule had been, the Emperor had never behaved as brutally towards his opponents within France as did the Bourbons in the second half of 1815. To some extent, the execution of men such as Marshal Ney served to discourage potential rebellion or unrest, but the lasting legacy was one of bitterness and enduring hostility. As soon as the groups targeted by King Louis and his followers got a chance, they would take their revenge.

Many French people who were spared the 'White Terror' suffered instead in 1815 at the hands of the hundreds of thousands of Allied soldiers who occupied their country that summer and autumn. As in 1814, the British and the Russian regular troops generally behaved well, but many Cossacks and Prussians used the opportunity to settle old scores or simply to engage in rape or looting. Indeed, in the Prussian case, it seemed almost to be official policy to treat the French ruthlessly. Certainly Blücher showed little concern over his soldiers' behaviour.

The Prussians also took the lead in pressing for a draconian peace with France. In an anticipatory echo of a future Franco-Prussian settlement, Frederick William and his government argued that the French should be stripped of the north-eastern territories of Alsace and Lorraine, and even parts of Burgundy and Franche-Comté. Such a dramatic amputation would inevitably upset the delicate balance of power in western and central Europe that the British and Russians both favoured and had been trying to restore at Vienna, so the Tsar and Castlereagh successfully united to oppose these harsh demands.

Even so, the second treaty of Paris, signed on 20 November 1815, did strip France of some territory, though only those lands along her northern and south-eastern borders which she had been granted in 1814 but had not possessed at the start of 1792. More punitive were the massive indemnity of 700 million francs, payable in fifteen regular instalments over five years, inflicted upon the country and the imposition of a 150,000-strong army of occupation, to be headed by the Duke of Wellington, which was scheduled to remain on French soil at French expense until the indemnity was paid off. Together, the cost of meeting these obligations was to hinder severely French post-war economic recovery.

The same day that the second treaty of Paris was signed, the four Allied powers also committed themselves to a pact pledging them to contribute at least 60,000 men each if at any point over the next twenty years the French tried to overturn any part of the peace settlement imposed upon Europe in 1815. With France having come so close to achieving a lasting European hegemony under Napoleon, the other major powers were determined not to allow that possibility to arise again, as well as to try to contain the 'dangerous ideas' spawned by the Revolution within their country of origin.

Five months before the agreements concerning France were concluded, indeed a week before the Waterloo campaign had commenced, the European settlement had been finalized at Vienna. We have already seen how the Allied powers had resolved the trickiest question confronting them even before Napoleon had escaped from Elba, but his return helped maintain a spirit of cooperation that allowed the Congress of Vienna to publish its final act on 8 June 1815.

It is easiest to deal with the settlement area by area. In Scandinavia, the cession of Norway to Sweden was officially sanctioned, although the Swedes were forced to yield Swedish Pomerania to the Danes as compensation. Denmark swiftly swapped this territory with Prussia for territory on the lower Elbe, land which the Prussians would take back by force of arms later in the century.

Prussia was returned all her territory west of the Elbe that she had lost in 1807, mostly to the short-lived kingdom of Westphalia, and also gained a large portion of the former French lands on the western bank of the Rhine. Berlin had to settle for forty per cent of Saxony and received neither of the kingdom's two main cities, Dresden and Leipzig, but it was given back the Posen region of its former Polish territories by Russia (the north-western section of the now defunct Grand Duchy of Warsaw).

In the Low Countries, Belgium was united with Holland to form the kingdom of the Netherlands, to be ruled by the Dutch House of Orange. By turning two small European regions into one medium-sized state a more effective barrier to any possible future French expansion northwards would be created. It was partly for this reason that William of Orange was also made Grand Duke of Luxembourg, although this was mostly done simply to prevent the Prussians from gaining control over the area.

Switzerland was another country that was to act as a buffer to potential French expansionism. Strengthened by the return of the cantons annexed to France by Napoleon, the Swiss were given a 'new' constitution (essentially a rehash of Napoleon's popular arrangement of 1803) and their neutrality was confirmed.

In Italy, it was to a large extent a question of turning back the clock to the 1790s. In the north-west, the kingdom of Piedmont was restored and given the strip of coastal territory centred on Genoa in order to improve its ability to act as a bulwark against potential French expansionism in the peninsula. In the south, Murat had resolved a dispute between the Austrians and Britain and Bourbon France over who should rule the kingdom of Naples with his precipitate action in the spring, although Metternich had already decided to dispense with the former marshal who had betrayed the Emperor to fight alongside the Austrians in 1814 anyway. The Neapolitan Bourbons were restored to their former possessions on the mainland, just as the Spanish Bourbons had been put back on the throne in Madrid. North of Naples, the Papal States were resurrected in central Italy, while north of there, a cluster of statelets were created or recreated. These included the Grand Duchy of Tuscany, ruled by a Habsburg, and the Duchy of Parma, which was granted to Napoleon's ex-Empress, Marie-Louise, though only for her lifetime. Upon her death, it was to revert to yet another branch of the Bourbons.

The rest of Italy, the large regions of Lombardy and the Venetia which made up most of the north of the peninsula, was given directly to Austria. This was not only recompense for the Habsburg's contribution to Napoleon's defeat, but also a means of making Austrian influence dominant throughout Italy, thereby helping to keep French influence out of the area and strengthening Austria as a balance to the other Continental powers. The Habsburgs also got the former Illyrian Provinces and the Tyrolese lands they had been forced by Bonaparte to cede to Bavaria. They did not, however, get back the chunk of Polish territory they had yielded to the Grand Duchy of Warsaw in 1809.

In Germany, the Allies sensibly decided not to try to restore the great majority of mini-states, independent cities and bishoprics that Napoleon had swept away. Indeed, barring a few relatively minor territorial adjustments, southern Germany broadly remained as the Emperor had left it. There was more change in northern Germany, thanks largely to the dismantling of the Kingdom of Westphalia and the reversal of France's annexation of the lands bordering the North Sea and the Baltic. Hanover was restored to the King of England and the old Hanseatic cities, including Hamburg and Lübeck, regained their earlier independence. In the end, thirty-five states and four free cities made up the new Germany. They were grouped in the German Confederation, a sort of heir to Napoleon's *Rheinbund*, which was nominally headed, as had been the old Holy Roman Empire, by Austria, although Prussia's predominance was tacitly acknowledged in northern Germany. Again, this institution was largely aimed at blocking any possible future French expansionism.

Russia's reward for her role in bringing down Napoleon was the bulk of the former Grand Duchy of Warsaw. Rather than simply annexing the region, though, Alexander indulged in something of a liberal affectation. He restored a kingdom of Poland with himself as its ruler, the two realms being indissolubly linked in the person of the Tsar-King and his successors. He even pledged to grant the Poles a constitution, which was more than he would give the Russians. The Austrians were initially alarmed at Alexander's apparent desire to play the constitutional monarch and appeal to Polish nationalism, fearing that the new kingdom of Poland might spark unrest in their own Polish lands, but it soon became clear that they had little to worry about. Rather than including all or even any of the former Polish territory annexed by Russia during the reign of Catherine the Great in the restored kingdom, the Tsar restricted his new realm to the lands of the defunct Grand Duchy, a bitter blow to Polish nationalists. He was more generous regarding the promised constitution, though even here its limitations swiftly became apparent. On paper, a relatively progressive arrangement for the government of Poland was drawn up. There was to be a lower house, for example, elected by a fairly broad franchise (there were more voters in Poland after 1815 than there were in France, even though the population was over ten times smaller) and the Poles were given the freedom to practise their Catholic religion unhindered. Although the legislature had to be convened at least every two years, it could only be called by the Tsar, who could veto any of its resolutions and dismiss it at will. Nor could it initiate legislation when it sat, but only comment upon what was put before it. Real power in the kingdom of Poland thus resided with the King-Tsar and his personal representative, who during Alexander's reign was his reactionary brother Constantine. Congress Poland, as it became known, was certainly no more independent than, say, Napoleon's Kingdom of Italy and rather less independent than the former Grand Duchy of Warsaw. Even so, as early as 1820, the Tsar's spokesman at a meeting of the Polish legislature was to be found warning the members of the lower house, 'You will bear in mind, gentlemen, that you have been granted the constitution and that it is possible to take it away from you'. The legislature did not meet again until 1825 and after that until 1830. In that year, the Poles rebelled against Alexander's successor, seeking greater independence and freedom, only to be crushed by Russian arms. The constitution was torn up and any semblance of Polish self-rule destroyed.

Just as the Russians made gains in 1815 in what was for them the key area, so did the British. Territorially, they kept several valuable overseas possessions taken from the Dutch – Ceylon (Sri Lanka), the Cape of Good Hope, and some islands in the West Indies – to add to their acquisitions from the French. In the North Sea, the former Danish island of Heligoland, not far off the German coast, was retained, while in the Mediterranean, British control of Malta and the Ionian Islands, both captured from the French, was confirmed. These gains all helped to cement British mastery of the world's seas and trade, but even more important for that was the restoration of a balance of power on the Continent. Although the four Continental powers were by no means individually matched, Russia being clearly more powerful than Prussia, for example, the system set up in 1814–15 was designed to prevent any one country dominating a combination of the others and establishing a hegemony comparable to that briefly enjoyed by Napoleonic France. This limited the potential of every Continental power, but particularly the French, to challenge the wealthy, industrializing, colonially-dominant British either navally or economically, leaving Britain able to become the superpower of the nineteenth century. Only when the system established in 1814–15 completely broke down, and Prussia unified the rest of Germany under her, did the British face another major challenge from within Europe to the predominance of her navy and economy.

In some ways, Britain was the biggest winner from what, for convenience, we might call the Vienna system, but there were others who did well out of it. Most obviously, there were the restored monarchs and their followers, notably the Bourbons in France, Spain and Italy. Then there were the lesser powers which made territorial gains, including Sweden, Holland and Piedmont. All the great powers, of course, barring France, did well out of the system, though to varying degrees. Although Russia initially seemed to emerge from the settlement having done particularly well in her acquisition of most of the Grand Duchy of Warsaw, Prussia and Austria may have done better over the longer term. Berlin might not have gained as much territory as it had hoped, but Prussia had been fully restored and recognized as one of the five great powers, and was in a position, in time, to become the nucleus of a new German state that would become the most powerful on the Continent. Austria, on the other hand, was a state in decline, a fact which her repeated defeats by the French Republic and Empire had eventually rammed home. For her, the Vienna system represented a chance to halt the decay, to regain influence in Germany, Italy and the Balkans, and to use the opportunity provided by the years of relative peace which followed the Napoleonic Wars to suppress any threat, real or imagined, to the continued survival of the hotchpotch, multinational Austrian Empire and its ruling elite.

When we talk about Austria, Prussia, Russia and others as being winners from the Vienna system, what we really mean, of course, is the rulers and elite of those countries. For the great majority of Europeans, the settlement of 1814–15 did little to improve their lot. Indeed, in some cases, such as the Poles of Congress Poland, the Saxons in the lands annexed by Prussia, and the Italians in Lombardy and Venetia, who saw relatively progressive rule by Viceroy Eugène replaced by more reactionary government by the Habsburgs, it is perfectly possible to argue that things clearly got worse after 1815.

Defenders of the Vienna system, though, contend that all Europeans ultimately benefited from it in that it secured decades of peace after so many years of war. A couple of points need to be made in connection with this claim. First, there may have been no further great power conflicts until the Crimean War in the 1850s, but there were certainly a good number of disturbances, revolts and minor wars throughout Europe in the intervening four decades, many of them directly related to the Vienna settlement, such as rebellions in Belgium against the Dutch, in Poland against the Russians, and in Spain and Naples against the Bourbons. Secondly, although the balance of power on the Continent, re-established in 1814–15, possibly contributed something to the decision of great powers not to resort to war with each other again over points of dispute until the 1850s, it was not the key factor behind the temporary avoidance of major conflict. More significant were the sheer cost of the French Revolutionary and Napoleonic Wars and the shared belief among the great powers' ruling elites post-1815 that a major war might open the door to their overthrow, as it potentially had between 1806 and 1812.* Over time, fear of the possible cost of war and of its potential

---

* Napoleon on St Helena rued not having deposed the ruling families of both Prussia and Austria when he had had the chance, and Alexander never forgot the incredible tension of 1812.

for upheaval dimmed and great power conflicts erupted again, culminating, of course, in the cataclysm of the First World War.

If the contribution of the Vienna settlement to the maintenance of great power peace for almost four decades was arguably minimal, though, it at least did more than the construct initiated in autumn 1815 by Tsar Alexander. We have seen how Alexander had become an increasingly religious man during the ordeal of 1812, and his Christian zeal reached its peak in the summer of Waterloo when he met and came under the influence of the Latvian mystic, Baroness von Krüdener. Even before she appeared on the scene, however, he had been looking for a way to tie the European settlement in with his religious convictions. In December 1814, for example, he had tentatively suggested to his allies that their alliance should be explicitly based upon 'the immutable principles of Christian religion', which were the 'only foundation of the political order and of the social order with which sovereigns, making common cause, will refine their principles of state and guarantee the relations between the peoples entrusted to them by Providence'. The impact of von Krüdener was thus to give the Tsar the motivation to push his own beliefs harder. The result was the Holy Alliance of September 1815. Signed initially by the monarchs of Russia, Austria and Prussia, it was soon joined by every European ruler except the Pope, who refused to associate himself with Protestant and Orthodox Christians, and the Prince Regent, who claimed that the English constitution forbade him from signing. The large number of adherents said much for Alexander's standing at this time, but probably even more about the vague ambiguity of its terms, which allowed everyone to interpret it pretty much as they wished. Essentially, the Holy Alliance, which pledged its signatories to treat each other in accordance with 'the sublime truths which the Holy Religion of Our Saviour teaches', was just a fuzzy declaration of Christian brotherhood, justifiably dismissed in private by Castlereagh as a 'piece of sublime mysticism and nonsense' and by Metternich as a 'loud sounding nothing'. If it had any practical significance in the years after 1815, it was as an excuse for repression in the name of Christian order, though such repression would surely have taken place had the alliance not existed anyway.

Europe after 1815 was not the same as Europe before 1789 or 1799, but the bulk of its rulers did aspire to preserve, indeed to revive, the *ancien régime*, both in terms of a balance of power among the Continental powers and of the society and politics of European states. Although things could never be the same after the French Revolution and Napoleon, the fundamental political hue of post-1815 Europe was undoubtedly reactionary. For this reason, it can justifiably be said to have been a new, old Europe.

The story of the next ten, indeed twenty, thirty, forty years was largely one of the attempt by Europe's ruling elite to maintain the Vienna system, both internationally and domestically, in the face of radical new forces, like liberalism and nationalism. Initially, the continent's statesmen did pretty well in keeping things as they wanted them. Metternich clamped down on liberals and nationalists in Germany, and progressive rebellions against arbitrary royal authority in Naples, Piedmont and Spain were all crushed in the early 1820s, with the supposedly liberal Tsar playing a leading role in encouraging Austrian and French troops to march into these other countries and reassert royal power. Never was Alexander more a reactionary, more Catherine the Great's grandson, than when he asserted in 1821 that rebels and revolutionaries constituted an 'empire of evil' that was 'more powerful than the might of Napoleon'.

For Russia and her ruler, the final decade of Alexander's reign – he died of a fever in December 1825 aged just 47 – were a period of gratifying prominence on the international stage; a prominence, in fact, that was not checked until Russia's defeat in the Crimean War, and even then was not reversed utterly. The key part the Russians played in defeating Napoleonic France cemented their position as a major player in European affairs. Indeed, Russia came to be seen after 1815 increasingly as Europe's new great land power, superseding both Austria and France. Yet there remained a degree of insecurity in St Petersburg, evinced partly by Alexander's efforts to rehabilitate France and foster good relations with her as a potential ally against either Austria or Britain. It was only at the Tsar's insistence, for example, that French delegates were allowed to attend the great power congress held at Aix-la-Chapelle (modern Aachen) in autumn 1818, and once there Alexander took the lead in persuading his allies to end the occupation of France two years early and reduce the balance of the indemnity the French had left to pay. He even managed to turn the Quadruple Alliance into a quintuple one by securing France's accession to it on the grounds that, as she was once more ruled by an established royal dynasty that shared the outlook and aims of the bulk of Europe's other ruling elites, she could be relied upon to uphold the peace and stability of the continent.

The Tsar had some formidable rivals for the position of Europe's leading statesman post-1815, particularly the wily Austrian Metternich, Castlereagh, and his successor as British foreign secretary, George Canning, yet it is fair to claim that he remained the foremost European figure right up to his untimely death. Germans, Italians, Spaniards, French; all appealed for his support over a range of issues. When a group of Bonapartists were hatching a plot in 1818 to try to get their hero freed from St Helena, they did not plan to kidnap Metternich or a British statesman, but Alexander, believing that only he could deliver what they wanted (the plot was foiled).

Needless to say, the Tsar loved being seen as Europe's leading figure and cherished his self-image as the continent's arbiter and ultimate guarantor of peace and security. Indeed, this even played a part in averting, or rather postponing, another Russo-Turkish war. In 1821, a Greek by the name of Alexander Ypsilantis who was serving as a general in the Russian Army invaded the Danubian principality of Moldavia on his own initiative at the head of a band of émigré Greek nationalists and called upon Christians throughout south-east Europe to rise up against their Ottoman overlords. Ypsilantis and his 'army' were soon routed by the Turks, but not before the Greeks in Greece itself had launched a far more serious rebellion. Pressure mounted in Russia for Alexander to come to the Greeks' aid, not least from his foreign minister Capodistrias, especially when atrocities began to be committed on both sides. This was a perfect opportunity, Capodistrias and others told the Tsar, to take over the Principalities and establish Russian predominance amongst the Orthodox Christians of south-east Europe. The prized jewel of Constantinople might even fall. Yet Alexander demurred, to the surprise and relief of the Turks and much of the rest of Europe. He argued that it would set an unfortunate example for Russia to support the Greek rebels at a time when it was necessary to crush those who challenged established authority elsewhere in Europe. More serious than that, there was no telling how long and arduous a new war against the Ottoman Empire might be. The Turks certainly looked to be on the back foot in the early 1820s, but Russo-Turkish conflicts had a nasty habit of proving more protracted and costly than expected. Russia was still recovering from the huge strain of the Napoleonic Wars and the last thing she needed was another expensive struggle. Most worrying of all, though, was the damage a major Russian intervention might do to European peace and stability. Any attempt to extend dramatically Russia's influence in south-east Europe was likely to be fiercely opposed, quite possibly militarily, by the Austrians, the British and probably the French too. That would open a can of worms that the Tsar was not at all sure he wanted to open. It would also make a mockery of Alexander's claim to be Europe's leading force for peace and stability, and it was concern for this, as well as the more practical issues, that led Russia's ruler to resist the temptation and pressure to wade in on the side of the Greeks. Instead, he worked with the other great powers, especially the British, to try to find a diplomatic solution to the crisis in south-east Europe. He failed, but at least he did not provoke a major European war. His successor, his brother Nicholas, did eventually go to war with the Turks in 1828–29, securing additional territory for Russia along the Black Sea coast and in the Caucasus, and increasing Russian influence over the Principalities. The other great powers allowed Nicholas to get away with this much, although the British and French ensured that they joined with Russia in forcing the Turks to grant the Greeks full independence in 1832 in order to prevent Russian influence from predominating in Greece. Distrust of Russia remained, however, and culminated just over twenty years later in the Crimean War, a conflict fought by Britain and France largely to reverse and restrict the expansion of Russian territory and influence at the Turks' expense.

The France which fought the Crimean War was once again led by a Bonaparte emperor, Napoleon's nephew, Louis Napoleon. His victory could perhaps be seen in part as some kind of retribution for his uncle's defeat in 1812, but it was not witnessed by the great man himself. By the time the conflict broke out, Napoleon I had been dead for over three decades.

The few years the former Emperor spent on St Helena were pretty miserable ones. The island is a desolate, black rock even smaller than Elba in size, hundreds of miles from anywhere, and frequently battered by wind and rain. Its climate is anything but conducive to good health and seems to have contributed to Bonaparte's frequent illnesses during his final years. Yet the real bane of Napoleon's life was the petty-minded man the British government appointed governor of St Helena. Sir Hudson Lowe seems to have viewed his job as to make Napoleon's life as difficult and unpleasant as possible. He restricted his prisoner's movement around the island and kept him under almost constant surveillance, even though there was no realistic chance of the former Emperor escaping as the Royal Navy maintained a constant patrol in St Helena's waters. It was the mark of the man that Lowe refused to pass on a book sent to his eminent captive as it was inscribed to Emperor Napoleon rather than General Bonaparte, the name by which the British government had always insisted upon referring to their great adversary. He even at one point refused to allow Napoleon to order a new pair of shoes until the old ones had been handed over to him first. All the Allied commissioners sent to St Helena to monitor Napoleon's captivity for their governments, including Count Alexander Balmain for Russia, thought Lowe a small-minded, insufferable man and disapproved of his treatment of the former Emperor, but unfortunately the Governor's word was final on this British-owned rock.

Two things kept Napoleon going on St Helena. The first was the hope that he might be released or at least moved somewhere more hospitable. This was dashed in 1818 at the congress of Aix-la-Chapelle, when the Allies determined to keep him where he was. The other was the opportunity his captivity provided for him to set out his own version of his life and career for posterity. Through records of conversations with those who shared his exile and accounts of events which he dictated to them, Bonaparte endeavoured to establish a favourable image of himself and his career at the same time as his enemies in Europe were doing their best to blacken his name, thereby fuelling the intense historical controversy that has raged over him ever since. The Napoleonic legend that emerged from St Helena was obviously highly biased, but it was not as utterly distorted as some have claimed. Napoleon admitted, for example, to having made a number of crucial mistakes in his career, most notably in the Iberian Peninsula and Russia. Nor was his insistence that he was far from solely responsible for all the wars he fought unreasonable, as this book has endeavoured to show.

It was inevitable that Napoleon would comment often in exile upon Russia, and he rightly acknowledged that she had played a key role in his downfall. While he was prepared to admit to having made errors in his campaigns against the Russians, particularly in 1812, he showed no willingness to accept that he had made serious diplomatic mistakes in his relationship with Russia when she and France had been allies. Perhaps it was just too painful to admit to having blown the greatest opportunity he had had to secure lasting French hegemony over most of Europe.

Interestingly, and to his credit, Napoleon showed no real bitterness towards either Tsar Alexander or his country. Indeed, he commented at one point that 'Russia ought always to make common cause with France'. Whether the Russians really needed to, though, Bonaparte doubted, for his frequent remarks about Russia's new standing, and predictions concerning her future, made it clear that he saw the land of the Tsars as the dominant force in post-Napoleonic Europe. Referring to St Petersburg, he averred, 'It is there that the fate of Europe is decided', while of Tsar Alexander he commented, 'If I die here, he will be my real heir in Europe'. The ex-Emperor argued that Russia's huge size and population gave her great advantages over the other powers of the Continent, especially as she was so difficult to defeat on her own soil. He predicted, moreover, that the Russians would exploit these advantages 'to acquire universal dominion'. Several times, he asserted that Russia would march on Constantinople and he also prophesied that she would challenge the British for control of the Indian subcontinent and its neighbouring regions. Nor could an attempt to conquer Europe be ruled out: 'in less than ten years', he remarked at one point, 'all Europe may perhaps be overrun with Cossacks'. Such a prospect was not encouraging. 'Who can avoid shuddering,' he observed, 'at the thought of such a vast mass, unassailable either on the flanks or in the rear, descending upon us with impunity; if triumphant, overwhelming everything in its course; or if defeated, retiring amidst the cold and desolation that may be called its forces of reserve; and possessing every facility of issuing forth again at a future opportunity.' So serious was the threat, Napoleon believed, that it led him to engage in a moment of naïve speculation. If no one else could stop them, 'I may be wanted to check the power of the Russians'. Of course, his services would probably be declined and, in any event, he would not live forever. He concluded, therefore, that the likelihood was that Russia 'will in the end become mistress of the world.'

There is no doubt that Bonaparte overestimated the power of early nineteenth century Russia and exaggerated the aims of her rulers of that period. She was, like the rest of the great powers, expansionist, but did not have the potential or the desire to overrun the rest of Europe. Constantinople, though, was an aim, and Russia would challenge British dominance in south Asia later in the nineteenth century in what became known as the 'Great Game'. Jumping forward to the twentieth century, the Russians did, of course, take over eastern Europe, and it is possible that but for the American commitment to defend the western half of the Continent, they might have overrun that region as well. There is a wonderful anecdote about Stalin conversing with his Western allies in the immediate aftermath of victory over Hitler's Germany. When it was suggested to the Soviet dictator that he must be relieved and delighted that his forces had finally made it all the way to Berlin, he apparently replied with a wry smile that Tsar Alexander had got as far as Paris. Perhaps the tease revealed a worrying ambition.

Napoleon died in early May 1821, aged just fifty-one. The official post-mortem recorded that he had died of stomach cancer, but it is almost certain that this was rigged by the British. He had, after all, been very fat when he had died, hardly a symptom of a wasting disease such as cancer. A more likely cause of death, therefore, is hepatitis, an illness to which the climatic conditions of St Helena were conducive. Concern that it may have been this that accounted for Bonaparte's premature demise would certainly explain the British authorities' desire to advance the notion of stomach cancer, for they had been repeatedly criticized for keeping the former Emperor on an island that was harmful to his health. Also possible, though, is that Napoleon was poisoned by one of his entourage, the Comte de Montholon, in the pay and on the orders of Bourbon extremists in France led by Louis XVIII's brother, the ultra-reactionary Comte d'Artois. Bonaparte's recorded symptoms fit this theory best, and if it is sensible to be generally wary of conspiracy theories, that does not mean that they are not sometimes true.

Napoleon was initially buried in an unmarked grave on St Helena. In a final act of pettiness, Lowe refused to allow the word 'Emperor' to be inscribed on the stone, so, rather than bow to his wishes and have 'General Bonaparte' carved instead, Napoleon's entourage chose to leave it blank. Just under twenty years later, however, in 1840, with a less Francophobic government in charge in Britain and the reactionary Bourbons having been overthrown in France, London acceded to the forcefully expressed wish of the French people to have the body of the Emperor returned to them. Napoleon was therefore disinterred and transported back to Paris, where, with full ceremony, he was reburied in the heart of the church of Les Invalides, a hospital dedicated to looking after injured soldiers. He remains there to this day, enclosed in a magnificent tomb made of red porphyry presented to the French nation by Tsar Nicholas, ruler of the country and brother of the man who had arguably been most responsible for the Emperor's demise. Even in death, the intimate connection between Napoleon and Russia endures.

22

Napoleon, Russia and Europe

The period covered by this book was a truly seminal one for France, Russia, indeed the whole of Europe. History is not an immutable process. It is not written in stone. Individual figures, individual events do matter, sometimes profoundly. The story of Napoleon, and especially of his relationship with Russia, is a classic example of this. Probably no other man than Bonaparte could have come so close to achieving a lasting French hegemony in Europe, to building a new Rome; quite possibly no other country than Russia could have prevented him doing so. True, the Emperor never managed to defeat Britain, his most inveterate foe, but then the British did not have the means to defeat him either. The idea that France was somehow strangled by the Royal Navy's blockade is utter nonsense. Economic warfare harmed both the British and the French, but it was only potentially lethal to a Britain which normally conducted the bulk of her trade with the Continent rather than to a France which dominated the European mainland. Bonaparte could only be definitively defeated on land, and while the British could certainly exacerbate French difficulties in the Iberian Peninsula, the 'Spanish Ulcer' was unlikely ever to kill the Napoleonic Empire. Indeed, it only became quite as damaging as it did thanks to events elsewhere in Europe. But for Austria going to war with France in 1809, the Emperor might well have broken the back of resistance to French rule south of the Pyrenees and chased the British permanently from Iberia. Without the disastrous Russian campaign, the critical reverses Napoleon's forces suffered in Spain in 1812–13 would almost certainly never have happened.

To be sure, it would be erroneous to argue that Britain did not play a major role in the ultimate defeat of the France of the First Empire, but the point is that it is even more mistaken to imagine that everyone else who fought Bonaparte was a bit-part actor in the drama compared to John Bull. The truth is that it took a coalition of all four non-French great powers to bring the Emperor down, with each playing an important role. That such a coalition came into being, however, that it was capable of beating the mighty Napoleon and his armies, and that it pursued victory to the point of totally dismantling the French Empire and dethroning its ruler owes more to Russia and her Tsar than to anyone else. There are not many dates that have profound importance in the history of an entire continent, of the entire world even, but 1812 is undoubtedly one of them. As the

Emperor later reflected on St Helena, the war with Russia 'was the last effort that remained to France. Her fate, and that of the new European System, depended on the struggle. Russia was the last resource of England. The peace of the whole world rested with Russia.' Without a Russian triumph in 1812, without the scale of loss endured by the *Grande Armée* in Russia, without Alexander's decision to pursue the war west of the Niemen, without his determination to eschew peace short of Bonaparte's complete submission, the course of European history would have been very different. Russia was the one Continental power capable of resisting Napoleon and she was the heart of the alliance which defeated him.

The great irony, of course, is that Russia was also a key factor in Bonaparte's rise to pre-eminence and his potential partner in securing lasting French hegemony over most of Europe. Had Catherine the Great sent an army west in 1793, the nascent French Republic might well have been crushed and Napoleon left as a mere historical footnote, if that. Conversely, but for Tsar Paul deciding to go to war with France half a decade later, the country would not have been left facing the crisis which justified the coup d'état of 1799 that brought Bonaparte to power. Over the following years, Russia continued to play a pivotal role in Napoleon's life. Her withdrawal from the Second Coalition greatly facilitated the French victories of 1800 that cemented the First Consul's rule. Her increasingly anti-British attitude was a major factor in London's decision to agree to peace in 1801, a development which further strengthened Bonaparte's hold on power in France. A few years later, it was stunning successes against Russian armies at Austerlitz and Friedland that, in combination with other great triumphs at Ulm and Jena-Auerstädt, paved the way for Napoleon to make himself master of Europe.

Having achieved hegemony over most of the Continent by 1807, the alliance formed with Russia at Tilsit was probably the best means the Emperor had of making it endure. There was no overriding reason why a Franco-Russian partnership could not have endured, provided each side felt they were getting a fair deal from the arrangement. Napoleon's stubbornness over the Polish and Turkish questions in particular wrecked the whole arrangement. He perhaps never made a more costly mistake. It is fascinating (if ultimately futile) to speculate how history might have developed had Bonaparte not committed those errors. How long might the Tilsit system have lasted? Or the Napoleonic Empire? Would there be a Germany or an Italy as we know them today? What would have happened to the Ottoman Empire? Would Britain have sued for peace or even been invaded? Would Russia ever have fallen to communism? How would mainland Europe have developed politically? The questions are almost endless and the answers only guesses at best.

The collapse of the Russo-French alliance left Napoleon in an awkward position. He could (and arguably should) have done nothing. He might have left the initiative to the Russians. If they wanted to attack his Empire, let them. They would hopefully be soundly beaten and thrown back across the Niemen. The problem with this was that there would be an indefinite tension on the Empire's north-eastern frontier, akin perhaps to the situation which obtained in central Europe after the Second World War. This would be economically and psychologically draining. Over time, moreover, the position of Russia *vis-à-vis* France might alter in the former's favour. The Russians might win over Prussia and Austria, for example, and attack the Napoleonic Empire when its founder was either past his military prime or dead. It was these concerns that led Bonaparte to contemplate rebuilding the old kingdom of Poland as a *cordon sanitaire* between Russia and the rest of Europe, and to do it sooner rather than later. As he explained in a memorandum in April 1812, 'The French Empire is now in the enjoyment of the full energy of her existence: if she does not, at this moment, complete the political constitution of Europe, tomorrow she may lose the advantages of her situation, and fail in her enterprises.' Still, the resurrection of the kingdom of Poland, particularly within its most extensive borders, would be a major undertaking, as Napoleon himself realised only too well. That is why he showed some reluctance to invade Russia, why he never stated his ultimate aims publicly, and why he probably would have forsaken his ideal goals for a peace deal with the Tsar that left Russia pretty much in tact but acknowledged a position of inferiority to the Napoleonic Empire and an intention to live peacefully with it.

Could the Emperor have succeeded in 1812, either in reconstructing the kingdom of Poland or in getting the Russians to accept a position of inferiority? There are no incontrovertible grounds for ruling either possibility out. And how would a French victory have shaped the course of European history? Napoleon himself answered this question on St Helena:

> Peace concluded at Moscow would have fulfilled and wound up my hostile expeditions. It would have been, with respect to the grand cause, the term of casualties and the commencement of security. A new horizon, new undertakings, would have unfolded themselves, adapted, in every respect, to the well-being and prosperity of all. The foundation of the European system would have been laid, and my only remaining task would have been its organisation.

He went on to state that he envisaged the birth of a European nation with the same laws, the same money, the same weights and measures. He even maintained that his own authoritarian rule would have given way under his son to a more constitutional form of government. It was a remarkable vision and it is not hard to see why many, both those in favour of and against the notion, see Bonaparte as one of the inspirations behind the idea of a European superstate.

Of course, Napoleon was seeking on St Helena to portray as favourable an image of himself and his career as possible, and there is therefore good reason to question the rosiness of the picture he painted. That does not mean, however, that there might not have been at least some truth behind the vision he put forward. There are simply too many variables to argue with any degree of certainty how European history would have unfolded in the wake of a French defeat of Russia, but it is by no means inconceivable that peace might have returned to the continent and that those areas dominated by France would have become increasingly integrated. Whether this would have been better for the majority of Europeans than what happened in reality is, of course, impossible to say.*

It is easier to comment upon how the actual course events took affected the international history of Europe post-1815. The most obvious fact is that the continent remained one of many separate states which continued to jostle and compete with one another, often by means of war and sometimes at catastrophic cost. Thankfully, much progress has been made towards removing military conflict from relations between European nations since the end of the Second World War.

The Allied victory of 1814–15 also did much to determine the fate of each of the various great powers. Britain was left in a position to become an unmatched superpower for much of the nineteenth century, Prussia was able in time to build a united Germany with her at its heart which would dominate the history of Europe in the first half of the twentieth century, and the Austrian Empire was able to continue to play an important part on the European scene until the First World War. But what of Russia and France?

The standing of Tsarist Russia was never higher than it was in the final years and aftermath of the Napoleonic Wars, and she remained a major player on the international stage over the following century and, as the Soviet Union, beyond. And yet her ultimate victory over Napoleon was very much a mixed blessing for it stifled the movement for reform which Russia very much needed. Alexander talked of reform after 1815 as he had before, but again he did practically nothing. Probably the only thing that might have paved the way for the kind of far-reaching changes that the country required was a heavy military defeat on her own soil. This, after all, is what spurred reform undertaken in Prussia and Austria in the early nineteenth century, not to mention what finally goaded Tsar Alexander II to introduce a series of changes in Russia, including the long-overdue abolition of serfdom, in the years following the Crimean War. In the end, though, the second Alexander's reforms were not enough to save Tsarist Russia. Having been repeatedly checked in her ambitions towards the Ottoman Empire and humiliated by losing a war to Japan in 1904–05, she entered the First World War still a backwards country compared to the likes of Germany, France

---

* Adam Zamoyski has written a thought-provoking counterfactual essay which considers what might have happened had Napoleon defeated Russia published in A. Roberts (ed.), *What Might Have Been* (London, 2004).

and Britain, and her institutions proved incapable of meeting the demands of total war. Two revolutions in 1917 overthrew the monarchy, replaced it with a communist regime, and led to Russia signing a draconian and humiliating peace treaty with Wilhelmine Germany that was only overturned thanks to the ultimate victory of Britain, France and the United States over Russia's conquerors. Following that narrow escape, the new Russian leaders embarked upon a massive program of change over the next twenty years which, despite inflicting much suffering on a great many people, at least enabled the Soviet Union to survive and emerge triumphant from the Nazi onslaught. Indeed, in international terms, the Communists elevated Russia to a position which even Tsar Alexander I had not reached. Their failure after the Second World War to construct an economy capable of sufficiently addressing the everyday needs and desires of the Soviet people as well as of meeting the demands of a military superpower, however, eventually led to their fall, the break-up of the Soviet/Russian Empire, and the considerable diminution of Russia's importance on the international stage.

France's post-1815 history has been every bit as much of a rollercoaster ride as that of Russia. Although she soon began to recover from the international nadir of 1814–15, it became clear over the next few decades that France was but a shadow of the power she had once been under the Emperor. The French could do little in the face of British and other opposition to get Belgium reincorporated within their frontiers when she rebelled against Dutch rule in 1830, for example, having to settle instead for her becoming an independent country. Things improved considerably, if temporarily, in the 1850s and early 1860s under the Second Empire of Napoleon's nephew, Louis Napoleon. Victory over Russia in the Crimean War and over Austria in the Italian War of Liberation did much to restore French military prestige as well as to increase French influence in the Near East and regain France the regions of Nice and Savoy that she had lost in 1815. The conquest of Algeria was also completed at this time and other overseas French colonies, such as Senegal and Cambodia, were established. Just as France seemed to be re-emerging as the greatest power on the European mainland, however, swift and crushing defeat at Prussian hands in 1870 not only humiliated the French army and resulted in the loss of the provinces of Alsace and Lorraine, but also led to the creation of a unified Germany that was clearly more powerful both economically and militarily than France. The republican regime that replaced the toppled Louis Napoleon at this point thus took over a country whose standing as a great power had perhaps never been lower, yet once again France's international status slowly recovered. The overseas empire expanded in the last decades of the nineteenth century and by 1914 was exceeded in size only by the mighty British Empire. An alliance with the Russians and an entente with the British further strengthened the French position internationally, and while Russia was defeated in the First World War and underwent a revolution that made her a pariah, France emerged from the cataclysm as one of the 'Big Three'. The United States' subsequent retreat into isolationism left the French as effective leaders alongside the British of the new League of Nations, but France's lofty international standing in the 1920s and 1930s exceeded her actual power in a way it never had under Napoleon. Whereas Soviet Russia avoided defeat at Hitler's hands and came out of the Second World War a superpower, therefore, France was vanquished by the Nazis and, despite regaining her liberty in time to claim a role as one of the victorious Allied powers, lost any real credibility as a great power. She endeavoured, mostly unsuccessfully, to regain some of her lost status in the post-war years, but even though she managed to hold on to a permanent seat on the United Nations Security Council, eventually the truth sank in. Since the 1950s, French leaders have turned increasingly to the European Union (European (Economic) Community as was) as the means to restore their country, in cooperation with others, to a leading position in international affairs once more.

And so perhaps in some regards the broad outline of the European system envisaged by Napoleon is becoming a reality some two centuries after he bestrode the continent as its colossus. Europe is becoming more and more integrated, with the same currency, the same weights and measures, and increasingly similar laws. Modern France is certainly not the dominating force she was in the system in the Emperor's day, but she holds a position of considerable significance within it. Excluded from the system, of course, is Russia, just as she was in Bonaparte's time. She remains a not quite fully European country, and as such is unlikely ever to become an intrinsic part of an integrated Europe. Yet if the story of Napoleon and Russia has any lesson to teach us, it is that it is better to find some way of working with the Russians as partners than to treat them as rivals. The Emperor himself failed to appreciate this, and it ultimately cost him everything.

Bibliographical Essay

The following is not intended to be an exhaustive list of all materials relating to Napoleon or to France, Russia and Europe in the Napoleonic era, but rather a guide for those who wish to investigate aspects of the story told in this book further or from a different angle. For ease of use, it is divided into various categories. Given that this volume has been written in English for an English-speaking audience, priority has naturally been accorded to works in English, but studies in French have been included where the literature in English is thin. For the same reason, books that were originally published in French but have been translated into English appear here in the latter form, although readers should be warned that sometimes the translated versions are abridged.

BIOGRAPHIES

Biographies are generally a good way to explore an historical era and their inevitable focus upon a particular individual has advantages as well as drawbacks. The Napoleonic period is well-served by biography overall, although some figures have received considerably more attention than others.

FRANCE

Given that Napoleon was one of the most intriguing, important and controversial individuals ever to have lived, it is no surprise that a glut of biographies of him have been written in the two centuries since he bestrode the world's stage. In some ways, the best account of his life (in English at any rate and possibly in any language) remains John Holland Rose's *The Life of Napoleon I*, 2 vols (London, 1902). Some have criticized the work as being rather too favourable to its subject, but this arguably says more about their view of Napoleon than it does Rose's. In reality, this hefty study is a pretty balanced account of Bonaparte's career and is still a fine read more than a century since its original publication. Perhaps the best modern biography of Napoleon is Frank McLynn's *Napoleon: a Biography* (London, 1998). Unlike many English-speaking authors, McLynn makes a genuine effort to avoid nationalistic bias and to provide an even-handed judgement on Napoleon the man and on his career. Some of his arguments are maybe stronger than others, but they are never dull. Another modern study that is highly recommended is *Napoleon: A Political Life* (New York, 2004) by Steven Englund. As the title suggests, the emphasis of the work is less on the military side of Napoleon's career than is typical for biographies of the great man, and that gives the author room to explore the other aspects of Bonaparte's life in more depth. On Napoleon's domestic policy and relationship with the French, the book is unsurpassed and is full of fascinating insights on the man and his place in history. On international affairs, however, which are admittedly not Englund's main concern, the study is less convincing, seeming to lean rather too heavily and uncritically on the work of Paul Schroeder (see below). Still, overall, the book remains a first-rate work, although its rather academic tone and assumption of a certain degree of prior knowledge of the period means that it should not perhaps be the first biography of Napoleon one reads.

Contrasting with Englund's work, in its emphasis and style anyway, is R. B. Asprey's *The Rise and Fall of Napoleon Bonaparte*, 2 vols (London, 2000–1). Written by a former marine, it is little surprise that it is the military side of Napoleon that shines through here. Although a little simplistic (and at times downright wrong) regarding political issues, Asprey is a fine relater of campaigns and battles and has succeeded in writing a decent account of Bonaparte's life, which avoids the crudely negative caricaturisations of some other works written in English. Felix Markham's *Napoleon* (London, 1963) is still a decent (and fairly short) read some four decades on, while R. B. Jones *Napoleon: Man and Myth* (London, 1977) is another reasonable, short book. J. M. Thompson's *Napoleon Bonaparte* (Oxford, 1988) makes some interesting points, albeit in a rather dry fashion, and Jean Tulard's *Napoleon: the Myth of the Saviour* (London, 1984) is an important study by a modern French scholar.

Of course there have always been books which have sought either to excoriate or exalt Napoleon and no bibliography would be complete without mention of a few such works. Aside from some memoirists, perhaps the most negative vision of Napoleon conjured up by a Frenchman is to be found in P. Lanfrey's *The History of Napoleon the First*, 4 vols (London, 1871–9) in which it seems the main character could do almost nothing right. This is pretty much the line taken by Corelli Barnett in his *Bonaparte* (London, 1978), a book which seeks to give as little credit as possible to Napoleon for any of the successes he or France enjoyed during his period of prominence. Like Barnett, Alan Schom concentrates mostly on military affairs in his hefty work, *Napoleon Bonaparte* (London, 1998) and again finds his subject lacking in the skill generally attributed to him. It is Napoleon the man that takes a particular pounding in Schom's book, though, with what seems at times like every negative thing ever said about Napoleon (regardless of whether it was true or not) being repeated. The absence of rejoinders of a more positive nature gives the lie to the author's extraordinary claim to have written a balanced account of Napoleon's life. Paul Johnson is another to have written a stridently anti-Napoleonic text in recent years. Despite his short study being entitled *Napoleon* (London, 2002), Johnson, like Barnett, seems incapable of referring to his subject by his first name. Perhaps this is merely a result of the evident loathing the author feels for Napoleon, whom he presents more as a caricature than a real person, or maybe it is a subtle attempt to strengthen one of the main propositions of his book, namely that (Napoleon) Bonaparte was the prototype for (Adolf) Hitler, (Joseph) Stalin and any other twentieth century dictatorial madman one would care to mention. To say that the link between Napoleon and his regime and Hitler, Stalin etc. and their regimes is overplayed by Johnson is an understatement (Englund's excellent book is a fine antidote to such notions). If one feels the need to read any of these virulently anti-Napoleonic works, one should also be sure to read a highly laudatory account of Bonaparte's character and career. Vincent Cronin's *Napoleon* (London, 1971) is often heralded as one such book, though in reality the level of its praise for the Emperor never matches the depth of denunciation achieved by Schom, Barnett or Johnson. For that, one might turn to B. Weider & E. Gueguen *Napoleon: the Man who Shaped Europe* (Staplehurst, 2000), a truly hagiographical recent study.

Although ostensibly a biography, Georges Lefebvre's *Napoleon*, 2 vols (London, 1969) is in some ways more an account of the Napoleonic era than of Bonaparte's life. Lefebvre wrote from the perspective of a French Marxist but his work is less undermined by this than one might imagine. Although highly critical of Napoleon, sometimes unreasonably so, he at least recognizes that he was not solely to blame for all the conflicts and other regrettable occurrences of the Napoleonic period. Another notable 'biography' is Geoffrey Ellis's *Napoleon* (London, 1997). Focusing heavily upon how Napoleon ruled, Ellis's book is very academic in tone and not for the faint-hearted, but it raises some interesting questions.

Although many general biographies of Napoleon concentrate heavily upon his military career, there is still probably nothing to match David Chandler's magisterial *The Campaigns of Napoleon* (London, 1995) as an examination of Bonaparte the soldier. Chandler explains expertly just how and why Napoleon was such a brilliant commander, and his account of the many campaigns the great man fought is both comprehensive and adroit. Although a little wayward with statistics on occasion, Chandler's book is rightly viewed as a masterpiece of Napoleonic historiography. A much briefer, and somewhat drier, account of Napoleon's generalship and campaigns is provided by J. Marshall-Cornwall in *Napoleon as Military Commander* (New York, 1998). More provocative is Owen Connelly's *Blundering to Glory: Napoleon's Military Campaigns* (Wilmington, Del., 1987). Not as negative an analysis of Napoleon's generalship as the title would suggest, this book provides an interesting alternative view of Bonaparte's military skill.

Authors have always struggled to come to grips with Napoleon's highly complex character but John Holland Rose arguably did as well as anyone in his *The Personality of Napoleon* (London, 1912), a fascinating read. Along similar lines, J. C. Herold, *The Mind of Napoleon: a Selection from his Written and Spoken Words* (New York, 1955) can be rather insightful. Napoleon's relationship with his family has been exhaustively studied by F. Masson in *Napoléon et sa famille*, 13 vols (Paris, 1897–1919), while his relationship with his wives has been entertainingly told by Evangeline Bruce in *Napoleon and Josephine* (London, 1995) and Alan Palmer in *Napoleon and Marie-Louise* (London, 2001). *Napoleon In Love* (London, 1969) by R. F. Delderfield, a master storyteller, provides a marvellous account of Bonaparte's various female entanglements, which has been recently augmented, though not surpassed, by Christopher Hibbert's *Napoleon: His Wives and Women* (London, 2002). A fascinating, if contentious, take on the final years of Napoleon's rule and life is provided by D. Hamilton-Williams, *The Fall of Napoleon: the Final Betrayal* (London, 1999), a provocative work which will especially appeal to those into conspiracy theories. Stephen Coote's *Napoleon and the Hundred Days* (London, 2004) provides a highly readable, if at times excessively glib or even plain wrong, account of the events of 1815, while Alan Schom's *One Hundred Days: Napoleon's Road to Waterloo* (Oxford, 1993), upon which Coote's book is heavily based, is better than his biography of the Emperor but still marred by the author's excessive bias. For those with French, *Les Cent-Jours ou l'esprit de sacrifice* by the French statesman, Dominique de Villepin, is well worth a look and provides a perspective on the Hundred Days that many English-speakers may find fresh. On Napoleon's period in exile on St Helena, there is F. Giles's *Napoleon Bonaparte: England's Prisoner* (London, 2001) and Jean-Paul Kauffman's poignant *The Dark Room at Longwood* (London, 1999). *Napoleon: the Final Verdict* (London, 1996) by P. J. Haythornthwaite *et al.* is, despite the rather absurdly bold title, a solid collection of essays on the man and his era. Finally, it seems that no bibliography of Napoleon is complete without reference to P. Geyl's *Napoleon: For and Against* (London, 1949). An account of Napoleonic historiography rather than of the man himself, it is not for the casual reader, but what it sets out to do, it does very well. In similar vein, R. S. Alexander's *Napoleon* (London, 2001) provides a highly academic but interesting account of how Bonaparte has been viewed at different times by different people.

Moving on to Napoleon's family, Desmond Seward's *Napoleon's Family* (London, 1986) provides a decent introduction, although Masson remains the definitive work. Josephine and Marie-Louise are well-covered in the books by Bruce and Palmer already mentioned. For those interested in Joseph Bonaparte, one might try Owen Connelly, *The Gentle Bonaparte: A Biography of Joseph,*

Napoleon's Elder Brother (New York, 1968) or M. Ross, *The Reluctant King: Joseph Bonaparte, King of the Two Sicilies and Spain* (London, 1976). Jerome's life is covered, in part anyway, by G. J. Lamar's *Jerome Bonaparte: the war years, 1800–1815* (London, 2000). More significant a figure than either in some ways was Napoleon's stepson and Viceroy of Italy, Eugène de Beauharnais. There is a very good account of this fine young man's short life in Carola Oman's *Napoleon's Viceroy: Eugène de Beauharnais* (London, 1966), while those with French might look at F. de Bernardy, *Eugène de Beauharnais* (Paris, 1973).

Given that Napoleon was effectively his own foreign minister, especially in later years, it is unsurprising that the only one of his chief diplomats to have received much attention from historians is that great survivor Talleyrand. The most readable biography of him in English is probably A. Duff Cooper's *Talleyrand* (London, 1932), although he is more than a little kind to the shifty and self-serving Talleyrand. J. F. Bernard, *Talleyrand: a Biography* (London, 1973) provides another accessible account, while P. G. Dwyer, *Talleyrand* (London, 2002) is a more academic study; insightful but harder work.

The popularity of military history means that Napoleon's military subordinates have been better served biographically than his diplomatic minions. For those wishing to discover a little about each of the twenty-six marshals, D. G. Chandler (ed.), *Napoleon's Marshals* (London, 1998) is an excellent starting point, containing, as it does, brief biographies of every member of the Emperor's Marshalate. *The March of the Twenty-Six: the Story of Napoleon's Marshals* (London, 1962) by R. F. Delderfield is a cracking read which paints vivid portraits of every marshal and was, fortunately, recently republished. A. G. Macdonell's *Napoleon and his Marshals* (London, 1934) has also been republished in recent years and provides another highly accessible account, although it is stronger on Napoleon's relationship with his marshals than on biographical detail of the marshals themselves. Peter Young, *Napoleon's Marshals* (Reading, 1973) can also be read with profit and R. W. Phipps's *The Armies of the First French Republic and the Rise of the Marshals of Napoleon I*, 5 vols (London, 1926–39) gives a detailed account of the marshals' early careers.

As far as biographies of individual marshals are concerned, some have been covered more widely than others. There is only one biography of the brilliant Davout in English, for example, but fortunately it is a very good one; J. G. Gallaher's *The Iron Marshal: a Biography of Louis N. Davout* (London, 2000). For greater detail, those with French might consult H. Vigier, *Davout, maréchal d'Empire, duc d'Auerstädt, prince d'Eckmühl, 1770–1823*, 2 vols (Paris, 1898). Ney, on the other hand, has had lots written about him. The best works in English are *The Bravest of the Brave: Michel Ney, Marshal of France, Duke of Elchingen, Prince of the Moskowa, 1769–1815* (London, 1912) by A. H. Atteridge, and *Marshal Ney: the Romance and the Real* (Tunbridge Wells, 1982) by R. Horricks. Recent works in French include F. Hulot, *Le maréchal Ney* (Paris, 2000) and E. Perrin, *Le maréchal Ney* (Paris, 1993). As well as chronicling Ney's life, A. H. Atteridge produced a fine biography of Murat entitled *Joachim Murat, Marshal of France and King of Naples* (London, 1911). M. Dupont's *Murat: cavalier, maréchal de France, prince et roi* (Paris, 1980) is a useful modern French study. For a long time neither Lannes nor Soult had works about them in English but that has changed with the publication of M. S. Chrisawn's *The Emperor's Friend: Marshal Jean Lannes* (London, 2001) and P. Hayman's *Soult: Napoleon's Maligned Marshal* (London, 1990). The last quarter century has also seen a number of biographies of both these marshals published in French, among them J. C. Damamme, *Lannes, maréchal d'Empire* (Paris, 1987), L. Willette, *Le maréchal Lannes, un d'Artagnan sous l'Empire* (Paris, 1979), F. Hulot, *Le maréchal Soult* (Paris, 2003) and N. Gotteri, *Le maréchal Soult* (Paris, 2000). The best biography of Masséna is probably James Marshall-Cornwall's, *Massena* (Oxford, 1965), while those wishing to learn more about Napoleon's chief of staff might read S. J. Watson, *By Command of the Emperor: a life of Marshal Berthier* (London, 1957). That thorn in Napoleon's side Bernadotte has been recently studied by Alan Palmer in his highly readable *Bernadotte: Napoleon's Marshal, Sweden's King* (London, 1990), but the definitive biography of the Gascon turncoat remains the hefty three-volume work of D. P. Barton: *Bernadotte, the First Phase 1763–99* (London, 1914); *Bernadotte and Napoleon 1799–1810* (London, 1921); and *Bernadotte, Prince and King 1810–44* (London, 1925). Neither Marmont nor Poniatowski have yet been served by an English-speaking biographer, but accounts of their lives can be found in French in R. Christophe, *Le maréchal Marmont, duc de Raguse* (Paris, 1968) and S. Askenazi, *Le prince Joseph Poniatowski, maréchal de France* (Paris, 1921).

RUSSIA

Although Russia's rulers during this period have not received the same level of attention as Napoleon, they have been far from ignored. Of the many works on Catherine the Great, two of the best in English are John T. Alexander, *Catherine the Great: life and legend* (Oxford, 1989) and Isabel de Madariaga, *Catherine the Great: a short history* (Yale, 1993). Both are fairly academic in tone, however, and more accessible, though perhaps less insightful, is Henri Troyat's *Catherine the Great* (Oxford, 1979). The short reign of Paul I has meant that he has been less troubled by biographers than either his mother or son, but there do exist a few works in English. R. E. McGrew, *Paul I of Russia* (Oxford, 1992) is a solid, informative study, while H. Ragsdale (ed.), *Paul I: a Reassessment of his Life and Reign* (Pittsburgh, 1979) provides some interesting examinations of aspects of the man and his rule. It was Paul's son Alexander, though, that had most impact upon Napoleon's life and career, and there are several decent studies of him in

English. Although short and quite academic in tone, Janet Hartley's *Alexander I* (London, 1994) is a good survey. Less penetrating perhaps, but eminently readable and very worthwhile all the same are Alan Palmer, *Alexander I: Tsar of War and Peace* (London, 1974), Henri Troyat, *Alexander of Russia* (London, 1984) and M. Dziewanowski, *Alexander I: Russia's Mysterious Tsar* (New York, 1990). A. McConnel's *Alexander I: Paternalistic Reformer* (Arlington Heights, Ill., 1970) is also useful and L. I. Strakhovsky's, *Alexander I of Russia: the Man who Defeated Napoleon* (London, 1949) provides a Russian view of the enigmatic tsar.

Russian statesmen of the era have been even less well-served by English-speaking biographers than French diplomats, but fortunately P. K. Grimsted in *The Foreign Ministers of Alexander I: Political Attitudes and the Conduct of Russian Diplomacy, 1801–1825* (Berkeley, 1969) has provided brief accounts of each of Tsar Alexander's key foreign policy subordinates. *A Man of Honour: Adam Czartoryski as a Statesman of Russia and Poland, 1795–1831* (Oxford, 1993) by W. H. Zawadzki is a more detailed biography of Alexander's Polish friend, who is also the focus of Marian Kukiel's *Czartoryski and European Unity, 1770–1861* (Princeton, 1955).

There is a little more available for the English-speaker in terms of Russia's military leaders, but not much. Suvorov's life has been fairly well chronicled by P. Longworth in *The Art of Victory: the Life and Achievements of Generalissimo Suvorov, 1729–1800* (London, 1965), while K. Osipov's *Alexander Suvorov: a biography* (London, 1944) gives a Russian version of this warrior's career. M. Josselson's *The Commander: a life of Barclay de Tolly* (Oxford, 1980) does much to put that dour, Baltic soldier in his rightful place in the history of the period. One searches in vain for English biographies of Wittgenstein, Bennigsen or Miloradovich, but Kutuzov has been covered, more than a little flatteringly, in *The Fox of the North: the life of Kutuzov, general of 'War and Peace'* (London, 1976) by Roger Parkinson. S. Nabokov, *Koutouzov, le vainqueur de Napoléon* (Paris, 1990) is an interesting account for those who can read French.

OTHERS

In international affairs, Pitt the Younger, Castlereagh and Metternich all played key roles during the Napoleonic period and biographies in English can be found of all of them. The wily Austrian is covered with Alan Palmer's usual skill in *Metternich: Councillor of Europe* (London, 1972), while C. Bartlett, *Castlereagh* (London, 1966) and J. Derry, *Castlereagh* (London, 1976) are both solid accounts of another major figure. Despite his failure to emulate his subject and attain Britain's top political post, former Conservative leader William Hague has produced a well-written, if predictably (over) positive, biography of a Tory hero in *William Pitt the Younger: a biography* (London, 2004).

Turning to military affairs, there is a veritable flood of biographies of Wellington in English. The best is perhaps Elizabeth Longford's two-volume study, *Wellington: Years of the Sword* (London, 1969) and *Wellington: Pillar of State* (London, 1972). Richard Holmes's recent *Wellington: the Iron Duke* (London, 2002) is highly readable, if a little rose-tinted at times, and Andrew Roberts has produced good and generally pretty even-handed characterizations of both Wellington and his greatest opponent in *Napoleon and Wellington* (London, 2001). Those interested in that other great British hero of the period, Horatio Nelson, might turn to Andrew Lambert's *Nelson: Britannia's God of War* (London, 2004), a very favourable but persuasive biography which is excellent on Nelson the commander, or, for a more detailed account of the admiral's personal life, to Christopher Hibbert's *Nelson: A Personal History* (London, 1994). On that dogged old warhorse Blücher, Roger Parkinson has produced a very good study in *The Hussar General: the life of Blücher, man of Waterloo* (London, 1975), while G. Rothenberg, an expert on the Austrian military during this period, has written *Napoleon's Great Adversaries: the Archduke Charles and the Austrian Army, 1792–1814* (London, 1982).

GENERAL HISTORIES

The critical importance and fascination of the late eighteenth and early nineteenth centuries has ensured that the period has been well researched by historians and there are a range of good studies available. F. L. Ford, *Europe 1780–1830*, 2nd edn (London, 1989) is an accessible, not too long and judicious survey. G. Rudé, *Revolutionary Europe, 1783–1815* (London, 1964), Owen Connelly, *The French Revolution, Napoleonic Era* (New York, 1979) and C. W. Crawley (ed.), *New Cambridge Modern History, IX: War and Peace in an Age of Upheaval, 1793–1830* (Cambridge, 1965) all cover much the same period and each is worth a look. For a Marxist perspective on the era, Eric Hobsbawm's *The Age of Revolution, 1789–1848* (London, 1962) is a readable account which does not wear its political bias as polemically as one might fear.

Taking a broader temporal perspective, I. Collins, *The Age of Progress: a Survey of European History between 1789 and 1870* (London, 1964) is interesting, while Paul Kennedy's masterly opus, *The Rise and Fall of the Great Powers: economic change and military conflict from 1500–2000* (London, 1989), has something valuable to say about every period it covers. D. McKay & H. Scott, *The Rise of the Great Powers, 1648–1815* (London, 1983) is a solid general survey of European grand politics.

Focusing more specifically upon Napoleonic Europe, J. C. Herold's *The Age of Napoleon* (London, 1964) remains a good review and the more recent *The Age of Napoleon* (London, 2004) by Alistair Horne is as well-written and accessible an account as that author always produces. More academic are Michael Broers's *Europe Under Napoleon, 1799–1815* (London, 1996), a thought-provoking book which deepens our understanding of the Napoleonic Empire, and P. G. Dwyer (ed.), *Napoleon and Europe* (London, 2001), an eclectic mix of essays on various aspects of the era, which are generally insightful, if at times a little dry. For those looking for a short survey, D. G. Wright, *Napoleon and Europe* (London, 1984) and A. Stiles, *Napoleon, France and Europe* (London, 1993) both do a very good job of covering the period within very limited space.

Two important works on the Napoleonic Empire were produced in the early 1990s. Although short, and at times as dry as dust, Geoffrey Ellis's *The Napoleonic Empire* (London, 1991) is a scholarly study which is considerably better at pointing out the disadvantages of Bonaparte's empire than its more positive contributions. A little more accessible, and arguably more balanced, is Stuart Woolf's *Napoleon's Integration of Europe* (London, 1991). On the Continental System, the best work in English remains E. F. Heckscher, *The Continental System* (London, 1922).

Turning to general studies of warfare in the Napoleonic era, there are a range of books dealing with the mechanics of conflict, some rather better than others. Among the best are Gunther Rothenberg's *The Art of Warfare in the Age of Napoleon* (London, 1977), Brent Nosworthy's *Battle Tactics of Napoleon and his Enemies* (London, 1995) and Rory Muir's *Tactics and the Experience of Battle in the Age of Napoleon* (Yale, 2000), although each will only really be appreciated by serious military enthusiasts. More accessible to the interested non-specialist might be Michael Glover's *Warfare in the Age of Bonaparte* (London, 1980). *The Wars of Napoleon* (London, 1995) by Charles Esdaile contains a series of chapters dealing with various aspects of warfare, socio-economic and political as well as purely military, and makes some very interesting observations, although the author is arguably more that a little biased against Napoleon.

EUROPE IN THE NAPOLEONIC ERA

FRANCE

Anyone interested in learning about French domestic history during the period covered by this book might consult F. Furet, *Revolutionary France, 1770–1880* (Oxford, 1988), a wide-ranging study which takes the story past the Second Empire of Napoleon III and into the Third Republic. D.M.G. Sutherland's *France, 1789–1815: Revolution and Counter-Revolution* (London, 1985) focuses more specifically on the Revolutionary and Napoleonic eras.

Works on the French Revolution and the 1790s in France abound, with opinions on events ranging as widely as they do on Napoleon himself. William Doyle's *The Oxford History of the French Revolution* (Oxford, 1989) is a pretty detailed, well-written and generally fairly accessible survey that is more even-handed than some accounts written by English-speakers. Simon Schama's *Citizens: A Chronicle of the French Revolution* (London, 1989) has been widely heralded as a wonderful read, although some may find the author's style a little florid. Certainly, Schama has a great skill for storytelling and relates many a fascinating anecdote, but one ultimately might be left asking whether he has quite got the point of the Revolution. A robust (and, for an English-speaker, atypical) defence of the French Revolution has been provided by Mark Steel in *Vive La Revolution* (London, 2003). Although the author is a comedian by profession, his history is sound (if a little prone to his strongly left-wing bias at times) and he has written a highly entertaining account of the great events of the late 1780s and early 1790s that is strongly recommended to anyone inclined to view the Revolution as little more than anarchy, war and the guillotine. Two good, short studies of the Revolution have been provided by D. Townson, *France in Revolution* (London, 1990) and D. G. Wright, *Revolution and Terror in France, 1789–1795*, 2nd edn (London, 1990). Anyone who still doubts the counter-revolutionary convictions of the French monarchy and its determination to reverse the Revolution should read Munro Price's *The Fall of the French Monarchy* (London, 2002).

France under Napoleon has been studied less than France in the 1790s, but there is still a plethora of works. L. Bergeron, *France under Napoleon* (Princeton, 1981) is widely seen as a standard text on the subject and M. Lyons, *Napoleon Bonaparte and the Legacy of the French Revolution* (London, 1994) makes some interesting points. Louis Madelin provides a pro-Napoleon analysis in *The Consulate and the Empire*, 2 vols (London, 1934–6), a study originally produced in French. Almost a century earlier, Adolphe Thiers, a French statesman, wrote his monumental *History of the Consulate and Empire*, 20 vols (London, 1845–62), a fairly even-handed, if rather Anglophobic, work which will reward those with the stamina to take it on.

Of books in English on the French military in this era, J. R. Elting's *Swords Around a Throne: Napoleon's Grande Armée* (New York, 1988) might well be called definitive. Certainly, he leaves few stones unturned in his examination of Napoleon's military machine. A good feel for the experience of the French soldiers of the era can be gained from Alan Forrest's *Napoleon's Men: the Soldiers of the Revolution and Empire* (London, 2002).

RUSSIA

As Russia may seem less familiar to many English-speakers than France, a perusal of G. Hosking, *Russia and the Russians: a History* (London, 2001) will provide a good, broad base of knowledge and understanding. On Russian expansion and decline, D. Lieven's *Empire: the Russian Empire and its Rivals* (London, 2000) is very thought-provoking, on empires in general as well as on Russia specifically.

Perhaps the best book on Russia in the late eighteenth century is Isabel de Madariaga, *Russia in the Age of Catherine the Great* (London, 1981), while D. Saunders, *Russia in the Age of Reaction and Reform 1801–1881* (London, 1992), H. Seton-Watson, *The Russian Empire, 1801–1917* (Oxford, 1967) and E. Thaden, *Russia since 1801: the Making of a New Society* (New York, 1971) take the story on through the nineteenth century. Alan Palmer has written a brief, informative and typically accessible account of Russia during the Napoleonic period in *Russia in War and Peace* (London, 1972). A. M. Martin, *Romantics, Reformers, Reactionaries: Russian Conservative Thought and Politics in the Reign of Alexander I* (DeKalb, Ill., 1997) is an insightful work, but not for the uninitiated.

On the Russian military, J. L. Keep, *Soldiers of the Tsar: Army and Society in Russia, 1462–1874* (Oxford, 1985) is a very good study, which can be supplemented by the relevant parts of R. Higham & F. Kagan (eds), *The Military History of Tsarist Russia* (Boston, Mass., 2001). R. Wilson, *Brief Remarks on the Character and Composition of the Russian Army* (London, 1810) is an interesting account from a British general who observed Tsar Alexander's army at first hand.

OTHER COUNTRIES

Although the real key to understanding Napoleonic France's rise and fall may lie, as this book has suggested, in Napoleon's relationship with Russia rather than Britain, there is no denying the crucial importance of the British to the history of the period. C. Bayly, *Imperial Meridian: the British Empire and the World, 1780–1830* (London, 1989) gives a good overview, while H. T. Dickinson (ed.), *Britain and the French Revolution* (London, 1979) offers some interesting observations. R. Glover, *Britain at Bay* (London, 1973) is an account of British efforts to protect themselves against the threat from France. *British Strategy in the Napoleonic Wars, 1803–15* (Manchester, 1992) by C. D. Hall is a valuable study and the relevant part of A. D. Harvey's excellent *Collision of Empires: Britain in Three World Wars, 1793–1945* (London, 1993) is definitely worth a read.

On Austria, C. A. Macartney, *The Habsburg Empire, 1790–1918* (London, 1969) is informative and accessible. R. Okey provides a more recent study in *The Habsburg Monarchy, c. 1765–1918: from Enlightenment to Eclipse* (London, 2000). Prussia is dealt with well in P. G. Dwyer, *The Rise of Prussia, 1700–1830* (London, 2001) and is also examined, along with the rest of Germany, in J. J. Sheehan's much lauded *German History, 1770–1866* (Oxford, 1989) and T. Nipperdey's *Germany from Napoleon to Bismarck, 1800–1866* (Dublin, 1996).

Those wishing to find out more about the Ottoman Empire might try to get hold of J. Kinross, *The Ottoman Centuries: the Rise and Fall of the Turkish Empire* (London, 1977) or, for a more focused study, W. Johnson & C. Bell, *The Ottoman Empire and the Napoleonic Wars* (Leeds, 1988) or S. J. Shaw, *Between Old and New: The Ottoman Empire Under Sultan Selim III, 1798–1807* (Cambridge, Mass., 1971). South-east Europe in this period is covered in B. Jelavich, *History of the Balkans: Eighteenth and Nineteenth Centuries* (Cambridge, 1983).

Another area crucial to Franco-Russian relations was Poland. The standard work in English on this country is *God's Playground: a History of Poland*, 2 vols (Oxford, 1981) by Norman Davies (the first volume goes as far as 1795, the second takes the story on from there). Also worth reading are W. F. Reddaway *et al.* (eds), *The Cambridge History of Poland: from Augustus II to Pilsudski, 1697–1935* (Cambridge, 1941) and P. Wandycz, *The Lands of Partitioned Poland, 1795–1918* (Seattle, 1974). Adam Zamoyski's *The Polish Way: a Thousand-Year History of the Poles and their Culture* (London, 1987) is very readable.

The role of Sweden in Russo-French relations was not perhaps as crucial as that of Poland or the Ottoman Empire, but it was significant nonetheless. More can be learnt about the country which was prepared to make a king of one of Napoleon's less worthy marshals in I. Andersson, *A History of Sweden* (London, 1955) or F. Scott, *Sweden: the Nation's History* (Minneapolis, 1977).

MILITARY CAMPAIGNS

Campaign histories, though not to everyone's taste, are always popular with military enthusiasts and David Chandler's *The Campaigns of Napoleon* (London, 1995) is a veritable classic of the form. Briefer, though still highly admirable, histories of the Napoleonic Wars are provided by Gunther Rothenberg in *The Napoleonic Wars* (London, 2000) and David Gates in *The Napoleonic Wars 1803–1815* (London, 1997). Russell Weigley takes a longer perspective in his excellent *The Age of Battles: the Quest for Decisive Warfare from Breitenfeld to Waterloo* (London, 1993) and there are some terrific maps in V. J. Esposito & R. Elting, *A Military History and Atlas of the Napoleonic Wars* (New York, 1964). For a Russian perspective on the wars, A. A. Lobanov-Rostovsky, *Russia and Europe, 1789–1825* (Durham, N.C., 1947) is a very valuable, and well-written, source.

T.C.W. Blanning provides a good general history of the conflicts of the 1790s in *The French Revolutionary Wars, 1787–1802* (London, 1996), while R. W. Phipps's epic *The Armies of the First French Republic and the Rise of the Marshals of Napoleon I*, 5 vols (London, 1926–39) is full of interesting detail. Chandler's tome is particularly good on Napoleon's first Italian campaign, but M. Boycott-Brown has devoted greater space to it in his recent *The Road to Rivoli: Napoleon's First Campaign* (London, 2001). The War of the Second Coalition is given a sound overall treatment by A. B. Rodger in *The War of the Second Coalition, 1798 to 1801: A Strategic Commentary* (Oxford, 1964), but he is stronger on some aspects of that conflict than others. For the story of Napoleon's Egyptian campaign, see J. C. Herold, *Bonaparte in Egypt* (London, 1963). P. Fregosi covers all extra-European clashes during the Napoleonic Era in *Dreams of Empire: Napoleon and the First World War 1792–1815* (London, 1989), while Christopher Duffy gives a sterling account of Suvorov's 1799 campaign in *Eagles over the Alps: Suvorov in Italy and Switzerland, 1799* (Chicago, 1999). On Bonaparte's second Italian campaign and the battle of Marengo, there is less in English than one might expect, but D. Hollins's short book, *Marengo 1800: Napoleon's Day of Fate* (Oxford, 2000), is a worthy study.

Following the renewal of war between France and Britain in 1803, much of the actual fighting, limited as it was, took place in the Mediterranean and this is the subject of Piers Mackesy's *The War in the Mediterranean, 1803–10* (London, 1957). Much more significant, of course, were the major campaigns fought in central and eastern Europe between 1805 and 1807. Alistair Horne has covered these in his usual engaging and elegant style in *Napoleon, Master of Europe 1805–1807* (London, 1979), while his *How Far from Austerlitz?: Napoleon, 1805–1815* (London, 1997) provides both an extended narrative of the Emperor's greatest victory and an entertaining run through the remainder of the campaigns of the Napoleonic era. The best account of Austerlitz in English remains Christopher Duffy's *Austerlitz 1805* (London, 1977), but I. Castle, *Austerlitz 1805: the Fate of Empires* (Oxford, 2002) is another solid version. *Napoleon's Conquest of Prussia, 1806* (London, 1972), a reprint of a book originally written in the early twentieth century, is the first (chronologically) of a number of Napoleonic campaign studies written by F. L. Petre. Although not the easiest of books to read, they have the merits of being thorough and detailed. *The Jena Campaign, 1806* (London, 1998) by F. N. Maude is another reprint of an old book which has similar advantages and drawbacks to Petre's work. For an in-depth account of the Emperor's campaigns in eastern Prussia/Poland in 1806–07 one must again turn to F. L. Petre and his *Napoleon's Campaign in Poland, 1806–1807* (London, 2001). H. T. Parker provides us with a solid narrative of the battle of Friedland (as well as of Aspern-Essling and, inevitably, Waterloo) in *Three Napoleonic Battles* (Durham, N.C., 1983).

The Peninsular War has spawned an industry of its own in English, but much of what has been produced distorts the history of the Napoleonic period, either by inflating the significance of Wellington and the British Army to eventual victory in Iberia (not that they were unimportant), by granting the 'Spanish Ulcer' a greater weight in accounting for Napoleon's eventual defeat than is really merited (not that it was by any means inconsequential) or by portraying the Iberian guerrillas in a rather more favourable light than the vast majority of them deserve. Fortunately, there have also been some very good studies of the Peninsular War produced, among them Charles Esdaile's *The Peninsular War: a New History* (London, 2002), which is particularly strong on the Spanish aspect of the conflict, if a little unfair to Napoleon at times, and David Gates's judicious *The Spanish Ulcer: a History of the Peninsular War* (London, 1986).

Napoleon's campaign against Austria in 1809 is beginning to get more attention in the English-speaking world than it used to. For a long time, F. L. Petre's *Napoleon and the Archduke Charles: a History of the Franco-Austrian Campaign in the Valley of the Danube in 1809* (London, 1909) was the only specific study of any significance in English, but recent years have seen the publication of J. R. Arnold's *Napoleon Conquers Austria: the 1809 Campaign for Vienna* (London, 1995) and Gunther Rothenberg's (inaccurately titled) *The Emperor's Last Victory: Napoleon and the Battle of Wagram* (London, 2004).

The most important, and certainly the most monumental, of Napoleon's campaigns was, of course, that in Russia in 1812 and much of the best work available on this in English has been written in the past quarter century. Adam Zamoyski's *1812: Napoleon's Fatal March on Moscow* (London, 2004) is an excellent example of skilfully constructed narrative history and is full of fascinating anecdotes. As an account of the soldiers' experience of the campaign it is probably unsurpassed, for although Paul Britten Austin's colossal *1812: Napoleon's Invasion of Russia* (London, 2000) contains even more detail than Zamoyski's lengthy work, it is a less accessible read. Shorter (though still extensive) versions of the momentous events of 1812 are available in Curtis Cate's excellent *The War of the Two Emperors: the Duel between Napoleon and Alexander – Russia, 1812* (New York, 1985), Richard Riehn's *1812: Napoleon's Russian Campaign* (New York, 1991) and the ever-enjoyable Alan Palmer's *Napoleon in Russia* (London, 1967). R. F. Delderfield, that most easy-to-read of Napoleonic scholars, turned his attention to events in Russia in *The Retreat from Moscow* (London, 1967), while Christopher Duffy's *Borodino: Napoleon against Russia, 1812* (London, 1972) is possibly the best account of that battle in English. For a Russian (or should that be Soviet?) perspective, one might try E. Tarle's *Napoleon's Invasion of Russia, 1812* (London, 1942).

Despite his cataclysmic defeat in Russia, Napoleon's cause was not an entirely lost one at the start of 1813 and it took three further major campaigns to dethrone him. The story of those campaigns is told with verve and panache by R. F. Delderfield in *Imperial Sunset: the Fall of Napoleon, 1813–14* (London, 1968). More academic and detailed, though less enjoyable, are F. L. Petre's *Napoleon's Last Campaign in Germany, 1813* (London, 1974) and *Napoleon at Bay, 1814* (London, 1914), the first of which deals with the two German campaigns of 1813, the latter with the defence of France. M. Leggiere, *Napoleon and Berlin: the Napoleonic Wars in Prussia, 1813* (London, 2002) is a recent, interesting study of events in Germany in 1813. The battles of Lützen and Bautzen, especially the latter, were far more significant than is generally appreciated, even if only because of what they failed to achieve, and they are examined in Peter Hofschroer's short but useful *Lützen and Bautzen 1813: the Turning Point* (Oxford, 2001). The same author turned his attention to the largest clash of the entire Napoleonic Wars in *Leipzig 1813: the Battle of the Nations* (London, 1993), an engagement studied in some detail, if perhaps a little lifelessly overall, by Digby Smith in *1813 – Leipzig: Napoleon and the Battle of the Nations* (London, 2001).

And so, inexorably, we come to Waterloo, one of the most interesting campaigns of all time, but also one whose significance has too often been blown out of all proportion. In English there are quite probably more books on Waterloo than on all the other campaigns and battles of the Napoleonic Wars combined. D. Howarth, *Waterloo: A Near Run Thing* (London, 2003), Lord Chalfont (ed.), *Waterloo: Battle of Three Armies* (London, 1979) and E. Saunders, *The Hundred Days* (London, 1964) are all good accounts, while Peter Hofschroer's *1815: The Waterloo Campaign – The German Victory* (London, 2004) provides a provocative but much needed antidote to the common belief that Wellington and his 'British' army essentially won the battle on their own.

Finally, although naval warfare has not featured very much in this book, anyone interested in war at sea in this period will find good introductory texts in N. Miller, *Broadsides: The Age of Fighting Sail, 1775–1815* (New York, 2000), Andrew Lambert, *War at Sea in the Age of Sail* (London, 2000) and C.N. Parkinson, *Britannia Rules: The Classic Age of Naval History, 1793–1815* (London, 1977).

FOREIGN AFFAIRS AND DIPLOMACY

The purpose of war is – or at least should be – to achieve the goals of foreign policy, a fact that (contrary to what some historians have claimed) Napoleon did appreciate, even if at times he failed to make warfare realize his aims. The convoluted nature of diplomacy and foreign policy means that most popular historians have rather shied away from them, leaving them to the academics to discuss in books that are often primarily read by other academics. This is unfortunate as it leads to views commonly held by non-academics being somewhat simplistic or uneven, the idea that the Napoleonic Wars were the sole responsibility of one supposedly half-deranged, jumped-up little Corsican being a prime example of that. Most of the works cited in this section, therefore, are not among the most readily accessible to a general readership, but that is not at all to say that they are not worth the effort required to work through them.

Among the more accessible general studies of foreign affairs in this period is S. T. Ross, *European Diplomatic History 1789–1815* (New York, 1969), but the book which has come in recent years to be seen as something of a standard work is the more academic Paul W. Schroeder's *The Transformation of European Politics, 1763–1848* (Oxford, 1994), which devotes the bulk of its attention to the late eighteenth and early nineteenth centuries. Schroeder's work is certainly very admirable in a number of ways and is clearly the product of many, many years of painstaking research, but one feels compelled to suggest that he is perhaps too sympathetic at times in his interpretation of the foreign policies of Napoleon's enemies, especially the Austrians, and too damning, simplistic even, in his condemnation of Bonaparte's foreign policy (indeed, he pretty much argues he didn't have one as such). Of course, many will agree with Schroeder's interpretation, for which he certainly puts up a solid enough case, but even if one is inclined to disagree with it, as this author is, his book remains a highly valuable work as a chronicle of the complex and shifting diplomatic manoeuvrings of the era.

Albert Sorel's *L'Europe et la Révolution française*, 8 vols (Paris, 1885–1904), available in English in abridged form as *Europe and the French Revolution: the Political Traditions of the Old Regime* (London, 1969), offers an interpretation of the foreign affairs of the period which is much more positive towards Napoleon. Ultimately, his interpretation is probably as questionable as Schroeder's, but like him, he makes his case well. Adolphe Thiers in his *History of the Consulate and Empire*, 20 vols (London, 1845–62) covers foreign policy as well as domestic issues, while André Fugier's *La Révolution française et l'Empire napoléonien* (Paris, 1954) is a more manageable French study.

Although most general studies of foreign affairs in the period focus quite heavily upon Napoleon's own role and aims, R. B. Mowat, in his very readable *The Diplomacy of Napoleon* (London, 1924), concentrates even more explicitly upon the great man. Less accessible (particularly if one does not have French) is Edouard Driault's multi-volume *Napoléon et l'Europe*, 5 vols (Paris, 1910–27). This is a pretty even-handed work overall, critical of Napoleon at times, admiring at others. E. Bourgeois, in his drearily titled *Manuel historique de politique étrangère*, vol. 2 (Paris, 1898), set out an interesting but ultimately unconvincing interpretation of Bonaparte's foreign policy, which argued that everything he did was geared towards the construction of a major French empire in the East. *The Genesis of Napoleonic Imperialism* (Cambridge, Mass., 1938) by H. C. Deutsch is a useful study, while H. Butterfield's *The Peace Tactics of Napoleon, 1806–1808* (Cambridge, 1929) provides an interesting snapshot of Napoleonic diplomacy.

Work in English specifically on Russian foreign policy in the era is, predictably, limited. Although the author argues that her book is not a study of Russian diplomacy *per se*, P. K. Grimsted, *The Foreign Ministers of Alexander I: Political Attitudes and the Conduct of Russian Diplomacy, 1801–1825* (Berkeley, 1969) does shed some light on the subject. Much can also be gleaned from A. A.

Lobanov-Rostovsky's *Russia and Europe, 1789–1825* (Durham, N.C., 1947). N. E. Saul, *Russia and the Mediterranean, 1797–1807* (Chicago, 1970) is valuable for understanding that aspect of Russian foreign policy.

Books explicitly on Franco-Russian relations are very few and far between. Hugh Ragsdale's *Détente in the Napoleonic Era: Bonaparte and the Russians* (Lawrence, Kansas, 1980) is less comprehensive than the title suggests, focusing solely upon the early years of the Consulate, but this short work is of considerable value. For Russo-French relations from Tilsit to the invasion of Russia, Albert Vandal's *Napoléon et Alexandre Ier, l'alliance russe sous le premier Empire*, 3 vols (Paris, 1891–6) is useful but flawed. Influenced perhaps by the pre-eminence of Britain throughout the nineteenth century, Vandal somehow contrives to portray Franco-Russian relations almost as an adjunct to what he sees as the critical relationship between France and the United Kingdom. His interpretation of Napoleon's aims and actions can also be a little naively favourable at times.

On the outbreak of European war in the early 1790s, T.C.W. Blanning's *The Origins of the French Revolutionary Wars* (London, 1986) is a valuable study, although some of his interpretations might be questioned (but then isn't that always the case when dealing with so complex and controversial an issue as the outbreak of war?). The fate of the Ottoman Empire on the international stage during its period of long decline is the subject of M. S. Anderson's excellent *The Eastern Question, 1774–1923* (London, 1966). V. J. Puryear looks more closely at Bonaparte's own attitude to the Turkish question in *Napoleon and the Dardanelles* (Berkeley, Calif., 1951), while P. F. Shupp's focus is even narrower in *The European Powers and the Near Eastern Question, 1806–1807* (New York, 1931). For Britain's foreign policy in the period, M. Chamberlain, *Pax Britannica? British Foreign Policy, 1789–1914* (London, 1988) is useful, while Metternich's diplomacy is addressed in considerable detail in E. Kraehe's very scholarly two-volume work, *Metternich's German Policy, I: the Contest Against Napoleon 1799–1814* (Princeton, 1963) and *Metternich's German Policy, II: the Congress of Vienna 1814–1815* (Princeton, 1983). More generally on the Congress of Vienna, H. Nicolson, *The Congress of Vienna: a Study in Allied Unity, 1812–1822* (London, 1946) is a very readable account. R. B. Mowat, *A History of European Diplomacy 1815–1914* (London, 1922) also covers the congress, as well as foreign affairs in its aftermath.

MEMOIRS

The Napoleonic era unsurprisingly threw up a plethora of memoirs, some of distinctly greater value and reliability than others, some much more enjoyable to read than others. On the French side, Armand de Caulaincourt's recollections, published in English as *Memoirs of General de Caulaincourt, Duke of Vicenza*, 3 vols (London, 1950), are generally considered to be a pretty reliable, as well as an important and fascinating, source. His predecessor as Napoleon's foreign minister, Hugues Bernard Maret, also left memoirs, although these are only available in French as *Souvenirs intimes de la Révolution et de l'Empire*, 2 vols (Brussels, 1843), their non-translation into English hinting at their lesser significance than the recollections of Caulaincourt. Inevitably, Talleyrand wrote memoirs (published in English as *Memoirs*, 5 vols (London, 1891–2) by C. M. de Talleyrand) to try to convince posterity of his own wisdom and far-sightedness, and while interesting, their reliability is as dubious as one would expect. That part-time diplomat (if such a word can really be used to describe him) General Savary published his recollection of events in *Memoirs of the Duke of Rovigo*, 4 vols (London, 1828).

Fewer senior French military figures than one might anticipate left memoirs, partly, of course, because a good number of them died before they could do much about it. Given the less than glorious role he played at the end of the Napoleonic period, Marmont was understandably keen to give history his own version of events and did so in the *Mémoires du duc de Raguse*, 9 vols (Paris, 1857). Needless to say, they are not the most trustworthy account one will ever read. More reliable, though rather dull, are Macdonald's memoirs, available in English as *Recollections of Marshal Macdonald*, 2 vols (London, 1892). Both Oudinot and St Cyr left their own take on events for posterity in N.C.V. Oudinot, *Memoirs of Marshal Oudinot, duc de Reggio* (London, 1896) and L. G. St Cyr, *Mémoires*, 4 vols (Paris, 1831) respectively, while *Memoirs of Marshal Ney*, 2 vols (London, 1833), published posthumously, are much less valuable than one might hope as they focus on his early career and military thoughts. For senior military memoirs of real value and insight, one needs to turn to individuals a step or two down from the Marshalate. Both J.B.A.M. de Marbot, *Memoirs of Baron de Marbot* (London, 1988) and P. de Ségur, *Memoirs and Recollections of Count Ségur*, 3 vols (London, 1825–7) are of great interest and pretty sound reliability. J. Rapp, *Memoirs of General Count Rapp, First Aide-de-camp to Napoleon* (Cambridge, 1985) is also worth consulting.

Many of those who lived their lives in even closer proximity to Napoleon than his senior military subordinates left recollections; most of them favourable to the great man. A.J.F. Fain, *Napoleon: How He Did It – the Memoirs of Baron Fain, First Secretary of the Emperor's Cabinet* (San Francisco, 1998) are particularly flattering, but not without value. Another secretary, Claude François Méneval, recorded his memories in *Memoirs to Serve for the History of Napoleon I from 1802 to 1815*, 3 vols (London, 1894). An even more personal portrait is provided by two of Bonaparte's valets in L. Constant Wairy, *Memoirs of Constant, the Emperor Napoleon's Head Valet*, 4 vols (London, 1896) and L.J.N. Marchand,

In Napoleon's Shadow: being the first English language edition of the complete memoirs of Louis-Joseph Marchand, valet and friend of the Emperor, 1811–1821 (San Francisco, 1998).

Napoleon himself did not formally produce memoirs, but his period of exile on St Helena gave him the opportunity to present his version of events to history via members of his entourage. The most important work to emerge from those years was Emmanuel de Las Cases's *Mémorial de Sainte Hélène*, 4 vols (London, 1823), but there is also Charles Tristan de Montholon's *History of the Captivity of Napoleon*, 4 vols (London, 1846), Gaspard Gourgaud's *Talks of Napoleon at St. Helena* (London, 1904) and Henri Gratien Bertrand's *Napoleon at St. Helena*, 2 vols (London, 1953). All these books of course carry a heavy bias towards Napoleon and contain much of questionable veracity, but there are also moments of perhaps surprising honesty and frankness, and it is possible that they provide a more reliable picture of Bonaparte's aims and views than his detractors allow. Ultimately, how one views these books is likely to be a reflection of how one views Napoleon himself. Those inclined to lambaste him at every turn will dismiss them as a wholly unreliable *ex post facto* apologia, those who take a highly favourable view of the man will tend to see them as a trustworthy explanation of Napoleon's career, while those with a more balanced view will see them as flawed accounts that nevertheless contain important insights.

Turning to the memoirs of senior figures on the Russian side, the literature is less extensive, particularly for those without Russian. In English, there are *Memoirs of Prince A. Czartoryski and his correspondence with Alexander I*, 2 vols (London, 1888) and *In the Service of the Tsar against Napoleon: the memoirs of Denis Davidov, 1806–1814* (London, 1999), while available in French are *Mémoires du général Bennigsen*, 3 vols (Paris, 1907–08), *Mémoires de l'amiral Paul Tchitchagof*, (Paris, 1909) and *Mémoires de Langeron, général d'infanterie dans l'armée russe* (Paris, 1902). *Private Diary of Travels, Personal Services, and Public Events during Mission and Employment with the European Armies in the Campaigns of 1812, 1813 and 1814*, 2 vols (London, 1861) by the British general Sir Robert Wilson provides an interesting, if not always entirely reliable, picture from the perspective of a man who had access to the Russian, and later Allied, high command. Regarding international politics, *Memoirs of Prince Metternich*, Vols I & II (London, 1880) are a little more trustworthy than Talleyrand's recollections, but not much.

Interest in the personal memoirs of ordinary soldiers, NCOs and lower ranking officers has burgeoned in recent years, but the quality of such sources varies greatly and far more is available to English-speakers from those who served in Napoleon's armies than from those who fought for Russia. Among the best are J. R. Coignet, *Note-books of Captain Coignet, Soldier of the Empire 1799–1816* (London, 1998), A.J.B.F. Bourgogne, *Memoirs of Sergeant Bourgogne 1812–13*

(London, 1996), H. von Brandt, *In the Legions of Napoleon: the Memoirs of a Polish Officer in Spain and Russia, 1808–1813* (London, 1999) and F. J. Hausmann, *A Soldier for Napoleon: the Campaigns of Lieutenant Franz Joseph Hausmann, 7th Bavarian Infantry* (London, 1998).

Finally, a few words on specific memoirs of 1812. That momentous campaign was observed at first hand, and later described and analysed, by one of the greatest military theorists of all time, the Prussian Karl von Clausewitz, but his *The Campaign of 1812 in Russia* (London, 1992) is a work that will only be appreciated by those who are truly passionate about military history. Much more readable is P. de Ségur's *Napoleon's Expedition to Russia*, (London, 2003). General Wilson also provided a specific account of the great campaign in his *Narrative of Events during the Invasion of Russia* (London, 1860). At a more junior level, E. Labaume, *1812: Through Fire and Ice with Napoleon, a French Officer's Memoir of the Campaign in Russia* (London, 2002) and H. A. Vossler, *With Napoleon in Russia: the Diary of Lieutenant H. A. Vossler, a Soldier of the Grand Army* (London, 1998) are both enlightening. As the title suggests, A. Brett-James's, *1812: Eyewitness Accounts of Napoleon's Defeat in Russia* (London, 1966) provides a range of recollections of various incidents from a number of participants (he did much the same for the Leipzig campaign in *Europe against Napoleon: the Leipzig Campaign, 1813, from Eyewitness Accounts* (London, 1970)).

PRIMARY SOURCES

It is highly unlikely that many general readers will wish to consult primary sources relating to Napoleon's relations with Russia, but in case any do, the following are suggested. On the French side, there has been a wealth of material published from Bonaparte's own voluminous correspondence in a variety of forms. The biggest, and most important, are the thirty-two volumes of the *Correspondance de Napoléon I* (Paris, 1858–70), but there are also the *Supplément à la correspondance de Napoléon I* (Paris 1887), the *Lettres inédites de Napoléon I*, 3 vols (Paris, 1897–98), the *Dernières lettres inédites de Napoléon I*, 2 vols (Paris, 1903), and the *Lettres inédites de Napoléon I à Marie-Louise, écrites de 1810 à 1814* (Paris, 1935). Far more accessible, though obviously much less extensive, are J. M. Thompson (ed.), *Napoleon's Letters* (London, 1998) and J. C. Herold, *The Mind of Napoleon: a Selection from his Written and Spoken Words* (New York, 1955). *Napoleon on Napoleon: an Autobiography of the Emperor* (London, 1992) by S. de Chair is an interesting work compiled from a wide range of Napoleon's own written words.

Though technically not a primary source itself, S. Tatishchev's *Alexandre Ier et Napoléon d'après leur correspondance inédite 1801–1812* (Paris, 1891) is full of valuable primary material, while more of Alexander's correspondence can be found in *Correspondance inédite de l'Empereur Alexandre Ier avec sa soeur la Grande-Duchesse Catherine* (St Petersburg, 1910) and A. J. Czartoryski, *Memoirs of Prince A. Czartoryski and his correspondence with Alexander I*, 2 vols (London, 1888). Further Russian (and French) primary sources have been published in N. Mikhailovich (ed.), *Les relations diplomatiques de la Russie et de la France d'après les rapports des ambassadeurs d'Alexandre et de Napoléon 1808–1812*, 6 vols (St Petersburg, 1905–8) and A. Trachevsky (ed.), *Les relations diplomatiques de la France et de la Russie à l'époque de Napoléon Ier*, 4 vols (St Petersburg, 1890–93).

MISCELLANEOUS

To help make sense of what can at times seem a veritable maelstrom of personalities and events, a number of reference works on the Napoleonic era have been produced. Among the best are D. G. Chandler, *Dictionary of the Napoleonic Wars* (Herts., 1999), O. Connelly (ed.), *Historical Dictionary of Napoleonic France* (Westport, Conn., 1985) and C. Emsley, *The Longman Companion to Napoleonic Europe* (London, 1993).

Finally, mention must be made of what is undoubtedly the most famous (and, by implication, possibly the most important) book ever written on Napoleon and Russia. This is, of course, Leo Tolstoy's mammoth oeuvre, *War and Peace*. While it undoubtedly deserves its reputation as one of the great works of world literature, one feels compelled to make one or two criticisms from an historical standpoint. Although Tolstoy made greater efforts to ensure that he got his facts right (and was more successful in doing so) than many subsequent historical novelists, his historical interpretation is at times rather questionable. His depiction of Kutuzov as the hero of 1812, for example, while not entirely indefensible, would be challenged by many historians. Even more debatable is Tolstoy's general historical outlook, which attaches little significance to the actions of individuals in the unfurling of history. Still, to criticize *War and Peace* too severely would perhaps be churlish. For all its flaws, it remains a story that has stood the test of time and which continues to interest people in the Napoleonic period. And that is no bad thing.

Index